Seasons Past

Seasons Past

by
DAMON RICE

Praeger Publishers
New York

CREDITS

Extract from "Polo Grounds" from *Collected Poems of Rolfe Humphries*, © 1965 by Indiana University Press and reprinted by permission of the publisher.

Lines from "True and False Unicorn," from *A Long Undressing* by James Boughton (New York: Jargon Society, 1971), used by permission of the poet.

Endpaper montage: Photographs of Yankee Stadium and Polo Grounds, United Press International; Ebbets Field aerial view, *New York Daily News*; Ebbets Field exterior, Wide World Photos; scorecards and yearbooks courtesy of the National Baseball Hall of Fame, David Shableski, and Harold Parrott.

Published in the United States of America in 1976
by Praeger Publishers, Inc.
111 Fourth Avenue
New York, N.Y. 10003

© 1976 by Praeger Publishers, Inc.

Library of Congress Cataloging in Publication Data

Rice, Damon.
    Seasons past.

    1. Baseball—United States—History. I. Title.
GV863.A1R52   796.357′0973   74-1739
ISBN 0-275-05890-5

Printed in the United States of America

Time is of the essence. The crowd and players
Are the same age always, but the man in the crowd
Is older every season. Come on, play ball!

Rolfe Humphries, "Polo Grounds"

Prologue

I happen to be a baseball fan. Not just your casual follower of the game, but a true fanatic. Lately I've heard a lot of baloney about baseball's being a dead sport, and I've listened to all sorts of proposals for "reviving" the game. Most of that kind of talk comes from baseball people who are suffering from a football complex. They've jealously watched pro football's recent rise in popularity, and now they're looking for ways to put more "action" into baseball—to make it more *like* football, if you can imagine anything that stupid. Baseball probably comes closer to perfection than any other game. It has an uncanny symmetry, just the right balance between excitement and relaxation, the two basic ingredients of all good entertainment. The moguls of baseball should stop thinking up ways to tamper with the game and start paying attention to their fans. Otherwise, the game *will* be dead. But I am already off on a sidetrack. Right now I have a story to tell. It will show you why baseball is such an important part of me—why it's in my blood.

To start with, I grew up in a town with three great ball clubs—teams that were colorful when they lost and awesome when they won. Even when my own team was buried in the second division, I always had a pennant race to get excited about. But there's more to baseball than the changing standings of any one season. In my boyhood as a fan I became totally involved in the exploits of my special heroes. At times I was so absorbed in their fortunes I would even forget to ask for my allowance. When Cookie Lavagetto, Mel Ott, or Joe DiMaggio was on deck, I could feel their toes wiggle as they got ready to step up to the plate. They say baseball is suffering from a shortage of heroes today; maybe so, but I had my share when I was a kid. In those days the game centered upon its supermen, and I got to see them all *in person* several times a season, because I was lucky enough to live in New York.

Occasionally I run into a fan whose feelings about baseball are almost as strong as my own. Whenever that happens, I ask my newfound friend where he grew up. Invariably the answer is Chicago, or Boston, or Cincinnati, or one of the seven other cities where baseball flourished and stood its ground from 1903 until 1952. I conclude from this, and from other informal observations over the years, that the fine art of following baseball is essentially an urban skill; most of the game's truly exceptional fans were brought up in big cities, where they developed and refined their rare talent by suffering at close hand the agonies of one long season after another, from early childhood into adolescence and beyond.

What I'm trying to say is that an appreciation for baseball does not come easily or naturally. Unlike football, a spectacle that can instantly spark almost anyone's interest, baseball requires its fans to come out to the park equipped with a solid grounding in the fundamentals of the game. By "fundamentals" I mean not only a knowledge of rules and strategies but also an understanding of baseball's reliance on records and statistics, a sense of the sport's history, and even a penchant for singling out certain players—heroes, if you will—to root for with extra gusto.

Without at least a partial grasp of these basic elements of the game, it's simply not possible to enjoy baseball. Imagine a nonfan sitting through a no-hitter—an event very few of us get to witness even once. To the casual spectator this must be the dullest of all possible contests. Nothing of interest happens on the field, because most of the action takes place *in the minds* of the players and fans. An observer who can't feel the tension build as each inning of goose eggs goes up on the scoreboard doesn't belong in the ball park. Better he should go to the beach and wait for the Dolphins, the Vikings, and the Jets. If he's past high school age, the chances are just about nil that he'll ever warm up to baseball.

Because baseball doesn't rely wholly on spectacle, because there's more to the sport than readily meets the eye, it's not surprising that it lacks immediate spectator appeal. The typical fan is made, not born; as I said, he usually comes from an old big city, where he began following the game at an early age. I grew up in Brooklyn. My father first took me to Ebbets Field when I was seven, so I could easily qualify as a typical fan. But the point I'm trying to make is that I'm not typical: For me baseball is not just an interest, it's a passion. To explain this, it won't do just to tell you about my childhood; I'll have to go back even further. You see, I *was* born a fan. My family not only lived and breathed baseball but made it a religion.

My father sometimes carried his love of baseball to ridiculous extremes. He was a gentle, fun-loving man, and whenever his friends talked about him they began or ended by saying, "He *means* well." But Pop let baseball get the best of him. Whenever he had a dollar bill in his pocket he was off to the ball park, even if he could ill afford to give up an afternoon's pay. One March he vanished for two weeks because he just had to see spring training for himself. We had our share of lean times, but we also had moments of great joy, because Pop had a terrific knack for tossing aside his own troubles and getting us to toss ours aside too, especially in my early days. In a flash he could hurry us all out the door for a picnic in Prospect Park, a trip to Coney Island, or an excursion on the Staten Island Ferry. But, for me, the greatest moments of all were when he and I were sitting together in the upper deck at Ebbets Field, in the bleachers at Yankee Stadium, or behind third base at the Polo Grounds.

Uncle Harry (not to be confused with the Harry Rice who played in the big leagues in the twenties and early thirties) was more stable than my father but no less a fan. Even though Harry held down the same bookkeeper's job for a good part of his life, he spent as much time as my father, if not more, keeping up with the game. On any given day he could tell you the exact batting average of every player in the American League and the ERA of every starting pitcher in the majors. If you had time to sit down for a few beers, he would give you his "line" on each team in both circuits. Every night, sometimes for five or six hours, he would record all the statistics and work out all the equations that went into his "line," which measured a team's overall statistical performance against its place in the standings. If Boston had a won-lost percentage of .602 and was two games in first, but Harry evaluated the team at .548, he would pronounce that the Braves were playing over their heads and give you a date when they would be back in second or third place. If you disagreed and cared to make a wager, he would gladly take your action, and usually your money as well.

My uncle and my father were a remarkable combination—the perfect blend of statistics and emotion. Together they taught me all the baseball I know. But Uncle Harry holds a special place in my heart for still another reason. From the time I was eleven until I was seventeen, he lived in an apartment house facing Bedford Avenue, across from Ebbets Field. If you were a Dodger fan, you might even remember the place. It was right behind the scoreboard, and it had a large sign advertising "MARLIN BLADES AND SHAVE CREAM" between the top row of windows and the roof. From that roof you could get a fair view of the game, especially with opera glasses and a radio to give you Red Barber's play-by-play. During the years that Uncle Harry and Aunt Ellen lived there, I always had a catbird seat for the action when I was too broke to pay my way into the park.

My grandfather, Fletcher "The Bird" Rice, was the only member of my family who ever played professional baseball. You can find his record in *The Baseball Encyclopedia*, where he's listed simply as "Fletcher."

He was fast and wiry and might have been a star if he'd been able to hang in there against a curve ball. If you think the curve is a twentieth-century invention you're sadly mistaken; by the 1870s there were several pitchers around throwing breaking stuff, and those who pitched to old Fletch had his number. That's why his big league career lasted only one season—1872, when he batted .250 for the Brooklyn Eckfords.

He died eight years before I was born, but it's easy to see from photos taken during the last years of his life that Fletcher was an amazing character. You would guess from those pictures that he was a banker or a captain of industry, possibly a blueblood, maybe even a Boston Brahmin. But behind that aristocratic face with its elegant white moustache was a card shark, a boozer, and a hustler who could more than hold his own in an era when hustling was a cutthroat profession. It is with Fletcher Rice that my story really begins.

BOOK ONE
Fletcher

> Unfortunately, the early history of professionalism in the metropolis is darkened with the records of crooked work.
>
> *The Dime Base-Ball Player*, 1881

1

The records of the Bureau of Statistics in Hoboken, New Jersey, reveal that my grandfather was born in that city on June 19, 1846. Fletcher's father worked in Manhattan, commuting each day on the Barclay Street Ferry to his job as a teller with the City Bank, where his immediate supervisor was one Benjamin Cartwright, who may have been the brother of Alexander Cartwright, the man who organized and laid down the rules for the New York Knickerbockers, America's first baseball club. Whether or not my great-grandfather's boss was related to the "inventor of baseball' is an interesting speculation, but it is more important that my grandfather grew up in Hoboken. The Knickerbockers practiced and played their home games less than two miles from Fletcher's house in a beautiful park on the banks of the Hudson known as the Elysian Fields. It was there that young Fletcher was infected forever by the baseball bug, watching the Knicks take the field to practice as well as to answer the challenges of their archrivals from upper Manhattan, the New York Gothams.

Before the Civil War baseball was a regional game. Each section of the country had its own rules, and movement toward standardization was painfully slow. Membership in most clubs was limited to "gentlemen"—players with more than their share of leisure time. They had no interest at all in spreading the game beyond their own domains, which, after all, could only lead to opening up baseball to the working classes. When standardization did come about it came not through compromise but by universal adoption of the rules of the "New York Game," the version of baseball played by the clubs that proliferated in and around New York City during the 1850s.

7

In the spring of 1858 Fletcher's father took a position with the Brooklyn Savings Bank, and the family moved from New Jersey to the town that was rapidly becoming the capital of the baseball world. The Brooklyn Excelsiors, Atlantics, Eckfords, and Putnams were four of the best and most famous teams of the day. Another club to be reckoned with, the New York Mutuals, also played its home games in the City of Churches.

Dreams of young boys don't change. Just as I and my father before me secretly longed to make it someday to the big leagues, so too did my grandfather envision himself as a budding star. As Fletcher approached his teens, he began to believe he would make it as a ballplayer, not just for one of Brooklyn's many neighborhood clubs, but for a team with national standing. His first choice was the Atlantics, but four or five other clubs would do almost as well. This wasn't exactly a pipe dream: Fletcher was the best player in his grammar school, and during the summers he played regularly with much older boys, always excelling as a fielder and holding his own at the plate.

In the spring of 1860 it began to appear that his dream would come true, for his reputation brought him to the attention of the Stars, a club in South Brooklyn that acted informally as a farm team for the famous Excelsiors. The Stars were looking to beef up their roster because the previous winter they had lost a number of players to the Excelsiors, including Jim Creighton, who would soon go on to become the most famous pitcher of the early Civil War period. Even though Fletcher was not yet fourteen, he was invited to come to the Stars' grounds for a tryout.

He practiced with the Stars at shortstop and second base for two weeks in April 1860. While he dazzled the team with his play in the field, he had trouble getting his bat around against a quality of pitching he'd never seen before. In one practice game he went 0 for 4 with two strikeouts but made up for it with three unbelievable catches, leaping stabs of liners that rose from the bat like surefire extra-base hits. One of the Stars remarked at the end of the game, "Young Fletcher there flies into the air like a bird," and from that moment on he became "The Bird" to everyone who knew him in baseball. He gained a nickname, but he failed to win a job. When the two weeks were up he was sent home for more seasoning. He needed to work on his swing.

Fletcher did not lose heart; he was convinced he had what it took. With a little bit of hard work, he'd surely be on his way. That summer he applied himself as never before, and soon his fellow players came to respect his hitting almost as much as his fielding. One day it occurred to him that it wasn't enough just to hit, run, and field well; to *win* you also had to understand the game itself. Overnight Fletcher became a serious student of baseball. Whenever he had the opportunity, he went out to watch his favorite team, the Brooklyn Atlantics. The Atlantics had known better years, but they were still one of the best teams around, with the most loyal and rabid fans in all of Brooklyn. During that summer of 1860, the Atlantics clashed with the Excelsiors in three bitterly contested matches that demonstrated, if nothing else, how exciting and unpredictable baseball can be.

In June 1860 the Excelsiors took off on baseball's first extended road trip. They visited several cities in upstate New York, soundly trouncing all local teams. Smug and confident, they returned to Brooklyn for a game with the Atlantics on July 20. It was no contest; the Excelsiors won, 23–4, and immediately hit the road again, this time to Baltimore and Philadelphia. When they returned still undefeated, the general view was that they were invincible. Nonetheless, the Atlantics agreed to face them again, and a game was scheduled for August 10. The betting line established the Excelsiors as overwhelming favorites, and Fletcher's father, for one, saw no reason why the game should be played at all.

As the day drew near, interest started to mount, especially among fans of the Atlantics, who were certain their team had played the first game on an off day. Fletcher had no doubts at all his team could do the job, and he tried to persuade his father to come out with him to the game and be proved wrong. "Sorry, son," was the reply, "but I have more important things to do with my time than waste an afternoon at a lopsided baseball contest." And lopsided it was for the first three innings, as the Atlantics fell behind, 8–0. Slowly, though, Fletcher's team picked up momentum, until the seventh inning when, down 12–6, they shelled Creighton for five runs on nine hits and went on to win, 15–14, breaking the Excelsiors' winning streak. A rubber match was immediately scheduled for August 23 in neutral territory—the new home field of the Brooklyn Putnams.

Fletcher's father suddenly lost his indifference. After all, this third game had more than just local importance. The winners not only would be the champions of Brooklyn but would also be recognized as the leading team in the East. "This time I *will* take you to the game," Fletcher's father told him, "and my friend Mr. Danser will come with us. I've told him what a promising player you are, and how you predicted the Atlantics would win. He's very anxious to meet you."

How or when Fletcher's father had met Mr. Matt Danser is a mystery. I have good reason to believe the two men were more than just friends, but I've yet to find any solid clues, in either our family papers or the public record, to confirm my suspicion that there were business dealings between them. I *do* know that my great-grandfather left his post at the Brooklyn Savings Bank in the fall of 1859 and that he never worked at a regular job again, right up to his death in 1868.

During those nine years, while a confidant and frequent companion of Mr. Danser, he became a regular bettor at horse races and baseball games and had more money than ever before in his life. Danser was a professional gambler—the sort known today as a high roller—with excellent connections in Tammany Hall.

When Fletcher and his dad arrived at Gates and Lafayette avenues, the site of the Putnams' field, Matt Danser was waiting to escort them to their seats. He had somehow managed to obtain space on the reporters' plank, which, it soon became apparent, held more impostors than bona fide members of the press. The air grew heavy with excitement as the crowd increased to more than twenty thousand, an enormous figure for pre–Civil War days. As Fletcher settled into his seat he began to feel uneasy. He had never been to a ball park with such a raucous, unruly crowd.

Throughout the crowd were pockets of gambling activity as bettors scrambled to get a last-minute piece of the action. From all corners of the field spectators were shouting insults and obscenities at the players, with the Excelsiors taking most of the abuse. Soon the gallery behind first base began screaming for the game to begin, and as their chants spread to the rest of the crowd the Atlantics ran out to their positions on the diamond.

"Do you remain convinced the Atlantics will win?" Danser asked Fletcher as the game got under way.

"I'm certain of it," Fletcher replied.

"If the rumors I hear are true," his father added, "the Excelsiors will not be allowed to win—in a close contest."

"Do you believe that?" Danser asked, smiling slyly.

"I can't say I *dis*believe it. Where do you have your money, Matt?"

"My hopes are riding with the Atlantics," he affirmed with feigned seriousness. The two men were, of course, alluding to the possibility of a fix. If the fix *was* on, Matt Danser knew about it.

The crowd remained restless and unruly, but despite several outbreaks of catcalls and insults the teams managed to play four and a half innings of baseball. Then, in the bottom of the fifth, trouble began. The Atlantics came to bat behind, 8–4, but quickly rallied for two runs. They appeared to be on their way to making it a new ball game when McMahon, their centerfielder, overran third and was called out. The play wasn't particularly close, but it ended the rally and infuriated the Atlantics' fans, who decided to make the umpire their scapegoat. When the Excelsiors came to bat in the top of the sixth, the crowd began hollering for a new umpire. It seemed that violence might erupt at any moment. J. B. Leggett, the Excelsiors' catcher and team captain, came over to the crowd to appeal for order.

"If this doesn't stop," he shouted through a megaphone standing just twenty feet from Fletcher, "the Excelsiors will leave the field!"

The roar of the crow diminished, but as Leggett turned away it started up again even louder. He spun around, called his players together, and then led the Excelsiors up the sidelines to a six-horse stagecoach that was waiting to take them home. Leggett handed the ball to one of the Atlantics and said a few words. Then he and his teammates climbed aboard the coach and were followed off the grounds by a band of shouting, threatening roughnecks. The two teams would never meet again.

For several minutes Danser and Fletcher's father stood in their places without uttering a word, their faces betraying more than a little concern. Then, as word drifted through the crowd that Leggett had given the Atlantics a tie, the two men loosened up, smiled, and began to make small talk. As they were leaving the ground Fletcher began to wonder how much money Danser had wagered on the contest, and whether his father had also placed a bet. Fletcher wanted to be a player more than anything else in the world, but it was beyond him why anyone would want to waste money gambling on baseball. Like the game itself he was young and filled with ideals. His father's hints about the possibility of a fix had gone over his head. One day he would learn that innocence is a gambler's greatest ally.

Fletcher spent all of the next winter longing for spring to arrive. In his dreams he performed fantastic feats—plays he would surely repeat on the diamond as soon as the cold weather was gone. In his heart he just *knew* he was destined for greatness, and he began setting his sights beyond "junior" teams such as the Stars. He convinced himself he would settle for nothing less than the likes of the Excelsiors or the Atlantics.

As April arrived Fletcher was hard at work writing letters to the major clubs around New York. He was certain a tryout was all he would need. But on April 12 his dreams were blown away. The Confederates attacked Fort Sumter. Overnight young men everywhere began answering the call to arms. The baseball clubs, their rosters depleted, curtailed activities for the duration.

In June Fletcher left school. For the next year he drifted between odd jobs, played an occasional pickup game of baseball, and followed closely the news of the war. It soon became obvious the struggle to preserve the Union would go on for a long time. As he read of fierce battles in unheard-of places such as Bull Run, Ball's Bluff, Pea Ridge, and Shiloh, Fletcher decided he would join up as soon as he was sixteen. His mother and father tried desperately to dissuade him, but they succeeded for only a few months. In September 1862, shortly after Lee defeated Pope in the Second Battle of Bull Run, the 5th New York Infantry, the Duryee Zouaves, sent a detail to New York to recruit for the regiment. Fletcher, armed with his mother's reluctant letter of consent, reported for induction at Camp Washington on Staten Island. As it turned out there were more recruits than the "Old Fifth" could use, so Fletcher became part of a new regiment, the 165th New York Volunteer Infantry, which soon became known as the Second Duryee Zouaves. The new outfit trained on Staten Island through that fall, and in December it was assigned to action in the Louisiana campaign. On December 18, 1862, the 165th boarded the steamer *Merrimac* bound for Hilton Head, South Carolina—the only stop en route to battle.

Although baseball went into limbo on the home front, it flourished in the field throughout the war. Whenever there was a prolonged lull in combat, some foresighted soldier would inevitably produce a ball from his knapsack. On Christmas Day, 1862, Fletcher's regiment challenged a team of "all-stars" from other Union outfits camped on Hilton Head Island. Private Rice played shortstop, and it was probably his finest hour ever as a ballplayer. Before a crowd of more than ten thousand soldiers Fletcher went five for five and made like a bird for three fantastic catches. Three days later the 165th broke camp and sailed off to war, leaving baseball heroics behind for a more critical brand of heroism.

The Second Zouaves spent all of the next year in Louisiana, seeing their most important action at the Battle of Port Hudson in May 1863. Later in the war they fought in Virginia, in the battles of Deep Bottom and Cedar Creek. Fletcher never failed to display bravery in the face of enemy fire, and when his unit was mustered out of the active army in September 1865 he was not only well-decorated but had become one of the youngest sergeants in the Union ranks.

By the time Fletcher returned to civilian life, baseball was well on the way to its prewar level of popularity. As players returned to their teams, and as the public found time to enjoy the new peace, the leading clubs quickly took up where they had left off. The gamblers were also back in full strength and more brazen than ever. Now there was open talk about the probability, if not the certainty, that many games were being thrown. The Brooklyn Eckfords became known for their suspicious tactics, and other teams became suspect because of disreputable bosses. The New York Mutuals fell into the hands of Boss Tweed, and a new team from upstate, the Troy Haymakers, was controlled by John "Old Smoke" Morrissey, one of the most notorious gamblers in the country.

Morrissey, who first gained fame as heavyweight champion of America, would use his Tammany connections to get elected to the House of Representatives in 1866. He owned the most lavish casino in all of Manhattan and had plans to build another opulent gambling hall in Saratoga Springs. He even operated the betting pools at the Saratoga racetrack. Throwing games was then known as "hippodroming." A particularly blatant example of the practice took place only a few weeks after Fletcher's discharge. To the amazement of everyone except the gamblers who had taken the long odds, the Eckfords defeated the Mutuals, 28–11. It turned out that three of the Mutuals had thrown the game. By rights the culprits should have been barred from baseball forever, but Boss Tweed took care of his boys.

While gambling was fouling the atmosphere around baseball, the game itself was undergoing crucial changes. New rules and strategies were evolving. Each year saw a marked improvement in the quality of the players, especially on the most prominent teams, where it became customary to pay salaries to the more indispensable members of the lineup.

As yet no team was 100 percent professional, but almost every major club had at least two or three paid players on its roster. Players like Fletcher, solid but not outstanding, didn't have a chance to win a place on a top team. For the next three years Fletch worked at a variety of jobs, sometimes managing to find action as a stand-in for indisposed players on lesser aggregations, such as the Brooklyn Peconics and the Brooklyn Powhatans. He remained an avid fan, however, rooting for his Atlantics whenever possible. On August 17, 1868, he was on hand at the Union Grounds in Brooklyn for the most exciting game of the 1868 season. In a contest billed as a "grand championship match," the Atlantics staved off a late inning rally to beat the Mutuals, 12–11, before more than fifteen thousand fans.

Fletcher's father died in the fall of 1868. It became clear very quickly that the old man had been less than prudent with his recently found riches. There was barely enough money to get his widow through the winter, which meant that by spring her son would have to take over her support. So Fletcher gave up his last remaining hopes of being a ballplayer and decided to look for a situation with good prospects. Aware that such a job would not be easy to find, he searched his brain for a place to start and thought of Mr. Danser. He dashed off a letter of inquiry. A few days later came an invitation to join Mr. Danser at his club for lunch.

"What happened to your ambition to be a baseball player?" was Danser's first question.

"I'm afraid it wasn't very realistic to begin with," Fletcher replied, "and now it's out of the question."

"Oh, I don't know about that. How brazen are you?"

"Quite brazen, if I have to be."

"Good. Come and see me before the baseball season opens."

Fletcher probably would not have gone along with Danser had he known then what the gambler had in mind. By the time he reported for his mysterious assignment his mother was flat broke, so there was no turning back.

Danser had found him a spot on the Atlantics as a substitute outfielder. It didn't matter that substitutes almost never played. Fletcher's main duties would be off the diamond. He was to make friends with the players—not only the Atlantics but their opponents as well—and be on the lookout for an opening, however small, that could lead to a fix. When he discovered such a possibility he could either pursue it himself or call upon Danser for help. Would he ever get to play? Probably not, but there was always a chance. Anyway, he found himself earning $25 a week.

The season of 1869 opened, and Fletcher quickly discovered he couldn't stomach his new job. Still, he couldn't afford to give up the money, so he began to engage in a very dangerous practice—telling his boss the fix was on when it wasn't. He turned out to be a skillful handicapper. From May to July he successfully predicted the winning side in four important contests. In one case he was helped out by the Cincinnati Red Stockings, who that year became the first all-professional team and didn't lose a game all season. In June they came to New York and mowed down, on successive days, the Mutuals, 4–2; the Atlantics, 32–10; and the Eckfords, 24–5. Fletcher's prediction that the Reds would beat the Atlantics didn't exactly require clairvoyance, but it won bets for Mr. Danser, and that was all that mattered.

At six o'clock on the evening of August 1 the Atlantics boarded the steamboat *Connecticut* at Pier 44 in Manhattan, bound for Troy, New York. They were on their way to the first of two successive Monday contests with the Haymakers, a team that was gaining a reputation as one of the toughest in the East. Fletcher felt his team would be no match for the Troy club; before leaving he passed the word to Danser that the Haymakers would win the first game. The Brooklynites arrived in Troy at nine the next morning, several hours before game time. While his teammates were settling into the American Hotel—a well-known gamblers' haunt—Fletcher decided to drop into the saloon for a glass of beer.

"I understand your line of vision includes the future," he heard someone mutter just as the waiter brought the lager. Fletcher looked to an adjacent table, where he caught the eye of a thin man with dark brilliantined hair and an elegant moustache.

"Who are you?" Fletcher asked. "And what's that supposed to mean?"

"Hamilton Baker is the name," the man said moving over to Fletcher's table.

"Well, what can I do for you, Mr. Baker?"

"As I said, I understand you have a knack for predicting the future. My employer could almost surely use your services."

"And who would that be?"

"Perhaps I can persuade you to stay behind when your team goes back to New York. If you would care to spend a few extra days in these parts, I'm sure I can arrange an appointment."

So his reputation as a "handicapper" was beginning to spread. Baker looked like a man who had Trouble for a bedfellow, but Fletcher's curiosity was stronger than his common sense. Besides, he was beginning to enjoy money.

"All right. The club sails back on the morning steamer. I'm sure no one will miss me."

"Why don't you stay the week? You can rejoin the team for next Monday's game in Saratoga."

"Sure, why not?"

"You'll be hearing from me, Mr. Rice," Baker said picking up his hat and walking out of the room.

In the early afternoon the Atlantics boarded carriages for Lansingburgh, where the Haymakers played their home games. A crowd of eight thousand, quite a turnout for such a rural setting, showed up. Once again Fletcher successfully predicted the outcome. The Haymakers won, 17–10. Only a few of his teammates were even curious when they discovered he was not with them for the trip back to New York.

Fletcher spent most of that week drinking beer and rocking on the front porch of the American Hotel. He began to wonder whether Baker would indeed show up. If not it would be no great loss. On Monday the team was due back for the second game of the series, scheduled to be played at the racetrack in Saratoga. If nothing happened, well, the week had been pleasant enough, and it hadn't cost a cent. The hotel manager assured him that all his bills would be picked up by Mr. Baker. So Fletcher had nothing to do but relax and wonder what Baker had up his sleeve.

On Saturday evening, around supper time, Fletcher looked up from his rocking chair to see Baker standing before him. "Sorry I didn't get back to you sooner," Baker began, "but I work nights and sleep days, which doesn't leave much time in between. Are you up for spending the night out?"

"Damn right I am."

It would turn out to be a most eye-opening evening, a night Fletcher would look back upon as a turning point. Baker took him down to Albany to an elegant bagnio—a full-service brothel—where they helped themselves to all the whisky, fine food, and wine they could stomach. And yes, they helped themselves to women too, though Fletcher found it difficult to make a choice; the young ladies at his disposal were unlike any he had ever met, except perhaps in his fantasies. He finally singled out an especially delicate young woman named Kate, and he returned to her bedroom three times, the last time to finish out the night. The whisky finally got the better of him. He awoke to find Baker shaking him.

"Come on, Fletch, you have a train to catch."

"A train?" he asked groggily, trying to find the floor with his feet. He turned to see that Kate was also in the bed, snoring softly, oblivious to the activity around her. It would be many hours before she would have to get up.

"That's right, so let's get moving."

"What about breakfast? My head's killing me."

"There'll be time enough for that."

The station was only a short walk from the whorehouse. As it happened, they barely made the early train to Saratoga Springs. It was a short trip, and when they pulled in, just before nine o'clock, an open carriage was waiting.

"I'll leave you now. Good luck," Baker said as Fletcher climbed into the carriage. The driver slapped the reins across the horse's rump, and the coach lurched down the street. A few minutes later Fletcher was deposited before a side door of the Saratoga Club House, the Honorable John Morrissey's newly opened gambling emporium, the most extravagantly appointed establishment of its kind in the world.

Fletcher was escorted into a private dining room, where he was served a breakfast of porterhouse steak, stewed kidneys, a perfect omelet, and a cup of delicious mocha. The night before, Baker had opened Fletcher's eyes to life's sensual pleasures; now, barely awake, he was taking in more of the same. During breakfast he tried to look out the door of the little room to see what was going on. All he saw was an empty corner of the grand saloon with nothing but covered gaming tables. It was Sunday, and the casino was closed.

Presently Fletcher's waiter, a distinguished colored gentleman, beckoned him to come along and led him across the deep, flowered carpets of the great public gambling hall, past gaudy bronzes and wood panels adorned with sensuous carvings, and into a picturebook Victorian reception room. At the far end, sitting in an easy chair by an open window and puffing contentedly on a Reina Victoria cigar, was "Old Smoke" Morrissey himself. Fully bearded, broad-shouldered and deep-chested, a picture of robustness, the congressman displayed that special charisma given only to the Irish.

"Well, Mr. Rice. Come over here and take a seat," Morrissey bellowed. Fletcher quickly obeyed.

"What can I do for you, sir?" Fletcher asked.

"Well, that remains to be seen. I understand you're a business associate of Matt Danser. Is that correct?"

"Yes, it is—in a manner of speaking."

"Good. I've had business dealings with Danser myself. In fact, we were partners once. He can be trusted, and that's the most important thing you can say about a man."

"I suppose you're right."

"Of course I am. Now, Mr. Rice, how would you like to do a little job for me?"

"I suppose so. That is, if it's all right with Mr. Danser."

16

"Don't you worry about him."

"All right, then, what do you want me to do?"

"Take up where you left off with Matt. Well, almost. The assignment I have in mind will probably be more difficult than anything you've tackled thus far."

That was an understatement. Morrissey explained that his baseball team was scheduled to play the Red Stockings in Cincinnati on August 27. Fletcher's job would be to get the Reds to ruin their historic season by lying down for the Haymakers. The Reds would be heavy favorites. If Troy could manage to win, Old Smoke and his cronies would collect a bundle.

"It sounds like an intriguing proposition. Quite a challenge," Fletcher said. "Let me give it a try." He hardly hesitated. The lure of wine and women had done him in.

"Excellent. Oh, to let Mr. Danser know you won't be working for him for a while, why don't you send him a wire?"

"What shall I say?"

"Tell him the game tomorrow will be an easy victory for the Atlantics."

"But last week they were beaten by the Haymakers, and by a good score."

"Of course. The odds should be very favorable indeed. Oh, here's a thousand dollars—for expenses," Morrissey said, handing Fletcher an envelope. "There'll be another thousand when the Red Stockings lose." Old Smoke stood up, shook Fletcher's hand, and left the room.

That afternoon Fletcher sent a cryptic telegram he knew Danser would understand. He then took a room and spent the day wandering around the Spa waiting for his teammates to arrive. He began to see the Atlantics as somehow pathetic, sailing up the Hudson ready to play their hearts out in a game they couldn't lose if they tried. What fun was that? The business he was drifting into didn't give a damn about fun. Money was the long and the short of everything.

The game was scheduled for four o'clock Monday afternoon and was preceded by a full card of horse racing. It was Fletcher's first visit to a track, and he thoroughly enjoyed it. His betting instincts were remarkably sound, and he managed to win a few dollars. The baseball contest that followed was a joke. The Atlantics opened up with eight runs in the top of the first and went on to beat the carefree Haymakers, 25–11.

Two weeks later Fletcher found himself in the Gibson House in Cincinnati, trying to figure out how to approach the Red Stockings. The game was still four days away, but the city was already buzzing, and Fletcher was far from the only stranger in town with a keen interest in the outcome.

His first idea was to seek the aid of the umpire, John Brockway, who played for Cincinnati's other team, the Buckeyes. Fletcher found Brockway in a saloon where the Buckeyes often gathered to talk baseball and drink beer. As soon as he realized what Fletcher was up to, Brockway threatened to beat the daylights out of him if he didn't get lost. Further, he warned that any close decisions were likely to go to the Reds. So Fletcher's first attempt at hippodroming ended in dismal failure. Instead of improving his team's prospects, he'd made them worse.

Gun-shy from the Brockway fiasco, Fletcher stayed close to his hotel until the day before the game. Suddenly he realized the Haymakers would be in town in just a few hours. He had to think of something. Rumors about heavy betting were everywhere, and he even overheard someone speculate that Old Smoke had more than $50,000 riding on the contest. That bit of news made Fletch's palms wet up like frogs' asses on a lily pad. He came to one very obvious conclusion: There was no way he could bribe Harry and George Wright, the leaders and stars of the team. That meant the Reds were bound to score runs, and the only way to beat them was to score more runs. Now that *could* be accomplished with a little help from Asa Brainard, the Cincinnati pitcher. Fletcher decided to pin his hopes on one bribe. He would try to get to Brainard.

Fletcher made a few inquiries and found out where Brainard lived. He then sent a bellboy from the hotel around to the pitcher's room with a sealed envelope containing the following message:

> In one hour you will receive $200.
> Also instructions for earning
> an additional $300.

The boy soon returned to report that Brainard had come to the door, opened and read the note, and gone back into his room without saying a word. Fletcher waited an hour and then dispatched the messenger with a second envelope containing $200 in bank notes and this offer:

> If "Haymakers" score ten or more
> runs in 1st and 2nd innings, you get
> $300 regardless of final outcome.

This time the messenger reported that Brainard had taken the envelope into his room without opening it. Fletcher had done what he could do—maybe he had bought the Haymakers a leg up, maybe not, but at least he had tried. As he milled around the hotel lobby the word got around that the Haymakers' train had arrived and the team was on its way to the Gibson House that very moment.

Someone said that Old Smoke himself was traveling with his boys. That news didn't exactly thrill Fletcher. The last thing he wanted was to be within a hundred miles of Morrissey if the Haymakers took a shellacking. But when the players came bursting into the hotel behind their president, Jim McKeon, Fletcher could see that it was a case of mistaken identity. A spectator down at the station had jumped to the conclusion that McKeon was Old Smoke. The Haymakers settled into the hotel, spent the day relaxing, and went to bed right after supper to get as much rest as possible. For Fletcher it wasn't a restful night.

Every train that pulled into Cincinnati the next morning was filled with baseball fans. The town was tingling with suspense, because everyone knew the Haymakers could give the Red Stockings a fight. Interest in the contest was so great that two thousand extra seats were put up. Western Union even ran a telegraph line out to the grounds to give folks back in the city a play-by-play account of the action. At 3:20 in the afternoon the Haymakers took the field, and it was obvious from the outset that this wasn't going to be an ordinary game. For reasons that escaped everyone in the grandstand, the Haymakers put Fisher, their ace pitcher, at second base and began the game with Bearman in the box. Fletcher had seen Bearman pitch before and had very little confidence in his abilities. Even if the Haymakers *were* spotted ten runs, the Red Stockings were certain to breathe heavily down Troy's neck.

Much to everyone's surprise, Bearman held the Reds scoreless in the top of the first. In the bottom half of the inning the Haymakers scored six runs, but Fletcher didn't get a single easy breath, because Cincinnati came up with ten in the second. When Troy bounced right back with seven runs of its own in the second, Fletcher was out an additional $300 but still a long way from victory. By the end of the fourth the score was tied at thirteen apiece, and in a wild and woolly fifth inning that had the crowd on its feet for every play each team scored four runs to make it 17–17.

Fisher was now pitching for Troy, and Fletcher was beginning to feel his team had a chance. Not only had they scored seventeen runs off the "invincible" Red Stockings, but Fisher appeared to be in excellent form, and the Haymakers had the advantage of batting last. There was, however, one small problem: Mr. Brockway was being true to his word. He was handing every close decision to the Reds. The Haymakers were getting credit only for clean hits and easy putouts. Six of the Cincinnati runs in the second had come after a close "safe" call that Fletcher was certain should have been the third out.

In the top of the sixth the game came to a sudden, surprising conclusion. McVey, at bat for the Reds, slashed a foul tip down between the feet of Craver, the Haymakers' catcher. The rules of the time stipulated that if the catcher caught a foul tip on the first bounce the batter was out. Craver dropped down, scooped up the ball, and asked Brockway for a decision.

"Not out," the umpire said.

"What do you mean?" shouted Craver. "I had it on one bounce!"

"The ball was dead when you picked it up," Brockway replied.

"And you're blind as a bat! You've been calling plays against us ever since this damn game began!"

Jim McKeon stood up from the Troy bench and called Craver over. "What the hell is going on?" McKeon asked.

"That was an out," Craver replied. "Enough is enough."

"In that case, bring the boys off the field," McKeon ordered. "We'll not pitch another ball today."

As quickly as that, the game was over. To the taunts and catcalls of the crowd the Haymakers quit the game, leaving behind a 17–17 tie— the one blemish on what otherwise would have been a perfect season for the Red Stockings. In December of that year, at baseball's national convention, someone proposed that twenty runs be added to the Reds' score, but the resolution was tabled. The tie remains in the books to this day.

By the time the angry crowd swarmed over the ropes and onto the field, the Haymakers' omnibus was on its way back to town, with Fletcher along for the ride. At the hotel they learned that the game scheduled between the Haymakers and the Buckeyes for the following day had been called off because the other Cincinnati club would not be seen on the same field with the "cheaters" from Troy. The next day the Haymakers took off for a game in Louisville, and Fletcher headed back to Brooklyn. Before he left he sent Brainard the $300.

Waiting for Fletcher in Brooklyn was a message from Old Smoke. Congressman Morrissey happened to be in New York for a few days; he was at his gambling establishment at 5 West Twenty-fourth Street. He wondered whether Fletcher would mind dropping over to discuss a few items of business they failed to cover in their last meeting. "My God," Fletcher thought, "the Irishman is blaming *me* because the Haymakers didn't win." He still had $400 of Morrissey's money, which he had already decided to return.

That evening, anxious to face the music, he headed right for Manhattan, where he was suddenly cast into a glittering world that made him very aware of his own insignificance. Because he happened to enter the casino behind a group of swells, the doorman failed to notice that he wasn't properly dressed. It wasn't until he had been standing for several minutes behind a faro table, spellbound by the insouciant dexterity of the dealer and astounded by the enormous wagers, that a floor boss spotted his inappropriate attire. He quietly invited him to leave the premises.

Fletcher explained that he was there to see Mr. Morrissey, but the bouncer found that hard to believe. After Fletcher repeated his story half a dozen times he was finally taken upstairs, where he waited for more than an hour before being ushered in to see the great man.

Morrissey appeared genuinely pleased to see Fletcher. He began the interview by asking several questions about the game in Cincinnati. Fletcher answered them carefully, trying hard to point out that he had done everything he could to ensure victory, having arranged for the Haymakers' thirteen runs in the first two innings. It soon became clear that the congressman did not want his money back, nor did he hold Fletch responsible for Troy's failure to win.

Old Smoke had summoned Fletcher to offer him another assignment. The Haymakers were about to travel to Baltimore for two games—one with the Pastime Club, a third-rate team, and the other with the Maryland Club, champions of the South.

The plan was simple. Morrissey's team would lose to the Pastimers, creating very favorable odds for the game against Maryland. Fletcher's job was to go to Baltimore with a bundle of Old Smoke's money, wait for odds on the second contest, and place as many wagers as possible on the Haymakers. It was a sweet proposition. If the plan failed it was no skin off Fletch's hide; if it succeeded he would receive 5 percent of Morrissey's winnings.

It was not an offer a money-hungry young man could refuse. Before long Fletcher found himself in Baltimore watching the Haymakers do what they could do best—lose a baseball game convincingly.

After Troy lost to the Pastime Club there were plenty of pigeons in Baltimore, all puffed with civic pride, ready to lay odds on Maryland. Fletcher worked the saloons, a few private clubs, and of course the pool-sellers. Before he was finished he had committed $10,000 of Morrissey's money to a Haymaker win. Miraculously, the team returned to form, beating the pants off the Marylanders, 25–12. Collecting the winnings was not that easy, for a number of losers, well aware they'd been had, either refused to pay or offered to settle for even money.

Young Fletcher, not having a great deal of clout so distant from his sponsor, took what he could and still returned to New York with more than $16,000 in winnings, bringing him a neat profit of $800. With the money he had left from Cincinnati he now found himself with more than a thousand dollars—a small fortune for 1869.

He got his money just in the nick of time. A few weeks later the stock market crashed. Morrissey lost $800,000 and was unable to continue hippodroming the Haymakers. It was sobering to think of one man losing all that money overnight. Fletch decided to give up gambling. He had enough money to take care of himself and his mother for more than a year. It was time to relax and think about an honest future.

Fletch not only took the whole winter off, he devoted almost all of the following spring and summer to baseball. When he wasn't practicing with the boys in the neighborhood, he was out at the Capitoline Grounds watching his former teammates in action. The Cincinnati Red

Stockings, who had extended their undefeated streak into the new season, came to Brooklyn on June 14, 1870, to meet the Atlantics. The Reds had just defeated the Mutuals, and the Atlantics had lost their last outing to the Forest City club from Rockford, Illinois. That didn't keep Fletcher and almost ten thousand other fans from going out to the ball park on a sweltering early summer afternoon. As Fletcher watched Brainard blank the Atlantics in the first inning, he couldn't help but wonder about his bribe. What had the pitcher done with the $500? There was no way to find out except to ask him point-blank. That, of course, was out of the question. As the game progressed, it became obvious that the Reds were not at their best. By the bottom of the fourth the Atlantics were ahead, 4–3, and at the end of nine innings the teams were deadlocked, 5–5.

"It must be my presence," Fletcher thought, laughing to himself, "I always bring the Red Stockings a tie." The game appeared to be over. The Atlantics, happy to have a draw, went into the clubhouse, and the crowd got up to leave. But the Reds were still on the field, and Harry Wright was in a heated argument with the umpire.

Fletcher could see that Cincinnati would not accept another tie without a fight. After some discussion the Atlantics were summoned back onto the diamond, and, to the great delight of the crowd, play was resumed. In the tenth the Reds pulled a trick that would be illegal under today's rules. The Atlantics had men on first and second when Smith, their third baseman, hit a pop-up to George Wright at short. Wright trapped the ball and flipped it to Waterman at third for the force; Waterman then threw to second for an inning-ending double play.

In the top of the eleventh things looked very gloomy as the Reds picked up two runs. But in the bottom half of the inning the Atlantics put on a terrific rally. They tied the score, and for a while their boisterous fans put a halt to the game. As soon as play resumed, Bob Ferguson, on first, advanced to second on an error by Gould, the Reds' first baseman. Gould ran down the ball and threw wild into left field trying to stop Ferguson, who then darted home, ending the game and bringing defeat at last to baseball's first great dynasty. At the close of the season the Cincinnati club was to disband. George and Harry Wright, along with Gould and McVey, would head for Boston to establish a new dynasty of Red Stockings.

Over that summer of 1870 Fletcher slowly discovered that gambling was still in his blood. Not far from the Capitoline Grounds was a betting room—a place where fans could buy into the pools for upcoming games. At first Fletcher went there to check the odds, to see how closely his own judgment followed the betting line. As the summer wore on, he started placing wagers himself. He soon discovered he knew more about the competing teams than those who were selling the pools. By the end of the season he had won enough money to stay afloat for another winter; slowly but inevitably, he was being sapped of every incentive to find a steady job.

As if that were not enough, he also took to drinking that summer. There was a saloon right on the Capitoline Grounds. Many of his fellow gamblers hung out there before and after the games, and it didn't take an idle man with money in his pockets long to join them. The beer and whisky made him light of heart and brought back to mind a night that was playing an important part in his fantasies. Whenever he had a few drinks under his belt he thought of that time with Kate. Someday he would go back to Albany.

Creeping professionalism was becoming a serious problem for baseball. It was no secret that the way to draw crowds was to win, and Cincinnati had shown that the way to build a winning team was to recruit the best available talent. But the most promising players were seldom gentlemen of leisure. If a man was to devote the better part of the year to hitting and throwing a baseball, he would have to be paid.

As more teams added salaried players to their rosters, baseball split into two camps—clubs still dedicated to amateurism, and those committed to a profit. As the 1871 season approached, it became clear that the differences between the two groups were irreconcilable.

On St. Patrick's Day representatives from ten pro clubs met in Collier's Saloon at Broadway and Thirteenth Street in Manhattan to form the first professional league. The organization was named the National Association of Professional Baseball Players, and a month later it began its first season. The only club from New York to join was the Mutuals, but in the middle of the 1871 season the Brooklyn Eckfords took the place of the Fort Wayne club, and in 1872 the Atlantics also entered the new league.

The summer of 1871 was a sad time for Fletcher. His talent for handicapping abandoned him; by the end of the season he was heavily in debt. Finally, in late September, his mother died. Cut away from its only mooring, his life was set adrift.

He groped through the following winter. When spring arrived he was in desperate straits. He was even willing to take back his old job with the Atlantics, and he wrote to Matt Danser to see if it was available. The reply was several weeks in coming. The gist of it was that times were changing, and the Atlantics no longer had a spot on their roster for a player like Fletcher. But if something else should come up, Danser would be in touch.

Alone, in debt, and out of work in 1872, Fletcher found himself hanging around Jim McCloud's place. Jim was a pool-seller who operated down the street from the Union Grounds, the field in Brooklyn where the Mutuals and Eckfords played their home games. Even though Fletch had no money to bet, his fascination with gambling, now stronger than ever, compelled him to keep up on the pools. He was certain he could cash in if only he could come up with a new stake.

On May 9 Fletcher's old friends from Cincinnati, now the Boston Red Stockings, came to Brooklyn for a game with the Eckfords. The Boston team was off to such a roaring start it was doubtful that even the 1871 champion Athletics could hold them back this year. From his seat in the stands Fletcher recognized McVey, Gould, and, of course, the Wright brothers.

Brainard was not with the team; Boston's ace pitcher was young Al Spalding, the best hurler in the game. To no one's surprise Boston demolished Brooklyn that day. The score was 20–0—a shutout, or, in the slang of the period, the Eckfords were "Chicagoed."

There was very little gambling that day. Even at 100 to 30 it was not easy to find a Brooklyn fan foolish enough to bet against the Red Stockings. So Fletcher skipped his usual postgame visit to the betting rooms and went instead to a nearby saloon. Finishing his first beer, he noticed a familiar face next to him at the bar. It belonged to Big Jim Clinton, the young, inexperienced manager of the Eckfords.

"Another whisky," Clinton said, beckoning to the bartender.

"I don't blame you for taking a drink after the drubbing your boys took this afternoon," piped up Fletcher, half trying to get Clinton's goat.

"What the hell do you do with a team that muffs every second chance in the field?" Big Jim asked, obviously happy to find a sympathetic ear.

"Find some new players, I guess."

"With what? We barely have enough money to take the team out of town. How the hell are we going to pay for new players? Besides, all the best men are already under contract." He paused, swigged his whisky, and finally took a long look at his listener. Suddenly his eyes lit up. "Say, don't I know you?" he asked.

"I don't know. Do you?" Fletcher replied.

"Sure, you're Fletcher the Bird. When I was a kid I used to watch you play down in South Brooklyn. You had great hands."

"I still do."

For the rest of the evening the two young men swapped baseball stories, lamented that the game had fallen upon such dark times, and got stinking drunk. Parting, Big Jim offered Fletch a job with the club. The Eckfords had to be the worst defensive team in baseball—ancestors of the gremlin-infested Dodgers of the 1920s and 1930s, not to mention the Mets of the early 1960s. Clinton's idea was to have either his shortstop or his third baseman fake an injury whenever the team was ahead in the late innings and put in Fletcher to help protect the lead. It was a tactic that one day would become part of every manager's defensive repertoire.

When Fletcher reported for practice he was more than a little worried that Big Jim would plead drunkenness and renege on the offer. But it turned out the manager was completely serious. The pay would be $20 a week, except when the Eckfords were out of town; the team couldn't afford to take any extra players on the road. It wasn't long before Fletch was back in shape, dazzling everyone with his lightning moves and steel-trap hands. He even took batting practice, proving he had spunk but confirming that hitting was not his forte.

Fletcher soon discovered why he had been lucky enough to land a job with the Eckfords. They were one of the most hapless aggregations ever to step onto a big league diamond. Through May, June, and July they lost every single league game and managed to drop a few exhibition contests as well, including an ignominious 13–5 loss to Yale. Unfortunately, the team was seldom ahead in the late innings, so Fletcher didn't get many chances to shore up the infield. But he was called upon to play the outfield in two games, and he surprised himself and everyone else by getting two hits in eight trips to the plate, for a lifetime average of .250.

As the season wore on it became clear the National Association was in bad shape. Three teams dropped out of the race—the Washington Olympics, the Middletown Mansfields, and the Troy Haymakers. After the stockholders of the Troy club met in late July to disband the team, the Eckfords picked up most of the Haymaker lineup, putting several of the original members of the Eckfords out of work.

Clinton was among those let go, but Jimmy Wood, the new manager, decided to keep Fletcher around, not for his playing abilities but because of his gambling contacts. Before the season was over one team or another was certain to hand the Eckfords a phony victory. Fletcher was told to keep his eyes and ears open; as soon as he had an inkling the fix might be on, he was to report back to Wood. A wager on the Eckfords could bring a handsome return. The owners appeared ready to go to any lengths to save the team from going under.

On August 19 the Atlantics came to the Union Grounds for a league game with the Eckfords. The betting line favored the Atlantics, but not by a wide margin. Fletcher wondered whether this might be the day. As the teams came on the field for pregame practice, he surveyed the grandstand to look for someone who could verify his hunch. Right behind first base he spotted just that someone—Matt Danser himself. Fletch ran over to say hello.

"Well, well," Danser said as Fletcher reached him, "my old friend Mr. Rice. I'm glad to see you back in uniform, though I must say you could have chosen a better outfit."

"Beggars can't be choosers."

"No, I guess not. How have you been?"

"Not too bad. Yourself?"

"Well, things have been slow for a while, but now they're picking up again."

"Are you saying there's an advantage to be gained this afternoon?"

"There's *always* an advantage to be gained. Even when the opening is well hidden. But you know that better than I."

"Well, yes. But what about today?"

"Today? Why don't you ask the gentleman standing behind you?"

Fletcher turned around to discover his former teammate Bob Ferguson, playing manager of the Atlantics and now president of the National Association, trying to listen in on the conversation.

"Oh, hello, Bob," Fletch said, breaking into a guilty smile.

"Rice, will you please come with me?" Ferguson ordered.

"All right. See you again, Matt," Fletcher said, turning to follow Ferguson, who was leading him over to Jimmy Wood.

"Jim, I've just found Rice here openly consorting with gamblers," Ferguson began as the two men came up to the Eckfords' manager. "I've always suspected he was involved in hippodroming, even back in '69, when he was hanging around our club."

"Aren't you jumping to conclusions?" Wood asked.

"Maybe, but we can't afford to give these gamblers the benefit of the doubt anymore. They're ruining the game. I want Rice off the field and out of uniform. Not just today, but for good."

"Say, wait a minute," Fletcher began, but then felt his protest trailing off. His goose was cooked to a crisp, and he knew it. The Eckfords would never fight the league president over a third-rater who had no business on the roster. Ferguson knew it too, which is why he decided to use Fletch as an example. In any case, he suddenly turned his back on Wood and Fletcher and stormed back over to Danser.

"Danser, all I can say is you are a dirty son of a bitch! Only an SOB would work as hard as you do to destroy this game," he screamed at the top of his lungs. Then, a few rows back, he spotted Jim McCloud. "McCloud, that goes for you too! Next time I see you selling pools I'm getting my bat and bashing your head in!"

Fletcher changed into his street clothes and joined the crowd in center field. For the time being he was too interested in the game to feel sorry for himself. It turned out to be one hell of a contest. The Eckfords squeaked out a 4–3 win in ten innings, their first league victory of the season. No one could claim the fix was on that afternoon; the Atlantics fought hard all the way, trying to avoid the disgrace of losing to their sorry fellow Brooklynites.

After the game Fletch got around to thinking about Ferguson's tirade. Bob had a point, no doubt about it. Games were being thrown all over the place, fans were losing interest, and attendance was terrible. But why get sore at little old Fletch? The Eckfords were a joke—they were *too bad* to hippodrome. But their fellow tenants at the Union Grounds, the Mutuals, weighed many games against the odds. If Bob really wanted to start picking bones, he should do it with them.

Later that afternoon Fletcher had a beer with Jim McCloud, who confided he was having a great year, mostly because of the Mutuals. The New York club was expert at playing either side of a fix, and the gamblers had won big on three games between the Mutuals and the league's defending champs, the Philadelphia Athletics. The really big payoff came on June 1, when, at odds of 100 to 40 against them, the Mutuals beat the A's, 3–2, at the Union Grounds. In July, down in Philadelphia, the Athletics lost again to the New Yorkers twice in one week, 5–0 and 11–6. By then the odds had tightened up, but it was difficult to get too excited about the betting line when you were wagering on a sure thing. "And there's more of this easy money to come," Jim explained. "You know, Fletch, I could use a man with your knowledge and experience. Now that you're available, why not come to work for me?"

"I'd be happy to," Fletcher replied. He didn't think twice. It looked as though gambling would be his life's work, and he'd served his apprenticeship well.

The relationship between Fletcher and Jim McCloud was a good one. Each man respected the other, and each worked hard to hold up his end of the bargain. Fletch quickly demonstrated a special talent for setting odds, auctioning the pools, and keeping the necessary records. Jim became the front man; he drummed up business, kept close to the gamblers' grapevine, and stayed out late drinking with the players. The business was more profitable than Fletcher could ever have imagined.

Fletcher worked with Jim for five years, and during that time he watched the slow, painful death of the National Association. The Eckfords dropped out of the league at the end of the 1872 season, but the Atlantics and Mutuals stayed around to watch Harry Wright's Red Stockings walk away with four straight pennants. The monotony of Boston's success contributed somewhat to the yearly decline in fan interest, but there were other, more profound reasons, such as gambling and drunkenness.

The clubs, unwilling or unable to clear the air, fell back on the only solution they knew—trying to perk up attendance by fielding better ball teams. They began to raid each other for star players. Encouraging members of other clubs to jump their contracts, known as "revolving," only added to the chaos. By the end of the 1875 season every team was on the verge of bankruptcy.

Into this dismal state of affairs came William A. Hulbert, the new president of the Chicago White Stockings. Hulbert, an ardent Midwest chauvinist, had two items on his agenda when he took control of the Chicago club—to build a winning team and to wrest control of baseball from the game's Eastern Establishment.

His first move made it clear he meant business. In June 1875 he traveled to Boston, where he offered contracts for 1876 to four of the champion Red Stockings stars—Al Spalding, their pitching ace, and Ross Barnes, Deacon White, and Cal McVey, three of the top four hitters in the league. All four agreed to jump to Chicago. Then Hulbert and Spalding went to Philadelphia, where they signed up Ezra Sutton and Cap Anson of the Athletics. With these great players on their roster, the White Stockings were almost certain to become the new champions.

Hulbert had, of course, violated the National Association's rule against tampering, but the league was too weak to do anything about it. The raided clubs had no choice but to take their lumps.

Firmly established as a man to be reckoned with, Hulbert was now ready to move toward his next objective—a new professional association. That fall, with the eager help of Spalding, Hulbert drafted a constitution for the proposed league. In January 1876 he and Spalding held a secret meeting in Louisville with representatives from the St. Louis, Cincinnati, and Louisville teams. Hulbert unveiled his new constitution and, appealing to the Midwestern pride of the others, invited them to join in forming the nucleus of a new association. His proposals quickly won approval, and he returned to Chicago armed with authority to negotiate with other clubs interested in breaking away from the old order.

Hulbert had set one goal above all others—solvency for his new league. The National Association contained more impoverished teams than wealthy ones; the weaker sisters, often unable to take their scheduled road trips, placed the burden of keeping the pennant race alive upon those clubs able and willing to travel. To avoid this problem Hulbert determined to keep the new association small and completely free of deadwood. He vowed if any club failed to play out its schedule it would, as prescribed by the rules, be expelled.

A four-member league was, however, too small. To get it off the ground Hulbert needed to recruit additional members. With this in mind he personally invited the presidents of the strongest Eastern clubs to meet with him in New York on February 2 at the Grand Central Hotel on Broadway, just ten blocks south of the spot where the National Association was founded five years earlier.

A nasty, snowy morning did not deter representatives from the Mutuals, Red Stockings, Athletics, and Hartfords from showing up at Hulbert's room to find out what he had in mind. As soon as his last guest arrived Hulbert locked the door behind him and quickly outlined his plan. Everyone agreed it was excellent.

So, almost without argument, the National League of Professional Baseball Clubs came into being. One could not have guessed it at the time, but the league would prove more durable than the building where it was born. Ninety-seven years after that wintry day, on August 3, 1973, the old place, later named the University Hotel, collapsed without warning. More than one hundred fifty persons were left homeless. A plaque commemorating the birthplace of major league baseball disappeared in the rubble.

One of Hulbert's professed reasons for founding the National League was to rid baseball of gambling. Indeed, his new constitution expressly forbade all forms of betting on club grounds. But when he sent out his invitations to the February meeting, Hulbert was careful to include Bill Cammeyer of the Mutuals. The New Yorkers were the most notorious hippodromers in the National Association, and Hulbert had no reason to believe they would mend their ways as part of the new league. If fixing continued, the New York club would be in on it. But the Mutuals, despite their unsavory reputation, did have a loyal following, and it was unthinkable that the new league would begin without an entry from New York. So the Mutuals, complete with crooked players, took part in the National League's inaugural season. To improve the team's image, Cammeyer outfitted his players in bright new uniforms with red stockings and changed its name to the *Brooklyn* Mutuals. As the season wore on it became obvious these cosmetics would fool no one.

As expected, the Chicago White Stockings walked away with the first National League pennant in 1876, winning by six games. Also as expected, the summer was marred by several suspicious contests, most of them involving the Mutuals and the Athletics.

It was another profitable season for Fletch and Jim; the pickings were especially easy because McCloud had two of the Mutuals—Al Nichols and Bill Craver—in his hip pocket. But attendance at the Union Grounds continued to decline. When the time came for the Mutuals' final western swing, the club found itself in deep financial trouble. Cammeyer, figuring the new league would be just as lax in enforcing rules as the National Association had been, decided to cancel the road trip.

The Athletics, in even worse shape, also reneged on their last scheduled visit to the Midwest. Hulbert was furious. That December, at the league's first annual meeting, both clubs were expelled. The convenient reason for removing the errant clubs was their failure to play out the schedule; it was no accident, however, that the action ridded the league of its two problem children. So New York, the best baseball town in the country, was suddenly without a National League team.

As the 1877 season approached, Fletcher slipped into a deep depression. Not only were the Mutuals gone, but the police had decided to crack down on gambling. They closed the betting rooms in New York, forcing the gamblers to move their operations to New Jersey. Overnight, Hoboken became the gambling capital of the East. Jim and Fletch moved into a second-floor loft above a saloon near the waterfront. The neighborhood was dismal, and so was their new place of business. The ceiling was black with soot, and the glow from the hissing gas lamps revealed cracked and peeling walls. Fletcher had come down a long way from the lush carpets and crystal chandeliers of Old Smoke's Club House.

Fletcher had returned to the town of his birth, and not in a manner that would have made his father proud. He was making great money, but it brought very little comfort. All he could see on the horizon was a tawdry existence on the fringe of society. His dismal prospects sent him back to the bottle more often than before.

Jim McCloud, sensing his partner's despair, tried to cheer Fletcher up. Bill Cammeyer had persuaded the Hartford club to play its 1877 home games on the Union Grounds, so Brooklyn would have a team after all. And Hoboken could have been worse. There was plenty of betting action, especially now that they'd branched out into the horses.

But Fletch found it difficult to get worked up over the Hartford Brooklyns (or were they the Brooklyn Hartfords?), even though they were a respectable team. His drinking began to affect his work—so much so that by July Jim wanted Fletcher out of his hair.

One day Fletch was sipping a whisky at his desk in the barren little back room that served as the office. McCloud slammed shut the account book he'd been inspecting and stared over at his partner. "Fletch, old boy," Jim began, "I think what you need is a vacation. Why don't you spend the rest of the month up in Saratoga?"

Fletcher perked up at Jim's suggestion. Saratoga! How long had it been? Eight years. He had been a punk then. At least now he had money in his pockets—enough to look people like Old Smoke straight in the eye. Hell, yes, he would go to Saratoga!

He outfitted himself with an entire new wardrobe, complete with evening dress, and just before his journey he visited Jim McCloud's barber in Earle's Hotel on Canal Street in New York, where he had the works—hair wash and trim, manicure, and shave. Stepping out into the July sunshine, Fletch felt ready to hobnob with anyone, even those swells up in Saratoga.

The Grand Union Hotel in Saratoga Springs was the most impressive building Fletcher had ever seen. He checked in early on Saturday morning, July 21, and immediately went for breakfast in the main dining room, a massive hall that could accommodate more than a thousand persons at a single sitting. After filling his stomach he took a long stroll around the hotel's grounds, observing with great care the dress and appearance of the other guests. Shortly before noon he left for the race course.

It was the first day of the meeting, and he was anxious to bet on a horse running in the Travers whose potential was not reflected in the odds. At the track Fletcher found a pool-seller doing a very brisk business, and he had no trouble placing a $100 bet. His horse was Baden

Baden, winner of two previous stake races, including something called the Kentucky Derby.

Baden Baden won all right, and when the day's races were over Fletch was $700 ahead. He returned to the Grand Union, changed, took a leisurely dinner, and then decided to test his luck at faro over at the Club House. It wasn't only the lure of the tables that took him to the casino. He still remembered how insignificant he had felt on that day long ago when Mr. Morrissey had summoned him to Saratoga. Now he was back, he had a bankroll, and he was no longer a kid. He hoped he would run into Morrissey that night and that Old Smoke would recognize how far his protégé had come.

Fletcher entered the Club House around nine o'clock, purchased $1,000 in chips, and took the one remaining seat at a faro table that was attracting a lot of attention.

In faro the dealer lays down two cards in each turn. Suits have no meaning; the rank of the first card down loses, the rank of the second wins. To bet on a card to win you place your chips on the proper rank on the betting layout. If you think a card will lose you "copper" your wager by placing a penny on top of your bet. Fletcher was fumbling with his chips, trying to make up his mind, when the dealer, giving him the fish eye, said politely, "Sir, you must have a bet up to sit at this table." As he coppered $100 on the six Fletcher took a good look at this guy who was giving him the lip. The dealer was none other than Hamilton Baker. The two men recognized each other at the same instant, but neither uttered a sound. The first card down was a six.

When Fletch got up from the table he was richer by $700 more. He went into the same private room where he had waited for his interview with Morrissey, sat down to a glass of brandy, and lit up a cigar. It wasn't long before Baker appeared at the door. "Well, if it isn't the Bird," he said. "It's good to see you again. How long do you plan to be here at the Spa?"

And so an old friendship was renewed. Baker joined Fletch for a drink, and the two men laughed about the raucous night they'd spent together in Albany. As he thought back on it, Fletcher was reminded that it had been quite a while since he'd had his ashes hauled. Baker said this was no problem. In fact old Kate, Fletch's girl that evening, now had a house of her own down in Troy. They could go there sometime during the next week.

Fletcher thought that was a terrific idea. He'd had dozens of lustful thoughts about Kate over the past eight years, and he was eager to see if the real thing would measure up to his fantasies. Later in the conversation he asked Hamilton what had happened to Morrissey. "I'm afraid the Irishman isn't well these days," Baker replied. "But, you know, I bet he'd be happy to see you again. Why don't we visit him tomorrow?"

31

The next afternoon they met on the front porch of the Adelphi Hotel, where Morrissey was staying. Upstairs they were ushered in by Old Smoke's wife, who made them promise not to stay too long. The old man was lying on the parlor sofa, propped up on cushions and wrapped in a woollen shawl. He was so fat his fleshy cheeks and drooping jowls completely disguised the handsome face Fletcher remembered.

"Well, Rice, good to see you again," Old Smoke rasped. "It looks like things are going well for you." His barely audible voice was punctuated by gasps from the asthma that was choking off his life.

"Why yes, I hope so, sir." Fletcher replied.

"I ran into Fletcher here at my faro table," Baker remarked.

"Did you win?" Morrissey asked.

"Yes I did."

"Good. People are always saying my tables are crooked. Baker here will tell you that's a lie. My decks are honest and I have nothing but straight men on my payroll. Isn't that right, Baker?"

"Right. And that's why we're here. We need a new faro dealer, and I think Rice would be perfect for the job," Baker said, much to Fletcher's amazement.

"Well, then, by all means hire him," Morrissey answered slowly. He was a very tired, very sick man. The conversation drifted on for five or ten minutes more, and then the two visitors took their leave.

"Did you really mean that about a job?" Fletcher asked as soon as they reached the street.

"Sure. Do you know what I make here? Forty-five hundred dollars a month plus fifteen percent of the take. There's plenty of money to be made for someone I can trust. How about it?"

"Let me think it over for a few days."

On Tuesday night they visited Kate's down in Troy. At first she didn't remember Fletch, and she suggested he'd be much happier with one of the younger girls, rather than with the madam herself.

But the Bird was persistent. Finally Kate invited him to her room where, just as before, he wound up staying the night. Happily, she *was* as good as he'd remembered. Baker returned to Saratoga the next morning, but Fletch hung around the whorehouse till the end of the week, staying pleasantly drunk and keeping his stoker as clean as a whistle.

His only concern was whether or not to take Baker up on his offer. By the time he got back to the Grand Union he was ready to give it a try. If the job didn't show much promise after a month or two, he could always return to Hoboken. So he wrote McCloud to say he was having such a wonderful time that he might not be back till September.

August was a delightful month. Fletcher went down to see Kate at least once a week, and he dealt faro every second night. The dexterity that made him a good shortstop stood him in good stead. He was soon as proficient as all but the very best dealers in the Club House. Life was fun again for the first time in a very long while. He began to look down on pool-selling, which, after all, was a mighty crooked business. The cards he dealt had no stake in the game. That was a lot more than you could say for baseball players.

Fletcher did not, however, lose track of baseball. The newspapers filled him in on the National League race, which was boiling down to a three-way contest among Louisville, Boston, and Hartford. By the middle of August the Louisvilles had jumped to a comfortable lead, and the so-called smart money was riding on them.

Then something very peculiar happened. On August 17 Louisville arrived in Boston for the start of the team's last eastern road trip, which included four games each with the Red Stockings and the Hartfords. Louisville lost one game in Boston and then went to Brooklyn, where it suffered two more losses and a tie. Fletcher, examining the box scores, noticed that Al Nichols had joined the Louisville club and was filling in for Bill Hague at third. Bill Craver had been the regular second baseman all season, so Louisville's team now had two old Mutuals protecting half the infield. And these were not just any old Mutuals—they were the very men Jim McCloud claimed to have in his hip pocket.

When Louisville lost its next four games and dropped below Boston into second place, Fletcher was certain the fix was on and that his partner was behind it. During the first week of September he sent McCloud this wire:

> CAN YOU EXPLAIN KENTUCKY DISASTER?
> FLETCH

Jim's reply read as follows:

> KENTUCKY DISASTER OPENED RICH HOBOKEN
> LODE. COMING HOME SOON? SASH

"Sash" was McCloud's code word meaning a game was definitely fixed. Fletcher didn't guess it at the time, but Craver and Nichols were not the only players throwing those games. Two other members of the Louisville squad—Jim Devlin and George Hall—were also involved. The full story, destined to shock the entire country, would not come out until that November. All four players would be banned from the game for life, and public confidence in professional ball would sink to a new low.

Fletcher was sitting right on top of baseball's biggest scandal of the century, and he didn't even know it. He did know he'd had enough of McCloud and the rest of the Hoboken crowd. He thought for a few days and then wired back the following answer:

> STAYING HERE. HAVE FUN SASHING
> BY YOURSELF. FARO

33

It wasn't long before the Saratoga season came to a close. The swells went home, the tables in the Club House were covered, and the gambling paraphernalia was put under lock and key for another year.

Baker left to spend the winter in Nevada, in the Comstock Lode country where he won his first fortune and made his name as a sharp man with a faro deck. Fletcher found himself facing a long, cold winter in upstate New York. For some that would have been a dismal prospect, but he looked upon his exile from the city as an opportunity to take a hard look at himself. Perhaps he would discover why, at the ripe age of thirty-one, he still wasn't ready to take on a family and an honest job. He would also have to come to terms with the peculiar fact that he'd fallen in love with a whore. Soon after he said goodby to Hamilton Baker, Fletch moved down to Troy to spend the winter with Kate. They lived together in her private apartment on the top floor of the brothel. He arranged his comings and goings to avoid the hours of peak traffic downstairs.

The winter was peaceful and comfortable, and Fletcher savored it to the last before spring finally won out. One sunny morning in April Kate suddenly dashed upstairs, took the last burned-out logs from the fireplace, pulled back the curtains, and threw open the windows. Later that day Fletcher read in the papers that Morrissey was already back in Saratoga. Soon Hamilton would be there too. It promised to be a happy summer. But on Wednesday, the first of May, something happened that dampened Fletcher's spirits. Old Smoke finally died.

Kate came to Fletcher with the news. After she told him she broke into tears. "He was a great man, Mr. Morrissey," she said. "He was one of us, born right here, and he fought his way up from the streets. I met him once. He was a real somebody."

That Friday night Old Smoke's body was brought to a house on River Street in Troy, where it was viewed by more than five thousand mourners. Kate and Fletcher were among those who filed by to pay their last respects.

Just before the opening of the season Fletcher went up to Saratoga to see whether he still had a job. He arrived at the Club House half expecting to find the place boarded up or draped in black bunting. Instead the doors were wide open, and maids, carpenters, and painters were hard at work putting everything in shape for the summer. A workman informed him the place had been taken over by two men—Mr. Charles Read and Mr. Albert Spencer. Fletch didn't know Spencer, but he'd heard of Charlie Read before. Down in New Orleans, during the Civil War, he had been the proprietor of a rather notorious gambling place. After wandering all through the Club House, Fletch found Spencer in one of the private card rooms on the second floor and walked in to introduce himself. "Oh yes, Rice," Spencer said standing to shake hands. "I'm glad you're here. Have you had any word from Hamilton Baker?"

"No, I haven't," Fletch replied.

"That's strange. He should be here by now. Do you know where he spent the winter?"

"In Nevada, I believe."

"*Nevada?* Well, he's probably having some trouble making connections. I'm sure he'll be here in a few days."

"I'm sure he will too. . . . Oh, Mr. Spencer?"

"Yes, Rice?"

"Will you be wanting me to deal faro this year?"

"Why, of course. You're one of our top men."

A month went by. Baker finally showed up, full of tales about the bawdy West. The season was still young and the action at the Club House was light, so Hamilton figured he hadn't lost much—until Spencer informed him he would no longer get his percentage. His salary would remain the same, but his cut of the take was out. The new owners had an unhappy faro dealer on their hands, but they figured correctly that he would stick around. The money was still too good to pass up. Hell, Rice was happy making a third of Baker's salary.

Fletcher's thoughts turned to baseball, but he found it difficult to muster much interest. The Hartfords had dropped out of the National League, again leaving New York without a professional team. Despite his self-imposed exile, Fletch was still a New Yorker at heart, and he deeply resented the league's rejection of his home town.

Even though baseball in New York was in a sad state, Fletch did not fall out of love with the game. Indeed, with the coming of spring he had thoughts about getting out on the field again himself. The Troy Haymakers were back in business, and, even though the team had lost its national reputation, it was said to be a pretty fair club.

One morning he went over to the Phoenix Hotel in Lansingburgh, the team's headquarters, to see whether the Haymakers would let an old Eckford work out with them. It didn't take long to make friends with the players and to wangle an invitation to take part in their practice sessions. He spent the summer shuttling back and forth between Saratoga and Troy; when he wasn't dealing faro at the Spa, he was either in bed with Kate or out on the diamond trying to relive the past.

The following winter, in an earnest effort to recapture its lost greatness, the Troy baseball club enlarged its grandstand, resodded the infield, built a new clubhouse, and began recruiting topflight players. These moves were designed to qualify the club for admission to the National League, and they succeeded. The league's 1879 season began with teams in four new cities—Buffalo, Cleveland, Syracuse, and Troy. Suddenly Fletcher found himself back in a big league town.

The new Haymakers, now called the Troy City Club to play down the team's long association with the small town of Lansingburgh, had plenty of spirit, but they were no match for the established clubs in the league. Still, Fletcher rooted for them with all the fervor he could muster, and he pressed himself to the limit during practice. This won him the admiration of the players, and many of them became his friends.

The new summer was turning out even better than the last, making Fletch wonder if he'd ever be ready to go back to the big city. He felt bad that the Haymakers were losing, but they were a new team in a tough league. It would take a few years before they'd be ready to make a serious bid for the pennant.

Unfortunately, the owners didn't share his patience. One morning Fletcher reported to practice to find that Hustling Horace Phillips, the manager, was gone. Fletch came trotting onto the field with his customary enthusiasm and was startled as hell by the sight of the last man he ever wanted to see in Troy. The new manager, unaware of Fletch's arrangement with the club, was just as surprised. It took a few minutes before Bob Ferguson knew what to say. "Rice," he finally began, "I thought I was rid of you years ago. Get off this field right now, and please do me the very big favor of not coming back." Speechless, Fletcher turned around and headed slowly for home. Ferguson's nickname was "Death to Flying Things." Well, he certainly had killed the Bird.

Fletcher followed the Haymakers closely for the rest of the season, despite his feelings toward their manager. His rooting did not prevent them from finishing seventh in a pennant race won by the Providence Grays. The next year, 1880, aided by first-class pitching from Tim Keefe and Mickey Welch, the Haymakers moved up to fourth. They were beginning to show promise; Fletch was heartened, but in September his attention was diverted by some very interesting news from New York.

A new independent professional team, the Metropolitans, had suddenly appeared, playing many of their games in Manhattan in a ball park at One Hundred Tenth Street and Fifth Avenue called the Polo Grounds. Large crowds, including curious players from National League teams, were coming out to the games, proving that baseball interest was alive and well in the big city. Fletcher was especially glad to see that the team was playing good baseball.

During their short autumn season they appeared in twenty-four games, winning sixteen, losing only seven, and tying one. This record included a six-game series with the Haymakers, which was split at three games apiece. The following season, 1881, while the Haymakers dropped to fifth, the Mets played a full schedule of 151 games against college, outside professional, and National League teams. Their overall record was eighty-one victories, sixty-eight defeats, and two ties—not bad at all for a newly organized ball club. Their only weakness was in sixty games against National League competition; of these they won eighteen and lost forty-two. Still, the Mets in little more than a year had gained the reputation as the best club in the country outside the league.

Clearly, the return of professional baseball to New York was an idea whose time had come. But the arrival of the Mets was not the result of careful planning; it happened quite by accident when two very different men—John B. Day and James J. Mutrie—happened to sit next to each other at an amateur game in Prospect Park. Day was a wealthy business-man from Manhattan. Mutrie was a newcomer to New York, a young man from Boston who once played for the New Bedford team and then went on to manage the Brockton club to the 1879 championship of the Massachusetts Association.

Mutrie was trying to prove himself as a pitcher in Brooklyn. He had just been knocked out of the box, which is why he happened to be in the grandstand and not on the field. The two struck up a conversation, and Mutrie, never suspecting he was speaking to a possible benefactor, out-lined his wild scheme to start and manage his own ball club. He was convinced it could be done; he would make up for his lack of money with gumption and hard work.

Day was taken with Mutrie and impressed by his enthusiasm—so much so that he offered to back the plan. They formed the Metropolitan Exhibition Company, and Mutrie set out to recruit a team. He soon lined up a number of promising players, and the Mets opened for busi-ness in Brooklyn, playing most of their early games at the Union Grounds, which was by then slated for demolition. The team needed a new home.

One morning Day's bootblack told him about the Polo Grounds. The idea of bringing baseball to Manhattan made great sense; late in Sep-tember 1880 the Mets opened in their new park and were an instant success.

In the spring of 1882 a new major league, the American Association, came into being. The top clubs in the National League had proved that baseball could be not only profitable but also a valuable source of civic pride. Several cities, locked out by Boss Hulbert's "closed door" policy, were eager to field first-rate teams of their own. The obvious answer was a second league.

The new circuit offered three amenities forbidden by the National League—Sunday baseball, alcoholic beverages, and twenty-five-cent ad-missions. The owners most instrumental in bringing booze back to base-ball were Chris Von der Ahe of the St. Louis Browns, a saloonkeeper, and Harry Von der Horst of the Baltimore Orioles, a brewer. Fans and the press had long been critical of the National League's required fifty-cent admission price, so the American Association decided to exploit this weakness by cutting its price in half. Another exploitable weakness was the league's continued boycott of Philadelphia and New York, two cities that could give the fledgling circuit enormous prestige. The Association managed to bring in Philadelphia for its inaugural season and tried very hard to get the Metropolitans to represent New York. But for the time being John Day was content to keep his options open.

As the 1882 National League season progressed, Fletcher became aware of two inescapable facts. He knew that, no matter how tight the race would get, Chicago, under the inspired leadership of Cap Anson, was destined to win its third pennant in a row. He could also see that the Haymakers, who were playing mediocre ball before very small crowds, were not long for the majors. Fletch no longer hated the White Stockings, partly because Hulbert had died earlier that year but also because there was no way to get around the fact that Anson—the team's manager and star first baseman and the league's 1881 batting king—was probably the greatest player he'd ever seen. Anson was more than a superstar. He was a genuine folk hero—a man whose legend spread far beyond Chicago to all corners of the country. Fletch attended every game the White Stockings played in Troy from 1880 through 1882.

Fletcher's premonition that the Haymakers were heading for a fall brought him around to thinking about his own situation, which, on the surface at least, appeared just as rosy as when he began his life upstate five years before. But those years were all blending into one another, leaving him with the feeling that nothing new was happening anymore.

He was bored, and his thoughts were turning toward the city. If for no other reason than to get away from Kate for a while, he would take a trip to New York as soon as the Saratoga season came to a close. Kate had turned thirty that July, and now, fully believing she'd given Fletcher the five choicest years of her life, she was hinting strongly that it would be nice to get married. He couldn't conceive of such a thing. How could she think for a minute he would marry a common whore? Unfortunately, Fletch had fallen out of touch with himself. He had no idea how much he loved her.

On a particularly sultry afternoon in July, Fletcher was perspiring his way through a day off when one of Kate's girls came up to the apartment to tell him he had two visitors. The callers turned out to be Hamilton Baker and Barney Devlin, a short, red-nosed friend of Baker's from New York.

"What the hell brings you down here on a hot day like today?" Fletch asked as Hamilton and his companion, their shirts glued to their chests by sweat, came in and sat down.

"An important proposition," Baker replied.

"What do you mean?"

"Fletcher, what do you know about Read and Spencer?" Baker asked.

"Not much, only that they're cheapskates. Read once ran a gambling club down in New Orleans."

"Did you know he was a convicted murderer who got a phony pardon a few days before he was sentenced to hang?"

"No, but so what?"

"Well, I just want you to be aware you're working for a no-account son of a bitch who spends every Sunday in church to hide his true colors. If something unfortunate should happen to him, he'd only deserve it."

"Who says something unfortunate is going to happen to him?"

"We do," Devlin piped in.

"Look, Fletch," Baker went on, "we have a little plan. Our idea is to help ourselves to some of the Club House's riches."

"How the hell do you propose to do that?" Fletch asked, his heart starting to flutter.

"We're going to deal Barney a few winning hands. When it comes time to call the turn, our friend here is going to have quite a winning streak."

"Calling the turn" is the final phase of faro. When the deck is down to the last three cards, the players are invited to guess the exact order in which these cards will fall. A correct bet pays four to one. Baker's plan was to shuffle three specific cards to the back of the deck, signal Devlin they were in place before starting the deal, and have Barney make $100 bets until the "turn," at which point he would raise his wager to $2,500. Five hits would wipe out the house's $50,000 reserve for extraordinary losses. By moving quickly back and forth from Hamilton's table to Fletcher's table, Devlin could make the kill in less than an hour. With luck the house wouldn't smell a rat until they were all out of town.

The proposition scared the hell out of Fletch. Had he not been quite so bored, he probably wouldn't have gone along. But now he was thinking about getting back to New York, a town where a man was nothing without money in his pockets. So a few days later Hamilton began teaching Fletch how to trick shuffle. By early August they were ready to make their move.

They picked August 12 as the night for the job. It was the biggest Saturday of the racing season—a very busy evening at the Club House. Fletcher felt as though everyone in the casino could read his thoughts as he took his station and began to deal. More than an hour passed before his nerves were suddenly shaken by a loud outburst of applause from the opposite side of the room. Barney had made the first kill, and the spectators around the table were giving him a hand.

A few seconds later Fletch watched Devlin make his way through the crowd and take a seat across from him. As he shuffled, Fletcher tapped out his signals in this sequence: middle card, low card, high card. He finished making the deck, placed it in the dealing box, and started the game. Barney played according to plan, making $100 bets and breaking even. Finally they got down to the last three cards.

"It's a cat-hop—a three, another three, and a queen," announced the case keeper, whose job it is to keep track of the cards as they are played by moving beads on an abacus-like counting board. Something had gone wrong. Fletch thought he had put a two of spades in the middle position, not a three. A "cat-hop"—a pair among the last three cards—reduces the odds on the "turn" to two to one. Barney correctly inferred that the queen was the last card, but his confidence in his confederate was so shaken that he bet only $500. When the hand was over Devlin went back across the casino to the greener pastures of Baker's table.

Fletcher continued to deal. His motion became quite erratic, but no one at the table seemed to notice. He waited nervously for Barney to return. More than an hour went by without a sign of his accomplice. Then there was another burst of applause from the other side of the casino; ten minutes later came a second outbreak, and ten minutes after that a third. Fletch realized that his partners were going ahead without him. He was hurt that a single slip-up had shaken their confidence. But, more than that, he was worried what might happen if Read and Spencer figured out what was going on. And from the noises across the room, it was hard to see how they could fail to notice they were being cheated blind.

The long evening finally came to an end. Fletch nervously closed down his table and began looking for Hamilton. His friend was not in the Club House, so Fletch hurried over to Baker's room, where they had planned to meet if it became necessary to split up. The place was empty. It didn't look as if Hamilton had been there since before going to work. Something was wrong, but what? Had Devlin and Baker taken off with the loot? That was possible, but Fletcher found it hard to believe of Baker. There was nothing to do but lie down and wait.

It was ten the next morning before Fletcher, waking from a fitful sleep, was fully convinced neither Baker nor Devlin would be returning. It was his Sunday off, so he headed down to Troy. He arrived at the whorehouse late in the afternoon. As he opened the door, Kate rushed over and beckoned him to follow her upstairs. "I was worried about you," she said as they reached the door to her apartment. "Where in God's name have you been?"

"Waiting for Hamilton."

"Well, you should have waited here. Come inside, but let me warn you now you won't like what you're going to see."

She opened the door. Inside Fletcher heard a low, agonizing groan. He ran into the bedroom to find Hamilton half-naked on the bed, being attended by a physician. Baker's face had been reduced to a lump of open flesh, and there were large welts on his arms and chest. The doctor was wrapping his hands in bandages.

"Jesus, what happened?" Fletch asked, his eyes filling with tears.

"He was given a first-class beating, that's what's happened," the doctor replied. Baker gave a nod in Fletcher's direction, but it was obvious he was in too much pain to talk just then.

"Will he be all right?"

"I don't know about these hands," the doctor replied. "They're in very bad condition—there isn't a finger left in one piece."

"Those dirty bastards!" Fletcher said backing away. He went downstairs to the bar for a stiff drink.

By the end of the week Hamilton was strong enough to tell his story. It seems Barney returned to Baker's table after Fletcher's blunder and wouldn't move. Hamilton, expecting his confederate to leave again after winning the first hand, held back on any further signs for fear the case keeper, or someone else around the table, might figure out what was going on. But when an hour went by and Barney still wouldn't budge, Baker, anxious not to throw away the opportunity, signaled the winning combination three rounds in a row. Even then the casino wasn't aware of what had happened.

Devlin, his brow covered with nervous perspiration, had presented every last one of his $52,000 worth of chips to the cashier. He was led back into the office, where Spencer himself opened the safe and gave him the money. As soon as Barney had stuffed all the cash in his pockets, he leaped out the door like a frightened rabbit. It was only then that Spencer summoned his partner, who was home in bed.

It didn't take Read long to figure out what had taken place. He called Baker into the office and listened to the expected denials. He then introduced Hamilton to three roughs, who escorted him into a carriage and drove him down to the north side of Albany. There, by the side of the railroad tracks, they pummeled his hands, chest, and head with rocks and then left him bleeding in a ditch. Over the next several hours, he somehow managed to make it to Kate's. The money? They could safely assume Barney had helped himself to it all.

The season was almost over, but Fletch wanted nothing further to do with Read or Spencer, even though he was sure they didn't suspect him of taking part in the scheme. He went up to Saratoga one more time to pick up his pay and gather his belongings, and he returned to Troy the same day. Hamilton stayed in Kate's apartment growing stronger by the day, but it was clear the damage done by what he referred to as his "railroad accident" would never completely mend. His hands were so badly mangled he could barely write his name, let alone deal faro.

One day in mid-September Fletcher came back from a walk to find Hamilton packing his belongings. "What's going on?" Fletch asked.

"I'm getting ready to leave."

"So soon?"

"Yeah, it's time to move on."

"Where are you going?"

"New York first. Then back to Nevada."

"You mind if I join you as far as New York?"

41

"Not at all. Glad to have you along."

The decision was made. That evening, as soon as the nightly callers began to keep Kate occupied, the two men went down the back stairs and out the kitchen door. Fletch left behind a silly farewell note and just like that walked out on the woman who'd given him the choicest years of her life.

The rivalry between New York and
Brooklyn as regards baseball is unparal-
leled in the history of the national game.

New York Times, October 18, 1889

2

Hamilton Baker was no stranger to New York. He had spent many a
winter dealing faro in Old Smoke's club in Manhattan and had made
quite a few friends in the sporting world. Now he was hoping one of his
connections might help Fletcher find a job. A good place to look was
the Old Home Plate, a restaurant on Twenty-seventh Street, just three
blocks up Fifth Avenue from Morrissey's old casino. It was a hangout
for theater people, sports celebrities, and your better class of gambler. A
few days after Hamilton and Fletch arrived in New York they dropped
by to see whether any of Baker's acquaintances were around. As they
came through the door, they were greeted by Nick Engel, the owner.

"Bake! Good to see you," Engel began, offering his hand. "Jesus, are
you banged up. What the hell happened?"

"Believe it or not, I fell off a train," Hamilton replied. "I'd like you
to meet Fletcher Rice. He played for the old Eckfords."

"An old Eckford, huh? Those were the good old days. What brings
you to town, Bake? Are you still up at the Club House, now that Old
Smoke's gone?"

"We just quit. I'm heading back West, to God's country. Fletcher
here is looking for a job. Do you know anyone who could use a good
faro dealer?"

"Faro? Doesn't that have something to do with gambling? Don't you
know gambling is illegal in New York?" Engel broke into laughter over
his own joke. "Do you know Charlie Byrne over there?" he asked, pointing to a table where two gentlemen were sitting.

"I don't think so. Which one is he?" Hamilton asked.

"The ordinary-looking one. The fellow with the wild moustache wearing white tie is Jim Mutrie, the manager of the Metropolitans. Byrne runs a gaming house down on Ann Street. I'm sure he's always on the lookout for experienced dealers. Come on, I'll introduce you." They walked over to the table. "Excuse me, Charlie," Engel began, "I'd like you to meet two friends of mine from Saratoga, Hamilton Baker and Fletcher Rice. They've just finished dealing faro at the Club House, and Rice here is looking for work."

"You men are from Saratoga?" Mutrie interrupted, rising from his seat. "Do you know anything about the Haymakers?"

"Quite a bit. I went to watch them play every chance I could get," Fletcher replied.

"Rice here played with the old Eckfords," Engel remarked, trying to make an opening in the conversation for Byrne.

"Is that right?" Mutrie went on. "Then you must know your baseball."

"I hope so," Fletch said.

"What do you think of the Troy club? They didn't make a very good showing this year, did they?" Mutrie asked.

"No, but they have some first-rate players. They'll do better next year— if they're still in the league," Fletch replied.

"What do you think of Keefe? Is he as good as they say he is? His record leaves something to be desired," Mutrie continued.

"Tim Keefe would be one of the best in the game, if he had some batting behind him. That goes for Mickey Welch, too."

"Is that right? Who else's abilities do you respect?" Mutrie asked.

"Well, Buck Ewing is a fine third baseman, and he's an excellent catcher as well. I'd put him right up there with the best of them."

"You don't say. So you believe there's quite a bit of talent on the Troy roster," concluded Mutrie.

"Perhaps, Jim, you'd like to engage Rice here to help you manage the Metropolitans," Engel interjected with every bit of sarcasm he could muster.

"You never can tell. Listen, why don't you and your friend join us, Mr. Rice?" Mutrie asked, pulling out the two empty chairs at the table. He then turned to Byrne and said, "Well, Charlie, I'll give you first crack at this old Eckford. Can you use a good faro dealer?"

"Possibly. Nice to meet you gentlemen. I'm Charles Byrne," he said extending his arm to shake hands with Fletcher and Hamilton. "How long have you been dealing faro, Mr. Rice?"

"Five years, Mr. Byrne. I like to think I'm one of the best."

"Well, then, come by my club tomorrow and we'll give you a try."

Fletch and Hamilton stayed at the table for the better part of an hour. They had a good conversation, but at times it was hard for anyone but Mutrie to get a word in edgewise. His enthusiasm had no limits, so there was nothing to do but ride along with it. The talk centered on baseball and the turf, with Mutrie invariably bringing the topic back to the Haymakers. They finally came to a lull in the conversation, and Byrne took the opportunity to ask the newcomers if they would mind very much letting him and Jim finish up the private business they'd come there to discuss. Fletch left the Old Home Plate happy. He had found a job and had made friends with the manager of the Mets. Hamilton was also pleased: With Fletcher's future settled, he was free to move on. Early the next morning he set out on the first leg of his long journey to the West.

Less than a week after Fletcher's visit to Nick Engel's restaurant, the National League held a special meeting in Philadelphia. The main item on the agenda was the expulsion of the Worcester and Troy clubs for "want of success, both financially and in the contest for the championship." The American Association, playing in larger cities to better crowds, had emerged in its inaugural season as a legitimate major league and a very satisfactory alternative to the Senior Circuit. With the prospect of a war for players, and with its prestige clearly on the line, the National League felt compelled to get rid of deadwood. The Haymakers didn't stand a chance.

All summer long Fletch had heard rumors that the Metropolitans would join the National League that December. But now the American Association appeared to be a better bet, and fans began to speculate that Day and Mutrie would enter their team in the new league instead. One rumor led to another, and it wasn't long before there was talk that the Metropolitan Exhibition Company was about to form another pro team in Brooklyn. If that were true, Mutrie would need plenty of new ballplayers, which might explain Jim's unusual interest in the Haymakers. Rather than dwell on all these questions, Fletch turned his attention to the closing weeks of the season. For the Mets it was another successful year. They played 162 games, winning 101, losing 57, and tying only 4. Chicago did indeed win the National League pennant, edging out Providence by three games. And the Haymakers said goodby forever to the big leagues, playing their final league game against Worcester before a crowd of twenty-five diehards.

Fletcher was happy to be in New York. He missed Kate—so much that once or twice he almost wrote to ask her to join him—but he thoroughly enjoyed city life. His job at the Ann Street casino was working out well; he and Charlie Byrne got along fine, the hours were good, and the pay, while not as high as at the Club House, was more than adequate. As the new year drew closer, he felt like a man with a lot to look forward to.

Not long after Fletch started his new job, stories about a new Brooklyn baseball club began appearing in the papers, and the man most often mentioned as the head of the venture was none other than Charles

H. Byrne. Fletch was tempted to ask his boss if the reports were true, but he decided to keep his curiosity to himself. If a new team were in the offing, the official word would come out soon enough. It was exhilarating to think that Brooklyn, the home of baseball for so many years, might again have a team of its own.

The prospect of a new club raised some interesting questions: Where would the team play? Would the club join a league or start out as an independent like the Mets? And what about Jim Mutrie and John Day—were they somehow involved? Finally, Fletch could restrain himself no longer.

One afternoon he barged into his boss's office to ask Charlie if he were indeed the man behind the new Brooklyn team. "I sure am," Byrne replied with a wide grin. "Say, Fletcher, you're a baseball man. How'd you like to join me and a friend of mine for supper? We'll fill you in on the details, and maybe you can give us your reactions to what we're up to."

"Sounds great," Fletch said. He wouldn't have missed that meal for a season's pass to the Polo Grounds.

They met in Mouquin's Restaurant on Fulton Street. Charlie's friend was a fellow named George Taylor, who worked as an editor for the *New York Tribune*. Over supper Byrne explained that George had come to him some months earlier with the idea of starting a pro club in Brooklyn. It took Charlie some time to warm up to the idea, but now he was extremely enthusiastic—not only had he agreed to be the principal backer, but he'd also persuaded two of his friends, Joseph Doyle and Gus Abell, to put up the rest of the money needed to get the project off the ground. Fletch knew both of the other investors. Doyle owned a piece of the gambling house on Ann Street. Abell, whom Fletch had seen a number of times at the Club House in Saratoga, was the proprietor of the famous casino on the Narragansett Pier in Rhode Island. There was no doubt in Fletcher's mind that Brooklyn was ready for a new professional team; he was only sorry he didn't have any money to invest in the project.

Before supper was over, Fletch had the answers to all of his questions. The Brooklyn club would not apply to one of the major leagues but would join instead a new minor professional league called the Interstate Association. It would be a modest beginning, but, if things went well, who could tell what might happen? As for John Day and Jim Mutrie, they had nothing at all to do with the venture. Charlie's meeting with Jim at the Old Home Plate had been a fishing expedition for both men. Byrne was trying to get some free advice on how to start a baseball team, and Mutrie was curious to find out whether the reports he'd heard about a new Brooklyn club were true. Neither man had learned much, but enough people saw them together to start spinning the sails of the rumor mill.

Taylor, who had to get to work, left before Charlie and Fletch were quite finished eating. They stayed around longer than they'd planned, reminiscing about the days when Brooklyn was the baseball capital of the world and expressing their hopes that the new team would return to the city at least a small portion of its lost greatness. "By the way, Fletch, you're from Brooklyn—do you know the old Washington Pond?" Charlie asked as they got up to leave.

"Sure. It's in South Brooklyn, at Third Street and Fourth Avenue. I used to skate there when I was a kid."

"What would you think about putting our new ball park there?"

"That's a great idea. The trolley line goes right by. It'll be an easy place to get to," Fletch replied. Byrne, who was in real estate as well as gambling, already knew he'd picked a good site, but he was happy to have Fletcher confirm his opinion. By the following spring the area would be encircled by grandstands and bleachers, and the pond would be transformed into a baseball diamond. In keeping with the site's history, Byrne would name his field Washington Park. It was located on the very ground where George Washington fought the Battle of Long Island.

While Byrne and his friends were working to bring baseball back to Brooklyn, John Day and Jim Mutrie were making plans of their own— plans that would bring Manhattan not one but two major league teams. They did not enter the Mets in the National League but placed the club instead in the up-and-coming American Association, which in late 1882 looked very much like the league of the future.

The National League, seriously threatened by the association's sudden popularity and prosperity, realized it could no longer indulge itself by continuing to boycott New York and Philadelphia. At the league's annual meeting that December, both were invited to join. The New York franchise was awarded to none other than the Metropolitan Exhibition Company. So John Day, in the first case of what later became known as "syndicate baseball," hedged his bets by becoming the owner of New York clubs in both major leagues.

To stock their National League team, Day and Mutrie took over the dead Troy franchise and filled out their new roster with several stars from the Haymakers, including Buck Ewing, Roger Connor, Mickey Welch, and Del Gillespie. Mutrie, who planned to stay on as manager of the Metropolitans, needed a new pitcher and catcher for his own team, so Tim Keefe and Bill Holbert were sent to the Mets. As the season of 1883 approached, New York, a baseball wasteland for five years, found itself with an embarrassment of riches.

The Polo Grounds could easily have handled both New York clubs, but Day decided to give each team its own playing field. His reason was to provide National League patrons with better accommodations for the extra quarter it would cost them to see a game. So in the spring work began on a new diamond for the Metropolitans at the Sixth Avenue end of the Polo Grounds. Because the Mets' fans would be getting their baseball at bargain prices, Day had no desire to provide them with much in the way of extras. Their end of the field wasn't ready until the middle of May, and every corner was cut to keep costs down. Raw garbage was used as land fill. A shabby canvas fence was put up to separate the Mets from their National League rivals. If ever a ball club was relegated to the status of second-class citizens it was the old Metropolitans.

Fletcher had a great deal of difficulty trying to decide whether to place his loyalties with the Metropolitans or with the new National League club. As the season got under way, he found himself trying to root for both teams. It was easy to identify with the National League club, because so many of the players were former Haymakers. But he couldn't help sympathizing with the Mets, who were so suddenly and harshly cast in the role of underdogs. In April the two clubs squared off for a series of exhibition contests, and as the Mets lost one game after another, Fletch's frustration became close to unbearable. The team was playing very good baseball but getting none of the breaks. By the time the Metropolitans had lost twelve straight games to National League clubs, including six to their fellow New Yorkers, Fletch was a diehard Met fan. When his team finally pulled out a 3–1 win over their rivals from the greener end of the Polo Grounds, Fletcher was as happy as if they'd won the American Association pennant.

That summer Fletch lived on a steady diet of baseball. While his heart went out to the Metropolitans, he had to concede that the National Leaguers were a better team. Still, the Mets were a hell of a lot of fun.

Mutrie managed wearing a high hat and tails, and during games he would roam through the stands yelling words of encouragement to his players and the fans alike. At one point in the season he even hired John L. Sullivan, the heavyweight champion, to pitch for the Mets in exhibition games. Old John L. couldn't throw a baseball worth a damn, but what did that matter? He added a comic element to the game and attracted fans who normally wouldn't have bothered coming out to the park to see a contest that didn't figure in the standings.

In those days every club played a heavy exhibition schedule. The only reason for these games was revenue; if a touch of show business could help sell tickets, what was wrong with that? The early Mets were aware of something few baseball people over the years have grasped: Folks go out to the ball park for one reason—to be entertained.

Even though he spent most of his free time at the Polo Grounds, Fletch didn't forget about the new club over in Brooklyn. It was a bit tough, though, getting excited about the race in the Interstate Association. Brooklyn finished with a record of forty-four victories and twenty-eight losses to edge out Harrisburg by two games. At the close of the season the Interstate Association collapsed; the Brooklyn club, the only member to survive, joined the American Association that December.

So the start of the 1884 season saw greater New York with three major league teams—two in the city itself and one in Brooklyn. Fletcher believed it was no less than his home town deserved. In the years ahead his feelings would be shared by generations of baseball fans.

The Metropolitans, though cast in the role of lowly stepbrothers to the National Leaguers, were destined to have one shining hour before heading down the path toward oblivion. As the 1884 season began to unfold, it became apparent the Providence Grays, behind the amazing pitching of Old Hoss Radbourne, would walk away with the National League flag. The New York club spent the entire campaign in the middle of the pack and wound up tied with Chicago for fourth place. Meanwhile, over in the American Association, Brooklyn dropped deep into the second division, finishing ninth in a thirteen-team race. But the Mets, who were in the thick of things from the start, battled for the lead with Louisville and Columbus through all of July and August, then pulled ahead by five games in September and finished the race six and a half games in front. They also did well in exhibition matches with their rivals from the Polo Grounds, winning five of ten with the New York club. At the end of the regular season the Mets, now ready to take on the world, challenged Providence to a two-out-of-three-game series for the "championship of the United States." Frank Bancroft, the manager of the National League winners, was happy to accept, and what was in effect the first World Series began on October 23.

The idea of a showdown series between the pennant winners of the two major leagues had captured Fletcher's imagination ever since the American Association appeared on the scene. Now the Series was not only a reality, but a New York team would be taking part! Fletcher had trouble sleeping the night before the Series opener. He woke up very early and went right up to the Polo Grounds, even though it was several hours before game time. The morning was damp, windy, and very cold—hardly ideal weather for baseball.

Alone in the park except for two members of the Providence team who were having a catch in the pitching lane, he took a seat in the grandstand and settled down for the long wait. As he looked down on the field he recognized the two players as Hoss Radbourne and Sandy Nava, the Grays' second-string catcher. Old Hoss was standing a third of the way between home plate and the pitcher's box and was delivering the ball to Nava with a slow, painful motion. As the morning went on, Radbourne edged backward a step at a time until, after more than an hour of practice, he was able to reach the plate from the official distance, which was fifty feet. From there Hoss continued moving back until just before noon, when he was finally able to reach home plate from center field on a fly. Fletch was observing a warmup drill that Radbourne went through before every game of his big league career. The leading pitcher in the National League, a man who won sixty games and lost only twelve that year, had a lame arm!

Only two thousand fans showed for the first World Series game. Not only was the crowd disappointing, but so was the performance of the Mets. Tim Keefe felt uneasy throwing to any catcher other than Bill Holbert, his regular battery mate. But Holbert was out of action that day; his replacement, Charlie Reipschlager, unsettled Keefe to the point that he began throwing the game away.

In the first inning he hit two batters. Both came around to score with the help of a couple of wild pitches and a passed ball. In the third another runner was given a free ticket home on a wild pitch, and in the seventh Keefe gave up three runs on four clean hits. Meanwhile Radbourne pitched a shutout, allowing only two hits as he coasted to a 6–0 victory.

The second game was a much better contest. With Holbert back behind the plate Keefe returned to form, pitching well in every inning but the fifth, when he gave up a three-run homer. He would have been spared even those runs if it hadn't been for a terrible call. When a runner tried to steal second, Holbert threw him out by a mile. At least that's what everyone thought, except for one man—the umpire. Unfortunately the three runs were more than Radbourne needed; he held the Mets to only three hits and won the game, 3–1.

The third game of the series, played on a particularly cold day, was merely a formality, since the Grays had already won the championship. Fletch delayed going to the Polo Grounds until just before starting time and arrived to find the park almost empty. Only three hundred fans had come out, and when the Providence players saw the size of the crowd they at first refused to play. Mutrie finally persuaded his opponents to take the field by letting them choose the umpire.

The Grays took excellent advantage of the concession—they chose Tim Keefe, thereby taking the Mets' most valuable player out of the lineup. Mutrie sent an untried pitcher named Buck Becannon to the box and assigned the catching chores to good old Charlie Reipschlager.

The game was a disaster. All by himself Charlie committed six of the Mets' nine errors, and he also gave up two passed balls. At the end of six innings, with the Grays ahead, 11–2, Keefe took his teammates out of their misery by calling the game "on account of darkness."

In three games the Mets had managed to score only three runs on eleven hits. Clearly they were no match for the National League champs. But at least they'd had their moment of glory.

As fickle as the Mets' fans may have been in supporting them in the World Series, they didn't hold a candle to the team's owners. The club had just completed a season that was a success on the field but very disappointing at the gate. The Metropolitan Exhibition Company's profits from its National League franchise had been largely drained away by the Mets' losses.

Day and Mutrie had two options. They could stop treating the team like a stepchild and give it their full support, or they could get rid of it. Eventually they chose the second, but first they made a move that clearly demonstrated they had no further use for the club. In the spring of 1885 they transferred the Mets' two best players—Tim Keefe and Dude Esterbrook, the star third baseman—to their National League team. To accomplish this they pulled a trick that outraged the other owners in the American Association. A player was not permitted to sign with a new club until ten days after the termination of his old contract, so theoretically he would be free to entertain offers from every club that might wish to bid for his services.

To make sure no one else could get their hands on his two stars, Mutrie took them on a cruise to Bermuda. When they returned, the waiting period was over. The new contracts were signed, and the players were safely on the roster of the New York club. The transfer had a dramatic effect on the fortunes of the two teams. The National Leaguers, now managed by Mutrie, climbed to second place, finishing just two games behind Chicago, while the Metropolitans, playing their final season at the ragged end of the Polo Grounds, plummeted all the way down to seventh, thirty-three games off the pace.

After the 1885 campaign, Day sold the Mets to Erastus Wiman's Staten Island Amusement Company. For two summers the team played at the St. George Playgrounds on Staten Island, where it became part of a lineup of attractions that included a circus, fireworks displays, and Buffalo Bill's Wild West Show. Finally, in 1887, Charlie Byrne bought the team, assigned the best players to his Brooklyn club, and returned the franchise to the American Association.

Although the team came to a sad end, it had made a lasting contribution to baseball and had coined a nickname that one day would be revived by another club given the task of rejuvenating the game in New York City.

During the summer of 1885, fans began referring to New York's National League team as the "Giants," supposedly because so many of the players were unusually tall. They may have appeared imposing on the diamond, but in reality the average height of the team was only 5 foot, 10 inches, hardly gigantic even for the 1880s. Only two players, both old Haymakers, were taller than six feet—Roger Connor, who was 6 foot, 3 inches, and Del Gillespie, at 6 feet, 1½ inches.

It's possible these two men were dubbed Giants first, and then the nickname spread to the rest of the team. In any event, Jim Mutrie loved the name and began using it in his chants to the crowd. As he marched around the Polo Grounds he would often stop and yell, "Who are the people? The Giant fans are the people!" About the same time the Brooklyn team, destined to have many nicknames over the years, became known as the Trolley Dodgers, a reference to the fact that Brooklyn's pedestrians, to survive, spent a lot of time doing just that.

Fletcher was living in the Broadway Central Hotel, the new name for the hostelry where the National League had been founded a decade earlier. Many of the Giants also lived there, so while Fletch tried to divide his loyalties equally between the Brooklyn and New York teams, he found it difficult not to favor the Giants. He already knew some of the players, including Tim Keefe, Roger Connor, and Mickey Welch, from his days in Troy, so it didn't take him long to meet the other members of the club. One player who became his friend was Monte Ward, the star outfielder and shortstop who had come to the Giants from Providence in 1883. When Ward was not out courting his fiancée, the beautiful actress Helen Dauvray, he and Fletch would sometimes have dinner together or sit around the lobby of the Broadway Central swapping baseball lore.

One day Monte invited Fletcher to join him and his fiancée for supper after the ball game in Roberts Road House, a fashionable restaurant just across the street from the Polo Grounds. Fletch arrived to discover that Helen had brought along a friend—a very frail but not unattractive young actress by the name of Matilda Morgan. Immediately taken with the woman, Fletcher did his best to charm her. His dapper attire and worldly ways made an excellent impression; she never suspected for a moment he might be engaged in any but the most respectable kind of work.

The evening was a great success. By the time they parted, Fletcher was well on his way to winning Matilda's heart. Later, when he told her he earned his living in a gambling hall, she began to have her doubts. But Fletch pursued her month after month without letup. In December 1887, just a few days before Christmas, they were married. Fletcher bought a house in the Park Slope section of Brooklyn and brought his bride to the city where he had grown to love baseball.

In 1888, when four members of the Trolley Dodgers all got married within a matter of weeks, the team became known as the Bridegrooms. The Grooms got off to a sluggish start in the American Association race, but by June they began to click, prompting their manager, Bill McGunnigle, to boast that his players now worked together "like well-oiled machinery."

By the middle of July Brooklyn was battling for first place with the St. Louis Browns, who had already won three pennants in a row. In August the Bridegrooms stumbled badly, winning only eight of twenty games, and they dropped back to fourth. But the team played solid baseball in September and October, to wind up in second place, six and a half games behind the Browns.

Meanwhile, over in the National League, the Giants also got off to a weak start in 1888, failing to hit their stride until July, when they won eighteen and lost only five. At one point they put together a ten-game winning streak, after which a pundit remarked that "the change of the playing of the club has had a magical effect upon Manager Mutrie. 'Handsome Jeems' has at last stopped pulling his beard and as a result his moustache is bushy and fierce again."

The Giants went on to win the pennant, beating out Chicago by nine games. At the close of the regular season the Browns and Giants faced each other in a ten-game World Series that added up to quite a road show. The teams played three games in the Polo Grounds, one in Brooklyn, another in the Polo Grounds, one in Philadelphia, and the last four in St. Louis. When it was all over, the Giants had given the Browns a pretty good trouncing. New York got magnificent pitching from Tim Keefe and won six of the first eight games, including two laughers by scores of 12–5 and 11–3.

Thus the last two contests in St. Louis became meaningless exhibition contests that the Giants, by taking their stars out of the lineup, allowed the Browns to win, 14–11 and 18–7.

Through all of 1888, Fletcher heard rumors that Brooklyn would resign from the American Association and join the National League for the 1889 campaign. There was no doubt that Charlie Byrne was becoming disenchanted with the association, largely because Chris Von der Ahe, along with some of the other owners, had grown to resent him for supposedly assuming too much power in the association's councils. Actually, the other clubs were jealous because Byrne, through shrewd deals and hard work, had quickly built his team into one of the best in the league. Despite the growing tension between Byrne and the anti-Brooklyn faction, Charlie decided to stay with the association for at least another year. He hoped the conflict with his fellow owners could be resolved, but his main reason for sticking it out was that the association permitted Sunday baseball.

Although Sunday games were illegal in Brooklyn, the Grooms were allowed to play them at Ridgewood Park in Queens. Large crowds came out almost every week, providing the club with an important source of revenue. A switch to the National League, which still banned games on

Sundays, would create financial uncertainties Byrne was not yet willing to face.

For the Giants, 1889 meant a move to a new Polo Grounds. For many years the city had made it clear that one day the section of One Hundred Eleventh Street enclosed by the old ball park would become a public thoroughfare. Now that time had come, forcing John Day to shift to a new location at Eighth Avenue and One Hundred Fifty-fifth Street. And for Fletcher Rice, 1889 meant becoming a father for the first time. His first son, Harry, was born in April of that year, just a few days after the opening of the baseball season.

Fletcher followed the 1889 campaign with great interest and enthusiasm, dividing his loyalties and his time just about evenly between New York and Brooklyn. The Giants, who began the season playing their home games in Jersey City and on Staten Island, finally moved into their new Polo Grounds on July 8 and went on to win the National League pennant for a second year. They defeated the Boston team, now known as the Beaneaters, in a close race that went right down to the wire. Things were just as tight over in the association, where the Browns and the Grooms were again going at it tooth and nail. Von der Ahe had inflamed the rivalry by accusing Byrne of bribing certain umpires. The St. Louis owner's scurrilous charges only inspired Brooklyn to try to win at all costs. The Grooms took the pennant on the final day of the season and won the right to face the Giants in the World Series.

As the Series approached, the baseball world was buzzing with rumors of impending turmoil. Once again there was widespread speculation that Brooklyn, along with Cincinnati, would jump to the National League. John Day, asked if the reports were true, replied, "No, sir. Not while I have a voice in the league, and I think I have something to say in the councils. We want no gamblers in our organization, and Byrne will never get in with his club while I'm in it." Fletcher, outraged that the Giants' owner would slur a fine man like Charlie Byrne, found himself hoping the Grooms would beat the pants off the Giants in the Series. The substance of another, more disturbing rumor was that the Brotherhood of Baseball Players, a union that included most players with National League contracts, was about to break away and form a league of its own. If that were to happen, the entire structure of professional baseball might collapse. A week before the Series, Monte Ward, the president of the Brotherhood, met with John Day to announce that he and most of his teammates were indeed planning to start their own club. Ward claimed they had plenty of financial backing and had already leased land for a new ball park right next door to the Polo Grounds under Coogan's Bluff. On October 18, as Brooklyn came to Manhattan to meet the

Giants for the championship of the world, the future of baseball was filled with dark shadows of uncertainty.

Mutrie, who set up the general rules for the Series, stipulated that the games would alternate between the Polo Grounds and Washington Park and that the first club to win six contests would be the champion. Unlike previous years, unnecessary games would not be played. As the crowd began forming for the opening game, Fletcher, one of the first to arrive, was overcome with excitement. He couldn't remember being so nervous about a ball game since that long ago day when the Reds took on the Haymakers. He was especially worried because his old enemy, Bob Ferguson, had been chosen as one of the umpires. If anyone could bring Brooklyn bad luck it was Death to Flying Things.

Fletch pondered the Bridegrooms' prospects and decided that everything hinged on Parisian Bob. If Bob Caruthers could hold the fierce Giant bats in check, Brooklyn might just walk away with the championship. McGunnigle, however, did not start the Series with Bob but instead put Bill "Adonis" Terry, another fine pitcher, in the box. The game began well for the Grooms; they held the Giants scoreless in the top of the first and then shelled Tim Keefe's curve balls for five runs in their half of the inning.

The crowd of more than eight thousand included twice as many Giant rooters as Brooklyn fans, but what the contingent from across the river lacked in size it made up for with volume. At the end of six innings the gap between the two teams had been narrowed to only one run, with Brooklyn leading, 6–5.

Just then one of the Giant fans shouted, "Hey, this is the lucky seventh! Let's all stretch for luck!" The New York rooters slowly rose to their feet and then, in the words of one observer, "settled down, just as long grass bends to the breath of the zephyr." The Giants responded by immediately scoring five runs, and a baseball tradition—the seventh inning stretch—was born.

The Bridegrooms came back with two runs in the bottom of the seventh and four more in the eighth; then, much to the displeasure of the Giants, the Grooms began stalling. Before long many of the spectators, bored with the delays, began roaming down to the sidelines and then out onto the diamond. Ferguson called the game on account of darkness, and Brooklyn became the winner, 12–10.

The attendance at game two was sixteen thousand—Washington Park's second largest crowd up to that time. Caruthers pitched for the Grooms and did an excellent job, but his efforts were sabotaged by his catcher, Joe Visner. In addition to committing three errors, Visner made several terrible throws to second, allowing the Giants to steal that base almost at will. The final score was 6–2 in favor of New York. Before the third game Buck Ewing, captain of the Giants, boasted, "It's a hundred dollars to a toothpick that we win today!" His odds turned out to be inaccurate.

By the ninth inning Brooklyn was ahead, 8–7, but the Giants had the bases loaded with only one out. Just then John Gaffney, the umpire, called the game because of darkness. The Giants were livid, but that didn't prevent Gaffney from calling the next game for the same reason, again with the Grooms in the lead, this time by the score of 10–7.

John Day was at his boiling point as he told the press, "Three times have we lost in this series through trickery and we shall do so no more. Unless the Brooklyn club plays on its merits the same as the New Yorks are doing, the Series will end at once. This kind of ballplaying and umpiring are enough to kill the game. I do not mind losing games on their merit, but I do mind being robbed of them."

Jim Mutrie, less concerned than Day about games that were already history, predicted his team would take the lead in the Series by the end of the week. Very few fans took him seriously, even after the fifth contest, which the Giants won easily, 11–3.

Fletcher was one Brooklyn fan who was worried. He realized that the Grooms had suddenly become vulnerable. Their first-string catcher, Bob Clark, sprained his ankle during the fifth game, leaving the backstop chores to Visner and to Doc Bushong, who was also losing his touch. In game six, the loss of Clark came immediately into play. The contest developed into a thrilling pitchers' duel between Adonis Terry and Hank O'Day. In the ninth inning Brooklyn was ahead, 1–0, and New York was down to its last out when Monte Ward hit a single, stole second and third on Visner, and scored when Roger Connor smashed a drive that Davis, the Grooms' shortstop, couldn't handle. Fletcher's heart sank as the game went into extra innings; New York scored a run in the eleventh, and Brooklyn went down to defeat, 2–1. In the next two games the Giants' bats came alive early; they scored eight times in the second inning of the seventh game and went on to win, 11–7, and then came right back with nine runs in the first two innings of the eighth to lay the foundation for a 16–7 victory. New York had now won four games in a row; they were ahead in the Series five games to three. Mutrie's prediction had come true.

The final game, played at the Polo Grounds on a cold, miserable day before a crowd of only three thousand, matched Terry against O'Day once again. It was sudden death for the Bridegrooms—a situation that filled the park with more tension than Fletcher was able to endure. He calmed down a bit when the Grooms scored twice in the top half of the first, but the Giants scored one run in their half of the inning, sending Fletch to the men's room to relieve himself. He did not return to his seat until the fourth inning; by then each pitcher had found his groove, and neither team had scored again. The Giants tied the game in the sixth, took the lead by one run on an error by Bushong in the seventh, and went on to win, 4–2. Crestfallen, Fletcher watched helplessly as the Giant fans jumped for joy at the final out. They surged onto the field and joined their heroes in the chant, "We are the people!"

Then they crowded around the Polo Grounds' victory gong and sent out a deafening peal that announced the game's outcome to everyone for blocks around. Fletcher went home to spend the winter brooding over Bob Clark's sprained ankle and Parisian Bob Caruthers's bad luck.

Early in November several members of the Brotherhood convened in New York to launch their new league, the Players' National League of Base Ball Clubs. There were many reasons for their drastic action, all stemming from the Brotherhood's long-standing contention that the league treated its players as chattels, buying and selling with no regard for the needs and wishes of the players themselves.

The situation came to a head over two rules that were particularly repugnant to the Brotherhood. The first was the reserve rule, which gave an owner complete control over his players until he no longer required their services. The second rule was the classification code, which allowed owners to evaluate each player not only for his ability to play baseball but also for his conduct off the field. This evaluation became the basis for each player's "classification" into one of five salary categories from $2,500 a year on down.

Together the two rules meant that in the game of labor relations the owners held all the cards. Not only were players the exclusive property of the clubs to which they belonged, but their salaries were determined by a scheme that, aside from being totally arbitrary, allowed no room at all for bargaining. When the Brotherhood, which had tried for four years to get the owners to compromise on the reserve clause, was rewarded for its efforts in 1888 with the classification code, Monte Ward and his followers decided enough was enough. So they prepared to go into business for themselves.

Ten days later the National League and the American Association held their annual meetings at the Fifth Avenue Hotel in New York. The league, deeply troubled by the revolt of the players, decided to strengthen its own ranks at the association's expense by finally offering membership to Brooklyn and Cincinnati. Charlie Byrne, who had taken all the guff from Von der Ahe and his clique that he could, gladly accepted the invitation.

On the morning of November 14, he walked out of the parlor where the association was in session and joined his partner, Gus Abell, in the hall; the two representatives of the Brooklyn club, along with Aaron Stern and Harry Sterne of Cincinnati, then strolled down to the National League's meeting room, where they were welcomed with open arms. Even John Day was happy to let bygones be bygones. He, along with Byrne and Stern, sent out for baskets of wine, and everyone toasted Brooklyn and Cincinnati, "wishing them prosperity among their new associates."

Then Day, John Rogers, and Al Spalding were assigned the task of preparing a press release to let the public in on the good news. It was no coincidence that these were the very men who constituted the National League's war committee, just formed to lead the battle against the Brotherhood.

The team that suffered the most from the coming of the Players' League was the Giants. Almost all the stars left the club. Monte Ward went across the river to manage and play short for the Brooklyn entry in the upstart circuit; Roger Connor, Buck Ewing, Hank O'Day, and Tim Keefe all jumped to the Brotherhood's New York club, which also became known as the "Giants." Of the old club's front-line players only Mickey Welch and Silent Mike Tiernan, the great outfielder who batted .335 in 1889, remained loyal to Day and Mutrie. The Bridegrooms' roster, on the other hand, was barely touched by the rival league. For one thing fewer players in the American Association belonged to the Brotherhood; more important, Charlie Byrne paid his men top salaries and commanded more loyalty from his team than any other owner in the majors.

The season of 1890 was a financial disaster for every club in New York. The Giants, decimated by the players' revolt, barely managed to field a team. They struggled through the season with a band of players purchased from the Indianapolis club and finished in sixth place, twenty-four games out.

One of the players from Indianapolis, Amos Rusie, a pitcher with a tremendous fastball, became the workhorse of the Giant staff. Pitching for a weak team he managed to chalk up twenty-nine victories against thirty losses and established himself as a fixture in New York. The Players' League "Giants" fared somewhat better, coming in third, eight games behind the pennant-winning Boston club.

Over in Brooklyn the Bridegrooms, playing with an unscathed lineup, won the National League flag easily, beating out Chicago by six games. The great Monte Ward managed the Grooms' counterparts in the Players' League into second place, six and a half games in back of Boston.

For part of the summer Brooklyn was plagued with still another major league club, an American Association entry that didn't even make it through the season. With five clubs vying for support in one metropolitan area, it wasn't surprising that none made money. Even the Grooms, the proud winners of the National League pennant, failed to turn a profit. Charlie Byrne hoped to recoup some of his losses in the World Series against Louisville, the champs of the association. But attendance was so bad after seven games, with the teams deadlocked at three victories apiece and one tie, the Series was discontinued. Even Brooklyn's great fans found it hard to get excited over a "World Series" that, by excluding the Players' League, was at best a watered-down version of the Fall Classic.

That year Fletcher gave up on New York and became a diehard Brooklyn fan. There were a number of reasons for his decision. To begin with, he was still smarting from the Grooms' frustrating loss to the Giants in the 1889 World Series. Also, as was obvious, New York's recent misfortunes had left Brooklyn with by far the better team. But there were personal reasons as well. Over the previous few years Charlie Byrne had introduced Fletcher to most of the members of the Washington Park staff, and many of them had become his friends.

One of Fletcher's favorite people was Charles Hercules Ebbets, a young man who worked in the business office and wore other hats as well, including those of ticket-seller and program-hawker. Whenever Charlie came upon Fletch while making his rounds through the stands he would stop to watch a batter or two. Fletcher never failed to be impressed by Ebbets's enthusiasm and energy.

"Charlie, you could do a lot better than you're doing here," Fletch would often say. "Don't make the same mistake I made. Baseball will never get you anywhere. Why don't you get started in a profession with a future?" But Charlie would just smile, get up, and resume selling his scorecards.

In the fall of 1890, the backers of the Players' League began looking for ways to protect themselves from further losses. In October Wendell Goodwin and Eddie Talcott, representing the Brotherhood clubs in Brooklyn and New York, approached the National League with an offer to consolidate their teams with the Bridegrooms and the Giants. The League agreed to entertain their proposals, and before long the Pittsburgh and Chicago clubs in the rival circuit were also negotiating mergers with their National League counterparts.

The back of the rebellion had been broken, and by December the Players' League collapsed. A year later the American Association, never able to recover from the loss of Brooklyn and Cincinnati, also faded into oblivion. Its four strongest franchises—Baltimore, St. Louis, Louisville, and Washington—joined the National League, which suddenly found itself the lone victor holding all the spoils of war.

The consolidation of the Brooklyn and New York Players' League clubs with the Grooms and the Giants had a profound effect upon the balance of power within both organizations. George Chauncey, the principal owner of Brooklyn's Brotherhood club, agreed to invest in the Grooms, but on two conditions. He wanted to move the club from Washington Park to his own Eastern Park, the home of his former team in the Players' League. His second condition was that Monte Ward be named manager of the Grooms. Charlie Byrne had no trouble agreeing to the first proposal, even though it meant going out to East New York, a remote section of Brooklyn. But he felt terrible about the prospect of having to fire Bill McGunnigle, who had just won his second pennant in a row. Still, he needed money so desperately he had no choice but to accept Chauncey's terms.

Meanwhile, in New York, John Day was in even worse financial shape. To save the Giants from bankruptcy, he had been forced to sell off a large piece of the club. Still not out of deep water, Day now had no choice but to offer a block of stock to Eddie Talcott, who also stipulated that the manager would have to go. Day was able to protect Mutrie for a year, but after the 1891 season he gave in and allowed Talcott to name Pat Powers as Jim's successor.

That same year also saw the Giants move next door to Brotherhood Park, which became the third and last field to be called the Polo Grounds. A year later Day himself was sent packing by Talcott and John T. Brush, another stockholder. With Mutrie and Day gone, the era of the Giants' inception was over.

During the early 1890s Fletcher and his wife began to have marital difficulties. After the honeymoon period, Matilda began to miss the gay life in the world of the theater and started resenting Fletcher for having taken her to Brooklyn, which she considered the sticks. She did not particularly enjoy being a mother, even though she claimed she loved her son, Harry. But what irritated her most about married life was her growing belief that her husband was a very silly man. His job—dealing cards in a gambling den—might have been all right for an adventurous young fellow, but Fletcher was approaching fifty.

And then there was his childish passion for baseball, a game that made no sense to her at all—except when it came to admiring handsome young players like Monte Ward. Perhaps Matilda was feeling a strain that was inevitable for a woman married to a man almost fifteen years her senior. Whatever the reason, she began to convey her unhappiness to Fletcher—not by harsh words but by subtle, and sometimes not so subtle, deeds and actions. Fletcher's first response was despair. After giving the matter some thought he pulled himself together and went to work on the problem. The upshot of his efforts was that Matilda's second son, Alexander Rice, was born in the fall of 1892.

Now that the National League was the only circuit, the high costs of competing for players and fans were eliminated, and most clubs began turning healthy profits. While the situation was great for the owners, it didn't make the fans very happy. Two great ball clubs, the Beaneaters and the Orioles, won all the pennants from 1891 to 1898. While Boston and Baltimore followers enjoyed an abundance of riches, fans elsewhere lived on vain hopes and old memories.

From Fletcher's point of view, the most unfortunate aspect of the National League's monopoly was the discontinuance of the World Series. In an effort to find a substitute for the Fall Classic, William C. Temple, onetime owner of the Pittsburgh team, sponsored the Temple Cup Series between the first- and second-place finishers in the pennant race. The winner of the four-of-seven series took home an ornate silver trophy and 65 percent of the proceeds, the remainder going to the losing team. Fletcher got some enjoyment out of the Temple Cup contests, especially in 1894, when the Giants, after finishing three games behind Baltimore in the regular season, swept the Orioles with four straight victories, two each by Amos Rusie and Jouett Meekin. But for the most part Fletcher looked upon the Temple games, which lasted only four seasons, as a tepid substitute for the old World Series.

The years leading up to the turn of the century were a time of great upheaval for baseball in Brooklyn and in New York. Both clubs underwent changes in ownership, and both teams went through a succession of field managers. The Bridegrooms, who were now all proud fathers, obviously needed a new nickname; they became known as Ward's Wonders, an appellation that was short-lived because Monte Ward, longing for the bright lights and gay life of Manhattan, left Brooklyn in 1893 to become manager of the Giants. His successor was Dave Foutz. Some fans began referring to the team as Foutz's Fillies, while others went back to calling the club the Trolley Dodgers, or just plain Dodgers.

Over in New York, Ward lasted only two seasons. In 1894, right after his team's impressive Temple Cup victory, he announced his retirement. Actually he'd been fired by Eddie Talcott, who hired George Davis as the new manager. Then Talcott himself left the club, selling out to one Andrew Freedman, a Tammany politician, destined to become one of the most despised figures in the history of baseball.

What can one say about Andrew Freedman? He was arrogant, ruthless, miserly, stubborn, egotistical, and completely unpredictable.

He was also brilliant. After his death, when it became known that he'd left $4 million to charity, people also began saying that he was misunderstood. In any case, he ran the Giants for seven years, and during that time he watched the club plunge from second place to the lower depths of the second division. The team reached its nadir in 1899, when it finished the season forty-two games behind first-place Brooklyn. To say that Freedman himself was responsible for his club's demise is not conjecture but hard fact. His policies, both on and off the field, left the Giants in such chaos that there was no way at all they could be expected to win ball games.

George Davis lasted only two months as manager of the Giants. Freedman replaced him with Jack Doyle in June 1895, and before the season was finished he fired Doyle too, replacing him with Harvey Watkins. In seven years Freedman had thirteen different managers; some of them, including Cap Anson and Buck Ewing, were among the greats of the game.

Others were not so great, but Watkins deserves special recognition as the most unqualified man ever to run a big league ball club. Freedman discovered old Harvey at the Barnum & Bailey circus, where his most important duty was feeding the goldfish in the business office.

The lack of regard Freedman had for managers was equaled, if not surpassed, by his attitude toward players. His most famous player dispute was with Amos Rusie, the Hoosier Thunderbolt, who was the mainstay of the Giants' pitching staff throughout the 1890s. In 1896 Rusie, whom Freedman had harassed with a $200 fine at the end of the previous season, demanded a salary of $5,000, more than twice the league's $2,400 pay ceiling. When Freedman refused to give in, the tenacious Rusie remained a holdout for the entire season.

Most Giant fans sided with Amos, and many decided to boycott the Polo Grounds until his return. The following year the owners of the eleven other clubs, who all had a stake in keeping the New York franchise healthy, came up with Rusie's back pay. When he returned to the pitcher's box in 1897 Amos posted a record of twenty-nine wins and eight losses, with an ERA of 2.54.

Under Dave Foutz, Brooklyn fell upon hard times, finishing no higher than fifth during the four seasons he managed the club. In 1897 Charlie Byrne replaced Foutz with Billy Barnie, who also failed to return the team to its former greatness. Nonetheless, Fletcher remained a diehard Brooklyn fan, suffering the agonies of the present while contemplating the glories that were surely waiting in the not-too-distant future. But while he outwardly displayed unswerving loyalty to Brooklyn, Fletch also secretly admired another team—the Baltimore Orioles.

The Orioles were more than a team, they were an event—the embodiment of a revolution that profoundly altered the basic strategies, and hence the very nature of baseball. They were, of course, a fantastically talented ball club, and they believed in winning, whatever the cost. Ned Hanlon, the Birds' brilliant manager, exploited these traits to the fullest; through skill, drive, and intelligence the Orioles changed baseball from a boy's game to a man's art. It was Hanlon, for example, who discovered that the most effective way to combat the curveball is to put in left-handed batters against right-handed pitchers and vice versa. Baltimore's other contributions to baseball tactics included perfecting the hit-and-run, the bunt, the squeeze, base-stealing, and the sacrifice—all plays that rely not on brawn but on speed, agility, and alertness. These new tactics gave the opposition fits. At the start of the 1894 season the

Orioles, in a four-game series with New York, successfully executed the hit-and-run thirteen times in a row. The Giants lost every one of those games, prompting a very disgusted Monte Ward to remark, "This isn't baseball the Orioles are playing, it's an entirely new game."

The players who created that "new game" were all destined to write their own chapters in the legends of baseball. The Orioles' leadoff batter was John McGraw, the feisty third baseman and captain of the club. Aside from being a great hitter—his lifetime batting average was .334— he was one of the best baserunners of his day. During his career he stole 436 bases and earned a reputation as a man who, once on base, would invariably find a way to score.

McGraw would rather chew a can of nails than lose a ball game. He protected third base with a vengeance, and when fair play would not do the job he had no qualms about resorting to chicanery. Passing runners were often thrown off stride by a sudden bump from his shoulder, and a man tagging up to come home on a fly to the outfield had to look behind him to make sure McGraw wasn't holding onto his belt.

The second man in the lineup was Wee Willie Keeler, probably the greatest bat handler of all time. Willie, who boasted that he could "hit 'em where they ain't," was indeed able to place the ball with remarkable accuracy. It was Keeler, batting with McGraw on first, who made the hit-and-run play an Oriole trademark. He also perfected the Baltimore chop—a sharp hit down in front of the plate that bounces so high the runner reaches first base before the fielder has time to make the play.

Willie had lightning speed, especially going down to first; he was an excellent right fielder and during his career hit .345, the fifth best lifetime batting average in the majors. A fierce competitor, he once ripped up his arm ramming it through a barbed-wire fence to make a game-saving catch.

The Orioles' catcher was Wilbert Robinson, the only man ever to get seven hits in a nine-inning game. Robbie was a solid backstop who, during Baltimore's golden years, had three superb seasons at the plate; he hit .334 in 1893, .353 in 1894, and .347 in 1896.

Other standouts were Big Dan Brouthers, the first baseman, who began his career with the Haymakers, came to Baltimore from Brooklyn in 1894, and batted .347 in his one season as an Oriole; Hughie Jennings, the short-fused shortstop, who led the team in batting in 1896 with a .401 average; and Joe Kelley, the left fielder, who batted cleanup. Of the players mentioned here, only Kelley has still to reach the Hall of Fame.

Fletcher, an old student of baseball, understood better than most how dramatically Baltimore was changing the game. Some critics accused the Orioles of poor sportsmanship, especially when it came out they used "special tactics," including these beauts: hiding an extra ball in the high outfield grass to use when the real ball got away from the defense; raising the level of the third-base line to keep bunts from going foul; with an Oriole on third, driving the pitcher crazy by sending the third-base coach dashing toward the plate; and sloping the first-base line to provide the speedy Baltimore runners with a downhill start.

These devices, obviously outside the rules, served notice to all challengers that the Orioles played to win. Fletcher admired them as much for their determination as for their skill, and he couldn't help wishing their traits would somehow rub off on the Trolley Dodgers. His wish would soon be granted.

Around New Year's Day, 1898, Charlie Ebbets, now secretary of the Brooklyn club, managed to acquire a financial interest by buying stock from George Chauncey and Gus Abell. Then, in January, Charlie Byrne died. Ebbets suddenly found himself president, and he immediately began looking for ways to bring the moribund franchise back to life. His first move was to pull out of East New York and return to South Brooklyn, where the club had flourished before the revolt of the Brotherhood.

He acquired land at First Street and Third Avenue and built a new Washington Park, complete with a modern grandstand that could seat twelve thousand. The plant was constructed in record time; by opening day everything was in shape, giving Ebbets reason to believe his first season as president would be a success.

He couldn't have been more wrong. The Trolley Dodgers got off to such a miserable start that by June Ebbets fired Billy Barnie and named Mike Griffin, his center fielder, as the new manager. When Griffin lost three out of his first four games Charlie took over the helm himself; he spent the last two-thirds of the season sitting on the bench directing the team from under his top hat. His record as a manager was considerably worse than mediocre; he won thirty-eight games and lost sixty-eight, for a winning percentage of .358.

Brooklyn wound up the season in tenth place, its worst showing since joining the National League. Ebbets had no illusions about his abilities as manager; he knew he belonged in the front office, not on the field. Then, out of the blue, help came. The bearer was Harry Von der Horst, owner of the Orioles.

By 1898 Baltimore fans, perhaps bored by their team's long string of successful seasons, had lost interest. The club was losing money, and Von der Horst was unhappy about having to make up the deficits. He had a great product, but people in Baltimore weren't buying, so he began looking to move Oriole baseball somewhere else.

Brooklyn, with the most rabid fans in the league, would surely support a winning team. Von der Horst went to Abell and Ebbets with a proposal. In exchange for a large piece of the Brooklyn club, he would give them Ned Hanlon, several key members of the Baltimore lineup, and a small percentage of Oriole stock. Once again "syndicate baseball" was rearing its ugly head.

Despite the possible conflict of interests, the deal went through, and overnight Brooklyn had a pennant contender. Among the players to switch clubs were Willie Keeler, Hughie Jennings, and Joe Kelley. John McGraw and Wilbert Robinson, partners in a saloon in Baltimore known as the Diamond, refused to leave town. McGraw became player–manager of the Orioles, and Robbie stayed on as catcher.

In 1899 the Trolley Dodgers received a new name. At the time there was a famous troupe on the vaudeville circuit known as Hanlon's Superbas; when a sportswriter began referring to the team as the Superbas, the public soon followed. Von der Horst's juggling act may have given the club an idiotic nickname, but that was a small price to pay for the best lineup in baseball.

The death of Charlie Byrne had a devastating effect upon the life of Fletcher Rice. The Ann Street casino closed down, putting Fletch out of work for the first time in over fifteen years. He was fifty-one years old, hardly an easy time in life to be seeking new employment.

But losing his job was only the beginning of his woes. A few months later Matilda left him. He woke up one morning to find her packing. She explained she'd had all she could stand of married life; her youth would soon be gone, and she had no intention of squandering even one more precious day in Brooklyn. Now that Fletcher was no longer employed, he would have plenty of time to look after the boys. As soon as she was situated in New York she would send him her address; he was not to bother her needlessly, but if an emergency were to arise he could, of course, get in touch with her.

Fletcher pleaded with her. He promised to begin searching at once for an honest job, and he even offered to sell the house and move the whole family to Manhattan. But Matilda had been brooding a long time; now that she'd finally made up her mind to move, nothing was going to hold her back. Fletcher at last gave up. Even though his stomach was tied in knots, he went to find a carriage and then sent his wife on her way.

So Fletcher, with no job and no prospects, was left to look after two young boys. He had a small cushion of money—enough to keep him out of the poorhouse for at least a year. Matilda's departure left him feeling so sorry for himself that he lost any desire he might have had to go out and find a job. Instead, he found escape in baseball.

That summer he and his sons went to nearly every Brooklyn home game. When the Superbas were out of town, Fletch would take the boys on the long trek up to the Polo Grounds to see the Giants in action. The only place where Fletcher completely forgot his troubles was Washington Park. As he watched the great Ned Hanlon lead the reborn

Brooklyn team to its first of two pennants in a row, he drifted back to happier days.

It didn't surprise Fletch that his sons quickly became ardent baseball fans. Alex, only six, followed the lead of his father and rooted for Brooklyn. Harry, at ten, already had a mind of his own and decided he preferred the Giants. His second favorite team was Baltimore, because his special hero was John McGraw. The Orioles' manager won Harry's admiration during a game in Brooklyn late in the 1899 season, about the time the Superbas clinched the pennant. Bill "Wagon Tongue" Keister, the Baltimore shortstop, was on first when McGraw, on the coaching lines, called to the Brooklyn pitcher, Brickyard Kennedy, to let him see the ball. Time had not been called; when Kennedy tossed the ball over McGraw jumped out of the way. It rolled all the way to the grandstand fence. Keister dashed over to second and later scored. "That goddamn moth-eaten trick!" Fletcher cried out in disgust. But Harry loved it, and McGraw was his hero.

Suddenly the season ended. Fletcher no longer had a refuge from the grim realities of his situation. The new year would bring in the twentieth century, an era some people were looking forward to with great expectations. But for Fletcher each tick of the clock brought closer the day sometime in January when his money would run out.

Ban Johnson may possibly put an
American League team in Weehauken
or Hackensack, but not in New York.
He has no more chance of placing a
team on Manhattan Island or the Bronx
than a pig has of making a point lace
coat for King Edward.

Big Jim Kennedy, 1902

3

The cold drizzles of late autumn did little to lift Fletcher's spirits. Knowing little about running a household or rearing two boys, he hired a housekeeper. Elizabeth was a handsome widow in her late thirties, but Fletcher took little notice of her. Aside from an occasional catch with Harry and Alex, Fletch confined his activities to sipping bourbon and reading newspaper accounts from the hot stove league.

In December Phoney Martin and Marty Swandell, two of his old teammates from the Eckfords, possibly aware of Fletch's despondency, sent him a note asking him to join them for a holiday dinner. They met in the Tenderloin, a West Side area of Manhattan famous for its resorts and disorderly houses. Fletcher, having spent the afternoon at the barbershop, was a picture of trimmed and manicured elegance.

It was a pleasant meal, and the three swapped many good baseball tales of days gone by. Marty and Phoney finally excused themselves, saying they had business early the next morning. Fletcher was well aware they had to get home to their wives.

Feeling a warm glow from the evening's wine and the unaccustomed fellowship, Fletcher strolled along Sixth Avenue. Muted sounds of merrymaking drifted out from nearly every building. Deciding to take advantage of his evening dress, he presented himself at the entrance to one of the palaces of chance.

"Evening, Sam," he said to the liveried Negro who opened the door. "Remember me? Fletcher Rice. I used to deal faro in Ann Street."

Sam grinned and opened the door wide. "Going to try your luck from the wrong side of the table, Mr. Rice?"

"I may indeed," Fletcher replied as he made his way up the heavily carpeted stairs. He picked up a brandy at the bar and wandered through the crowd of holiday plungers, nodding greetings to familiar faces. Not having the wherewithal to try his luck, he contented himself with watching the action at one of the roulette wheels.

Suddenly there was a burst of applause from the far side of the room. His curiosity aroused, Fletcher eased slowly in the general direction of a crowd gathered at one of the tables. From the back, he watched the faro dealer. Under the green eyeshade the young man's eyes darted nervously from side to side. The crowd's attention was riveted on the game, but something about the dealer's face caught Fletcher's eye. He could not see the table itself, but when the dealer brushed the perspiration from his upper lip, Fletcher noticed that the hand was shaking.

A corridor opened in the crowd, and Fletcher quickly stepped into it. As he reached the table, the spectators again broke into applause, startling the young dealer. At the end of the table a portly, red-faced man with a bulbous nose was gathering in a large pile of $100 chips. Time and other enemies had left their marks on the face, but it took Fletcher no time at all to identify it. He pointed a finger at the man and yelled out: "Cheat! I know that man—he's a cheat!"

Barney Devlin bolted for the door, overturning the table and scattering chips in the process, but before he could escape two large men materialized and escorted him from the room. Within moments the dealer, shaking in his boots, had likewise been convoyed through the door.

Still infuriated by the memory of Hamilton Baker's broken body, Fletcher went to refill his glass. Before he reached the bar, a man appeared at his elbow and whispered, "The proprietor requests a word." Fletcher nodded and followed the man upstairs to the private quarters. He knocked twice on an ornately carved door, opened it, and motioned to Fletcher to enter.

Smoothing his salt-and-pepper moustache, Fletcher stepped into an airy salon and hesitated at the edge of an oriental carpet. The room was ringed by marble statuary, and on three of the walls hung large oil paintings, two Flemish, one Italian. The fourth wall consisted mainly of French doors, which opened onto a terrace. In front of the doors, at a leather-top desk, sat Frank Farrell.

Farrell tilted his head and squinted at Fletch. "You have a familiar look, sir," he said after a moment.

"Fletcher Rice. Until recently I worked for Mr. Charles Byrne."

"Rest his soul."

"And you've seen me in the Club House in Saratoga, where I was also employed, Mr. Farrell."

"You know me, then."

"Only by name, sir." This brought a smile from Farrell. Mystery was his stock in trade. Although much was suspected about his activities, little was known, and virtually nothing could be proved. A popular joke among those in the sporting world was that Farrell was "John Doe himself," a reference to Farrell's knack for keeping his name from appearing in print.

Fletcher, however, knew more about Farrell than he was letting on. He knew that this short, stocky son of the Tenderloin was closely associated with former police chief William S. Devery. Their friendship had begun when Farrell was a barkeep at Sixth Avenue and Thirtieth Street and Devery was chief of the precinct house half a block away. He knew Farrell owned a number of race horses and was, along with Richard Canfield, John Daly, and Sol Lichtenstein, one of the "Big Four" of the gambling world. He had heard rumors that Farrell was the primary force in a syndicate that controlled two-thirds of all the gambling houses and poolrooms in New York City. That Big Bill Devery wasn't Farrell's only powerful friend was a foregone conclusion.

After studying Fletcher for a full minute, Farrell motioned for him to be seated. "I owe you a good turn, Mr. Rice. Another minute and that thimblerigger would have made off with the velvet."

Fletcher responded quickly: "Well, sir, I guess you'll be needing a new faro dealer."

"How did you know the man was cheating?" Farrell asked after a moment.

Fletch hesitated. "Let us say I know something of his history."

Farrell chuckled. "I'll wager you know a good deal of history." Then he slammed his fist on the desk. "Here's the deal," he said. "I can put a man of your experience and appearance to better use than dealing cards. Five hundred a week and plenty of bonuses." Farrell produced a wallet and peeled off a pair of $1,000 bills. "Your first bonus. Meet me here at eleven tomorrow morning and I'll fill you in on your duties. And, needless to say, the fewer people who know you're in with me, the more valuable you'll be."

The two men shook hands, and a somewhat numb Fletcher Rice started for the door. "One more thing, Rice," Farrell called after him. "I act on the square with everybody—and I make damn sure everybody does the same to me."

So, as the twentieth century began, Fletcher had a new position—utility man for Frank Farrell. He never again saw or heard of Barney Devlin, and he made it a point not to discover what fate had befallen Devlin at the hands of Farrell's hirelings. Fletcher's new job—if it could be called that—consisted mainly of "being around," as Farrell had put it. In the evenings Fletch would don black tie and mingle with the crowds at one or all of Farrell's establishments. If things were slow at a particular table, Fletch would shill—using house money, of course—until the table had filled with genuine players. Otherwise he socialized, kept an eye out for shady deals and known cheats, kept track of the comings, goings, fortunes, and misfortunes of high-rolling swells, and generally stayed on top of things.

Through diligence and constant association with members of the uppermost echelon of the sporting world, Fletcher soon became an expert on horse racing, boxing, bicycle racing, and even tennis. And, of course, his new associations gave Fletcher a better opportunity than ever before to study the inner workings of the baseball world. Within two months, Farrell had come to regard Fletch as one of his most reliable advisers.

When the 1900 season opened, Fletch found ample time to attend the home games of both the high-flying Superbas and the hapless Giants. Occasionally Harry or Alex or both would accompany him, but since Fletch made it a practice to check out the action in the betting parlors before and after the games, he usually found it more expedient to travel solo. Besides, the boys were getting old enough to look after themselves.

In June 1900 the players, fed up with the imperial ways of the owners, held a meeting at Sturtevant House in New York City and formed the Protective Association of Professional Baseball Players. After listening to a message delivered by an emissary of Samuel Gompers, the newborn association politely refused an invitation to join the American Federation of Labor. The owners, secure in their ivory towers, took little notice of the group's activities.

As the 1900 season came to an end, Hanlon's sublime Superbas, led by Willie Keeler, won the pennant with relative ease, while Freedman's ridiculous Giants finished last, a solid twenty-three games back.

That October the National Agreement, the supreme law of baseball for the preceding five years, expired. Three months later, in late January 1901, Byron Bancroft Johnson, president of the American League—formerly the Western League—pompously announced that his organization was assigning itself major league status. The new eight-team league, which intended to play a 140-game schedule, consisted of the Baltimore Orioles, the Boston Invaders, the Chicago White Sox, the Cleveland Babes—also called the Blues—the Detroit Tigers, the Milwaukee Brewers, the Philadelphia Athletics, and the Washington Senators.

Almost precisely three months later, on April 24, 1901, more than ten thousand customers passed through the turnstiles at Comiskey Park to see the White Sox down the Blues, 8–2, in the new league's first game. The White Sox went on to win the pennant behind a 24–7 season by right-hander Clark Griffith, who also managed the club. Griffith had much to do with the fact that the Sox outdrew their crosstown rivals, the Cubs, just as Cy Young, the new league's leading pitcher with thirty-three wins, was the main reason the Invaders outdrew their hometown rivals, the Beaneaters.

Fletcher had spent the 1901 season just as he had the previous season, dividing his time among Washington Park, the Polo Grounds, and the betting parlors. With all the new action caused by the new league, he had all he could do to keep up with the sports gossip and the welter of statistics. Even though Wee Willie hit .355 and Wild Bill Donovan was the winningest pitcher in the league, the best Brooklyn could do was a fairly distant third place behind the pennant-winning Pittsburgh Pirates, led by the hard hitting of Honus Wagner and the pitching of twenty-game winners Deacon Phillippe and Happy Jack Chesbro. The Giants finished a whopping thirty-seven games out of first place, but there was a bright spot, as Harry pointed out to Fletcher: Christy Mathewson, at age twenty-two, notched twenty victories in his first complete season.

On February 18, 1902, the estate of Josephine Peyton was sold at auction. Twelve parcels of real estate, valued at $377,800, were purchased by one John J. Byrne, who happened to be related to Big Bill Devery. A friend who had been present confided to Fletcher that Byrne had been closely attended by Uncle Big Bill, who had poked his nephew in the ribs approximately twelve times during the proceedings. One of the twelve parcels was an elegant house on Thirty-third Street.

Several days later, Farrell told Fletch he was planning to open a new gambling house, "the splendor and extent of which will not be exceeded by any similar establishment in the world." Opening was set for late summer, and Fletcher was to be instrumental in planning, coordinating, and supervising the preparation of the new casino, to be housed at 33 West Thirty-third Street, almost next door to the Waldorf Astoria.

In early June of that year Farrell became very interested in the progress of Ban Johnson and the American League. In addition to his responsibilities with the new casino, Fletcher also found himself charged with collecting and analyzing all details of the deepening struggle between the two major leagues.

By early August Farrell's new palace of chance was near completion, but circumstances began to worry Fletcher. Right-minded citizens and rabble-rousing politicians were making the going rough for the gambling world. A series of raids in July and early August had closed down a number of the resorts and poolrooms. Farrell himself had faith in his connections and noted that the raids were affecting only the penny-ante operators.

Devery, meanwhile, was running for the Democratic leadership of the Ninth District. On August 5, the *New York Times* labeled Devery a brigand, asserting he was "unfitted for any useful vocation, trusted by no one with anything at risk, and lacking every moral and mental quality which would recommend him to public confidence."

The date for the opening was set for August 30, to coincide with the running of the Futurity, a race that would draw wealthy sportsmen from throughout the country. The carving of the $30,000 marble stairway—the stoneworker had been laboring diligently for nearly eight months—was finished by mid-August, and Fletch watched as workmen carefully uncrated the priceless sculptures and placed them on the pedestals that lined the majestic sweep of steps. By late Friday, $50,000 worth of food and champagne had been delivered, and all was ready.

On Saturday Fletcher rose late, ate a light lunch prepared by Elizabeth, and arrived at the Sheepshead Bay racecourse in time for the first race. He placed several wagers but spent most of the afternoon circulating through the crowd. From time to time he would approach one of the nattier spectators, nod greetings, and then whisper several words into the person's ear. He even invited strangers when the cut of their clothes and the bulge of their wallets told him they would be welcome guests at Farrell's new establishment. After the final race he returned home to rest and dress for the evening's festivities.

When Fletcher approached 33 West Thirty-third, the house was brightly lighted. Two policemen were keeping watch over the gawking crowd. "Evening, Jake," Fletch said to one of them as he passed. "What's going on?"

"A housewarming, Mr. Rice," the young officer replied with a wink.

Fletch climbed the stairs to the entrance and rang the bell. The huge bronze door swung open, revealing Sam, who was sporting a new set of evening clothes.

"You look particularly resplendent this evening, Mr. Smith," Fletch bantered, proffering a calling card.

"Thank you, Mr. Rice," Sam said with a smile, accepting the card and then sliding it through a grating in the second door. Within moments the second bronze door opened, and Fletcher entered the finest reception room in all of New York. Presenting his hat and walking stick to a butler, he admired the marble stairway for a moment, then stepped into the elevator, which carried him to the second floor. His calling card had preceded him, and as he stepped from the elevator a second butler announced in a booming basso, "Mr. Fletcher Rice." Fletch bowed slightly, accepted a glass of champagne from a passing waiter, and surveyed the crowd.

The room was filled with roulette and faro tables surrounded by stuffed leather chairs. Fine oil paintings lined the walls, and the scene was given warmth by clusters of incandescent bulbs, all hidden from view by the hand-carved cornice that extended around the ceiling. In the dining room, beneath two shimmering chandeliers, a table thirty feet in length was heaped with gourmet viands. The light from two candelabra reflected merrily in the cut glass, crystal, and silver that lined the white linen.

Spotting Farrell in deep conversation with Joe Gordon, a small, dignified coal merchant, Fletcher smiled across the room and raised his glass. Farrell returned the salute.

The gaming tables were not to be open this night, and before long the formal atmosphere and trivial conversation began to bore Fletcher. Securing a bottle of bourbon, he climbed the back stairs past the third-floor apartment of Billy Burbridge, the manager, to the private rooms on the fourth floor. "We need a place," Farrell had said with a wink, "for those who become drowsy when the action is light." Snores of the overindulgent were already coming from two of the rooms. Finding an empty room, Fletcher removed his tie, collar, and shoes, poured a tumbler of bourbon, and crawled onto the four-poster. He began to think about Matilda. In a short time, he began to think about Kate. Just before he fell asleep, he realized he was thinking about Elizabeth.

Fletcher spent the next day lounging about the new club. He, Burbridge, and all the servants ignored the incessant ringing of the doorbell by curious persons, several of whom were reporters.

Late Monday morning, Fletcher and Billy Burbridge breakfasted on iced champagne and the first oysters of the season. As they were finishing, the butler announced the presence of Captain Sheehan of the Tenderloin precinct house. Sheehan joined them and accepted a cup of coffee.

"Listen, Billy," he said, "sorry to bother you, but the damn reporters are worrying me to death. Damn thing's all over the morning papers. 'Cap'n Sheehan,' they sez, 'what in the world's goin' on?' 'Don't know anything about it,' I sez, and I give 'em this." Sheehan demonstrated a shrug. "Say, you got any more o' them ersters?" Billy beckoned to a servant. "Quite a shindig the chief's throwin', eh?"

Sheehan was referring to the fact that Devery, in an attempt to secure votes in the upcoming election, had that morning presented the longshoremen and other working men of the Tenderloin with two 850-pound roast oxen, two hundred half-barrels of beer, eighteen thousand loaves of Vienna bread, and a speech. "Last I heard there was ten thousand souls on hand."

Sheehan sucked the last oyster shell dry and stood up. "Got to go tell them damn reporters this here is a private residence. Listen, Billy, with all this damn stink I just might have to raid this damn place. Before you open up you put a man over by Astor Court in his shirtsleeves. You know, one up, one down. Don't you go openin' till I get word to him."

That evening Fletcher removed his coat, rolled his right shirtsleeve up to above the elbow, and took a seat on a barrel that was standing in front of Astor Court. For nearly an hour he peered into the face of each passerby. Finally a large, jovial-looking man came along. As he passed the barrel, he caught Fletch's eye and nodded once in the affirmative. After waiting a few minutes, Fletcher jumped down from the barrel, strolled past the house, and nodded to Sam, who was peeking through the cheesecloth curtains. Sam immediately began admitting patrons. Earlier that day Fletcher had received a hand-carried note from Farrell:

Eschew things not tested by time.

John Doe

Fletch went straight home. Two days later he read with amusement a letter from Farrell printed in the *Times*. Farrell emphatically denied any connection with the alleged gambling house. The editorial page of the same paper mentioned that William S. Devery was a "vulgar wretch" and a "cheap Falstaff."

Reasoning that it might be wise to eschew all gambling spots, time-tested or not, Fletcher spent the fall attending ball games and reading about the machinations of the two leagues, now locked in mortal combat. Brooklyn, again led by Willie Keeler, played .543 ball in 1902 but finished twenty-seven and a half games behind a clearly superior first-place Pittsburgh. Even though the denizens of the Polo Grounds finished in the cellar, fifty-three and a half games out, Harry assured Fletcher that the Giants had a bright future.

In the Junior Circuit, Connie Mack's Athletics won the pennant, led by perhaps the flakiest ballplayer of all time, wacky Rube Waddell, a twenty-four-game winner.

In the fall of 1902, New York City was sure that Ban Johnson planned to land an American League entry on Manhattan Island itself.

Following Farrell's instructions, Fletcher had made it a point to keep abreast of the development of the American League. He now knew as much about the American League as anyone other than Ban Johnson himself.

Ban Johnson *was* the American League. He was a forceful man, a relatively fair man, and he was possessed of a lack of scruples adequate to ensure his success. He was known to drink, often to excess, but never to the detriment of his dealings. Johnson had attended both Oberlin and Marietta colleges. At both schools he distinguished himself as a catcher, but injuries prevented his pursuing a career as a ballplayer.

After a short stay in law school, Johnson became a sports reporter for the *Commercial-Gazette* in Cincinnati. He soon became a drinking crony of Charles Comiskey, then the manager of the Reds. It took Johnson little time to earn the hatred of John T. Brush, owner of the Reds. He accomplished this by pointing out in his newspaper stories that Brush was a pinchpenny, a scoundrel, and a generally ungifted person.

Johnson and Comiskey may have hatched the idea of the American League as early as 1893. In November of that year, Comiskey singlehandedly persuaded the owners of the newly reorganized Western League to install his pal Ban Johnson, who had virtually no credentials, as secretary, treasurer, and president of the league. It so happened that Brush owned a team in the Western League. He got wind of what was afoot and had already packed his monkey wrench when Comiskey waylaid him and conjured up a vision of the idyllic life he would lead once Johnson had vacated Cincinnati. Since it was out of the question for him to support Johnson's election bid, Brush conveniently missed the train that would have taken him to the meeting in Detroit, where Johnson was elected.

Comiskey's contract with the Reds was effective through the 1894 season. When the agreement terminated, Charlie turned down Brush's new offer. Instead, he bought the Sioux City franchise of the Western League and moved it to St. Paul. Brush told the world Charlie was crazy, but he was beginning to suspect he had been flimflammed.

In 1899 the Columbus franchise was moved to Buffalo. After the season that year, the Nationals dropped Baltimore, Cleveland, Louisville, and Washington. Johnson was overjoyed, but he moved cautiously. The first step was to give the league the sound if not the substance of a major. There was no question that the league was a minor, since the Nationals were still drafting its best players under the provisions of the National Agreement. The Western League's club owners met that October in Chicago and voted to drop the restrictive word "Western" and replace it with the more expansive "American."

Johnson's next step was to secure financial backing. To do this, he traveled to Cleveland, where he enlisted the aid of Charles J. Somers and John F. Kilfoyl. Kilfoyl had amassed a fortune through shrewd dealings in real estate. Somers had sown his inheritance from the family coal business, nurtured it well, and reaped millions. Within hours the fast-talking Johnson had their support.

His war chest overflowing, Johnson confidently moved the Grand Rapids franchise into Cleveland and Comiskey's St. Paul franchise into Chicago. The Cubs' management was less than delighted that Comiskey had crashed their party, but there was little it could do. The alternatives were to accept Comiskey's presence or to start a war. Since Johnson was making a great show of abiding by the National Agreement, the Cubs could count on little support from the rest of the league in a showdown.

When the National Agreement expired in October 1900, Johnson made no move to renew it. The president of the National League, Nick Young, sent Johnson a letter ordering him to cough up his dues. Johnson wrote back that he felt a personal meeting and discussion were in order. Young's reply was silence.

Johnson had been dealt an ace when the players formed the Players' Protective Association in June 1900. In December of that year the owners of the Nationals met. Most of the meeting was taken up by wrangling. Still confident of their monopoly, the owners showed no inclination to grant the association any of its demands—which basically were the abolition of the reserve clause, the guarantee of higher salaries, and the cessation of the practice of farming out players to other teams without the players' consent.

Convinced of the owners' intransigence, the players sent two representatives—Hughie Jennings and Chief Zimmer—to find out where Johnson stood on these issues. They found Johnson in Philadelphia. While the enemy owners were occupied bickering at one another, Johnson and Connie Mack had stolen into Philadelphia to install an American League club to compete with the Phillies.

Johnson welcomed Jennings and Zimmer with open arms, promised to recognize the association, and agreed to honor all their demands. The two players in turn informed Johnson that the majority of stars in the National League were more than willing to listen to offers.

About six weeks later, in late January 1901, the American League owners met in Chicago and voted unanimously to become a major league. The Buffalo franchise was moved to Boston, again financed by Charlie Somers. The Indianapolis, Minneapolis, and Kansas City franchises were dropped. The placing of teams in Washington and Baltimore made the league's invasion of the East complete.

Johnson compiled a list of approximately fifty players he coveted for the American League and commissioned a band of raiders to bring them into the fold. Before opening day of the 1901 season, all but one of the players on the list had signed with the Americans. Among those who jumped to the new league were Cy Young, Clark Griffith, John McGraw, Joe McGinnity, and Nap Lajoie.

Comiskey's White Sox won the first pennant of the new league. During the first season of the war, 1901, the Nationals drew approximately 2 million spectators, while the Americans were drawing approximately 1.7 million. In Boston and Philadelphia—two of the three cities in which the leagues met head-on—the American entries emerged victorious in the race to attract supporters.

By 1902, the National League found itself in dire straits. Not only was attendance off, but teams were being forced to bid competitively for the services of ballplayers. The Nationals, long accustomed to being the only game in town, were not faring well in the bidding war. Every team in the league found itself missing from four to ten of its top players— every team, that is, except Pittsburgh. Because Johnson thought Barney Dreyfuss could be persuaded to bring his team into the American League, he had followed a hands-off policy with the Bucs. Roster intact, the Pirates won with relative ease in 1901 and frolicked to the flag in 1902, winning seven of every ten games they played.

When the 1902 season ended and accountings were made, the Americans had won the battle of the turnstiles, outdrawing the Nationals by more than a half million.

Meanwhile, rumors were flying in New York. It was generally believed that Johnson would attempt to place a team not only in Manhattan but in Pittsburgh as well. The wise money was saying the New York entry would be backed by Senator Tim Sullivan, that the business manager would be Big Jim Kennedy, a well-known sports promoter, and that the playing field would be on any one of a dozen sites—several of which were imaginary.

The unwanted publicity concerning the new casino had forced Farrell to postpone its opening. Two days before Halloween, the House with the Bronze Doors suffered another setback. When a reporter gained access to the building and began to ask bothersome questions, two of Burbridge's men contused and concussed him a good bit. The story in the *Times* the next day, while expressing outrage at the incident, mentioned only that the house was "said to be owned by a wealthy gambler." John Doe had done it again.

By early November there was no longer even a lingering doubt that Johnson intended to place a team in New York City. It was generally accepted that Comiskey would donate Clark Griffith to manage and pitch for the New York Americans. Speculation was rampant that Wee Willie Keeler would jump from Brooklyn to the American entry. The consensus was still that Big Jim Kennedy would head the operation and that Tim Sullivan was backing the deal. A new name, however, was being mentioned along with Sullivan—Frank Farrell. It was agreed that between them the two men had enormous power.

It would take nothing less than enormous power to ensure the success of the venture. John Brush had vowed to thwart the attempted invasion of his turf. Whenever Johnson showed interest in a particular location, Brush's spies would report the news to him. Brush would feed the information to Andrew Freedman, who would then pull wires in Tammany Hall. Within a day or so the property would be sliced up by streets or declared a city park.

Clark Griffith was paying regular visits to Manhattan, and it was reported that the Old Fox had already signed several well-known players. It was also reported that the "enormous power" behind the New York Americans considered giving Brush a taste of his own by cutting streets through the Polo Grounds. It was decided, however, that such a move would alienate the fans, who were solidly behind the Americans.

On the first day of December the House with the Bronze Doors was raided. The only person arrested was Sam Smith. Ten days later, when Sam was arraigned, the Negro doorman was defended by former New York Governor Black and former Assistant D.A. O'Reilly. He was released on $1,000 bail, and the case was quietly buried. The incident did, however, persuade Farrell to dissociate himself entirely from the house and look for action elsewhere.

What that new action was to be was confirmed to Fletcher in early December. Jim Kennedy had just returned from Europe, where he had been supervising his bicycle-racing enterprises, and it seemed that Big Jim's wind had changed direction. He now disclaimed any association with the New York Americans and proclaimed loudly that Johnson's efforts were doomed. Whether Kennedy had been forced out or bought out, Fletcher never learned. On Sunday, December 8, Fletcher received word that Farrell wished to see him.

"I'm about to have a business conference, Fletch," Farrell told him. "I want you to sit in the corner and back up my memory."

Shortly, two men arrived. The first was Joe Vila of the *New York Sun*, one of the better-known sportswriters of the day, who introduced his companion—Byron Bancroft Johnson. Johnson was a large man—Fletcher guessed about two hundred fifty pounds—who projected energy and confidence. He punctuated his remarks by slamming a fist against an open palm or anything else within reach.

"Mr. Farrell," Johnson began, "it's a pleasure to meet you at last. You must forgive my insisting on this meeting, but frankly I was beginning to suspect that Joe here was working for Freedman or the National League, trying to stall me until it was too late.

"Let me fill you in. As you probably know, at our league meeting in Detroit last spring, my club presidents gave me carte blanche in my endeavors to place a team in this city. We've lost our shirts in Baltimore, so we're ready to move the franchise here. I have felt all along that we will not be on equal footing with the Nationals until we've fielded a ball club in the metropolis of the United States.

"There has been some difficulty in securing a suitable site for a playing field. I have, however, signed a lease for land at One Hundred Sixty-eighth Street and Broadway. The land is owned by a charitable organization, so Freedman and his Tammany cronies will play hell trying to run streets through it. My prospective backers, however, enthusiastic at first, are now half-hearted, if not invisible."

"I will back a baseball team in New York City," Farrell said.

"It will cost a good deal of money and you'll have a hell of a fight on your hands."

"I have money," Farrell said quietly, "and I do not object to fighting." He handed a check to Johnson. "Here is my guarantee."

Johnson looked at the check. "Twenty-five thousand is a large amount," he said.

"Ban," Vila said, smiling, "Frank drops that much on a horse race."

"All right," Johnson said. Heaving his bulk from the chair he strode

78

to Farrell's desk and pounded it with his fist. "Done!" The two men shook hands. "I spoke with Frank Robison on the train that brought me here. He was en route to the National League meeting, which is taking place here this week. Robison is tired of the fight and intends to urge the other owners to sue for peace. However, I wish to keep this evening's transaction secret for the time being. We may yet need a bombshell to explode within the ranks of the Nationals."

The National League meeting of 1902 took place December 9 through 12 at the Victoria Hotel in New York City. None of the owners noticed the teenage hotel employee, hired specially for the occasion, who from time to time left off emptying ashtrays and busing dishes to hurry behind a potted palm and scribble notes. It was Harry Rice.

When the breathless messenger arrived with the note from Harry, Fletcher gave him a dollar and read with interest:

> Dear Poppa,
>
> *Robison:* "Am tired of fight that can only result in continued loss & ultimate ruin."
> *Col. Rogers:* "Agree."
> *Herrmann:* "Can see no necessity for continuing war for sake of pride & stubbornness."
> *Brush:* "Nothing to say @ present."
> *Ebbets:* "Either way."
> *Dreyfuss:* "Ditto."
> *Soden:* "2 teams no good in Bos. Let's fight."
> *Brush:* "Fight it out. Willing to stake reputation & existence AL has no grounds on Manhat. AL not sincere in wanting peace. Put to test & put NL right in public eye."
>
> Peace faction jumped @ chance. Rogers composed resolution offering to negotiate. Passed unan. Negotiating comm. formed. Herrmann named chair., 'cause new to OB & has no enemies. Robison & Hart also named, 'cause friendly with AL owners. Adjourning soon.
>
> Love,
> Harry

Fletcher pocketed the note and hurried off to the Hotel Criterion to inform Ban of the developments. He entered the hotel behind three men. As he reached the center of the lobby, Fletcher suddenly swerved and headed into the hotel bar. The three men were August Herrmann, Frank DeHaas Robison, and Joseph A. Hart. They had evidently walked the twelve blocks from the Hotel Victoria to see Johnson in person.

From his vantage point in the bar, Fletcher watched as the three men approached Johnson and John Kilfoyl, who were just finishing their evening meal in the dining room. Johnson appeared surprised, but the conversation seemed amicable. After several minutes Johnson and Kilfoyle rose, and the entire group made for the bar. Fletch sidled into a dark corner.

As the group entered, Johnson called for several bottles of champagne. When they arrived and all the glasses were filled, Johnson raised his.

"To your good health, gentlemen. And to peace. You shall have my formal reply within twenty-four hours."

Before leaving New York, Johnson met again with the National League peace committee. He also announced to the press that the New York Americans had backing, a playing field, and several star players, including Griffith, Keeler, Dave Fultz, and Jack Chesbro.

The negotiating committees of the two leagues met in January in Cincinnati. The Nationals' arbitration team consisted of the three men who had visited Johnson at the Hotel Criterion and Harry Pulliam, who had been elected league president at the New York meeting. The Americans were represented by Johnson, Comiskey, Somers, and Killilea.

By mid-January 1903 peace had come. Even John Brush—the main supporter of a plan to form a single twelve-team league with Johnson as president—was ostensibly supporting the treaty. Under the agreement the Nationals were to allow the Americans to invade New York unmolested. In return, the Americans pledged to stay out of Pittsburgh. Each league retained its eight-team format, and the committees worked out nonconflicting schedules in those cases where rival-league clubs shared a home town.

The committees created the National Commission, a three-man panel, to be the supreme governing body of organized baseball. The commission was to comprise the presidents of each league and a third, elected, member. August Herrmann, the new owner of the Reds, was selected to rule, along with Johnson and Pulliam.

The American League agreed to institute the foul-strike rule, which the Nationals had been using since 1901. Before the adoption of this hotly contested rule, foul balls had counted as neither balls nor strikes.

One of the stickier problems facing the two negotiating committees was the disposition of disputed players, of whom there were sixteen. Fletcher was particularly pleased with this aspect of the agreement, since two of the nine athletes ultimately awarded to the American League were Willie Keeler and Dave Fultz.

Frank Farrell was also pleased, both with the results of the Cincinnati meetings and with the situation in general. True, the Oriole franchise, which Johnson had sold him for about $18,000, did not bring with it a great deal of baseball talent, but Johnson and the other magnates of the American League were doing nearly everything in their power to see that Farrell would field a representative team in New York.

In early February 1903, Farrell, Clark Griffith, and Fletcher journeyed to Washington Heights to inspect the site of the ball park to be. Farrell grimaced as he looked about. There were outcroppings of rock, stands of trees, ravines, a brook, and a swamp.

Several days later, five hundred workmen descended on the grounds. Before they could begin to construct the wooden grandstand that would hold fifteen thousand, the workmen would have to blast out some twelve thousand cubic yards of rock and haul in thirty thousand cubic yards of fill.

John Brush was not yet resigned to the American League presence in the city. Petitions, claiming the ball park would attract an undesirable element and demanding that streets be cut through the property, were circulated throughout the neighborhood. Farrell and Devery were equal to the challenge and managed to thwart Brush's last-gasp sabotage attempts. Brush, of course, denied any knowledge of the maneuverings, much less involvement.

In March the newspapers published a list of stockholders in the club. Farrell's name was among those mentioned, but Devery's name was absent. Joe Gordon, who had held several minor political offices and had owned stock in Day's Metropolitans—and who also happened to be John Day's brother-in-law—was named president of the club.

Gordon announced that he owned controlling interest in the team and would be solely responsible for determining its destiny. When a reporter spotted Big Bill inspecting the construction progress, Devery protested, "Me a backer! I only wished I did own some stock in a baseball club. I'm a poor man and don't own stock in anything. Besides, how could I pitch a ball with this stomach?" The New York sporting world, however, was well aware that Devery had kicked in $100,000. He and Farrell owned the majority of the stock, if not all of it.

The team was training in Atlanta, and the word was they would be pennant contenders from the first. Wee Willie was giving his teammates pointers in batsmanship, and the Old Fox, Clark Griffith, was sharing his baseball wisdom. The gossip from the South had it that the New York uniforms were "the swellest thing in the business" and "louder than Bowery hose." Griff had designed them. His players said he was drugged at the time.

On April 18 the blasting was finally finished and the workmen began to construct the grandstand from the enormous pile of lumber that had been stacked next to the cement foundation. Five days later, on April 23, the New York Americans played their maiden contest in Washington. The Senators won the game, 3–1.

On May 30, 1903, Fletcher attended the home opener. The opponents were again the Senators. Each of the 16,243 spectators passing through the turnstiles, equipped with automatic counting devices, was presented with a miniature American flag. As Fletch moved toward his box in the unfinished grandstand, he tipped his hat to Farrell and Devery, who were already seated in their box and trying to look inconspicuous.

In right field there was a deep gully that the workmen had not yet had time to fill. A rope stretched around the outfield. Any ball hit past it would go as a ground-rule double. The crowd, however, seemed forgiving of the rough condition of the park. They were aware of the struggle that had faced the new club.

The day was clear and hot, but the stiff breeze that snapped the colorful flags and bunting kept the temperature at a comfortable level. Far below the playing field, the sun glinted on the Hudson. The 69th Regiment Band struck up the "Washington Post March" in deference to the visiting team and began to lead the march to the grandstand. A beaming Ban Johnson and a dapper Joe Gordon, his white moustache immaculately trimmed and his bald head protected by a derby, followed the band and led the two teams to the foul line in front of the stands.

As the last note faded, the fans waved their miniature flags and uttered a roar that rolled down Washington Heights and across the river, reverberated off the New Jersey Palisades, and echoed back to the playing field. The teams broke ranks and began their warmups as the band plunged into "Yankee Doodle."

The New Yorkers were resplendent in their white uniforms, white flannel hats with black facing, and maroon jackets with mother-of-pearl buttons. The Senators wore white shirts and blue pants.

As the band finished "Yankee Doodle" and began to move off the field, a fan sitting near Fletcher groused, "They oughta played 'God Save the King.' Highlanders! Goddamn limey name for a bunch of good Yankee boys." They were being called the Highlanders because their playing field was one of the highest points in Manhattan and because a well-known British military unit of the era was Gordon's Highlanders. The team was also being called the Hilltoppers, the Porch-Climbers, and the Burglars, the latter two nicknames a reference to the team's somewhat surreptitious entry into the city.

A still beaming Ban Johnson threw the ball in to catcher Jack O'Connor, and the game began. After Happy Jack Chesbro, stolen from Pittsburgh in one of the final raids before the peace, held the Senators scoreless in the first, Wee Willie got things started for the Highlanders by popping a clean hit and subsequently scoring. The New Yorkers added runs in the second, fifth, and seventh innings. In control from the beginning, the Highlanders took the game, 6–2.

After their auspicious home opener, the Highlanders skidded. Griff managed to regroup his boys in midseason and brought them home in the first division. The Highlanders finished the season fourth, with a better than .500 winning percentage. Chesbro won twenty-one, and the Old Fox put himself in the box often enough to notch fourteen victories.

Owners Dreyfuss of Pittsburgh and Killilea of Boston agreed to match their two pennant-winning teams in a nine-game postseason series. The Pirates won three of the first four games, but the Pilgrims—"Invaders" proved to be a short-lived nickname—came back to sweep four straight, winning the World Championship, five games to three.

For the 1904 campaign Griffith beefed up the team by strengthening his pitching staff and picking up catcher Red Kleinow and outfielders John Anderson and Patsy Dougherty. The story of the year was Chesbro. Grim-visaged Happy Jack started fifty-one games, completing forty-eight and winning forty-one, a single-season record no other pitcher has ever been able to match.

On October 7 the Yankees (that grousing fan had proved prophetic—the team was now being referred to as the Yankees almost as often as it was the Highlanders) were in first place by a half game. Three days later, on the final day of the season, they found themselves trailing Boston by one and a half games. And on that day, October 10, 1904, the Pilgrims arrived at Hilltop Park to play a doubleheader. If the Yankees could win both games they would own the flag. The Giants had already clinched the National League pennant, but Brush had made it clear that his team would not condescend to play a series against the champions of the American League.

It was a brisk fall day when Fletcher, along with nearly thirty-thousand other spectators, made his way into the grandstand. He stopped by the box where Farrell and Devery sat, handed over an envelope containing records of the bets the two men had made and booked, chatted briefly with Farrell, and then moved down several boxes to his own seat.

When Fletcher looked back, he saw that the two men had called Griffith over and were talking to him. Their continual second-guessing was a source of irritation to the Old Fox. He listened, stonefaced, then trotted back onto the field.

The controlled tension in the grandstand erupted into wild cheering when Jack Chesbro placed his 5-foot, 9-inch frame in the box and began throwing warmups. After all, Happy Jack had sent enemies down to defeat forty-one times that season. His opponent, Bill Dineen, one of the heroes of the 1903 World Series, had notched a paltry total of twenty-two wins.

It was a pitchers' duel all the way, and the excitement mounted as the line of goose eggs lengthened on the scoreboard. In the third inning Chesbro smashed a triple to no avail. In the fifth the Yankees finally staged a rally. They put together two walks and three hits, and when the inning ended they owned a two-run lead.

Boston came back to score two in the seventh, deadlocking the game. Fletcher fidgeted through the scoreless eighth. Then the Pilgrims came to bat in the top of the ninth. Lou Criger, the Boston catcher, ripped a single to start things off. He moved to second on a sacrifice bunt and took third on a slow roller to the right side of the infield.

Fletcher squirmed in his seat and stared hard to see whether Chesbro, an expert spitballer, would load the next pitch. Happy Jack glanced at Criger on third, went into his motion, and delivered. Red Kleinow, the catcher, had no chance. He leaped into the air, but the ball sailed a good ten feet over his outstretched mitt. Criger chugged down the third base line and scored easily.

The New Yorkers came up empty in their half of the ninth, and it was all over. A dejected Fletcher Rice did not remain to see the Yankees go on to win the second game, 1–0. He trudged numbly from the park. He had been sure his team would win it all. So sure that he was now $5,000 poorer.

As the years of the century's first decade ticked away, Fletcher passed his sixtieth birthday. His hair and moustache were now silver. Because of his relationship with Elizabeth—a relationship that had developed shortly after the opening of the House with the Bronze Doors—he never considered remarrying. For her part, Elizabeth endured the tongue-clucking of Park Slope as much out of affection for the boys as for Fletcher. Just as Matilda had, Elizabeth frowned on Fletcher's drinking habits, abhorred his fascination with gambling, and found him, at times, a silly man.

The standout performer for the 1905 Highlanders was Hal Chase, their newly acquired first baseman. Chase was a big, handsome natural athlete who is often mentioned as the greatest first baseman of all time. In sacrifice situations, Prince Hal astounded opponents by charging the plate, scooping up the bunt, and rifling the ball to second to start the double play.

In a game with Cleveland, Nap Lajoie, who had heard of Chase's plate-charging technique, faked a bunt and tried to take off Hal's head with a screaming line drive. Chase, only a few feet from the batter's box, calmly speared the ball and pegged to Jimmy Williams at second, doubling the runner.

But Chase's easygoing ways also made enemies. Many players and fans objected to his appearing in public unshaven, tieless, and wearing sandals. On off days Chase would often play with semipro teams to pick up extra money. During the offseason he played with so-called outlaw leagues in California, his home state, under an assumed name.

He also hustled extra bucks at shooting, golfing, boxing, or anything that required skill or strength. Although his detractors were soon saying that the Prince was not averse to fixing games if the price was right, his affable way, quick smile, and stupendous talent gained him many admirers and increased the crowds at Hilltop Park.

The 1905 Yanks finished in sixth place. Aside from the exploits of Prince Hal, the only bright spots were Willie Keeler, who with a .302

batting average was one of only two players in the league to break the magic .300 mark, and Jack Chesbro, who won twenty games, well off his previous season's pace but still more than respectable.

In 1906 both Chesbro and Al Orth had twenty-game-plus seasons, and Keeler, Chase, and Kid Elberfeld all batted over .300. But the best the New Yorkers could do was a second-place finish, three games behind the Hitless Wonders of Chicago. The White Sox went on to win the World Championship from their hometown rivals, the Cubs, in six games.

The following season—a season that saw a twenty-year-old Detroit slugger named Ty Cobb win his first batting championship—the Yankees slipped to fifth. In that same year, 1907, Farrell and Devery came out into the open. They dismissed figurehead Joe Gordon and took over the front-office reins themselves.

Farrell's and Devery's taking open control of the team signaled the beginning of a dismal era for the Yankees. Midway through the 1908 season the volume of second-guessing, needling, and interference reached a critical mass—Clark Griffith resigned in disgust. The owners then made Norman Arthur Elberfeld, the Tabasco Kid, the first of a long line of managerial scapegoats. The Kid quickly lived up to his nickname, alienating many of the players, including Hal Chase, who jumped the team and popped up weeks later as a member of the Stockton Club in the California State League. The Highlanders finished dead last, thirty-nine and a half games out.

For the 1909 season, Farrell and Devery coaxed their star first baseman back from California and hired George Stallings, who had managed in Detroit and Newark, as manager. Stallings, who was to become the miracle man of the Miracle Braves in 1914, could manage only parlor tricks with the Yankees. They finished fifth.

In 1910 baseball officially became the national pastime when President Taft threw out the first ball on the opening day of the season. The ball he tossed out was of a new variety, having a cork center surrounded by ⅛ inch of rubber. The new ball was livelier, held its shape better, and had an immediate if not overwhelming effect on the number and distance of hits.

Stallings piloted the Yanks to a .555 season, but, almost inevitably, there was dissension in the ranks. Toward the end of the season the team was on a road trip when suddenly Hal Chase disappeared. When the team returned home, the reason for Chase's absence became evident. Prince Hal had cornered Farrell and delivered an ultimatum—either he or Stallings would have to go. When Stallings, who had gotten his fill of front-office meddling, heard the news, he saved Farrell from having to make a decision. He exploded like a skyrocket and came down in environs other than those of New York City. Farrell immediately named Chase manager.

Under Prince Hal the Highlanders won nine of their last eleven games. Even though they finished with a .583 winning percentage, the team ended up fourteen and a half games behind first-place Philadelphia, the first team in the history of the American League to win more than a hundred games.

As the 1910 season came to an end, baseball fever was running high in New York. The Athletics and the Cubs were preparing to square off in the World Series, but the Big Apple was staging a fall classic all its own: At long last the Yankees and the Giants were going to meet. John Brush had relented and allowed his manager, John McGraw, to test his team against the crew from the Hilltop in a best-of-seven series. Hughie Jennings, who had motored all the way from Detroit to cover the clash for the *New York World*, called the teams dead even and predicted the team that got the jump would win it all.

On the morning of October 13, 1910, Farrell and Brush each deposited $10,000 good-faith money with Thomas Lynch, president of the National League, who was acting on behalf of the National Commission. By the midafternoon game time, some twenty-five thousand fans—Fletcher Rice included—had jammed the Polo Grounds to see the Yanks' young ace, Russell Ford, purveyor of the "mystery pitch," go against Christy "Big Six" Mathewson, the acknowledged king of the hill. The crowd was in a festive mood, although Highlander supporters and Giant fans pelted one another with balls of wadded newspaper, and the atmosphere was jovial and friendly.

The crowd gave an enthusiastic cheer when the ailing John Brush, looking frail in his spectacles and soft cap, was driven in his car across the outfield. For his part, Farrell remained seated in his box, his snapbrim pulled low over his eyes.

The crowd roared again when the two teams took the field, increased the din when they lined up and shook hands, and nearly brought down the grandstand when the boyish Chase and the stocky McGraw clasped hands near home plate for the benefit of photographers. When Hughie Jennings took his place in the pressbox, he was forced to take a number of bows before the crowd would finally let him be seated for good.

Mathewson received a tremendous ovation as he began his warmups. He then proceeded to retire the Yankees with little effort. When stocky little Russ Ford made his way to the box, the crowd greeted him with equal enthusiasm. Ford, possessed of a spitter he could break either way and a fine curve, showed the form with which he had chalked up twenty-six victories that season by easily putting down the Giant side.

In the top of the second, Highlander shortstop Jack Knight cracked a leadoff single between short and third. Several pitches later, Mathewson, with a beautiful move to first, caught Knight far off the bag. Knight simply dug for second, and when Fred Merkle threw the ball five feet over Al Bridwell's outstretched glove, Knight moved on to third. Unflustered, Big Six bore down and struck out Frank LaPorte and Birdie

Cree. Catcher Ed Sweeney swung late on an inside fastball, caught the ball on the handle of the bat, and sent a high pop into the area behind first base. Matty had already started off the field when Merkle fell down, missing the ball, and Knight scored.

The Yankees led, 1–0, until the sixth. In that inning, the Giants' Josh Devore beat out a bunt for a single and then stole second. Larry Doyle laid down a sacrifice bunt, moving Devore to third, and was out on a close call at first.

McGraw, enraged, stormed onto the field. When umpires Klem and Evans jointly ordered him back to the bench, a gleeful Fletcher couldn't help calling out, "Stop squealing, Muggsy!" The other Yankee fans took up the cry and bellowed it at McGraw until he was back in his place, livid. The glee was short-lived. Cree fumbled a fly ball off the bat of Red Murray, and Devore scampered home with the tying run.

The game remained a 1–1 pitchers' duel until the eighth. As twilight began to settle over the Polo Grounds, Mathewson led off the Giant half of the inning with a single to right. Devore then laid down his second bunt single of the game. Doyle, the next batter, also bunted. Chase fielded the ball brilliantly and fired a perfect strike to third, but Jimmy Austin bobbled the throw and the bases were loaded. Ford quieted the frenzy of the Giant rooters by fanning Fred Snodgrass and forcing Murray to hit a shallow fly. Two out, bases loaded.

Bridwell then executed what Fletcher later called "another goddamn old Baltimore trick" by refusing to get out of the way of one of Ford's spitballs. As Bridwell hopped about holding his right ankle, Matty dented the plate with the go-ahead run. Art Devlin, Merkle, and Chief Meyers followed with singles to score three more runs before Mathewson popped up to end the rally he had started. Russ Ford had struck out nine, but Matty had struck out fourteen and won the game, 5–1. Mathewson was still king of the hill.

The next day it was the Yankee fans' turn to cheer. Little Jack Warhop pitted his 14–14 record against the 15–12 credentials of Hooks Wiltse. In the ninth inning, with the score tied, 4–4, Wiltse walked Chase to force in the winning run. Hooks, the willowy southpaw of Coogan's Bluff, howled with dismay and fury, slammed his glove to the ground, heaved his hat to the wind, turned 360 degrees shaking his clenched fists at the world, and then shambled from the field, slope-shouldered and dejected.

Hilltop Park was pandemonium. Hats, jackets, waistcoats, and small change filled the air. Hal Chase was the man of the hour, and thousands of fans pursued him, anxious to touch him adoringly and bear him from the field. Prince Hal skipped nimbly away from the multitude. In front of the clubhouse he paused and turned back. He waved, lifted his hat, and laughed with pure joy before disappearing.

At the Polo Grounds the next day, nearly thirty thousand fans watched as the Giants built up a 5–1 lead in six innings. In the top of the seventh, as fog and twilight gloom began to settle over the arena, the Highlanders loaded the bases with nobody out. McGraw then made a move that no one could argue with. He pulled pitcher Louis Drucke and replaced him with Mathewson. Big Six allowed three Yankees to cross the plate before he put out the fire, but the Giants went on to win, 6–4.

After resting on Sunday, the two teams resumed hostilities on Monday and played to a 5–5 tie, the game being called on account of darkness after ten innings. In the fifth game of the series, Mathewson was again the flagbearer for the Giants, Ray Fisher for the Yankees. Matty pitched masterfully, allowing only one run, and that unearned. Fisher, with an extremely slow motion, allowed the Giants to steal six bases and sealed his doom by delivering two home-run pitches. The Giants won the game, 5–1.

The sixth game, played at Hilltop Park, was a slugfest in which the two teams combined for twenty-four hits and thirty total bases. The Yankees' 10–2 victory was highlighted by another brilliant, if not magical, play by Hal Chase. In the seventh Snodgrass smoked one down the third base line. Austin made a fine stop but then threw the ball well over Chase's head. Hal simply ran up his invisible stepladder and stabbed the ball, which was on its way to the twentieth row of the grandstand. Chase then somehow managed to get his foot back down to the bag a full step ahead of Snodgrass. The Yankee fans went wild. The Giant fans, several of whom had been heckling the Yankees' star and manager, acknowledged the play with conspicuous silence.

After a day of rain the seventh game was played at the Polo Grounds. The Highlanders drew first blood, scoring a run in the third. But in their half of the inning the Giants struck back. Jack Warhop was in the box for the Yankees. The Irish Indian delivered one of his underhand shoots, and Larry Doyle smacked it into the upper section of the right-field grandstand for a three-run homer. The Yanks got to Mathewson for two more in the seventh, but errors and sloppy fielding allowed the Giants three more runs. The final was Giants 6, Yankees 3. The Giants had won the series, four games to two.

Fletcher refused to be discouraged by the loss. The series had been a financial and popular success, and the Yankees had won a moral victory. They had earned respect in the eyes of the New York fans and in the eyes of the Giants themselves, who had expected to steamroller the upstart Hilltoppers. And, Fletcher reasoned, the main difference had been Mathewson—three complete-game victories and three innings of respectable relief. Without Matty, Fletcher thought, the series just might have gone the other way. One person who would never buy that argument was Harry. Fletcher wisely decided not to discuss the Yankee defeat with his older son.

In April 1911 the Polo Grounds suffered severe damage as a result of fire. Having formed a tentative friendship with the Yankees, the Giants became their temporary tenants at Hilltop Park.

That year, the Yanks won seventy-six and lost seventy-six, finishing sixth. Although Chase had the quick mind and baseball knowledge to make him the perfect manager, his cavalier ways made it impossible for him to run a tight ship. The Giants, meanwhile, finished the season—a season in which Honus Wagner of Pittsburgh won his eighth and final batting crown—back in the Polo Grounds and in first place.

Recognizing Chase's lack of credibility as a leader, Farrell and Devery brought in Harry Wolverton to manage, allowing Chase to concentrate on his feats at first base and at bat. Wolverton, fresh from the minors, tilted his sombrero over his eyes, chomped a big cigar, and told New York he would take the Yanks to the top. Colorful Harry unfortunately got his directions mixed up, and the Yankees finished the 1912 season in the cellar, fifty-five games out.

Another dismal season behind them, Farrell and Devery once more began their search for the magic manager who would dispel their woes. This time they had help. Ban Johnson was not at all pleased with the showing of the New York Americans. He felt the continued success of the American League was to a large degree contingent on the success of the Gotham entry.

Following the 1912 season, Frank Chance, the Peerless Leader of the Chicago Cubs, had retired to his home in Glendora, California. Pulling strings, Johnson managed Chance's release from the National League and then arranged a meeting between Farrell and Chance in early January 1913.

Johnson was so anxious that Chance sign to manage the Yankees, he skipped the meeting of the National Commission in Cincinnati, pleading lumbago, to be present at the Chicago conference between the Yank owner and the retired Cub. Chance arrived in Chicago saying he had no intention of signing. After listening to the persuasive Johnson and reading the terms of the even more persuasive contract—three years at $25,000 per year, plus 5 percent of the profits—he decided sunny California could wait a while.

Hal Chase immediately announced he had nothing but admiration for the former great first baseman, that he would give Chance his best, and that he wanted an opportunity to play second base. Even though Chase was a left-handed thrower, he had played second base as well as first for the Los Angeles team of the Pacific Coast League before signing with the Highlanders. Even so, some observers felt the Prince was simply hedging his bets and trying to protect himself. Others, however, said that Chase could play any position on any team, was bored and looking for a challenge, and was being gracious. Unfortunately, Chase sprained his ankle during spring training in Bermuda. The injury and other complications prevented him from proving that a left-hander could be a great second baseman.

The lease on Highland Park having expired, Farrell decided it was time to find more suitable grounds. Big Bill Devery, who had busied himself with real estate dealings since his abortive foray into politics, secured land at Kingsbridge, Broadway and Two Hundred Twenty-fifth Street. While the new park was being constructed, the Yankees would need temporary quarters. John Brush volunteered to become Farrell's landlord. Farrell quickly accepted, and the Yankees moved into the Polo Grounds.

Before the new season was two months old, Prince Hal and the Peerless Leader ran afoul of each other. Chance, who in the 1907 World Series had had a finger broken by a pitch from Wild Bill Donovan and had simply spit tobacco juice on it and continued to play, had stopped a number of high hard ones with the left side of his head. As a result, he was nearly deaf in his left ear.

Aside from his prodigious physical talents, Hal Chase had a gift for mimicry. Hal often entertained his teammates in the dugout with impressions of Chance, always taking care to be on Chance's deaf side. One day Chance caught him.

On June 2, 1913, headlines told the sporting world that the great Hal Chase had been traded to the Chicago White Sox for Rollie Zeider and Babe Borton. The reason the Yankee management gave out was that Chase, once reliable at bat, could no longer hit, though he was still without peer in the field.

For Chicago that season, Chase hit .286—the highest average on the White Sox roster—and drove in thirty-nine runs. Zeider and Borton batted .233 and .130 respectively and drove in thirty-three runs between them. Borton refused to be shipped down to the Jersey City team and was eventually sold to Montreal at his own request. In mid-July Farrell petitioned Ban Johnson for redress from the White Sox, claiming Zeider had been spiked two weeks before the trade. It was a good try, but it didn't work. The truth was, Zeider had bunions and spent most of his short career with the Yankees on the bench, resting his tender feet.

The Yankees finished seventh, thirty-eight games out of first place.

After the 1913 season, the Federal League, an independent minor, announced that it was now a major league and would not honor the reserve clause of the other two majors. The new league's biggest asset was money. It had the backing of a number of millionaire industrialists, including Philip de Catesby Ball, Charles Weeghman, Robert Ward, and Harry Sinclair. The eight teams—Baltimore, Brooklyn, Buffalo, Chicago, Indianapolis, Kansas City, Pittsburgh, and St. Louis—opened the 1914 season in seven new ball parks. The Brooklyn entry played in old Washington Park. The Chifeds, who soon became known as the Chicago Whales, played their home games in an arena that would later become Wrigley Field.

The Feds, called the Lunch Room Circuit by detractors because one of the league's principal backers, Charles Weeghman of Chicago, owned a chain of restaurants, began the season with a number of established stars from the other two leagues. As the season progressed, they gained more. Hal Chase was, not surprisingly, one of the first to go. In early June he gave the White Sox ten days' written notice before jumping to the Buffeds. Other jumpers included Joe Tinker, Three Finger Brown, Al Bridwell, and Russ Ford.

The Indianapolis team won the first championship of the league behind the pitching of Cy Falkenberg, another jumper, and the slugging of young Benny Kauff. Innovations help new leagues, and one of the Feds' new wrinkles was the keeping of two sets of batting averages, one against right-handed pitchers and one against lefties. Kauff, a lefty who led the league in batting with a .370 mark, batted .422 against lefties, .352 against righties.

In the National League the miracle Boston Braves caught fire in mid-July and stormed out of fifth place to overtake McGraw's Giants and win the pennant by ten and a half games. The Braves then swept four straight from Mack's powerhouse Athletics, leaving the Tall Tactician mumbling mildly.

The Yankees, meanwhile, still unable to play .500 ball, stumbled to a sixth-place tie. With seventeen games left in the season, the Peerless Leader, never cozy with the team owners since the Chase fiasco, finally succumbed to meddlemania, just as so many before him. He took a poke at Devery and went home to California. Shortstop Roger Peckinpaugh took over the reins until the end of the season.

Chance's boilover was the last straw for Ban Johnson. He wanted a winner in New York and was prepared to go to almost any lengths to get it. Johnson got help from, of all people, John McGraw, who sent millionaires Jacob Ruppert and Tillinghast L'Hommedieu Huston his way.

After two months of negotiations, during which Johnson promised the two prospective buyers complete cooperation from the league in rebuilding the team, Ruppert and Huston bought the club for approximately half a million dollars. Ruppert and Huston had wanted Hughie Jennings of Detroit for their manager, but Detroit owner Navin balked. There was a limit to his cooperativeness. Jennings recommended his good friend Wild Bill Donovan, who had managed Providence to the pennant of the International League the year before.

Fletcher was sitting in the lobby of the Hotel Wolcott when Johnson, Huston, and Farrell emerged to make the announcement of the sale.

Johnson said a number of nice things about Farrell and emphasized that he had not forced him out. Then Huston stepped in front of the reporters.

"The New York Americans," he said, "will play next season at the Polo Grounds, but Colonel Ruppert and myself have plans to build an immense park to house our team. Mr. Wild Bill Donovan will manage the team, and he will in no way be hampered by any official of the club."

Johnson was in a hurry to return to Chicago, where the Federals were about to file an antitrust suit against Organized Baseball in the United States District Court. Kenesaw Mountain Landis, the presiding judge, had recently fined Standard Oil $29 million for monopolistic behavior. Before Johnson left, Fletcher had a word with him.

"It looks as though baseball is in trouble, Ban," he said. "That trust-buster is going to ruin the game."

Johnson winked. "Don't you worry, Fletcher," he said. "The Flapjack League will get little satisfaction from Judge Landis. He's a dyed-in-the-wool fan and has played the game himself. The game is safe in his hands."

After Johnson had left, Fletcher and Farrell repaired to the hotel bar for a much-needed drink. The two men sat in morose silence for a long time. Finally Farrell shrugged helplessly. "What could I do, Fletch? I needed money, and the Czar wanted me out."

"You did the right thing, Frank," Fletcher said softly.

As it turned out, Johnson's announcement had been premature. It took nearly another week of negotiating, mainly between lawyers for the two sides, before the transfer of stock was effected. On January 11, 1915, Ruppert and Huston officially became the owners of the New York American League Baseball Club.

Relations between Farrell and Devery had become strained. After the sale the two men divided the money and went their separate ways. Even though Fletcher, Joe Vila, and other friends tried repeatedly to bring them together, they never spoke to each other again. Devery died in 1919, Farrell in 1926. Both were penniless at death.

In 1915 Joe Tinker's Chicago Whales, who got their nickname from a contest staged by owner Weeghman, nosed out the Sloufeds to win the Federal League pennant. Benny Kauff, sold to John Ward's Brooklyn Tip Tops, again led the league in batting. It was a successful year for the league, but the high salaries caused by the war were a huge financial drain. And Judge Landis had been sitting on the antitrust case for nearly a year, urging the two parties to negotiate privately.

When it became clear that to continue the war would be foolish, oil millionaire Harry Sinclair, later to become involved in the Teapot Dome scandal, pulled a tactical move that has become common practice in league wars. After negotiating with Devery for the Kingsbridge property, Sinclair took an option on land at One Hundred Forty-fourth Street and

Lenox Avenue and announced he was bringing a Federal League team into Manhattan.

Sinclair proceeded to take out a two-year lease on a luxurious suite of offices in a Manhattan skyscraper. He applied to the city fathers to have the streets on his property closed off. He even went so far as to display blueprints for a proposed forty-thousand-seat ball park in a store window on Forty-second Street. Sinclair had no intention of moving into New York, but the National Commission took the bait.

The warring factions met in Cincinnati in December 1915 and worked out a peace treaty. Organized Baseball paid the Federals half a million dollars to give up the ghost. Weeghman was allowed to purchase the Cubs, and Phil Ball bought the St. Louis Americans. In one of the most outrageous acts of flesh-peddling since the Civil War, Harry Sinclair obtained the contracts of nearly all the Federal players not belonging to Weeghman or Ball and auctioned them off.

In the American League in 1915 Boston had nosed out Detroit for the pennant. Connie Mack, never a loose man with the dollar, had reacted to the high salaries caused by the war by selling off the stars of the team that had won the 1914 pennant. The Mackmen of 1915 played .283 ball and finished in the cellar, fifty-eight and a half games out. Boston went on to whip the Phillies in the World Series.

As for Donovan's revamped Yankees, they bettered their previous season's win total by one game and finished fifth. It was, however, the beginning of a new era for the Yankees, as even Fletcher grudgingly admitted. As a minor part of the sale contract, Farrell had secured a lifetime Yankee pass for Fletcher. Looking ahead to his seventieth birthday, a white-haired and somewhat frail Fletcher Rice couldn't help but wonder how much use he would get from it.

BOOK TWO

Alex and Harry

Sportsmanship and easygoing methods
are all right, but it is the prospect of a
hot fight that brings out the crowds.

John J. McGraw

4

In late June 1902 Andrew Freedman, in the twilight of his career as president of the Giants, sent Fred Knowles, the secretary of the club, on a special mission to Baltimore. His assignment was to persuade John McGraw to become the Giants' new manager.

A heavy rain was falling as Knowles's train pulled into the station. The Giant executive hailed a cab, rode out to McGraw's house, and invited the pilot of the Orioles for a ride. John agreed, and for more than four hours the cab plowed through puddles and circled the wet, deserted streets of Baltimore, while Knowles recited the many virtues of New York and the National League. But when the ride was over John could only say, "Tell Freedman I can't give him a definite answer. I need time to think it over."

John had a lot on his mind. Before the start of the 1902 season Ban Johnson had told him the American League planned to drop the Orioles and transfer the franchise to New York City in 1903. To make room in the league for a team in Manhattan one of the present clubs would have to go, and Baltimore, which was in deep financial trouble, was the obvious choice. McGraw, led to believe he would be manager of the transplanted team, had visited New York on June 4, 1902, to discuss the situation with Frank Farrell. He and Farrell met at the Gravesend racetrack in Brooklyn, where they talked about the possibility of building an American League ball park on a vacant lot at One Hundred Eleventh Street between First Avenue and the East River. Farrell agreed to lease the land if it was available.

A short while after the meeting Fletcher Rice arrived at the track with some papers for Farrell to sign. While he was there Fletch took the opportunity to place a few wagers and to have a brief conversation with the famous third baseman and manager of the Orioles.

"My oldest boy thinks you're the best tactician in the game today," Fletcher told McGraw.

"Is that right?" John replied. "Well, it looks like he'll soon have an opportunity to see me in the flesh."

"Really?"

"Yes, indeed. Farrell stands ready to back me for any amount. If we can get ground we'll put Freedman out of business. Baseball has been bad in Baltimore, and we intend to dump that city as soon as we can make arrangements to come here."

While McGraw was boasting about his plan to bring the Orioles to New York, he secretly feared that Ban Johnson was going to dump *him* along with the Baltimore franchise. He and Johnson had never been on the best of terms, and John knew the bad blood between them could boil over at any moment. The source of their feud can be found in Johnson's first bulletin to the American League clubs. In May 1901 he gave notice to all owners, managers, and players that "CLEAN BALL is the MAIN PLANK in the American League platform, and the clubs must stand by it religiously. There must be no profanity on the ball field. The umpires are agents of the League and must be treated with respect. I will suspend any manager or player who uses profane or vulgar language to an Umpire, and that suspension will remain in force until such time as the offender can learn to bridle his tongue."

John McGraw looked upon Ban Johnson's edict as just so much palaver. He meant to lead his team in the best tradition of the Orioles. If umpires made stupid calls, nothing was going to stop him from telling them where to get off.

On the field he disputed their decisions with the most profane and vulgar language he could think of, and publicly he accused them of gross incompetence. His players eagerly joined the fray, and Johnson, determined to stamp out this "rowdyism," punished the Orioles with so many fines and suspensions that McGraw accused the American League "Czar" of tearing his team to pieces.

Then, early in the 1902 season, John got into a mean rhubarb during a two-game series with Detroit. In the first game Joe "Iron Man" Mc-Ginnity was trying in vain to pick off Dick Harley, the Detroit left fielder, who had reached third. Every time McGinnity threw over to McGraw, Harley jumped back on the bag and shouted an insult at the Oriole pitcher. Finally John decided he'd listened to enough mouthing off; he ran over and stamped his spikes right into his adversary's foot.

The next day Harley was out for blood, and he got it. He reached first, stole second, and wasted no time trying for third. As he barreled toward McGraw, Roger Bresnahan, the Orioles' catcher, threw to John for an easy out. But Harley just picked up speed and came into third base with his spikes high in the air. He ripped into John's knee, opening up a gash that sent blood gushing over his leg. Immediately the two went at each other, fists flying.

McGraw's injury kept him out of action till the end of June. His knee began slipping out of its socket, and John knew his playing days were numbered. On his first day back in the lineup he managed to get into a heated discussion with the umpire. The ump threw him out of the game, and when John refused to leave the field the contest was declared a forfeit. Ban Johnson then suspended him indefinitely. So McGraw had good reason to suspect he would never be allowed to carry the American League banner into New York.

Soon after his meeting with Farrell, McGraw learned that the plot of land on the East River had been condemned and would become a public park. There was a strong possibility that Andrew Freedman had pulled strings at Tammany Hall to keep the site out of the hands of the American League. John suddenly found himself caught between two iron-willed men—Freedman and Ban Johnson.

For more than a year Freedman had been trying to lure McGraw to the Giants, but until then John had little interest in working for a man who hired managers one day and fired them the next. But now he faced the possibility of being dumped by Johnson and being stranded in Baltimore with nothing to keep him busy except the Diamond Café. With his career as a player almost over, he had to take steps to protect his future as a manager. If Freedman would give him a free hand to run the Giants his own way, he would be a lot better off moving to New York than facing uncertainty in Baltimore. However, before he could negotiate with Freedman in good faith, he needed a release from his contract with the Orioles. Luckily, he had an excellent bargaining weapon.

The team was so broke that McGraw had been paying some of the players' salaries out of his own pocket, and he had already put up close to $7,000. He called a special meeting of the club's board of directors and asked his fellow owners either to come up with the money he had advanced or give him his unconditional release. They chose the latter, and John sent word to Freedman he was ready to make a deal.

Much to McGraw's surprise, Freedman willingly gave in to all of his demands. John would have complete control to hire, fire, and trade players, and he would be protected by a four-year contract calling for a salary of $11,000 a year.

If Freedman's eagerness to please his new manager seemed out of character, it was actually quite understandable. For even while he was negotiating with McGraw, he was already planning to get out of baseball and turn the club over to John T. Brush. On July 9 McGraw was in

New York to sign his contract. He told the press, "I appreciate the kindliness which has prompted the Baltimore Club to give me the release I asked for, and I wish to assure them publicly that in consideration of their kindness I shall not tamper with the Baltimore Club's players." He kept his promise for little more than a week.

On July 19 the papers broke the surprising news that McGraw had acquired 201 of the 400 outstanding shares of Baltimore stock and that four Orioles—pitchers Joe McGinnity and John Cronin, first baseman Dan McGann, and catcher Roger Bresnahan—had been transferred to the Giants. To acquire the stock, which was actually paid for by Freedman, McGraw had gone through some slick maneuvering. First he traded his half of the Diamond Café for Oriole stock held by Wilbert Robinson. Then he "sold" his original stock plus the shares obtained from Robbie to John J. Mahon. Mahon, who owned some stock of his own, then bought the shares held by Father John G. Boland, a Baltimore priest.

The stock in Mahon's hands now represented a controlling interest in the club; the shares were turned over to Joseph C. France, Freedman's attorney in Baltimore, who passed them on to Brush, who was then chairman of the executive committee of the National League. With McGraw as the central figure, the National League, in an effort to kill Ban Johnson's plans to invade New York, had taken over control of an American League club.

Johnson, trying to appear unperturbed by the curious turn of events, told the papers, "McGraw was one of the hardest men in the league to control, and now that he has left I cannot see how the American League has lost anything. I hope that McGraw will make good where he is going. We like rivalry."

The news of John McGraw's arrival in New York filled Harry Rice with joy and high hopes. "Watch the Giants now," he told his younger brother. "With ol' John in charge, they'll soon push your Superbas right into the cellar."

"Oh yeah?" said Alex, the diehard Brooklyn fan. "I'll bet on Hanlon any day. All Muggsy's gonna do is start a lot of fights and stir up trouble."

"And win ball games. You watch. New York will take the pennant next year."

Harry's prediction was mighty brash. The day McGraw joined the Giants they were in last place, thirty-three and a half games behind first-place Pittsburgh. Even with the players brought from Baltimore it was too late to do much for the team that year. The club was demoralized and totally without motivation. John knew it would take time and hard work to build a winning club. First he would have to discard the deadwood and replace it with his kind of men—alert, aggressive, and eager to improve themselves. He was lucky to have one man who more than satisfied those requirements. His name was Christy Mathewson.

When McGraw arrived in New York he was shocked to discover that his predecessor, Horace Fogel, had been playing Mathewson at first base. John, an expert at sizing up talent, had already recognized that Matty "was pretty nearly the perfect type of a great pitching machine." But the gangly young hurler had two basic problems—his control was weak and he hadn't yet learned how to pitch to a batter's weakness.

This second fault became painfully evident in a game against Chicago shortly after McGraw joined the club. The Giants were ahead, 2–1, in the ninth with an opposing runner on base when Jimmy Slagle, a great fastball hitter but a sucker for a curve, came to the plate. Instead of working on the batter with breaking stuff, Matty dished up a fat, letter-high fastball that Slagle promptly smashed out of the park to end the game.

Under McGraw's tutelage, Mathewson soon learned every strength and weakness of every batter in the league. He went on to build an overpowering arsenal of pitches, including a change of pace, a magnificent curve, an occasional spitter, and his famous fadeaway—now called a screwball. And he also became one of the greatest control artists of all time. In 1908 he averaged less than one base on balls a game, and in 1913 he pitched sixty-eight consecutive innings without a walk. One day McGraw would look back and say, "There never was another pitcher like Mathewson. I doubt if there ever will be."

McGraw was also looking to beef up his new team in other departments. In his search for talent he picked up George Browne, an outfielder from Philadelphia, and Jack Warner, a catcher on Boston's American League club. The Giants climbed all the way to second place in 1903, winding up six and a half games behind the Pirates.

The next winter, in what he later described as "the most successful deal I ever made," McGraw sent Charlie Babb and Jack Cronin to the Superbas for Bill Dahlen, the great Brooklyn shortstop. Midway through the 1904 season he strengthened his outfield by acquiring "Turkey Mike" Donlin from Cincinnati.

In less than two years John had transformed the Giants into a team to be reckoned with, displaying competent hitting, excellent fielding, and Mathewson and McGinnity—the most powerful pitching combination in the league. As the 1904 season got under way it became clear that Harry Rice's prediction wasn't all that far-fetched. It stood a good chance of coming true only a year late.

Harry's brother, Alex, was a moody eleven-year-old. When he heard the news about Bill Dahlen he broke into tears. "That no good Ned

Hanlon," he cried to his brother. "First McGinnity and then Keeler and now he's even lost Dahlen. We'll never win another pennant!"

"Don't worry, little brother," Harry replied. "Muggsy will put Dahlen to good use."

Alex ran upstairs to his room, slammed the door, and ripped up his collection of Brooklyn scorecards. It wasn't quite fair of him to lay all the blame on Hanlon, but the Superba lineup had indeed been sapped of much of its strength. In the war with the American League McGraw had spirited away McGinnity to the Orioles, Fielder Jones went to the White Sox, and Lave Cross jumped to the Athletics. Then, in the peace settlement between the leagues, Keeler was awarded to the Highlanders. And now, in what Alex saw as a very dumb trade, Dahlen was on his way to the Giants. The Superbas had slid to fifth place in 1903; the following year, after the Dahlen trade, they dropped another notch.

As early as July 1904 the Giants made it clear they were the club to beat in the National League. As they widened their lead to seven games, New York fans, convinced their team was the best in baseball, began looking forward to the World Series. Because Pittsburgh had accepted Boston's challenge the year before, everyone assumed the Fall Classic was once again a regular feature of the game. Indeed, the peace treaty between the leagues stipulated that the two pennant-winners would meet in a postseason championship series.

Both Harry and Alex, National Leaguers to the core, anxiously awaited the windup of the regular schedule. They boasted to their turncoat father that McGraw and his men would have no difficulty avenging the Pirates' embarrassing loss the year before. But Fletcher just laughed at his sons and confidently predicted the Highlanders would win the seesaw battle they were waging with the Boston Pilgrims and then prove they were the best team not only in the world, but in New York as well.

During that July, however, there were reports in the press that Brush—who had opposed the peace agreement and continued to despise the American League—would not let his club play in the World Series. Most fans disregarded this. The season had a long way to go, the Giants were still not certain of victory, and if they did win it was impossible to believe that John McGraw would shrink from a good fight.

But then, on July 27, McGraw himself told reporters, "The Giants will not play a postseason series with the American League champions. The reasons for my decision are that Ban Johnson has not been on the level with me personally, and the American League management has been crooked more than once. Johnson thought he could do better by dropping Baltimore and invading New York. The method he used to queer me was to suspend me indefinitely and otherwise prosecute me by jobs he framed up with his umpires. Finally it got so rank that I could stand it no longer, and I threw in the sponge.

"Now I have the whip hand. My team will have nothing to do with the American League as long as I have a word to say, and no influence to bear upon me by the National League people can make me change my mind."

Alex and Harry were astonished. They couldn't believe McGraw would turn his back on the Giants' loyal followers just to fan the fires of his old feud with Johnson. They speculated that Brush was the real villain and that McGraw's remarks were made under orders from his boss. Fletcher didn't see it that way. "I always knew Muggsy had a yellow streak," he said, much to the irritation of his sons. "The bastard is scared to death the Giants might get their hides tanned by Griffith and his boys."

Ban Johnson dismissed McGraw's outburst: "No thoughtful patron of baseball can weigh seriously the wild vaporings of this discredited player who was canned out of the American League," Johnson remarked. He believed it was Brush who didn't want the club to take part in the Series. As the season progressed and the Giants tightened their grip on the pennant, rumors came out of the clubhouse that the players intended to meet the American League champions with or without the consent of their superiors. One player told the press, "Our manager is not afraid of any team on earth, but he is being held back by the powers that be."

In late August the Giants took off on their last western road trip. During that swing they won twelve and lost two, and they returned to New York on September 4 with the pennant clinched. Meanwhile, the battle royal between the Highlanders and Pilgrims continued, with first place exchanging hands every few days. In late September the Highlanders briefly took the lead, and they issued a formal World Series challenge to the Giants. In turn, Brush released a "manifesto" in which he declared, "There is nothing in the constitution or playing rules of the National League which requires its victorious club to submit its championship honors to a contest with a victorious club in a minor league."

For the time being Alex's and Harry's hopes for a World Series in New York were shattered. But the following winter Brush himself formulated the rules and procedures that were to govern World Series play from 1905 to the present. As the new season got under way the Giants, eager to prove they could lick the American League, set out to win their second pennant in a row.

By 1905 the Giants, swaggering confidently into every rival city, had become the most hated team in the National League. They were particularly unpopular in Pittsburgh, where as early as July of 1904 the local papers had accused the New Yorkers of displaying a "rowdy spirit" and being "stuck up."

One reporter characterized McGraw as a loudmouth who taunted Pirate fans with expressions outside "the bounds of propriety." The bad feelings between the two teams intensified over the next year until, in a game in 1905, McGraw got into one of his fierce umpire rows. During his tirade John unleashed several wicked insults at Barney Dreyfuss, president of the Pittsburgh club. McGraw's slanderous remarks earned him a $150 fine and the hatred of all loyal Pirate rooters. From then on, whenever the Giants visited Pittsburgh they entered an inferno. As they rode in carriages from their hotel to the ball park, they would often be bombarded with stones, trash, and rotten vegetables. Describing that 1905 team McGraw would later say, "They thought they could beat anybody and they generally could. As a result of this fighting instinct we got into much trouble."

In Brooklyn the Superbas had fallen on grim times. They were on their way to the cellar, and Ned Hanlon, not on the best terms with Ebbets, appeared to be on his way out. It was especially frustrating for Alex Rice to watch his brother's team enjoy such fantastic success while his own club wallowed in the second division. It's hardly surprising that the Giants were no more popular in Brooklyn than in Pittsburgh. Their record against the Superbas in 1905 was 15–7, and every one of those fifteen wins was a bitter blow to the Washington Park faithful. One day that summer McGraw was arguing with an umpire in front of Charlie Ebbets's box; when Charlie stood up and tried to get into the discussion McGraw blurted out what sounded like an obscenity.

"Did you call me a bastard?" the shocked Ebbets demanded.

The Giant manager strolled over to the railing and yelled in Charlie's face, "No. I called you a son of a bitch!" The insult was heard by everyone for rows around. From that day on Ebbets and McGraw were bitter enemies.

McGraw and his men may have been hated outside of New York, but they were the darlings of Manhattan. That year they were in first place by only two games at the end of August, but during September they widened their lead to eight and a half and won the pennant easily. Over in the American League Philadelphia and Chicago struggled down to the wire, with the Athletics finally winning out by two games. As the World Series approached, New York went baseball crazy. The stage was set for a meeting of the two greatest minds in baseball—Connie Mack and John McGraw.

With the Series drawing closer, baseball discussions in the Rice household became heated. "I have to go with Philadelphia," Fletcher said. "Rube Waddell and Eddie Plank are the best hurlers in baseball. They'll mow down the Giants just as sure as you live."

"What about Mathewson and McGinnity?" his sons argued. "Between them they won fifty-two games."

"I'm not saying they aren't good. I'm only saying the Athletics are better," their father replied.

"How do you know Waddell is going to play?" Harry asked his old man the day before the opening game.

"Connie Mack said so. I read it in this morning's paper."

But Waddell's participation was very much in doubt. Rube was a brilliant pitcher. His record was 24–11 that year, but his bizarre behavior off the diamond convinced many followers of baseball he was crazy.

Some days he just said to hell with the ball game and went fishing; on others he took off to tend bar in a Camden saloon. One afternoon, while the crowd was waiting for him to come to the pitcher's box, he was under the stands playing marbles with a bunch of kids.

During the first week of September, on a train heading back to Philadelphia from Boston, Rube and Andy Coakley, another pitcher, took part in a bit of horseplay. Waddell was thrown against the door of the Athletics' car while trying to smash Coakley's straw hat. He supposedly suffered a bruised shoulder, and for the rest of the season he complained his muscles ached so much that his pitching arm was useless. When neither the team doctor nor the trainer could find anything wrong with him, Mack and the other players accused him of malingering.

At one point a rumor erupted that New York gamblers were paying Waddell to stay out of the Series. When Rube heard the accusation he remarked indignantly that if he *were* crooked he could "serve the gamblers' purposes better and quicker by playing than laying off."

The first game of the Series was played on October 9. That morning the Giants rode to Philadelphia in a special car hooked onto a regular train. In their entourage were a number of New York celebrities, including Gentleman Jim Corbett, the boxing champion, and Louis Mann, a famous vaudevillian.

Elsewhere on the train, in one of the public cars, were Alex, Harry, and their father. Throughout the journey Fletcher and his sons argued over which team had the better pitching. They all conceded it would be a pitchers' series, but no one could really tell who had the superior staff. Even the usually outspoken McGraw was not willing to brag that his hurlers were better than Mack's. The day before he had said, "We can beat the Philadelphians in batting, and furthermore we can beat them running the bases. The only question left open for argument, then, is pitching. They might put it on us there, but I don't believe it."

The train arrived in Philadelphia at 10:00 A.M. Fletcher and his boys alighted from their car and then stepped to one side as McGraw, arm in arm with Corbett and Mann, came strutting up the platform with the team right at his heels. As the Giant manager passed, Fletcher yelled out, "Hey John, the smart money is still with the Athletics. What do you think of that?"

McGraw stopped, took a long look at Fletcher, and then said with a laugh, "What would one of Farrell's mob know about smart money? I thought you boys were all back in New York crying about the High-landers. Sixth place isn't much of a showing. Well, just to show you my heart's in the right place, I'll give you a tip. The odds are too big. Take even money!"

"I guess he told you," Harry said to his father. Fletcher just smiled and watched McGraw and his followers hurry away. While the Giants climbed into carriages for their ride to the Continental Hotel, Fletch and his boys took a trolley out to the park. They were smart to go early. By game time the stands would be overflowing. Some ten thousand fans would be turned away.

The Giant rooters congregated in a corner of the grandstand. At precisely 2:15 the New Yorkers appeared on the field, and the stands buzzed with excitement. The Giants were nattily attired in brand new uniforms—*black*, of all colors, with white caps, belts, and socks. The Athletics, in uniforms frayed and soiled from a long season, looked a bit pathetic next to the invaders from New York. If anyone knew how to gain a psychological advantage, however small, it was John McGraw.

The manager of the Giants joined the umpires and Lave Cross, the A's captain, at home plate to go over the ground rules. Suddenly Cross pulled something out of newspaper wrapping and handed it to McGraw. It was a miniature white elephant. Some years earlier, when asked about the prospects of the American League team in Philadelphia, McGraw had predicted, "Connie Mack will have a white elephant on his hands." John accepted Cross's gift with a chuckle, did a little jig step, and returned to his bench. The game was ready to begin, with Eddie Plank, the ace southpaw, going against Christy Mathewson. It was now apparent that Waddell would not appear in the Series.

Both sides were scoreless for the first four innings. Then, in the top of the fourth, Mathewson led off with a clean single, and the Giant rooters roared, "Go get 'em, boys. Cinch the game here!" Harry and Alex, sensing that this might be the Giant's inning, opened a package they had carried all the way from New York and produced a chunk of charcoal and some sheets of manila paper, six by four feet. Roger Bresnahan came up to the plate and hit a grounder to Monte Cross at third, who forced Matty at second. To atone for his weak turn at bat, Roger promptly stole second, and Harry and Alex lifted a sign that read:

ROGER, THOU ARTFUL DODGER,
THEY CATCH THEE NOT.

Mike Donlin was the next batter up. When he swung and missed Plank's first pitch, Fletcher's boys raised this message:

WHAT? A STRIKE FOR MIKE? IT CANNOT BE.

Donlin agreed. He drilled a single between third and short, and Bresnahan came around to score the first run of the Series. Then Dan McGann walked, and Sam Mertes hit a fly deep to center field. Bris Lord made a valiant effort to reach the ball; he lunged into the air, held it for a second, but then fell back into the roped-off crowd. He came up empty-handed, allowing Donlin to race home. Mathewson held the A's completely in check the rest of the way; the Giants scored another run in the ninth, and New York came out on top, 3–0.

That evening, on the train back to New York, Harry and his father analyzed every element of the game. Fletcher conceded that Mathewson had pitched brilliantly, but he argued that Waddell would have done better than Plank.

"Maybe so," Harry remarked, "but Philadelphia didn't score a single run. What could Waddell do about that? Matty had them completely fooled. His control was perfect and his curves went every which way. He only gave up four hits and not even one base on balls. I'm sorry, Pop, but I think the days are numbered for your American Leaguers."

The next day New York was in a carnival mood as twenty-five thousand fans jammed into the Polo Grounds and several thousand more stood along the tracks of the elevated line hoping to cheer the Giants to victory. The crowd waved hundreds of flags and let out a tremendous roar as McGraw, then Mathewson, crossed the field from the clubhouse to the home bench.

The game promised to be another pitcher's duel, with Iron Man McGinnity facing Chief Bender, whom one pundit described as "the swarthy aboriginal speed incubator." It was New York's misfortune that the wily Chippewa's arm hatched many an untouchable fastball that day. Following Matty's example Bender held the opposition to four hits and no runs, while the A's managed to score three times. With the series now even at one game apiece, Fletcher was convinced the American League was on the road to victory.

The weather turned bitter cold for game three in Philadelphia, but the change of climate did not hinder the Giants. Once again Matty took to the box, and once again he was brilliant. He mixed his pitches with such skill that he completely befuddled the Athletic batters. New York, meanwhile, scored nine runs, five of them on errors by Dan Murphy, the A's second baseman. It was a sad day for Andy Coakley, who pitched well despite the lopsided score. After the game McGraw boasted, "Any club that beats us has to beat our pitching," articulating one of the key axioms of baseball—good pitching will always stop good hitting.

The Series returned to New York for the next two contests. McGinnity faced Plank in game four, which developed into a classic pitchers' battle. Plank gave up only one unearned run, which came in the fourth when Monte Cross and Lave Cross both made errors on routine grounders. The Iron Man did Eddie one better, holding the opposition scoreless by quickly closing the door whenever the A's put men on base.

The tough 1–0 loss left Connie Mack with his back to the wall. His team had now been shut out in three games, causing a New York press-box wit to remark that "goose eggs are becoming as staple an item of Father Penn's diet as scrapple."

It turned out there was enough fat in the fire to cook up yet another goose egg. In the sixth game Matty defeated Bender, 2–0. The Giants were champions of the world. Fletcher Rice had a good part of those eggs on his face.

At the final out of the Series the Polo Grounds broke into pandemonium. Fans in the grandstand threw their seat cushions at spectators on the field, who immediately sent them flying back. The band struck up a victory march and led several thousand delirious rooters in a dance around the diamond. Some of the Giants came out onto the second floor porch of the clubhouse in right center field and threw their caps and gloves down into the crowd, causing a wild scramble for souvenirs. Fletcher got caught up in the celebration. He caught Roger Bresnahan's cap on a fly, but before he could stuff it into his pocket a boy rushed by him and pulled it away. Alex tried to run after the thief, but he vanished into the crowd. The players soon disappeared into the clubhouse, and Fletch and his sons slowly made their way to the elevated and the first leg of the long journey back to Brooklyn.

For Fletcher, who had burned his bridges when he threw in with the American League, the series was a bitter disappointment. In later years he would often say, "Things would have been a lot different if Waddell had gone up against Mathewson."

Alex, on the other hand, was pleased the National League had won, but he still found it hard to cast aside his basic dislike for the Giants. For Harry New York's victory was the happiest moment of his life. He had observed McGraw's brand of baseball long enough to know it was only a matter of time before the Giants would become the undisputed world champions. Now his prediction had come true! Watching his team trounce the highly esteemed Athletics not only brought joy to his heart but gave him great confidence in his own powers of reasoning.

As Harry reflected on the Series, he continued to be amazed by Matty's remarkable performance—three shutouts in three starts. It was a feat that surely would never be equaled. But there was more to the Giants than fine pitching. They played for John McGraw, which meant they always had an edge on the competition. The Giant manager was the leading practitioner of what became known as the "inside" game. An outgrowth of the baseball of the old Orioles, its elements included an ironclad defense and an offense that produced runs by playing the percentages of the moment.

While the Giants were enjoying their perch on top of the world, Charlie Ebbets was having his problems. Before the start of the season

Harry Von der Horst, who died during that summer, had sold his stock to Henry W. Medicus, a friend of Ebbets who owned a prosperous furniture business in Brooklyn. Ned Hanlon had a strong desire to move the Superbas to Baltimore and had tried unsuccessfully to get Von der Horst to sell the stock to *him*.

Several months later, at the end of the 1905 season, Hanlon took part in a scheme to get the National League to drop Brooklyn in favor of a new Baltimore franchise. In the middle of September a report came out of Cincinnati that Hanlon was there to purchase players for a new Oriole team. Then Ban Johnson and Connie Mack gleefully got into the act. They both confidently predicted that big league ball would return to Baltimore the following year. Hanlon was apparently trying to damage Ebbets's credibility with the National League.

It was well known that Brooklyn had suffered a deficit of almost $25,000 that season. If the other owners lost faith in the ability of Ebbets and Medicus to make good the losses, Hanlon figured there was a chance the league would let Brooklyn go and take Baltimore in. Fortunately for Brooklyn fans, it was a tepid scheme. It soon became clear that Medicus had the resources and the desire to back Charlie all the way.

Despite his difficulties with Hanlon, Ebbets was reluctant to dump him. Ned was respected as one of the most knowledgeable men in baseball; he had brought great glory to Brooklyn in the past, and he was by no means solely responsible for the club's dismal showing of late. As Hanlon himself put it, "When you get right down to it Brooklyn would have been lucky to do much better this year. The team never has had a first baseman, most of the time hasn't been possessed of a second baseman, part of the time has been without a shortstop, and all the time has had a third baseman who has played in great style one day only to fall down a little in the next."

There was no doubt the Superbas needed new players, but the immediate question facing Ebbets and Medicus was whether or not to go with Hanlon another year. They finally decided it was time for a change.

Just as Hanlon was expecting to have his contract renewed, he learned that Patsy Donovan—who had previously managed in Washington, Pittsburgh, and St. Louis—was coming to Brooklyn to take over the Superbas. For Hanlon it was no tragedy; Cincinnati had been trying to get him for more than a year and quickly signed him up.

Donovan's first move was to trade Brooklyn's star left fielder, Jimmy Sheckard, to the Cubs for two other outfielders, Billy Maloney and Jack McCarthy. Most Brooklyn fans were not sorry to see Sheckard go, but Alex Rice saw the move as another bad trade. He said to his brother, "Maybe Jimmy didn't have his best year. He's sure to be back in form next season. And where will he be? In Chicago, playing against us."

Not only did Sheckard move to Chicago, so too did the seat of power in the National League. During the next five seasons the Cubs, featuring the double-play team of Tinker to Evers to Chance, won four pennants and two World Series, while the Giants finished second three times, third once, and fourth once. Patsy Donovan turned out to be of little help to Brooklyn. He stayed with the club through the 1908 campaign, but he never finished higher than fifth.

The Giants' victory in the World Series had no effect upon John Mc-Graw's arrogance. On the field he remained as pugnacious and fiery as ever. His war with the umpires went on, and once, in 1906, he actually denied admission to the Polo Grounds to Johnny Johnstone, an umpire he particularly despised. In New Orleans the following spring he forfeited two exhibition contests with the Athletics when he refused to let his team play unless Chief Zimmer, the umpire assigned to the games, was replaced.

In April 1908 Dan McGann, the first baseman McGraw had traded to the Braves at the end of the previous season, attacked the Giant manager in the Copley Square Hotel in Boston. McGraw got his shoulder bruised and his hat crushed in return for having called McGann an "ice wagon" after the ex-Giant hit into a double play. A few months later McGraw, along with Joe McGinnity, started a riot over a dispute that began not on the field but in the stands.

John was under a three-day suspension for an argument with Johnstone during which he horribly insulted the ump by calling him a "piece of cheese." He was watching the first game of a doubleheader from a cubby hole under the grandstand when the trouble began.

Since he wasn't pitching that day, McGinnity had decided to take in the games from the stands. The Giants were leading in the third inning when it began to rain. When the downpour made the grounds unplayable, the contest was called, and ushers began passing out rain checks. One fan, a very small fellow, raised a fuss, demanding a check that guaranteed admission to a doubleheader. Two Pinkerton guards were called to remove the unhappy patron; when they began to rough him up, McGinnity came to his rescue. From out of nowhere McGraw appeared, and he and the Iron Man began slugging it out with the guards. A bunch of spectators then decided to help out the two Giants; pretty soon a riot was under way, and the city police had to be called in.

With each new brawl McGraw became more popular with his fans and more despised by his enemies. But while John's critics abhorred his "hoodlum tactics," there wasn't much they could do about them. Rival fans and sportswriters took joy in calling him "Muggsy," a nickname they knew he hated. But the use of that label was hardly calculated to bring the Giant manager into line. He despised the name because it belonged to a notorious barfly and roughneck who hung around Baltimore in the days when he first came to the Orioles. McGraw resented being compared to a mug.

To some of his critics, however, that's exactly what he was. Joe Vila wrote at the start of the 1907 season that "McGraw, with a team of four-flushers, intends to browbeat the umpires, terrorize and frighten them, so that they will give him the best of it; also that the same thug tactics employed to intimidate visiting players and spectators who are inclined to jeer, will be in evidence again. . . . It is a case of win, no matter how!"

It was indeed a case of winning at all costs. For McGraw, victory was the only point of the game. But, while the Giants continued to play good baseball from 1905 to 1910, the Cubs played even better. In 1906 New York had ninety-six victories and still finished *twenty games* behind Chicago. The only pennant the Cubs lost during those years was to the Pirates in 1909. The Giants came close only once—in 1908. To this day, Harry Rice believes his team actually won the flag that year. The record books tell a different story.

The 1908 season was when Harry began to immerse himself in statistics. The previous winter he had taken a job as an apprentice bookkeeper with the accounting firm of Kaplan, Cohen and Cohan, whose offices were located on Court Street in downtown Brooklyn. Some people look upon bookkeeping as dull, tedious work, but Harry found it quite pleasant. There was something nice about shutting out the world and dwelling on figures. He saw each ledger entry as a tiny piece to a puzzle—one element in a pattern that would reveal whether a business he was helping to audit would turn out a success, a failure, or a mediocrity.

It wasn't surprising that Harry's sudden interest in numbers should carry over to baseball. At the start of the 1908 season he set up ledgers to record simple batting and pitching statistics for the entire National League, and he also began recording the inning-by-inning performance of the Giants. Harry observed every move the Giants made during that campaign. When it was all over, he was in a good position to look back and see whether his team was indeed a victim of fate, a single decision by an umpire, or one bonehead play by a substitute first baseman.

In the years to follow, the 1908 National League campaign would be for Harry a constant source of frustration and fascination. During the next several winters he would play that season over many times, searching for moves McGraw might have made differently. He found it difficult to buy the contention made again and again in the press that a single misplay had undone the collective efforts of an entire summer of baseball.

As it happened, he found all sorts of plays that the Giants, if given another chance, might have turned into golden opportunities. In the end, however, it all came down to the absurdly simple fact that they had lost one game too many. Perhaps that game came at the very start of the season, when the overconfident New Yorkers opened the Polo Grounds by losing three out of four to Brooklyn. Perhaps it came in a double-header they lost to the Cubs on September 22. Perhaps. Perhaps. No matter how hard Harry searched for explanations, he always came back to the bizarre events that took place in the Polo Grounds on September 23, 1908. On that morning, as a result of their two losses to Chicago the day before, the Giants were in first place by only six percentage points. The standings were:

	W	L	Pct	GB
New York	87	50	.635	—
Chicago	90	53	.629	—
Pittsburgh	88	54	.619	1½

The Cubs, three games down in the loss column, were still not in great shape. As one reporter put it, "It will require an earthquake to dislodge the Giants." Then came the tremor.

Harry and Alex had planned to go to the doubleheader the previous day, but when Harry learned that Three Finger Brown—the most fear-some hurler in the league, as far as Harry was concerned—would be in the box for the second game, he persuaded Alex to wait a day and watch Mathewson go up against Pfiester. So it was somewhat by accident that they were on hand that fateful afternoon.

Harry managed to get off from work early, so he and his brother arrived at the Polo Grounds in plenty of time to get excellent seats half-way down the line between third base and the left-field corner. The contest developed into what one observer called "a bang-up, all a-quiver game." Mathewson pitched well, holding the Cubs to only five hits while striking out nine. He did, however, give up a run in the fifth when Joe Tinker homered. The Giants were having their troubles with Pfiester but managed to tie the game in the sixth. Buck Herzog singled to third and reached second when Harry Steinfeldt made a bad throw trying to save the play. Bresnahan then bunted Herzog to third, and Donlin sin-gled him home. That's the way things stood until the bottom of the ninth. The skies were starting to darken, but Harry guessed there was enough time for two or three extra innings.

Cy Seymour opened the Giants' final inning by grounding out, Evers to Chance. Then Art Devlin lined a single up the middle, and the Polo Grounds came alive. Moose McCormick followed with a depressing grounder that Evers tossed to Tinker, forcing Devlin at second.

"Who's up next?" Alex asked his brother.

"Oh, it's Merkle," Harry replied. "Guess we'll have to wait till the tenth."

Fred Merkle was a substitute who wouldn't even have been in the game if Fred Tenney, the regular first baseman, hadn't awoken with a backache. To the crowd's joyous surprise Merkle slashed a long drive down the right-field line. The ball was fair by a few feet and looked like a sure double, but Fred wisely held at first since the only runner who mattered was McCormick, who had scampered around to third. The next batter up was Al Bridwell, the Giants' shortstop.

"Ol' Al's gonna pull us through," Harry said. "I just know it!" But his heart was chugging like a locomotive.

Bridwell stepped into the box but backed out, unhappy with Merkle's long lead. Fred got back to the bag, and Bridwell moved up to the plate. Pfiester's next pitch was a belt-high fastball right down the middle that Bridwell lined past Bob Emslie, the second base umpire, into right center for a clean single. McCormick skipped happily home with the winning run, and the game was over.

"We did it! We did it!" Harry shouted as he slapped his brother's back and jumped up and down. The crowd around them clapped and hollered and whistled, and then fans from everywhere in the stands began swarming onto the field.

"What's going on between third and second?" Alex asked as he and Harry were moving down toward the diamond.

"I don't know," Harry replied.

Two players who weren't even in the game, Joe McGinnity and Rube Kroh, a Chicago pitcher, were grappling for the ball, which Solly Hofman had pegged in from the outfield. The Iron Man managed to snatch it away and fling it right toward Harry and Alex.

"Here it comes!" Alex shouted. He lunged for the ball but lost out to a burly Negro who reached above his head and caught it with one hand.

By the time Harry and Alex got onto the field Johnny Evers had somehow produced another ball. He stepped on second base several times and then began shouting at Bob Emslie. Whatever it was Evers was arguing about, the umpire wasn't buying it. Then Evers pulled Hank O'Day, the senior arbiter, into the discussion. Alex and Harry joined a crowd that was forming around the argument.

"Didn't you see it?" Evers was protesting. "Merkle never touched second. That means he's been forced out and the run doesn't count."

"Baloney!" someone in the crowd cried out.

"That's a bunch of hot air!" Harry yelled.

"Go to hell, Evers. You lowdown son of a bitch!" a third man shouted.

The crowd started pressing in on Evers and the umps. "Well, what about it, O'Day?" someone asked.

But O'Day wasn't saying anything. The crowd got hotter and began moving closer. A number of fans hurled insults at O'Day and threatened to bust his head in if he didn't put an end to this nonsense. The situation was at the boiling point when the police rushed in and escorted the two umpires to safety under the grandstand. After several minutes, a rumor began spreading through the crowd that O'Day had indeed called Merkle out at second.

"What does that mean?" Alex asked his brother.

"Not a goddamn thing," Harry replied, his voice cracking from anger and frustration. "Who cares if Merkle didn't touch second? We scored the winning run and that's all that counts. They'll never get away with such a rotten trick."

But the Cubs did indeed get away with Evers's trick. The rules state that a run cannot score on a force out that ends an inning. *If* Merkle was forced out, the run clearly did not count.

The Giants protested O'Day's decision to Harry Pulliam, president of the National League, who upheld the ruling of his umpire. The game was a tie and would be played over if its outcome would have a bearing on the final standings. New York appealed to the league's board of directors; Chicago filed a counter appeal, claiming the Giants had forfeited the game on two counts—first because of McGinnity's interference with a ball in play, and second because New York had refused to play the game over as part of a doubleheader the next day. The directors sustained Pulliam's verdict. They ordered that the game be played again on October 8, if necessary.

As fate would have it, New York and Chicago finished their remaining games in a dead heat for first place. Despite several injuries the Giants played good ball right up to the end, winning fifteen and losing six. But the Cubs played even better; they won eight and lost only three. So the work of an entire season came down to a game the New York fans and players were convinced they'd already won.

Many of the Giants were opposed to playing the game over. McGraw himself wasn't sure what to do and told his men the night before the contest, "I don't care whether you fellows play this game or not. You can take a vote."

The team argued the matter for some time and then decided to send a group of representatives to discuss the matter with John T. Brush, who was sick in bed at the Lambs Club. Christy Mathewson, the group's leader, explained the players' dilemma to the Giants' owner. It was obvious Brush wanted them to play, but he said, "You boys can play the game or not. But I shouldn't think you would stop now after making all this fight."

The players talked it over for a few minutes, and then Matty told Brush, "We'll play."

"I'm glad," their boss replied. "And say, boys, I want to tell you something. Win or lose I'm putting up ten thousand in bonus money for the team."

Alex and Harry woke at dawn on Thursday morning, October 8. It was a beautiful fall day. The sky was clear, the air was fresh, and the leaves were only a few days away from their peak autumn colors. Elizabeth served them a hearty breakfast of fried eggs, ham, and waffles. Then she packed a lunchpail with fried chicken, German potato salad, grapes, and apples.

Harry and Alex took the El to the Polo Grounds, which was already packed almost to capacity when they got there. They managed to fight their way into the stadium and find two seats just before the police closed the gates. Somewhere outside the park was Fletcher, who found it impossible to gain admission even though he had a box seat ticket right behind first base. As game time approached, thousands of locked-out fans crowded onto whatever perches they could find outside the park, whether on the elevated tracks, up on Coogan's Bluff, or on the roof of the grandstand. Two men fell to their deaths from the elevated platform to the street below. Their vantage points were quickly occupied by two other intrepid fans.

The Cubs took a short batting practice that was interrupted when McGinnity and Chance got into a fistfight. The tension on the field quickly spread; fights and loud arguments were breaking out all over the stands. Finally it was game time. Mathewson took his place in the box, and one, two, three he disposed of the top of Chicago's lineup.

"I think Matty's got it today," Alex told his brother.

"Maybe," Harry said. "But something isn't right with his delivery."

The Giants scored a run in the bottom of the first, and Harry told himself everything was going to be all right. But then Three Finger Brown was brought in to put out the fire, which he did, filling Harry with gloom. In the second, Matty again held the Cubs scoreless, but in the third they broke the game wide open with four runs.

Meanwhile Brown continued to mystify the Giant batters. His one lapse was in the seventh, when he allowed the bases to load up with no outs. But then the three-fingered wizard bore down, allowing only one run on a fly to the outfield. All hope for New York was lost. The final score was 4–2.

"What happened?" Alex asked as he and Harry were leaving the park.

"Matty didn't have it today," his brother answered. "His curves were flat. He couldn't put a thing on the ball. The minute Brown came into the game it was all over."

So destiny, or fate, or whatever, robbed New York of a well-earned pennant. Over the years the contention that the Giants were the "real champions of the National League" was to ignite many a baseball argument. The Merkle incident left Harry with a bitter taste that remained with him a long time. Nonetheless, his exhaustive study of the 1908 campaign did lead him to the conclusion that the Giants had played over their heads for a good part of the year. John McGraw had kept the club alive.

Harry agreed with the writer of an article in the November 1908 issue of *Baseball Magazine* who argued that "it was the wonderful work of this man, then almost alone, that kept the Giants among the contenders all year. I venture to say that with Chance at the helm of the New York team this season, or Fred Clarke, or any of the other managers, the Giants would have been extremely lucky to finish fourth."

Over the next few seasons McGraw broke up his old team and began building for the future. Matty remained his ace hurler, but elsewhere around the diamond there were several new faces. Larry Doyle had already replaced Billy Gilbert at second, and now Fred Merkle—whom John never blamed for his lapse on the basepaths—became the regular first baseman.

Chief Meyers took over for Roger Bresnahan behind the plate; Fred Snodgrass became the left fielder; and Buck Herzog was installed at third. In 1908 McGraw purchased Rube Marquard from the Indianapolis Club in the American Association (a minor league) for $11,000. At that time it was the highest price ever paid for a baseball player.

Marquard got off to a slow start. His record was five and thirteen in 1909 and four and four in 1910. Some critics were calling him the $11,000 lemon, but McGraw stayed with him. Marquard repaid his manager's confidence by winning more than twenty games in each of the next three seasons. In 1912 he led the league in wins with a record of twenty-six and eleven.

In Brooklyn, Charlie Ebbets was also searching for a winning combination. In 1909 he fired Patsy Donovan and named his right fielder, Harry Lumley, as manager. The next year, after the Superbas finished sixth, Ebbets replaced Lumley with Bill Dahlen. Juggling managers could not, however, solve Brooklyn's basic problem—a severe shortage of playing talent. Two standout players—Nap Rucker, the tireless pitcher, and Zack Wheat, the great left fielder—did join the team during the period, but the first division still remained way over the Dodgers' heads.

Early in 1909 Harry Pulliam, suffering from nervous exhaustion brought on by the pressures of office, committed suicide. His successor as president of the National League was John A. Heydler, who had held the post of secretary-treasurer. In December of that year, at the league's annual meetings in New York, Heydler was opposed for reelection by Robert W. Brown, a newspaper owner from Louisville, and Monte Ward, now a respected attorney.

None of the candidates was able to win enough support to get the job. John T. Brush resolved the stalemate by proposing Thomas J. Lynch, who had been a National League umpire in the 1880s and 1890s. Brush, echoing his manager's sentiments, claimed that what was now needed more than anything else was a man who could control the umpires. Whether or not his argument was valid, Lynch, with his reputation as "a man of nerve and independence," got the job.

At those same meetings Barney Dreyfuss gave a lavish dinner in the ballroom of the Waldorf Astoria to celebrate the victory of his Pirates in the World Series. The *Sporting News* called the affair "one of the biggest social events ever known in the history of baseball." Barney's guest list included two hundred of the greatest names in the game. On hand were such luminaries as Frank Farrell, Ned Hanlon, Christy Mathewson, John McGraw, Willie Keeler, Cap Anson, and Charlie Comiskey. John T. Brush, scheduled to give a toast, became indisposed at the last minute and could not attend. The title of his talk was to have been "A Prophecy."

Charlie Ebbets was asked to stand in for the Giants' owner. He rose to give a kind of prophecy of his own. As the champagne flowed, he talked about some of the problems facing the two major leagues, and then he remarked, "Baseball is in its infancy." To many of those present it was a silly statement. At least a few of the great men assembled there must have known those were the most meaningful words spoken that night.

It was around 1910 that Harry began to worry about his kid brother. Alex was seventeen, an age when one should be taking on, or at least preparing for, the responsibilities of adulthood. But Alex saw no reason to bother himself with weighty problems such as completing his education or finding a position.

He had already dropped out of school half a dozen times and been fired from three jobs. The only thing that sparked his interest was the Brooklyn baseball club. A large part of the problem was his father's doing. Fletcher's duties for Frank Farrell kept him in New York most of the time. Whenever he was home in Brooklyn he tried to make up for being a poor father by giving his youngest son conscience money. Sometimes it would be a dollar or two, but more often it would be ten or twenty. The result was that Alex, who spent his days either loafing or watching ball games, had more money than Harry, who worked hard every day for a salary of $18.50 a week.

That spring, during the first week of May, Alex suddenly disappeared. After two days Harry telephoned Fletcher. "Oh, don't worry about Alex," his father said. "He's just trying to prove he's a man. If he wants to strike out on his own, well, that's his affair. He'll be back when his money runs out."

Harry was disturbed by his father's indifference. After all, Alex was pretty helpless. He had never in his life been called upon to fend for himself. For all they knew he was in jail or in a hospital somewhere.

One morning Harry and Elizabeth discussed the problem over breakfast.

"Liz, where do you think Alex is?" Harry asked.

"Oh, I don't know. Maybe he's found a woman."

"I doubt that. Suppose he's in trouble?"

"If he is, there's nothing we can do about it until he gets in touch with us," Elizabeth said.

"I can't understand Pop's attitude."

"I can. Don't think your father isn't worried. I know he is. But Fletcher has given up trying to come to grips with his problems. He hides from them and hopes they'll go away. Alex is the same way. It's very difficult to help people like that. It's hard to love them too."

While Elizabeth was talking, Harry was examining her features. How old was she? Somewhere in her forties. She was still a handsome woman. A perfect wife for someone. And yet here she was, taking care of a big old house that no one really wanted to live in. What a waste of beauty and stored-up love.

On a hot, muggy evening in early June, Harry came home from work to find his brother sitting in the parlor. Alex looked up from his newspaper and said, "Hello, Harry." Then he went back to reading as though he hadn't been gone for more than an hour.

"Where the hell have you been?" Harry asked.

"Here and there," Alex replied indifferently. "But mostly Pittsburgh, Cincinnati, Chicago, and St. Louis. It was great fun."

"What in God's name were you doing?"

"Following the Superbas around. It's something I've wanted to do for as long as I can remember."

A few days later Elizabeth gave Fletcher a piece of her mind. She told him Alex needed parental guidance, and she suggested he sit down and have a heart-to-heart talk with his son. She also said it would be a good idea if he stopped letting him have so much spending money. Fletcher thanked her for her concern and promised to heed her advice, but he could not face up to his duties as a father. He went right on giving Alex money, and Alex, in turn, went right on loafing and drifting.

The baseball season ended, winter came, and another baseball season came around. For a while Harry tried to keep tabs on his brother, but then he became occupied with other matters. At his church's Christmas bazaar he met an attractive young schoolteacher named Ellen Watchman. She was tall and dark, and quite taken with Harry. He quickly decided the most important thing in his life was to make her his wife. So while he continued to worry about his brother, he began devoting most of his free time to his budding courtship.

With the coming of spring, John Brush decided to spruce up the Giants' ball park. New bleachers were put up in left field, and the grandstand received a fresh coat of paint. As the new season got under way, Harry told himself this was the year the Giants would make it back on top. Then, early in the morning on April 14, 1911, disaster struck the Polo Grounds. Just after midnight a watchman on the elevated line adjacent to the park saw flames shooting up from the stands. He sounded the alarm, but by the time firemen arrived the grandstands around the diamond were already a pile of rubble, and the blaze had spread to the left-field bleachers. Only the clubhouse, the right-field bleachers, and a portion of the seats in center field could be saved. With the season but a few days old, the Giants found themselves without a ball park.

Luckily for the Giants, the Yankees offered to share their field until the Polo Grounds could be rebuilt. While McGraw's men played their home games at Hilltop Park, work began on what was to become the most modern baseball plant in the country.

In June, after winding up a successful road trip, McGraw said of the other teams in the league, "We have them all beaten to a frazzle." That may have been his opinion, but the standings didn't confirm it, and neither the Cubs nor the Pirates were inclined to agree. It was still anybody's race. On June 28, the Giants moved back into the Polo Grounds, still only partially rebuilt, and Matty celebrated the homecoming by shutting out Boston, 3–0. A reporter on hand commented that "one feature of the new stand . . . is that stamping can no longer be used as a means of applause. The concrete floor deadens the sound of the feet so that now a greater tax will be put on the hands and throat." The Giants were giving their fans plenty to yell and clap about. As the stadium grew up around the field, McGraw kept his team near the front of a race that Harry prayed would end with New York taking its first pennant in six years.

Then, in the first week of August, the Giants went sour. After losing three straight in Pittsburgh, they went on to Chicago, where they dropped the first of a three-game series. The team was tense and exhausted, and everyone had lost his sense of humor. "The man we need right now is old Robbie," McGraw told a bunch of reporters in the hotel lobby. "Say, you newspaper boys, go and fix up a message to him, will you?" After a few minutes of composing, the journalists sent McGraw's old pal Wilbert Robinson this wire:

> COME ON FIRST TRAIN AND BE IN FOR THE
> BIG FINISH. TEAM IS ABOUT TO GO TO
> PIECES THROUGH WORRY. COME ALONG
> AND HELP STRAIGHTEN OUT THEIR NERVES.
> THEY WON'T EVEN PLAY POKER. MC GRAW

While the Giants were losing another game to the Cubs, Robbie, who had retired from baseball some years earlier, was on a train to Chicago. For two seasons he had gone south with the club for spring training, so he knew the players well and was liked by them all. He was waiting at the hotel when the team got back from the ball park, and he immediately went to work.

The first man he ran into was Chief Meyers. "What the hell's the matter with you?" Robbie asked. "You're working too hard. Now cut out this training and come with me." He escorted the Chief into the hotel bar and bought him a glass of brandy. Then Robinson sought out Marquard. He slipped Rube a bottle of ale and then took him and Meyers to a vaudeville show.

The next morning Robbie organized a pool tournament. Then he took Fred Snodgrass and Fred Merkle shopping for new clothes. By game time that afternoon the Giants were as loose as a flock of geese. With Marquard in the box they demolished the Cubs, 16–5.

Wilbert Robinson was not the only newcomer to the Giants that season; 1911 was also the year Charles Victor Faust cast his spell upon the club. That spring, in his hometown of Marion, Kansas, Faust had visited a fortune teller. "You will become the greatest baseball pitcher the world has ever known," the soothsayer told the thirty-year-old man. "You will lead the New York Giants to the pennant, and then you will meet a beautiful girl named Lulu. She will become your wife, and you will be the father of a long line of baseball heroes." Faust took the words very much to heart. He learned the Giants would be in St. Louis to play the Cardinals in the middle of June, so he traveled across Missouri with every expectation of joining the team.

McGraw was on the bench watching batting practice just before the final game in St. Louis when Faust approached him and introduced himself. He told John of the fortune teller's prediction and said he would be happy to join the club and help win the pennant. McGraw was far too superstitious to dismiss the young man out of hand. "So you're a pitcher," the Giant manager said. "All right, let's see what you've got." John picked up a catcher's mitt and started warming up the strange Kansan.

It was painfully obvious after half a dozen pitches that he had nothing at all on the ball. McGraw sent Faust to the plate. He hit a puny dribbler to the infield and then ran around the bases, sliding awkwardly into each bag and kicking up dust all over his new Sunday suit. The players all got a good laugh out of the gag. When Faust left the field, they never expected to see him again. That night, on the train to Boston, they were astonished to discover that he had joined the team. "Charlie here is going to help us win the flag," McGraw told his men.

Charlie Faust soon earned a reputation as a jinx killer. The Giants went right into a winning streak. As the season progressed, Faust displayed an uncanny ability to predict the outcomes of games and series. He warmed up to pitch every afternoon that summer, always figuring McGraw was just about ready to give him his chance. He never received a salary, but John made sure he had more than enough money in his pockets to cover expenses. In September—whether aided by Faust's good luck or by Robbie's good cheer—the Giants finally pulled away from the Pirates and Cubs. On October 4, at Washington Park in Brooklyn, they clinched the pennant. The Superbas, in a last-ditch effort to thwart their archenemies, called Nap Rucker back from his honeymoon to pitch against Mathewson. It was no use. The Giants won, 2–0, and the flag was theirs.

On the last day of the season, in the second game of a doubleheader at the Polo Grounds, Charlie Faust got his chance. In a contest won by the Superbas, 5–2, he entered the game in the top of the ninth. The Brooklyn players took exaggerated swings at Charlie's puny deliveries, and the side was quickly out. In the bottom half of the inning, Faust took his turn at bat. Eddie Dent, the Brooklyn pitcher, put Charlie on base by grazing him with a slow curve; then the Superbas let him steal second, third, and home. One reporter described the inning as "pure burlesque." Perhaps so, but Charlie Faust had made it to the big leagues.

The Athletics were champs of the American League in 1911. Once again McGraw outfitted his team in those sinister black uniforms for the World Series, and once again Matty and Chief Bender faced each other in the first game. On October 14, a record crowd for a Series—almost forty thousand fans—crammed into the Polo Grounds for the opening contest. As Matty made his way to the box, Harry, who went to the game alone, crossed his fingers in the hope that the Giant hurler could keep alive his string of World Series shutouts. That dream was shattered in the second inning, when Frank Baker scored from third on a single by Harry Davis. The Giants tied the game in the fourth and took the lead in the seventh after Chief Meyers hit a double to left and was sent home on a single by Josh Devore. Matty held the A's the rest of the way, and New York won, 2–1.

Harry was now certain his team could make it. Eddie Plank was scheduled to pitch for the Athletics in the second game, and Harry figured the Giants, with Marquard pitching, would treat Eddie just as harshly as they had six years earlier.

Harry's job kept him in Brooklyn that day, so he followed the action on a scoreboard set up in front of the office of the *Brooklyn Eagle*. The game began inauspiciously for the Giants. Marquard allowed a run to score in the first on a wild pitch. New York tied the game in the second, and the score remained 1–1 until the sixth, when, with two out and no one on, Eddie Collins of the A's hit a drive down the left-field line that fell fair by less than two feet. Collins pulled into second with a double, and Frank Baker strolled up to the plate. He had gone two for four in the first game and was an excellent fastball hitter. Chief Meyers signaled Marquard for a curve, which came in for a strike. A second curve went wide for a ball. Meyers asked for still another breaking ball, but Rube decided to fool Baker with a fastball.

It was a mistake. Baker lofted a drive over the right-field fence, and the Athletics had a 3–1 lead. The Giants failed to score after that, and the Series was all tied up at one game apiece.

The teams returned to the Polo Grounds for game three, which pitted Mathewson against Jack Coombs. The Giants got on the score-board early with a run in the third. Matty pitched brilliantly, keeping the A's off balance and holding the dangerous Baker in check with slow curves. The game moved into the top of the ninth with the score still 1–0.

Collins led off with a slow grounder for an easy out, and up came Baker. Out in the right-field stands Harry Rice squirmed in his seat. "Now, Matty, damn it, don't give him *anything* but curves," he pleaded.

Mathewson appeared to be obliging. The count went to two balls and a strike. Then Baker's bat cracked sharply. "Oh no!" Harry cried out as the ball sailed over his head and landed several rows behind him.

Mathewson retired the rest of the side with little difficulty and walked dejectedly to the dugout. "I gave Baker a high fast one," he told Mc-Graw. "I've been in this business a long time and have no excuse."

The game went into extra innings. In the top of the eleventh, Collins singled to left with one down. Then Baker hit a sharp grounder to Herzog. Buck's throw to first was wild, allowing Collins to reach third as Baker moved over to second. The next batter, Murphy, punched an easy roller to short, but a nervous Art Fletcher bobbled the ball and Collins dashed home with the tie-breaking run. Harry Davis then drilled Matty's first pitch to right; the single sent Baker in with the A's second, and final, tally of the inning. The Giants made a good try in their half of the eleventh; they managed to score once, but the rally died and Philadelphia had a 3–2 victory.

The Series moved back to Philadelphia, where it was interrupted by a steady downpour that lasted six days. McGraw saw the rain as a bit of luck, for it gave his ace pitcher a long, badly needed rest. When play resumed on October 24, Matty appeared ready to go. He was given his third start in four games. New York began well, tapping Chief Bender for two runs in the top of the first. But in the fourth, Baker, the thorn in the Giants' side, once again sparked an Athletic rally. He led off with a double and scored the first of three runs in the inning.

In the fifth, Baker drove in Philadelphia's fourth run with another double to deep right. Bender blanked New York the rest of the way, making the final score 4–2. The Giants were now down in the Series, three games to one.

In the fifth contest McGraw's men proved they still had some fight left. In the ninth inning they extracted two runs from the jaws of defeat and tied the game at three all. They went on to chalk up a single tally in the tenth to win, 4–3.

That proved to be the end of the line for the Giants. In game six the A's tagged Red Ames, the Giant's starter, for four runs in the fourth inning, and when the contest was over Philadelphia had destroyed New York, 13–2. Mack and McGraw were all even at one World Series apiece.

For Harry the Series was a sad revelation. The Giants were no longer the supermen of 1905. It would have been easy to blame their downfall on those two ill-timed fastballs that turned Frank Baker into Home Run Baker. But those two bad pitches went right to the heart of the problem. Matty was getting older and was losing his touch. Marquard, despite his flashes of brilliance, would always have an erratic streak. Harry worried a lot about such things.

On March 4, 1912, Alex attended one of the most important events in the history of Brooklyn—the ground-breaking ceremonies for Ebbets Field. For Charlie Ebbets the new ball park was a dream come true. To finance the project he had bought out Henry Medicus's stock and then sold 50 percent of the club to Steve and Ed McKeever, two brothers who were prosperous Brooklyn contractors.

The McKeevers put up $100,000 for their interest in the Superbas. Two corporations were formed; the Ebbets–McKeever Exhibition Company owned the park, and the Brooklyn National League Baseball Club operated the team. The site Ebbets chose was in a shantytown in Flatbush that went by many unpleasant names, including Pigtown, Goatville, Tin Can Alley, and Crow Hill. On the surface it was not an especially promising piece of property, but Charlie could see that the neighborhood was growing and improving, and he noted that public transportation to the area was quite good.

At the ground-breaking ceremonies Charlie Ebbets was handed a silver spade. As he ceremoniously drove it into the ground, someone yelled out, "Dig up a couple of new players, Charlie!" The crowd broke into laughter, and Alex Rice, author of the remark, doffed his hat and made a little bow.

The need for a new ball park was vividly demonstrated on opening day at Washington Park. More than thirty thousand spectators squeezed into the rattletrap enclosure to see the Superbas and the Giants square off for another season of bitter rivalry. Fans were everywhere—along the foul lines, in the outfield, and on top of each other in the stands. Marquard went against Rucker, and the Giants had a field day, scoring eighteen runs in six innings. The large crowd was so unruly and potentially dangerous that Bill Klem, the umpire, called the game "on account of darkness" in the bottom of the sixth. The final score was 18–3. Alex was trounced as badly as the Superbas. Caught in the crush of the crowd, he suffered a sprained ankle and a chipped tooth.

That opening day pretty well told the story of the 1912 campaign. The Superbas played terrible baseball all season and wound up in seventh place, while the Giants took the lead in May and coasted to their second straight pennant, finishing ten games in front of the second-place Pirates.

Along the way Rube Marquard tied the major league record of nineteen straight victories set by Tim Keefe of the Giants in 1888. Alex had very little to yell about that year, but one afternoon in September his hopes for the future were given a lift by the appearance of a promising young rookie. In a game against Pittsburgh this new outfielder got four hits and a walk. That night over dinner Alex couldn't stop talking about the Superbas' find.

"What did you say his name was?" Harry asked.

"Charlie Stengel. You watch. He'll help Brooklyn win the pennant next year."

The World Series of 1912 between the Giants and the Red Sox was poorly played but terribly exciting. The opposing managers—John McGraw and Jake Stahl—were a study in contrasts. As one observer put it, the Little Napoleon, as McGraw was now called, was "older, craftier, more resourceful, aggressive, slightly domineering, keen, alert, and decisive in all his actions." Stahl, who not only managed but also played first base, was described as "younger, more optimistic, energetic, courteous, considerate, popular, and a favorite with his players and with the public." The betting odds favored Boston, and even Harry Rice, who was still brooding over the Giants' humiliating loss to the A's the year before, lacked the confidence to lay a few bucks on New York.

The Series opened at the Polo Grounds with Jeff Tesreau pitching for the Giants against Boston's ace fastballer, Smokey Joe Wood. McGraw wanted to save his best hurler for the next day's game in Boston, figuring Mathewson's cool and experience would be important assets in enemy territory. The strategy backfired. The Giants lost the first contest, 4–3. Game two ended in a 6–6 tie; it was called because of darkness after eleven innings, forcing the teams to remain in Boston to play it over. The Giants were still a game behind, and their ace pitcher's first start had been wasted.

The next hurler in their rotation was Marquard. Rube managed to save the third game by squeaking out a 2–1 victory, but then Boston won two in a row, 3–1 and 2–1. The Giants dug themselves out of a hole by outplaying the Red Sox, 5–2, and then crushing them, 11–4. Each team now had three victories, and everything had come down to the eighth and final game.

Harry traveled to Boston for the deciding contest on October 16. It was a cold, bleak day; as he made his way from the train station to the ball park he congratulated himself for heeding Elizabeth's suggestion to wear a warm coat. Much to his surprise, the crowd was fairly small. It may have been the weather, or perhaps the Boston fans were discouraged by the Giants' momentum. Whatever the reason, only seventeen thousand fans were on hand, including two thousand rooters from New York. Christy Mathewson and Hugh Bedient were named the starting pitchers. The Giants scored first with a run in the third, but in the fifth they were deprived of two more runs when Harry Hooper, the Red Sox right fielder, made one of the great plays of the Series.

With Josh Devore on first, Larry Doyle sent a wicked drive to right center. Hooper chased it all the way back to the fence, dived into the crowd, and plucked the ball out of thin air to rob Doyle of a homer. Matty, pitching with everything he had left in the final hours of a long season, held the Red Sox scoreless till the top of the seventh. In that inning, after one out, Jake Stahl popped a Texas League single into shallow center. Then Heinie Wagner walked, and Hick Cady hit an easy pop up to Art Fletcher at short. Now there were two outs and it was Bedient's turn to bat.

Stahl yelled in from second base for Olaf Henriksen to come in as a pinch hitter. The "hard-hitting Dane" hit a double down the third base line that tied the score, and then Hooper flied out to Snodgrass to end the inning.

Neither team scored again through the ninth, so the extra game of the Series was sent into extra innings. Batting against Wood, who had come in to relieve Bedient, the Giants scored a run in the top of the tenth when Red Murray doubled to left and Fred Merkle drove him home with a single over the head of Steve Yerkes, the Boston second baseman. "*Finally*, another Series for McGraw," Harry told himself as Matty went out to polish off the last three outs.

The first batter up was Clyde Engle, batting for Wood. The Boston fans groaned as Engle sent a high lazy fly into left center; Fred Snodgrass waved Red Murray off, got his range, and pulled the ball in—momentarily. It dribbled out of his glove and fell to the ground. Engle was safe at second.

Harry Hooper, the next batter, fouled off a bunt and then hit a blast to deep center field. As Hooper himself put it years later, "Ninety-nine times out of a hundred no outfielder could possibly come close to that ball. But in some way, I don't know how, Snodgrass ran like the wind, and dang if he didn't catch it. I think he *outran* the ball. Robbed me of a sure triple." Snodgrass also came within a hair of doubling off Engle, who just made it back to second ahead of the throw. At this point Harry Rice, trying to shake off the tension, moved to a new seat. Rattled by Hooper's drive, Matty lost his range and walked Yerkes. Then Tris Speaker, Boston's great center fielder, came up to the plate. On the first pitch he hit a pop foul near first that Fred Merkle should have handled with ease. But Merkle stayed at his position as if in a daze while Chief Meyers scampered up the line and lunged in vain for the ball. It was utter folly to give Speaker a second chance. He promptly singled to right sending Engle in with the tying run and moving Yerkes over to third. Larry Gardner then flied out to Josh Devore in right; the peg home was not in time to prevent Yerkes from crossing the plate. The game was over, and so was the Series.

A rich period in the history of the New York Giants came to an end on November 26, 1912, when John T. Brush died. He had been ill a long time and had decided to spend the winter recuperating in sunny California. He was on the way there in his private railroad car when, passing through Missouri, he succumbed to a stroke.

Brush's widow and two daughters became the new owners of the Giants. Harry N. Hempstead, Brush's son-in-law, had joined the front office a short time before to be groomed for the presidency. It now became necessary for him to take over the club before his training period was over. There would be no changes in policy; McGraw would remain in full control of the team.

On Saturday, April 5, 1913, the Yankees invaded Brooklyn for a very special exhibition contest. That was the day Ebbets Field opened its gates for the first time. Alex dragged Harry and Ellen to the game. At first Ellen didn't want to go, but she decided that if she was going to marry Harry it would be a good idea to learn something about baseball. As they entered the park through the main entrance at the corner of Cedar Place and Sullivan Street, Ellen marveled at the ornate marble rotunda that was Charlie Ebbets's pride and joy. Harry and Alex were both impressed with the new stadium, and they agreed Ebbets had fulfilled his promise to "make the new playground one of the most attractive in the world."

A crowd of twenty-five thousand fans—a record for an exhibition game—bought tickets to see the magnificent new park, and ten thousand more were turned away. The enterprising owner of a plot of land on Dead End Hill, a bluff that looked down on the diamond from behind left field, had set up bleachers of his own and sold seats for a quarter each to five-hundred fans who failed to get into the park.

As the huge crowd grew restless and began to cry "play ball," Charlie Ebbets and Ed McKeever and his wife strolled out to the flagpole in center field for the opening ceremonies. The American flag was unfurled and hoisted to the strains of "The Star Spangled Banner," and then Genevieve Ebbets, Charlie's daughter, threw out the first ball, making a fine peg to umpire Bob Emslie.

Then Ebbets led his team across the field as the band played "Here

Comes Your Daddy Now." It was a festive occasion, and hardly anyone could disagree with the observer who remarked that "when Mr. Ebbets stages one of these dedication affairs he is right in there with the dignity and the glitter and history making."

When the lineups were announced, Alex grinned in approval. His new hero, Charles "Casey" Stengel, had taken the job of center fielder away from Herb Moran. The starting pitchers were Nap Rucker and Ray Caldwell.

The game marked Frank Chance's first appearance in New York as manager of the Yanks, as well as Hal Chase's debut at second base. Prince Hal moved to the middle of the diamond to allow Chance to play his customary position at first. Both pitchers got off to good starts.

The game was scoreless until the fifth inning, when Stengel, batting with the bases empty, hit a drive to deep left center. Harry Wolter ran after it at full speed with his back to the diamond. Alex bellowed with glee as the ball dropped a few feet ahead of the center fielder; it bounced up, hit Wolter's foot, and rolled all the way to the fence. Meanwhile Stengel rounded third and came across the plate with an inside-the-park home run.

In the sixth Jake Daubert, the Superbas' star first baseman, also homered, and the game went into the ninth with Brooklyn ahead, 2–0. Then the Yankees, batting against Frank Allen, who'd replaced the tiring Rucker in the sixth, came to life. Chase walked, Chance singled, and Ed Sweeney, the Yanks' catcher, laid down a perfect bunt. Allen fielded the ball and threw in desperation to Daubert. The throw was wide by several feet, the ball went flying into the right-field corner, and Chase and Chance rushed home with the tying runs.

In the bottom of the ninth, Zack Wheat led off against Ray Fisher, the new Yankee pitcher. Zack placed a bunt in front of the plate and Ed Sweeney threw the ball away, allowing Wheat to reach second. Daubert also bunted, sacrificing the runner to third. Then Red Smith, Brooklyn's third baseman, lined a single into left center that drove in the winning tally. As Alex, Harry, and Ellen were leaving Ebbets Field, Alex boasted, "I told you this was the year. The Superbas are going to be in the thick of things."

The optimism of Alex Rice proved to be ill-founded. The Superbas lost their first three regular season games in Ebbets Field to the Phillies, each by 1–0. Brooklyn's sour start was a preview of the campaign to come. Despite the team's apparent promise the Superbas remained in contention only until July, when they slid into the second division for good.

The bright spot in the season was the hitting of Jake Daubert, who won the National League batting crown with a .350 average. Brooklyn finished the campaign in sixth place, thirty-four and a half games off the mark.

The Giants, meanwhile, recovered from a shaky start, began climbing in June, and by midseason had built up a powerful head of steam that carried them to their third pennant in a row. They finished twelve and a half games in front of the Phillies. The Athletics won the flag in the American League, setting up a "rubber" World Series between McGraw and Connie Mack.

On September 26, in a game between the Giants and the Superbas, Fred Snodgrass had caught a spike on the bag while crossing first, tearing up a leg muscle. Fred made it into only one game the rest of the season and did not recover in time to be of much use in the World Series.

Then, a few nights before the first game, Larry Doyle crashed his car into a tree in Central Park. The auto was a total wreck, and Larry was damned lucky to walk away from the accident in one piece. His shoulder was badly bruised, and his ability to play was severely hampered.

So as the Series got under way, McGraw had a lot to worry about. When Frank Baker hit another homer off Rube Marquard in the fifth inning of the first game, McGraw knew he was in trouble. The A's won that opener, 6–4; during the game Fred Merkle sprained his ankle and played the rest of the Series with it swollen to twice its normal size.

Then Chief Meyers, warming up for the second game, fractured a finger. The injury was so painful the Giant catcher left the field biting his lip to keep from breaking into tears. With so many starting players hobbled, it was a wonder the Giants had any spirit left. But in the second game Matty again faced Eddie Plank, and again the great New York hurler pitched one of his shutouts against the Athletics. It took ten innings before the Giants could score; Matty himself batted in the first run of the game in the top of the tenth, and New York wound up with a 3–0 victory.

From then on the Series belonged to Philadelphia. The A's won the next three, and New York lost its third World Series in a row. Harry Rice was depressed for weeks. He choked, as if on a nasty pill, when he read in *Baseball Magazine* that "those dear Giants were overwhelmingly trimmed, thrashed, and annihilated. Once more the American League had triumphed, and once more the good old National is bowed in dust and ashes."

As usual, Harry spent several weeks pondering every important play of the Series. One play in particular made no sense. In the third inning of the fourth game the Giants had one out and no one on and were behind, 1–0. Snodgrass, so lame he could hardly walk, attempted to bunt for a base hit. Chief Bender threw Fred out by a mile, and McGraw immediately pulled the injured center fielder out of the game.

After the play Harry scratched his head in bewilderment and continued to puzzle over it well into the fall. How could McGraw expect Snodgrass to beat out a bunt by limping to first base? It just didn't figure.

What Harry didn't know was that Wilbert Robinson, coaching at first base, had misread one of McGraw's signals. The mistake caused a fierce row between Robbie and the Little Napoleon.

The evening following the Series, the two men went out to dinner and argued bitterly about the play. John accused Wilbert of making a bonehead move, and Robbie answered by saying it was an insult to his intelligence to think he would have taken it upon himself to ask a player in Snodgrass's condition to bunt. They wound up drinking beer in the old Hofbrau House on into the early hours of the morning. Finally McGraw, unable to contain his fury, told Robbie, "You're through. You're through with this ball club."

Robinson had been the Giants' pitching coach since the day in 1911 he came to Chicago to lift the players' spirits. He had done wonders with Rube Marquard and had a large hand in developing Jeff Tesreau. John and Robbie had been great pals and business partners for the better part of two decades. Because of one petty misunderstanding Robinson was now out of a job. The two old friends were destined to be bitter enemies for almost all their remaining years.

At the close of the 1913 season McGraw not only got rid of Robbie but also saw the last of Charlie Faust. The zany Kansan, who had become known as "Victory" Faust, had remained with the Giants as their mascot through the 1912 campaign.

One day someone told McGraw about another "eccentric" in Chicago who had been for years the butt of a long, tired practical joke by a number of Cook County politicians. The man was told he was destined for a high political office, perhaps even the presidency of the United States. Finally, it all went to the fellow's head—he went berserk and murdered Carter Harrison, Chicago's mayor.

The story gave the Little Napoleon the willies. He began to see a wild, evil glint in Victory's eyes. One day he politely asked Charlie if he wouldn't mind going home. But in 1913 Faust popped up again several times, always begging for another chance to show his stuff. Over the next winter McGraw and a number of Giants joined a contingent of major league players on a tour around the world. By the time they returned Faust had disappeared. He surfaced in an insane asylum in Portland, Oregon, in the spring of 1914. A year later Victory died.

By November 1913 everyone knew that Bill Dahlen was through as manager of the Superbas. The only question was who would get the job. The pundits were tossing around several names, including Roger Bresnahan, Hughie Jennings, and Jake Stahl. But when Charlie Ebbets announced his choice it came as a complete surprise.

He picked a man everyone thought was headed in one capacity or another for the new Federal League team in Baltimore. The new Brooklyn pilot was none other than Wilbert Robinson.

Ebbets had learned of Robbie's clash with McGraw. Charlie figured if anyone had the drive and desire to beat the Giants—and the rest of the league in the process—Robinson was the man. Portly, jolly, and always of gentle disposition, Robbie didn't look much like a man who could command the loyalty and respect of a ball team. Yet he was an old Oriole and a learned disciple of John McGraw. When asked about his plans for the team, Robbie replied, "The main thing I have to do with the Brooklyn club is develop some pitchers." If he could accomplish that, he would surely give Alex something to cheer about.

On April 19, 1914, a week after Harry Rice's twenty-fifth birthday, Ellen and Harry were married. The reception was held in Manhattan at the old Waldorf Astoria Hotel at Fifth Avenue and Thirty-fourth Street. Fletcher was madly in love with his new daughter-in-law, and he decided to give her the most lavish wedding money could buy. It was the last thing Ellen really wanted, but she and Harry decided it would be best to let Fletcher have his way.

The old boy cut quite a figure in his cutaway coat as he paraded to the ballroom arm-in-arm with the bride and groom past the marble archways and over the lush Oriental rugs of Peacock Alley, the Waldorf's grand passageway.

More than five hundred guests showed up for the occasion—a remarkable number considering that Ellen and Harry, between them, invited fewer than twenty-five family members and friends. It was Fletcher's big day. Frank Farrell dropped by to offer a toast. In the reception line were many notables: bigwigs and lesser wags from Tammany Hall; swells from the racing set and highbrow gamblers; a large contingent of "New York's Finest"; most of the regular crowd from Dinty Moore's Restaurant, Fletch's favorite watering hole; some members of the Yankees, including Roy Hartzell, Birdie Cree, and Ray Keating; and even a few players from the Washington Senators, in town for a four-game series with the Yanks.

Along the walls were long tables heaped with food: turkeys, hams, roasts, oysters, smoked salmon, and salads of every description. To quench his guests' thirst, Fletcher provided five barrels of beer, a bottle of V.S.O.P. brandy for every table, and champagne—fifty cases of Möet & Chandon Imperial Crown Brut.

Fletcher escorted Elizabeth, absolutely stunning in a green silk gown she'd made especially for the occasion. The twelve-piece orchestra began by playing the "Artists' Life Waltz." Harry and Ellen took to the dance floor, and a few minutes later Fletch and Elizabeth joined them, moving with a precision and grace that prompted applause. Everyone remarked that the elder Mr. Rice and his mystery woman made a striking couple.

Long after the bride and bridegroom had left for Grand Central to catch their Pullman for Niagara Falls, and several hours after Ellen's parents had retired to their suite for the night, the party was still going strong. At the stroke of each new hour Fletcher commissioned the orchestra to play for another sixty minutes; the crowd dwindled hour by hour, until at last only Fletcher, Elizabeth, and Alex remained.

"Come to bed, Liz," Fletcher finally said. "Let's call it a night while there's still something left in these old bones."

The orchestra limped through a good-night waltz. Fletch gave the conductor a generous tip, and then he and Elizabeth went upstairs. Alex sat by himself sipping champagne in the debris of the evening until the sun began filtering into the hall. When the porters and waiters finally came in to clean up, he pulled his coat over his shoulders, stepped out into the brisk air of the early morning, and strolled down Fifth Avenue to Madison Square.

After a long walk he drifted into a subway and headed back to Brooklyn. That afternoon he could be found behind third base at Ebbets Field beseeching the Superbas to kill the Giants.

It was 1914, the year George Stallings managed the Miracle Braves to their first pennant in sixteen years. Boston was in the cellar as late in the season as July 19, and then the club went on a wild winning binge. The Braves knocked the Giants out of first place on September 8 and then won the pennant by ten and a half games over New York. The Superbas finished fifth, nineteen and a half games in back of Boston.

It was also the year the Federal League claimed major league status. Robert B. Ward, owner of the baking company that made Tip Top Bread, leased and refurbished old Washington Park for a Brooklyn entry in the new circuit. Not surprisingly, the team became known as the Tip Tops. While the Brooklyn Feds weren't much of a club—they also finished fifth that year, eleven and a half games behind pennant-winning Indianapolis—they did draw some fans away from the Superbas. Charlie Ebbets still had a good year at the box office, but he was accustomed to running the only game in town.

In the spring of 1915 the Superbas set up their training camp in Daytona Beach, Florida. Also in Daytona that spring was an attractive young aviatrix named Ruth Law. She had been hired by local merchants to give exhibition flights and take tourists on joy rides in her Wright model B plane. Some years earlier, Gabby Street, a catcher with the Washington Senators, had caught a baseball tossed from the observation window of the Washington Monument, 500 feet above the ground. Robbie, an old catcher himself, mentioned he wanted to take a crack at breaking Street's record; so someone on the Brooklyn club sent Miss Law a message asking if she would mind dropping a baseball on the Superbas' playing field from an altitude of 525 feet.

She was happy to comply, and at the appointed hour her flying machine appeared over the Daytona ball park. The Brooklyn manager stood in the middle of the field waiting to make the catch. Sure enough, out of the plane came a small round object. As it fell toward the ground Robbie put his mitt up and got ready to make the grab.

As Casey Stengel later described it, the missile "caromed off the edge of the mitt and hit him right in the chest. And he spun around and then fell over, like in a Western picture where you see an Indian that's out on the hill, and they shoot him and he goes around in a circle and falls dead."

The worried players rushed to Robbie's side. They found him lying on the ground with a pulpy, gooey substance splattered over his chest and face. Then everyone broke into laughter.

The story of Wilbert Robinson and the grapefruit has, over the years, become legend. As the tale goes, Casey Stengel was the mastermind of the practical joke. Supposedly he gave the grapefruit to Frank Kelly, the club's trainer, and it was Kelly who went up in the plane and actually performed the dirty deed.

Generations of writers and fans have had a lot of laughs embellishing that basic version of the story. Some years ago, however, Ruth Law remembered the event this way: "Time arrived for the demonstration, my plane was rolled out on the beach, and I was ready to fly. But alas, I had forgotten to bring along the ball from the Clarendon Hotel several miles down the beach. What to do? Time was running out; no time to send anyone for the ball. While I was considering the dilemma, a young man working in my outfit brought me a small grapefruit that he intended to have with his lunch and suggested that I drop that." The young woman flyer didn't see all that much difference between a grapefruit and a baseball, so she went up and tossed Robbie the fruit. She didn't know she was also tossing him enough raspberries to last the rest of his life.

In 1915 Benny Kauff came to Brooklyn. The slugging outfielder's .370 batting average the year before was the highest in the Federal League. His team, the pennant-winning Indianapolis Hoosiers, collapsed at the end of the 1914 season. The franchise was moved to Newark, and Benny was transferred to the Brooklyn Tip Tops.

John McGraw tried to lure him to the Giants with the promise of a $5,000 bonus, but Kauff stayed with the Feds, even though he was unhappy about the way he was treated by Robert Ward. Benny's salary at Indianapolis had been $6,000 a year. Ward wanted him to play for $4,000, and agreed to the higher figure only when he discovered Kauff was flirting with McGraw.

Benny once again won the Federal League batting title, this time with a .342 mark. Even Alex Rice went over to Washington Park to see him in action, and although Alex didn't think much of the Feds, he sure would have liked to see Kauff, "the Ty Cobb of the Federal League," playing for the Superbas. Charlie Ebbets and Wilbert Robinson would have liked that too, but it was not to be. When the Federal League folded, Harry Sinclair peddled Kauff's contract to the Giants for $35,000. Benny, who refused to jump the year before largely because he thought of himself as a "Federal League man," didn't get one cent out of the deal.

The National League campaign of 1915 gave Alex quite a bit to yell about. Brooklyn stayed in contention most of the season and was in second place as late as September 15. Philadelphia won the pennant, Boston finished second, and Brooklyn came in third, ten games in back of the Phillies. The Giants, meanwhile, wound up dead last. It was the first time Brooklyn finished ahead of the Giants since 1902. McGraw, anxious to begin building for the future, sold Rube Marquard to the Superbas toward the end of the season.

Those were happy times for Harry and Ellen. Fletcher insisted that they live in the house in Brooklyn, and he even paid to have the top floor converted into a private apartment for them. At work Harry was promoted to a senior bookkeeper, allowing Ellen to leave her teaching job to become a housewife.

Downstairs Elizabeth became less of a fixture. Harry suspected she was spending many of her nights in Fletcher's small suite in the Broadway Central Hotel.

Alex remained a problem child. Every few months he announced he had either found a terrific job or was working on a scheme that was bound to make them all stinking rich. His enthusiasm always died after a few weeks, and then he would keep to himself and remain silent until his next bright idea came along.

By the spring of 1916 the war in Europe, now almost two years old, began inching closer to the United States. Dismayed by the reckless attacks of German U-boats on passenger and freight ships and discouraged by the failure of either side of the conflict to respond to his proposal for a peace conference, President Wilson began implementing a program of military preparedness. If war were to come, the United States wanted to be ready.

The Rice family was divided on the question of whether or not America should enter the conflict. Fletcher believed France and England were the natural allies of the United States, and he was all for getting in there and wiping out the Hun.

Harry, on the other hand, was an ardent isolationist. As far as he was concerned both sides were equally to blame. In any case, the dispute was none of America's business. As Alex saw it, neither side of the argument had much merit. War was an inescapable feature of the human condition. The issues surrounding particular wars were never of much consequence. The only important question a citizen had to ask was whether or not he personally—regardless of motives—was ready to join the ranks.

Harry was shocked by Alex's attitude. "You're growing up to be a cynic," Harry told his brother one night after dinner. "Don't you believe in the principles that went into the founding of our country?"

"I haven't thought about it. Not since grade school," Alex replied. "In any case, let's stop wasting our breath. This discussion is pointless. What's your feeling about the Robins? Robbie says if they can get some hitting they'll be right up there in the fight for the pennant."

Harry was in no mood to discuss baseball. He and Ellen went upstairs, leaving Alex to ponder the possibilities of the new season by himself. In honor of Wilbert Robinson the Brooklyn team was now nicknamed the Robins, though some fans and journalists preferred to call them the Dodgers. Alex was thinking about the great job Robbie had done with the club's pitching. Now, if only the hitting could get back up to snuff. And, come to think of it, the Robins could also do with a little luck.

On paper the 1916 Robins didn't look particularly imposing. In addition to Marquard, Robbie had now brought Chief Meyers over from the Giants. It was a bit hard to see how the Chief, discarded by McGraw, could be of much help to Brooklyn. Alex was still happy to see him on the roster. He knew Meyers was the one catcher who could keep Marquard settled down. But the Chief had batted only .232 in 1915. There wasn't much chance he could aid the attack.

Hitting was definitely Brooklyn's problem. The previous season Casey Stengel had dropped from .316 to .237, Zack Wheat had slumped from .319 to .258, and Jake Daubert, who led the league with a .329 average in 1914, fell off to .301 in 1915. The Robins may have been in first place in May, but it would be a long campaign, and it was difficult to see how they could beat out the two previous pennant winners, Philadelphia and Boston.

Most baseball experts expected Brooklyn to drop out of the race any day, but Robbie's boys hung in there all season. An important ingredient in the club's success was the hitting of the top three batsmen. Stengel was back up to .279, Wheat rebounded to .312, and Daubert's average had risen to .316.

Brooklyn's pitching that year was excellent. Jeff Pfeffer's record for the season was 25–11; Larry Cheney's, 18–12; Marquard's, 13–6; Jack Coombs's, 12–8; and Sherry Smith helped the cause with 12 wins against 10 losses.

As the race moved into September, the Robins still were right up with the Phillies and Braves. On September 9 Brooklyn dislodged Philadelphia from first place. Alex was beside himself with joy. After sixteen years his team finally had a chance. He got a tremendous kick out of ribbing Harry about the continuing misfortunes of the Giants. "Don't count your chickens so soon, little brother," Harry warned. "Brooklyn hasn't won it yet."

Over at the Polo Grounds, the Giants were undergoing profound changes. It was a bitter pill for their fans to swallow, but Christy Mathewson, now thirty-five years old and in his seventeenth campaign, was washed up as a pitcher. In midseason Matty was traded to Cincinnati, where he replaced Buck Herzog as manager.

McGraw hadn't cast his old friend aside; he let him go because Mathewson was eager to try his hand at managing. As far as John was concerned, Matty could have remained with the Giants as a coach forever. The trade brought Herzog back to New York.

Buck never had much love for the Little Napoleon, but each man respected the other's baseball talents, and McGraw was convinced Herzog could help the team in the infield. During that season McGraw sent Larry Doyle to Chicago and Fred Merkle to Brooklyn. New faces on the Giants, in addition to Benny Kauff, included two other refugees from the Federal League—Fred "Spitball" Anderson and Bill Rariden, a catcher; other additions to the team were Slim Sallee, a pitcher who came over from the Cardinals, and Heinie Zimmerman, a third baseman from the Cubs who led the league that year in RBIs.

By the end of the campaign the Giants began to jell. On September 7 they defeated Brooklyn, 4–1, and then went on to set a record of twenty-six consecutive wins before losing the second half of a twin bill to the Braves on September 30. Despite their remarkable stretch drive, the New Yorkers finished the season in fourth place.

When Alex kidded his brother about the Giants' mediocre showing, Harry replied, "Well, last year McGraw finished last. Now he's moved halfway up the ladder to fourth. That can only mean that next year he'll be back up on top."

On October 3 Brooklyn's magic number was three. The second-place Phillies were scheduled to meet the Braves in a doubleheader that afternoon, and the Robins were playing host to the Giants at Ebbets Field. So it was conceivable that Brooklyn could clinch the flag before the day was out. John McGraw was hellbent to thwart Wilbert Robinson's pennant hopes.

When the Robins began shelling Rube Benton, New York's starting pitcher, the Little Napoleon quickly replaced him with Pol Perritt. But it didn't look like the Giants' day. Easy grounders mysteriously rolled through the infield for safe hits. Perritt, who knew better, kept going into a full windup with runners on, giving the Robins golden opportunities to steal bases.

It didn't take a genius to figure out what was going on. McGraw's men were lying down to help old Robbie win the pennant. In the fifth inning, when Perritt continued to ignore McGraw's signals to pitch from the stretch, the Little Napoleon stormed off the bench in a rage, leaving his Giants to lose the game on their own, 9–6. Meanwhile the Phillies lost both of their games, and Brooklyn had its first championship since the days of Ned Hanlon.

Afterward McGraw explained his early departure. "I do not like indifferent playing of this kind after the hard work we have had this season. I refused to be connected with it." The following day, instead of returning to Ebbets Field to lead his team against the Robins, John went to the Polo Grounds to watch the Yankees play the Senators.

When asked about the Giant manager's display of temper, Robbie remarked, "McGraw's assertions are very unsportsmanlike. He knows very well that the Dodgers are superior to the Giants. The Dodgers defeated them in a majority of the games in which they met this season, and when they came over here Monday, they encountered the best team in the league, and it is only natural that the best team should win again."

The winners of the American League flag were the Red Sox, the defending world champions. Alex had only four days to savor the Robins' victory. On October 7 he took a train to Boston for the opening games of the World Series.

To accommodate the large crowds, the contests in Boston were played at Braves Field instead of Fenway Park. In the first game Robbie went with his old hand Rube Marquard, while Bill Carrigan, manager of the Sox, sent Ernie Shore to the box. As game time approached the happy, confident home crowd broke into a chorus of "Tessie"—a song Boston rooters had sung to celebrate victory ever since the Series of 1903.

The game began slowly. The American Leaguers scored first and were leading, 2–1, in the seventh when they opened things up by tapping Marquard for three big runs. They scored once more in the eighth and held a comfortable 6–1 lead going into the ninth. Suddenly Brooklyn came alive. The Robins scored four runs and had the bases loaded when Jake Daubert, hitless for the day and obviously overdue, came to the plate. Jake smashed a deep grounder to short but was out by a step at first. The rally had fizzled and Boston had escaped with a 6–5 win.

Damon Runyon summed up Alex's sentiments perfectly in the *New York American*. He wrote: "The old fault of the Dodgers that was characteristic of them through the National League drive was marked in them today. The men seemed fearful that they were going to lose, instead of confident that they were going to win, which was the attitude of the Red Sox." He was describing a state of mind that would plague Dodger fans and players for years to come.

Game two in Boston was a remarkable pitching duel between two left-handers—Sherry Smith and a very able young hurler named Babe Ruth. Brooklyn scored a run on a homer by Hy Myers in the first, Boston tied the game in the third, and the deadlock remained unbroken all the way to the fourteenth inning, when the Red Sox squeaked out the winning run with a walk, a sacrifice, and a pinch single. Alex was most impressed by Ruth and hoped the Robins wouldn't see any more of him for the remainder of the Series. His wish was granted.

Just before game time for the third contest, played at Ebbets Field, Jake Daubert rubbed his bat for luck over the dome of a bald fan sitting in a field box. The ritual worked—Jake went three for four, and Brooklyn won the ball game, 4–3. The Robins made light work of the submarine pitches of Carl Mays, the Red Sox starting pitcher. Brooklyn got seven hits and three runs off him before he was removed for a pinch hitter in the fifth.

That, however, was the Robins' last gasp. The magic spell was much too short and not all that sweet. Boston wrapped up the Series in the next two days by winning, 6–2 and 4–1.

The fourth game, though, did have one great moment for Brooklyn. Nap Rucker made the final appearance of a remarkable career. He came in in the eighth inning, and, to the cheers of the Flatbush regulars, held the Red Sox scoreless in the losing cause.

Rucker's entire career had been spent pitching his heart out for second-rate Brooklyn teams. In ten seasons he won 135 games and lost 136, and his lifetime ERA was 2.42. He will probably never be admitted to the Hall of Fame, though he surely was one of the great pitchers in the history of the game.

Casey Stengel once said of Rucker: "He was very graceful. Everything he did was in rhythm. He had a beautiful-looking curve, and he also had a beautiful fastball. In batting practice he'd say, 'See if you can get a hit off me,' and I couldn't do it. But it was good practice."

Alex came home from the Series broken-hearted. "Well, Harry," he said to his brother, who was a good deal more charitable than he might have been, "at least Casey had a good Series. He led the team with a .346 average." Stengel was still Alex's special hero.

A few weeks after Brooklyn's inglorious showing in the World Series Alex pulled another disappearing act. For the first few weeks of his absence neither Harry nor Elizabeth expressed much concern, but when a month went by without any word, even Fletcher began to get worried. Thanksgiving came, and as the family sat down to dinner everyone's eyes looked to Alex's vacant chair.

"Don't you think we should report Alex's disappearance to the police?" Ellen asked Fletcher, who was sitting glumly at the head of the table, his gaze off in the distance.

"I suppose we have to," Fletcher answered in a voice that had grown very hoarse in recent months. "Damn it, I know Alex is all right. The minute I tell the cops to start looking for him, he's sure to turn up. And then won't my face be red."

"Good. You'll have a red face, and the rest of us will have peace of mind," Harry said.

"All right. All right. Let's enjoy our dinner," Fletcher replied sticking his fork into Elizabeth's chestnut dressing.

The next morning Fletcher went down to the precinct house and filed a missing person report. Alex did not materialize. Christmas came, and then New Year's, but there was still no sign of Harry's kid brother. Then late in January a letter arrived. It was postmarked Paris:

> 21 rue Raynouard, Paris
> New Year's Day, 1917

Dear Harry

Surprise! I am alive and in Paris. My decision to come here was made on the spur of the moment, so I barely had time to grab a few belongings, let alone go through a dozen farewells. I sailed from New York on the *Rochambeau* the last Saturday in October. Sorry to have been incommunicado for so long, but I've been waiting for six weeks for some good news, which finally arrived a few days ago. I've been accepted in the Aviation Section of the French Foreign Legion. So it won't be long before your brother will be right in the thick of the war.

Yesterday I went to the Legion's very dingy *Bureau de Recrutement* near the Invalides for my medical exam. Quite an experience, because I went through the tests with several volunteers for the Legion's infantry. What an unusual lot of characters they were, including negroes, a few Europeans—Austrians I think, and two swarthy gentlemen who didn't speak French, or English, or any other civilized tongue, from what I could gather. Well, I won't see any more of them. They're headed for the trenches while I'm on my way to the skies.

I leave for flying school in a few days. It will be good to get out of this hostel. The beds are too short and it's much too damp here. Nice old gardens surround the place, though, must be lovely in the spring. Paris has been quite an experience. Until my money ran out I was living life to the fullest—plenty of wine, song, and *women*, if you know what I mean.

Which reminds me, when you break the news to Pop, please ask him to send me some money. Cable it to American Express, Paris, and I'll pick it up when I get my first permission. Believe me, my pay as an aviator will not be enough to live on.

> Love,
> Alex

The members of the family responded to Alex's news in different ways. Fletcher, who still had vivid memories of his own days in combat, put up an especially brave front, claiming that if he were a young man he would have acted precisely as Alex had. Harry thought it was a crime that his brother should be risking his neck in someone else's war. And Elizabeth, who always had a warm spot in her heart for "her little Alex," said a tearful prayer each night for his safe return.

Several months went by before Alex was heard from again. The United States was in the war by the time this letter arrived:

Ecole D'Aviation Militaire
Avord, Cher, France
May 31, 1917

Harry

This has been one hell of a winter (excuse my French). The weather here was cold and raw, and right after my arrival I came down with the grippe, which laid me low for almost a month. Well, today I was *breveted*, which means I am now a full-fledged *pilote*. My training was in the Bleriot—the most difficult machine to fly, which should stand me in good stead when I reach the front. My last test for brevet was two triangle flights between Avord, Chateauroux, and Romarantin. My first trip went off without a hitch, but on the second go-round I had quite a bit of trouble with bad weather and an engine that did not run as well as it might. I was lost for more than an hour on the last leg, but landed safely if a bit rattled. The experience did not dampen my love for flying, which is fascinating sport.

I expect to go to Pau soon, where I'll learn to fly the Nieuport and get some practice in combat tactics.

Love to all,
Alex

P.S. Harry, please get a hold of a *Spalding's Guide* for me, will you? Also, tell Pop the money was gratefully appreciated, but now I need a little more. How are my Robins doing?

Unfortunately, the Robins were not doing well. When Harry received Alex's letter, Brooklyn was in fifth place, already six and a half games behind New York, the league leader. The rejuvenated Giants, sparked by the pitching of three left-handers—Slim Sallee, Rube Benton, and Ferdie Schupp—were on their way to the pennant, while the Robins, suddenly a collection of has-beens, were headed for seventh place. Alex's next letter arrived in Brooklyn in early August:

Hotel de la Bonne Rencontre
Plessis-Belleville
July 12, 1917

Harry

Am now awaiting assignment to my *escadrille*. Pau was a wonderful place, right at the base of the Pyrenees, with beautiful scenery to admire while practicing my acrobatics—*vrilles, renversements,* and *virages.* There was a large American colony in Pau, so I got a chance to meet and talk with some folks from the States. I even found a few baseball fans, though most of the talk is about

the war, and about prospects for victory now that America is in it.
I should be at the front in a few days. I look forward to flying
the Spad, which is quite a machine. Tell Pop and Liz not to worry.

Affectionately,
Alex

The Giants won the 1917 National League pennant by ten games, and
went on to face the Chicago White Sox, managed by Pants Rowland,
in the World Series. The key players on the White Sox squad were Eddie
Collins, the crafty second baseman; Joe Jackson, the slugging left fielder
who had an off year at the plate, batting only .301; and Eddie Cicotte,
the league-leading pitcher with twenty-eight wins, whose weirdly rising
shine ball (which he defined as "a ball which is discolored on one side
and unusually smooth on the other") was considered illegal by most fans
east of Lake Michigan.

For the first time the Series was a contest between the two largest
cities in the land, and interest around the country was unusually high.
And, of course, many fans were off fighting a war. Before the Fall Classic
began, John K. Tener, president of the National League, proclaimed
that "news of the games will be flashed, as fast as the cables can carry it,
to our soldiers in France. Not even the close proximity of the firing line
and the uncertainty which is the very essence of warfare, can deaden the
love for baseball which still animates the spirit of our soldiers three thousand miles away."

One soldier whose spirit would not be instantly animated by news of
the Series was Alex Rice. Flying for France, he was isolated from all
things American, including ball scores. It would be several weeks before
he would learn of the Giants' fate.

Harry, however, was safe at home to witness the outcome of John
McGraw's fifth Series. Because he was married, Harry had escaped the
draft, which suited him fine since he didn't believe in the war anyway.

The Series began in Chicago, where the first two games were disastrous for the Giants. In game one Slim Sallee pitched a great ball game,
holding the White Sox to two runs on seven hits. But Cicotte gave up
only one run, also on seven hits, to lead Chicago to a 2–1 victory. In the
second contest the White Sox romped over New York, 7–2. So McGraw
and his boys returned to Manhattan in the hole. The first game in New
York was postponed a day by rain—weather that perfectly suited Harry's
mood.

In game three Rube Benton pitched brilliantly, scattering five hits over
the nine innings to defeat Cicotte, 2–0. The Polo Grounds broke into joy
at the final out. As one reporter put it, "the captains of industry in the
boxes, the Broadwayites, the visiting buyers from Iowa, and plain ordinary New Yorkers who crowded the lower stand and bleachers all jumped

to their feet, threw up their hats and yelled themselves hoarse at the Giants' triumph."

In the fourth contest Benny Kauff, who had gone 0 for 13 thus far in the Series, broke the ice—and a scoreless tie—with a homer off Red Faber in the fourth. In the eighth Benny homered again with a man on board. Ferdie Schupp pitched masterfully, shutting out Chicago for the second day in a row as New York won, 5–0.

The Series was all tied up, and the betting line swung over to the Giants' favor. As the gamblers saw it, Pants Rowland was overworking Cicotte. The teams headed back to Chicago, and Harry hurried to get his money down on New York.

In game five McGraw committed a managerial blunder that Harry couldn't believe. The Giants had the game in the bag. They were ahead, 5–2, going into the bottom of the seventh when Sallee began to tire. Pol Perritt was all warmed up in the bullpen and ready to go, but the Little Napoleon stubbornly stayed with his starter. Sallee was tagged for three runs in the seventh and two more in the eighth before Perritt was finally brought in. It was too late to save the game. The White Sox scored once again and won, 8–5.

The clubs now returned to New York. The stage was set for one of the most controversial plays in history.

It happened in the fourth inning of the sixth game. Neither team had scored; the contest promised to be an exciting duel between Rube Benton and Red Faber.

Eddie Collins led off the inning for Chicago. He hit a grounder to Heinie Zimmerman at third, whose throw to first was wild, allowing Collins to get on. Joe Jackson sent a fly to right field, where Dave Robertson juggled the ball and then let it drop, putting Jackson on first and allowing Collins to get all the way to third.

Happy Felsch came to bat. With Collins taking a long lead, Happy slapped a fast bounder back to the box. Benton fielded the ball smoothly and turned to find Collins trapped halfway down the line. Instead of throwing to Bill Rariden, his catcher, he ran over toward the runner, who was waving wildly for Jackson and Felsch to get around to third and second while the getting was good.

Rariden started moving up the line to run Collins down. Walter Holke, the Giant first baseman, remained at his position, which meant no one was guarding home. Finally Benton threw to Zimmerman. Collins reversed gears and dashed by Rariden, giving him an open field to the plate. Heinie, with nobody to throw to, raced desperately after Collins, who was by far the faster man. Naturally he won the footrace and scored the first run of the game.

It was a comical sight—Heinie lunging down the line after Collins— but the humor of it was lost on the New York crowd. Fans were still booing and shaking their fists at Heinie as the next batter, Chick Gandil, came to the plate. He quickly singled home the other two runners. That broke the back of the Giants. The White Sox went on to win, 4–2. John McGraw had lost his fourth World Series in a row.

Once again a fluke play had done the Giants in, once again one player had been singled out as the goat. The next morning the *New York Times* reported that "instead of crowning a new baseball king, Manhattan placed a clown's cap on the head of Heinie Zimmerman from the Bronx." According to *Baseball Magazine* "the Merkle bone of 1908, compared to this one, was as ice cream compared to yellow mud."

As Harry read these and other attacks on Heinie he had to laugh. People were always looking for a scapegoat. Zimmerman, with no one to throw to, did the only thing he could do—chase the runner. His teammates—Benton, Rariden, and Holke—committed the unforgivable sin of leaving the plate unguarded.

It was a failure of the team to execute fundamentals, and the only one to blame for that was John McGraw. All winter long Harry wondered whether the Little Napoleon had lost his touch.

The war went on. Alex kept right on going too. In December he sent this letter to the family:

> Escadrille Spad 15
> Christmas Day, 1917

Father, Harry, Ellen, and Liz

Sorry to have been so shamefully long between letters. I'm now *Sergent* Rice, although it's a bit of a mystery to me why I was singled out for promotion. At any event I've been lucky to say the least, having knocked two Boches out of the sky. My machine is extremely dependable (knock on wood for me very hard) and our current duty, patrolling the lines near the Argonne, isn't as hazardous as it might be. My biggest complaint is the winter flying. It is freezing up there this time of the year, and no amount of extra clothing seems to help.

I will remain a French aviator only until the spring. After that I will probably transfer to the U.S. Army, hopefully as a first lieutenant. After that, who knows? Perhaps I'll be home in time to see Brooklyn win the 1918 pennant.

> Much love,
> Alex

P.S. Don't forget to send me *Spalding's Guide* when it comes out in March. By then I'll be starved for baseball news.

Over the winter the Robins made a trade that infuriated Alex when he finally got the word. They sent Casey Stengel to Pittsburgh. Early in the season, on the day he returned to Ebbets Field in a Pirate uniform, Casey pulled a prank that secured his reputation as one of baseball's comedians.

As he strutted to take his first turn at bat the Brooklyn fans, who just a few months before had looked upon him as one of their darlings, booed and heckled him. He stopped and began motioning that there was something in his eye. The umpire called time.

Casey turned to the stands, doffed his cap, and bowed to the crowd. As he made his gesture a sparrow flew off his head and circled the field. The crowd gave a long gasp of astonishment and then broke into laughter and applause.

Casey had been handed the bird by his old pal Leon Cadore, a Brooklyn pitcher who'd caught the sparrow in the bullpen. After the game Robbie remarked that Stengel had "birds in his garret." Harry wrote his brother about the prank, and Alex thought it was hilarious.

As it turned out, Alex did not end up in the Army. He was transferred from the Lafayette Flying Corps to the U.S. Navy in March 1918. Much to his chagrin he received a commission as an ensign, not as a lieutenant j.g. He was assigned to the Naval Air Station at Dunkirk, and he remained in Europe several months after the armistice was signed in November. He didn't miss much of a season. The Cubs won the National League pennant, the Giants finished second, ten and a half games back, and Brooklyn wound up in fifth, twenty-five and a half lengths off the pace.

Toward the end of 1918 Harry Hempstead, on behalf of John Brush's heirs, made it known that the controlling interest in the Giants was for sale. Among those rumored interested in purchasing the club were Harry Sinclair, George M. Cohan, and George W. Loft, the candy manufacturer.

But when, in January of 1919, the news broke that "the most costly franchise in baseball has changed hands," the name of the new owner came as a complete surprise. He was Charles A. Stoneham, a stranger to the game. As part of the deal, John McGraw was given the opportunity to buy a small piece of the club. Another new minority stockholder was Judge Francis X. McQuade, a pal of McGraw's who, in recent years, had hung around the Giants' spring training camp and joined the team on several road trips.

Who was this Stoneham, and how did he come to the Giants? The first reports in the press identified him as a "well-known broker of Wall Street." In reality he was the proprietor of a "bucket shop"—an establishment that accepted orders to buy or sell stock but did not execute the transactions, instead holding onto the money in the hopes of cashing in on the customers' bad hunches.

In other words, Stoneham was a bookmaker; he made his fortune by taking bets on stocks instead of horses. It was a shady business, and it put him in touch with shady characters. One of his partners was Arnold Rothstein, a gambler who had once bribed Judge McQuade in a case involving a shooting in one of his casinos, a place called the Partridge Club. Rothstein acted as the go-between in the sale of the Giants.

Under the new regime Stoneham became the president of the club, McGraw was named vice-president in addition to being field manager, and McQuade was elected treasurer. In a release to the press, the new owners vowed to "conduct the affairs of the club on the same liberal lines that have obtained in the past."

Alex spent the winter in France and finally came home in April 1919. Everyone in the family hoped he would now begin to make something of his life. One thing was certain. He would savor every inning of the new baseball campaign.

Prohibition has been a big saving for a
lot of fellows. Where they used to have
to go to the corner, now they only have
to go downstairs.

Will Rogers

Bing! The loud, sharp crack, as the
swiftly moving ball met the still more
swiftly moving bat, told the spectators
that it was a heavy hit.

From *The Home-Run King*,
a novel by Babe Ruth (1920)

5

"Dammit, Alex, stop ogling every female we pass. A uniform and a
Croix de Guerre don't make you a Fairbanks. Besides, these Brooklyn
girls aren't like the mademoiselles you're used to."

Harry and Alex were edging through the midday bustle of downtown
Brooklyn.

"Ahh, you old married guys are all alike. Jealous as hell." The dinging
bell and the rumbling wheels of a passing trolley drowned out Harry's
retort. Laughing, their arms around each other's shoulders, the two
brothers turned into Gage and Tollner for lunch. They found a table
in a far corner of the long, mirrored, gas-lit hall and ordered a couple
of lagers.

"Your health, hero," Harry said, raising his stein. As they drank Harry
looked into his brother's face. Two years of war had left their mark.
Alex was thinner, gaunter, and his eyes—the startling blue eyes that
glowed improbably below a shock of dark hair—were not the eyes that
Harry remembered. The amusement was still there, the twinkle, but
there was also sadness and a touch of resignation.

Alex, meanwhile, was engaged in similar musings. Harry's lighter
brown hair, a legacy from his mother, was beginning to thin. In his
brother's eyes, a less intense blue than his own, Alex could read only
contentment and acceptance. Both Rice boys had always been slender,
even wiry, but in the five years since his marriage Harry had fleshed out
a bit. But Harry wasn't heavy, Alex decided. Simply content. In his cheap,
ready-made business suit, Harry had the look of a man who had come
as far as he wanted to, as far as he needed.

Both men realized they were staring at each other. Harry laughed.

"You have a lean and hungry look, commodore," he said. "Let's get some food." After they had ordered, Harry looked at Alex and cleared his throat. "Look, Alex, I don't want to sound like a big brother, but . . . well, what I mean is, do you have any plans? Don't you think it's about time you settled down, got a job, made something of yourself?"

Alex smiled. "As a matter of fact, I do have a sort of plan."

Uncomfortable, Harry shifted his weight in the chair. He had intended to be firm with his little brother, to set him straight. But Alex's new confidence and air of authority made the task more difficult than he had expected. "Well, uh, do you mind if I ask what it is?"

"Not at all. I plan to settle down, get a job, and make something of myself."

"Really? Alex that's—aw, you're just ragging me."

"No, I'm serious. I've frozen my ass off at five thousand feet defending the likes of you for almost no pay, and now I'm going to be one of you and get paid for it."

Harry was having a difficult time finding words. He had spent most of the morning in his office going over the various arguments he planned to use to persuade his brother to mend his ways. He had expected a long conversation, making a number of cogent points, skillfully parrying Alex's objections, until in the end Alex would grudgingly admit that Harry had been right all along. The ease with which he had gained his victory unsettled him, perhaps even disappointed him.

But when he said, "I'm glad, Alex, I really am," he meant it. "Do you have any idea where you can find a job?"

"No," Alex said, still smiling, "but I have a hunch you do."

Grinning and red-faced, Harry produced a business card from his vest pocket. Alex read:

JACOBSEN & SONS
SHIP CHANDLERS
10 WHITEHALL STREET
NEW YORK, NEW YORK

"I keep their books," Harry said, "and I found out that they need a clerk. You have an appointment Monday morning at nine o'clock. Ask for Tor Jacobsen. He's one of the sons."

Just then a patron brushed against a passing waiter, knocking two rolls off his tray.

With a quick motion, Alex scooped them both before they touched the floor, placed them on his plate, and winked at the waiter. Harry shook his head in admiration. "You've got Pop's hands," he said. Which reminded him of his second order of business. "Alex," he said, "I'm worried about the old guy. His mind wanders, he gets confused, he forgets things. And he doesn't get around so well anymore."

Alex shrugged slightly. "He's an old man, Harry. It happens to us all. If we're lucky."

"I know he's an old man. That's my point. He's got no business living alone. He hardly ever comes to visit Ellen and Elizabeth and me. He says he's busy, but I think it's just because it's too hard on him to make the trip. He ought to move back to Park Slope where we can take care of him." Alex nodded. "Go talk to him, Alex. He'll listen to you. Get him to come back."

The following day Alex journeyed to the Broadway Central Hotel in Manhattan prepared to wheedle, trick, and if necessary sandbag his father into renewing Brooklyn citizenship. But Alex found himself playing the role that Harry had played the day before—trying to argue with someone who had no argument, to persuade someone who didn't need persuading.

Fletcher chuckled to himself after he let a perplexed but pleased Alex out of his suite. Fletcher had decided weeks before to move back to Park Slope but had thought it best to wait till his sons had properly importuned him. Young people liked to think everything was their idea.

Fletcher's decision to return to Brooklyn had little to do with his advanced years and the state of his health, despite what his sons thought. The simple fact was he could no longer afford to support himself in the style to which he had become accustomed since Frank Farrell had made him a fairly wealthy man.

The money had been so abundant and Farrell so generous that even with his prodigal ways Fletcher had managed, almost by accident, to put aside enough to see himself comfortably through the past five years. But in those five years the cost of necessities, not to mention luxuries, had become exorbitant. That very morning, during their daily telephone conversation, Elizabeth had bewailed the fact that eggs were up to sixty-two cents a dozen, butter to sixty-one cents a pound. When Farrell sold the Yankees prices had been half that.

So it was economic necessity that was sending Fletch back to Brooklyn—that and loneliness. The old duffers who sat around in the over-stuffed chairs in the Broadway Central's lobby were poor company. They complained too much. No moxie. Fletch preferred young people, even though they were hard to keep up with.

The sale of the Yankees to Ruppert and Huston had been the signal for Fletcher's retirement. For several years before the transaction, Fletcher's age and the changing times had made his services less valuable and less necessary to Farrell. The Poolroom King had kept Fletcher on the payroll mostly for the sake of friendship.

But Fletcher didn't mind being retired. He had money and a lifetime pass to Yankee Stadium. The first season of the new ownership, 1915, he attended every home game, with the exception of several in the fall when the chill in the air hurt his bones and the team was already well out of the race. He naturally felt sad that he was no longer connected with the team. But he also was eager to see what miracles might be wrought by the two millionaire owners.

Colonel Jacob Ruppert, the new team president, was an aristocrat on paper and in fact. Every article of clothing the colonel wore, from his shoes to his underwear to his hat, was custom made.

Assisted by his valet, Ruppert often turned out in as many as three or four tasteful, immaculate outfits a day. He belonged to the 7th Regiment, the "Silk Stocking" regiment, and gained his military title when he was appointed an aide to Governor Hill of New York.

Soon after leaving high school, Ruppert had gone to work in his father's brewery. His first job was washing beer kegs, working twelve hours a day for a weekly salary of $10. At age twenty-three he became general manager of the brewery, at twenty-nine the president.

He belonged to a long list of the finest clubs, the Jockey and New York Yacht included, and had found time to build a reputation as a sportsman, even though he ran several businesses besides the brewery and had served four terms in Congress.

Colonel Jake owned a stable of thoroughbred race horses; bred trotters, St. Bernards, and Boston Terriers; and collected Chinese porcelains, jade, and canvases of the Barbizon school.

Ruppert had played baseball as a boy and loved the game, but there were those who doubted the depth of his understanding of the sport. Once, during spring training, he expressed concern that his players weren't hitting the ball. The manager told him to relax, that the pitchers were simply ahead of the batters. Several days later, when a friend commented on the lack of thunder, Ruppert happily assured him, "Don't worry. It's just that the pitchers are ahead of the hitters. Next month it will be the other way around."

So Ruppert was a man of wealth, breeding, and high social standing. But Fletcher didn't care a damn about all that. The colonel had another quality that appealed to Fletcher. Ruppert liked to win.

Captain Tillingham L'Hommedieu Huston was a perfect counterpoint to his partner. Where Ruppert was natty, Huston was baggy. He often wore the same suit for a week at a time, and his dusty, ever-present derby soon earned him the nickname "The Man in the Iron Hat."

Where Ruppert was cool and reserved, Huston was brash and outgoing. A civil engineer in Ohio at the outbreak of the Spanish-American War, Huston organized a company of engineers and led them to Cuba. After the war, he stayed on in Cuba and organized his own engineering firm, accumulating a fortune dredging harbors and building sea walls, roads, railroads, public buildings, and private residences.

When John McGraw brought his Giants to Cuba for spring training, the two men were introduced. Their mutual enthusiasm for baseball and bottled spirits sparked an immediate and strong friendship. When Ruppert and Huston plunged nearly a quarter million dollars each to buy the homeless, managerless, starless Yankees, it was McGraw who provided advice, even going so far as to secure the services of his friend Harry Sparrow as business manager.

Not that the captain and the colonel weren't businessmen themselves. Cap Huston was a self-made millionaire, and Ruppert had increased the family fortune severalfold—even though he had once poured $75,000 into a "salted" gold mine in Kansas. But had these two hard-headed businessmen known what they were getting into, chances are that Ban Johnson would have been obliged to look elsewhere for new blood. At the celebration marking the one-year anniversary of their ownership of the Yankees, Huston and Ruppert looked into each other's eyes and simultaneously shouted, "Sucker!"

But just a few weeks later the captain and the colonel proved they were in the game to stay. They purchased Home Run Baker from Connie Mack for $37,500. Baker had spent the 1915 season living on his farm in Maryland and playing ball with a semipro team in Upland, Pennsylvania.

Some reports had it that Baker, wanting a reward for not jumping to the Federal League, had held out for a higher salary in 1915, prompting Mack to tighten up on his checkbook and let the slugger cool his heels for the entire season. Another story was that Mack, in the process of peddling the members of his $100,000 Infield to recoup losses suffered during the Federal league war, had sold Baker to the Yankees, but Baker had refused to report.

Another version, the least likely, was that Baker was tired of the exigencies of traveling with a ball club and wanted to spend more time on his farm. In any event, as of mid-Febrary 1916, Home Run Baker was a member of the New York Americans.

Yankee fans had two reasons to celebrate. For the first time since Hal Chase had enchanted Hilltop crowds, the Yankees had a gate attraction, a star of the first magnitude. More important, a precedent had been set. It had been known from the beginning that the new owners had a great deal of money. It was now apparent they were willing to spread it around to build a winner.

But, even though Baker belted ten homers in only 100 games, and Bob Shawkey, obtained earlier from the A's, posted a 24–14 record, the best Wild Bill's boys could do in 1916 was a fourth-place finish.

The day after the United States declared war in April 1917, Cap Huston enlisted. It wasn't long before Cap had obtained the services of several army sergeants to put the Yankee players through close-order and manual of arms drills—using baseball bats for rifles—before each game. By the time Huston sailed for France on August 1, Yankee pennant hopes had gone west. After a sixth-place finish, twenty-eight and a half games out, Wild Bill Donovan found himself headed in the same direction, toward his California home. "You're a good man, Donovans," Ruppert told him, "but somebody's got to go."

From across the water Huston let it be known that his choice to be the new Yankee pilot was his old friend and drinking buddy, Wilbert Robinson. But Ban Johnson had another idea; he was still anxious to see a winner in New York and had an ulterior motive besides. Branch Rickey had recently been lured from the American to the National League, and Johnson wanted to retaliate.

"Get Miller Huggins," he told Ruppert. "You'll get a good man and we'll be taking a good man away from the enemy."

So Ruppert got Miller Huggins. Little Hug, 5 foot, 6 inches and 140 pounds, had been a star second baseman and leadoff batter for the Cincinnati Reds and the St. Louis Cardinals. He had managed the Cards since 1913, and, though the team's record was short of spectacular, Huggins had worked wonders considering the material he had available. He was a frail, introspective man who had few friends, but his courage, determination, and resourcefulness were widely respected. Early in his playing days Huggins had discovered that his small stature made it almost impossible to reach curve balls thrown by righties. He spent the winter swinging at a ball suspended from his basement ceiling by twine and reported the following spring as a left-handed hitter.

When Huston learned that his recommendation had been ignored and Ban Johnson's—a man for whom Cap had little affection—followed, he roared like a wounded bear. The wound was never to heal.

Taking Huston's lead, sportswriters and fans reviled the little man— he had stabbed Wild Bill in the back and stolen his job. He was drab and colorless and no match for the mighty McGraw; he was a second-rate manager from a second-rate team. Not that anyone in his right mind would claim that the Yankees were a first-rate team.

Unruffled, Huggins engineered one of the wholesale trades for which he became noted, sending five players—pitchers Urban Shocker and Nick Cullop, infielders Fritz Maisel and Joe Gedeon, and catcher Les Nunamaker—to the Browns for second baseman Derrill Pratt. To make the trade appear more even, the Browns tossed in Eddie Plank, but no one was surprised when the veteran hurler failed to report. Huggins later commented that he knew he couldn't help the team by adding players, so "I did it by breaking up the doggonedest second-base combination I ever saw—and it took the Browns five years to recover!" He later admitted, however, that he had made a mistake in giving up Shocker.

Luckily for Huggins, his new team's fourth-place finish was all but ignored in a season that found the ranks of major league baseball decimated by the call to arms. After an abbreviated season, ending on Labor Day, the Red Sox, behind the pitching of Babe Ruth—who ran his Series scoreless innings streak to twenty-nine and two-thirds, a major league record that was to stand for forty-three years—and Carl Mays, defeated the Cubs four games to two in a World Series that took place only at the indulgence of Secretary of War Newton Baker.

Fletcher enjoyed the 1918 season. There were days when he could urge his creaking body no farther than his favorite chair in the hotel lobby, but for the most part he managed to reach the Polo Grounds by game time or the second inning at the latest, depending on how much "Kentucky sleeping medicine" he had imbibed the night before. These days he enjoyed baking his aching joints in the summer sun as much as watching the game, and he often woke with a start to find that the score had changed drastically.

He especially enjoyed watching McGraw's old nemesis, Home Run Baker, who hit six of the team's twenty home runs that year and batted .306. Baker used a fifty-two-ounce, virtually untapered chunk of wood that resembled a wagon tongue. Once, in Philadelphia, Hank Gowdy had borrowed one of Baker's bats, gone hitless for a week, and then handed it back, saying, "Here, take your damn tree back. I've hit all the wind out of Shibe Park with it."

And Fletch enjoyed observing Miller Huggins. He felt an immediate warmth for the wan little man who, in a uniform that seemed two sizes too large, his jaw puffed out with loose-leaf chewing tobacco, had to crane his neck to bawl out his players, all of whom towered over him. And in mid-January, when Cap Huston—who was now a colonel but still preferred to be called Cap—returned from Europe and indicated in unmistakable terms that he would never accept the presence of the new manager, Fletch became an even more avid Hug supporter. He figured the little guy needed all the help he could get. He was right.

Nothing could have pleased Fletcher more than Alex's safe return from the war. He couldn't help feeling that his son had been a bit foolhardy—but, what the hell, hadn't he himself gone off to war when he was young and had the chance? "Chip off the old block," he had told his cronies. "Got a lot of sand." But his sleep had been troubled. Now, however, as the spring of 1919 approached, Fletcher was at peace. He was once more ensconced in the house on Ninth Street in Park Slope, both his sons were gainfully employed, and Harry had promised to make him a grandfather soon, God and nature willing.

As the baseball season approached, the teams were once more at full strength, having reclaimed their stars from the armed services. Interest in the game was at its highest point in nearly a decade. The American people had put the grim realities of war, and the sacrifices it demanded, behind them. They were ready to have some fun.

Fletcher was determined to attend every Yankee home game. "Got to get enough baseball to last me a while," he told Elizabeth. On week-ends, Harry and Alex would join Fletcher for at least one game. Fletcher's baseball appetite was so insatiable that he often accompanied the boys even when the Giants were in town.

On a Saturday in July the three were shuffling through the crowd on Eighth Avenue on their way into the Polo Grounds to watch the McGrawmen. "How about that kid Ruth?" Harry remarked as they neared the gate. "Hit two home runs in the same game the other day in Philly."

"Yeah," Alex said, "he can really pop the old horsehide. Ed Barrow sure was smart to let him play outfield this year. What's the record, anyway?"

"American League record, Socks Seybold, sixteen, 1902. Major League record, Gavvy Cravath, twenty-four, 1915," Harry intoned.

Alex grinned and winked at Fletcher, who seemed not to be paying attention. "What was Seybold's mother's maiden name?"

Harry looked narrowly at Alex. "Smith," he said evenly, "Mary Smith."

"You made that up."

"Care to place a wager?"

"No, but you made it up, anyway." Fletcher muttered something. "What's that, Pop?" Alex asked.

"I said *no finesse!* Babe Ruth isn't a ballplayer, he's a carnival act!"

As Alex and Harry laughed, Fletcher forged ahead. Presenting their tickets to the wizened gatekeeper, the three men passed through the turnstile. Suddenly Fletcher stopped and let his cane fall. Alex retrieved it and jumped to his father's side. "Pop! What's the matter?" he asked anxiously.

Without uttering a sound, Fletch turned and walked back to the turnstile, stopping directly in front of the gatekeeper. The old man eyed Fletcher warily. Fletcher finally spoke.

"You're Jim Mutrie," he said.

"Yes, that's right," the old man said slowly, still unsure what to make of the situation.

"Jim!" Fletcher cried, "what the hell are you doing here?"

"Why, I'm taking tickets. That's what I'm paid to do."

"Don't you remember me? I'm Fletcher Rice. We met at the Old Home Plate back in '82. I was just down from Saratoga."

Mutrie frowned, then brightened. "Of course. Now I remember," he said, extending his hand. "And how are things going for you, Mr. Rice? Still interested in the turf?"

Fletcher shook his head. "No, Jim, baseball. Mainly just watch baseball games these days. But what are you doing here? Is this some kind of joke?" But Fletcher knew it wasn't a joke. He could tell from Mutrie's frayed clothing, his demeanor.

"Well, Mr. Rice," Mutrie said, looking down at the scuffed tip of one of his shoes, "times change, you know. I've got a little newsstand out on Staten Island, but with the cost of things, well, I fill in here from time to time. Say, it might interest you to know that the man I fill in for is John Day. Guess you could say we're still partners, sort of."

"John Day!" Fletcher gasped.

"Like I said, Mr. Rice, times change. Back in—'82, you say?—those were the good times."

"They were at that, Jim. They certainly were." There was an uncomfortable pause. "Well, look, Jim, I'm out in Park Slope. Easy to find. If there's anything I can . . . look me up, will you?"

Mutrie squared his shoulders and looked directly into Fletcher's eyes. "Don't you worry about me. I'll get by all right. Nice to see you again."

Fletcher nodded slowly and walked back to his sons. Alex was still holding his father's cane. Falling into step beside Fletcher, each son took an elbow to help support him.

"Who was that?" Alex asked.

"That man," Fletcher said, shaking his head as though to clear it, "along with John Day, once owned the ball club you've come here to watch today. And the New York Mets, to boot! And now he's . . . now they're both . . ." Fletcher shrugged helplessly.

"I don't think he remembered you, Pop," Harry said.

"And why the hell should he?" Fletcher snapped. The two brothers exchanged glances and remained silent for the rest of the afternoon. Throughout the game, Fletcher stared morosely into space. Harry had to nudge him when the game was over.

"Come on, Pop. It's time to go." Fletcher rose and followed his sons from the park. When the subway train reached Forty-second Street, he stood up.

"I'll see you boys at home. Got some business to attend to."

"We'll go with you," Harry said, rising.

"No, no." Fletcher motioned for him to sit. "Something to take care of. Private anyway. I'll see you at home. May miss dinner." The doors closed behind him. Harry and Alex watched apprehensively as their father propelled his thin, bent frame through the crowd on the platform. The train pulled out of the station.

When Fletcher reached the street, he walked over to Broadway and turned into the first saloon. Hanging his cane on the edge of the bar, he tugged his hat firmly onto his head and ordered a double bourbon.

"Handsome Jeems," Fletcher muttered as the barkeep set the glass before him.

"Beg pardon, sir?"

Fletcher looked at the bartender. "Young man," he said, "are you aware that Jim Mutrie and John Day are gatekeepers at the Polo Grounds?"

"No, sir, I wasn't."

"Well they are."

The bartender moved to the far end of the bar, where two men in work clothes were drinking. He shrugged and held out his hands, palms up. The men grinned and shook their heads.

Fletcher took no notice. He was seeing a picture of Jim Mutrie, a straight, erect Jim Mutrie, spiffy in a new suit of clothes, the moustache dark and bristling. But another picture kept crowding into his mind—the shabby, sagging gatekeeper, eyes downcast, the moustache white and drooping. Fletcher looked down at the hand that held his glass. He looked at the swollen knuckles, the blue latticework of veins that threaded through the white spots on the leathery skin. He ordered another double. Staring into the whisky he thought about his life—and the women in his life. By the time he ordered his third, an idea was forming.

Fletcher awoke the next morning in his own bed, sandpaper in his mouth and a gong in his head. He lay quietly, trying to focus on the ceiling. He had a vague memory of the bartender helping him into a cab. After that, nothing. Then he remembered his idea. He rose, donned his robe, and walked down the hall to Elizabeth's room.

The door was open. When he entered, he found Elizabeth tearfully writing a note. Her closets were empty, and her ragged old suitcase was by the door.

"What's going on?" he asked.

Elizabeth turned toward him, anger and hurt showing on her face. "I'm going to Cincinnati to live with my sister," she said. "I can't spend my life worrying about an old fool like you."

"No you're not," Fletcher said. "You're not going anywhere. Sit down here on the bed. I want to tell you about a thought I had last night."

A week later Elizabeth and Fletcher were married.

And some time later, much to Fletcher's satisfaction, Charles Stoneham, owner of the Giants, provided Mutrie with a pension, and the National League, at the behest of Charlie Ebbets, did likewise for John Day.

For nearly two weeks Fletcher led the euphoric life of a newlywed. Then, in late July 1919, the Yankees made a move that brought excitement to the Rice household and caused a furor throughout the baseball world. They signed ace pitcher Carl Mays, who had jumped the Red Sox team back on July 12. Mays had been having a terrible year, winning five while losing eleven.

Game after game Mays had watched the mighty bats of the defending world champs whiffing at air, piling up goose eggs, while his adversaries were piling up unearned runs. In his final game with the Red Sox, Mays was losing, 5–0, to Chicago—four of the runs unearned. Although it was only the second inning when he was relieved, Mays had already built a head of steam strong enough to carry him straight from the mound in

Chicago to his apartment in Boston. Once there, he quickly packed a bag, hopped in his Marmon roadster, and drove to Pennsylvania to do some hunting and fishing.

Ruppert and Huston, a step ahead of a number of other clubs, located Mays by telephone, obtained a verbal commitment from him, and then anted up $40,000 and two players, Alan Russell and Bob McGraw.

When news of the transaction reached Ban Johnson, the old tyrant flew into a rage. He suspended Mays and nullified the trade. Some observers hinted darkly that Johnson had more than a passing interest in the Cleveland club, which had also been negotiating with Red Sox owner Frazee. Some simply said that years of boozing had deadened the Czar's sensibilities, while others felt that Johnson was in the right, even if he was acting in a typically autocratic manner.

Whatever the reason, the two colonels were not about to acquiesce quietly to Johnson's edict. They took their case to court, much to the shock of the old school, and obtained an injunction against Johnson's action from Judge Robert F. Wagner, father of a future mayor of New York City. On August 7 Carl Mays pitched and won his first game as a Yankee. He went on to pitch eleven consecutive complete games and finish the season with nine wins and three losses for New York.

The Yankees were glad to have Mays aboard—all except one. On his first day with the team, Mays made the rounds of the locker room, shaking hands and exchanging pleasantries with his new teammates. As he approached Truck Hannah, the Yankees' massive catcher, Hannah spun and smacked Mays across the chest, driving him to the opposite wall. Hannah vaulted a table and charged, but when he reached Mays he was grinning and extending a welcoming hand. "We're even," he said.

"What was that all about?" someone asked Mays.

Mays explained that he was always fastidious about his personal appearance on the field. "But every time I'd go up to bat when I was pitching against the Yankees, Hannah would squat down there underneath the bat with that big quid of his and he'd splatter tobacco juice all over my shoes. So every time he'd come up to bat I'd deck him."

In mid-August, Fletcher was seated in his box at the Polo Grounds, alternately watching Mays pitch and explaining to the man next to him how Mays had ruined his arm in the minors, seen Iron Man Joe McGinnity pitch, and decided he would learn to pitch underhand—though, of course, the Iron Man was a sidearmer, you know, whereas this boy throws the ball straight under. Fletcher broke off when Alex entered the box and sat next to him.

"What are you doing here, son? Take the day off?"

"No, Pop. I turned in my arm garters and eyeshade."

"You quit?"

"I just sort of left. I was sitting there at my desk, the sun streaming through the window, reading the *Sporting News*. This fella came by, looked at my paper, looked out the window, and said, 'Nice day for a ball game, ain't it?' I said, 'Damn right it is.' And here I am."

"I suppose you know what you're doing, Alex. But jobs are hard to find these days."

"I've already got one. Last night I was up at Jack's—you know, the saloon on Sixth Avenue and Forty-third? Jack Dunston, the owner, and his barkeep were having a row, and the barkeep told him he could have his job, could do it himself, there wasn't any future in it anyhow.

"I offered to step behind the bar and take over, which I did. On my way up here I stopped by and asked for the job. I start tonight. Twenty a week plus extras. That's three more than I was making at Jacobsen's, and I don't have to worry about some ship out in Hoboken not getting its twelve crates of laundry soap."

Fletcher chuckled and turned his attention back to the game. It was the bottom of the ninth, and Carl Mays was batting with two strikes. There were two out and a runner on second. Umpire Evans called strike three. Mays whirled and stared at Evans in disbelief. Then he lofted his bat down the right-field foul line; it spiraled lazily through the air and fell just short of the foul pole. Evans thumbed Mays out of the game, even though it was over.

"That boy," Fletcher confided to Alex, "has a temper."

On September 24, 1919, the Red Sox were in town, playing the second game of a two-game series with the Yanks. Four days earlier, on Babe Ruth Day in Fenway Park, where Cap Huston had been the honored guest of his old friend Harry Frazee, the Bambino had stroked one over the left center field fence to tie the major league home run record.

That record, it turned out, did not belong to Gavvy Cravath with his twenty-four blasts, as Harry had believed, but to a little-known player named Ed Williamson. With four-bag fever mounting, one of baseball's amateur historians had ferreted out the fact that Williamson had socked twenty-seven homers in 1884—most of them over a 215-foot right-field fence, to be sure, but twenty-seven nonetheless.

Fletcher and a large crowd watched as Bob Shawkey offered Ruth an off-speed curve that hung slightly. The Babe waited out the pitch and then swung smoothly, almost effortlessly. The ball rose toward right field, rose high into the afternoon sun, and, some claimed, was still rising when it cleared the double-deck stand. Shoeless Joe Jackson had once parked one on the roof of that grandstand, but the Babe's clout had cleared it completely, bounding crazily through the rocks, weeds, and discarded tin cans in the field beyond. It was the longest hit in the history of the Polo Grounds.

After the game, Fletcher stopped by Jack's for a beer and a visit with Alex. Fletcher felt comfortable in Jack's. The place never closed, and it was in many ways a direct descendant of the Old Home Plate. The clientele was made up for the most part of writers, politicians, and sporting figures who ran the gamut from bookmakers to headliners.

Not long after Fletcher had settled in at the bar, there was a sudden commotion near the front door. Babe Ruth, in the flesh, along with several of his teammates, had just entered. A crowd of men immediately surrounded the Babe, pumping his arm, pounding his back. Ruth, in a rumpled soft cap and old sweater, finally disengaged himself from the crowd and moved to the bar. Every man in the place—except Fletcher—clamored for the honor of buying the Babe a beer.

"Like to oblige all you fellas," he said, as Alex placed a foaming stein before him, "but I gotta catch a train."

"Here's to the Sultan of Swat," a man at the end of the bar shouted, holding aloft his glass, "the greatest ballplayer of all time!"

"Applesauce!" Fletcher sniffed, as Ruth downed the beer with two mighty gulps. "Where's the finesse? Any baboon can swing from his heels all the time. Couldn't hold a candle to Wee Willie Keeler. Willie could slap 'em around. He could hit 'em where they ain't!"

Ruth, his face clouded, stepped around the one man that separated him from Fletcher. He wiped his mouth with the sleeve of his sweater and glared sternly down at the old man. Then his big, round face broke into a grin. "Well, pop," he said, "one place they ain't is in the right-field bleachers!" He let go a laugh and made for the door. Most of the men in the bar followed him onto the street, where they waved and shouted farewells.

That September the Yankees, for the first time in memory, found themselves in a pennant race. When it was all over, the Chicago White Sox had nosed out the Cleveland Indians by three and a half games and the Yankees by seven and a half. But the Yankees' 80–59 record for a .576 winning percentage was a source of encouragement for New York fans.

In the National League, the Cincinnati Reds had edged the Giants to walk off with the flag. The baseball world was mildly surprised when the underdog Reds won the best-of-nine Series, five games to three.

While Yankee fans were still savoring their winning season and anticipating even better things to come, Ban Johnson hurled down another thunderbolt from his Olympus in Chicago. From August on, the two colonels had obtained an injunction in every city where Carl Mays pitched. Johnsonian fiat now nullified Mays's nine wins, dropping the Yankees from third to fourth place and out of their World Series money.

Ruppert and Huston paid their players out of their own pockets and then filed a half-million-dollar damage suit against the league. Then they joined forces with Harry Frazee and Charlie Comiskey, whom Johnson had long since alienated, to drive Johnson out of the game.

At the league meeting, which took place in Chicago in February 1920, the Yankees' position was upheld, the club moved back to third place, and the World Series share was handed over. In addition, a two-man panel comprising Clark Griffith and Ruppert was set up to review Johnson's major fines and suspensions. It was a serious defeat for the father of the American League, a defeat from which he would never recover.

But the Yankees themselves had already dropped the biggest bombshell of all when they announced on January 5, 1920, the purchase of Babe Ruth from the Red Sox for $125,000. Ruth had not only hit twenty-nine homers—four of them grand slams—but had also led the league in runs scored and runs batted in while batting .322. He had been the heart of the Red Sox club, and Boston fans were shocked, outraged, and sorrowful.

The Babe himself was less than enthusiastic about the idea of moving to New York, away from his cigar factory and friends. But when Frazee, in an effort to cover his tracks, gave out to the press that Ruth's drinking and wild behavior had all but ruined the Sox, Babe's feelings began to change. He announced that he was glad he'd been sold and would play for the Yankees if only to show up Frazee.

"Frazee is not good enough to own any ball club," Ruth said. He went on to tell that on Babe Ruth Day the previous season, not only had he been obliged to pay for Mrs. Ruth's ticket, but after the game Frazee had given him a cheap cigar and a thank-you. "That's a fair example of his liberality," the Babe snorted.

The fact was, Frazee had little with which to be liberal. He was more interested in show business than in baseball, and his ventures on the boards were faring poorly. Several years later he would make a fortune on *No, No, Nanette!*, but at that time he was financially strapped. As part of the purchase agreement, Ruppert had loaned Frazee $300,000, receiving a mortgage on Fenway Park in return. In the years to come, cynics would say—not without cause—that Frazee paid off his loan by sending his best players to the Yankees.

The arrival of 1920 found Fletcher in a nagging depression. His body, now almost seventy-five years old, had become a network of swollen joints and frozen muscles. He was still able to get around, to stop in one of his old haunts now and then for a drink, but it required a certain amount of effort, effort that took something away from the pleasures of sitting down to a cold beer. He longed for his old friends, but most of them were gone. He still enjoyed tipping a glass or two, but it would have been a lot nicer if he could count on being joined by someone who went back to the old days. As much as he loved Elizabeth, she wasn't much of a gabber, and she certainly wasn't interested in listening to him reminisce about how it was before she knew him.

It wasn't that old Fletch wanted the present to go away, but he just couldn't get comfortable living in it. More than once Harry tried to educate his father about the social and technological advances that would soon "revolutionize the world." But Fletcher had no time to concern himself with the future. He was interested in simple daily pleasures. Now, with the coming of Prohibition, it looked as though a good part of what the old boy thrived on would vanish overnight. So it wasn't exactly surprising that Fletcher was depressed.

New York, along with the other states and localities that were not already dry, was scheduled to climb aboard the water wagon at midnight on Friday, January 16, 1920. The talk around the city was that there would be one hell of a wake for John Barleycorn. Many saloonkeepers announced plans to stay open all through Thursday night and keep the booze flowing right up to the final minute on Friday. Fletcher, who had no intention of missing the celebration, pleaded with Elizabeth to join him on the final toot of his life.

"Look, Liz," he said on Thursday afternoon, "you've been telling me to slow down on the sauce ever since the first day you walked into this house. Well, this is my last night of booze. Come with me tonight, and I promise you an evening you'll never forget."

"That's exactly what I'm worried about," Elizabeth replied. "If you think I'm going into New York to be with all those hooligans drinking themselves silly, you're sadly mistaken."

"The place I have in mind is holding a very elegant affair. I thought we'd go to Reisenweber's, where they're having a funeral ball for John Barleycorn. It's five dollars to get in, so I don't think you'll see any riffraff."

"Fletcher, I really am surprised at you. Seventy-four years old and trying to behave like a lad of twenty. Look at you! You need a cane to get around, and you're talking about going to a ball. I wish you'd stay home and let Prohibition start a few days early."

"I can't say anything, then, to make you change your mind?"

"I wouldn't go with you for love nor money," Elizabeth exclaimed. "If you want to make a fool of yourself, go right ahead. But don't expect me to feel sorry for you when you come home with your head pounding like an anvil."

As much as she hated to see him go off on such a fool's errand, she knew there was no way to stop him. If there was one thing you could say about Fletcher, it was that he was set in his ways. He left the house sometime in the middle of the afternoon. As Elizabeth stood by the window watching her man slowly make his way toward the subway, she had second thoughts about not joining him.

Fletcher's first stop was Mouquin's, the venerable restaurant on Fulton Street in Manhattan where he had taken many a beer and hot meal when he worked for Charlie Byrne. He was joined at the bar by Emil, the headwaiter who had worked for the Mouquin family for more than twenty-eight years.

"Well, Emil, these are crazy times, wouldn't you say?" Fletch said with a sigh as he made ready to take his first swig of the evening.

"They certainly are, Mr. Rice."

"What's going to happen to this old place?" Fletcher asked.

"Tomorrow's our last night. Mr. Mouquin is closing the doors. He says he's going to open somewhere else, but I'll believe it when I see it."

"Things just aren't going to be the same, are they, Emil?" Fletcher asked, ordering another beer with a wave of his hand. "Say, do you know the definition of a Prohibitionist?" Without waiting for an answer, he gave the punch line. "A man with water on the brain and rye in the cellar!"

Emil tried to muster a smile, but it fell upon Fletcher to supply his own laughter. Before long the headwaiter returned to his duties. Fletcher emptied his glass and headed uptown to Jack's.

As his taxi sped up Broadway, Fletch suddenly decided to take a quick tour of the Tenderloin. After that, he dropped in at Maxim's, then Reisenweber's, where the walls and ceilings were draped in black crepe.

The funeral for John Barleycorn was held in a room called Paradise. It was at Reisenweber's that Fletcher decided to switch from beer to whisky. He visited more than half a dozen places that night, and it was well past ten by the time he arrived at Jack's.

Behind the bar, which was lined three deep with merrymakers, Alex was working feverishly. He took a moment to greet his old man and offer him a drink.

"Pop, I can't talk to you now," he said, turning to fill a waiter's order. "Look, come back after midnight when things begin to quiet down. I don't know when I'm going to get off, but as soon as I do I'll take you home."

No one had time for Fletcher. There he was, trying to get into the swing of New York's final drinking spree, and the evening was passing him by.

He was nothing but an old man taking up space at the bar; to most of the drinkers around him he was invisible. Fletcher waved goodby to his son, left the restaurant, and hailed a cab. He rode down to the Broadway Central, checked in for the night, and had the bellhop bring a bottle up to his room.

"Tonight wasn't very exciting," he said to himself as he broke the seal, "but tomorrow should be quite another matter." He had visions of Broadway crowded with old friends, all lifting their glasses to memories of seasons past.

On Saturday morning Harry got a telephone call from Stanley Bell, the assistant manager of the Broadway Central. It was Mr. Bell who had attended to Fletcher's needs when he was a resident of the hotel.

"Mr. Rice," the caller began, "your father checked in two nights ago, bolted his door, and hasn't come out since. We're just a little concerned, his being an old man and all, and we'd like your permission to break into his room."

"Of course, Stan, go ahead. I'll be there as soon as possible."

Harry went downstairs to talk to Elizabeth, beside herself with worry. Fletcher had promised to come home Friday night at the very latest. She had regretted not going with him from the moment he departed, and now she was blaming herself for whatever might have happened to him. Harry wanted her to stay home while he went to investigate, but Elizabeth insisted on accompanying him. They set off for Manhattan prepared for the worst.

They arrived at the hotel to find Stanley Bell waiting for them in the lobby. Bell's expression told them all they needed to know. Elizabeth broke into tears even before he spoke the dreaded words. The two men escorted her into the manager's office. Harry went up to Fletcher's room. A doctor was just leaving as Harry entered. Fletcher was lying on the bed fully clothed. His face bore an expression of indifference, as if to say, "Well, what did you expect?"

Without knowing why, Harry went through his father's pockets and emptied their contents onto the nightstand. He produced a set of keys, several coins, a wad of dollar bills, a silver pill box, and a curious little wooden object. On closer inspection Harry discovered it was a souvenir from Reisenweber's funeral ball—a miniature wooden coffin that bore the inscription:

JOHN BARLEYCORN, ESQ.
Born ?   Died Jan. 16, 1920
R.I.P.

Alex was not around to learn of his father's fate. After Jack's bar closed for good, he and some of his fellow bartenders from around Broadway carted several cases of booze out to a hotel in Brighton Beach, where they proceeded to get soused, stewed, and pickled for almost a week.

By the time he returned home the following Friday, Fletcher had already been laid to rest in Greenwood Cemetery. The news shocked Alex even more than he would have guessed. Unlike Harry, who took it philosophically, Alex grieved throughout the winter and into spring. Not even the opening of the baseball season could shake him out of his depression.

⊖

By the middle of the summer, Alex's spirits were brightened by the surprising performance of the Brooklyn team.

After finishing a lowly sixth in 1919, the Robins had suddenly come alive and were battling with Cincinnati for first place. Uncle Robbie had managed to put together the best pitching staff in the majors. To begin with, he had two of the most accomplished spitballers in the game, Burleigh Grimes and Clarence Mitchell.

The spitter had been outlawed earlier that year, but there had been special dispensation for the seventeen pitchers in the majors who already threw it. No one in baseball wanted to cut short the careers of the several great hurlers who relied on loading the ball, especially since the arguments against the pitch did not always center on whether or not it was immoral to doctor a baseball with a foreign substance.

Many critics of the wet ball were against it simply because certain spitball artists preceded each delivery with an uncouth ritual that often included splattering the ball in full view of the crowd. It was hardly the kind of behavior calculated to sell hot dogs.

In 1920, Grimes, who had come to Brooklyn as part of the deal that sent Casey Stengel to Pittsburgh, enjoyed one of the best seasons of his long career. Before the campaign was over he would win twenty-three games and lose only eleven, posting a .676 winning percentage, the best in the league. He formed the backbone of a mound staff that included, in addition to Mitchell and Cadore, Jeff Pfeffer, Sherry Smith, Al Mamaux, and the ageless Rube Marquard.

As Alex got caught up in the season, he began to realize that Brooklyn, with its excellent pitching depth, had a good chance of winning the pennant. Following the progress of the campaign became far more important than finding a new job. And so he fell back into his old ways. Only this time he didn't have his father to bail him out.

Over at the Polo Grounds the story was a little different. The Giants, hampered by erratic pitching, languished in the second division for the first half of the season. Then, in the middle of July, Frankie Frisch, out sick for several weeks, came back into the lineup at third base.

His return had a magical effect on the club. In just three weeks, McGraw's men climbed from the cellar to third place, and all at once the National League had a three-team race. Harry and Alex began acting like kids again; they quarreled playfully over which club was stronger at each position, and they got into long arguments over who was the better manager—Wilbert Robinson or John McGraw. Alex contended that Robbie was a master at developing pitchers, and pitching was the name of the game.

Harry countered that McGraw towered over his Brooklyn rival; not only could the Little Napoleon develop players at all positions, but, equally important, he was a tactical genius. The debate continued throughout the summer. Harry, meanwhile, secretly searched the box scores and season statistics for signs of strengths and weaknesses in the two clubs.

Four or five weeks before the end of the campaign, he concluded that it was not going to be the Giants' year. Instead of revealing his findings to his brother, he kept the argument going loud and strong.

Shortly after the Giants began coming out of the doldrums, John McGraw, as pugnacious as ever, got into the most bizarre scrape of his stormy career. The Little Napoleon had earned a reputation for always standing ready to back up his mouth with his fists.

In 1913 he had knocked out Ad Brennan, a pitcher with the Phillies. The following year, in spring training, McGraw was decked by Pat Newman, manager of the Houston team. And in June 1917, in a game against the Reds, Muggsy had assaulted Bill "Lord" Byron, an umpire who had the annoying habit of humming tunes while he waited for a pitcher's next delivery. His attack on Byron cost the Giant manager a $500 fine and a sixteen-day suspension. John McGraw was certainly no stranger to violence, but not even he could have expected the weird incident that took place at the Lambs Club, his refuge in New York City.

Sometime in the early hours of Sunday morning, August 8, 1920, John McGraw arrived at the Lambs to have a few drinks and to engage in friendly conversation with some of his old pals. Although Prohibition was supposedly in full force, a man's club remained a sanctuary where he could still raise a glass of whisky without fear of the law.

The Little Napoleon strutted into the grill room, where half a dozen members were sitting around drinking and shooting the breeze. In one corner, two men were playing cards. One of the men was John C. Slavin, a friend of McGraw's who was a comedian on the musical stage. The other card player was William C. Boyd, one of Broadway's most celebrated leading men. McGraw, already well in his cups, mistook Boyd for Walter Knight, another actor, whom the Giant manager couldn't abide. Earlier that year, McGraw had provoked Knight into a noisy argument in the club's rooms; as a result, the house committee had suspended John's membership for three months.

On seeing Boyd, McGraw walked to the table and let fly a string of insults and obscenities. Boyd, stunned by the unexpected barrage of invective, stood and told McGraw to shut his mouth.

Suddenly fists were flying. It was quickly apparent that Boyd was no pussyfoot. He pummeled his adversary to the ground, leaving him with a tremendous shiner and a swollen forehead.

Once Muggsy had been subdued, Slavin and Winfield Liggett, a resident of the club, escorted him home in a taxi. As the three men emerged from a cab in front of McGraw's apartment house at Broadway and One Hundred Ninth Street, each insisted on paying the fare. An argument erupted, and McGraw shoved Liggett back into the taxi. McGraw then disappeared into his apartment building. As Liggett got out of the car for the second time, he discovered Slavin out cold on the pavement. With the help of the cab driver, Liggett tried to revive the unconscious man; when he would not come around, they rushed him to St. Luke's Hospital in critical condition.

When the police investigated the incident, no one involved could explain how Slavin had been knocked out. According to McGraw, he and his companions had "parted on most friendly terms." Liggett and the cabbie backed up McGraw's story. The cops seemed willing to believe that Slavin, who remained unconscious for several days, had somehow slipped and fallen, knocking his head on the sidewalk.

If that were the case, his injuries were indeed extraordinary. He had a fractured skull, a cut lip, and a badly bitten tongue, and he had lost two front teeth. While her husband was in the hospital, Mrs. Slavin exclaimed, "I can't understand how, if he only fell, his clothing could have gotten into such a state or how he could have become so bruised."

Somehow poor Slavin was forgotten in the storm of publicity that followed the incident. Prohibition agents joined the investigation, and Chief Agent James S. Shevlin searched the Lambs Club for intoxicating beverages. The chairman of the club's house committee expressed shock when told that liquor had been openly consumed on the club's premises. He claimed that "any liquor in this club could have been brought in only in a bottle or in the members' stomachs." The committee quickly investigated the matter; McGraw was summoned to appear for a hearing, but he failed to show up. After listening to Boyd's side of the story, the committee concluded that Muggsy was completely to blame. He was thrown out of the Lambs.

For three years McGraw was barred from his club, but, after three hundred members had signed a petition calling for his reinstatement, he was invited back.

Perhaps a good part of McGraw's belligerence in 1920 was a result of the noises being made by the Giants' tenants at the Polo Grounds. Although the Giants were playing well, the Yankees were stealing their thunder. Thunder was the right word; the Babe was blasting homers with unprecedented, if not unbelievable, regularity.

A new, livelier ball had been quietly introduced into the American League at the beginning of the 1920 season. The National League would follow suit the next year. On July 15, batting against Bill Burwell of the Browns at the Polo Grounds, Ruth popped the explosive new horsehide into the stands to tie his own home run record of twenty-nine. Four days later, pitcher Dickie Kerr of the White Sox watched two of his pitches to Ruth exit the Polo Grounds. The Babe had thirty-one homers with barely half the season gone. "Inside" baseball was giving way to "outside" baseball, and fans were turning out in ever increasing numbers to watch the magic man make baseballs disappear.

On August 16 the pennant-contending Cleveland team arrived at the

Polo Grounds. When Carl Mays, pitching for the Yanks, took the mound in the top of fifth, he had already been roughed up for three runs.

The first batter in the inning was shortstop Ray Chapman, a great bunter and fastest man in the league. The count went to one and one. Muddy Ruel signaled for a fastball and placed the target low, directly over the plate. Chapman, a plate crowder, set himself.

At the top of his motion, Mays saw Chapman drop his right foot into push-bunting position. At the last instant Mays altered his delivery and smoked his fastball high and inside. There was a sharp crack as the ball dribbled out between first base and the pitcher's mound.

Mays bounded from the mound, scooped it, and fired to Wally Pipp at first. Pipp cocked his arm to start the ball around the infield, suddenly stopped in midmotion, and looked toward home plate. Every head in the park swung in the same direction. Chapman was on the ground, surrounded by Ruel, on-deck batter Tris Speaker, and several Cleveland players. The pitch had struck Chapman on the head. He got to his feet and, with the help of two teammates, walked to the bench. Harry Lunte took Chapman's place on first base and eventually scored what proved to be the winning run.

The next morning, at 5 A.M., Ray Chapman died.

Major league baseball's first and only fatality caused a furor. Mays was both attacked and defended. Writers, fans, players, and even baseball officials called for his banishment from the game. Overnight, Mays was a beanball pitcher.

True, he had dusted his share of batters, but then so had nearly every other major league hurler. Even statements by the Cleveland players—manager Tris Speaker, pitcher Ray Caldwell, and catcher Chet Thomas—affirming that the pitch had been a good pitch and that Chapman, seemingly mesmerized, had simply failed to get out of the way were insufficient to quiet the storm immediately, although it subsided as the season lengthened.

As September began, three teams—Chicago, Cleveland, and the Yankees—were scuffling for the American League pennant. But with two weeks remaining in the season, the Chicago White Sox team—not to mention Organized Baseball itself—was dealt a crippling blow. Eight members of the club—Eddie Cicotte, Joe Jackson, Lefty Williams, Swede Risberg, Chick Gandil, Happy Felsch, Fred McMullin, and Buck Weaver—were accused of throwing the 1919 World Series to the Cincinnati Reds.

The story developed that gamblers, possibly under the direction of Arnold Rothstein, had promised the players some $100,000 to lie down against the Reds. There were indications that Hal Chase—who had been suspended in 1918 from the Reds by Mathewson for "indifferent playing" and in 1919 from the Giants by McGraw for a blatant fix attempt—

had been one of the major figures in the fix and had won $40,000 in bets. The accusations against the eight "Black Sox" were never proved, but all were driven beyond the pale of Organized Baseball, suspended for life. Actually, Chase, along with Lee Magee and Heinie Zimmerman, had been expelled from the game shortly after the 1919 season for his involvement in the same fix attempt that had prompted McGraw to suspend him. Those at the seat of baseball's justice, however, had managed to keep the news from the public until the Black Sox ballyhoo.

The nucleus of its team banished, the White Sox faded and finished two games behind the pennant-winning Cleveland team. The Yankees wound up third, three games out, but all things considered the season was a stupendous success for them. For the first time ever they had outdrawn the mighty Giants, mainly as a result of Ruth.

The Bambino had belted a mind-boggling fifty-four homers and had led the majors in slugging percentage, RBIs, runs scored, and walks as well. He also managed to bat .376. Carl Mays, meanwhile, has posted a 26–11 record.

Despite the Giants' surge in the second half of the 1920 campaign, the Robins held onto first place and finished seven games ahead of their crosstown rivals. It was the first time since Brooklyn joined the league that the two New York Nationals had finished one, two in the season standings. Uncle Robbie's boys would now face the Indians in a World Series that would be played under a long, dark shadow. The Black Sox scandal left most fans wondering just how crooked the national pastime had become.

Because of the death of Ray Chapman, many fans around the country were rooting for the Indians. Sentimental considerations aside, the two clubs appeared evenly matched. Both Alex and Harry felt that the Robins had the edge in pitching, but they were willing to concede that Cleveland was slightly better in most other departments.

The two infields were about on a par, but the Indians' outfield of Charlie Jamieson, Tris Speaker, and Elmer Smith wielded stronger bats and provided a tighter defense than Brooklyn's trio of Zack Wheat, Hy Meyers, and Tommy Griffith. In the catching department, Alex agreed with his brother that there was no contest. Cleveland's Steve O'Neill was a far better backstop than Brooklyn's Otto Miller. As Alex left home for Ebbets Field on the morning of October 5, he felt certain that Uncle Robbie could give Tris Speaker, who both managed and played center field, a real run for his money.

If there was one decision made by Wilbert Robinson in the 1920 Series that invited second-guessing, it was his choice of Rube Marquard as starting pitcher for the opening game. Why would he bypass Burleigh Grimes, at the top of his form, for old Rube?

As Alex and Harry saw it, there were two reasons. First, Marquard was a veteran of four previous Series. But, more important, by going with a left-hander Robbie forced Speaker, who platooned every outfielder except himself, to replace Jamieson and Smith with Joe Evans and Joe Wood. The switch not only took away from the Indians' defense but also removed Smith, a .316 hitter, in favor of Wood, whose average was only .270.

Marquard was the first southpaw to start an opening game of the Fall Classic. Rube, whose Series record to that point was two and four, hadn't won a postseason game since way back in 1912. His opponent was Stan Coveleski, the Indians' cunning spitball artist.

Coveleski handcuffed the Robins, holding them to one run on five hits, as Cleveland won, 3–1. In game two, Brooklyn put its own spitball artist to work, as Grimes went up against Jim Bagby, the leading hurler in the American League that year with a record of thirty-one and twelve. Both pitchers held the opposition to seven hits, but Grimes was more effective with men on base and shut out the Indians, 3–0.

The opposing pitchers in the third contest were another Brooklyn left-hander, Sherry Smith, and Ray Caldwell. This time the Indians were completely baffled by southpaw pitching; Smith gave up only three hits as the Robins squeaked out a 2–1 win.

With the Robins leading two games to one, the action shifted to Cleveland for the next four games. The year 1920 was the second of three years that the Series was a five-of-nine affair; if more than seven games were needed, the scene would shift back to Ebbets Field for the final two.

Alex spent the last money he had in the world getting to Cleveland for the resumption of the Series. After game four, it began to appear that he'd made a bad investment. The Tribe knocked Cadore out of the box in the second inning and then coasted to a 5–1 victory.

The turning point in the Series came in the fifth game, which once again pitted Grimes against Bagby. This time the Indians had no trouble finding Burleigh's number. Charlie Jamieson led off the bottom of the first with a smash that went off the glove of Ed Konetchy, Brooklyn's first baseman, for a single. Then Bill Wambsganss singled to left. With men now on first and second, Tris Speaker laid down a sacrifice bunt. Grimes fell down trying to field the ball, and all hands were safe. Up came Elmer Smith. The count went to one ball and one strike, and then Elmer sent the ball soaring over the right-field fence for the first World Series grand-slam home run.

Robbie stayed with his starter until the fourth inning, when, with Doc Johnston on second and one out, Grimes gave Steve O'Neill an intentional pass to pitch to Bagby. The Cleveland pitcher answered the insult by sending a homer into the temporary stands in right center. It was the first home run by a pitcher in a World Series.

That ended the afternoon for Grimes, who was replaced by Clarence Mitchell, Brooklyn's southpaw spitballer. In the top of the fifth, it looked as though the Robins might get something going, even though they were behind, 7–0. Pete Kilduff, Brooklyn's second baseman, and Otto Miller started the inning with back-to-back singles. Then Mitchell, a good hitting pitcher, came up to bat for himself. Robbie put on the hit-and-run, and Mitchell sent a wicked shot over second base that looked like a sure hit.

Wambsganss leaped into the air and made a fantastic grab for the first out of the inning. As he came down, the Indian second baseman hesitated, as if not fully comprehending the unusual opportunity that was now staring him in the face. Instead of tossing the ball to Joe Sewell, his shortstop, he rushed over to second base and kicked the bag, eliminating Kilduff, who was almost to third. Then Wambsganss ran down the line between second and first and tagged out Miller, who was still trying to reverse gears. It took a few seconds for the crowd to realize what had happened. Then a great roar swelled from the stands. Wamby had completed an unassisted triple play! It was the only time the feat has ever been accomplished in the World Series, and it took the last ounce of starch out of the Robins. Cleveland laughed through the next four innings and won the game, 8–1.

In game six, Sherry Smith once again pitched brilliantly, allowing only one run on seven hits. But Duster Mails, a former Robin, did even better—he held the puny Brooklyn bats to only three hits as the Indians won, 3–0. The Series was over; Brooklyn's journey to Cleveland had been a total disaster. The only good thing Alex could say about his four days in the Midwest was that the Indian summer weather had been superb.

On the train back to New York, Alex pondered the Robins' many mistakes. It was impossible to see how things could have turned out differently. No amount of excuses could hide the fact that Brooklyn had received a first-class trouncing.

As his journey neared its end, Alex began thinking about his own situation. He was dead broke, and the long winter would soon be upon him. It was obvious that his first order of business was to hustle a job.

In late October 1920, while Alex was reading want ads and pounding the pavement, the Boston Red Sox were providing the Yankees with yet another pillar for the monumental baseball team they were building. Ed Barrow, manager of the Red Sox, became the business manager and secretary of the Yanks. It was Barrow who had stuck his neck out by making Ruth, an established pitching star, into an outfielder.

"Tell me what you need in the way of players and I'll get them for you," Ed told a hopeful but dubious Miller Huggins.

Hug's doubts were erased when Barrow engineered the swap that brought Waite Hoyt, Wally Schang, Harry Harper, and Mike McNally to the Yankees in exchange for Muddy Ruel, Herb Thormahlen, Del

Pratt, and Sam Vick. The deal was made with, not surprisingly, the Boston Red Sox.

By the time Barrow came to New York, Organized Baseball was in chaos. The winds of change had been blowing for some time, and the Black Sox scandal had whipped them to gale force. The only remaining question was what form the reorganization would take.

With power up for grabs, the magnates of baseball began to plot and politick with fervor. The National League approved in essence the Albert D. Lasker proposal, which called for the creation of the post of commissioner of baseball, to be filled by a man from outside the game.

Joining the Nationals in support of the measure were the *insurrectos* —Frazee of the Red Sox, Comiskey of the White Sox, and Ruppert and Huston of the Yankees. Having staggered Johnson in the Carl Mays affair, the insurrectos were now looking to drive the Czar completely out of baseball. When Johnson and the remainder of the American League teams, the Loyal Five, rejected the proposal, the insurrectos met with the National League and threatened to form a new twelve-team circuit, the open franchise, in Detroit, to be filled by a new team or by the first of the Loyal Five to defect.

Johnson and his loyalists decided not to call the bluff. On November 12, 1920, Judge Kennesaw Mountain Landis became baseball's first commissioner. The major leagues had offered him a yearly salary of $50,000, but Landis decided to retain his federal judgeship and asked the magnates to deduct his federal salary of $7,500. The difference was made up by means of an expense account, but the "official" salary, the figure released to the press, was $42,500.

Will Rogers, commenting on the appointment of Landis, twirled his lasso and drawled, "The game needed a touch of class and distinction at the moment, and somebody said, 'Get that old guy who sits behind first base all the time. He's out here every day, anyhow.' So they offered him a season's pass and he jumped at it."

The election of Landis sapped Ban Johnson's waning strength even further, leaving the former Czar on his last legs. Over the years Landis was to prove a competent despot in his own right, as he out-Johnsoned Johnson time and time again.

While baseball was refurbishing its image, Alex was finding that it was less than a snap for a twenty-eight-year-old former bartender to find a position with a future. During his several months of searching he had one or two offers, but nothing with very much promise. Surprisingly, Harry did not give his brother a hard time about his failure to get a job. It was obvious that Alex was trying to find work, and to Harry that was all that counted.

One day shortly after Thanksgiving, Alex got a call from Whitey

O'Day, one of the bartenders who had been along on the drinking spree at Brighton Beach.

"I hear you're looking for work," Whitey said.

"Damned right I am."

"Well, get over to Manhattan right now," Whitey implored, "I'll meet you in an hour under the Palace marquee. I know a guy who's looking for bartenders, and he's willing to pay top dollar."

"Bartenders?"

"Yeah, bartenders. The way things are going, it won't be long before this city is twice as wet as it was before the antisaloon biddies pushed through their holy amendment."

That afternoon Whitey escorted Alex to a garage at 223 West Fifty-third Street. The building was located in the shadow of the old Sixth Avenue El, which turned west to connect with the Ninth Avenue line.

They ducked inside the garage and made their way between the rows of parked autos to a door in the rear. Over a sign that read "Lavatory," someone had tacked a piece of cardboard bearing the words "Out of Order."

The two job applicants opened the door to discover a steel ladder that seemed to stretch upward for about three stories. They climbed to the top, where they came into a spacious loft with painted-over windows, high ceilings, and a creaky wooden floor. At one end of the large room, a bricklayer was putting up a new wall just a few feet in front of the outer wall of the building. Nearby two carpenters were constructing a long, oak-paneled bar. The whole place trembled as the El rumbled past the opaque windows and into the station. Alex and Whitey were greeted by Larry Silver, the proprietor of this unusual establishment. He was tall, skinny, bald, extremely nervous, and wearing a moustache that looked like the bristles from a well-used toothbrush.

"We were sent over by Heince, the waiter at Jack's," Whitey volunteered.

"You men are both experienced bartenders?" Silver asked, tugging at his maltreated lip hair.

"That's right," Alex replied.

"Good. You're hired. If Heince says you fellows are O.K., that's good enough for me. One thing I sure as hell can't do is advertise all over town. Can you start in two weeks?"

"You bet," answered Whitey.

And so Alex went to work in a speakeasy. From the day it opened the place attracted theater people—musicians, actors, first-nighters, and even a few critics. It became known as the Actors Club, and the word spread around Broadway that it was a congenial place for a drink or two. Very quickly the men who frequented the place began to bring female companions around, and Alex was called upon to mix all sorts of cocktails, from Manhattans and Bronxes to Tom and Jerrys, and a concoction known as Hotel Astor Number One Punch. Every Saturday night, Larry Silver provided music, usually a New Orleans jazz band. All things considered, Alex found his new life extremely pleasant. He and Whitey alternated their work schedules; one week Alex was on nights, the next he would work days. That meant when summer came he would have free afternoons to take in ball games.

The job had only one unpleasant aspect, the threat of a raid. Larry had, of course, taken several precautions. The booze supply, hidden behind the new brick wall, could be reached only from a secret trap door on the roof. Behind the bar was a chute that could, in less than two minutes, send all the bottles in current use smashing into the stones and rubble of the back alley.

As the months passed, Alex began to feel secure. But then, in the summer of 1921, something happened that made him nervous all over again—Izzy Epstein, the most notorious Prohibition agent in the East, arrested Jack Dunstan for selling liquor in his restaurant.

Even after the Eighteenth Amendment forced him to close his bar, Jack had gone right on providing drinks to his favorite customers. Epstein discovered Dunstan's cache of booze in a stronghold on the roof of an extension to the restaurant. The only way to get inside was by way of a fire-escape ladder that connected across an alley to a window in another building.

It just happened that the window led into Jack's private apartment. When Izzy and his men broke into the stronghold, they discovered more than $100,000 worth of top-drawer whisky and wine. Alex was unhappy to see his former employer fall into hard luck, but something else bothered him even more—Jack's was just ten blocks south of the Actors Club.

In 1921 the Robins fell apart completely, finishing in fifth place, sixteen and a half games back. As the campaign moved into the home stretch, it looked as though the Pirates were a cinch to win their first flag since 1909. But as late as August, Harry was still not ready to count the Giants out.

Over the season John McGraw had done a lot of tinkering with his lineup, trying to find a combination that would end his clubs' four-year pennant drought. In two trades with Philadelphia he acquired Johnny Rawlings, Irish Meusel, and none other than Casey Stengel. Casey, a real old-timer at the advanced age of thirty-one, had been traded to the Phillies the previous season. Hearing he was going back to New York, Ol' Case took off like a bat out of hell for Boston, where the Giants were playing the Braves. He wanted to reach the club before McGraw could change his mind.

Art Nehf, a Giant pitcher, happened to be near the outfield gate in

Braves Field when Casey arrived. Stengel, thinking himself unobserved as he came through the gate, performed a little dance, pounded his chest and arms, and muttered, "Wake up muscles! We're in New York now!"

On August 24, Pittsburgh, rolling along in first place, seven and a half games ahead of New York, invaded Coogan's Bluff for a five-game series. As Moon Gibson, the Pirate manager, figured it, all his team had to do was win two games and the pennant would be all but wrapped up. McGraw, on the other hand, knew he would have to pull a sweep to have any hopes of swiping away the flag.

The Pirates swaggered into the Polo Grounds fully expecting to make short work of the Giants. Even after they dropped both ends of the opening twin bill, they didn't appear perturbed. But the Giants couldn't be satisfied with just two wins, and they went on to take all five. By the time the Pirates moved across the East River for three games in Brooklyn, the Giants had fairly well kicked the swagger out of them.

The Bucs managed to salvage two wins over the Robins, but by then New York had the momentum. McGraw's men quickly took over first place and were two and a half games in the lead when they traveled to Forbes Field for three final victories that knocked Pittsburgh out of the race. The Giants, who finished four games in front, had won the flag by jumping all over the Pirates, beating them sixteen times while losing only six.

The free-spirited Yankees of 1921 gave Miller Huggins fits from spring training on. Ed Barrow, disturbed by stories of drunken carousing and all-night orgies that had taken place in Florida at the previous year's training camp, moved the site to Shreveport, Louisiana.

What Barrow had not reckoned on was that Shreveport was riding the crest of an oil boom and was a wide-open town. The Yanks, led by Ruth, took it upon themselves to prove that they could drink as hard, spend as freely, and connect with ladies as often as any newly rich wildcatter. "Yanks Training on Scotch" a headline in one New York newspaper announced.

But the Yankees were playing well, red eyes or not. The Bambino could still hit those "splendiferous spanks." Ruth's legend had already grown to mind-boggling proportions. He was a movie star, having appeared in *Headin' Home*, and was a merchandiser's dream.

Ruth's name or picture appeared on such items as sweatshirts, underwear, caps, shoes, notebooks, cigars, and cigarettes. And to top it off, the Babe Ruth byline was appearing over numerous stories and articles, all ghosted by a pool of writers.

When the Yanks played an exhibition, entire towns closed down at game time. If the Yankee train made a whistle stop at four in the morning, there would be hundreds of people on the platform, craning their necks in the mist to catch a glimpse of the superman.

As the season got under way, the Yanks proved their antics off the field did not prevent winning ball games. In fact, their carousing seemed to add to their awesomeness. Members of opposing teams stared in disbelief as the heart of the Yank order staggered bleary-eyed to the batting cage and proceeded to blast ball after ball in the general direction of outer space. In 1921, as well as for years to come, the Yankees would often win a game right there, demoralizing the opposition before the first pitch of the game.

Miller Huggins, of course, saw no value in liquor and late-night activity. He was thoroughly convinced that the Yanks could have and should have won the pennant in 1920. "We lacked but one thing," he said to a friend. "Hustle." Hug was grimly determined that his team would not fritter away another flag, but the roaring Yankees were almost more than he could handle.

The players, knowing that Huggins did not have the full support of the owners—that he was, in fact, despised by Cap Huston—openly defied the little man. Returning to their hotel in the wee hours, they would gather under Huggins's window and serenade him, chanting, "Huggins, come and get your drunken ballplayers."

When it was all over, Huggins's health had been seriously impaired, but the Yanks had won their first pennant, beating out a strong Cleveland team in the final weeks of the season. Ruth had hit fifty-nine homers, breaking that record for the third straight year, and had batted in 170 runs to lead both leagues. He had amassed 119 extra-base hits and 457 total bases, records that still stand. His batting average was a healthy .378.

Bob Meusel, meanwhile, was second in home runs with twenty-four, one more than George Kelly, the National League champ. Meusel was also runner-up to Ruth in runs batted in with 135, 9 more than the 126 collected by Rogers Hornsby to lead the National League. Mays, Hoyt, and Shawkey won twenty-seven, nineteen, and eighteen games respectively. The top ten pitchers on the Yanks' staff all boasted winning percentages better than .500.

The World Series of 1921 presented John McGraw with perhaps the greatest challenge of his career. In his last four attempts to capture the world championship he had been humiliated. Now he found himself facing not just any American League upstart, but the Yankees—a club with the audacity to outdraw the Giants in their own ball park for the second year in a row.

Harry and Alex, still loyal National Leaguers, were naturally rooting for McGraw. Along with most New Yorkers, they believed the two teams were evenly matched. In Jack Doyle's Billiard Academy, as well as out at Jamaica Race Track, most bettors were saying, "Even money and take your pick."

173

The opening game was played on October 5 before a crowd of only thirty thousand. Attendance was well below the Polo Grounds' capacity because thousands of fans had been discouraged by newspaper reports that tickets were impossible to come by. To make matters worse, it rained the previous night and into the morning, keeping away even more would-be spectators. Despite these adversities, the Rice brothers set out on the long journey from Park Slope to Coogan's Bluff, where they happily discovered that seats were plentiful.

Even though half the general admission seats in the upper grandstand were empty, there was little doubt that this was a great moment in baseball history. Looking down at the field boxes, Alex and Harry could see that such celebrities as Flo Ziegfeld, Irving Berlin, Norma Talmadge, George M. Cohan, Governors Miller of New York and Edwards of New Jersey, Harry Sinclair, Ned Hanlon, and Monte Ward had turned out to see the Gotham showdown.

Miller Huggins decided to spring Carl Mays on the Giants. It would be interesting to see whether Mays could baffle the McGrawmen with his submarine ball. The Little Napoleon named as his starter Shufflin' Phil Douglas, a spitballer who enjoyed booze a lot more than baseball. But when Phil had his mind off the bottle he could be as good a hurler as anyone in the big leagues. It was a curious matchup—the star-crossed Mays against Douglas the carouser.

Before the game McGraw stood for several seconds on the dugout steps, eying the short right-field wall. He knew all too well how familiar that target was to the Babe. The Giants were the "home" team that day. Just before Douglas started for the mound to begin the first inning, McGraw said to him, "Remember, don't give that big baboon anything but low curves."

In his initial appearance at the plate, Ruth, batting third in the order, singled home Elmer Miller from second for the first run of the Series. In the second inning the crowd got a chuckle when Irish Meusel flied out to his brother Bob. The score remained 1–0 until the top of the fifth, when Mike McNally reached third on a double and a sacrifice bunt. Then, before Douglas threw his first pitch to the next batter, Miller, McNally caught the Giant battery napping and stole home.

In the sixth the Yanks scored again, this time on a single by Roger Peckinpaugh, a passed ball, and a triple by Bob Meusel. His brother relayed the ball into first base, and Bob was declared out for missing the bag, but the run counted, and the Yankees went on to win, 3–0.

The game didn't give Giant rooters much to yell about. Actually, Douglas pitched pretty well, giving up only seven hits and striking out Ruth twice. But the Giant batters had very little luck with Mays. Only Frankie Frisch, who got four of his team's six hits, was able to get around on the submarine ball.

In the second game the Giants were the "visitors." They donned their road uniforms and switched dugouts with the Yankees. Young Waite Hoyt went against Art Nehf. Hoyt pitched flawlessly, giving up only two hits, as the Yanks once again came up with a 3–0 victory.

Now McGraw was in a real hole. Never before had a team lost the first two games and then gone on to win the Series. The Giants, responding to their predicament, came to life in game three—they exploded for twenty hits, a World Series record, and demolished their intrastadium rivals, 13–5.

In game four, with Douglas again facing Mays, the Giants edged the Yankees, 4–2. In the bottom of the ninth, Ruth finally gave the crowd what they were waiting for—he popped one into the right-field bleachers for his first World Series homer. Alex and Harry were delighted to see the blast wasted in a losing cause.

In the fifth game Hoyt once again handcuffed the Giants, as he outpitched Nehf and defeated the McGrawmen, 3–1. The Babe led off the Yank's fourth inning with a play that astonished almost everyone in the Polo Grounds: He laid a perfect bunt along the firstbase line and beat it out for a single. Nehf, visibly shaken by the play, piped a fastball to Meusel, who smashed a double to deep left field, scoring Ruth all the way from first.

As he came into the Yankee dugout, the Babe, suffering from an inflamed right elbow and a battered knee, collapsed on the bench. The game was halted while he was attended to, and the crowd cheered madly when he returned to his post in the outfield.

After the game the team doctor pulled Ruth out of the Series. That was good news for the Giants, who promptly evened the Series in game six. Jesse Barnes pitched well in relief of Fred Toney, who gave up five runs in the first two innings, and the Giants came back to win, 8–5.

What had begun as a five-out-of-nine Series was now reduced to a two-out-of-three affair. Game seven sent Phil Douglas shuffling back to the mound to face Carl Mays for the third time. It was another great pitching duel. The score was tied, 1–1, in the seventh, when, with two out, Johnny Rawlings reached first on an error by Aaron Ward, the Yankee second baseman. Frank Snyder, the Giant catcher, then doubled home the winning run. The 2–1 victory put McGraw just one game away from capturing his first World Series since 1905.

In game eight McGraw sent out Art Nehf to pitch against Waite Hoyt. The Little Napoleon figured that Nehf had been pitching too damn well to lose to anyone—even the precocious Hoyt—three times in a row. It was a chilly fall day, and the crowd of twenty-six thousand was even smaller than that of the opening contest. Many fans stayed home, saving their time and money, in the hope that there would be a game nine. Alex and Harry could not be kept away, and they witnessed one of the most thrilling games in World Series history.

In the top of the first, after George Burns had grounded out, Dave

Bancroft drew a walk. Frisch then fouled out to Wally Pipp, the Yankee first baseman. Ross Youngs followed with another base on balls, and then George Kelly topped an easy grounder to short that Peckinpaugh let roll right through his legs, allowing Bancroft to come in with the first run of the game. For the next eight innings, Nehf and Hoyt blanked the opposing batters. The score was still 1–0 when the Yanks came to bat in the bottom of the ninth. The crowd roared as Babe Ruth, who had been huddled under a sweater all afternoon, defied his doctor's orders and led off the inning batting for Pipp. But the Bambino grounded out to Kelly, leaving the Yankees two outs away from defeat. The next batter was Ward, who managed to coax a walk out of Nehf. "Oh, my God," Alex moaned to his brother. "Do you know who's up next?"

"I sure as hell do," Harry replied. The batter was none other than Home Run Baker. The Rice brothers exchanged grim glances. Nagging at them was the memory of Merkle, of Snodgrass, and of the damage Baker had done to the Giants in 1911 and 1913. Nehf's first pitch to the veteran slugger was a ball. Then a strike. After each delivery Snyder turned to the dugout to get the new sign from McGraw. The next pitch went for ball two. Then Baker fouled off a pair and took another wide one. The count was now three and two.

Ward was off and running but had to return when Baker sliced off another foul. Once again the runner was under way with the pitch; this time Baker smoked a line drive toward right that brought the Yankee fans to their feet. Somehow Rawlings got in front of the ball, knocked it down, and threw on his knees to Kelly at first for the second out of the inning. The Giant first baseman fired across the diamond to Frisch at third, who hurled himself in front of Ward. Ward charged into the bag like an angry bull. The two players collided and went sprawling. When Frankie came to his feet he was still holding the ball, and the Giants had finally won another world championship.

That first Subway Series gave fans a lot to debate about. According to Joe Vila, it proved that National League pitching was far superior to the hurling in the Junior Circuit. In his column he wrote, "When the Bambino and his ball smashing champions went up against the Giants' pitchers, Douglas, Barnes, and Nehf, the light was turned on and thousands realized how badly they had been fooled by the so-called supermen wearing Yankee uniforms." It was true that Murderers Row—Ruth, Meusel, Pipp, and Baker—hadn't shown much. Only the Babe had managed to bat over .300. But then the Giants hadn't exactly walked all over Hoyt and Mays. They were the first team ever to be shut out in the first two games of a World Series.

Judge Landis, having just attended his first World Series as the high potentate of baseball, was a bit grumpy after ceremoniously sitting through eight long ball games. Before leaving New York, he announced his recommendation that the old seven-game format be restored. A nine-game Series, he proclaimed, "overtaxes the patience of the public."

The Little Napoleon, never content to rest on his laurels, made a deal over the following winter that gave him what some fans still believe was the greatest infield of all time. McGraw purchased Heinie Groh, who had been a young second-stringer with the Giants ten years earlier, from Cincinnati for a sum reported to be more than $100,000, plus two players—George Burns and Mike Gonzalez. Groh was generally considered to be the best third baseman in the league. Frankie Frisch would now play second, and Johnny Rawlings would be benched.

As the 1922 season got under way, arguments raged over whether the new Giant combination of Groh, Bancroft, Frisch, and Kelly was better than either the Athletics' $100,000 Infield of 1911–14 or the Cubs' fabled quartet of Steinfeldt, Tinker, Evers, and Chance.

As far as Harry Rice was concerned, McGraw's foursome outclassed both the others. Even Johnny Evers, now a coach with the White Sox, agreed. He remarked, "In my opinion baseball has seen no infield as that of the Giants. I was a member of a pretty good quartet myself once, and I think I know an infield when I see one."

The loss of George Burns left McGraw with a big hole in center field. To plug the gap, he pulled Casey Stengel off the bench. Casey responded to the call with one of his best seasons ever, appearing in eighty-four games and batting .368.

Most of the Giants' problems that year centered on the pitching staff. Fred Toney lost his stuff and was sent to Boston as part of a deal that brought another pitcher, Hughie McQuillan, to New York. To get McQuillan, a hurler who had lots of promise but had yet to mature, Charles Stoneham paid the Braves $100,000.

McGraw's biggest headache was Shufflin' Phil Douglas, who continued to pitch well but also continued to disappear and get loaded. McGraw hired a private detective named O'Brien to watch over Douglas. The pitcher and his keeper quickly became friends, since O'Brien's solution to Phil's restlessness was to take him to a speakeasy and let him have a few drinks.

The Giant manager fired the detective when he learned of his approach, replacing him with Jesse Burkett, an old star from the 1890s who was a good friend of McGraw's. In early August, Douglas, miffed over his friend's dismissal, eluded his new keeper and disappeared for several days. When Burkett, with the aid of private detectives, finally found Phil, he put him in a sanatorium to dry out.

Five days later, when Douglas returned to the club, it was obvious that he was a very troubled man. One day he invaded the pressbox and picked a fight with a helpless reporter who had been crippled in the World War. A few days after that, Shufflin' Phil wrote a letter to Les Mann, an outfielder with the Cardinals, then battling with the Giants for first place. Douglas explained in his note that he was anxious to prevent McGraw from capturing the pennant, but he was afraid that if he stayed with the club the Giants would win. He was willing to abandon the club if the St. Louis players would make it worth his while. Mann turned the letter over to Branch Rickey, his manager, who sent it to Commissioner Landis. The judge, unable to find compassion in his heart for a man who was obviously ill, banished Douglas from baseball for life.

McGraw, within reach of his second pennant in a row, had suddenly lost one of the mainstays of his pitching staff. He sorely needed a replacement, and he found one in a manner that could hardly be believed. Jack Scott, a fine pitcher with the Braves the previous season, had been traded during the winter to Cincinnati. But, when he reported to the Reds for spring training, his arm had mysteriously gone lame.

The doctors who examined him pronounced that he would never pitch again, and Scott was given his unconditional release. He went home to North Carolina for a rest, but several weeks later he turned up at the Polo Grounds, where he told McGraw, "I think my arm's all right, and I want a chance to work out."

"I don't give a damn about your arm," McGraw replied. "Do you have any money?" He didn't, so the Giant manager gave him fifty dollars. Slowly Scott brought his arm around, and when Douglas was suspended the Little Napoleon made him a starter. Still not on the team payroll, Scott played for the bonuses McGraw gave him every time he won. He went on to post a record of eight and two.

By the end of August the Giants had a firm grip on first place, leading the Cubs by six games. The club coasted the rest of the way, winning the pennant by seven games over the Reds. John McGraw, taking his eighth league championship, was now firmly established as the winningest pilot in the history of the game.

And what happened to the Robins in 1922? *Baseball Magazine* summed it up this way: "Fat Robbie's men sank to sixth, with little chance to come out of that lowly station. Slowness on the bases, lack of timely hitting, and the failure of what had been a dazzling pitching staff, all contributed to the downfall of Brooklyn."

As for the Yankees, they picked up in 1922 right where they had left off the year before—hitting and drinking. They were, however, without two of their leaders in both categories. Following the 1921 World Series, Ruth and Meusel, along with a couple of lesser Yankees, had defied Judge Landis's direct orders and embarked on a barnstorming tour. Having earned nearly $100,000 on a similar tour the previous year, Ruth saw no reason that he shouldn't continue to earn an "honest buck." Even though Cap Huston tracked down Ruth on the road and persuaded him to abandon the tour, the irate Landis fined the players the amount of their World Series shares and declared them ineligible until May 20 of the following year. Undaunted, the Babe set out on a vaudeville tour. As a thespian, Ruth's expertise was roughly equivalent to that of a trained bear, but his natural charm and good humor won over audiences and left them begging for more.

Before returning to exile, Ruth and Meusel joined the team for spring training in New Orleans—Barrow seemed to have a knack for picking playgrounds—and a wonderful time was had by all. Just prior to the season Barrow acquired Whitey Witt, a speedy little player who could field and hit, to fill the gap in the outfield until the big bombers could return to base.

When the prodigals returned on May 20, nearly forty thousand fans packed the Polo Grounds to welcome them home. Ruth and Meusel were returning to a team that was several games ahead of the second-place St. Louis Browns, a position achieved largely through the fine play of Witt and the pitching of two newly acquired hurlers, Sad Sam Jones and Bullet Joe Bush.

Huggins put Ruth in right, Meusel in left, and the fleet Witt in center. As Jumping Joe Dugan—who later that year followed the well-worn path from the Red Sox to the Yankees—related to writer Kal Wagenheim, "One day, there was a long hit between Whitey and Ruth. 'Go grab it, Whitey!' Next one goes between Whitey and Meusel. 'Go get it, Whitey!' Next one's hit right over Whitey's head. He comes in, puffin', and Huggins calls him over. 'Whitey,' he says, 'I'm watchin' those two big stiffs. Keep chasin' 'em and I'll see that Colonel Ruppert gets you a bonus.' 'To hell with the bonus,' says Whitey, 'Tell him to buy me a bicycle!' "

As the season wore on, the Babe, now making the unheard-of sum of $52,000 a year, was displaying both ragged play and ragged temperament. Perhaps irritated by his lack of success at the plate, he fought with fans, with teammates, and with umpires. Ban Johnson repeatedly scolded, fined, and suspended the big man.

In mid-July, the Browns overtook the Yankees. Although the Yanks soon regained first place, they couldn't manage to shake the bothersome Browns. And when, on July 23, Frazee gave Barrow Jumping Joe Dugan and Elmer Smith for Chick Fewster, Elmer Miller, and Johnny Mitchell, the Browns screamed that the Yankees were trying to buy the pennant.

Dugan was possibly the best third baseman in the game, and Home Run Baker, who had held down the position for the Yanks since 1916, was beginning to wear out. In regard to Frazee's claim that no cash was involved in the deal, the *Boston Herald* retorted that "unless he got the equivalent of $50,000 or $75,000 he was sorely worsted." There was no doubt, the paper continued, that Dugan and Smith were sold to "the wealthy New York team" and that subs had been tossed in for camouflage purposes. The Yanks were allowed to keep Dugan and Smith, but the following year the baseball owners adopted a rule barring trades after June 1, except by the route of waivers.

On August 16, leading the Browns by a scant half game, the Yankees ventured into St. Louis for a three-game series billed as the "little world series." Trainloads of fans poured in. Scalpers were getting $45 for $2.50 reserved seats. Because extra wooden boxes had been built along the first and third base foul lines and the edges of the outfield roped off to create additional seating, the games would be played with special ground rules.

The Hugmen sent Bob Shawkey to face Urban Shocker, the former Yankee. The game developed into a tight defensive battle, with the Yanks scratching out single runs in the second and third innings. In the fourth, the St. Louis fans, who thus far had been occupying themselves by riding Ruth without mercy, nearly tore down the park when George Sisler spanked a double off Aaron Ward's shins to run his consecutive game hitting streak to forty, tying Ty Cobb's modern record. But it came to naught, and it wasn't until the sixth that the Browns managed to squeeze out their first run. Going into the bottom of the ninth, the score was 2–1, and the mood of the crowd was becoming ugly.

Eddie Foster, the leadoff batter, lofted a high fly to left center. As Meusel and Witt converged, a fan in the roped-off portion of the outfield stood, took dead aim, and hurled a pop bottle. The bottle spun through the air and, just as Meusel caught the ball, it hit Witt between the eyes. Whitey fell as though he had been axed.

There was a split second of frozen silence, and then all hell broke loose. The players of both teams and the umpires streamed toward the fallen Witt, the fans poured out of the stands, and a phalanx of mounted police galloped over from left field.

Witt lay unconscious, bleeding slightly. Yankee coach Charlie O'Leary, frightened by the frustrated fans, reached down and deftly smeared blood over Witt's entire face and then lifted him onto Freddy Hofman's shoulders. When the vanguard of stampeding fans saw the lifeless, gory Witt, they suddenly became quiet. Hofman packed Whitey to the clubhouse, and the mounted cops packed the fans back into the stands.

With Meusel in center and Elmer Smith in right, the Yankees quickly disposed of the two remaining batters and came away with a 2–1 victory.

Witt's injury was minor, but that fact did little to quiet the furor. Buck O'Neil, the New York columnist, stormed, "When you throw a pop bottle at Whitey Witt's head, you are throwing a pop bottle at the foundation of the national game!" The Browns and the St. Louis Rooters Club offered a reward of $550 for information. Not to be outdone, Ban Johnson confiscated the bottle as evidence and offered to pay $1,000 out of his own pocket for the arrest of the rascal who threw it.

Legend has it that the rewards were collected by a man who, with a straight face, claimed the dread article had been thrown onto the field earlier and that Witt had stepped on the neck of the bottle, thus flipping it up into his own face.

At any rate, the following day, when the bandaged Witt stepped up as leadoff batter, he was welcomed with a warm ovation by another record crowd of thirty-one thousand. But shortly the cheering was for Browns' pitcher Hub Pruett. His deceptive slow ball and slow curve baffled the Yankee batters. Meanwhile, Waite Hoyt was being shelled, but a tight Yankee defense was holding the Browns at bay. In the sixth Ruth, who'd already swatted his share of air, got a good look at one of Pruett's slow balls and lofted it out of Sportsman's Park onto Grand Boulevard.

The Browns came back in their half of the sixth to score three runs. In the eighth St. Louis put away the game by scoring twice more, and the fans nearly leveled the park when Ken Williams hit his thirty-eighth homer of the season to take the league lead in that department. The Browns were now only one-half game behind.

The third day dawned bright, as yet another record crowd, thirty-two thousand, crammed into the bandbox. Bullet Joe Bush and Dixie Davis quickly settled into a classic pitchers' duel.

By the bottom of the seventh the Brown's owned a 2–0 lead. But in the Yankee eighth, after Witt had grounded out, Dugan knocked the ball to the left center fence for two bases. The crowd became uneasy as Ruth stepped in. The Babe looked at a third strike and returned to the dugout to thunderous catcalls and jeers. Wally Pipp came up and promptly cracked a shrieker through the box. The ball caromed off Davis's glove. Marty McManus retrieved it and, showing poor judgment and an even worse arm, fired the ball past Sisler at first. The crowd groaned as Jumping Joe pounced on the plate and Pipp streaked safely into second.

Two out, the tying run on second, and big Bob Meusel was the batter. Davis ran the count to two and two, and came in with a roundhouse curve. The bat remained on Meusel's shoulder, the ball dipped over the heart of the plate, and the inning was over.

The Browns took the field for the first of the ninth still clinging to a 2–1 lead. The leadoff batter, Wally Schang, copied Pipp's earlier trick and singled off the glove of Davis. Huggins then pulled Aaron Ward in favor of left-handed-hitting Elmer Smith. Browns manager Lee Fohl countered by replacing Davis with yesterday's hero, lefty Hub Pruett. When the youngster had completed his warmups, Hug called Smith back and sent righty Mike McNally to the plate. The Browns infield closed in for the bunt, the pitch got away from Hank Severeid, and Schang scampered along to second. Then, with the infield back, McNally outfoxed the Browns by dropping a perfect bunt. All hands were safe. After Pruett walked Deacon Scott to fill the bases, Urban Shocker came on in relief.

A pall had settled over Sportsman's Park. The next batter was Bullet Joe Bush, a fine hitter. After examining several of Shocker's deliveries, Bush sent a sizzler into the hole between first and second. McManus made a diving stop, came to his knees, and threw wildly homeward. The ball skidded crazily through the infield. Severeid dug it out of the dirt and lunged in front of the runner. Schang was out.

No warm ovation welcomed Whitey Witt this time as he stepped in. Whitey silenced the St. Louis partisans once and for all by drilling his third single of the day, scoring McNally and Scott. Dugan followed by hitting into a double play, but the Yanks set down the Browns in order in the bottom of the ninth, taking away a 3–2 victory and a one-and-a-half game lead.

The Browns, down but not out, played excellent ball throughout the late summer but could never again overtake the Yankees, who finally won the pennant by a margin of one game.

While the rest of the country was left out in the cold, New York got ready to monopolize its second straight Series. This time the Yankees were clearly the betting favorites, with much of the wagering focusing on how Babe Ruth would perform.

Alex, although still loyal to the National League, had a hunch that the Bambino would walk away with all the batting honors. To Harry's horror, Alex bet $500 that the Babe would get the most homers, the most extra-base hits, and hit for the highest average in the Series.

Radio had made its World Series debut the previous year. A reporter in the Polo Grounds pressbox had relayed his account of the games by telephone to station WJZ in Newark, New Jersey, where an announcer repeated the play-by-play. In 1922 radio came into its own. WJZ put Grantland Rice and his microphone right into the Polo Grounds.

And so round two of the battle for Gotham got under way. In the first game Miller Huggins sent his ace, Bullet Joe Bush, to the mound; McGraw went with Art Nehf. Hoping to tire the Yankee starter, the Little Napoleon told his players, "Wait out Bush." But Bullet Joe figured out what was going on, got ahead of the batters by putting his first pitches over, and blanked the Giants for the first seven innings.

Meanwhile, the Yankees scored twice. In the sixth Ruth singled Joe Dugan home from second, and in the seventh, Bob Meusel came in from third on a sacrifice fly to center by Aaron Ward.

As the Giants came to bat in the bottom of the eighth, McGraw told his leadoff hitter, Dave Bancroft, to swing at the first pitch. Bancroft lashed a single to right. Groh followed with another base hit to right, also on the first pitch. Then Frisch, who by all conventional logic should have sacrificed, pounced on Bush's first pitch and smacked a single to left. With the bases loaded, Irish Meusel, having received the same instructions from McGraw, came to the plate. He tied up the ball game with a drive that skimmed over Bush's fingertips into center field.

With no one out and men on first and third, Huggins sent in Waite Hoyt to relieve the badly bitten Bullet Joe. The next batter was Ross Youngs; he hit a long drive to center that Whitey Witt caught up with at the last moment, but Frisch came home easily with the go-ahead run. Hoyt struck out the next two batters, George Kelly and Casey Stengel. Rosy Ryan, who had come in for Nehf in the top of the eighth, held the Yanks scoreless in the ninth, and the Giants won the opening game.

The only game Harry and Alex were able to get tickets for was the second one, played on Thursday, October 5. It turned out to be one of the most frustrating and controversial contests in Series history. With Jesse Barnes pitching for the Giants and Bob Shawkey on the mound for the Yankees, the Giants jumped to a 3–0 lead in the top of the first.

The Yanks fought back slowly, picking up one run in their half of the first and another in the fourth before finally tying things up with a tally in the eighth. The game remained deadlocked through nine frames.

As the teams prepared to go into extra innings, umpire George Hildebrand had a little chat with Commissioner Landis, stationed as usual in his front-row box. Play resumed, but neither team scored in the tenth. After the inning, Hildebrand and his colleague Bill Klem called the game "on account of darkness."

Harry looked at his pocket watch. It was 4:45. Then he looked at the sky, still blue and filled with light, although the shadows off the grandstands were spreading onto the field. "Called on account of *darkness?*" Harry asked his brother. "They can't be serious."

"I'm afraid they are, Harry," Alex replied. "It's the stupidest thing I ever heard of."

As they reached the field, Harry and Alex came upon Judge Landis's box, where the commissioner and his wife were standing, surrounded by angry fans.

"Crook! Robber!" several people called out.

"Baseball's a crooked game! Bring back the Chicago White Sox!" Alex piped up, masking his laughter with cupped hands.

"Barnum was right! We're all suckers!" Harry yelled.

The judge was determined not to be intimidated by the crowd. He escorted his wife across the diamond, threatened all the way by a mob of jeering fans. As he reached the right-field exit, he turned back for a moment. "You're all cowards!" he cried out to his tormentors.

Landis, of course, had nothing to do with the decision to halt the game. It was Klem who had suggested to Hildebrand that the time had come to stop play. Klem reasoned that the pace of the game had been slow all afternoon, and it might not be possible to complete another full inning before dark. Whatever the merits of the umpires' decision, Landis was anxious to show the fans that the game had not been called just to squeeze an extra gate out of the Series. He ordered that the day's receipts, more than $120,000, be donated to charity.

The only misfortune to befall either club in game two was suffered by the Giants. In the second inning, Casey Stengel aggravated a charley horse beating out a base hit and was out for the rest of the Series. "That was too damn bad," Alex said later. "Case got off to such a great start— two for five. He deserved to be in there all the way."

In game three, McGraw sent Jack Scott, the refugee from the scrap heap, to pitch against Waite Hoyt. Scott held the Yankees to four hits and no runs for a 3–0 victory.

During the game the Giant fans began to razz the Babe, who in three games had managed only two hits in twelve trips to the plate. Yankee rooters quickly came to the Bambino's support, and fistfights broke out in the bleachers.

The Babe was also taking plenty of abuse from the enemy bench. Several of the Giant players yelled "Hey, Nigger!" every time he came to the plate. It was an epithet he particularly hated. Johnny Rawlings, the loudest of Ruth's tormentors, took great glee in bringing the Babe's blood to a boil.

Scott's 3–0 victory was the culmination of one of the great comebacks in the history of the game. As *Baseball Magazine* put it, "You will go far and search many forgotten records to find a parallel to the pitcher who was all through in June yet became the pitching sensation of the following World's Series."

After the game, Ruth, accompanied by Meusel, invaded the Giant clubhouse to have it out with Rawlings. The Babe marched over to the infielder and threatened to beat the hell out of him if he didn't begin to guard his tongue.

It wasn't long before Jesse Barnes was in the middle of the controversy, accusing Ruth of hurling worse insults at him while he was pitching the day before. The argument was about to become a fight when Hughie Jennings, McGraw's old teammate and now a Giant coach, entered the locker room.

He ordered the two Yankees out, and they sheepishly obeyed. When he reached the door, the Babe paused and turned back. "Listen, fellas," he said, "I'm sorry this happened. I don't mind being called a son of a bitch or a bastard, but from now on lay off that personal stuff!"

The final two games of the Series were played in miserable, rainy weather. By the time the fourth was over, the sky was a damned sight murkier than it had been when game two had been called. It was an especially gloomy day for the Yankees, as Hughie McQuillan beat Carl Mays, 4–3. The next day the Series came to a close as Art Nehf once again defeated Bullet Joe, this time by the score of 5–3.

Even for National League fans such as Alex and Harry the puny showing of the Yankees was a disappointment. Ruth had failed to produce, and the Yanks had fallen to pieces. The Babe got only two hits in the entire Series—a single and a double—and he wound up with a batting average of .118. The Little Napoleon explained the Bambino's poor showing this way: "I signaled for every ball that was pitched to Ruth. We pitched but nine curves and three fastballs to him throughout the Series. All the rest were slow balls. Of those twelve, eleven set the big fellow on his ear. He got just one foul off those twelve strikes. And usually we crossed him with the curve when there were men on bases."

Alex, out five hundred bucks, dashed off the following poem and sent it to *Baseball Magazine*:

HE HIT .118!

Lives of great guys
Oft remind us
That they sometimes
Fail their trust.
Ruth, for instance,
In the Series.
Holy Moses!
What a bust!

For John McGraw it was another sweet victory. After every game he had his cronies up to his suite at the Waldorf until the early hours of the morning. As Westbrook Pegler described the scene years later, each night, when the carousing was finally over, the Little Napoleon's guests would emerge from the suite "hurtling, bruised and disheveled, like bums out of a barrel house."

Such behavior had become commonplace during those early years of the Prohibition era. Indeed, the Yankees and Giants encouraged it by establishing a joint "press headquarters" on the mezzanine of the Commodore Hotel. All during the Series, mounds of food and cases of booze were there for the taking. Reporters, friends of the two clubs, and anyone else who could wangle an invitation addressed themselves to the liquor with, as Pegler remembered it, "that pathetic and unforgettable greediness of the time when every true American tried to drink his fill in the belief that the chance would never come again."

It was there, in front of the press bar at the Commodore, that the rift between Ruppert and Huston over Miller Huggins reached its critical point. Huston had quietly but grimly traveled to the Commodore after the final game of the Series.

Once at the bar, he quietly and grimly began to try to drink away the memory of the ignominious defeat. But the liquor only added to the pressure, and he finally exploded. Letting out a shriek, he cleared the bar top with a sweep of his arm. Stomping furiously among the broken glass and spilled drinks, Huston thundered, "Miller Huggins has managed his last Yankee ball game! He's through! Through! Through!"

But when reporters cornered Ruppert, he stood behind little Hug. "I will not fire a man who has just brought the Yankees two pennants," he stated firmly. The die was cast. Someone had to go. That someone would soon turn out to be Huston.

To Harry, always the statistician, the interesting thing about the 1922 Series was the way the number "3" kept repeating itself. The Giants won the first and third games by the score of 3–0. Game two was a 3–3 tie. In the fourth game, the Yankees scored three and lost. In the final game, the Giants scored three times in the eighth inning to win the game, while the Yankees again scored three runs in a losing cause. What did it all mean? Harry wasn't sure, but he spent most of the winter searching for hidden meanings in those unexplained recurrences of baseball's most significant number.

In 1923, Alex was destined once again to watch Uncle Robbie's flock flounder in the second division. Brooklyn fielded a ragged team that year and again finished in sixth place. But Alex saw hope for the future in the brilliant pitching of Dazzy Vance, a thirty-two-year-old castoff from the Yankees who had spent most of his career hurling for minor league clubs in Columbus, Toledo, Sacramento, and New Orleans.

During the 1921 season, Nap Rucker, on a scouting trip for Charlie Ebbetts, saw Dazzy pitch and reported back that the tall, rangy old-timer had a few good years left in him. Vance was famous around the league for his wildness, so Charlie wasn't all that interested. He was, however, eager to sign Hank DeBerry, a catcher on the New Orleans club. After some haggling, Ebbets agreed to take both players for $10,000.

Flatbush worked like a tonic on Dazzy. He pitched well in 1922 and 1923, winning eighteen games in each season while leading the league in strikeouts. By the end of the 1923 season, Robbie was boasting that the Dazzler had "more stuff than any other pitcher in the National League."

The Giants went into first place on opening day of 1923 and never left it, although they were given a run for their money by the Reds, a team with three twenty-game winners—Dolf Luque, Pete Donohue, and Eppa Rixey.

McGraw, with a much weaker mound staff, got his wins by yanking men out of the box at the drop of a hat, often using five or six hurlers in a single game. The Little Napoleon added two talented players to his roster that year. Travis Jackson, a young infielder called up from Little Rock, played superbly, filling in at short when Dave Bancroft was sidelined with pneumonia for part of the season. The other newcomer was Jack Bentley, a pitcher McGraw bought from Baltimore in the International League for $65,000. Bentley held out for a piece of the purchase price, reported late, and got off to a slow start. By the middle of the race he found his stride, and his 13–6 record contributed greatly to the pennant-winning cause.

McGraw also picked up an outfielder named Jimmy O'Connell from San Francisco in the Pacific Coast League. O'Connell was promising enough to warrant a whopping purchase price of $75,000, but he didn't measure up. By the end of the campaign he was spending most of his time on the bench.

McGraw was at the peak of his career. On his way to a third straight pennant, he was now widely recognized as the greatest manager in history. And yet, in New York, right on his own turf, he and his team were forced to share the spotlight with Ruth and the Yankees.

From the Polo Grounds McGraw could look across the Harlem River at the magnificent new ball park that Jacob Ruppert had built for the Babe. McGraw hated Yankee Stadium, standing there in all its majesty, looking down on the Giants' quaint old ball park. He persuaded Charles Stoneham to refurbish the Polo Grounds. Construction went on throughout the 1923 season, as the horseshoe grandstand was enlarged to form an oval that extended out to Eighth Avenue and surrounded most of the outfield.

To a large extent McGraw had himself to blame for the existence of Yankee Stadium. In 1920, after the Yanks had outdrawn the Giants by 100,000 on their way to becoming the first team ever to draw more than a million fans in one year, McGraw and Stoneham had decided that the Yankees were getting too big for their ball park.

After Stoneham had informed the two colonels by letter that he wanted them to leave, McGraw made a famous and fateful statement. "The Yankees," Muggsy said, "will have to build a park in Queens or some other out-of-the-way place. Let them go away and wither on the vine."

After inspecting a number of sites, Ruppert and Huston settled on a spot in the Bronx. The land, over which the Harlem River often meandered, was located between One Hundred Sixty-first Street and One Hundred Fifty-seventh Street and was bordered by River Avenue on the east and Doughty Street on the west. Best of all, it was hardly more than the distance of a Ruthian blast from the Polo Grounds.

After the colonels had purchased the ten-acre site from the estate of William Waldorf Astor for $600,000, Huston put his engineering skill and experience to work. Cap visited every major league park in the country and then worked out plans for the stadium with the architects of the White Construction Company. Work began in February 1922 and continued at a frenzied pace to ensure the stadium would be ready for opening day.

On April 18, 1923, a crowd of 74,200 fans, the largest ever to see a ball game, jammed into Yankee Stadium for its grand opening. More than twenty-five thousand were turned away at the gate. Celebrities dotted the crowd. John Philip Sousa himself led the 7th Regiment Band, and Governor Al Smith threw out the first ball to Wally Schang.

The umpire was Tommy Connolly, the same man who officiated the opening game at old Hilltop Park. Bob Shawkey, senior member of the pitching staff, threw the first official pitch, and Whitey Witt was the first Yankee to notch an official at bat. The Yanks made it an auspicious inauguration by beating the Red Sox 4–1, and the Babe baptized the park with a three-run homer in the third.

The Yankees of 1923 were awesome. The pitching staff, already strong, had been shored even more by the acquisition of Herb Pennock from, of course, the Red Sox in a preseason deal. Home Run Baker had retired in February, but Joe Dugan was a more than adequate replacement.

When the 1923 season was a month old, Jacob Ruppert announced that he had paid $1.5 million to Huston for Cap's share of the Yankee ownership. Ruppert sent a terse telegram to his team on the road:

I AM NOW SOLE OWNER OF THE YANKEES.
MILLER HUGGINS IS MY MANAGER.

At last little Hug was on firm ground.

With the Ruppert takeover, the Yankee's image began to jell. Had Huston bought out Ruppert, there's no telling what changes the jovial, shaggy engineer might have wrought, aside from immediately firing Miller Huggins. But it was Ruppert, the meticulous blueblood, who was in charge.

One of his first moves was to purchase two extra sets of uniforms. Ruppert wanted his players to win, but he wanted them to be clean and natty while doing so. The colonel would eventually introduce the Yankee pinstripes—chosen because they made the portly Ruth appear more svelte—and would mold the team into the image he preferred, that of dignified, well-bred businessmen, whose business was winning ball games.

The Yankees breezed through the 1923 season, clinching on September 20 and eventually winning by sixteen games over second-place Detroit. Ruth enjoyed what many called his best season ever, hitting forty-one homers to lead the league, batting .393, knocking in 130 runs, and setting a record that still stands by collecting 170 bases on balls.

The stage was set for the third straight Subway Series. On October 10, 1923, a record crowd for a World Series crammed into Yankee Stadium to see Waite Hoyt square off against Solemn John Watson of the Giants in what the *Times* called the greatest game ever played between championship teams. Among the fifty-eight thousand fans were Alex and Harry, both fervently hoping that McGraw would capture his third straight Series crown.

After Hoyt blanked the Giants in the first inning, the Yanks began to rough up Solemn John. Leadoff batter Whitey Witt lined out, but Joe Dugan followed with a walk. Ruth screamed a grounder to Heinie Groh at third. Groh, having trouble finding the handle, managed to nip Dugan at second, but Ruth was safe on a fielder's choice. The next batter was Bob Meusel, who ripped a double to center, scoring Ruth. Pipp's fly ended the inning, but the Yanks had a one-run lead.

The Giants nearly got something going in the second when Casey Stengel, playing with a bruised heel, hit a long fly down the right-field line. But Ruth snagged the ball as it was dropping into the corner to rob Stengel of extra bases.

When the Yanks came to bat in the second, Aaron Ward jumped on the first pitch of the inning and hammered it to left for a single. Wally Schang followed with a single to center. Deacon Scott's bunt along the first base line was hit a bit too hard, allowing first baseman George Kelly to make the putout unassisted, but both runners advanced on the sacrifice. After Hoyt fanned, little Whitey Witt popped one over second base, scoring Ward and Schang. The Yankees held a 3–0 lead.

In the Giant third, John McGraw, who refused to venture from the dugout throughout the Series, began to strut the stuff that had made him the acknowledged wizard of baseball. Kelly lined the first pitch to center for a single. After catcher Hank Gowdy walked, McGraw began his moves by sending in Freddie Maguire to run for Gowdy and Jack Bentley to bat for Watson, the pitcher.

Bentley looped a Texas Leaguer over second, but Kelly, who had waited to see whether the ball would be caught, had to stop at third. With the bases loaded, McGraw sent in Dinty Gearin to run for Bentley. At this point, a fan who was sitting in front of Alex and Harry and who'd been scribbling, erasing, and scribbling the changes furiously on his scorecard threw down his pencil. Jumping to his feet, he cupped his hands and shouted, "Hey, Muggsy! If you don't have any mercy on the Yanks, think of *us!*"

Dave Bancroft stepped in and hit a grounder to Scott, who threw to Ward at second, forcing Gearin but allowing Kelly to score the Giant's first run. With Maguire on third and Bancroft on first, an overconfident Hoyt ignored the stretch and went into a windup. Bancroft stole second.

Heinie Groh then sliced a liner down the right-field line that got past Ruth for a triple, scoring Maguire and Bancroft. A stonefaced Huggins pulled Hoyt and replaced him with Bush. Bullet Joe eventually put out the fire, but not before Frankie Frisch had singled home Groh to make the score Giants 4, Yankees 3.

The Giants' new battery, Rosy Ryan and Frank Snyder, coasted through the third, but in the fourth it looked as though the Yankees were about to rise again. Schang led off with a walk. After Scott struck out, Bush belted a double along the left-field line, Schang stopping at third. The next batter was Witt. Whitey looked at a couple and then hit a bouncer back to Ryan. The pitcher stabbed the ball, chased Schang partway back to third, and then threw to Groh who made the putout on Schang. Bush, meanwhile, had slid safely into third, and Witt was digging for second. Groh wheeled and fired to Frisch. The back of Frankie's glove was touching the bag as the ball popped into it. Witt was out by inches, and the inning was over.

In the fifth the Yanks threatened again. With one out, Ruth choked up on the bat and clipped one down the left-field line. The ball and the Babe arrived at third base simultaneously, and Ruth was safe with a triple. Meusel then blooped to short right. Youngs sprinted in from right, Frisch sprinted out from second. The Babe hesitated at third. Nearly everyone in the park could read his mind. If Youngs made the catch, Ruth was a dead duck. But if Frisch, his back to the infield, hauled it in, the play was the Babe's. At the last moment, Youngs veered off and Frisch made a spectacular leaping catch. The Babe thundered homeward. What Ruth couldn't see was that, as Frisch caught the ball, he whirled in midair and fired toward home. Frankie didn't get much on the ball, but he made up for the lack of zip with quickness of release and accuracy. On the second bounce the ball was in front of the plate, and a fraction of a second later Ruth was not only out but down, taking two bounces himself—one off big Frank Snyder and one off the ground.

But the Yankees would not be denied. In the seventh, with one out and Bush on first, Dugan ripped a triple to right center, scoring Bush and tying the game. Then the Babe stepped up. Alex and Harry exchanged glances of apprehension. Even though Ruth was choking up about three inches on the bat to counteract the bad pitches he was seeing, the Giants' infield, out of respect for his awesome power, still had to play back.

With only one out, it looked as though almost anything Ruth hit would score the go-ahead run. The Rice brothers' hearts sank as the ball met the bat and became a subliminal white streak heading toward right field. First baseman Kelly dived into the air and somehow, miraculously, knocked the ball down. He scrambled to his knees, found the ball, and hummed it to Snyder. Dugan was out by a step on what many experts, McGraw among them, called the best play they had ever seen in baseball.

The game went into the ninth inning still tied at 4–4. Youngs led off the inning and lined to Witt. Irish Meusel grounded out to Dugan. With two out, Casey Stengel stepped in. Ol' Case worked the count to three and two. On the next pitch, he hit the ball on a line to left center. It knifed between Witt and Meusel and rolled to the fence. Casey was off to the races. Witt retrieved the ball and flipped it to Meusel, owner of the strongest arm in baseball, who fired it toward the plate.

Casey slid into home and up on one knee in the same motion. He was already giving the crowd a "nothin' to it" wave with his right hand when the ball thudded into Schang's mitt. Here is how Damon Runyon described the play in the *New York American*:

> This is the way old Casey Stengel ran, running his home run home to a Giant victory by a score of 5 to 4 in the first game of the World's Series of 1923.
>
> This is the way old Casey Stengel ran, running his home run home when two were out in the ninth inning and the score was tied and the ball was bounding inside the Yankee yard.
>
> > This is the way—
> > His mouth wide open.
> > His warped old legs bending beneath
> >   him at every stride.
> > His arms flying back and forth like
> >   those of a man swimming with a
> >   crawl stroke.
> > His flanks heaving, his breath whistling,
> >   his head far back . . .
> > The warped old legs, twisted and bent
> >   by many a year of baseball campaigning,
> >   just barely held out under
> >   Casey Stengel until he reached the
> >   plate running his home run home.

Stengel himself explained that, if he was less than graceful rounding the bases, it was because of the rubber pad he was wearing to protect his bruised heel. "As I was making the turn at second base I had the feeling that this shoe with the heel pad was going to come off. So I commenced dragging the shoe, and everybody said afterward that I looked like an old man out there."

Casey, actually at the ripe old age of thirty-three, had just married and had not yet met his in-laws. Although no one really believed that anything could worry him, Casey claimed he was afraid that his new relatives would think their daughter had married a decrepit old derelict.

The crowd in Yankee Stadium for the opener had been equally divided between Giant and Yankee rooters, but the Polo Grounds crowd for the second game was openly pro-Giants. Everyone loved the Babe, however. As one sportswriter put it, "the cheers were 50 percent Giants, 50 percent Ruth." Babe earned his hurrahs by parking one over and another into the right-field stands as the Yanks downed the Giants, 4–2.

But the next day, back at Yankee Stadium, Art Nehf held the Yanks to just six hits in shutting them out, 1–0. The offensive hero of the day was once again Ol' Case, who homered into the right-field stands in the seventh inning for the only run of the game. Having taken more than his share of abuse from the Yank bench jockeys and fans, Stengel toured the bases with his thumb held to his nose, fingers wiggling. Casey's silent eloquence earned him applause from Giant rooters and a stern reprimand from Judge Landis.

In game four, played at the Polo Grounds, the Yankees slammed five pitchers to win, 8–4. "It was a rotten game for a good team to lose," was all McGraw could say.

With the Series tied at two games each, nearly sixty-three thousand fans, another all-time record, filled Yankee Stadium for the fifth game. Jumping Joe Dugan tied a Series record by getting four hits as he and the Yanks jumped all over four Giant pitchers and crushed the McGrawmen, 8–1. On the brink of defeat and with the glaring weakness in their hurling department exposed, the Giants pinned all their hopes on Art Nehf, the only Giant pitcher who had thus far been able to stand off the Yankee bats.

Harry and Alex, who had been among the estimated fifty thousand potential spectators turned away from Yankee Stadium the day before, had no trouble finding seats in the Polo Grounds for the sixth game. Many Giant fans had given up and stayed home. When Ruth began the festivities by spanking a homer his first time at bat, the Rice brothers began to wish that they too had stayed away.

But Nehf, with his great speed, side-breaking curve, and pinpoint control, quickly took charge of the Yankees. The Giants scored once in their half of the first and then rapped Herb Pennock for single runs in the fourth, fifth, and sixth innings. Going into the eighth, the Giants led, 4–1.

Nehf, seeming stronger with each inning, had allowed only two hits. The Yankee leadoff batter in the eighth, Aaron Ward, hit a weak fly to Kelly for the first out. The next batter, Wally Schang, dug in a little too near the plate to suit Nehf. The first pitch was high, hard, and very close to Schang's ear. As Wally scrambled to get out of the way, the ball hit the bat and bounded over third base for a single. Scott followed with a smash single past Kelly at first, Schang reaching third on the play.

Alex nudged Harry, who was studying his scorecard. "What's wrong with Nehf?" he asked. Harry squinted down at the figure on the mound. Sure enough, the man who moments before had been the master of all he surveyed had undergone a change. His face was ashen, his shoulders hunched. He even seemed smaller.

Freddy Hofman, pinch-hitting for Pennock, stepped into the batter's box. Nehf walked him on four straight pitches. Bullet Joe Bush batted for Witt. Nehf walked Bush as well, forcing in a run. McGraw, who evidently had been thinking that even a gutted Nehf was better than anything else available, changed his mind, pulled Nehf, and inserted Rosy Ryan. Ryan promptly walked Dugan on four pitches, forcing in another run.

The score was 4–3, one out, bases loaded, and the batter was Babe Ruth. Harry and Alex rose to their feet, along with the rest of the crowd.

The Babe stepped confidently into the box. And struck out. The roar of the crowd died suddenly as Bob Meusel strode to the plate. The Giants weren't out of the woods yet. Ryan curved the first pitch over for a called strike. Meusel swung on the second delivery and knocked the ball back through the box and into center field. Cunningham fielded the ball and fired to third. The ball took a bad bounce, skidded past Groh, and rolled to the grandstand. Hinkey Haines, running for Hofman, scored from third. Ernie Johnson, running for Bush, scored from second, and Dugan, doing his own legwork, scored from first. Meusel slid safely into third.

Sad Sam Jones came on for the Yankees in the eighth and had little trouble putting down the remainder of the Giant batters. With their 6–4 victory, the Yankees had at last become world champions. The Yankee Colossus had come of age.

John McGraw, his twenty-year ambition of winning three Series in a row thwarted, took defeat gracefully. "The best team won," he said. He went on to praise the gameness of his club and then ended on a melancholy note. "The old guard dies," the Little Napoleon admitted, "but it never surrenders."

At the start of the 1924 campaign, Alex said to his brother, "Well, Harry, this is destined to be Brooklyn's year. We won in '16 and again in '20. Every four years."

"Malarkey," Harry replied. "The Robins will be damn lucky to finish in the first division."

Logic was certainly not on Alex's side. And as the season began to unfold, neither was the playing of the Robins. From April to late August, while the Giants sailed along in first, Brooklyn stayed in the middle of the pack.

As usual, John McGraw had made a number of important changes in his roster. Over the winter, Casey Stengel and Dave Bancroft had been traded to Boston. Travis Jackson was now the regular shortstop, and on the bench were two players from the Toledo club who were destined to have bright futures with the Giants. One was an eighteen-year-old infielder named Fred Lindstrom. The other, Bill Terry, had been called up briefly the year before and then sent back to the minors for more seasoning. McGraw and Terry didn't care much for each other, but the Giant manager was well aware of Terry's talents and was grooming him to be his next first baseman.

The dislike the two men had for each other began the day they met. At the time Terry was out of professional baseball. He had quit the minors to take a job with Standard Oil in Memphis, but he was keeping in shape by playing for the plant team. On a tip from Tom Watkins, owner of the Memphis club, McGraw sent for Terry and offered him a

Giant contract. "Excuse me if I don't fall all over myself," Bill told the Little Napoleon, "but I'm not going to move to New York just to play for the Giants. If you want me, you'll have to make it worth my while." McGraw couldn't believe his ears. The nerve of this bushleaguer, threatening to pass up the chance of a lifetime. The two men parted without coming to an agreement, but a few weeks later Terry received from McGraw a contract offer that he couldn't turn down.

The Yanks, meanwhile, their championship team virtually intact, looked like surefire winners. As the season began, there were only two major changes. Earle Combs had come up from Louisville, where he had batted .380, and had replaced Witt in center. But Combs broke his leg after only eleven games, and Witt reclaimed his spot. The other change was one that would hurt the Yankees. The fiery Carl Mays had never pitched again for the Yankees after Ruppert became sole owner and gave Huggins free rein. During the off season, Mays was sold for the waiver price to Cincinnati, where he won twenty games to lead the Reds' staff.

The irrepressible Ruth had a great year on the field and a great time off it. In the course of making numerous public appearances, the Babe demonstrated a knack for incisive political thought and impeccable diplomacy when brought to bay by a serious young reporter. "Mister Ruth," the journalist inquired, "what do you think of the Chinese situation?"

"The hell with it," was the Babe's considered opinion.

Although the Yanks played good ball throughout the season, the Senators, led by aging Walter Johnson, stayed right with them. As the race came down to the wire, the Yanks pulled out all the stops, winning eighteen of twenty-two in September.

It wasn't enough, however, to overcome the white-hot Senators, who clinched on the next to last day of the season. Ruth led the league with forty-six homers and a .378 batting average. He also paced the league in hits, walks, runs scored, total bases, slugging percentage, and strikeouts. But the Yankees finished second, two games off the pace.

In the last week of August, the National League race suddenly got hot. Brooklyn moved up to challenge the Giants, and Alex, relishing the prospect of spoiling McGraw's bid for a record fourth straight pennant, told his brother, "We're gonna make it!"

Harry couldn't believe what was happening. It just didn't figure. But four of the Robins were having sensational seasons. Dazzy Vance was having the best year of his career; when the race was over he would have a record of 28–6, with a 2.16 ERA. Burleigh Grimes, still throwing those spitters, was compiling a 22–13 record.

Thirty-six-year-old Zack Wheat was batting .375, and Jack Fournier— a first baseman who had come to Brooklyn from the Cardinals the previous year—was on his way to hitting a league-leading twenty-seven homers while batting .334. Over the weekend of August 29, the Robins beat the Giants three straight.

On September 6, Brooklyn reached first place, but only for three hours—the Giants lost the first half of a doubleheader to the Phillies but came back to win the second game and regain the lead. The next day, before a wild crowd at Ebbets Field, Brooklyn played host to New York for a single game. Excitement was at such a fever pitch that the riot squad was called in to disperse the fans who had been locked out of the packed park and who repeatedly tried to storm the gates. Several hundred actually did gain admission by breaking down the gate in left field.

At the end of seven innings the score was tied, 3–3. In the top of the eighth, the Giants exploded for five runs. The Robins came back with a run in the eighth and three more in the ninth before finally succumbing to Hughie McQuillan, pitching in relief of Jack Bentley.

Nonetheless, Uncle Robbie stayed right on the Little Napoleon's tail, and when, on September 20, McGraw announced that injuries would keep both Groh and Frisch out of the lineup for the remainder of the season, Alex thought the Robins were in.

On Monday morning, September 22, the Giants' lead was down to a half game, and they were about to start a tough three-game series with the third-place Pirates. Somehow, even without two key members of the infield, New York managed to sweep the three-game set and pull one and a half games in front with only three games with Philadelphia left to play. McGraw's magic number was now two, and Brooklyn's hopes were just about dead. The Giants won their first game with the Phillies while the Robins lost to the Braves, and New York had clinched the pennant.

A few days later a strange incident came to light, an incident that marred McGraw's great season and spread a cloud of scandal over the World Series. Before the start of the pennant-clinching game with Philadelphia, Jimmy O'Connell had approached Heinie Sand, the Phillies' shortstop, and offered him $500 if he wouldn't "bear down too hard" that day. Sand immediately reported the attempted bribe to Art Fletcher, his manager, and it wasn't long before Judge Landis was investigating the matter. Under interrogation, O'Connell quickly admitted that he had indeed made the bribe offer.

"Who put you up to it?" the commissioner asked.

"Why, Cozy Dolan," O'Connell answered. "That was on Saturday morning before the game. He said the whole team would chip in to make up the $500. Frankie Frisch, Pep Youngs, and George Kelly all knew about it. When I told Pep what Dolan had said about the money, Youngs said, 'Go to it!' Then I told Frisch, and Frank said to me, 'Give Sand anything he wants.'"

Dolan was one of the Giant coaches, an old buddy of McGraw's who was disliked by most of the team. They referred to him as Muggsy's private detective, because they suspected him of tattling to McGraw whenever he saw a player breaking one of the club's rules. When he was brought before Landis to answer O'Connell's charges, all Dolan would say to the judge, over and over again, was "I can't remember. I can't remember."

Landis then interviewed Frisch, Youngs, and Kelly and came away satisfied that none of the three was involved in the plot. He expelled O'Connell and Dolan for life, then left for Washington to attend the opening game of the World Series. John Heydler, president of the National League, announced, "As far as I am concerned, I think the entire investigation is closed." But Ban Johnson, eager to get in a few good licks against his old enemies Landis and McGraw, accused the commissioner of failing to get to the bottom of the matter.

"I can't understand why these men did what they did," McGraw said, "when the chances were 100 to 1 that New York would win the pennant. The only explanation I can give is that they are a couple of saps. If you search the country over you probably couldn't find two bigger ones."

For several reasons, most Americans outside of New York City were pulling for the underdog Senators to win the 1924 World Series. For one thing, the stink of the Dolan-O'Connell affair had rubbed off on the rest of the Giant team. For another, New York had monopolized the Fall Classic for three seasons.

Here at last was a chance for another city to get into the act. And this wasn't just any city—it was the nation's capital, which had never been represented in the Series. And while the Little Napoleon was respected as much as he was despised around the leagues, the Senators had on their club two of the most popular men in the game. One was twenty-seven-year-old Bucky Harris, the manager and second baseman. The other was Walter Johnson, now almost at the end of his fabulous career. He had waited eighteen summers for a chance to pitch in the Series.

Johnson, nervous and not at his best, started the opening game against Art Nehf. After the regulation nine, the score was tied, 2–2, but the Giants finally scored twice in the top of the twelfth and won the game, 4–3. In game two, Tom Zachary of the Senators defeated Jack Bentley, and once again the final score was 4–3. The teams continued to alternate victories, with Johnson losing again in the fifth game, until each side had three wins.

Through the first six games, one of Bucky Harris's biggest problems had been trying to contain Bill Terry, who had gone six for twelve against the Senators' right-handers. As part of a strategy to force McGraw to remove Terry from the lineup, Harris named Curly Ogden, a mediocre right-hander, as the starting pitcher of the seventh and deciding game, played in Griffith Stadium in Washington.

McGraw went with Virgil Barnes, who had been with the Giants for five years but had always pitched in the shadow of his brother, Jesse. Jesse had been traded to the Braves the previous year, and now it was Virgil's turn in the spotlight.

"What the hell is going on? Why is Harris starting Ogden?" Alex asked Harry. They were at the 104th Field Artillery Armory at Broadway and Sixty-eighth Street in Manhattan. Two thousand fans, including the banished Jimmy O'Connell and his wife, were on hand to follow the action on a large scoreboard constructed especially for the Series.

"You watch," Harry replied. "Before the inning is over, Ogden will be out of there."

Sure enough, after striking out Lindstrom and walking Frisch, Ogden left the game in favor of George Mogridge, a southpaw. In the sixth inning, with the Giants down, 1–0, on a homer by Bucky Harris, McGraw finally pulled Terry out of the game and sent Irish Meusel to bat in his place.

Harris immediately replaced Mogridge with right-handed Firpo Marberry. With men on first and third, Meusel lifted a sacrifice fly that tied the game. For the time being, Harris's strategy had backfired. The Giants scored two more runs on errors by Joe Judge at first and Ossie Bluege at short. New York was now ahead, 3–1. But Alex and Harry were thinking about the old Giant jinx, and in the bottom of the eighth inning it appeared.

With one out, Nemo Liebold, batting for Tommy Taylor, doubled. Then Muddy Ruel, the Senator's catcher, singled for his first hit of the Series. All at once the tying runs were on base. Bennie Tate, pinch-hitting for Marberry, followed with a walk to load the bases. After Mule Shirley came in to run for Tate, Earl McNeely hit a short fly to Irish Meusel.

The runners held, and now there were two out. Bucky Harris was the next batter. He drilled a sharp single over Freddie Lindstrom's head to tie up the game, and the Washington crowd went crazy. The delirious fans threw confetti, newspapers, and even hats and coats onto the field. One observer remarked that the outfield "looked like the first snow of winter." It took several minutes for the commotion to subside. Then McGraw sent in Art Nehf to put out the fire.

In the top of the ninth Harris called on Walter Johnson to come in and win the ball game. Johnson managed, by the skin of his teeth, to hold the Giants scoreless for four innings. Then, in the bottom of the twelfth, with Bentley now on the mound for New York, the Senators got something started.

With one out, Muddy Ruel popped a high foul in back of the plate. Hank Gowdy, the Giant catcher, threw off his mask. As he followed the ball with his eyes, he tripped over the mask, fell, and muffed the play. Ruel took advantage of his new lease on life by ripping a double down the left-field line.

Walter Johnson came to bat and hit an easy grounder to Travis Jackson at short. Jackson fumbled, and Johnson was safe at first. Instead of the inning's being over, the Senators had two baserunners, one in scoring position, and only one out. Earl McNeely then came to the plate and hit what looked like a simple grounder to Lindstrom at third. The Giant third baseman stood poised to make the play for out number two, when suddenly the ball took a freak hop and sailed over his head, allowing Ruel to dash home with the winning run.

For the overjoyed hometown fans, the Senators' sudden victory was like a miracle; for John McGraw, it was yet another lesson in baseball's unpredictability.

As the Rice brothers left the armory, Harry suddenly realized he wasn't all that unhappy that the Giants had gone down to defeat. Perhaps it was the recent scandal. Maybe he had been affected by the widespread sympathy for Walter Johnson and the Senators. Or perhaps he was just plain tired of John McGraw. Whatever the reason, he turned to his brother and said, "Starting next year, Alex, I'm going to pull for the Yankees."

And one can relish the varied idiocy of
human action during a panic to the full,
for while it is a time of great tragedy,
nothing is being lost but money.

John Kenneth Galbraith,
The Great Crash

But ball teams are like human beings.
They are born, live and die. Time takes
care of all things.

Ed Barrow, *My Fifty Years in Baseball*

6

In early April 1925 Charlie Ebbets, suffering more than usual from a
heart condition that had bothered him for many years, left the Robins'
spring training camp in Clearwater and returned to New York, to be
confined to his suite at the Waldorf Astoria. Early in the morning of
April 18, he fell into a deep sleep, awoke briefly, and then died.

The funeral was held two days later at Trinity Church in Brooklyn.
It was a cold, rainy day, but that didn't stop thousands from swarming
into the streets around the church to pay their last respects to the man
who had done so much for their borough. Before heading to Greenwood Cemetery, the cortege drove past Ebbets Field and the site of
Washington Park.

For Alex it was a sad day indeed. He watched the funeral procession
from in front of the Ebbets Field rotunda and then retired to a nearby
speakeasy to brood and drink. On the wall behind the bar was a black
wreath, and just below the wreath the bartender had tacked a clipping
from that day's *Brooklyn Eagle*: "It cannot be denied that the Spaldings,
Reaches, Wrights, William A. Hulbert, and others of the 1876 period,
when the National League was formed, had a rare vision, but we venture
to say that Ebbets saw even further ahead than they did."

Ed McKeever was named the new president of the club. While at the
funeral, however, he caught a bad cold that developed into influenza.
On April 29, he too passed away. A month later the stockholders, evenly
divided between the Ebbets heirs and the McKeever interests, elected
Wilbert Robinson president. Robinson was a compromise choice, and it
was clearly understood that along with his new duties he would continue

to run the team. Shortly after his election, Robbie named Zack Wheat the club's assistant manager.

The Rice family also had a death that spring. In May, after being laid up in bed for the better part of a year, Elizabeth passed away. Her death severed Harry's and Alex's last link to their father and the past.

As for the future, it was beginning to appear that Fletcher's tree would wither and die. Harry was now thirty-six years old. He and Ellen had been married for more than ten years and were still childless. Alex was thirty-two and as yet showed no inclination to settle down. The women in his life were either casual girlfriends or Broadway one-night stands. As far as anyone who knew Alex could tell, he had never been involved in a serious love affair.

On a hot Sunday morning in July, Whitey O'Day telephoned Alex to invite him to spend a day at Coney Island. Alex thought it was a splendid idea. He hopped right on the subway and in less than an hour met his friend at the Washington Baths.

As it happened, Whitey had not come alone. He had brought along a young woman named Sally Friarson. Alex's first impression of her was that she was a bit stuck on herself. She was cute all right, but nothing out of the ordinary. However, when she suddenly produced a picnic basket filled with all sorts of sandwiches and fresh fruit, he began to think a little better of her. In any case, Alex's opinion of Sally didn't matter much. It was obvious that Whitey was completely taken with her.

The three spent the early part of the afternoon on the beach. After polishing off Sally's lunch, they sunned themselves for an hour or so, and then they played awhile in the surf. Sally suggested they get dressed and take in some of the rides at Steeplechase Park. Whitey was less than keen on the idea, but it didn't take her long to win him over.

When Sally emerged from the bath house, Alex saw at once that her appearance could hardly be called ordinary. She was a very striking woman. Though not particularly tall, she was slender enough to wear gracefully the waistless fashions of the day. Her auburn hair was shingled, her dress came to just below her knees, and she wore a touch of rouge.

Whether or not she could be called a flapper was hard to say. She still resisted the temptation to take up drinking or smoking, and she did not roll her flesh-colored silk stockings down below her kneecaps. And yet there was something about her that told Alex she had an adventurous spirit. He wondered how old she was. Twenty-two, maybe twenty-three. But certainly no more than twenty-five, he decided.

It turned out that Whitey was frightened to death of the rides, so it fell upon Alex to take Sally on such attractions as the Steeplechase horses, the giant slide, and the Human Pool Table. Whitey and Alex stood on the sidelines as Sally got in line to ride the Whirlpool, a whirling concave disk of polished wood with a large hump in its center.

Women and men were not permitted to go on this contraption together. The ticket taker announced the next turn for ladies only. Alex watched with great interest as Sally and the other fearless girls walked over a gangplank and sat on the hump. The gangplank was raised away, and very slowly the disk began to spin. As it picked up speed, centrifugal force sucked the lasses one by one into the wooden maelstrom. Sally was the last to go, and she was pulled into the lap of a rather plump young girl whose boyfriend, a sailor standing next to Whitey, burst into applause and wild laughter.

It was hard for a young man not to be impressed by the sight of all those young women of different shapes and sizes all tangled together, their arms and legs spread out in every direction.

Turning away from the dizzying scene, Whitey asked Alex, "How can she do it? It makes me sick just looking at that thing."

The Whirlpool slowed and came to a stop. Sally bounced down the steps and joined her two escorts.

"How do you feel?" Alex asked.

"Fine," she replied. "Why don't we go have some supper?"

They walked down the Boardwalk to Feltman's Garden, where they feasted on steamed clams and hot dogs. After supper they took a stroll along the Bowery—Coney's tawdry midway. It was a street filled with penny arcades, weight guessers, chambers of horrors, fortune tellers, shooting galleries, games of chance, gravity rides, and shadowy doorways that led into smoke-filled speakeasies.

The air was ripe with every smell imaginable, from Shetland ponies' dung to dimestore perfume. Alex and his friends were ballyed into the crowds in front of several grind shows, but none of the talkers' spiels could entice them to part with their money to find out what was happening on the inside.

Sally thought it all very exciting, but Alex was less enchanted with the scene. He remembered another Coney Island—a glittering resort with elegant hotels such as the Oriental and the Brighton Beach, not to mention three racetracks to which America's finest stables brought their horses. Alex thought of his father. How miserable Fletcher would be if he could see what had become of Brooklyn's showplace. The coming of the subway had opened Coney Island to the masses. It wasn't surprising, but it was still a shame that the place was now pandering to such common tastes.

Whitey wanted to take Sally dancing. Alex saw he was in danger of wearing out his welcome, so he thanked his friends for a lovely day and headed home. The subway ride was very disturbing. He couldn't get Sally out of his mind. She was pretty, she was bright, and she had taste. Above all, she knew how to have a good time. Why in God's name, he asked himself with no small amount of self-pity, did she have to be his best friend's girl?

While Eros was tinkering with Alex's peace of mind, the baseball gods were being equally unkind to brother Harry. His newly adopted team, the Yankees, began and ended the year disastrously. The first setback occurred in early April as the team was making its way northward.

Stepping from a train, Babe Ruth collapsed onto the marble floor of a North Carolina train depot, victim of "the bellyache heard round the world." It has since been conjectured that the Babe's ache was centered somewhat lower than his belly and that penicillin—had it existed—was a more accurate prescription than bicarbonate of soda. Even though the thousands of followers of Freud, Jung, Adler, and Watson, the prophets of the newly popular science of psychology, dutifully parroted the themes that inhibitions were the root of all evil and *sin* was an outdated term, lingering Victorianism may have converted a case of the clap into stomach trouble.

Whatever the Babe's ailment, he was a very sick man. When he emerged from St. Vincent's Hospital in New York after a stay of nearly a month, he had shed thirty pounds. It required nearly another full month of convalescence before he could return to the Yankees.

During Ruth's absence, veteran shortstop Everett "Deacon" Scott was benched in favor of Pee Wee Wanninger, a good-field, no-hit youngster. Back on May 2, 1923, Secretary of the Treasury Edwin Denby had presented the Deacon with a gold medal in recognition of his having appeared in 1,000 consecutive baseball games. To many, Scott's award signaled not only a great achievement, but the end of an era. Certainly no modern player would ever be tough enough, determined enough, even to threaten Scott's mark.

Besides Wanninger there was another new face in the Yankee dugout. Lou Gehrig had secretly signed with the Yanks in 1923 while still playing for Columbia University and had spent two years in the minors. On May 31, about three weeks after Scott, his streak extended to 1,307 games, went to the bench, Huggins called on Gehrig to pinch-hit for Wanninger in the eighth inning of a game against the Senators.

The next day, the day that Ruth made his triumphant return, first baseman Wally Pipp told Huggins he wanted to sit down. Pipp had been skulled during batting practice several days earlier and was bothered by recurring headaches. So the big guy from Columbia, the kid who in 1924 had searched New Orleans in vain for a soda jerk job to support himself during spring training, started at first.

But the crowd's attention was on the recovered Ruth, who narrowly missed a home run, smacked a single, and made a spectacular catch. Though he hit a double and a single, the powerful but somewhat clumsy youngster at first was barely noticed. Nobody dreamed that Columbia Lou, soon to be known as the Iron Horse, had just taken his second step on the road to nearly doubling Scott's consecutive game record.

Earle Combs had returned sporting two good legs, and a short time later Whitey Witt, along with the Deacon, was released.

Despite the presence of two new sluggers, Gehrig and Combs, the Yankee offense sputtered. Ruth was having a terrible year and had become even more belligerent in his dealings with Miller Huggins. In a game in Chicago, with two on and none out in the first inning, Hug flashed the hit sign to Ruth. The Babe bunted.

In the ninth inning, with one out and two on, the Yanks were trailing by a run. Huggins called for a sacrifice, but Ruth swung away and hit into a double play, ending the game. Huggins might have been able to live with Ruth's insubordination, but there was more.

According to Huggins, the Babe "refused to get in shape and insisted on breaking training rules. It hurt me to see him wasting his opportunity. I had envied big fellows all my life, and had nursed my strength like a miser, and here was a hitting marvel, still half-sick, but throwing youth and strength in all directions."

Finally Ruth pushed Hug too far. From St. Louis, Huggins put in a call to Ed Barrow. "I'm going to fine the big fellow," Hug told him. "I'm going to fine him five thousand dollars and I don't want the colonel to back down on it." Barrow assured him that Ruppert would back him to the hilt.

On August 29, 1925, every newspaper in the country carried the story. Huggins had not only fined Ruth $5,000, he had suspended the Babe indefinitely. Ruth was furious, but Ruppert was as good as Barrow's word and stood behind the manager.

After a week or so Ruth apologized to Huggins and begged to be allowed to play. According to Huggins, "I treated him like dirt." Eventually, however, Huggins broke down and reinstated Ruth. The Babe finished the season in a blaze, but it wasn't enough to help the faltering Yankees, who finished in seventh place, a woeful twenty-eight and a half games behind the pennant-winning Washington Senators.

In their postseason autopsies, many journalists reckoned that Ruth was through, over the hill. After all, the Sultan of Swat was nearly thirty-two, and it was no secret that he had packed a lot of living into those years. Despairing over the fallen Yankees and the possible end of the Ruthian era, few persons noticed that during the season Ed Barrow had purchased two players who would leave their marks on New York baseball—Tony Lazzeri and Leo Durocher.

For a brief moment during the last half of the 1925 baseball season it began to appear as if John McGraw might just win his fifth pennant in a row. Earlier in the campaign, illness had put the Little Napoleon out of action, but he recovered in plenty of time to lead his club down the homestretch.

At the start of August, after spending all of July in second place, the Giants grabbed the lead from the Pirates. Harry was briefly tempted to give up on the hapless Yanks, but when the Giants quickly dropped back into second he resolved to stick with the American League. Pittsburgh never again relinquished the lead and went on to capture the flag by eight and a half games.

"Say," Alex remarked to Harry, "your rooting for the Yankees had a wonderful effect on them. Do me a favor. Next year root for Pittsburgh as well."

The Giants had proved they were still a power in the circuit, but the Robins, who looked good on paper, fell completely apart that year. Dazzy Vance came up with another excellent season, winding up with a record of 22–9, and Zack Wheat batted a sizzling .359.

Still, the club did not win ball games. A large part of the problem was the ineffective pitching of Grimes. Burleigh was the losingest pitcher in the league; his spitter stopped playing tricks on the batters; he wound up with an 11–19 record.

In the early months of the campaign, Wilbert Robinson had stayed away from the bench, allowing Zack Wheat to run the team. But in midseason, when Robbie suddenly reappeared in the dugout, many fans saw it as a sign that he was dissatisfied with Wheat's performance.

Robbie quickly explained that he alone was the manager of the team. His only reason for having been temporarily away from the bench was to concentrate on learning his new duties as president. Whatever the reasons for his absence, his return did not help the club. It was a sad year indeed for Uncle Robbie, who had figured at the start of the season that he had a good shot at the pennant.

That summer, for the first time since his return from France, Alex found his mind drifting from the daily happenings of the baseball season. Other things were occupying his thoughts.

There was, for example, the Scopes trial, which took place in July 1925. Alex had always loved a circus, so it wasn't surprising that he followed closely each new development in the historic confrontation between Clarence Darrow and William Jennings Bryan. By the time the trial was over the Robins were in third place, eight and a half games back and fading.

It wasn't until the start of the World Series between the Pirates and the Senators that Alex's interest in baseball perked up again. But just as the Series got under way, the baseball world was shocked and saddened by the death of Christy Mathewson. Matty had been fighting a long battle against tuberculosis and was thought to be on the road to recovery.

Suddenly his weakened body was attacked by pneumonia. On October 7 he died without warning. He was forty-five years old.

The big question in the 1925 World Series was whether Walter Johnson could once again save the day for the Senators. As in 1924, it took seven games to reach a decision. Johnson was the winning pitcher in two of Washington's three victories, so Bucky Harris had good reason to send the old master in to pitch the final game. Pitching in a steady downpour and working from a mound that was so muddy it provided almost no footing, Johnson managed to hold the Bucs at bay for seven innings.

But in the seventh, Kiki Cuyler broke the game wide open by doubling for the Pirates with the bases loaded, and Pittsburgh won, 9–7. Both Harry and Alex had been pulling for old Walter to repeat his stellar performance of the year before, but it was not to be. Without knowing whether it was Matty's death or Johnson's downfall that jogged his memory, Alex found himself silently reciting these lines from a poem memorized in the distant past:

> Now you will not swell the rout
> Of lads that wore their honours out,
> Runners whom renown outran
> And the name died before the man.

At the Actors Club, Whitey and Alex divided the day into two shifts. The first began at noon and ended at eight; the second ran from eight to closing, usually around three in the morning. On a Friday afternoon a few weeks after the Series, Alex was at the Astor Theater watching Lon Chaney in *The Phantom of the Opera* while Whitey was working the day shift at the club. There were only a few customers in the place when the downstairs buzzer signaled that someone was on the way up. When Whitey went to the entrance shaft and peered down, he saw a man with an enormous block of ice on his shoulder slowly making his way up the ladder.

"What's going on?" Whitey called down.

"Ice delivery," answered the man, sweating profusely and stopping to rest on every rung.

"We got ice this morning."

"I know," the man grunted. "Your boss just called me up. Big party here tonight. At least fifty guests."

"All right, come on up."

"Where do you want it?" the iceman gasped as he finally reached the top of the ladder. Whitey pointed to the swinging door in the back that led to the kitchen. A minute later, the iceman came out of the kitchen, sat at the bar, and ordered a shot of whisky. "How much?" he asked.

"Fifty cents," Whitey answered. Whitey turned his back to ring up the sale on the cash register.

"Well, here it goes!" the iceman said. But instead of drinking the whisky, he poured it into his pencil pocket, where it entered a funnel and flowed down a tube into a small bottle hidden in his jacket lining. Then he lit up a cigar, which he sat puffing.

"Have another?" Whitey asked, turning back.

"No thanks," the iceman replied. He tapped the ash from his cigar and looked at Whitey. "My boy," he said, "I'm afraid I've got a little bad news for you."

"Oh, what's that?"

"You're under arrest."

Whitey had been snookered by Izzy Epstein, dry agent *par excellence*.

By the time Alex arrived for work, the door in the garage that led to the club had been padlocked. Above the padlock was a sign announcing that the premises had been raided.

"Son of a bitch," Alex said out loud, the words echoing back at him from the walls of the empty garage. But as he began to think the situation over, he realized that things weren't all that terrible. Up to now, he and Whitey had been damned lucky. After all, the place had escaped being raided for five years. And there were now so many speakeasies in New York that they would have no trouble at all finding new jobs.

"Hello, Alex." Startled, Alex wheeled quickly and discovered Sally, wearing evening clothes and a warm smile.

"Hello, Sally. Hey, you look terrific. I'm afraid the club has been raided."

"So I see. I was supposed to meet Whitey after work. Where do you think he is?"

"Probably in the hoosegow. Do you want me to call the precinct house?"

"Would you? I'd certainly appreciate it."

Alex went to a pay phone in a corner of the garage, made the call, and came back over to her. "They didn't hold him," he reported. "He's probably gone over to your place to pick you up. You must have just missed him."

"Oh, for crying out loud. I was looking forward to having fun tonight. Now I'll have to trudge all the way back over to Brooklyn."

"Why don't you call your roommate and leave a message for Whitey to meet you somewhere? I'll take care of you till he arrives."

"That's a great idea. Where shall we go?"

"How about the Epicure?"

"That sounds perfect," Sally replied, moving toward the phone booth.

It was only a short cab ride to the Epicure, a posh speak in the Fifties, just across Fifth Avenue. The trip was, however, long enough to give Alex a chance to find out more about the stunning young woman who had fallen so suddenly into his clutches.

She was just twenty-three and had been in New York for about a year.

Her hometown was Washington, Pennsylvania, where she had entered the world, gone to grammar and high school, and then taken a job as a sales clerk in her father's dry goods store. A few years later, a young doctor had moved to town.

Although he was neither handsome nor charming, most of the young women in those parts cast longing eyes upon him. He began casting around too, and he soon singled out Sally as the girl for him. After a suitable courtship he asked her to marry him. At first she was somewhat taken with the idea, but when the talk inevitably came around to actually setting a date she began to get cold feet. One balmy autumn afternoon in 1924, she packed her bag, strolled down to the depot, and boarded a train for New York. When she arrived, she moved in with an old high school girlfriend who lived in Brooklyn Heights.

Sally quickly found a job in the millinery department of Loeser's, a department store in downtown Brooklyn. Her friend happened to be secretary to a lawyer in the same building on Court Street where Harry's office was located.

The Epicure was bigger, snootier, and a lot more fun than the Actors Club. In the foyer Sally and Alex were greeted by a school of goldfish bubbling their way through the rocks and weeds of an enormous aquarium. The decor included thick red carpets and palm trees set in real silver pots. Upstairs was a mahogany-paneled bar where serious drinkers could indulge themselves in comparative solitude. On this particular evening, Alex decided to remain on the main floor. He and Sally were seated by the captain in the largest of the three dining rooms, where they could watch and listen as the Negro orchestra knocked out tunes in stop-time while the couples on the dance floor embraced in what Sally laughingly called a "tomcat crouch." Even though Alex was now out of work, he treated his guest and himself to sirloin steaks and genuine French champagne.

Whitey never showed. After dinner Alex cautiously invited Sally to dance. She accepted without hesitation, and as each tune blended into the next he found that her body was becoming more and more attuned to his. The people around them seemed to float out of their way as they moved around the dance floor.

She held onto him with particular firmness, never missing a step, following his uncertain foxtrot with assurance and poise. He begged the evening not to end. The clock responded by ticking away at a furious pace. Before either was aware of it, it was three in the morning, time for all good Epicureans to call it a night.

The late hour prompted Alex to offer to take Sally home in a cab. She gratefully accepted. As the car sped downtown and across Brooklyn Bridge, he panicked. What should he do now? If he didn't speak up, if he didn't make an overture, he might lose her forever.

But suppose she thought him a cad for trying to horn in on his best friend? Still, he had to say something. Friendship didn't matter any more. All that mattered was Sally.

"How much do you care about Whitey?" he finally blurted out as the cab rumbled up Pierrepont Street and came to a stop at her front door.

"Quite a lot," she answered. His heart dropped like a brick falling off the back of a truck.

"Do you want to marry him?"

"I hadn't thought about it," she answered with a smile that betrayed her fib.

"In that case you're still free to play the field?"

"I suppose so."

"Well, then, ah, how about playing the field with me?"

"I'd love to," she said, and then she planted a decisive kiss squarely on his astonished lips.

Alex's happiness was marred only by the twinge of guilt he felt every time he thought about Whitey. After several dates, Sally broke the news to Whitey that someone else had entered her life.

It didn't take him long to figure out who that someone was. But the doors of the Actors Club had been closed for good, so Alex and Whitey had no trouble avoiding the embarrassment of running into each other. As it turned out, Alex never laid eyes on his former friend again.

That fall, while Alex was busy courting Sally, his brother's head was often buried in the financial pages of the daily newspapers. The market was beginning to take off, and Harry was eager to learn as much as possible about the impending boom. On Sunday, November 15, 1925, the *New York Times* reported, "For the first time in six years the attention of the whole community has been directed to a speculative craze of immense proportions on Wall Street, with what the stock exchange calls the 'outside public' visibly and on the largest scale infected by the speculative mania."

Harry tried to persuade Alex to take a job with a brokerage house. He argued that it was about time Alex found himself a legitimate position. Where better to look for work than on Wall Street, where there were more opportunities than people?

But Alex was happy tending bar, even with all the risks. He soon found a job working the graveyard shift at a speakeasy in the Fifties called the Dizzy Club. It was a rather pleasant place, even though the owner, a former cop named Lou, had plastered the walls with corny slogans such as "KEEP YOUR TEMPER, WE DON'T WANT IT"; "THE GIRL YOU BRING IN IS THE GIRL YOU'LL TAKE OUT"; and "A ROLLING TOMATO GATHERS NO MAYONNAISE."

Alex's first night on the job was marred by a minor riot that came about when a group of raccoon-coated Princeton men became drunk and obnoxious and were summarily decked by Al the bouncer. Al, a strapping coffee-colored man who claimed to be a Hindu and absolutely not a Negro, whomped the sorry collegians into the floorboards and then threw them out onto the pavement. Most nights, though, the Dizzy Club was a pleasant, easy place to work. In time it would become one of the most venerable of New York's speakeasies.

On Christmas Eve that year, Sally and Alex arrived at the front door of Sam and Mae Friarson's comfortable house in Washington, Pennsylvania. They rang the bell and waited anxiously as Sam, robust and cheerful at the peak of his middle years, came to the door. He stood speechless, staring at his daughter and the strange young man, their arms filled with gaily wrapped presents.

"Well, Daddy, aren't you going to ask us in? It's cold out here. Besides, I want you to meet your new son-in-law."

And so, at last, there was again hope that Fletcher's tree would grow a new branch.

For five years Alex had been living on and off in Manhattan, most recently in a tiny flat in Greenwich Village. When he and Sally returned from Pennsylvania after New Year's, they moved into the family house in Park Slope. They took the apartment that Fletcher had given to Harry and his bride so many years before.

For some time now, Harry and Ellen had lived downstairs, sleeping in the master bedroom. They were delighted to share the house with the newlyweds. Sally and Ellen quickly became good friends, and Harry and Alex drew closer than at any time since before the World War. They were indeed one happy family. In later years Alex would look back on those early days of his marriage as by far the best time in his life.

At the start of the 1926 season Alex had almost no confidence in his team. Key players were getting old, with stars such as Wheat, Fournier, Vance, and Grimes all well into their thirties. Uncle Robbie picked up one more veteran that spring when he purchased Rabbit Maranville from the Cubs on waivers. Alex thought it was totally senseless to add still another old-timer.

In the early going of the campaign, two players kept the club alive— Jesse Petty, the only southpaw on the pitching staff, and Babe Herman, a newcomer from the Pacific Coast League. Herman played both in the outfield and at first base, where he filled in for Fournier, who sprained his ankle early in the season.

Babe quickly surprised Uncle Robbie and the fans with his remarkable ability to hit major league pitching. A left-handed batter, he sprayed hits to all fields and did almost as well against southpaws as against righties. Two months into the season his .362 average was third in the league behind Kiki Cuyler's .367 and Pie Traynor's .364. Babe would finish the year farther down in the pack, but even his .319 final average made him one of the Robins' big finds of recent years.

Ironically, Uncle Robbie had acquired Herman not to make him part of the team but to complete a deal with the Minneapolis club for an infielder named Johnny Butler. Seattle had originally offered Babe to the Reds for $7,500; when Cincinnati's acceptance telegram went astray, Brooklyn's bid was accepted, and Robbie sent Herman to Minneapolis. But Mike Kelley, the Minneapolis owner, refused to take him, so he wound up in Brooklyn, where he became a legend. It was in 1926 that the Daffy Dodgers—also known as the Daffiness Boys—were born. Babe Herman was the daffiest of them all, with Uncle Robbie a close second.

Why did the Dodgers become known as the Daffiness Boys? Because they were the zaniest, most unpredictable, most gremlin-infested team in the history of baseball. They dreamed up new ways how not to play the game. In a few years they would be firmly established as the laughingstock of baseball.

It is difficult to pinpoint the exact time when the team became the Daffy Dodgers. Perhaps it was when Uncle Robbie made a fool of himself by starting a pointless, self-destructive feud with the *New York Sun*. On Saturday, June 5, 1926, a cartoon with the heading "VALUABLE ROBINS" appeared in the sports pages of the *Sun*. It had sketches of four Brooklyn stars, with the caption: "Wheat is paid $16,000 a year; Fournier draws down $15,000; Vance gets over $15,800; Grimes, $15,000." Dominating the cartoon was a likeness of Jesse Petty. In an adjoining column, the cartoonist, Feg Murray, explained that "Petty became the 'first Robin of spring' by pitching a one-hit shutout against the Giants on opening day. So far this year his speed, curves, and control have been worth far more to the club than Vance's, yet you'll not notice Jess's name included among the quartet who draw the big salaries. Next year he probably won't overlook such a petty detail."

Murray had a valid point. Vance had managed to win his first game of the season only the day before, and Grimes was struggling along with a record of three and four. But when Wilbert Robinson read the *Sun* that evening he blew a gasket and lost a few screws in the process. He was certain Joe Vila had put Murray up to drawing the cartoon. Robbie believed Vila was trying to spite him by demoralizing the team's most successful hurler. For two days the Brooklyn manager fumed and fussed. Finally he called Vila's boss, Keats Speed, the *Sun*'s managing editor. When Speed picked up the phone he was stunned and nearly deafened by a barrage of profanities and accusations.

"Calm down, Wilbert," Speed said when he finally got the gist of the complaint. "The cartoon wasn't all *that* bad. Maybe it'll help get Vance and Grimes back on the right track."

But Robbie could not be appeased. He screamed, "Maybe you bastards would like to know the bat boy's salary!" At that point, Speed hung up. Two days later, at the bottom of page one of the *Sun*, the following headline appeared:

DONOHUE FACES DAZZY
VANCE IN BOX
Reds and Dodgers Start
Series in Brooklyn

To a fan of today, that headline wouldn't have much significance. But it signaled an important change of policy for the *Sun*. Every newspaper in New York referred to the Brooklyn team as the Robins, but now one of the most influential papers in town had gone back to "Dodgers"—the old name that was occasionally used by veteran scribes to break up the monotony of writing "Robins" too often in the same story. On the sports pages of that issue of the *Sun* came the real zinger, a boxed item:

> The Bat Boy's Salary
> Wilbert Robinson of the Brooklyn baseball club called up THE SUN Monday to protest violently because this paper correctly printed the salaries paid to several Brooklyn players. He said maybe the salary of the bat boy would interest the public.
> THE SUN doesn't care what Robinson earns.
> S.

Never again during Uncle Robbie's tenure as manager would the *Sun* refer to Wilbert Robinson by name. He became the anonymous "manager of the Dodgers." Robbie's battle with Vila and Speed turned out to be the beginning of his demise. It sparked a bitter feud with old Steve McKeever, who thought Robbie had behaved like an ass; it damaged the club's relations with the press; and it hurt Robbie's standing with many fans. One could certainly make the case that the Brooklyn manager was losing his marbles. If there were any doubts that daffiness was invading Ebbets Field, fate was waiting in the wings to dispel them.

Alex and Harry happened to be at Ebbets Field on August 5, 1926. That afternoon Zack Wheat hit the ball out of the park, pulled a muscle rounding first, staggered into second, and sat down on the bag. After five minutes, Rabbit Maranville went out to run for Wheat, but Zack finally managed to get up and limp home.

"How would you have scored that if Maranville had gone in?" Harry asked his brother.

"It's still a homer," Alex replied.

"Oh, yeah? How could that be if Wheat didn't actually score the run?"

"Well, then, it's a double, with a run batted in."

"But the ball went out of the park on a fly."

"I give up."

"The scorers were mighty lucky they didn't have to dope that one out," Harry remarked. "Damnedest thing I ever saw." Ten days later he would have to eat those words.

On Sunday, August 15, the Braves were in Brooklyn for a double-header. In the seventh inning of the first game, with the score tied, 1–1, the Robins had the bases loaded—Hank DeBerry was on third, Dazzy Vance on second, and Chick Fewster on first. There was one out. Babe Herman came to the plate and hit a sharp drive off the right-field wall— a solid double. DeBerry came in with the go-ahead run. Vance thought Jimmy Welsh, the Boston right fielder, might have a shot at the ball; he held up until it made the wall and then took off for third, rounded the bag, and headed home. By then the ball had been relayed in. Seeing he had no chance to score, Vance dashed back to third. Meanwhile, Fewster and Herman had been barreling around the base paths heedless of the location of the ball or the progress of the other runners.

As Vance returned to third from one side, Fewster pulled in from the other, and right behind him came Herman. Three men were standing on a single base! Babe turned around and started back to second; Fewster, who figured he was out, disgustedly left the bag and was tagged out by Eddie Taylor, the Braves' third baseman. Taylor then tossed to Doc Gautreau at second, who put the tag on Herman.

"Now *that* was the damnedest thing *I* ever saw," Alex told his brother. The crowd was in an uproar. Some fans were goaning, but most were laughing. In the dugout, Robbie was shaking his head in disgust and disbelief. In spite of the buffoonery, Brooklyn won the game, 4–1, then took the nightcap as well. "First time all season," Robbie said later, "that the guys on this ball club ever got together on anything."

Members of the hot stove league still talk about that play. Many remember it as the time Babe Herman tripled into a triple play. Actually, he doubled into a double play. But no matter; that play, more than any other, symbolizes the zaniness that was Babe Herman and the daffiness that was the Dodgers.

The tales of Babe's ineptitude are countless. They recount lapses on the field and on the base paths almost too bizarre to be believed. Herman was never quite sure of himself when he was getting the range on a fly ball, and even though he *usually* snagged the ball, he became known as the only player in baseball who could make a spectacular catch out of a routine pop-up.

Some fans swear to this day that Babe once got hit on the head by a ball he was waiting to catch. One day writer Tom Meany asked him whether he had, in fact, ever been beaned by a fly. Babe indignantly replied that no such thing had ever happened. The day it did he would walk off the diamond for good.

"How about getting hit on the shoulder, Babe?" Meany asked.

"On the shoulder don't count," was the reply.

Off the diamond Babe was just as zany. One day he was asking a reporter to stop portraying him as a clown. After all, Herman complained, he was just a guy with a family trying to make a living. It wasn't fair of the press to damage his reputation by making him out to be a buffoon.

The reporter had just about bought the argument when Babe reached into his pocket, pulled out a cigar that was already lit, and began puffing away.

"All bets are off," the writer exclaimed. "A guy who carries lighted cigars in his pocket can't try to tell me he isn't a clown."

One thing Babe could do was hit. His lifetime average was .324. In 1930 he batted a sizzling .393 but still lost the batting title to Bill Terry, who hit .401. Trying to explain Babe's remarkable batting ability, Dazzy Vance once said, "He's a great hitter because he never thinks up there, and how can a pitcher outsmart a guy who doesn't think?"

Uncle Robbie, whose girth had inspired some writers to refer to him as "the Falstaffian Brooklyn manager," made his own contribution to the legend of the Daffy Dodgers. One incident involved Babe Herman's son Bobby. Robbie, very fond of the boy, often let him come into the dugout and sit on his lap. One afternoon the youngster climbed up on the manager's lap and suddenly found himself dumped right on the dugout boards.

"What's the matter, Uncle Robbie?" the boy asked, trying to hold back the tears.

Robbie scowled at him. "Why ain't your old man hittin'?"

In the 1926 season the Robins may have given their fans plenty of laughs, but they certainly didn't provide much to cheer about. The team wound up in sixth place, seventeen and a half games off the pace. More than anything else, it was a year of change for the Brooklyn club. In August another ancient player, thirty-six-year-old Max Carey, was purchased from Pittsburgh for the $4,000 waiver price.

For taking part in an uprising against Fred Clarke, the Pirates' vice-president, Max and two other players—Skeeter Bignee and Babe Adams—were given the ax. By the time Carey arrived in Brooklyn, the rumors were he was slated to be the Dodgers' next pilot.

As Max came in, three great old Robins were on their way out. Before the race was over, Zack Wheat, still suffering from the leg injury he received rounding first after hitting that homer, hung up his spikes and headed home to Polo, Missouri; he would wind up his career the following year playing on the Athletics for Connie Mack. Then, after the season came to a close, Robbie released Jack Fournier, who went on to play one more season with the Braves.

During the winter Robbie decided to get rid of Grimes. He knew his old enemy McGraw had his eye on Burleigh, so to keep his aging ace out of the Little Napoleon's clutches Uncle Robbie swapped him for a Phillies catcher named Butch Henline. No sooner had the deal become final than Philadelphia turned around and traded Burleigh to the Giants.

But 1926 was hardly kinder to John McGraw than it was to Wilbert Robinson. The Giants came in fifth, thirteen and a half games back, their first second-division finish since 1915. On paper the team looked like a potential champion, but it just couldn't win ball games.

A key player was lost when Ross Youngs became seriously ill and was forced to spend part of the season in the hospital. His illness turned out to be Bright's disease; it would claim his life in October 1927.

Morale on the Giants was lower than McGraw had ever seen it. He himself had become a big plunger in the Florida land boom, and a number of his players had tried to follow his lead. By the summer of 1926 the boom had turned to bust, and some Giants had lost their shirts. Word came out of the Giant clubhouse that "one player burned up all his savings on underwater land and has been on the verge of prostration."

In this gloomy atmosphere it was not easy to win ball games, and as the team sagged McGraw began riding his men, especially Frankie Frisch, whom he labeled the "Krauthead." Finally Frisch couldn't take any more; one night in St. Louis he checked out of the team's hotel and took a train back to New York. Deserting the club was a sin the Little Napoleon could never forgive. Frankie rejoined the lineup for the remainder of the season, but it was no secret he would be gone the following spring.

While the Robins and the Giants were floundering, the Yankees had gotten off to a fast start in 1926, young Tony Lazzeri providing the glue in a green infield that included Gehrig at first, Lazzeri at second, Mark Koenig at short, and Joe Dugan at third. After beating the Dodgers twelve times in a row in preseason, the Yanks took their winning ways into the season itself. As it turned out, the fast start became their salvation, as three teams—Cleveland, Philadelphia, and Washington—made late-season runs.

In August, after watching the Yankees dissipate their large lead, Harry began to think that he was a jinx. Even though the Yanks had recently won six in a row, he was anxious. On a rainy Saturday afternoon he was fretting over the week's statistics when Alex entered the room.

"I give up," he said, rubbing his eyes and pushing away the pile of papers. "The figures say the Yanks should win in a walk, but they're going to flop just to spite me."

"You're looking for sympathy from *me?*" Alex, whose Dodgers were already well out of it, asked. "No ball game today," Alex said, parting the lace curtains and peering at the wet street. "C'mon, Harry, what say we go over to Broadway and pay our respects to Valentino?"

At the time, the corpse of the recently deceased Rudolph Valentino was the object of one of the biggest publicity ballyhoos in history. His body was lying in state at the Frank Campbell funeral home, and a corps of press agents was making certain that no detail of the arrangements escaped public notice.

Unwilling to give up a good thing, the promoters prolonged the spectacle until the Board of Health finally ordered the coffin closed. Some thirty thousand persons had viewed the remains. When Valentino was finally laid to rest, some newspapers hit the streets carrying photos of a staged funeral cortege before the actual procession had even begun. The dashing actor had died bankrupt, but the promotion of his remains and the subsequent success of his posthumously issued films netted his estate more than half a million dollars.

"Not me," said Harry. "I heard the line was sixteen blocks long yesterday. Besides, I'd rather stay here and try to dope out the Yankees."

As it turned out, Harry had little to worry about. The Yankees clinched in September and ended up ahead of the second-place Indians by three games.

In the National League, meanwhile, Rogers Hornsby, the perennial batting champion, was demonstrating considerable managerial skill by leading the St. Louis Cardinals to their first pennant in history.

Herb Pennock held the Cards to just four hits as the Yankees took the first game of the World Series on October 2, but St. Louis came back to win the next two games. Waite Hoyt, with help from Ruth, downed the Cards in St. Louis on October 6 by a score of 10–2 to even the Series.

In that game the Babe smacked homers his first two times at bat. The next time up, he walked. When he came to bat the fourth time, Ruth took a ball, fouled off one, took another ball, and fouled off another. The Babe parked the next pitch into the seats in center field for a record-setting three home runs in one World Series game. Graham McNamee told a national radio audience, "They tell me this is the first ball ever hit in the center-field stand. That is a mile and a half from here!"

The following day, Herb Pennock gave the Yankees a 3–2 victory, leaving them one game away from their second world championship. Ruth again starred, making the defensive play of the Series when he spectacularly snagged a foul fly one-handed, then crashed into the box seats.

But the sixth game, on October 9, saw old Grover Cleveland "Pete" Alexander hold the Yankees to two runs while his teammates were piling up ten.

On October 10 the final game of the Series was played in Yankee Stadium. The pitchers were Jesse Haines, a knuckleballer, for the Cards and Waite Hoyt for the Yanks. Ruth put the Yankees on top, 1–0, in the third when he smacked his fourth home run of the Series. But the Cards came back with three runs of their own in the fourth. In the sixth a single by Joe Dugan and a double by Hank Severeid pulled the Yanks to within one run.

Haines's knuckler had been keeping the Yankee bats fairly well in check, but in the seventh inning he began to have trouble. A blister had been developing on the forefinger of his throwing hand. With two out, the blister finally broke. Before Hornsby caught on to the problem, the Yankees had filled the bases.

Hornsby jumped for the bullpen telephone and screamed for Alexander. Sportswriters have long given support to the story that Pete had celebrated his previous day's victory by drinking all night, that his head was throbbing, his eyes were bloodshot, and his breath was flammable.

Alexander himself later denied this, saying he took his time getting to the mound in order to let the young Lazzeri, the next batter, stew. Whatever the reason, it took Old Pete longer to traverse the distance between the bullpen and the mound than it had taken Haines to load the bases. And throughout the excruciatingly slow journey, the New York fans delivered a warm ovation for the aging great, who, nearing forty, was appearing in his first World Series.

Lazzeri was one for seven thus far against Alexander in the Series. Pete had been fooling the youngster with curve balls. Glancing briefly at each of the three baserunners, Pete delivered the first pitch. Sure enough, it was a curve, and Lazzeri swung and missed. Bob O'Farrell, the Cards' catcher, hand-carried the ball to Alexander and conferred with him briefly.

Evidently O'Farrell feared that Lazzeri was expecting the curve, because the next pitch was a high hard one. The crowd screamed hysterically as the ball exploded down the left-field line, then groaned as it tailed off and crashed into the bleachers ten feet on the wrong side of the foul pole.

Old Pete passed his hand over his face and muttered to himself. He had learned his lesson. The next pitch was another curve. Lazzeri took a mighty cut, but the ball broke sharply outside and he missed it completely.

Alexander retired the next five Yankees in order. With two out in the ninth, the batter was Ruth. Old Pete pitched carefully to the Babe, trying to work the corners, and wound up walking him. The next batter was Meusel. As Alexander delivered the first pitch, Ruth broke for second. O'Farrell fired to Hornsby, and Ruth was out by three steps. The Cards had won the Series.

Asked whatever possessed him to do such a thing, the Babe snorted, "Well, I wasn't doing any friggin' good where I was!"

In the early weeks of 1927 the Giants made one of the most sensational deals in baseball history—they acquired Rogers Hornsby from the Cards. Despite having just garnered the world championship, the Rajah was no favorite of Sam Breadon, the St. Louis owner.

Hornsby had been pressuring Breadon to fire Branch Rickey, the club's former manager, who was now vice-president. Rogers said he resented Rickey's "interference" in his running of the ball club, but rumor had it the main reason he wanted Rickey out was so he could get the VP title for himself.

The final break between Hornsby and Breadon took place during the 1926 pennant drive. Hornsby had asked his boss to cancel a series of exhibition games that he felt would jeopardize his team's chances to win the pennant. The Cards had just lost a heartbreaker to the Pirates when Breadon marched into the clubhouse—clearly the turf of the manager and his players—to deny Hornsby's request.

The Rajah was furious and gave the owner a tongue-lashing in front of the team. As Hornsby later remembered the scene, Breadon "was flushed and angry when he left the clubhouse. I believe he made up his mind then and there that, come pennant or last place, Hornsby wouldn't be with the Cardinals the next season, or any longer than was absolutely necessary."

Breadon knew trading his star would infuriate the St. Louis fans, but he was determined to get rid of this thorn in his side. When it came time to discuss a new contract, the negotiations bogged down—on the surface at least—over its duration. Hornsby had been playing and managing for two seasons under his $30,000-a-year player contract. Ilis argument, not hard to buy, was that "a manager who delivered without extra pay for two seasons and won the title ought to be assured of something better than a one-year future." Breadon refused to consider any contract other than one for a single year, although he was willing to up the salary to $50,000. He also added a few clauses that Hornsby believed were "put there because he knew I was hardheaded enough to refuse to sign."

Just before Christmas, realizing negotiations were going nowhere, Hornsby asked to be traded. Charles Stoneham, who had once offered $250,000 for the Rajah's contract, quickly made a deal with Breadon. Frankie Frisch and pitcher Jimmy Ring were sent to the Cardinals in exchange for one of the greatest right-handed batters in history. The Giant owner swore that no money was involved in the deal, but that was almost impossible to believe.

For a while it looked as though Hornsby might never play for the Giants. He was the second largest stockholder of the St. Louis club, and Judge Landis refused to let him play for New York until he had divested himself of his shares. Hornsby and Breadon were a long way apart on what would be a fair price for the stock. Finally, to break the deadlock, the other National League owners anted up the difference.

As the new season got under way, all eyes in New York fell on the new star second baseman of the Giants. Hornsby was a charmless, outspoken man who was not about to win any popularity contests. He quickly alienated many of his teammates, who felt he threw his weight around as though he owned the club.

For the first half of the season he failed to live up to expectations, and New York struggled along in the middle of the pack. But in August his bat came alive, and the team began to make its way up in the standings. McGraw, suffering from a sinus condition, let Hornsby manage the club on its final two road trips, and he did such an excellent job that he won the admiration of the entire team.

As a batter he wound up the season with a .361 average, second in the league behind Paul Waner's .380. Six batters in the Giant starting lineup that year—Bill Terry, Rogers Hornsby, Travis Jackson, Freddie Lindstrom, George Harper, and Edd Roush—hit better than .300. The pitching staff was a little weak, but McGraw got excellent work out of Burleigh Grimes, whose final record was 19–8, and Freddie Fitzsimmons, who won seventeen and lost ten.

On September 25 Hornsby led the Giants over to Ebbets Field, where thirty-two thousand fans were waiting to see whether their lowly Robins could throw a monkey wrench into the Giants' run for the pennant. Uncle Robbie sent Jesse Petty to the mound that day, and, as Alex later remembered the game, "Jesse pitched his arm off in his determination to beat the Giants." The contest was called because of darkness after seven scoreless innings. In the makeup game the following week, Dazzy Vance defeated the Giants, 10–5, and eliminated them from the race. New York finished the season in third place, just two games behind the pennant-winning Pirates.

Uncle Robbie derived only temporary pleasure from crushing the Little Napoleon's pennant hopes. Brooklyn once again ended up sixth, a whopping twenty-eight and a half games out. Nonetheless, the Robins managed to make money because of the amazing loyalty of their fans. At the end of the season, Thomas Rice wrote in the *Sporting News* that "for three years, despite miserable showings on the field, the Brooklyn fans had supported the club enough to ensure a profit."

Even more money could have been made if only Brooklyn had a bigger ball park. Unfortunately, Ebbets Field was bounded on all four sides by city streets and could never be expanded enough to fill the needs of "a borough of Brooklyn's size and enthusiasm." Focusing sharply on an issue that would come to a head thirty years later, Rice ended his article with this observation: "It all seems to prove that the late Charles H. Ebbets was a conservative man, after all. 'Baseball is still in its infancy,' declared the good Squire. Then he went out and built a ball park that went out of date within 15 years."

"They don't just beat you, they break your heart," was the way Joe Judge, the Senators' first baseman, summed up the 1927 Yankees. It was a year of miracles—Lindbergh's transatlantic flight, Al Jolson's talking picture, *The Jazz Singer*, the first demonstration of an almost frightening device, the television—and the Bronx Bombers were themselves a kind of miracle, the victors in 110 ball games for a .714 winning percentage.

Babe Ruth, now drawing a stunning $70,000 yearly, blasted his monumental sixty home runs. Close on his heels was Lou Gehrig with forty-seven, followed by Tony Lazzeri, who ranked third in the league with eighteen. In all, the Yanks hit 158 home runs. Second-place Philadelphia had the next highest total in the league with fifty-six.

The Yankees as a team also led the league in total hits, triples, RBIs, walks, batting average, slugging average—and strikeouts. In addition to the power of Murderers' Row, the Yanks sported an airtight infield, a superb outfield, and a first-class pitching staff.

The suprise of the Yankee hurlers was a thirty-year-old Oklahoman named Wilcey Moore, who had been signed virtually sight-unseen on the basis of his thirty wins in the South Atlantic League in 1926. One explanation for Moore's obscurity was that he had been only a fair pitcher until a line drive fractured his wrist. Trying to ease the residual pain of the injury, the tall, balding farm boy developed a sidearm motion, which in turn developed for him a great sinker pitch. Ed Barrow saw the results of that pitch in the fine print in the pages of the *Sporting News* and mailed Moore a contract, figuring any pitcher who could win thirty in the Sally League could win a few in the big time.

Barrow proved to be right, as Moore became the Yankees' first great relief pitcher, chalking up nineteen victories and posting the lowest earned run average in the league. Wilcey came within a gnat's eyelash of winning twenty. In September he was pitching against Detroit with two out in the ninth, when an error allowed the tying run to cross the plate.

Herb Pennock came in to relieve Moore, and the first pitch he threw was popped up to end the inning. Ruth led off in the bottom of the ninth, facing a fresh Detroit pitcher, and whacked the first delivery for a home run. The winning pitcher had thrown one pitch, the losing pitcher had thrown one pitch.

The Yankees breezed to the 1927 pennant, finishing nineteen games ahead of the second-place Athletics. They carried their momentum right into the Series, defeating National League champs Pittsburgh four straight. It was the shortest Series on record, because the 1914 Boston rout of Philadelphia had included an extra-inning game.

The 1927 season, besides producing what many have called the greatest team of all time, also saw the end of an era. Ban Johnson handed in his resignation. The trouble had begun following the 1926 season when Dutch Leonard wrote a letter accusing Ty Cobb and Tris Speaker of conspiring to fix a game.

Although convinced of their guilt, Johnson decided to let the two quietly retire. Judge Landis, however, heard of the case and exonerated Cobb and Speaker on the basis that Leonard, living in California, would not come east to testify against them. Landis either did not know, or refused to be bothered by the fact, that Leonard's sudden attack of shyness was brought on in large part by the Georgia Peach's threat to dismantle Leonard into parts small enough to pass through a keyhole if he ever saw him again.

When Landis released details of the case, excluding Cobb's demolition offer, to the press, Johnson exploded and announced publicly that neither man would ever play in the American League again. Because Johnson was in poor health, the baseball moguls were inclined to let this episode pass quietly.

Johnson disappeared for a while, but in a short time he was back, more tyrannical and arbitrary than before. The owners called a special meeting. While the meeting was in session, there was a light knock at the hotel room door. Seated at a table, the owners saw Johnson's shaking white hand deliver his pencil-written resignation to the man who had answered the knock.

But if an era was ending for baseball, a new one was beginning for the Rice family. In early August Sally called Alex into the backyard and gave him a bit of news that convinced him that 1927 was indeed a year of miracles. He was going to be a father. Hand in hand, they returned to the house to announce the glad tidings to Harry and Ellen, who were overjoyed. Harry immediately went to his special locker and broke out two bottles of champagne.

"Here's to the new member of the Rice family," Harry said, "and to the Coast Guard and the rum runners, without whose cooperation we could never get this wonderful bubbly."

Alex stared wistfully into his empty glass. "I hope he has Pop's hands," he said quietly.

On January 10, 1928, word came out of the New York Giants' headquarters on Forty-second Street that the day would bring a very important announcement. Many of the reporters assigned to cover the breaking story guessed that McGraw was going to announce his retirement and Rogers Hornsby would be named as successor.

It was 9:45 in the evening before the club secretary, James J. Tierney, came out of the inner offices to hand out the press release. As the *Times* described the scene, "had the ceiling of the room fallen down upon the heads of the astounded baseball writers there could have been no greater consternation." The statement, signed by both Charles Stoneham and John McGraw, read as follows:

> After due deliberation between President Stoneham and Manager McGraw and having in mind what we thought were the

best interests of the New York Giants, a trade was consummated today which involved Rogers Hornsby, second baseman of the Giants, whereby the Giants received Francis Hogan, a catcher, and James Welsh, outfielder, of the Boston Braves.

No cash was involved in the transaction.

It was a ridiculous trade. Shanty Hogan and Jimmy Welsh had each batted .288 the previous season, but two journeymen didn't equal one superstar, especially a player of Hornsby's remarkable abilities.

Why the Giants had given away the great Rajah was indeed a puzzle. John McGraw was not around to answer any questions. Knowing a storm would follow the announcement, he had signed the statement and then left for Havana. A few days later, when reporters caught up with him passing through Savannah, all the Little Napoleon would say was, "There's nothing to add to the announcement. The trade has been made and that's all there is to it."

There was widespread speculation that McGraw, feeling threatened by Hornsby, had persuaded Stoneham to get rid of the Rajah. But past events didn't back up that theory. The Little Napoleon had openly encouraged Hornsby to pilot the team during the pennant drive. In fact, all through one series in Pittsburgh, John had watched from the stands while Hornsby led the team from the dugout.

When asked why he wasn't at the helm, McGraw replied, "Because no one could possibly run the club better than it's being run now." The Little Napoleon was getting older—he was now fifty-four—but he was still a fighter. It just didn't figure that he would trade away a player who could help the Giants win ball games the way Hornsby could.

No, the central figure in the transaction was Jim Tierney—the man who had given the announcement of the trade to the press. Tierney, originally hired as club secretary because he was a pal of McGraw's, had successfully curried favor with Stoneham and was now the president's most trusted adviser. Over the past season, Hornsby, never one to mince words, had remarked on a few occasions that he was not particularly fond of Stoneham. Tierney carried these stories back to the boss, who became increasingly irritated. Then, during the pennant drive, Tierney and Hornsby got into an argument that sealed the Rajah's fate. After a game in Chicago that was blown because Travis Jackson muffed a grounder, Tierney complained bitterly to the acting manager about the sloppy play of the Giant shortstop.

Hornsby was furious. Errors are, after all, an inescapable part of baseball, even for a player of Jackson's great skill. Rogers tore into Tierney; he told him to stick to buying train tickets and booking hotel rooms and to stop poking his nose into areas that were none of his concern.

Some years later Hornsby revealed his suspicion that "as soon as Tierney got to the hotel room he called Charles Stoneham on the telephone and told him how the vulgar Hornsby had spoken so rudely to him." The great Rajah's release had nothing to do with baseball; it came about because the big jobs in the front office were filled by small men.

That spring Burleigh Grimes was also traded; he went to the Pirates in exchange for Vic Aldridge, a pitcher who turned out to be a total washout. Presumably that deal was also for "the best interests" of the team. Alex, who had taken a mild interest in the Giants now that the Dodgers had fallen on hard times, couldn't help but wonder, "for the best interests of *which* team?"

Once again, it was difficult to believe that McGraw had willingly thrown away his star hurler. It was painfully obvious that the Giant manager was losing his power. The days when he could make his own deals, pay his own prices, and buy and sell players at will were over. The Little Napoleon was no longer his own boss.

In the early hours of February 29, 1928, Sally entered Methodist-Episcopal Hospital in Brooklyn. At 12:15 P.M. she gave birth to an eight-pound, three-ounce boy, who was subsequently christened Damon Fletcher Rice. After he had calmed down, Alex sent a telegram to Harry.

RICE FAMILY COMPLETES DEAL FOR HOT PROS-PECT FROM SALLY LEAGUE. GREAT HANDS BUT NEEDS SEASONING.

Shortly after Damon's birth, Harry made one of the most important decisions of his life. Nervous because he was rapidly approaching his fortieth birthday, he decided that the time had come to take a crack at making something of his life. He left the small accounting firm in Brooklyn where he had worked for twenty years, beginning as an apprentice and advancing to the less than lofty position of chief bookkeeper.

Following the unheeded advice he had given to Alex a few years earlier, Harry decided to enter the world of high finance. To get his start, he took a job as a staff accountant for Loomis, Suffern and Fernald, a Manhattan CPA firm that had important Wall Street clients. His first assignment was to work on an audit of an investment company known as the American Founders Corporation. For several weeks he and the other members of the auditing team reported for work at the company's offices at 50 Pine Street, where Harry was quickly recognized as an alert, hard-working accountant. Before the audit had been completed, he was offered a job as a statistician in American Founders' economics department. Harry jumped at this new opportunity.

The American Founders Corporation was one company in a large network of investment trusts known as the American Founders Group. A creature of the 1920s, the investment trust was a company whose only activity was the buying and selling of securities. The theory was that a trust's large and diversified portfolio would be immune from fluctuations in the market that might adversely affect certain stocks or groups of stocks.

In other words, by purchasing shares in a company such as American Founders instead of ordinary common stocks, the little guy could protect himself against losing his shirt. By the late twenties, many investment trusts had begun to spawn other investment trusts, all owning shares in one another. Harry's employer was only one piece of a great paper pyramid that was propped up by the belief that the stock market as a whole was stronger than all its parts.

Harry's new boss was a man named Kris Ramnaes. Kris assigned to Harry all sorts of interesting tasks, such as preparing data on interest rates and commodity values or computing ratios of yield to market price. The economists in the department plugged Harry's figures into reports that the investment department used to determine the effects of general conditions on specific securities.

As Harry got deeper into his work, he became fascinated by its possibilities. He was anxious to find out whether in certain areas of human endeavor it was possible to predict future performance with a high degree of accuracy. All that was needed, he began to believe, were accurate, comprehensive data and a sound methodology. His thoughts shifted to baseball.

During the first week of June he tried an experiment. He scribbled his predictions for both major league pennant races on a scrap of paper, which he sealed in an envelope and then mailed to himself. As Harry saw it, the Yankees would capture the American League pennant by two and a half games, winning 101 and losing 53. The Cardinals would take the National League flag; their record would be 97 and 57, and they would finish four games ahead of the second-place club.

It was turning out to be an interesting season. John McGraw broke his leg in May and was out of action for six weeks. When he returned he quickly whipped his players into shape. Even though the Giants had been weakened by their two ridiculous trades, they didn't lose heart. The Cardinals were widely recognized as the power of the league in 1928, but as the season moved toward its conclusion the Giants began to give them a hell of a fight. In mid-August New York won three straight from St. Louis and took over first place by three percentage points.

Why were the Giants playing so much better on the field than seemed possible on paper? Because McGraw was getting standout performances up and down his lineup. Larry Benton, a pitcher who had come over from the Braves the previous year, was on his way to twenty-five victories. Freddie Fitzsimmons would win twenty and lose only nine. In the infield, Freddie Lindstrom and Bill Terry were both having fine years. Lefty O'Doul, who had come up to the majors as a pitcher, was making a name for himself as a slugging left fielder. But the key player on the team was young Mel Ott, who came into his own by hitting eighteen homers and compiling a .322 batting average.

Ott had joined the Giants two years earlier. The minute John Mc-Graw laid eyes on the seventeen-year-old from Gretna, Louisiana, he knew the youngster was destined for greatness. The Little Napoleon converted Mel from a catcher to an outfielder and used him as a backup man in 1926 and 1927. Casey Stengel was one of the many who questioned McGraw's handling of Ott. Casey, by then the manager of the Toledo Mud Hens, finally asked John why he was keeping the prodigy on the Giant roster instead of sending him to the minors where he could learn by playing every day.

"Neither you nor any other minor league manager is going to ruin that kid," bellowed Muggsy, shaking his fist at Ol' Case. "He stays with me!"

Contrary to all rules of good form, Ott raised his right foot as he swung into the ball. It may have been unorthodox, but it also worked, which was all McGraw cared about. He wasn't about to let another manager tamper with the kid's style.

So Ott spent two years warming the bench, waiting for his chance to become a regular. During that time McGraw became very fond of his protégé and soon began looking on him as a son. It was the first time he had felt that way about one of his players since Christy Mathewson.

The year 1928 also saw Carl Hubbell, another all-time great, first put on a Giant uniform. Carl was brought up in midseason from the Beaumont Exporters of the Texas League. Dick Kinsella, a Giant scout, had been impressed by the young southpaw's excellent control. A lefty who could consistently get the ball over the plate was a rarity in those days, so McGraw decided to give Hubbell a chance.

His first starting assignment was on July 26 in a game against the Pirates. Pittsburgh sent Burleigh Grimes to the mound that afternoon. Hubbell's screwball was shelled for seven runs in the second inning, and Grimes went on to defeat his old teammates for the fifth time in as many starts.

Despite Carl's inauspicious debut, McGraw sensed his new hurler had something. "I was lucky when McGraw gave me another chance," Carl recalled later. He won ten and lost six that year, and his arm kept the club in contention during the homestretch.

The Giants went as far as they could, but when the race was over, they were still two games behind the Cardinals. McGraw blamed his defeat on his broken leg. But if Hornsby, who led the league with a .387 batting average, and Grimes, who won twenty-five ball games for Pittsburgh, had been with the Giants that year, John McGraw would not have blown his last real shot at a pennant.

The Yankees leaped to a blazing start in 1928, and it looked as though they would once again run away from the field. At one point they led by seventeen games, but then the competitive edge began to dull. On top of complacency, Huggins had to combat the fact that a number of his men were playing the neon circuit, swilling the booze.

And, as if that weren't enough, the presence of cocky, hot-headed rookie shortstop Leo Durocher was causing dissension on the team. Huggins called him "the greatest infielder to ever smother a half-hop," but "The Lip" had a knack for alienating his teammates, who purposely tried to make him look bad on the field.

Meanwhile, Connie Mack's Athletics, led by slugger Al Simmons and ace pitcher Lefty Grove—and helped by two brilliant veterans, Tris Speaker and Ty Cobb—began to close the gap. On September 8 the Mackmen captured first place. The next day, an all-time record crowd of more than eighty-five thousand crammed into Yankee Stadium, which had been enlarged during the winter, to see the Yanks play the Athletics in a doubleheader. The Bombers put away the White Elephants twice, 3–0 and 7–3. The A's stayed hot, but the Yankees refused to be headed and finally clinched the pennant two days before the end of the season.

The Babe hit fifty-four homers and might well have broken his all-time record of sixty had it not been for the tight pennant race. During the last month of the season, when the Athletics had been breathing down the Yankees' necks, Ruth had shortened his grip and swung for left field. "You can break a home-run record with a last-place club," said the Babe, "but you can't get into a World Series except with a winner."

Gehrig had walloped twenty-seven homers and batted .374 to Ruth's .323. The pitching staff had come through once again, with George Pipgras—who led the league with twenty-four wins—Waite Hoyt, and Herb Pennock all having fine years. The only disappointment was Wilcey Moore, whose 4–4 record failed to come anywhere close to his previous year's performance.

Moore had reported to spring training with a bad arm, saying he had injured it falling off the roof of his barn. But those close to him knew the real story. As a reward for his great performances in relief in 1927, Miller Huggins had let Wilcey start the fourth game of the World Series. Moore won the game but threw his arm away in the process. He was never again the same.

The Cards and the Yankees squared off for the first game of their "grudge match" Series on October 4 in New York. The Yanks got their first taste of revenge for their 1926 defeat at the hands of the Cards by downing the St. Louis team, 4–1, behind superb pitching by Waite Hoyt. The next day, revenge was even sweeter as they downed Pete Alexander, 9–3. And when Tom Zachary, taking the injured Pennock's spot in the rotation, beat the Cards, 7–3, in the third game, it looked as though New York was a cinch to win its second Series in a row.

In the fourth game Hoyt faced Willie Sherdel, a twenty-one-game winner. The Cards struck first, scoring once in the third inning. In the fourth Ruth tied the score with a blast over the right-field pavilion. But in the Cards' half of the fourth, Hoyt tried to pick Rabbit Maranville off second. He wheeled and blazed the ball toward the bag, but there was no one there to catch it. Maranville galloped home, laughing.

The Cardinals led, 2–1, into the seventh inning. Then, with one away, Ruth stepped to the plate. Sherdel threw the Babe two slow curves for called strikes and then tried a "quick return." Immediately upon receiving the ball back from the catcher, he rifled it over the plate, catching Ruth unawares.

The Cardinals argued vociferously, much to Ruth's amusement, that the pitch should be called the third strike. Umpire Cy Pfirman, however, disallowed the pitch, saying that the quick return, fairly common in the National League but illegal in the American, had been barred from the Series by mutual agreement of the two clubs.

Sherdel then wasted two pitches, and with the count two and two Ruth blasted the next pitch over the right-field pavilion for the second time in a row. The Bambino pranced around the bases, waving derisively. Gehrig immediately followed with another four-bagger. Pete Alexander was called in to put out the fire, but the Yanks added two more runs before he could do so. It was all over for the Cards.

But it wasn't all over for the Babe. After surviving a bottle barrage in left field from disgruntled St. Louis fans, Ruth came up to bat once more in the top of the ninth. Young outfielder Cedric Durst had already made the score 6–2 with a homer of his own when Babe stepped in. With a count of one strike, Ruth parked Alexander's curve ball on top of the pavilion in right for his third homer of the game, equaling his own record for World Series play.

The Cards scored once in the bottom of the ninth, but with two outs Frankie Frisch lofted a high foul toward the left-field stands. Ruth galloped through a blizzard of flying scraps of newspaper, sandwich wrappings, and scorecards, snagged the ball out of the first row of seats, and, without hesitating, galloped straight to the clubhouse, holding the ball aloft for all the world to see.

This was only the third time that a team had swept the Series in four straight, and the Yankees had done it twice in a row. The feat was even more amazing in light of the fact that the Yankee dugout had looked like an outpatient ward.

In addition to Pennock's strained arm, Dugan had a knee injury, Ruth a charley horse, Lazzeri a bad shoulder, and Combs a bad leg. Of the catchers, three—including rookie Bill Dickey—were injured. Luckily, Benny Bengough had recovered sufficiently from an injury to play an outstanding Series.

The train ride back to New York was a hell-raiser, a marathon of shouting, singing, boozing, and back-thumping. When the players began ripping one another's shirts off, the Babe cornered Ruppert himself and in less than a second had left the colonel standing naked to the waist. Colonel Jake looked down at his shredded shirt, glanced at his bare chest, smiled benignly at the Babe, and asked, "Is dis usual, Roots?"

Almost before the train carrying the team had arrived in New York, a cry had gone out, a cry that would echo through the years: Break up the Yankees!

It wasn't until after the Series that Harry remembered to pull out the letter he had sent himself at the beginning of the season. One Sunday morning in October, he gave the envelope to Alex and said, "Take a look at the date of the postmark and then open it up." Alex was amazed at his brother's uncanny accuracy. The prediction for the Yankees was precisely correct—101 wins and a two-and-a-half-game margin. Harry had been slightly off on the Cardinals, but the forecast was impressive nonetheless.

"It's all done with mirrors," Harry told his brother.

Although eager to test his predictive skills in the stock market, Harry spent most of that autumn biding his time. Then, in November, shortly after Herbert Hoover had been elected president, a rally began that was quickly dubbed the "Hoover Bull Market." Prices started moving up, up, and farther up.

On November 26 Harry decided the time had come to get in. With Ellen's consent, he withdrew their fifteen years' worth of savings, $7,000, from the bank and invested it in a variety of stocks that he felt would make up a conservative portfolio. The issues that Harry purchased that day included American Can at 110, General Electric at 188¾, New York Central at 184, and U.S. Steel at 168. He took a flyer on Wright Aeronautical at 270 and hedged all his bets by purchasing a large block of American Founders at 68.

Harry paid only passing notice to a column that appeared in the financial pages of the *Times* that day. It observed that "among the numerous interesting psychological aspects of the present Stock Exchange speculation, not the least interesting is the fact that nobody troubles himself either to explain why these aerial flights of prices should occur, or how long they will continue before the rise will definitely cease, or what happens when it does."

Like so many speculators of the period, Harry was playing the market on margin. For most of his stocks he put up only 30 percent of the purchase price, using the stocks themselves as collateral on loans for the remaining 70 percent.

If prices went up, a margin investor could realize a handsome return on a relatively small investment. But if the prices plunged, the investor would be asked to answer a margin call—a request for more cash. If he were not able to produce the money in a hurry, his broker would probably sell him out at a loss.

Harry was well aware of this dire possibility. A few days after entering the market, he created an emergency fund by taking out a $12,000 mortgage on the house in Park Slope. He had more than a few qualms about borrowing on the old place; after all, Fletcher had paid for it in full long before the turn of the century. But this was only a temporary move.

Harry would pay off the note as soon as his holdings began to grow. Obviously there was no need to tell Ellen. It would only worry her.

It didn't take Harry long to dip into his reserves. On December 7 the market turned sharply downward. One glamour issue, the Radio Corporation of America, plunged all the way from 361 to 296. Sensing a bargain, Harry put half of his emergency fund into Radio stock. By New Year's he was congratulating himself on his perspicacity. The rally was under way again. This time there's no stopping it, he told himself. The year 1929 was definitely going to be the year of the bull.

That spring Harry once again mailed himself his predictions for the outcome of the new baseball season, but by the time the World Series rolled around he'd forgotten where he put the envelope. It was probably just as well, since he'd picked the wrong team in each league.

In any case, it wasn't much of a summer for baseball for either Harry or Alex. Brooklyn finished in sixth place for the fifth year in a row, and the Giants were a big disappointment after their strong showing in 1928. McGraw's men finished in third place, thirteen and a half games behind the Chicago Cubs—the latest team in the league to benefit from the services of Rogers Hornsby. Even the Yankees had an off year, finishing second in a race that brought Connie Mack his first pennant since 1914.

As the season wound down, the Yanks had lost even more than the flag. On September 20 Miller Huggins appeared at the stadium with an angry red blotch under his left eye. Little Hug seemed more pale and wan than usual. Just before game time he turned to one of his coaches, Art Fletcher. "Art," he said, "look after the team. I'm going home."

Five days later the Yankees were playing Boston in Fenway Park. Few of the fans, and none of the players, noticed when, during the third inning, the flag in center field fluttered slightly and slowly descended to half mast. After the fifth inning it was decided to break the news to the Yankee team.

A shudder when through the dugout as the tough, suntanned men thought of their frail little manager. The silence was finally broken by Earle Combs, who broke down and wept. A reporter started to ask Ruth a question, but the Babe silenced him with a menacing scowl.

Both teams gathered at home plate and observed, along with the seven thousand fans, one minute of silence. The Yankees shuffled silently back to their bench. Art Fletcher, the temporary leader, stood in front of the dugout, his hands in his hip pockets, and kicked at the dirt. "Well," he said finally, "let's get it over with." The Yankees won, 11–10, in ten innings.

It's doubtful Harry would have become involved in baseball that year even if the Yankees had won the pennant. His mind, both on and off the job, was totally preoccupied with the stock market. At work things were going very well for him. In June he received a fat raise and was promoted to the position of securities analyst. When Ellen asked how someone of his limited experience could work his way up the ladder so quickly, Harry replied, "These days things happen very fast on Wall Street."

As the summer wore on, the market climbed to giddy heights. By now Harry considered himself a skillful trader, and he was in and out of new stocks every day. He became obsessed with gaining as much leverage as possible, so he began increasing his use of margin. He had some loans that were for as much as 90 percent of the market value of his stock.

That summer the relationship between Alex and Harry took an odd turnaround. For the first time ever, Alex assumed the role of the brother worried about his sibling. There was no question that Harry's behavior had become a trifle bizarre. Some nights at the dinner table he would begin talking a mile a minute without stopping to catch a breath. On other occasions his eyes would become glazed and his mind would drift off. Alex didn't know what to make of it.

One day early in August, Harry mailed himself an unusual letter. The envelope, which was sent from his office in New York to his home address in Brooklyn, carried $3.55 worth of air mail postage. Inside was this message:

August 6, 1929

Dear Harry,

This letter comes to you around the world, Lakehurst, N.J. to Lakehurst, N.J. by German airship L.Z. 127, otherwise known as the "Graf Zeppelin."

Here's hoping you are happy and prosperous when you receive this, and that you know enough to get out of the market while the getting's good.

Good luck,
Harry

Labor Day that year was a real scorcher. The Rice family forwent its traditional outing at Brighton Beach and instead spent the day relaxing in the backyard of the house in Park Slope. In the early afternoon Ellen and Sally went inside to take naps, leaving the two brothers to watch over Damon, who was asleep in his carriage. As Alex studied Harry, who was sitting in his wicker chair with his thoughts a million miles away, he decided this was as good a time as any to find out what was troubling him.

"Harry, I've been worrying about you lately," Alex began. "You don't seem to be yourself."

"Oh?" Harry paused slightly to collect himself. "What do you mean?"

"I don't know. Your mind seems to be off in the clouds."

"Is that right?" Harry asked with no interest. He was thinking about the latest stock prices: American Can at 181, General Electric at 391, New York Central at 253, U.S. Steel at 257, American Founders at 118. And Radio, glorious Radio; its current price was 101, but it had split five for one since Harry had bought it. The stock he had purchased for 296 was now worth 505.

"Yes, that's right," said Alex, slightly annoyed.

"Well, you see, I have certain new responsibilities."

"What kind of responsibilities?"

"Last week I became a millionaire."

By the end of September, Harry was less of a tycoon. The market had begun to slide, and he had lost his status as a paper millionaire. There were still some good days, but most of the news coming off the ticker was bad.

Harry customarily reviewed his portfolio on Saturdays. Almost every week he found it necessary to make certain adjustments—to sell off some stocks to maintain adequate margins on the others. The bear raid gained momentum in October. Harry suffered one close call after another, but somehow he managed to protect his most important positions. Then, on October 24, the market was jolted by a wave of selling that erupted into a full-scale panic.

As prices began to plummet, margin calls went unanswered, causing more stock to be thrown into the market. The seriousness of the situation became painfully apparent when U.S. Steel dropped below its widely recognized support level of 200.

The ticker fell farther and farther behind the trading, making it impossible for a big plunger to know whether or not he was still solvent. The day would probably have ended in total disaster had not New York's most prominent bankers come to the rescue. At 1:30 P.M., Richard Whitney, vice-president of the New York Stock Exchange, went to the trading floor and bid 205 for 10,000 shares of U.S. Steel.

As he moved on to other trading posts to make similar bids, it became clear that the money barons had put up a vast sum of cash in the hopes of restoring confidence. At once the market rebounded; at the close prices were almost back to where they had been when that frightening day began. Nonetheless, when Harry calculated the value of his portfolio, the news was not good. Many of his less protected stocks had been sold out from under him. He was now only a quarter of a millionaire.

The confidence restored by the bankers was short-lived. The following Monday, October 28, was another horrendous day. Several of Harry's most important holdings were wiped out, including General Electric, which dropped 48 points. His portfolio was now down to less than $100,000, the bulk of which was tied up in Radio and U.S. Steel, and both were protected by perilously narrow margins. Badly shaken by the events of that unhappy Monday, Harry was not up to facing Ellen. He took a room at the Broadway Central and then went up to the Dizzy Club to have a few drinks with Alex.

"I hear Wall Street was pretty bad today. How did it go with you?" Alex asked when his brother appeared on the other side of the bar.

"Not good," Harry answered, "but it could have been worse. I'm still in the market, which is more than I can say for some of my friends. Kris Ramnaes was wiped out this morning."

"Cheer up. Things can only get better."

After a few drinks, Harry began to think maybe Alex was right. He loosened his tie and proceeded to get good and drunk. As the booze took its effect, he began to ignore his fears. By the time he got back to the hotel, he was able to fall asleep without worrying about tomorrow. Alex hadn't seen Harry so like his old self in more months than he cared to remember.

That night Harry overslept for the first time in his adult life. He never stayed in bed past 7 A.M., but at that hour on Tuesday he was still enjoying the most relaxing night's sleep he'd had all year. Just before 9 o'clock he finally opened his eyes and dragged himself out of bed.

Groggily he shaved and washed, went down to the dining room for breakfast, checked out of the hotel, and rode the subway downtown. By the time he reached his desk and began arranging the day's work, it was a minute or two past 10.

He hadn't been at his desk more than fifteen minutes when he heard people milling and shouting in the hall outside his office. Opening the door, he found that everyone on his floor was crowding into the reception room at the end of the corridor where quotations from the big board's ticker raced along a screen on the wall.

"Oh, my God," a man cried out. "I'm getting sick," someone else moaned. But most of Harry's fellow workers stood silently, as if mesmerized by the dancing numbers. Harry returned to his office and tried to call his broker. The line was busy. He tried again. Still busy. He needed someone to talk to, so he went looking for Kris Ramnaes. No luck. Kris hadn't bothered to come to work that day. He decided to call Ellen. No answer. Donning his coat and hat, he went down to the street. A minute after he left, a Western Union messenger arrived with a wire demanding more margin. It was just as well he didn't see it. Even if he had been able to come up with the money, it wouldn't have mattered. He had already been sold out.

At the moment the opening gong rang out in the New York Stock Exchange that fateful morning, a tidal wave of selling engulfed the trading floor. Stocks were dumped in such huge blocks that within a half hour more than 3 million shares—a full day's worth of trading—had changed hands. The market was crashing, turning a million dreams of riches into nightmares of penury. Steel sank to 167, Radio to 44½, General Electric to 210. The investment trusts showed the greatest vulnerability, some dropping to half or even one-third of their opening prices. The great paper pyramid had lost its underpinning and was collapsing under its own weight.

Harry walked over to Wall Street. A large crowd had gathered in front of the Stock Exchange. People were standing about as if waiting for something—they didn't quite know what—to happen. Harry stopped to listen in on a conversation.

"Surely the bankers will stop this madness," one man said to another.

"Oh, yeah?" his friend retorted. "The way I hear it, those bastards are the ones selling all the stocks!"

One group of men didn't know whether to laugh or cry. They were talking about a messenger boy who as a joke had put in a bid that morning to buy White Sewing Machine at 1. The night before, it had closed at 11. When no other buyers came forward, the boy actually picked up the stock for a dollar a share.

Harry fended off the despair that was attacking him from all sides. His first impulse was to go get loaded all over again. Surely the several speakeasies that served the financial community were already open, giving refuge to every frantic soul who had resisted the impulse to jump out a window. But there was really no point to picking up where he had left off the night before. He strolled down to Battery Park, where he sat on a bench facing the harbor. It took more than an hour to collect his thoughts. Then he walked to the Whitehall Street subway station and rode home to Brooklyn.

"What's the matter, Harry?" Ellen asked, her face filled with puzzlement at the sight of her husband walking through the front door in the middle of the day.

"Nothing of much importance. It's just that we were wiped out this morning."

The future of baseball? Why is there any doubt about it? When the present business troubles disappear, history will repeat itself more strikingly than ever, and baseball's hold on the sports-loving public will be stronger than in any of our past boom years.

Jacob Ruppert, 1933

We thought American business was the Rock of Gibraltar. We were the prosperous nation, and nothing could stop us now. A brownstone house was forever. You gave it to your kids and they put marble fronts on it. There was a feeling of continuity. If you made it, it was there forever. Suddenly the big dream exploded.

E. Y. (Yip) Harburg, in Studs Terkel's *Hard Times*

7

On a mild, sunny afternoon early in January 1930 Alex found himself strolling down Broadway. He had a few hours to kill before work, and he was thinking about taking in a show. He passed under the marquee of the Palace but could not be lured inside by a bill featuring George Jessel, Jack Benny, and Burns and Allen.

As he looked down toward Times Square, Alex couldn't help pondering the unbelievable changes that had taken place in the ten years since Prohibition came in. Were he alive, Fletcher wouldn't have known what to make of Broadway now. The great street bore little resemblance to the elegant thoroughfare of Fletcher's day. Gone were most of the majestic hotels that had sprung up during the Gilded Age. The Manhattan Hotel, where the Manhattan cocktail originated, closed its doors way back in 1921. A year later the stately Buckingham, immortalized in Edith Wharton's *The Age of Innocence*, was razed.

Gone too were the Knickerbocker, the Normandy, and the slightly bawdy Marlborough, where Anna Held had once received the press in a milk-filled bathtub. The hotels that remained were not the same. The Astor Bar—a great saloon in its day—had suffered the ignominy of being converted into a drugstore. And the Claridge, once swank beyond words, was now decidedly second-rate.

Deprived of the right to sell spirits, the proud old hotels went quickly into the red and one by one were forced to close their doors. In the process Broadway was transformed, as one observer put it, into "a raucous jungle of chop-suey restaurants, hot dog and hamburger shops, garish nightclubs, fruit juice stands, dime museums, flea circuses, penny arcades, and lunch counters advertising 'EATS.'"

Observing the scene around him as he made his way toward Forty-second Street, Alex couldn't help but agree with Wilson Mizner, a playwright of the day, who had recently commented that "the once great Broadway has become something of a heel, definitely run down." Everywhere in New York, from Coney Island to Times Square, the vestiges of Fletcher's world were vanishing. Of course, Prohibition wasn't all bad. After all, it gave Alex his livelihood, and it had replaced the old saloon with a much finer institution. For in the speakeasy the pleasures of drinking were greatly enhanced by the presence of women. As Heywood Broun would later put it, "I would like here and now to pay tribute to the newly enfranchised sex. Far from bringing a Puritanic repression into drinking places their presence served to enliven and heighten fellowship. Under repeal it may well be that drinking can never be quite the same."

On that day in 1930 Alex had not yet begun to think about repeal as a real possibility. Even though he and Harry knew Prohibition was a farce, and even though all their friends were avowed wets, the speakeasy and the bootlegger had become permanent parts of their lives.

Politicians in Washington seemed happier debating how best to enforce the Eighteenth Amendment rather than whether or not to get rid of it. It would be some months before the great issues of the thirties would begin coming into focus.

Neither Alex nor Harry had any notion that the country was on the brink of a catastrophe. To be sure, they looked upon the crash as a great personal calamity, but they both had their jobs, so they had little difficulty making the mortgage payments that had been forced upon them by Harry's recklessness. The hurricane of change whose clouds were loosely forming on the horizon was still only a zephyr.

During those first days of the new decade Alex's mind was filled with thoughts of his family. He was very proud of his healthy, happy son, soon to be two years old. He was beginning to grow weary of his work schedule, which kept him away from home almost every night. And he was constantly telling himself how lucky he had been to find Sally. A remarkable woman in so many ways, she had brought him more comfort and happiness than he ever imagined possible during the long days of his bachelorhood.

And then there was baseball. Even though the new season was three months away, there was plenty of juicy news coming out of the Brooklyn front office. Steve McKeever was trying to get rid of Wilbert Robinson once and for all. The two had not been speaking since Robbie's battle with the *Sun* in 1926. McKeever could barely contain his bitterness over the fact that a man he looked upon as a buffoon was not only manager of the club but also president, and had the team nicknamed after him to boot!

Robins, hell! As far as old Steve was concerned the team was still the Superbas. McKeever was now in his mid-seventies; some people were saying that he had become senile, but on one subject he was completely lucid—he wanted Wilbert Robinson out. And now that Robbie's contract had expired, Steve was ready to fight to get his way.

McKeever, however, controlled only 50 percent of the club's stock. The other half was in the hands of the Ebbets heirs, who wanted to sign Robbie to a three-year contract.

With the new season approaching, something had to be done quickly to resolve the impasse. Player contracts had to be negotiated, and plans for spring training had to be completed. The owners of the other clubs, fearful that the situation in Brooklyn might throw the whole league into turmoil, pressured John Heydler to find a solution to the problem.

In February the league president called both sides to a meeting at the Hotel Commodore, where he proposed this compromise: If Robinson would step down as president, he would receive a new two-year contract as manager. Neither McKeever nor Joe Gilleaudeau, Ebbet's son-in-law, was happy with the solution, but they both went along with it. The man named as the new president was Frank B. York, a Manhattan attorney who had grown up in Brooklyn and had been a lifelong fan of the team.

It was York who had brought Charlie Ebbets and the McKeever brothers together in 1911 when Ebbets was seeking capital to finance his new ball park. To avoid further deadlocks on the board of directors, Heydler further proposed that a neutral member be added. The job was given to Walter F. "Dutch" Carter, who happened to be the brother-in-law and law partner of Supreme Court Justice Charles Evans Hughes. Carter was also from Brooklyn; in his college days in the 1890s he had been a star pitcher at Yale.

York, on assuming the presidency, declared, "I am certainly not in favor of seeing the same old group that finished sixth last year stumble out of the dugout on opening day this spring." Uncle Robbie didn't need his new boss to tell him the club was badly in need of fresh talent.

By the start of the season there were indeed some new faces. There were two new infielders, Mickey Finn and Gordon Slade, purchased from Oakland in the Pacific Coast League. Shortstop Glenn Wright, who had come to Brooklyn the year before in a deal that sent Jesse Petty to the Pirates, sat out most of the 1929 season with a bad arm. Glenn had undergone a shoulder operation and had then spent most of the winter playing catch with his wife, hoping to bring his arm around. Now he was in the starting lineup and appeared to be in fine form.

Al Lopez, a young catcher who had spent the 1929 season in Atlanta gaining experience, had displaced Hank DeBerry as the first-string backstop. Lopez and Ray Phelps, a pitcher with a weird sidearm delivery, would, before the season was over, be referred to by *Baseball Magazine* as "the greatest young battery to come up to the majors in recent years." Dolf Luque, for more than a decade a mainstay on the Cincinnati pitching staff, had come over from the Reds on waivers.

No one could say that Robbie wasn't searching for a winning combination.

On opening day Alex only half believed that Brooklyn had even a prayer. As far as he was concerned, Uncle Robbie was pretty much over the hill, and so was the team. Alex was still a loyal member of the Flatbush Faithful, however, so he gave the Robins his full support, pulling for them as if they were true contenders.

The Robins, in turn, played like potential champions. For the first eight weeks of the season they flirted with the top of the standings and then, during the last week in May, beat the Giants—who had been struggling along in the middle of the pack—three games out of four.

Now, unbelievably, Brooklyn was tied for first place with St. Louis. On Memorial Day the Robins swept a doubleheader with the Phils and took sole possession of the lead. From then until the middle of August they spent most of the time on top of the National League.

The team's sudden success sparked a lively controversy between Brooklyn fans still loyal to Uncle Robbie and those such as Alex who felt the time had come for old Falstaff to hang up his flagon. If Robbie were indeed over the hill, how was it he was winning games with a team that everyone knew was mediocre at best?

Alex was almost ready to become a believer, but as the Robins hit the road in mid-August he still had some nagging doubts. For one thing Dazzy Vance's fastball wasn't popping, and he was losing a lot of close ball games. For another, both Joe McCarthy's Cubs and John McGraw's Giants could explode at any moment.

McGraw had lost one of his best players when Edd Roush, unhappy with Stoneham's final salary offer, held out for the entire season. But the Little Napoleon, always maneuvering, had strengthened his infield and added power to his lineup by trading Larry Benton to the Reds for Hughie Critz, one of the sharpest second basemen in the league. "Those goddamn Giants," Alex said to himself, "there's no way of telling what McGraw might do to upset the apple cart."

Sure enough, the cart toppled over, but in the Midwest, not in the Polo Grounds. On August 6 the Robins left Brooklyn three and a half games in first place. Their first stop was Pittsburgh, where they bowled over the Pirates twice before heading confidently to St. Louis for five contests with the Cards. Brooklyn won the first game and then lost four straight, blowing the final game by giving up three runs in the bottom of the ninth.

Suddenly the Cubs had taken over first place, and as it happened the next stop on the Robins' itinerary was Chicago, where they dropped the first contest, 3–2.

The misery went on. The club lost two out of the next three with the Cubs, three out of five with the Pirates, and then five straight to the Reds. On August 23 Brooklyn was in third place, five games back.

Meanwhile the Giants had gone on a hot streak and moved into second. Asked to assess the situation, Uucle Robbie remarked, "People don't think I worry because I'm fat. Fat people are supposed to be good-natured and sleep nights. I'll admit I'm fat. There's no use denying what the scales tell me. But I worried enough on this last trip. In fact, I was half sick. Sometimes I remember that I'm not as young as I used to be and a series of drubbings such as we got takes it out of your hide. For we lost a lot of heart-breakers."

The Giants' sudden rise was accomplished, for the most part, without the Little Napoleon at the helm. Coach Dave Bancroft was now leading the club, supposedly because McGraw was attending to the affairs of his brother, who had died in Toledo some months earlier.

Actually, John was not well. His physician had ordered him to take a long rest. McGraw's absence touched off all kinds of rumors. Some people said he was making a deal to manage the Yankees. Others were convinced he was part of a group that was planning to buy the Pirates from Barney Dreyfuss and that McGraw was slated to become the next Pittsburgh manager. Many fans suspected that Stoneham was at odds with McGraw and was planning to dump him when his contract expired in January.

In early September Stoneham decided to dispel all the rumors by signing John to a new five-year contract. The Little Napoleon wasn't finished yet.

Alex was already looking ahead to next year when, in the first week of September, the Robins unexpectedly came back to life. They put together an eleven-game winning streak, including three games over Chicago that knocked the Cubs right out of the race.

Frank York began taking orders for World Series tickets while denying rumors that if the Robins won they would play the Series in either Yankee Stadium or the Polo Grounds. Then Gabby Street's Cardinals, long ago counted out by their own fans, suddenly came out of nowhere. They took three games from New York, shoving the Giants into fourth place. On September 16 the Cards arrived at Ebbets Field a mere game behind the Robins, who were as surprised as anyone to find themselves back on top.

The first game of the series pitted Dazzy Vance against Wild Bill

Hallahan. Alex and Harry, viewing the action from a field box behind first base, were on pins and needles all afternoon as both hurlers held the opposition at bay until, at the end of the regulation nine, the contest was still scoreless.

As the Robins took the field in the top of the tenth, Alex began to lose heart. The Dazzler was pitching one hell of a ball game, apparently to no avail. In the tenth Gabby Street sent Andy High, a utility infielder, up to the plate as a pinch hitter.

Andy had once played for Brooklyn, but Uncle Robbie had cast him off back in 1925. The ex-Robin now repaid the insult by hitting a double, moving to third on a sacrifice bunt by Hallahan, and coming in to score the go-ahead run on a single by Taylor Douthit. The Robins failed to score in their half of the inning, and now they shared first place with the Cardinals.

In game two of the series, Andy High once again doubled home the winning tallies to give St. Louis a 5–3 victory. And in the final game another old Robin, Burleigh Grimes, defeated Ray Phelps, 4–3. Brooklyn was now two games back and fading.

The Cardinals went on to win the pennant by two games over the Cubs, the Giants finished third, five games back, and the Robins toppled to fourth, six games off the pace. Uncle Robbie had put on quite a show, but in the end his boys sank to their natural level.

As Harry explained the season to Alex, "Robbie got the absolute maximum out of his ball club. By rights he should have lost ten more games." That wasn't much consolation to a loyal fan who'd been waiting a decade for a pennant.

And Alex wasn't likely to receive much consoling from Harry anyway. Even if managerial magic had subtracted ten from the loss column and added ten to the win column, Harry's Yanks would still have finished out of the running in the 1930 season.

Having lost Miller Huggins, the Yankees had been in need of a new skipper. Barrow was turned down by Donie Bush, who'd managed the Senators and Pirates, and also by Eddie Collins. Looking closer to home, Barrow eyed Art Fletcher, the Yankee coach who had taken over after Hug's death. Art had managed the Phillies from 1923 through 1926—extremely lean years for Philadelphia. Because of his sad experiences, Fletcher had promised his wife that his managing days were over. He would remain with the Yankees as a coach for the next sixteen years, but as for the top job, it was a crisp "thanks, but no thanks."

While the managerial post was being tossed around like a hot potato, the Babe was beginning to build up some heat of his own. The legs were beginning to go, and Ruth felt that the Yankees owed him a little something. But when Babe approached the boss and asked for the job, Barrow turned him down flat. Ed was convinced that Ruth was unsuited to run a ball club because, after all, "Ruth couldn't manage himself."

The Babe could, however, find some consolation in his victory at the bargaining table. He first demanded $100,000 a year, a sum that thinned Ruppert's smile and thickened his German accent. Ruth backed down a little, but not much, publicly threatening to quit the game unless he received $85,000 a year on a three-year contract. He finally settled for a $160,000, two-year deal—with the stipulation that Ruppert return the $5,000 fine that Huggins had levied on the big fellow back in 1925. "So long as Huggins was alive, Roots, I'd never have given it back," said Colonel Jake, "but Miller's dead now and he'll never know."

Finally Barrow handed over the helm to Sailor Bob Shawkey, the veteran hurler who had been with the team for nearly fifteen years. Shawkey's tenure with the club appeared to be the perfect qualification, but it turned out to be his downfall. An easygoing sort, Sailor Bob was unable to establish authority. His former drinking buddies scoffed at his battlefield commission, and discipline was nonexistent.

Early in the season Shawkey and Waite Hoyt nearly came to blows after slugger Al Simmons parked one of Hoyt's pitches into the upper deck of the Philadelphia grandstand. As Hoyt entered the dugout, Shawkey asked him, "What'd you throw him?"

"A fastball."

"From now on, make him hit your curve."

Hoyt glared at the new manager. "Yeah? He'd hit my curve *over* the grandstand. Don't tell me how to pitch to Simmons. I'll pitch to him my way."

"You pitch the way I tell you or you won't pitch at all," Shawkey snapped.

A couple of weeks later, Shawkey traded Hoyt and Mark Koenig to Detroit for infielder Harry Wuestling, pitcher Owen Carroll, and outfielder Harry Rice.

In a trade that made more sense, Shawkey sent Cedric Durst to the Red Sox in exchange for Red Ruffing, who went on to post a 15–5 mound record for the Yanks. Ruffing was the only real bright spot on the staff. The best the Bombers could come up with was a third-place finish, sixteen games behind the pennant-winning Athletics.

It was apparent to the Yankee bosses that they needed a replacement for Sailor Bob. As the campaign was winding down, Barrow happened to run into Warren Brown, a Chicago sportswriter, at a boxing match. Brown, a friend of Joe McCarthy's, told Barrow that McCarthy was on his way out as manager of the Cubs, soon to be replaced by Rogers Hornsby.

By the time the move was made public in late September, Barrow had made up his mind. He sent Paul Krichell, the Yanks' ace scout, to track down McCarthy at the World Series in Philadelphia and bring him to New York.

When McCarthy met with Barrow and Ruppert in the colonel's Fifth

Avenue apartment, he proved to be a hardnosed bargainer. He repeatedly refused Ruppert's offers and demanded his own terms. Finally he jumped to his feet and stalked toward the door. Ruppert hurried after him, calling his name, and caught up with him as he was about to step into the elevator. The Yankees had a new manager. Later, Barrow asked McCarthy what he would have done if Ruppert had not called him back.

"What *could* I have done?" Joe said with a grin. "I'd-a just kept going."

Looking back on the 1930 campaign *Spalding's Guide* reported that "the National League not only had the best championship race in its history but it completed its most prosperous season." The main reason for the prosperity was the remarkable showing of the Dodgers. As Uncle Robbie had put it, "We've done our best to give the league a close pennant fight, and that's what the league wants. While we're about it, we've made a lot of money for the owners. And nobody I ever saw, owners or players or bat boys or fans, ever objected to money."

And while the Brooklyn club enjoyed a great season at the gate, it would have been even better if only Ebbets Field were larger. It was clear that one way or another the park would have to be expanded. For years Steve McKeever had tried to persuade the city to reroute Montgomery Street back onto the property the club owned on the other side of the street. That way the left-field and center-field grandstands could be enlarged. But no one at City Hall was willing to buy McKeever's argument that "a modern baseball plant in Brooklyn would be of civic benefit."

Now McKeever decided to expand the park from within and announced in October 1930, "the left-field wing of the present double-decked grandstand will be extended in a sweeping curve around and over the present wooden bleacher seats in left field." It was hoped that the new concrete stands would raise the capacity of the park to forty thousand. But once the work got under way, the engineers on the job realized that the expansion would bring the park's maximum attendance up to a mere thirty-five thousand fans—only half the hoped-for increase.

It may have been a prosperous year for the Dodgers, but the world outside of baseball became ever grimmer as 1930 wore on. In March, Frances Perkins, New York State's Industrial Commissioner, announced that unemployment was more severe than at any time since the state began keeping figures in 1914. By August the problem was so acute that the *New York Times* reported: "A large number of persons are in fact out of work, have little or no current incomes, have dependents, have bills to pay for food, housing and clothing. . . . The individual worries of the millions of unemployed are multiplied many times in terms of other millions who cannot escape dealings with the unemployed." By the end of the year the Depression was a reality almost no one in America was able to ignore.

Early in 1931 hard times finally hit the Rice household. Ever since the Crash people in Harry's company had been let go in dribs and drabs, until the firm was down to a skeleton crew. On Friday, February 27, Kris Ramnaes called Harry into his office to give him the unhappy news.

"The company is in terrible shape," Kris explained. "As soon as we've weathered the storm, I promise you'll be one of the first to be called back." Harry left without any resentments or even very many regrets. He had known for some time that this day was coming. Now that it had arrived there was no use crying about it. Something would turn up. He had no illusions about being invited back to American Founders. That was just as well, because later that afternoon Kris Ramnaes, who had spent the day giving people their walking papers, was himself given the ax.

During the first months of Harry's unemployment he went out every morning to search for a job, never returning home until the evening rush hour. He remembered with no small sense of irony how, so many years before, he had prodded his brother not to give up, to get out there and keep looking for work.

It wasn't until the middle of the summer that he began to lose heart. There simply were no jobs. To look for one was to play at charades. By stages Harry began staying home—first one day a week, then two, until finally he gave up altogether. It was then that Ellen began to share his desperation. As long as her man was out of the house she was able to convince herself that everything would turn out all right. Now that he was home, she too lost hope.

Alex, now the family's only breadwinner, tried to escape from his burdens that summer by immersing himself in baseball. The season gave him little to cheer about. Before the campaign began, Alex told Harry the Robins had a great chance to win the pennant. After all, Uncle Robbie had strengthened the team by picking up pitcher Joe Shaute from the Indians and slugger Lefty O'Doul from the Phillies.

In 1929 John McGraw had sent Lefty to Philadelphia; in two seasons there he had batted .398 and .383. Now he and Babe Herman, who hit .393 in 1930, would supposedly give Brooklyn all the power it could use. Other additions to the Robins' roster in 1931 included the old hurler Jack Quinn, who came up with the Yankees way back in 1909, and Van Lingle Mungo. Mungo—a rookie pitcher who, though wild, had an unbelievable fastball—was called up from Hartford in September.

All of these personnel changes went for naught. After a sluggish spring exhibition season that included a drunken junket to Havana, the Robins began the regular campaign by losing ten of their first twelve ball games. They never really were in the race, and they finished a very weak fourth, twenty-one games out of first.

The Giants fared somewhat better, winding up in second place, thirteen games behind the Cardinals.

Over in the American League the Yankees did not play well enough to allow Harry to forget his troubles. There were, of course, some great individual efforts. Ruth and Gehrig each hit forty-six homers. Young Lefty Gomez won twenty-one and lost nine, and his ERA of 2.63 was second best in the league behind Lefty Grove's 2.06. As a team the Yanks produced an unprecedented 1,067 runs, but they still came in second, losing the pennant to Philadelphia by thirteen and a half games. In the World Series the Cards defeated the A's four games to three, bringing the National League its first world championship in five years.

On October 23, 1931, the directors of the Brooklyn Baseball Club assembled in the board room in Ebbets Field. Several reporters, guessing something might be up, lounged outside the meeting room for four long hours; some whiled away the time shooting craps, while others pondered and discussed the question that was on everyone's mind: Would Wilbert Robinson's contract be renewed? Finally Frank York emerged from the inner sanctum and announced that the club had hired Max Carey to be its new manager. After eighteen years at the helm, Uncle Robbie was out. He was sent away, as one reporter put it, with "the board's more or less sincere good wishes for future health and happiness."

The reaction to Wilbert Robinson's release was generally favorable. Alex told Harry it was about time. Robbie himself, reached at his winter retreat at Dover Hall, Georgia, expressed surprise at the news but swallowed his pride and said, "If the directors want Carey as manager it's all right with me."

And so one of the most impressive careers in baseball came to an end. Only four men in the history of the game—Walt Alston, Cap Anson, Connie Mack, and John McGraw—have remained longer at the helm of a single club. Some people called Uncle Robbie a clown. At times he was a bit flaky, to be sure, but in his day he was a superb manager—a leader who could squeeze the last ounce of inspiration out of many an uninspired ballplayer.

He deserves his place in the Hall of Fame if only for his remarkable showing against the Giants. In his eighteen seasons at Brooklyn Uncle Robbie's teams finished in the first division only six times; during those same years John McGraw finished out of the first division only twice. And yet, in 392 games against the Little Napoleon, Uncle Robbie won 190, lost 197, and tied 5 for a .491 percentage.

After coming to the Dodgers from the Pirates in 1926, Max Carey had played regularly in the Brooklyn outfield during 1927 and 1928. But in

1929 he appeared in only nineteen games; his illustrious career was over, and he spent most of that season as a Dodger coach.

In 1930 Carey went back to Pittsburgh as a coach; he remained there only one season. He'd been out of work when the call came from Brooklyn.

Max appeared to be a good choice. He was recognized as one of the most intelligent players ever to wear a major league uniform. He had been a fine hitter, an excellent outfielder, and the best base-stealer in the National League. Tommy Holmes, writing in the *Sporting News*, accurately described the mood in Brooklyn when he wrote, "In Flatbush, Max comes face to face with one of the most loyal bands of fans in the country and he can walk off with both approaches to the Brooklyn Bridge, so far as they are concerned, if he makes good."

Holmes also suggested that, in light of the fact that Carey's name at birth was Maximilian Carnarius, the Robins be renicknamed the Canaries. But apparently the fans and the press had given up on birds, because the team soon became known once again as the Dodgers. One reference to our feathered friends would, however, become a permanent part of Brooklyn's baseball vocabulary. Some papers, especially the *Daily News*, would in the years ahead often refer to the team in headlines as "The Flock."

Alex, who approved wholeheartedly of Carey's appointment, was anxious to see what steps Max would take to strengthen the team. He didn't have to wait long. In January the new pilot brought Casey Stengel from the Toledo Mud Hens to be Brooklyn's assistant manager. Alex was delighted when he heard that his old hero was coming back to the Dodgers.

Stengel's appointment was also applauded by the *Sporting News*, which called him "a hard-bitten baseball warrior of the old school, with oodles of color, truckloads of fighting spirit and a rare sense of humor." In February Carey persuaded the Brooklyn management to purchase Hack Wilson from St. Louis for $45,000. Wilson, a heavy-hitting outfielder who began his career with the Giants in 1923, had been traded from the Cubs to the Cardinals a few weeks earlier.

Then, during spring training, Carey and York made a move that shocked most Brooklyn fans—they got rid of Babe Herman. They sent Herman, Wally Gilbert, and Ernie Lombardi to the Reds for infielders Joe Stripp and Tony Cuccinello and catcher Clyde Sukeforth.

Babe had been asked to take a salary cut from $19,000 down to $15,000 and had refused to report to Clearwater, Florida, for spring training. He remained at home in Los Angeles and spent most of the spring watching the Giants, who trained in Southern California that year, go through their preseason paces.

Now that the Dodgers had Wilson, Herman was dispensable. Some fans, on hearing about the trade, complained that Frank York was behaving like another Harry Frazee. The cry of outrage came as a bit of a surprise to the owners, because Herman had always been razzed by the home crowd more than all but the most hated rival players. Behind all that heckling was, no doubt, a great deal of affection.

As Alex viewed it, the trade made sense. First baseman Del Bissonette was injured and would be out for the entire season. Joe Stripp, the central player in the deal, was a versatile infielder who could fill Bissonette's shoes at first and also play third. Still, Alex couldn't help but feel downhearted at the thought of Babe Herman—the man *Baseball Magazine* described as having "more color than a Turkish rug"—playing for a team other than the Dodgers.

The Dodgers spent most of the 1932 season in the middle of the standings, coming on strong in the final weeks to finish in third place, nine games back. Lefty O'Doul won the league batting title with a .368 average, pitcher Watty Clark had the best year of his career with a 20–12 record, and Hack Wilson hit twenty-three homers. Alex felt that Carey had put the team in a good position to make a serious pennant bid in 1933. From the standpoint of the Dodger management, however, 1932 was not such a great year. No sooner had the club invested in the new outfield stands than attendance began to drop.

The Depression was no longer willing to overlook baseball. Many fans, Alex included, found it almost impossible to scrape up the price of admission. Frank York, blaming himself for the decline at the gate, literally walked off the job in October, leaving Steve McKeever to take over as president.

Time was running out on John McGraw. Suffering from a serious prostate condition, he was a very sick man. He had no business subjecting himself to the rigors of running a big league ball team. Nonetheless, as he left Los Angeles to begin the 1932 campaign, he was determined to win his first pennant in eight years. But after two months the Giants found themselves in the cellar. On the morning of June 3 John Kieran observed in his column in the *Times* that "on paper the Giants have a formidable team but, as has been pointed out so often, ball games are not played on paper. Even John McGraw is stumped for an answer to the question of what is wrong with the Giants, and if John McGraw doesn't know, who does?"

When Kieran wrote those words, McGraw had already decided to call it a career. His illness had forced him to leave the team during the first western road trip; on his return to New York his doctor told him he would have to confine his managing to the Polo Grounds. The Little Napoleon was not prepared to carry on in a half-baked manner. On Thursday, June 2, McGraw summoned Bill Terry into his office for a private conversation. Bill, who had not been on speaking terms with Mc-

Graw for some time, figured his manager was calling him onto the carpet. Terry had held out for a higher salary every spring since 1929, and McGraw, frustrated by the endless haggling, had tried to get rid of his temperamental first baseman several times.

In January 1931 he had offered Terry to Brooklyn for Babe Herman, and in December of the same year he had tried to send him to the Cubs for Kiki Cuyler. Then, in the spring of 1932, McGraw had told his perennial holdout he was free to offer himself to the Braves for pitcher Fred Frankhouse. Terry scowled at the Little Napoleon and said, "Make your own deals. I get enough blame just playing first base."

Terry entered the Old Man's office fully expecting an unpleasant confrontation. John looked up and told Bill to stand with his back to the door. "I don't want to close it," McGraw explained, "and I don't want anyone to know what I'm going to say."

Bill, puzzled, followed the instructions.

"I'm quitting," McGraw said. "If you want to be the new manager of this ball club, the job's yours. You can have a few days to think it over."

Terry, dumbfounded, stood in silence for several seconds and then, regaining his composure, replied, "I don't have to think about it. I'll take it."

The news of McGraw's resignation broke the following afternoon, June 3. As it happened, the Little Napoleon shared the headlines with Lou Gehrig, who on that same day tied the major league record by hitting four home runs in a single game against the A's.

The Rice brothers found it impossible to picture the Giants, or baseball for that matter, without John McGraw. Commenting on McGraw's departure, W. O. McGeehan of the *Herald Tribune* spoke for Alex and Harry as well as two generations of baseball fans when he wrote: "If I wanted to name anybody as the spirit of the American game incarnate I would think of John Joseph McGraw."

Bill Terry's first decision was to relax McGraw's rigid training rules. He hoped to loosen up his players and get the team rolling, but it soon became obvious that 1932 was not the Giants' year. They finished the season in sixth place, eighteen games behind the pennant-winning Cubs.

Joe McCarthy, meanwhile, was having better luck in his sophomore year as manager of the Yankees. In his first year McCarthy had quickly shown that he was Ruppert's kind of man by demanding that his players wear both jacket *and* tie whenever they were in public.

Because he wanted his men to concentrate on baseball, he outlawed card playing in the clubhouse—on Joe's orders, the card table was not only removed but chopped into splinters. He also banned shaving in the clubhouse, figuring that if his players knew they had to rise early enough to shave at home, they just might get to bed a bit earlier. He instituted no curfew, but the wily manager did hold a "breakfast check" on the road. The Yankees could stay up as late as they wished, but every one of them—Ruth included—was required to appear for breakfast by 8:30. Mc-

Carthy was always there, behind his morning paper, keeping a sharp eye out to see who was bright-eyed and who was bushed.

"I don't like to lose," Colonel Jake had told McCarthy early on. "Neither do I," was McCarthy's reply. He had brought the team in second in 1931. Ruppert had been able to accept that, but another second-place finish in 1932 might well have sent McCarthy packing. But Marse Joe had little worry about job security, as the Yanks seized first place in mid-May and never relinquished it, winding up thirteen games ahead of the second-place Athletics.

At the beginning of the 1932 season the Babe, for the first time in his career, had been forced to take a salary cut—to a mere $75,000. The haggling between Ruppert and Ruth was the source of a legendary exchange between the two:

"Roots, last year you earned more money than President Hoover."

"Hell, I had a better year than Hoover!"

Even though the Babe, now thirty-seven, had bouts with the grippe, bad legs, and mild appendicitis, causing him to miss some twenty games, he still managed to bat .341 and blast forty-one homers. But for the first time since 1925, Ruth lost the home run crown. Jimmy Foxx of the Athletics, "the new Babe Ruth," swatted fifty-eight four-baggers and walked away with the title.

The World Series with the Chicago Cubs was an anticlimax. When Charlie Grimm, who had taken over for the ousted Rogers Hornsby about two-thirds of the way through the campaign, brought his team into New York for the first game, about all the confident Yankees could find to get excited about was the presence of their former teammate, Mark Koenig.

The Cubs had brought Koenig up from the minors to help with their pennant drive. The switch-hitting shortstop had played thirty-one games for the Cubs, batted .353, and fielded brilliantly. There was no doubt that Koenig had been the key to the Cubs' taking the flag, yet his teammates voted him only a partial share of the World Series money. As the Cubs took the field for the first time, the Yanks, led by Ruth, greeted them raucously as cheapskates, penny pinchers, and nickel nursers.

The Yankees won the first two games easily and then traveled to Wrigley Field for the third. His first time at bat, in the first inning, Ruth made the score 3–0 by belting a Charlie Root pitch into the bleachers in right center. Gehrig followed with another homer. But when the Babe came to bat in the fifth inning, the Cubs had tied the score at four-all, and the tying run had scored when Ruth narrowly missed a shoetop catch—a fact that the hostile crowd was not about to let the Babe forget.

Root rifled one down the pipe for strike one. The crowd and the Chicago bench howled with glee. Grinning, Ruth elaborately indicated the count to the crowd by holding up one finger. Root then wasted two pitches before piping another one to make the count two and two. The crowd jeered wildly as the Babe held up two fingers. Then Ruth stepped out of the box and held up one finger. He could have been pointing to the vociferous Cubs bench. He could have been indicating that it takes only one pitch to get a hit. Or he could have been pointing to the center-field wall.

Whatever his signal meant, there was no doubt what he had in mind when he swung at the next pitch. The ball streaked high over the middle of center field and disappeared from the ball park. As the Babe rounded third, he held up four fingers and then doubled over in laughter.

It was all over for the Cubs. The Yanks swept four straight, making their record an almost unbelievable twelve straight Series victories. The Babe had played in his tenth World Series, a record he had long coveted, and had hit his fifteenth—and last—Series homer, a homer that would become a part of American folklore.

In November 1932 Harry and Alex were dealt the most serious setback of their lives. They lost Fletcher's house. During the several months since Harry had been fired, Alex struggled valiantly to hold onto the old place. But on his income there was no way to feed and clothe five persons and meet the mortgage payments as well. Finally, the bank foreclosed. The Rice brothers were forced to move both their families into a tiny one-bedroom apartment on the top floor of a brownstone on Ninth Street near Seventh Avenue in Park Slope.

Except for the sorrow over losing the family house, the Rices had little trouble adjusting to their new home. Alex, Sally, and young Damon shared the bedroom, while Harry and Ellen camped out in the living room. Alex, who spent most of his time at the Dizzy Club, wasn't bothered by the cramped quarters.

Harry was, however, understandably upset. He disliked being supported by his younger brother, but there was little he could do about it. He became more and more depressed. His appetite disappeared and he began to lose weight. He also had trouble sleeping, and often he would rise in the middle of the night and go for a long walk.

In an attempt to help his brother retain some pride, Alex turned most of his pay over to Harry, who paid the bills and managed the family budget. Although Harry usually wound up with several dollars left over each month, he allowed himself only one luxury—a daily newspaper. Through the paper Harry maintained a necessary if small connection with the outside world. He followed closely the developments of the nascent 1933 season, even though he knew full well that he would be attending few ball games that year.

In April 1933, beer—"the healthful temperance drink," according to Jacob Ruppert—was made legal. Colonel Jake celebrated the renaissance of the family business by putting up a quarter of a million dollars to help finance the second Byrd Antarctic expedition. When Byrd and his crew reached the Bay of Whales, they dumped two thousand empty Ruppert beer bottles, each containing a note, overboard. Colonel Jake solemnly declared that the bottles, presumably full when the voyage began, would teach scientists a great deal about ocean currents.

But the colonel was not so generous in matters concerning baseball. He sent the aging Ruth a contract for $50,000. "That's not a pay cut," the Babe sputtered, "that's an amputation!" Eventually, however, the Babe had to settle for $52,000.

A highlight of the 1933 season was the first All-Star Game, the brain-child of Arch Ward, sports editor of the *Chicago Tribune*. John Mc-Graw was lured out of retirement to manage the Nationals' dream team, while Connie Mack was at the helm for the Americans.

On July 6 fifty thousand fans ignored the Depression and filled Comiskey Park in Chicago to see this fantasy come true, the greats playing the greats. Some were undoubtedly disappointed when Mack kept a number of his greats on the bench, choosing to play tight, inside baseball once his team had gained the lead in the second inning. But the Babe, the man who had threatened inside baseball with obsolescence, gave the crowd its money's worth by belting a two-run homer in the third inning to ice the game for the Americans.

The Yankees played good ball throughout the season but lost the pennant to the red-hot Washington Senators, and the Babe once more lost the home run title to triple-crown-winner Jimmy Foxx.

The tribulations of 1933 made it difficult for the Rice brothers to concentrate on baseball. The sorry state of the Dodgers made it especially difficult for Alex. In February Dazzy Vance and Gordon Slade had been traded to the Cardinals.

Hundreds of fans, on hearing the news, called up the Dodger office to protest the trade. Over the previous eleven seasons Ol' Daz had become a Brooklyn institution. How could those bums in the front office just discard him like an old shoe?

But discard him they did, and in June another Brooklyn favorite, Lefty O'Doul, was also sent packing. He and Watty Clark were traded to the Giants for first baseman Sam Leslie. The Dodger fans now found themselves without any heroes, and they stayed away from Ebbets Field in droves.

In the past the Flatbush Faithful had supported a mediocre team because the Dodgers always had one or two players who captured a fan's imagination—Nap Rucker, Zack Wheat, and Burleigh Grimes, not to mention Babe Herman and Dazzy Vance. Now the club was made up of has-beens and would-bes.

One pundit described the 1933 Dodgers as "lethargic, listless, and philosophical." It was hardly surprising, especially in those hard times, that the same adjectives applied to the club's fans. In August Steve Mc-

Keever, hoping to give the club better leadership in the front office, fired general manager Dave Driscoll and replaced him with Bob Quinn, a former owner of the Boston Red Sox. The Dodgers finished in sixth place and lost a bundle of money. Alex saw a tiny ray of hope for the future in the pitching of Van Mungo; using his blazing fastball as his main weapon, young Mungo won sixteen games, lost fifteen, and posted an ERA of 2.72.

Some weeks before the 1933 season began Bill Terry was asked by a group of reporters how he expected the Giants to do that year. "I think we'll do third or better," Terry replied.

"Sure, Bill," one scribe piped up, "O.K., now that you've proved you have a sense of humor, tell us honestly—where do you think you'll finish?"

"I'm telling you guys, we're a cinch for the first division if Parmelee and Schumacher come through. Of course I'm taking Fitz and Hubbell for granted. If any of you think I'm kidding, put your money where your mouth is."

Several of the reporters accepted Bill's offer. They figured they were taking candy from a baby. The Giants would be lucky to finish fourth. They had no big guns except for Terry himself, and of course Ott.

Over the winter Terry had sold Shanty Hogan to the Braves and traded Freddie Lindstrom—who'd played center field for the past two seasons—to the Pirates. Travis Jackson was still trying to recover from a knee operation he'd undergone the previous fall. To fill Jackson's shoes Terry purchased shortstop Blondy Ryan from Buffalo. Other newcomers included Kiddo Davis, who replaced Lindstrom in center; Gus Mancuso, the new catcher; and Joe Moore, whom the *Sporting News* described as "a thin outfielder who looked hungry enough to be a Depression hero." It was hardly a star-studded roster. When, during the early part of the season, Terry fractured his wrist and was forced to remove himself from the lineup, the reporters were certain of their bets.

Terry was out for a month, but the Giants did not fall apart. They stayed close to the top of the standings until June and then surprised the experts by moving into first place. Despite challenges from a number of contenders, New York held onto the lead through July and August. Their amazing performance won the admiration of fans and the press alike, because, in an era famous for the long ball, the Giants were winning on pitching.

Carl Hubbell was having a remarkable year; he would win twenty-three games, ten of them by shutouts. Always reliable Freddie Fitzsimmons, the best knuckleballer in the league, was on his way to a sixteen and eleven record. And then there was Hal Schumacher, who turned in the most surprising performance on the staff. The previous year he'd been in twenty-seven games, winning five and losing six. Terry stayed with him, and in 1933 he came into his own. Relying primarily on a low fastball and an excellent curve, he would win nineteen and lose twelve. The fourth regular starter was Roy Parmelee, so wild the year before he'd been sent to Columbus to settle down. Now he had discovered the location of the strike zone, and he was hurling his way to a record of thirteen and eight. Other members of the pitching staff were forty-three-year-old Dolf Luque, who'd been brought over from the Dodgers in 1932, and former Cardinal Hi Bell.

No one who was in the Polo Grounds on July 2, 1933, will ever forget that day. The Giants were being challenged by the second-place Cardinals, who had just taken two of the first three in a five-game series with New York. The Giants' lead over St. Louis was now three and a half games; if the Cards could sweep the twin bill they would narrow the margin to only a game and a half.

The fifty thousand fans in the Polo Grounds witnessed one of the most remarkable pitching displays in baseball history. In the opener Terry sent Carl Hubbell up against right-hander Tex Carleton. The first nine innings went by without any scoring; neither starter was prepared to give an inch. It wasn't until the seventeenth frame that Carleton was removed for a pinch hitter. Hubbell kept going into the eighteenth, when Hughie Critz finally singled home Joe Moore from third, giving New York a 1–0 victory. Hubbell, in eighteen innings, was unbelievable. He allowed only six hits and not a single walk.

Gabby Street was now in a deep hole. The nightcap was a must game. In desperation he gave the nod to Dizzy Dean, who'd shut out the Giants only two days earlier. Terry sent in Roy Parmelee.

Dean held the Giants scoreless until the fourth, when Johnny Vergez powered a home run into the upper tier in left field to give New York a 1–0 lead. That ended the scoring. It was almost dark when the game finally came to an end.

Parmelee had given the Giants their second 1–0 shutout of the day and had increased the club's lead in the pennant race to five and a half lengths. The only sour note to an otherwise perfect day came in the second inning of the nightcap when Blondy Ryan was spiked by Joe Medwick. Ryan's wound, which required thirteen stitches, kept him out of action for almost two weeks.

The Giants hit the road, and without Ryan in the lineup they fell into a slump; they lost seven games in a row and watched their lead dwindle to two and a half games. Then, on July 12, Terry received a wire: "THEY CANNOT BEAT US. EN ROUTE. J. C. RYAN." In a few days Blondy was back at short wearing a special shin guard to protect his injured leg. The Giants snapped back to life and went on to capture the National League flag by five games. "They Cannot Beat Us" became the rallying cry of the 1933 Giants in much the same way "You Gotta Believe" became the slogan of the 1973 Mets.

The 1933 World Series reminded Alex and Harry of the last time the

Giants appeared in the Fall Classic, in 1924. Once again the Giants' opponents were the Senators, and once again the Washington manager was a hard-playing, fast-thinking infielder. Instead of Bucky Harris, the Senators had another boy wonder—twenty-six-year-old Joe Cronin. It was the first time since 1906—when Fielder Jones's White Sox defeated Frank Chance's Cubs—that two player–managers faced each other in a World Series. Most experts believed the Giants had won the pennant on a fluke, and the Senators were heavy favorites to repeat their triumph of 1924.

Poor as they were, Alex and Harry somehow managed to scrape up the price of two grandstand tickets for the opening game of the Series. They were not surprised, in that Depression year, to discover that there were empty seats scattered throughout the grandstands, while the bleachers were packed to capacity.

"The Senators are in for a big surprise if they think they're going to walk all over Carl. Wait till they get a look at his screwball," Alex said to his brother.

"Oh, I don't think they expect to walk all over him, but they sure as hell believe they're going to get to him before the afternoon is over," Harry replied, his voice filled with excitement. "This should be one fine ball game."

It was. Buddy Myer, the first batter, stepped in and watched carefully as Carl took his windup with the greatest of ease and then threw the ball with what appeared to be no effort at all. The deceptive motion caught the batter with his bat halfway into his swing, not sure whether to follow through or pull back. In quick order Carl struck Buddy out and then fanned the next two hitters—Goose Goslin and Heinie Manush—as well. In the bottom half of the inning Mel Ott homered with Joe Moore on to give the Giants a 2–0 lead. The first inning set the tone for the rest of the day. Ott went four for four that afternoon, and King Carl held the Senators to two runs as New York went on to win, 4–2.

In the second game Hal Schumacher faced General Crowder, Washington's veteran ace. After losing to King Carl the Senators were itching to get at Prince Hal, and they did manage to score first, getting a single run in the third. But in the sixth inning New York loaded the bases, and Lefty O'Doul, in his only appearance in the Series, hit a clean single up the middle to score two runs and give New York the lead. Alex, listening on the radio, stood up and gave out a loud cheer when the old Dodger made good. Before the inning was over the Giants scored six runs. Schumacher held the Senators scoreless the rest of the way as New York rolled to a 6–1 victory.

The scene shifted to Washington for game three. President Roosevelt came by to throw out the first ball and to watch Freddie Fitzsimmons pitch against Earl Whitehill. Freddie got off to a shaky start, giving up two runs in the first and one more in the second.

Then he settled down and held the Senators in check until the seventh, when he gave up one more run. The Giants were powerless all afternoon, and Freddie was removed for a pinch hitter in the eighth. Whitehill, a strong left-hander, allowed only five hits and no runs as Washington won the ball game, 4–0.

The following day Carl Hubbell and Monte Weaver clashed in another superbly pitched contest that the Giants won, 2–1, in eleven innings. The fifth game began with Schumacher once again facing Crowder. Both starters left in the sixth inning; Dolf Luque took over for New York and Jack Russell went to work for Washington.

With the score tied 3–3 the two relievers pitched flawlessly through the ninth inning, forcing the game into extra innings for the second day in a row. In the bottom of the tenth, with two out and no one on base, Mel Ott drilled the ball into left center. It tipped Fred Schulte's glove and then dropped into the seats to give the Giants the game and the Series.

John McGraw dragged himself to all five games. In Griffith Stadium, watching the action from the press box behind home plate, he appeared lost in a reverie as he munched his peanuts and quietly urged his old club on to victory.

Some fans, claiming the Giants were still "McGraw's team," were inclined to attribute the team's surprising finish to its old manager. McGraw didn't see it that way. In the Giant locker room, after offering Terry his congratulations, the Little Napoleon said, "I've had nothing to do with this. All of the praise belongs to Bill, a wonderful manager, and to the boys who backed him up on the field." Charles Stoneham agreed that the credit belonged to Terry. He quickly rewarded Bill by signing him to a five-year contract at $40,000 a year.

On December 5, 1933, Prohibition, after thirteen years, ten months, and nineteen days, was in its final hours. In one thousand newly licensed establishments, and in about one hundred thousand speakeasies, proprietors and customers alike sat listening to radios, waiting for word that liquor was legal. The Dizzy Club was no exception.

Alex, along with about ten customers, listened quietly as the radio hissed and squawked with static. "Hey, Al," a patron called, "you gonna make me one of them New Deal cocktails?" Alex smiled and didn't reply. At precisely 5:49½ P.M. Eastern Standard Time, the voice of acting Secretary of State William Phillips announced that the thirtieth state, Utah, had ratified the repeal amendment.

It was legal. The announcement was met with silence in the Dizzy Club. Finally Alex spoke. "Well," he said, "I guess the drinks are on the house." And he helped himself to one as well.

The reaction in the Dizzy Club was not unique. Throughout New

York, John Barleycorn's resurrection was greeted quietly. After all, for those who wanted it and could afford it, booze had never been easier to find than during Prohibition. Nonetheless, the city police, fearing a wild celebration, had placed wooden barricades and extra officers in Times Square. They needn't have bothered. The crowds were small, the mood was quiet.

It was dead at the Dizzy Club. Alex guessed that those few who did wish to celebrate were doing so in the new "legit" places, some of which were holding special parties. Up in Harlem a contest was going on to see who could tell drinks made with Prohibition stuff from those made with legal liquor. The Park Lane Hotel was offering a free drink to anyone who ordered "an authentic drink of any nation that cannot be produced from the rolling bar in full view of the customer."

But it was the Waldorf—the new Waldorf, the old having been demolished to make way for the Empire State Building—that was leading the way in drinking in the modern manner. The café in the old Waldorf had been a study in mahogany, a place where international bankers came to quaff rare whiskys, smoke fine cigars, and deal in millions.

The new café reflected the changes wrought by Prohibition, particularly the new drinking status of women. The ninety-foot-long café lounge was a symphony of blue mirrors and yellow shell. The floors were jade, the softly lit tables were of ultramarine glass and polished chromium, and all was in the "French manner."

But at the Dizzy Club business was so slow that Alex decided to close the place early. He had been helped in his decision by the drinks he had already put away and by the insistence of a customer that Alex accompany him to a party. After locking up, Alex hopped into his friend's Packard and they sped downtown and across the bridge to Brooklyn, nipping from a flask all the way.

When they entered the townhouse in Brooklyn Heights, the shindig was in high gear. The host was a party boss with whom Alex was only vaguely familiar. Alex helped himself to a tumbler of bourbon and found a seat on a staircase that provided a view of the general hubbub. Tinny music was blasting from a Victrola, and from somewhere off in another room came the sound of a piano.

The room was hot, smoky, and noisy. The chatter from at least a hundred partygoers was nearly deafening. A burly, red-faced man in shirtsleeves approached Alex.

"Hiya," he said, extending a meaty hand. "Who'd you work with last election?"

Alex looked at him blankly. "I'm a Dodger man," he said finally. Then he stood and walked to the door, buttoning his coat with his free hand. In the foyer he finished off the bourbon and hung the tumbler, upside down, on a coat tree.

The quiet of the night washed over him as he stepped outside. Jamming his hands into his coat pockets, Alex shuffled slowly through the cold air. For some reason, a reason he couldn't grasp, he was depressed.

He told himself he had every reason to be happy. After all, with the end of Prohibition there would be more work for bartenders—with no fear of the cops. On top of that, he had a loving wife and a healthy boy. But a feeling of dissatisfaction gnawed at him. There was something he should be doing, something he was leaving unfinished.

The clanging of a bell began to penetrate his thoughts. He realized he was walking in the middle of Fulton Street. He whirled and was blinded by the headlight of the speeding trolley. As he leaped to the side, the streetcar clipped him on the shoulder. He spun around, his arms flailing for balance. He hit an icy patch in the gutter, skidded, and shot into the air. His head rammed the curb.

He came to in a well-lighted place. A doctor was holding a small bottle under his nose. The cop standing behind the doctor was holding a handkerchief over the lower half of his face and dabbing at his eyes to ease the effect of the smelling salts. Alex inhaled deeply, trying to clear the cobwebs from his head. The base of his skull was throbbing, and he could barely move his right arm.

The doctor dismissed the cop and stitched up the gash in the back of Alex's head. When he had dressed the wound and examined the severely bruised shoulder, he handed Alex a sheet of paper. "Here," he said. "Take this to the emergency room at Kings County Hospital. We've got to get you X-rayed." Alex assured the doctor, who escorted him to a cab, that he would go straight to the hospital. Then he went home.

After a two-week convalescence, Alex returned to the Dizzy Club. But three days later he was back in bed. This time Harry himself saw to it that Alex had a thorough medical checkup. The family doctor told Alex he could do no work of any kind for at least three months.

Harry, who had all but given up his attempts to find work, became desperate. He scoured the city, but there was simply no work. The prospect of going on relief horrified Harry. He would rather starve.

The tiny apartment, once so cozy, now became dismal. With Alex in bed suffering from vicious headaches, the rest of the family tiptoed and spoke in whispers.

The telephone had been removed. Harry tacked cardboard over the windows to keep out the cold, and by February they had taken to heating only the kitchen to save on the gas bill. Their social life became nonexistent.

Sally and Ellen even gave up taking Damon to church; they had nothing for the plate and nothing suitable to wear. When a tube went in the Crosley, they were left without even the solace of the radio.

In March the situation eased slightly when Sally, over the protests of Alex and Harry, took a job as a hostess in a tea room. The exhaustion in her face after a seventy-two-hour work week brought tears to Alex's eyes, and the seven dollars she brought home every Saturday barely paid the rent. Meanwhile, Ellen had discovered that she could make three or four dollars a week giving bridge lessons to luckier ladies. "You know," she said to Harry in amazement, "most of them haven't even *heard* of the Depression!"

Two weeks after Sally began her job in the tea room, Alex pulled himself out of bed, dressed, and declared that he was going back to work. To his dismay, he found that the Dizzy Club had closed. For whatever reason, Lou had been unable or unwilling to obtain a liquor license. Worse yet, there seemed to be no spot for Alex anywhere. By cross-examining all the old acquaintances he could find, he did manage to find an occasional job, filling in for a sick bartender or working an occasional function at the St. George Hotel.

One temporary job looked as though it would turn into a permanent one when the man Alex was replacing suddenly died. But inexplicably, after two weeks behind the bar, Alex's new employer let him go. Privately Harry suspected that his brother was drinking, but he said nothing.

In late January 1934, Bill Terry once again sat down with a group of reporters to discuss the upcoming baseball season. This time none of the writers was willing to risk a nickel that the Giants wouldn't be in the thick of the race. Terry explained how he planned to use several of his players and answered questions on a variety of topics related to the fortunes of the Giants. When someone asked him what teams in the league would give him the most trouble, Bill replied, "Pittsburgh, St. Louis, and Chicago will be the teams we'll have to beat. I don't think the Braves will do as well as they did last year."

"And what about the Dodgers?" asked Roscoe McGowen, who covered Brooklyn for the *Times*.

"Haven't heard too much about them lately. I was just wondering whether they're still in the league," Terry quipped.

That cheap shot was quickly heard round Brooklyn, and it called every loyal Dodger rooter to arms. When Bob Quinn heard Terry's remark he was furious; he called every newspaper in town to protest the insult. "It shows a startling lack of diplomacy on the part of the manager of a championship ball club," Quinn wailed, "especially as Mr. Terry had his troubles last year with newspapermen because he was too sensitive about being picked for last place at the start of the season."

Alex was propped up in his easy chair, his head covered with his morning ice pack, when he read about Terry's jibe in the *Herald Tribune*.

"That dirty son of a bitch! That stupid bastard!" Alex screamed, jumping to his feet. The icebag slid off his head and knocked his coffee cup off the side table, sending it smashing to the floor. He kicked the side of his easy chair until his foot went through the fabric, trapping his slipper in the springs. "The audacity of that second-rate, over-the-hill, two-bit first baseman!" Damon began to bawl. "That no good bum! Is Brooklyn still in the league? The *gall* . . ."

Sally came running into the room. "Alex, will you please get hold of yourself!" Sally cried. He looked at her, quieted down at once, and slunk down into his chair again.

"What are we going to do?" Sally asked Ellen upon coming home from work that evening. "Alex was beginning to get better. Now it looks like he's losing his grip on himself. I wish he'd listen to us and go back to the doctor."

In February the word began spreading through the baseball world that Max Carey was about to be fired. Tommy Holmes, for one, didn't believe it. He wrote, "Rumors to the contrary, it's in the cards for Carey to remain at the helm all season. He isn't likely to resign voluntarily and the club isn't likely to pay off his $12,000 contract for the doubtful privilege of having another manager finish the job of piloting the boat into a second division dock."

No one could argue with Holmes's logic. And yet, no sooner had he filed his story than the rumors proved to be true. The news broke that Carey was out and that Casey Stengel, who at that moment was on board a train heading East from his home in Glendale, California, would be offered the job as soon as he arrived in New York.

Max heard the news in Florida, where he was busy preparing for spring training. "Why didn't they fire me at the end of the season so that I could scout around for a job?" Max asked bitterly.

When newsmen asked whether he thought Ol' Case would accept the offer, Carey replied, "I wouldn't blame Casey a bit if he took the job, but I don't think I would take it in the same circumstances if I were Casey."

Stengel, meanwhile, was under orders to stay clear of the press. He got off the train in Buffalo and flew into Newark, where a car was waiting to rush him to the New Yorker Hotel in Manhattan. Casey was hustled up a back staircase and ushered into a suite where Bob Quinn was waiting to offer him the job.

After he heard Quinn out, Casey said, "I understand Max's got another year to run on his contract."

"That's right," Quinn replied.

"Well, does he get the money or doesn't he?"

"That's not your worry. If you don't take this job, there are fifty others who will."

So Casey took it. And Carey would be paid his full salary for not managing the club. When Casey met the press he announced, "The first thing I want to say is that the Dodgers are still in the league. Tell that to Terry. I think I'll let our Mr. Van Mungo do a lot of arguing for me against the Giants this summer. When he starts heaving that fastball I'm quite sure he won't be easy to contradict."

"Carey says if he were in your shoes he wouldn't take the job," some-one piped up.

"Max didn't want me to take the job because he was afraid I'd start worrying if the team lost," Casey remarked with a wry smile. "I do worry, you know," he confessed as the reporters filled the room with laughter.

Two days later, as the first snowflakes of New York's second blizzard in a week began to fall, John McGraw passed away. He was only sixty years old. After funeral services in New York, his body was taken to Baltimore for burial.

Both Alex and Harry cried when they heard the news. Joe Vila, the only reporter in New York who'd been on the job when McGraw arrived from Baltimore thirty-two years earlier, wrote: "Millions of baseball fans, shocked and grieved by the death of John Joseph McGraw, will remember him as the manager of ten championship Giant teams and saviour of the National League. Those were McGraw's idols." Uncle Robbie, on learning of his fellow Oriole's passing, shook his head and said, "I can't say enough in his praise and words can't express how I feel about his death. Baseball has lost a great leader and a fine man." Before the year was out, Joe Vila and Wilbert Robinson would also be gone.

Brooklyn's owners were well aware that a new manager wouldn't have much effect on the team's fortunes; they had hired Stengel in the hopes that Ol' Case—a popular man in Brooklyn—would help the fans forget how miserable the team was. After two dismal seasons at the gate the club had gone deeply in hock to the Brooklyn Trust Company.

Bill Terry did more to stimulate fan interest in Brooklyn that year than the Dodger players and owners combined. His thoughtless crack about Brooklyn so infuriated the Flatbush Faithful that when the Giants came across the East River they were greeted by an army of hooting, hollering Dodger fans out for blood.

On Memorial Day, when the Giants invaded Ebbets Field for a doubleheader, five thousand fans were turned away. The Dodgers were, as usual, in sixth place, while the Giants were in third, only a game and a half behind the league-leading Cardinals.

The wild crowd did its very best to torment the New Yorkers; Terry got a chorus of catcalls every time he stuck his head out of the dugout, and the Dodgers got more vocal support than even a pennant winner could hope to expect. But Casey's boys were not up to the task. They lost both contests.

On September 1 it looked as if the Giants were going to waltz to the pennant. They were in first place, five and a half games ahead of St. Louis, and a few days later they extended their lead to seven games. But 1934 was the year of the Cardinals' Gas House Gang, that remarkable collection of spirited, highly talented, never-quit players, including the Dean brothers, Pepper Martin, Rip Collins, Joe Medwick, Leo Durocher, and of course Frankie Frisch, who managed the team and still played second base just about every day. The Cards began building a head of steam, and slowly, but steadily, the Giants fizzled. On September 21 the Gas House Gang met the Dodgers for a doubleheader at Ebbets Field; in the first game Dizzy Dean shut out Brooklyn 13–0, and in the nightcap his brother Paul pitched a 3–0 no-hitter.

New York's lead had now been cut to three games. A week later they found themselves in a flat-footed tie with the Cardinals. They had only two games left to play, both with the sixth-place Dodgers, a team that wasn't even in the league.

At last Brooklyn had a golden opportunity to get revenge against Terry. Ed Hughes, sports columnist for the *Eagle*, wrote: "Within the ensuing ninety-eight hours, weather permitting, Bill Terry will receive the answer to his sarcastic bon mot, 'Is Brooklyn still in the league.' The Dodgers—of all people—stand between the Giants and the National League pennant, not to mention, of course, the menacing figure of the St. Louis Cardinals. Little did the then self-sufficient Giant manager realize that the butt of his witticism would later assume such important proportions in his life."

As Alex saw it, the Dodgers just had to win. Although he was still suffering from excruciating headaches, nothing was going to keep him away from those two games at the Polo Grounds. To lose, and to hand the Giants the pennant on a silver platter, would be a fate worse than death.

The first game was played on Saturday, September 29. The Dodgers had already lost fourteen games to the Giants, so Bill Terry had every reason to believe his team would have an easy time. It rained all morning; the skies cleared by game time, but the bad weather reduced what should have been a sellout crowd to a modest turnout. Only 13,774 fans showed up, and most of them seemed to be from Brooklyn.

Armed with cowbells, klaxons, and strong lungs, the Dodger rooters gleefully invaded their archenemy's home turf. Stengel went with Mungo, even though his ace was suffering from a stubborn cold. Terry sent Parmelee to the mound. The first four innings were scoreless, although, as one observer put it, "the tension in the stands and on the field never relaxed for an instant."

Mungo led off the top of the fifth with a single and then scooted down to second on a passed ball. Buzz Boyle struck out. The next batter, Junior Frey, drilled a clean single up the middle and Mungo dashed home with the first run of the game. "We're gonna do it, we're gonna do it," Alex chanted to himself from his perch in the upper grandstand. All around him Dodger rooters were yelling, leaping, and clanging their bells and hooting their horns, making an unbelievable racket.

The Giants failed to score in their half of the inning. In the Dodger sixth Tony Cuccinello walked, Harry Taylor sacrificed him to second, and Joe Stripp received an intentional pass. Al Lopez flied out to George Watkins in center field for the second out. Up came Mungo. He punched a high outside pitch over Terry's head into right field to send Cuccinello in with the second run of the day. Once again the Brooklyn fans screamed with glee.

The Dodgers scored another run in the seventh. When, in the bottom of that inning, Watkins homered off Mungo's fastball to give New York its first run, the blast was received with tepid applause. Brooklyn scored two more runs in the ninth to win the ball game, 5–1.

Meanwhile the Cards beat the Reds 6–1, pushing the Giants a full game back with only one game left to play.

The next afternoon the Giants knocked Ray Benge out of the box in the first inning as they jumped to a 4–0 lead. For a moment it looked as if New York had a chance to force St. Louis into a playoff, but then the results of the Cards' first inning were posted on the scoreboard. Behind Dizzy Dean the Gas House Gang had scored two quick runs. The Giants, who knew damned well the hapless Reds weren't about to score two runs off Dean in a mere eight innings, gave up hope.

It just didn't matter when Brooklyn rallied to win the ball game. The campaign was over, and the Dodgers had converted a dismal year into a success, while the Giants had watched a fine season turn into a bitter defeat. "The Giants thought we gave 'em a beating Saturday and yesterday," Casey Stengel observed. "Well they were right. But I'm still sorry for them when I think of the beating they still have to take. Wait until those wives realize that they're not going to get those fur coats this year. I've been through it and I know."

Joe McCarthy, in an effort to win some furs for Yankee wives, had made a preseason attempt to refurbish his club for the 1934 campaign. He released two veterans, Herb Pennock and Joe Sewell. He purchased Don Heffner from Baltimore, where he had gained a reputation for a magic glove. He also brought Red Rolfe up from the minors. Lou Gehrig was an institution at first base, and Frankie Crosetti, who had joined the Yanks two years earlier, played a solid short. But throughout the season McCarthy experimented with the rest of his infield, moving Lazzeri, Rolfe, Heffner, and Jack Saltzgaver in, out, and around on a nearly daily basis. With Ruth, Combs, and Chapman, the outfield seemed fairly well set, but Combs was beginning to slow down a bit, and Babe—well, the Babe was nearing the end.

In 1933 he had failed to make the sportswriters' all-star team for the first time ever. As he entered his twenty-first season of baseball, his salary was a piddling $35,000. It was no secret that Ruth would have preferred managing a team to playing on one. He probably would have settled for any team, but he still felt that the team that played in the House That Ruth Built was rightfully his to manage. It was a feeling he made no effort to conceal.

The Yanks got off to a good start and moved ahead of the field in the early going, but by early July the Tigers had taken over the first slot.

On July 13, a Friday, the Babe both thrilled and disappointed twenty thousand fans in Detroit by parking home run 700 over the right-field wall. The blast meant the realization of a personal goal for the Babe, and it also put the Yankees back into first place over Detroit.

In late July the Yanks' hopes suffered a setback when Earle Combs crashed into the concrete wall in left center field of Sportsman's Park, fracturing his skull and ripping muscles in his throwing arm. For a time it looked as though the injury might prove fatal, and even after he began his recovery it was doubtful that the Kentucky Colonel would ever play again.

The Yanks and the Tigers continued to claw at each other, but on August 14 the Tigers invaded the Stadium and took away both ends of a doubleheader. There were still two months left in the season, but it was all over for the Yanks. They eventually finished in second place once more, seven games behind the Tigers.

But the season was not without its bright spots for the Yankees and their fans. Lou Gehrig whacked forty-nine homers, batted .363, and knocked in 165 runs to win the triple crown, a feat that Ruth had never been able to accomplish. Lefty Gomez, the free spirit who once claimed to have invented the revolving bowl for tired goldfish, returned to top form, leading the league in wins, twenty-six, and ERA, 2.33.

The year had been a disappointing one for Ruth. Weakening legs had forced him to sit out more than fifty ball games. The Babe finished the season with twenty-two home runs and a batting average of .288. But he had hit his seven hundredth home run and passed another milestone by collecting his two thousandth base on balls. Ruth had been greeted warmly wherever he went. As the campaign wound down, fans, sensing it would be his last, turned out in even larger numbers to say farewell to the aging superman.

The day after the season ended, Ruth approached Ruppert in his brewery office and demanded to know whether the colonel was satisfied with McCarthy as manager. When Ruppert responded in the affirmative, the Babe nodded. "That's all I wanted to know," he said. A few days later, Ruth was standing with several sportswriters on the platform at Union Station in St. Louis. When a railroad employee asked Ruth how the Yanks would do in 1935, the Babe snorted, "I don't give a damn what they do. I'm through with them."

The news of Ruth's retirement nearly overshadowed the World Series being played between the Detroit Tigers and the St. Louis Cards. In the seventh and deciding game, Ducky Medwick and Judge Landis combined to make baseball history. In the top of the sixth, with the Cards leading, 7–0, Medwick whacked a triple and slid hard into third base.

Marv Owen, guardian of that sack for the Tigers, took exception to Ducky's enthusiasm, and the two nearly came to blows. When Medwick tried to take his position in the outfield for the bottom of the sixth, the enraged fans at Navin Field, their team now trailing, 9–0, pelted him with an assortment of garbage.

After Ducky had been driven back for the third time, Landis called both Medwick and Owen to his box. After a brief consultation, Medwick was ejected from the game for his own protection. The move pacified the crowd but did nothing to help the Tigers, as the Gas House Gang took the game, 11–0. The Dean brothers had accounted for all the Cards' victories, notching two wins apiece.

As Thanksgiving of 1934 approached, the Rice family had to look hard to find anything to give thanks for. By cutting corners on the food budget for several weeks, shopping carefully, and using more than a little ingenuity, Ellen and Sally managed to spread a fairly attractive holiday feast. But neither Harry nor Alex was in a holiday mood, and the general atmosphere was glum. While the two women cleared away the remains of the meal, Harry and Alex divided up a day-old copy of the *Brooklyn Eagle*. They had been reading in silence for some time when Harry uttered a soft exclamation. Alex looked up questioningly.

"Old Man Kaplan died," Harry explained. Alex looked perplexed. "He was head of the firm I used to work for." Alex nodded. Unable to think of anything to say, he went back to reading his half of the paper. Harry stared at the wall, tapping his foot slowly. After a time, he went to the small desk in the corner of the room and wrote short notes of sympathy to Kaplan's widow and the two surviving partners in the firm, Cohen and Cohan.

The next morning, to save on postage, Harry decided to hike all the way down to Court Street and deliver the notes in person. Several hours later he burst through the apartment door, flushed and breathless from running up the stairs. The apartment was empty except for Alex, who was lying on the day bed in the living room.

"You sick or something?" Alex asked, raising his head.

"I've got something, all right," Harry said solemnly.

"What?"

"A job," Harry said, breaking into a grin.

Harry was once more an accountant, once more an employee of Kaplan, Cohen and Cohan. He was back at his old desk, earning exactly seven and a half dollars more per week than he had when he started in 1907. Meager though his twenty-five dollars a week may have seemed to some, to the Rice family it was a fortune. Hopefully, it was also a sign of good things to come.

On February 26, 1935, a press conference was called in Jake Ruppert's office at the brewery. Ruppert, Babe Ruth, and Emil Fuchs, owner of the Boston Braves, announced that the Babe was going to the Braves as player, assistant manager, and vice-president.

On the surface it seemed to be a giveaway—"Do you think I would sell this man?" Ruppert had responded to Fuchs's price inquiry—but secretly Ruppert was relieved to have the Babe off his hands. During the winter baseball meetings, Joe McCarthy had approached the colonel and offered to resign in favor of Ruth.

Ruppert told him to forget it. But the colonel had fretted over the ticklish problem of what to do with the Babe all winter. He was delighted to be rid of his dilemma, but he was also genuinely happy to see the big fellow find a place. Ruppert's refusal to put a price tag on the Babe was, in Harry's words, a high-tone move.

In 1929 the Yankees had become the first baseball team to sew numbers on the backs of the players' uniforms. The numbers corresponded to the player's position in the batting order. The third man in Murderers' Row had been Babe Ruth. When, on opening day of 1935, George Selkirk trotted out to right field wearing number 3, many of the denizens of Ruthville were offended. But the boos and hoots were not directed at Selkirk. They were aimed at the passing of time.

As for Joe McCarthy, he missed the Babe not at all. With the obstreperous living legend gone north, McCarthy felt that at last he could make the Yankees his own. And they did indeed get off to a fast start. Throughout June—the month in which the Babe hung up his spikes for good, having hit six homers and batted .181 for the Braves—the Yanks basked in first place.

Earle Combs was back, seemingly recovered, but by midseason it was apparent that the veteran had lost his edge. The Kentucky Colonel found himself a spot on the bench, and McCarthy alternated Myril Hoag and fleet-footed Jesse Hill in left, moving Ben Chapman to center. But Combs wasn't the only veteran having problems. Lefty Gomez couldn't find his stride, Crosetti was having difficulties, and Gehrig was having a subpar year.

All those problems added up to another bridesmaid finish, three games behind the flag-winning Tigers. McCarthy had now finished second in four out of his five seasons as Yankee skipper. Over his four second-place years, McCarthy had a total record of 368–238, for an overall winning percentage of .607. But as Alex told a disgruntled Harry, "Close only counts with horseshoes and skunks."

Although it was a tough year for Harry and his fellow Yankee fans, it was a milestone year for one member of the Rice clan.

On April 30, 1935, the Giants visited Brooklyn for their first game of the new season with the Dodgers. That was the day Alex took his son to his first ball game. Had it not been for the Depression, Damon surely wouldn't have had to wait until the ripe old age of seven to see the Dodgers in action.

Surprisingly, Brooklyn was in second place that day, only a half game behind New York. Even the Brooklyn fans knew that Casey's boys were playing over their heads. For the occasion of his son's initiation to Ebbets Field, Alex got seats in a field box just behind first base. He didn't want Damon to miss a thing. There was no score when, in the top of the second, Mel Ott strolled up to the plate.

"Damon, that's Mel Ott," Alex explained. "He's one of the best in the game. And he's a great guy even though he is a Giant."

Mel promptly hit a home run, giving the Giants a 1–0 lead. In the bottom of the third the Dodgers came back with six big runs. Every time a runner crossed the plate some guys sitting behind Alex and Damon tossed a bunch of firecrackers onto the field. Damon got more of a kick out of the pyrotechnics than the ballplaying, but he was still happy when the Dodgers won the game, 12–5. The winning pitcher that day was Watty Clark, back on the Brooklyn roster after being discarded by Bill Terry. The loser was Freddie Fitzsimmons, a hurler who usually walked all over the Dodgers. The previous year he had faced them six times and beaten them five.

"Well, son, that was quite a ball game, wouldn't you say?" Alex said to Damon as they left the ball park. "Casey picked right up where he left off at the end of last year." The following afternoon reality finally set in as the Giants defeated the Dodgers, 8–3.

New York held the National League lead until the middle of August, but then the Cardinals and the Cubs came on strong. The Giants began to fade, leaving most fans to believe that the Gas House Gang was headed for its second pennant in a row.

Then Charlie Grimm's Cubs put on one of the great finishing drives in history. From September 4 to September 27 they won twenty-one consecutive games and rushed to the finish line four games ahead of the Cardinals. The Giants finished third, eight and a half games back, and the Dodgers moved up a notch to fifth, ending the year twenty-nine and a half games off the pace. In the World Series the Tigers beat the Cubs, four games to two.

The most significant development of the 1935 season was the beginning of night baseball in the majors. The Cincinnati Reds, in deep financial trouble, desperately needed to draw fans to their ball park. There was little chance that the team, the perennial doormat of the league, could do it, so Larry MacPhail, the general manager, asked the National League for permission to experiment with night ball, which had already saved several minor league clubs from ruin.

The other owners reluctantly agreed, and on May 24 the Reds and the Phillies met in the first major league contest under the lights. More than twenty thousand fans jammed into Crosley Field; the Reds won, 2–1.

In the off-season between 1935 and 1936 both the Dodgers and the Giants found themselves in need of new leadership in their front offices. Bob Quinn left Brooklyn in December to return to Boston, where he became president of the Braves (or Bees, as they were called in those days). John Gorman, the Dodgers' road secretary, replaced Quinn as the club's business manager.

Then, in January, Charles Stoneham passed away. Thirty-two-year-old Horace Stoneham inherited his father's controlling interest in the Giants and quickly assumed the presidency, laying to rest rumors that the club would be sold. Jim Tierney resigned, and Eddie Brannick, who started with the club in 1905 as an errand boy, took over as secretary. Brannick was very popular with the press; his promotion was applauded as long overdue.

During the winter the Dodgers made some trades that proved, if nothing else, that the Brooklyn management was beginning to realize the team desperately needed a transfusion. In separate deals with the Braves the Dodgers picked up pitchers Fred Frankhouse and Ed Brandt and outfielder Randy Moore. And in a three-cornered deal with the Yankees and the Giants, the Dodgers got rookie first baseman Buddy Hassett and sent Sam Leslie back to the Polo Grounds, where Bill Terry, whose legs were giving out, needed a part-time first baseman.

Aside from Leslie, whom Bill would platoon with himself, the Giants' only new first-stringer was Burgess Whitehead, a second baseman picked up from the Cards for Roy Parmelee and Phil Weintraub. Whitehead and Dick Bartell, a fiery shortstop acquired from the Phils a year earlier, promised to give the Giants excellent protection around the keystone corner.

Harry just laughed when Alex told him the Dodgers were going to break into the first division that year. "You must be kidding, little brother," Harry said with a chuckle.

"Don't you think Frankhouse adds some punch to the Brooklyn pitching staff?" Alex asked.

"He would if he had some hitting behind him. But how the hell are the Dodgers going to get runs? With the Brooklyn bats to rely on even a good hurler is lucky to pitch .500 ball. Look at Mungo. With the Giants or the Cards or the Cubs he'd win twenty. With the Yankees he'd win twenty-five. As it is he'll be damn lucky to win sixteen or seventeen this year, and he'll probably lose twenty."

While it was generally agreed that the Dodgers' prospects for 1936 were as grim as ever, the Giants were impossible to dope out. Harry thought they had an outside chance to win the pennant, but many experts believed that Terry's men were now pretty much over the hill.

The 1936 Dodgers limped through the campaign and finished in seventh place, their worst showing since 1917. Brooklyn's biggest crisis of the year took place in June, when Van Mungo suddenly walked out.

The Dodgers were on the road at the time, and Mungo had just been roughed up badly in a contest with the Pirates.

His wildness had sent him to the showers in the second inning, and the Dodgers had gone on to lose the game, their sixth in a row, dropping them into the cellar. That evening, in the lobby of the Schenley Hotel in Pittsburgh, Mungo collared Casey Stengel and demanded to be traded.

Casey tried to explain that the owners of the club approved all trades, but Mungo would not be appeased. The next morning he was gone. He had flown back to New York, where he was popping off to the press that "the team was a bunch of inefficient semipros." He swore that he would quit baseball if he weren't traded.

Jim Mulvey, Steve McKeever's son-in-law and a vice-president of the club, sat down with Mungo and made him listen to reason. A few days later he rejoined his teammates, and in his first appearance he saved a game that ended the Dodgers' losing streak at nine. Mungo finished the season with a record of eighteen and nineteen. As Harry had pointed out, he would have been sensational with the right club.

On July 1 Terry's men were in fifth place, prompting Ed Hughes to observe in the *Brooklyn Eagle* that the Giants were "playing the forlorn, punch-drunk type of game supposedly the sole possession of our diabolically inventive Dodgers." Horace Stoneham, disgusted by his club's showing, moaned, "I guess the best thing that could happen would be if the team were torn to pieces and rebuilt from the ground up."

The Giants' obituary turned out to be premature. By the end of August they had won thirty-five out of their last forty ball games and found themselves in first place. They stayed hot through September and went on to capture the National League flag by five games over the Cubs. The victory was, of course, a team effort, but the big story of the year was the pitching of Carl Hubbell.

He won twenty-six games, lost only six, compiled a league-leading ERA of 2.31, and finished the season with sixteen consecutive victories. It was the first time since 1912—when Rube Marquard won twenty straight—that a National League pitcher had won that many games in a row. No wonder *Spalding's Guide* characterized King Carl as the man the other clubs found "as unwelcome as a midsummer downpour to July picnickers."

Across the Harlem River the story of the year was a kid named DiMaggio. Joe had been purchased from the San Francisco Seals of the Pacific Coast League two years earlier in a $25,000, five-player deal. In 1933, at eighteen, DiMaggio had hit safely in sixty-one consecutive games for the Seals and, according to some, had saved the league from bankruptcy. The price tag on the young outfielder would have been a great deal higher, but DiMaggio had injured his left knee in a freak accident—stepping from a cab—scaring away many of the prospective bidders. But

Yankee scout Bill Essick consulted with a doctor and then offered the youngster a contract. DiMaggio proved Essick's judgment sound by batting .398 in 1935, his last year with the Seals.

Yankee fans were forced to wait to get a look at their new prodigy. Joe injured a foot in spring training. While treating the injury with a diathermy machine, he sustained a bad burn. It wasn't until May 3 that Yankee rooters got their first glimpse of DiMaggio. Twenty-five thousand turned out to see the new Yankee outfield, which had DiMaggio in left—the sun field at Yankee Stadium—Chapman in center, and Selkirk in right. Earle Combs was now a Yankee coach.

DiMaggio pleased the curious crowd by whacking a single and a triple, helping the Yanks to a 14–5 victory over the St. Louis Browns.

In June, shortly after the arrival of the *Queen Mary* on her maiden voyage, Joe McCarthy traded Ben Chapman to Washington for Jake Powell. Alex snorted at the trade, but Harry thought he understood. McCarthy, like Huggins before him, didn't always judge a player strictly on physical ability. Powell was McCarthy's kind of man.

With Powell in left, DiMaggio in center, and Selkirk in right, the Yanks boasted their best outfield since Ruth, Meusel, and Combs. And the Yanks were once more the Bronx Bombers. The team as a whole batted an amazing .300 for the year. They were led by Bill Dickey with .362 and Lou Gehrig with .354.

Gehrig also hit forty-nine home runs to lead the league. Joe DiMaggio, getting his first look at big league pitching, batted .323 and hit twenty-nine homers. The Yankees moved into first place for good one week after DiMaggio entered the lineup. They clinched on September 9, the earliest date in American League history.

And so for the first time since 1923 the Fall Classic would be a Subway Series, or a Battle for Broadway, as it had been known in the days of John McGraw. The Little Napoleon was gone, and motor buses had recently replaced the trolleys on Broadway, but excitement was as high as it had been thirteen years earlier.

The first game of the Series was played on a cold, drizzly day at the Polo Grounds. Carl Hubbell went against Red Ruffing, and the Meal Ticket's screwball defused the Bombers. The final score was 6–1, the Yanks' only run coming on a third-inning homer by Selkirk.

When the teams reconvened the Yanks, behind Lefty Gomez, walloped the Giants, 18–4, in a game that saw a slew of records broken or equaled. Lazzeri hit a grand slam; Lazzeri and Dickey each drove in five runs; Crosetti scored four runs; and DiMaggio made all three put-outs in one inning, the ninth. The game also set records for runs by one team, total runs, bases on balls, and playing time. For the Giants, it was an inglorious way to enter the record books.

The scene shifted to Yankee Stadium for the third game. Freddie Fitzsimmons went for the Giants, and Bump Hadley was on the mound for the Yanks. Going into the eighth inning, the only scoring had been a Yankee homer by Gehrig and a Giant homer by Jimmy Ripple. With two out, Powell on third, and Ruffing—who had pinch-hit for Hadley—on first, Crosetti bounced one off Fitzsimmons's glove, and the winning run squeaked across as Fitz, probably the best fielding pitcher in baseball, watched with tears in his eyes.

In the fourth game Hubbell was back, facing Monte Pearson. But the Yanks seemed to have solved the mystery of Hubbell's screwball, and a record crowd of nearly sixty-seven thousand watched as the Yankees walked off with a 5–2 victory.

That evening, Sunday, October 4, John Gorman appeared at the World Series press headquarters at the Commodore to make an announcement that shocked and baffled the reporters who heard it. Casey Stengel had been fired. Only a few weeks earlier, both McKeever and Gorman had said that Ol' Case, who had another year to go on his contract, was in no danger of being let go. Now he was out, and the reason was "because he had not shown sufficiently successful results with the Dodgers."

Casey, like Carey before him, would be paid his entire salary of $13,000 for not managing the Dodgers. Tommy Holmes speculated that Burleigh Grimes would be named the new manager. A month later his guess would prove correct.

Alex couldn't believe the news. "Those jerks who run the Dodgers ought to be shot," he told Harry. "They know less about running a ball club than I know about knitting baby booties."

With the Yankees leading the Series, three games to one, the teams squared off for game five. The Giants, with Hal Schumacher on the mound, got off to a fast start, scoring three runs off Red Ruffing in the first inning. But the Yanks scratched back, and at the end of regulation play the score was tied at 4–4. In the bottom of the tenth, Joe Moore doubled, Dick Bartell moved him along to third with a sacrifice bunt, and Bill Terry delivered a long sacrifice fly to bring in the winning run and give the Giants new hope. Schumacher had pitched a brilliant game, striking out ten and stranding nine Yankee baserunners.

The Yankees went into game six at the Polo Grounds looking to end the Series. They knew that, if the Giants should prevail, Hubbell would be ready for the seventh game. After eight full innings, the Yanks were leading, 6–5.

DiMaggio opened the top of the ninth with a single. Gehrig followed with another safety, moving DiMadge to third. Dickey then grounded sharply to first. As DiMaggio broke for home, Terry fired the ball to third. Joe hesitated only briefly, continued his charge, and dived head first at the plate. Safe.

The run broke the Giants' back. The Bombers scampered home with six more runs that inning and went on to win, 13–5. The Yanks had won the Series four games to two, the same as in 1923. They had proved once again that they were the power of the majors by posting a .302 team batting average for the Series.

Lefty Gomez had added to his already formidable reputation as the flakiest pitcher in baseball. During the 18–4 romp in the second game, he had stepped off the rubber to gaze dreamily at a cargo plane as it droned over the stadium.

That winter was, perhaps, the darkest season of the Depression for the Rices. Just when the family was getting back on its feet, it suffered a bitter reversal. One afternoon in late November, Damon, dreaming that he was Babe Phelps batting against Carl Hubbell, played stickball long after a cold downpour should have sent him home. A few days later he developed a raw throat and a general feeling of malaise. He felt as if the objects and persons around him were adrift. His mother took his temperature, and when she read the thermometer her face turned white. It read 104 degrees.

Alex and Sally rushed their son to Victory Memorial Hospital, where the illness was diagnosed as pneumonia. Damon was placed in an isolation ward. He received serum therapy and was given oxygen several times a day. For more than a week, Sally was certain her son was going to die. When he finally came off the critical list, the doctors warned that recovery would take several months and that Damon would require constant care. Sally had no choice but to quit her job at the tea room.

Damon's world became a corner of the bedroom that was sealed off with mosquito netting. There were times when his dreams intruded on his reality, making it impossible to separate truth from illusion.

For the rest of the family, reality was inescapable. The financial burdens were heavier than ever, and they fell squarely on Harry. He went into debt to cover the medical expenses. As the winter passed, Alex's gratitude turned to resentment. He began to look upon his brother's generosity as a grand gesture designed to point up his own impotence.

The apartment was filled with undercurrents, undercurrents that even Damon could feel as he tossed and turned behind the netting.

It was April before he was strong enough to return to school. He had missed nearly all of the third grade. "Don't worry, m'boy," Alex told him the day he finally returned to the classroom. "You needed to give those other kids a headstart anyway."

Burleigh Grimes, better known as Ol' Stubblebeard, had his work cut out for him in 1937. He was determined to boost the Dodgers up into the first division. On paper the "Bums" appeared to be only slightly better than the year before. During the spring they had picked up outfielder

Heinie Manush. Although now thirty-five, Heinie could still hit the ball better than most of the Dodgers' other prospects. One youngster who did show promise was Cookie Lavagetto, whom Grimes could use at either third or short.

Ol' Stubblebeard was known as a hothead, and he quickly began to live up to his reputation. Midway through the season National League president Ford Frick found it necessary to call Burleigh on the carpet for unseemly behavior. But he kept right on feuding and fussing, and the Flatbush Faithful loved it.

Nowhere in the majors did the fans enjoy a good rhubarb more than in Brooklyn. But while Burleigh was free to let his own temper fly, he had one hell of a time trying to keep his ace pitcher on an even keel. Mungo began the season in fine pitching form but in a lousy state of mind. It wasn't long before he pulled another of his bad shows.

One night in May, while the team was on the road, he went out and got loaded. He arrived back at the hotel at 4 A.M. and barged into the room of Jimmy Bucher. When Bucher tried to get Van to go to bed he was greeted with flying fists. Before their teammates could arrive on the scene to pull Van and Jimmy apart, the furniture was smashed to bits and Mungo's eye was puffed up like an eight ball.

Gorman and Grimes had now taken enough from their prodigal hurler. They fined Van Lingle $1,000.

In June Grimes made two trades that he hoped would give him the help he needed to win that first division slot. He brought in two veteran hurlers well known to New York fans. One was aging Waite Hoyt, who came from the Pirates, and the other was none other than Freddie Fitzsimmons, whom Terry let go in exchange for Tom Baker. It was a sad day for Freddie, who in thirteen seasons at the Polo Grounds had come to look upon the Dodgers as mortal enemies. "I'll never forget riding across that bridge in a cab that afternoon," Freddie later confessed. "More than once I was tempted to tell the driver to turn around and go back." But Freddie went on and soon became a loyal Dodger and a favorite of the Brooklyn fans.

The All-Star Game was played in Washington that year, and Mungo was one of the hurlers chosen to represent the National League. The week before the midseason break Van complained to Grimes that his back was bothering him. Burleigh warned his ace not to take the game too seriously; after all, it was only an exhibition contest. If Van should be called upon to pitch, he was not to give it his all.

As it turned out, the American League batters had a field day; led by four Yankee sluggers—Gehrig, Rolfe, Dickey, and DiMadge—they defeated the Nationals, 8–3, with yet another Yankee, Gomez, notching his third All-Star win. The Senior Circuit went through four pitchers—Dizzy Dean, Carl Hubbell, Cy Blanton, and Lefty Grissom—before Van Lingle Mungo was called in. In two innings of relief he managed to throw his arm out. When he returned to the Dodgers, he began throwing with a cramped sidearm motion, and the opposing batters began knocking him out with depressing regularity. The team physician examined him and discovered his tonsils were inflamed. He was sent off to have them removed, but the operation did little to improve his arm. On August 19, in a game against the Phils, he made his first start in over a a month and was sent to the showers in the fourth inning.

By the end of August, after losing six straight games, Mungo walked out on the team. This time Grimes gave him an indefinite suspension. His record for the year was nine and eleven, but even if Mungo had been in good form all season Burleigh wouldn't have come close to a first division finish. The Dodgers lost five more games than the year before and finished in sixth place, thirty-three and a half games back.

Both the *Sporting News* and *Baseball Magazine* picked the Yanks and the Giants to repeat in 1937. The Yankees were expected to win in a breeze, and they did. The Giants, on the other hand, looked as though they would have some problems. Travis Jackson had finally retired, and Bill Terry had also removed himself from the active list. At third Terry installed Lou Chiozza, acquired from the Phillies over the winter.

In the pitching department the Giants were still looking for another starter, and Terry was pinning his hopes on Cliff Melton, a Yankee reject picked up from Baltimore. But as Harry and Alex could plainly see, this was not as strong a team as the year before. If Terry was to continue the remarkable success he had achieved in his first five years as manager, he would have to start rebuilding fast.

Amid all this uncertainty Carl Hubbell won his first eight outings to extend his regular-season winning streak to twenty-four games. It wasn't until Memorial Day, before a crowd of 61,756 fans at the Polo Grounds, that King Carl was finally overthrown. The Dodgers reached him for five runs in four innings, knocked him out of the box, and went on to win, 10–3. To that point in the season Terry's men had been struggling along in third place, but a week later, on Sunday, June 6, they knocked Pittsburgh out of first by taking both ends of a doubleheader from the Pirates.

New York remained in the lead until the end of the month, when the Cubs came on strong and pushed the Giants into second. Then Terry began to have serious problems. Hubbell went into a slump. Bartell and Mancuso were injured. Chiozza, though a good fielder, was a weaker hitter with the Giants than he had been with the Phils. Schumacher was another disappointment.

By the end of August the Cubs had extended their lead to seven games. Terry decided to take a desperate gamble; to get more power into his lineup he moved Mel Ott from right field to third base, put Jimmy Ripple in right, and sent Hank Leiber into center. Mel was not the slickest third baseman in the world, but he had plenty of heart. Cliff Melton answered the prayers of Bill and the fans by turning in a sensational rookie season. At the end of the campaign he would have a record of 20–9 with a 2.26 ERA.

As August moved along Chicago gave New York a helping hand by falling into a slow, steady slump. On September 1 the Giants regained first place by two percentage points, and a week later they extended their lead to three lengths. Chicago stayed close the rest of the way but couldn't make up the lost ground, and when the campaign was over New York had won the pennant by a three-game margin. Carl Hubbell wound up the year with twenty-two victories, four fewer than the year before.

A few days before the start of the World Series the Dodgers announced a curious trade. They sent four players—Joe Stripp, Johnny Cooney, Roy Henshaw, and Jimmy Bucher—to the Cardinals for Leo Durocher. Leo, who was staying at the Hotel Warwick in New York at the time, was furious when he read about the deal in the papers. As far as he was concerned Branch Rickey, vice-president of the Cards, might just as well have sent him to the Black Hole of Calcutta. Rickey was also in New York for the Series, and Leo quickly sought him out to gripe about the trade.

"Didn't think you were worth so much, Leo," Branch said when his former shortstop confronted him. "Imagine getting four men for you." Durocher groaned and moaned, and then Rickey gave him this advice: "Just go there and keep your nose clean. You have ambitions beyond being a player, haven't you?"

Alex couldn't believe the trade. Durocher was a flashy shortstop, no doubt about it, but he was also a puny hitter. That year he batted only .203. Three of the men traded for him had much higher averages. "What do you make of it, Harry?" he asked.

"I know the Dodger owners are stupid," Harry replied, "but they can't be *that* stupid. There's gotta be a method to their madness."

The next day the *Brooklyn Eagle* offered a plausible explanation for the trade: "Baseball men can't feature giving four players, including Bucher and Cooney, for Leo Durocher. Leo may be past his prime as a player, but if the Dodgers are looking for a 1939 manager mebbe the trade wasn't such a bum one at that."

As New York prepared itself for the second Subway Series in a row, most natives felt that the Yankees would have little trouble with the Giants. After all, the new Murderers' Row was back intact. Not only had DiMaggio led the league with forty-six homers while batting .346— Gehrig's figures were thirty-seven and .351—but Barrow had added to the thunder by purchasing young outfielder Tommy Henrich from the Cleveland organization. The Yanks boasted the only two twenty-game winners in the league in Gomez and Ruffing. Johnny "the Fireman" Murphy had posted a 13–4 record and had notched ten saves.

It didn't take the Yankee firepower long to assert itself. The Bombers blasted Carl Hubbell in the first game, 8–1, and then went on to take three of the next four, defeating the Giants in the Series, four games to one. Hubbell accounted for the Giants' only win, a 7–3 victory in game four, but by then even the most loyal of Giant fans knew it was all over.

Lefty Gomez collected two complete-game victories and recorded an ERA of 1.50 for the Series, while Pearson and Hadley notched the other two Yankee wins. The surprise batting hero of the Series was Tony Lazzeri, appearing for the last time in a Yankee uniform. Over the five games he hit a brisk .400.

By the end of 1937 the Brooklyn Baseball Club was on the verge of financial collapse. It owed the Brooklyn Trust Company a half million dollars, and its total indebtedness was more than $1,200,000. The Dodgers' shabby office at 215 Montague Street was a gloomy place indeed. Bill collectors and process servers were always around the anteroom, supposedly loyal employees often spent lunch hours hunting for new jobs, and at one point the telephone company even shut off service.

The Brooklyn Trust Company found itself in a rough position; it was reluctant to throw good money after bad, but if it didn't continue to shell out the club would almost surely go into bankruptcy. George V. McLaughlin, president of the bank, could see that the Dodgers badly needed a new general manager—someone who was forceful and imaginative and who had a good track record as a baseball executive.

He asked Ford Frick to recommend someone for the job. Frick, worried sick that one of his league's most important franchises might cease to exist, nominated Larry MacPhail. From 1933 to 1936, as general manager of the Reds, Larry had transformed the weakest property in the majors into a flourishing concern.

MacPhail was now out of baseball. He was working with his brother and father in the family investment business out in Michigan. When McLaughlin offered him the job he turned it down flat. As far as Larry was concerned the situation in Brooklyn "smelled to high heaven." McLaughlin, however, was not prepared to take no for an answer. He had a strong hunch that his man would come around if he were promised full authority to run the club without interference. McLaughlin laid down the law to old Steve McKeever, Jim Mulvey, and Joe Gilleaudeau. If MacPhail could be persuaded to take the job, they were to stay out of his way. Then McLaughlin committed the bank to putting up $200,000 in fresh working capital. It was an irresistible challenge. On January 19, 1938, the Brooklyn Dodgers announced that Leland Stanford MacPhail had agreed to become the club's new executive vice-president.

"What does 'executive vice-president' mean?" a reporter asked Mac-Phail.

"I have full charge of the club, its organization, and its farm system for a three-year term," Larry replied.

To be even more precise, it meant that, for the first time since the death of Charlie Ebbets, the Dodgers had a strong leader.

MacPhail cut quite a figure. He was forty-eight when he joined the Dodgers. He had bright red hair, a face full of freckles, and a voice that someone once compared to the call of a male moose. His ability to bray was important, because he was forever blowing his top—getting things done by putting the fear of God into his subordinates. But if he was loud, even truculent, he also had a sense of style. His wardrobe, for example, soon became the talk of New York. He appeared at Ebbets Field and elsewhere around town decked out in loud checked suits or elegant plaid sport jackets, bright ties, and custom-made silk shirts. He soon proved to be as shrewd as he was flamboyant. As Red Barber later described him, "Larry was not only dynamic and forceful and hot-tempered, he was also a beautiful, working, practicing diplomat. He got into no feuds with either faction of owners. Instead, he honey-toned both sides."

He honey-toned George McLaughlin as well. After spending the $200,000 loan to refurbish his ball park he walked into McLaughlin's office and announced, "I want fifty thousand more."

"What in God's name for?" McLaughlin asked.

"I need a first baseman," replied MacPhail. After less than five minutes of sweet talk he walked out of the bank with the full amount. He used the money to purchase Dolf Camilli from the Phils.

The Camilli deal, announced during the first week of spring training, made Alex sit up and take notice. Until then he'd had his doubts about the Dodgers' flashy new boss. One of MacPhail's first moves had been to sign up thirty-eight-year-old Kiki Cuyler, who'd been released by the Reds. All Alex could do was groan when he heard the news. The *last* thing Brooklyn needed was another aging outfielder. But Dolf Camilli, who'd batted .339 the year before and was a great first baseman, was another story. Maybe there was hope for the Dodgers after all.

The day after the Dodgers purchased Camilli they received a sad piece of news at their spring training camp. Steve McKeever was dead. The old judge, as he was affectionately known by everyone connected with the ball club, had caught pneumonia and succumbed to the inevitable. Harry felt a biting chill down his spine when he heard the news. Before too long Harry would himself reach the age of fifty.

That spring Sally learned from one of the customers in her tea room that the owner of a bar out in the Bay Ridge section of Brooklyn was looking for an experienced bartender to work part time. Alex was still not quite right—he could be attacked by a violent headache at any time, without warning—but he was going buggy hanging around the house, and was eager to take a crack at working two or maybe even three days a week.

He took the Fourth Avenue subway out to Bay Ridge and presented himself to the owner of the saloon, a place called the Web Café. Alex was hired on the spot. He worked two shifts, one on Saturday and the other on Sunday, and he earned $5 each day. It wasn't much, but it gave him something to contribute to the grocery kitty and provided him with a few extra bucks a week for luxuries. The first thing he treated himself and his son to was opening day at Ebbets Field. Alex gave Damon permission to play hooky, and they went out to watch the Dodgers begin another season against the Giants.

Alex couldn't believe it when he and Damon walked into the ball park. The old place, which had been deteriorating for more than a decade, looked like a million dollars. The seats had been painted, the walls of the refreshment stands were decorated with photographic murals, the bathrooms had new fixtures, and the infield had been resodded. Alex didn't know that the beautiful new lawn came from a Long Island polo field and cost fifty cents a square foot; he didn't know either that the members of the press now had a bar where they could escape from a dull game and get a beer or better on the house.

But he was impressed by everything he did see. When he and his son were ushered to their seats by a courteous young man in a smart green and gold uniform, Alex knew he was witnessing the beginning of a new era. In the past the so-called ushers had been little more than common thugs—men who took delight in treating patrons with contempt.

The Dodgers had plenty of scoring opportunities that afternoon, but in typical fashion they failed to cash in on them. The Giants won the ball game, 3–2. Damon, who at the age of ten was already well adjusted to the frustrations of being a Brooklyn fan, took the loss in stride even though he had to listen to his father curse the Dodgers all the way home. That opening day of 1938 took on a special meaning for Damon, because it was then that he made Cookie Lavagetto his own special hero. Cookie went three for three before leaving the game in the sixth after pulling a ligament sliding into third. For the rest of the season Damon followed Lavagetto's every move. The highlight of the campaign came in early June, when Cookie, hitting .355, briefly led the National League in batting.

The Dodgers had a fairly good infield that year, but that was about it. The pitching staff was a mess. Van Mungo remained on the club, but he still couldn't throw overhand, and his new sidearm motion made it impossible to get much on the ball. Grimes had a good catcher in Babe

Phelps, who could really slug a baseball, but during the season he fractured his thumb twice and appeared in only sixty-six games. Around Memorial Day, Leo Durocher was named field captain. It was difficult not to believe that Ol' Stubblebeard's days were numbered.

The Giants, meanwhile, got off to a blazing start. They won eighteen of their first twenty-one games, and it appeared that Bill Terry would cruise to his fourth pennant in only six full campaigns.

Larry MacPhail had vowed when he arrived in Brooklyn that he had no plans to bring night baseball to Ebbets Field. After watching his sorry ball club in action, he quickly changed his mind. He obtained permission from the league to schedule seven night games, got more money from the bank to install lights, and before the season was even half over was ready to introduce baseball under the lights to Brooklyn.

The first night game in New York City took place on Wednesday, June 15, 1938. The visiting team was the Reds, and as fate would have it the 38,748 fans—including Harry and Alex—who shoved their way into Ebbets Field that evening witnessed a display of pitching that remains to this day a major topic in hot stove circles.

The game was preceded by a card of special events that included a fireworks display and a 100-yard dash featuring Jesse Owens, the Olympic champion. Jesse, who spotted the fastest runners on the Reds and Dodgers to a ten-yard head start, finished a split second behind Ernie Koy, the Brooklyn center fielder.

The game got underway with Max Butcher hurling for the Dodgers against left-hander Johnny Vander Meer, who four days earlier had pitched a 3–0 no-hitter against the Boston Bees. The Dutch Master picked up right where he had left off, pitching one inning after another of no-hit baseball. The Dodger rooters, who began the game screaming for Vandy's hide, slowly turned against their team and started cheering the opposing pitcher. By the seventh inning, with Brooklyn down, 6–0, everyone in Ebbets Field was rooting for Vander Meer to hurl his second no-hitter. Harry and Alex gave out sighs of relief when Johnny retired the side in the seventh after issuing two walks. In the bottom of the ninth, after getting Buddy Hassett to ground out, Vander Meer once again had trouble finding the plate. He walked Babe Phelps and Cookie Lavagetto.

With a runner now in scoring position Grimes sent Goody Rosen in to run for Phelps. Dolf Camilli then came to the plate, and he too walked. Manager Bill McKechnie strolled out to the mound to calm his young hurler down. Then Ernie Koy sent a grounder down to third that Lew Riggs scooped up and tossed home to get the force on Rosen.

One more out to go. Up came Leo Durocher. The crowd was on its feet roaring encouragement to Vander Meer. Leo got the pitch he was looking for and hit a drive that veered foul into the left-field seats. On his next swing Lippy got a good piece of the ball and sent a line drive over second base that, in Leo's own words, "hung just long enough for Harry Craft to get under it in center field. I am not so sure many other center fielders could have caught it."

Vander Meer had his second straight no-hitter, and Brooklyn had ushered in night baseball in a manner that certainly befitted the flamboyant MacPhail.

The Dodgers' irrepressible showman had another scheme to boost attendance. Two days after he brought night baseball to Brooklyn MacPhail signed Babe Ruth to coach at first base and plop homers into Bedford Avenue during batting practice. The Babe joined the Dodgers on Sunday, June 19, for a doubleheader with the Cubs.

One writer estimated that fully half of the twenty thousand fans who showed up that day came expressly to see the Sultan of Swat appear in a baseball uniform for the first time in three years. He didn't hit any homers in batting practice, but he put on quite a show in the coach's box.

Bob Considine, in the *Daily Mirror*, described the Bambino's coaching style this way: "He slaps his fat hands together a lot, and his full fat lips holler encouragement in a resonant bass. He paces up and down on his impossible legs. Once he fell down in a particularly close play at first base."

Unfortunately, Ruth was more show than substance. The first man he sent down to second—Kiki Cuyler—was out by a mile. Later, with the bases full of Dodgers, Rip Collins, the Cubs' first baseman, let a ball get by him. At it rolled toward the Dodger dugout the Babe waved the runners around. Luckily they paid no heed; Collins got the ball on a fast carom off one of the field boxes and would have thrown out any of them by at least ten yards.

The arrival of Ruth intensified rumors that Burleigh Grimes was slated to be fired. The Babe confided to Durocher that "I'll be the boss around here before too long." Leo told the Bambino that he had a few aspirations of his own, and any other would-be managers had better line up behind *him*. A month or so later, in the ninth inning of another game against the Cubs, Durocher, swinging in desperation on a hit-and-run play, sent a squibbler down the first base line that went for a hit and scored Cookie Lavagetto all the way from first to win the ball game.

A writer asked Leo if it was Ruth who had put on the hit-and-run. Durocher said no, it was a private sign between him and Lavagetto. The next day, using that play as an example, the reporter wrote a piece that described the Babe as being "as useful as a wooden Indian" coaching first.

That afternoon, during a clubhouse meeting, Ruth picked a fight with Leo. The scuffle lasted only a few moments but it gave notice to MacPhail that there wasn't room on the same ball club for both the Bambino and the Lip.

Just down the street from the Rice family's flat was a friendly corner saloon known as Diamond's Café. The bar is still there; it hasn't changed in all these years. The place was then owned by Pat Diamond, a Tammany politician who ran the Eighth Assembly District in Brooklyn.

Now that Harry and Alex had a few extra coins in their pockets they enjoyed dropping in on the bar one or two nights a week to have a beer or two and discuss baseball with the other patrons, all avid fans of one New York team or another.

The bartender was usually Pat's son Bill, a Brooklyn fan who, like many Dodger rooters, found it difficult not to ridicule the ball club even though, in his heart of hearts, he would have given anything for the Flock to succeed. When Alex and Harry came in they would step up to the bar, order their drafts, and then go over the day's games with Bill.

Harry did most of the talking. He would offer his predictions for tomorrow's contests, analyze plays, and criticize different managers and players. Everyone enjoyed Harry's running commentary on the developing season as well as his forecasts of things to come. Ol' Harry Rice was known throughout the neighborhood as a perceptive observer of our national pastime.

In early July Larry MacPhail made a couple of trades that caused a bit of comment in Diamond's Café. He picked up catcher Gilly Campbell from the Reds and outfielder Tuck Stainback from the Phillies. The trades were of only passing interest. The big question on everyone's mind was—would the goddamn Dodgers *ever* beat the Giants? At the All-Star break New York had whipped Brooklyn ten straight and also had taken nine out of ten from the Phils. In other words, nearly half of the Giants forty-five wins had come from two ball clubs.

On July 12, Ol' Stubblebeard finally took one from Memphis Bill. At Ebbets Field the Dodgers mauled the Giants, 13–5. The victory was especially sweet because it knocked New York out of first place and gave the lead to the Pirates, if only by three percentage points.

That night Alex was in a particularly good mood. He dragged his brother down to Diamond's and proceeded to get polluted. Another Dodger fan, a post office worker named Robert Joyce, was likewise feeling no pain. Joyce, a buddy of Bill Diamond's, was glugging down the beers as fast as Bill could serve them up.

As he got drunker, Joyce began boasting that the Dodgers were one hell of a good ball team. "You guys watch," he bragged, "with these new trades the Brooks are gonna make it to the first division. Hell, they still have a shot at the pennant!"

"Come on, Bob," Bill remarked with a snicker, "that bunch of bums ain't going nowhere. They've found their spot already—sixth place."

"Oh yeah, just you wait and see," Bob replied, his face reddening. "What about those trades?"

"Tuck Stainback is a dud," piped up Frank Krug. An Albany man, Frank was vacationing in Brooklyn.

"I'll second that," said Harry.

"So will I," added Bob Eagan, another customer.

"Well . . . well . . . What about Campbell?" Joyce asked, his face screwed up in agitation.

"I'd say he's pretty much washed up," Krug replied.

The taunting got hotter, with almost everyone in the barroom getting in the act. Alex just stood there, sipping his beer quietly, feeling very sorry for Bob but not knowing quite what to say. After more than an hour, Joyce couldn't take any more; he stormed out of the place, and as he left he mumbled something about coming back and getting even.

Soon after he was gone Harry took Alex's arm, put it over his shoulder, and led his brother out the door, up the block, and into the flat. "Poor Alex," Harry thought as he put him to bed. "Not much spirit left."

Sometime after midnight Robert Joyce returned to Diamond's Café. He stormed into the bar, pulled out a revolver, and fired two shots at Bill Diamond, who was hit in the left side and slumped to the floor. Another shot went wild as Frank Krug and Charlie Miller, the waiter, jumped on the gunman and pulled him down.

Miller grabbed the weapon and went out into the street to find a cop. Then Joyce jumped up, pulled out another revolver, and ordered Krug and Eagan into the back room. Eagan ran into a telephone booth, and Krug tried to squeeze in behind him. Another shot rang out. It hit Krug in the head, killing him instantly.

"I'm going to kill you!" Joyce screamed at Eagan. "What's your name?"

"Eagan," Bob said trembling.

"I could kill you, but I won't." Then Joyce ran out into the street. A few minutes later the police arrived, called an ambulance for Bill Diamond, and went out to find the berserk Dodger fan. They picked him up about a block from the scene and booked him for murder. Joyce had taken the revolvers from the post office. He had his own key, and after letting himself in he broke into the gun locker and helped himself to two weapons. Then he returned to the bar and went amuck.

Bill Diamond was taken to Brooklyn's Methodist Episcopal Hospital, where he died two days later. The following February a jury convicted Joyce of murdering Diamond in the second degree, and a month later poor Bob pleaded guilty to the murder of Krug, also in the second degree.

Every old Dodger fan remembers how painful were the insults so glibly dished out by smug Giant and Yankee fans. Most of the Flatbush Faithful just took their lumps and waited till next year. A few got into fights. Robert Joyce carried his love for the Dodgers to a horrible extreme.

While the Dodgers were limping through the last half of the 1938 season on their way to another sixth-place finish, the Giants were suddenly afflicted with serious troubles of their own. Melton, after starting the season with six consecutive wins, went sour. He *seemed* to have good stuff, and he felt fine, but he just couldn't win ball games. Apparently Cliff had a bad case of second-year jitters.

And then there was Hal Schumacher. His herky-jerky motion had, over the years, chipped away at his elbow, which was now filled with so many bone fragments that he pitched only with great difficulty.

But the biggest disaster of all was Carl Hubbell, who also had a piece of bone in his pitching elbow. In late August he left the club to have it removed; the operation put him out of action for the remainder of the season. His final record for the year was a meager thirteen wins against ten losses, and his ERA was 3.07. Still, as long as Hubbell was on the team the Giants had managed to stay in contention. From the middle of July to the end of August they held second place behind the league-leading Pirates. They finished August on the road losing seven out of eleven games, and during the first week in September they toppled to fourth place.

They wound up the year in third, five games behind the Cubs, who came on to take all the marbles. Harry summed up the campaign well when he said to Alex, "Bill Terry has run his string out as far as it can go. You can bet that for the next few seasons, at least, the Giants are going to have one hell of a time keeping from sliding downhill."

In 1938 the Yankees fielded basically the same team they had the previous year. The only major change was at second base. Tony Lazzeri had gone off to be a player–coach for the Cubs.

His replacement was twenty-three-year-old Joe Gordon, who had come up through the Yankee farm system. For a while it seemed the Yankees would be without the services of Joe DiMaggio, who refused to report unless paid a salary of $25,000. Ruppert was unyielding, and Joe was just as obstinate, claiming that his new restaurant was doing so well he could hardly afford to leave San Francisco.

For some reason the fans, who had always supported Ruth in his holdouts, found fault with DiMaggio's actions. When Joe finally gave in and appeared in his first game on April 30, he was greeted by lusty boos. But it wasn't long before his hot bat, his graceful fielding, and his cool, even manner won back the admiration of the fans.

Partially because of DiMaggio's holdout, the Yankees got off to a slow start. But by the middle of July they had overtaken and passed Boston and Cleveland and moved into first place. The Bombers clinched on September 18. It was their tenth pennant. Only Connie Mack's Athletics had won as many American League flags.

The team's overall batting average was a mere .274, bettered by both Boston and Cleveland, which finished nine and a half and thirteen games back, respectively. In fact, five out of the other seven clubs in the league boasted higher team batting averages. But the window-breakers from the Bronx led the league in runs scored, home runs, RBIs, walks, and slugging average—and, not surprisingly, strikeouts. They also had the ace of the league, Red Ruffing, who chalked up a 21–7 season for a winning percentage of .750.

And it was off to Chicago to face the Cubs in the World Series. In the first game the Yanks pitted their ace against the ace of the National League, Bill Lee, and Ruffing came away with a 3–1 win.

Gabby Hartnett—alias Old Tomato Face or the Milford Freight— had taken over for Charlie Grimm as manager of the Cubs about midway through the season. Hartnett, who had not only managed well but hit the dramatic home run that put the Cubs into the Series, decided to send Dizzy Dean to the mound for the second game. Dizzy had been struck on the toe by a hard-hit ball in the 1936 All-Star Game—the same game in which Van Mungo had thrown away his arm.

Ol' Diz had tried to come back from the injury too soon and wound up throwing his arm away as well. The wily Branch Rickey had engineered a $200,000 deal that sent Dizzy to the Cubs. And now Ol' Diz, a legend in his own time—at least to hear *him* tell it—was facing the awesome bats of the Yankees, lame arm and all. Dean pitched gamely for seven innings, but in the eighth Crosetti banged a two-run homer to put the Yanks ahead, 4–3, and the following inning DiMaggio belted another two-run homer to ice the game for Lefty Gomez.

The Yanks proceeded to take the next two games, 5–2 and 8–3, behind Pearson and Ruffing to win their third straight Series.

In 1938 the Yankees had swept the World Series for the fourth time. Howard Hughes and his four-man crew had landed at Floyd Bennett Field after completing an around-the-top-of-the-world flight in the monoplane *New York World's Fair 1939* in the record time of three days, nineteen hours. On October 30 Orson Welles terrified the country with his "Mercury Theater" broadcast of *The War of the Worlds*. And soon after the turn of the year—thirteen days after, to be exact—an era ended for the New York Yankees. Colonel Jacob Ruppert died.

Even though thousands turned out for the funeral at St. Patrick's Cathedral, Ruppert's death had less impact on the baseball world than might have been expected. He had remained out of the public eye, and few fans had ever even seen him. He was often the butt of jokes—his lack of baseball knowledge, his German accent that thickened when he became excited.

But true baseball fans knew that Ruppert was a unique man. He had taken Farrell's and Devery's hapless Highlanders and turned them into an awesome force that rival cities wanted broken up.

The argument was that Ruppert's millions bought pennants, that fans wanted competition, not class. But Ruppert's estate was valued at a mere $7 million, not the $70 million it was popularly believed to be. Instead of breaking up the Yankees, Ruppert did everything in his power to make them even stronger. "I found out a long time ago," he once said, "that there is no charity in baseball. I want to win the pennant every year."

Ruppert died a bachelor. "Men marry only when they are lonely or in need of a housekeeper—I'm neither!" The Yankees were bequeathed to three women: Ruppert's nieces, Mrs. Helen Holleran and Mrs. Ruth Maguire, and Miss Helen Winthrope Weyent, a friend. A short time after Ruppert's death, Ed Barrow was named president of the club.

With the season over, all eyes turned to Brooklyn. As expected Burleigh Grimes was given the heave-ho. Now the big question was—who would replace him? In October Larry MacPhail announced that, after careful consideration of several candidates, Leo Durocher had been chosen to pilot the Dodgers in 1939.

When asked why Lippy was given the job, MacPhail replied, "Look at Leo's record. He has always been a team player, always a prominent figure in any mob scene that you ever saw on a ball field involving a team for which he played. He was captain of the Gas House Gang out in St. Louis and that was as aggressive and hard fighting a bunch as we've ever seen in the National League in our time. Besides all that he was captain of our team this year and, as such, has a running jump toward building the spirit that we like."

Babe Ruth was left out in the cold. He wrote a gracious letter to the newspapers in New York in which he thanked the Brooklyn fans and the Dodgers for what he described as "a happy interlude in my life." Then the Sultan of Swat retired from baseball.

When Larry MacPhail brought night baseball to Brooklyn he alienated the two other New York teams. Neither the Giants nor the Yankees had any desire to depart from their old ways, and they resented MacPhail for rocking the boat.

Another sensitive issue between the New York clubs had to do with radio. All three teams had agreed in 1935 to a five-year ban against broadcasting their games. Not long after the end of the 1938 season MacPhail said he was going to put the Dodgers on the air in 1939, even though the ban had another year to run.

Eddie Brannick of the Giants warned Larry that, if Brooklyn went through with its plan, the Giants would broadcast *their* games over a transmitter strong enough to blast the Dodgers into oblivion.

Brannick's threat enraged MacPhail. He quickly accepted an offer from General Mills to sponsor the Dodger games over WOR. At 50,000 watts, it was the most powerful station in town.

Larry insisted that the makers of Wheaties hire Red Barber as the Brooklyn announcer. Barber, who'd been broadcasting for the Cincinnati Reds since 1934 and doing the World Series since 1935, was widely regarded as an excellent play-by-play man.

It's generally believed that MacPhail had hired Barber in Cincinnati, but that's a myth. Red, who began his radio career at a small station in Gainesville, Florida, had been scouting around for a better job for some time, and in the course of the search had auditioned for a position with WLW in Cincinnati. As it happened WLW was part of the Crosley Radio Corporation, which was owned by Powel Crosley, who also owned the Reds. Someone in Crosley's organization figured it would be a good idea to broadcast the Reds' games, and Barber was called from Florida to try his hand at the job. Red, who announced the games over WLW's sister station, WSAI, was an instant success in Cincinnati.

In Brooklyn, however, it took him a while to catch on. Many Flatbush-ites had trouble at first figuring out what he was talking about—his Southern accent and colorful figures of speech took a bit of getting used to—but it wasn't long before his broadcasts became an essential feature of Brooklyn baseball.

The Yankees and Giants had no choice but to go on the air too, but Barber gave the Dodger games a special appeal.

Alex and Damon, like most Brooklyn fans, found that radio heightened the drama of the season. With every home game only a flick of the knob away, the campaign became a daily part of their lives, making defeats more bitter and victories more sweet. And because they never escaped being involved in the fortunes of the Dodgers, they went out to the ball park more often.

In March 1939 Harry Rice became a partner of Kaplan, Cohen and Cohan. A few weeks after Harry's promotion he and Ellen moved out of the flat to an apartment of their own on Stoddard Place in Flatbush. Shortly thereafter Alex also left Park Slope. He was now tending bar four and sometimes five days a week; to be near his job he moved his family out to Bay Ridge. They took the second floor of a decrepit old house on Shore Road. The place went back to the eighteenth century, and some of the neighbors told Damon that General Grant once stopped there while inspecting the Union Army garrison at Fort Hamilton.

The house may have been crumbling on its foundations, but Damon had a large room of his own that even had a fireplace. Privacy and freedom of movement had, until now, been unheard-of luxuries. Damon quickly and happily adapted himself to his new surroundings.

Less than a month after the family split up, Harry celebrated his fiftieth birthday. To commemorate the occasion Ellen threw a surprise party. Many old friends and acquaintances dropped by, and Alex came with a magnum of champagne. It was the first time Damon had been in his uncle's and aunt's new apartment. After all the toasts were over Harry took his nephew's arm and said, "Damon, I want you to come with me." They left the apartment and climbed the two flights to the roof.

"Holy cow!" Damon exclaimed as he took in the view.

They looked right down on Ebbets Field. The diamond was several hundred feet away, but it would still be possible, especially with binoculars, to follow a good deal of the action. Damon was the luckiest kid in Brooklyn.

Leo Durocher was made for Flatbush. Like MacPhail he was a hothead and a poor loser, a natty dresser, and the owner of a cunning baseball mind. Not only did he manage, he continued to play shortstop, and his hustle kept the infield on its toes even though as a batsman he had a well-deserved reputation as the "All-American Out."

Leo's heated disputes with the arbiters won him the admiration of the Brooklyn fans. The team had a new spirit, and the Flatbush Faithful rallied to its support. There were still plenty of weak spots on the roster, but it was clear that the Dodgers, with MacPhail and Durocher leading them, were no longer content to roll over and play dead.

During 1939 MacPhail picked up three players who would play important roles in the club's future: outfielder Dixie Walker came over from the Tigers on waivers; pitcher Whit Wyatt was purchased from Milwaukee; and Hugh Casey, another hurler, was drafted from Memphis.

On the last day of the season the Dodgers accomplished two remarkable feats—they went over the million mark in attendance (up from less than five hundred thousand two years earlier), and they clinched third place.

It was a happy summer for Damon. He spent many an afternoon watching the Dodgers from the roof of Harry's and Ellen's apartment house. What he couldn't see he picked up from Red Barber's play-by-play. Before every game Damon lugged Harry's old Crosley radio up to the roof and dropped three extension cords to his uncle's bedroom to plug it in. Damon and his father savored every Dodger win that year, and they delighted in every Giant defeat.

Except for a brief flurry in July when they reached second place, Terry's men were never really in the race. An axiom of baseball holds that to win a pennant a club should have at least two stoppers—pitchers who can win when it counts. In other seasons the Giants had Mathewson and Marquard or Hubbell and Schumacher. Now there was only Harry Gumbert.

King Carl and Prince Hal were both still on the roster, but neither performed up to old standards. Carl had a record of eleven and nine while Hal recorded thirteen victories against ten defeats. The Giants came in fifth—their first second-division finish since the debacle of 1932.

The National League flag was won by the Reds, a team that Larry MacPhail had molded. Larry now found himself in a curious position. The major obstacle between him and a pennant was a ball club of his own creation.

During Red Barber's first season as the voice of the Dodgers he took part in an event that received little attention at the time but became a landmark in the history of sports broadcasting. On August 26, 1939, the Cincinnati Reds were in Brooklyn for a doubleheader. Larry MacPhail added the opening game of the twin bill to his list of baseball "firsts" by allowing NBC to televise the action. In return, NBC installed a television receiver in the Ebbets Field press club so that reporters and members of the Dodger staff could get a good look at this newfangled contraption.

Barber left the radio chores to Al Helfer and announced the TV broadcast from a box on the third base side of the upper deck. Next to Red was one camera, which gave a general view of the diamond, and below him in the field boxes was a second camera for closeups of the action at the plate. Red did impromptu commercials for Wheaties, Ivory Soap, and Mobil gasoline during the game (which Cincinnati won, 5–2), and after the final out he went down to the field to interview manager Bill McKechnie and pitcher Bucky Walters of the Reds, as well as Leo Durocher, Dolf Camilli, Dixie Walker, and Whit Wyatt.

There were only a few hundred TV sets in existence. One of them was on exhibit in the RCA pavilion at the New York World's Fair, and so many people showed up to watch the game it became necessary to close the doors. It would be several years before baseball and television would become permanent bedfellows, but on that summer afternoon in Brooklyn a handful of broadcasting pioneers proved TV to be more than a curiosity.

During the winter of 1939, Joe McCarthy traded away Myril Hoag for a pitcher, Oral Hildebrand, and brought Charlie "King Kong" Keller up from the Newark team. At 5 foot, 10 inches and 185 pounds, Keller was built like a refrigerator. His long, powerful drives in spring training made him look ready-made to become a member of the Bronx window-breakers. Lefty Gomez, who confided to friends that Keller was the only ballplayer who had been scouted and signed by Frank "Bring 'Em Back Alive" Buck, sidled up to the young outfielder one day during spring practice. "Hey, kid," the irrepressible pitcher said, "I know you think all that muscle helps you hit, but maybe you should consider dropping a few pounds."

Keller looked at him incredulously. "No, seriously. When I first came up, Ed Barrow told me if I'd only put on some weight I could make the fans forget about Jack Chesbro, the first American League pitcher to win sixteen straight."

"Yeah?"

"Yeah. So I put on twenty pounds."

"What happened?"

"I made 'em forget Gomez."

But if Keller was a slugging silver lining, clouds were hanging over Lou Gehrig. The Iron Horse had finished the 1938 season with a batting average of .295, slipping below the .300 mark for the first time in twelve seasons. He seemed to be seeing the ball and making contact with it, but the explosiveness was gone from his bat.

On April 30 Lou made a routine play at first base. He stared into the infield dirt while teammates Johnny Murphy and Joe Gordon called, "Nice play, Lou." The Yankees then traveled to Detroit for their next game, on May 2. Lou approached McCarthy in the dugout before the game. "Joe," he said, "I'm benching myself."

After 2,130 consecutive games, Columbia Lou, the Iron Horse, was sitting one out. Seven weeks later, physicians at the Mayo Clinic announced that Lou would never again play baseball. In fact, although the doctors didn't say it, Lou's days were numbered. As a result of a rare neuromuscular disease, he would die within two years.

On July 4 the Yankees and New York honored Lou Gehrig. It was a special day, a day of joy and sorrow, a mixed aura of greatness and death hanging over the Stadium. "I consider myself the luckiest man on the face of this earth," said Lou, a catch in his voice.

The Yankees, saddened by their loss, were nonetheless relentless. They had taken over first place on May 11, and from there on it was a breeze. They easily won their fourth straight pennant, becoming the first American League team to do so and tying the Giants' streak of 1921 through 1924. The second-place Red Sox finished seventeen games back, but Beantown rooters were heartened by the emergence of a twenty-year-old rookie slugging star named Ted Williams. DiMaggio led the league with a batting average of .381, and Dickey, Selkirk, Keller, and Rolfe were all over .300. Red Ruffing not only posted a 21–7 pitching record but also batted .307.

The World Series with Cincinnati caused little excitement. Harry secured tickets for the first two games, but he couldn't persuade Alex to accompany him. "I'm tired of watching the Yankees win," Alex said.

"Okay, if that's the way you feel," Harry said. "But if you wait for your Bums to win a pennant, you may never see another World Series game." And he beat a hasty retreat.

Harry and Damon watched the Yankees win the first two games behind Ruffing and Pearson. The Bombers then traveled to Cincinnati and completed the sweep, Bump Hadley and Fireman Murphy collecting the wins. The Yanks had become the first major league team to win four straight Series and the first American League team to win eleven pennants. Over the four-year span, they had won sixteen of nineteen Series games, the last nine of them consecutively.

In 1940 Pee Wee Reese arrived in Brooklyn. This youngster from the Red Sox farm system was a crackerjack infielder and a determined batter.

Leo began to substitute Pee Wee for himself with very promising results. Then, on June 1, in a game in Chicago, Reese was beaned by Cub pitcher Jake Mooty. After three weeks in the hospital Pee Wee was back in the lineup, and Leo knew that his scrappy rookie was a man after his own heart.

The Dodgers got off to a great start that year. They began the season with nine straight wins and stayed in the thick of the race through the first two months of the campaign. From his first day in Brooklyn Larry MacPhail had been building toward a pennant, but logic told him his goal was still a year or two away.

Now, suddenly, he found himself with a bad case of pennant fever. He began looking for ways to beef up his club, and Branch Rickey of the Cardinals came up with a deal that was mighty tempting.

Rickey offered the Dodgers Joe "Ducky" Medwick, another member of the Gas House Gang and the winner of the National League's triple crown in 1937. Medwick was a fierce competitor. Dizzy Dean once complained that "that dawggoned Medwick don't fight fair. You try to argue with Joe and before you can say a dawggoned word, he bops you."

Larry MacPhail considered himself a pretty fair horse-trader, and he knew that if Rickey had placed Medwick on the market there was probably a catch. But Ducky was still only twenty-eight years old; surely he had a few good years left in him. Two months into the season he was batting .304, a sharp drop from his .332 of the year before. All Rickey was asking for his star left fielder was a paltry $132,500 plus four players, including Ernie Koy.

To show Larry what a nice guy he was, the Mahatma offered to throw in pitcher Curt Davis free of charge. After weighing the pros and cons MacPhail decided to depart this once from building for the future to get a man who might just help him win a pennant now.

On June 13 the news broke that Ducky was on his way to the Dodgers. MacPhail boasted, "We may go broke trying to pay for this fellow, but he is the man we wanted, and he is the player who is needed to give us a pennant contending club, which is what I promised the fans when I came to Brooklyn."

As soon as Alex heard about the trade he too was attacked by pennant fever. He called Harry to find out what the old baseball philosopher had to say about it. "Ducky Wucky can help the Dodgers," Harry opined, "but only if the other clubs don't get wise to his Achilles' heel."

"What do you mean?" Alex asked.

"Well, as I see it, Medwick's got to have a fatal flaw. From 1933 to 1937 he batted .387 in Ebbets Field. In 1938 Durocher left the Cards and came to the Dodgers. What happened then? Ol' Ducky's average in Brooklyn these last two years has been only .250. Leo has obviously tipped off the Dodger pitchers on how to throw to Medwick."

"So what? He's on the Dodgers now. It's a sure bet Leo isn't gonna tip off anyone else."

"Maybe not, little brother. But sooner or later the other clubs are going to catch on."

When Medwick joined the Dodgers he moved into the Hotel New Yorker, where Durocher also lived, and where the Cardinals bedded down in New York. Less than a week after Joe's arrival the Cards came to town, and one morning Leo and Joe ran into Bob Bowman, a St. Louis pitcher, in the hotel elevator. When Leo recognized the enemy hurler, who was scheduled to pitch that day, he made a wisecrack about Bob's puniness on the mound.

"I won't have any trouble getting *you* out, Leo," Bowman said.

"You won't get a chance to pitch to Leo," Medwick piped up. "We'll belt you out of there before you get that far down in the lineup."

As Bowman left the elevator he muttered something about "taking care of" both Leo and Joe when they came to the plate.

When Bowman went to the mound that afternoon he pitched as though he'd taken Medwick's prediction to heart. The first three batters to face him got hits, and two Dodgers had already crossed the plate by the time Ducky, batting cleanup, came up for his initial at bat. Bowman's first delivery to Medwick was a blazing fastball right at his head. Joe tried to escape, but it smacked him in the skull. He went down like a shot; as his shoulder blades landed on the ground his feet flew up in the air.

The stands and the playing field broke into an uproar. Players from both benches rushed onto the diamond, while the fans screamed insults at Bowman and his teammates. Somehow the umpires managed to keep the teams apart.

Medwick was quickly removed from the field on a stretcher. Then Larry MacPhail appeared on the steps of the Dodger dugout. He stormed across to the St. Louis bench where he called the Cardinals every vile name in the book and invited anyone who was interested to take a walk with him under the stands. Pepper Martin and Johnny Mize stood between MacPhail and their teammates. Billy Southworth, the Cards' manager, spirited Bowman away and sent him off to Manhattan in the care of two plainclothes detectives.

MacPhail finally ran out of steam and went back to the press club.

With calm restored the Cardinals proceeded to win the ball game, 7–5. The Dodgers had now been the victims of two nasty beanball incidents in less than a month.

Medwick stayed out of action only five days, but he was never his old self. He could still hit for average, but he almost always had trouble hanging in there in the clutch.

As the midway point in the season approached, Lippy's boys found themselves in a three-team race with the Reds and the Giants. On July 3, in a game at the Polo Grounds, Pee Wee Reese gave the Flatbush Faithful plenty to yell about. The Giants were leading, 3–1, going into the ninth; a win for New York would knock Brooklyn out of first and move the Giants to within a game of the idle Reds, who would take over the lead by default.

Suddenly the Flock tied the ball game with two quick runs, and then, with the bases loaded, Pee Wee lofted a high fly down the left-field line that hit the foul pole and dropped back on the field for a grand-slam homer, winning the game for Brooklyn, 7–3. Alex and Damon were giddy from the thrill of it all. The next morning, the Fourth of July, the standings showed that the Dodgers were still in first place.

"Well, Damon," Alex said, "if tradition has its way, we'll win the pennant. And over in the American League the Indians are out in front. Did I ever tell you about the time twenty years ago when I spent my last money in the world getting out to Cleveland to watch the Dodgers and the Indians in the Series? That was when Bill Wambsganss made that unassisted triple play. Wouldn't it be something if Brooklyn and Cleveland were in this year's World Series?"

If anyone had any doubts that Brooklyn was on the rise, all he had to do was take a look at the 1940 National League All-Star team. Six Dodgers—Durocher, Lavagetto, Medwick, Phelps, Wyatt, and Pete Coscarart—were named to the roster, more than from any other club. The midseason contest brought joy to the hearts of Senior Circuit rooters, as the Nationals beat the Americans, 4–0, in the first shutout since the game began in 1933.

After the All-Star break, the Reds, still the class of the National League, began to show their stuff. They took over first place and increased their lead week by week, winding up the season twelve games ahead of the second-place Dodgers. The Giants finished a distant sixth. All in all, it was a heartening season for Larry MacPhail and Leo Durocher, not to mention Alex and Damon Rice.

One incident that took place in 1940—another testimony to the zealousness of the Brooklyn fan—remains to be recounted. On September 16 the Reds played the Dodgers at Ebbets Field, and after nine innings the contest was all tied up, 3–3. In the top of the tenth, with runners on first and second and one out, Frank McCormick, the Reds' first baseman, hit a grounder to Johnny Hudson at short, who flipped the ball to second baseman Pete Coscarart.

Coscarart, in his haste to make the double play, dropped the ball, but umpire Bill Stewart ruled that the Dodger second bagger had held on long enough to complete the force out. The Reds began yelling bloody murder. They appealed the play to George Magerkurth, the ump at third, and George reversed the decision—all hands were safe. Leo Durocher ran out of the dugout and went at Magerkurth nose-to-nose.

It wasn't long before Lippy was tossed out of the ball game. When play resumed, Bill Baker hit a sacrifice fly to left that brought Mike McCormick, the Cincinnati center fielder, in from third with the winning run. After the final out, George Magerkurth stopped to talk to a friend on his way off the diamond. Suddenly an irate Dodger fan—twenty-one-year-old Frank Germano—leaped out of the stands and attacked the umpire. Magerkurth, who was 6 foot, 3 inches and weighed 230, towered over his stocky little assailant, but somehow, while the two men were exchanging swings, Germano managed to trip the ump and then jumped on top of him with his fists flying.

The two other umpires pulled the wild fan away, and the police quickly took him into custody. Frank was an ex-convict out on parole. Some sympathetic fans hired an attorney to defend him; only in Brooklyn would the lawyer's name turn out to be Louis J. Wacke. Despite the legal aid, Germano's misadventure put him right back into the clink. Two weeks later, the campaign came to a close.

For the Yankees, the season had been an unusual one. They got off to a ragged start, and by August 9 they were playing at an even .500. Then they caught fire and challenged the Indians and Tigers. When the smoke cleared on the next to last day of the season, Detroit was clutching the pennant. Cleveland was a game back, and the Bombers, two games off the pace, came in third, their lowest finish in a decade.

In the World Series of 1940, Cincinnati edged Detroit, four games to three. The hitting star of the Series was Jimmie Wilson, a thirty-nine-year-old coach who took over the catching duties for the Reds late in the season, after catcher Willard Hershberger committed suicide and Ernie Lombardi sprained an ankle.

That year the Christmas Eve gathering of the Rice family—a tradition that went back to the year Fletcher and Elizabeth were married—took place in Harry's and Ellen's apartment. Alex, Sally, and Damon took the subway from Bay Ridge to Flatbush laden with the kinds of presents that had become commonplace during the Depression. Sally had knitted a sweater for Ellen and made a silk tie for Harry. Alex had carved a pipe stand for his brother and bought Ellen a brush and comb set at

Woolworth's. Damon came bearing scented soap and a pouch of pipe tobacco.

Ellen's Christmas table was in sharp contrast to the meager holiday dinners of recent years. Alex couldn't resist a second helping of roast turkey, fresh cranberry sauce, chestnut-and-currant stuffing, and candied yams, all swimming in gravy. "Big brother," Alex commented as he sipped his third glass of imported claret, "you've outdone yourself. Whose books did you juggle to pay for this spread?"

After coffee, everyone repaired to the living room to trim the tree and open the presents. As soon as the ornaments and lights were in place, Damon eagerly offered to play Santa Claus. Before the others were settled, he picked out a package for himself. He ripped off the paper, opened the box, and found inside a note that read: "Look in the bedroom closet." Damon rushed into the bedroom, tore open the closet door, and discovered, to his amazement and glee, a brand new Schwinn bicycle complete with horn and headlight.

"Uncle Harry and Aunt Ellen!" he shouted. "It's the best present I ever got!" It was several minutes before he could bring himself to leave his new prize and return to the task of handing out gifts.

After Harry had unwrapped his new pipe stand and Ellen had thanked Damon for her soap, it was Sally's turn to open a small present. The tag revealed the giver only as "Santa Claus." She carefully untied the ribbon and removed the paper. Inside was a delicate, gold wristwatch. She turned to her husband and exclaimed, "Oh, Alex, I never expected anything so wonder—"

Alex stood quickly and went to the kitchen to pour himself a glass of beer. Sally looked at Harry and said, "You really shouldn't have."

The last present of the evening was to Alex from Harry. Alex fumbled with the large package for several minutes before finally producing his gift. It was a velvet smoking jacket, elegantly trimmed and handstitched. Leaving it in the box, he folded back the tissue and mumbled a thank-you.

In less than an hour Damon and his parents were on their way home. As they entered the Prospect Park subway station, they saw a young man, his jacket and trousers worn through at the elbows and knees, huddled in a corner trying to keep warm. Sally turned away. She had seen enough of this Depression.

"Say, mister, how about a nickel for Christmas?" the tramp asked.

Alex walked over to the lad, took the large box from under his arm, removed the smoking jacket, and placed it over the young man's shoulders. Then he rushed Sally and Damon through the turnstile.

While Damon was peddling his new bike through the ice-covered streets of Brooklyn, Joe McCarthy was preparing for the 1941 season.

He wasn't about to sit still for another third-place finish, so he gave the Yankees a new look. Over the winter, he sold Babe Dahlgren to the Boston Braves for the waiver price. "His arms were too short," was the only explanation McCarthy would offer. Joe assigned first base to Johnny Sturm, a rookie just up from Kansas City. There was another rookie from K.C. in camp, a twenty-three-year-old kid named Phil Rizzuto. Rizzuto, a floating ghost at short, could play the slow roller as well as any man who ever played the game. From the moment he took the field, it was obvious he was a big league shortstop. Gordon was moved back to second, and Rolfe remained at third. The outfield was Henrich, Keller, and DiMaggio.

DiMaggio. On May 15 he got a hit that was the beginning of one of the most stupendous records in baseball. Joltin' Joe kept on hitting, and on July 1 he tied Wee Willie Keeler's record of hitting safely in forty-four consecutive games. And Joe kept on hitting, putting more pressure on official scorers than they had ever experienced.

Damon, whose loyalties didn't exactly lie with the Yankees, couldn't help being excited by the streak. He was sitting in the rain with his Uncle Harry when DiMadge tied Keeler's mark. And he was there the next day, jumping and screaming with the rest of the Yankee fans when Joe broke the record. In Cleveland on July 17, it took brilliant plays by third baseman Ken Keltner and shortstop Lou Boudreau to end the streak at fifty-six. DiMadge, unruffled, turned around and hit safely in his next sixteen games.

Inspired by DiMaggio, the Yanks pulled away from the field. They clinched the pennant on September 4 and coasted to a seventeen-game final margin over second-place Boston. Once again Boston fans had to take solace in the performance of Ted Williams, who batted an amazing .406. The Yanks had made the 1941 Junior Circuit race a real yawner, but things were different over in the National League. It was a campaign that Damon would one day remember as the most exciting in the history of the league.

During the off-season, Larry MacPhail had strengthened the Dodgers by picking up two solid players—pitcher Kirby Higbe and catcher Mickey Owen. Higbe, who came over from Philadelphia, was a far better hurler than his 1940 record of fourteen and nineteen suggested. All season long he had come up on the short end of games that were blown by the Phils' puny batters.

Owen was purchased by the Cards to back up Babe Phelps. But the Blimp, claiming he was ill, refused to report to spring training in Havana. Actually, he was frightened to death of airplanes. Phelps did eventually join the club, but when, later in the season, he missed a train for a western road trip, Larry MacPhail got tired of Babe's shenanigans and suspended him.

The case came before Judge Landis, who gave the Blimp every opportunity to rejoin the team before finally placing him on the ineligible list. So, as it turned out, the deal for Mickey Owen became crucial to the Dodgers' pennant hopes.

The sensation of the Dodgers' training camp was Pete Reiser, who tore the cover off the ball all spring. Pete had come up from the minors toward the end of 1940. He played mostly at third base that year, and it was obvious he was not a great infielder.

Now Durocher was working Pete hard to improve his defensive skills in the hope of turning him into an accomplished outfielder. By the time the 1941 grapefruit season was over Reiser looked as if he was ready to try his hand at playing center field. Leo's plan was to move Dixie Walker out of center and onto the bench, and to use veteran Paul Waner, whom MacPhail had recently picked up from the Pirates, in right.

The fans back in Brooklyn couldn't believe it when they learned that Dixie, "the Peepul's Cherce," was not going to be a regular. Five thousand members of the Flatbush Faithful, including Alex and Damon, signed a telegram threatening to boycott Ebbets Field if Dixie didn't get his job back. Whether or not MacPhail and Durocher took the wire seriously, it wasn't long before Walker was back in the lineup. A minor injury put Reiser out of action for the first few games of the season, so Dixie was needed to take his place. Not long after Pete returned, Waner was sent packing, and Walker was moved into right field, where he was much more comfortable anyway. The Dodger outfield of Medwick, Reiser, and Walker gave the fans plenty to smile about.

As the season began, all of Brooklyn was afflicted with pennant fever. "Don't tell me we don't have one hell of a good chance to win it this year," Alex said to Harry.

"You know, Alex," Harry replied, "I think you're right. With Reiser hitting the ball the way he is right now, and with Wyatt and Higbe leading the mound staff, the Dodgers are going to be tough. The only real gap is at second base. Let's face it, Coscarart is through."

Coscarart *was* through as a first-stringer, no doubt about it. All spring MacPhail had been trying to wangle Billy Herman away from the Cubs, but so far he'd had no luck.

The Dodgers opened the season against the Giants at Ebbets Field. Alex, hunched over his radio with a cold glass of beer at the ready, figured the Giants were going to be pushovers. After all, Brooklyn had taken sixteen out of twenty-one from New York the year before.

"Let's rack this one up!" Durocher yelled to his men as they took the field. Alas, the Giants won, 6–4. They beat the Dodgers the next two games as well, prompting Bill Terry to boast, "What you see of my Giants is no flash in the pan." Alex listened in pain to all three games.

As soon as the Dodgers got the Giants off their backs they found themselves. They won fifteen of their next seventeen games. Then, on May 6, Larry MacPhail announced that he'd succeeded in getting Billy Herman. In return for the star second baseman he sent the Cubs outfielder Charlie Gilbert and third-string shortstop Johnny Hudson, plus, of course, a pile of cash.

"We can't miss now," Alex told his son. Damon was certainly inclined to agree, and so were the Dodgers. By the time July Fourth rolled around they were in first place, a game ahead of the Cards, while in the American League the Yanks were leading the Indians by two games.

"Wouldn't *that* be something," Alex said to Harry. "A Yankee-Dodger Series."

"Are you sure you could stand the strain?" Harry asked.

By the end of July the National League race was down to only two teams—the Cards and the Dodgers. It was painfully clear that Branch Rickey had rebuilt the Cards into a club that had the makings of another St. Louis dynasty.

The old Gas House Gang had been disbanded; in its place was a roster that included the likes of Johnny Mize, Marty Marion, Enos Slaughter, and a youngster by the name of Stan Musial. Throughout August Brooklyn and St. Louis battled away, exchanging the lead every few days.

As the tension mounted, Alex found it more and more difficult to get to work. He called in sick so often that he almost lost his job, but somehow he managed to hold on. Perhaps it was because Alex, on his lucid days, was an excellent bartender who worked hard keeping his patrons happy. And when they were happy they stayed around the Web Café and guzzled plenty of beer and whisky.

As the Cards and Dodgers got ready for the homestretch, Branch Rickey decided to shore up the Cardinal pitching staff by calling up young Howie Pollet from Houston in the Texas League. Pollet, a southpaw, was the pitching sensation of the minors that year. MacPhail, fuming, accused Rickey of running the minor leagues by calling up a hurler who could have helped Houston win the Texas League pennant. The Mahatma just laughed and reminded the press that a year earlier MacPhail had pulled Pete Reiser away from an Elmira club that was in the middle of a hot pennant race.

September arrived with no relief in sight. The National League flag would be won by the team that could hold up best under pressure. Just before leaving for their last western road trip of the year, the Dodgers took three straight from the Giants and pulled three full games ahead of the Cards.

The Giants, mired in fifth place, were winding up yet another terrible season, and their fans were disgusted when Terry's men, instead of playing the role of spoilers, actually aided the Dodgers' cause. A few weeks earlier Horace Stoneham had remarked that he was fed up with the club, causing Bill Terry to offer to tear up his contract. For the time being, at least, Stoneham refused to accept his resignation.

The Dodgers felt that they were holding most of the cards as they left New York on what Leo would later describe as "a haywire, hysterical road trip." The first stop was Chicago, where Brooklyn lost both ends of a doubleheader while the Cards were taking a pair from the Phils. The Dodgers' lead was now down to one lousy game. The next city on the schedule was St. Louis for three crucial contests.

In the opener Freddie Fitzsimmons, who'd just turned forty, huffed and puffed his way through a game that Brooklyn won, 6–4, in eleven innings. Hugh Casey came on to save the day by extinguishing an outbreak of St. Louis fire in the bottom of the eleventh. The next day Howie Pollet beat Curt Davis, 4–3, to tie up the series at a game apiece. The rubber game was a must for the Dodgers. A loss would put them in second place and would give momentum to the Cardinals.

Harry, Alex, and Damon listened to that game on the roof of Harry's apartment house. They brought up three chairs and a washtub filled with beer and Cokes, and they hooked up the old radio.

Looking down on Ebbets Field, empty and forlorn, they tuned in to a contest that might well decide whether or not the old park would soon play host to its first World Series in twenty-one years.

At 4:15 Red Barber came on the air to set the scene and announce the lineups. The Cardinals sent Mort Cooper to the mound to face Whit Wyatt.

Both began with excellent stuff. The first hit of the day didn't come until the bottom of the fifth, when Creepy Crespi led off with a double. Marty Marion, the next batter, hit a grounder to Reese who threw to third hoping to nail Crespi. The ball hit Creepy just as he was reaching the bag; before it could be retrieved the Cardinals had runners on second and third with no one out.

While Alex nervously sipped his beer and Damon squirmed in his chair, Wyatt struck out Gus Mancuso and Mort Cooper and then got Jimmy Brown to ground out to Camilli. In the fifth the Cards loaded up the bases but once again failed to score. Going into the eighth it was still 0–0, and the Dodgers still didn't have their first hit.

With one out in the eighth Dixie Walker rapped one off the right-field screen for a double. The next batter was Billy Herman. Walker Cooper, the Cardinal catcher, signaled to his brother Mort for a curve. Ol' Dixie out on second base stole the sign and flashed it back to Herman, whose eyes almost popped out of his head when he picked up the signal. Sure enough, down came a breaking ball. Billy drove it over the head of center fielder Johnny Hopp for another two-bagger. A run crossed the plate, and Wyatt hung in to win the ball game, 1–0. Leo later called the contest "one of the real pitching classics of baseball history, produced under pressure."

The victory, while sweet, did not comfort Alex and Damon. The Dodgers were far from out of the woods. They went on to Cincinnati, where they won their first game, 7–5. The next afternoon it took them seventeen innings to pull off a 5–1 win. The game was scoreless until the top of the seventeenth when Pete Reiser led off with a homer. The Reds then began to stall, hoping to get the game called on account of darkness. The rules then prohibited turning on the lights during a day game. Four more Dodger runs crossed the plate before Billy Herman finally fanned deliberately to get the third out. The Reds tallied once in their half of the inning, making the final score 5–1. The following afternoon the Dodgers lost to the Reds, 4–3, in eleven innings, and their lead was shaved to a game and a half.

On they went to Pittsburgh, where they went into the top of the ninth inning of the first game down, 3–1. Over in St. Louis the Cardinals were taking two from the Braves; a loss now would drop Brooklyn into second place. Augie Galan led off the ninth with a double, Reese singled him home, and then Reiser hit a booming triple to right center that put Brooklyn ahead, 4–3. The Dodgers scored two more times before the inning was over and won the ball game, 6–4.

The next day Brooklyn lost to the Bucs, 6–5, after Hugh Casey balked Vince DiMaggio in from third with the tying run in the bottom of the eighth. The balk call sent Lippy into a rage. He blasted umpire George Magerkurth for several minutes, finally went back into the dugout, and watched Casey, also fit to be tied, wing three straight fastballs right at Magerkurth's head! All three missed, but when the ump went to the mound to tell Hugh to cut it out, Durocher stormed off the bench, started up a brand new rhubarb, and was quickly thrown out of the game.

On his way to the clubhouse Leo smashed every light bulb in sight and heaved a chair through the transom of the umpires' dressing room. Not far behind Durocher were his teammates. While Lippy was throwing his tantrum, Alf Anderson was tripling home the winning run for the Pirates.

Two days later Alex took Damon to Philadelphia to watch a double-header against the Phillies. On the train Alex couldn't help but remember that long ago day in 1905 when Fletcher took him and Harry to see that great World Series contest between the Giants and the Athletics. Christy Mathewson had shut out Eddie Plank, 3–0. Alex was only twelve at the time; Damon was already thirteen. This visit to the City of Brotherly Love turned out to be as rewarding as the previous one. Wyatt and Higbe both notched up their twenty-first victories of the year as the Dodgers swept the twin bill.

"We're in," Alex told his son on the way home. "Even if the Bums only take four out of their last seven, the Cards will have to win seven out of eight to beat us." Alex was beginning to sound like his brother.

Five days later, in Boston, the Dodgers beat the Braves, 6–0, and clinched the pennant. Brooklyn threw a wild victory celebration that was a fitting conclusion to a zany pennant race.

Alex and Damon joined thousands of other fans at Grand Army Plaza for a parade down Flatbush Avenue and Fulton Street to Borough Hall. In the crowd were adults and children disguised as clowns, Indians, ballplayers, totem poles. One fat little man showed up as Leo the Lion. Howling Hilda Chester, the most famous of all Dodger fans, was there with her cowbell. Also on hand was Shorty Laurice with the Dodger Sym-Phony, a band that couldn't play a note but was always at Ebbets Field to support the Bums with plenty of noise. More than a million people participated in the celebration, either as marchers or as spectators. There were signs everywhere—"LIPPY FOR MAYOR," "DU-ROCHER FOR PRESIDENT," "MOIDER THEM YANKS." Alex was carrying a placard that said, "YES, MR. TERRY, WE'RE STILL IN THE LEAGUE."

The Dodgers, in open autos, led the procession into Borough Hall Square, where they were greeted by a thundering tribute that included a shower of confetti and ticker tape thrown out of the tall buildings along Court Street. The crowd nearly ripped the players' clothes off as they made their way up to the reviewing stand. The ceremonies were short and sweet, with Red Barber, Larry MacPhail, Leo Durocher, and several of the players coming to the microphone. The crowd milled around long after the Dodgers had gone.

Alex and Damon sat on the steps of Borough Hall until late in the afternoon. They were both so exhilarated by it all that they didn't want to leave. Finally Alex got up and said, "Come on, son, let's go home. Your mother has dinner waiting." Then he ran up to the top step of the historic building, cupped his hands around his mouth, and yelled out over the square, at the top of his lungs, "BRING ON THE YANKS!"

The betting line for the 1941 World Series favored the Yankees 2–1, but Brooklyn fans were quick to point out that the Dodgers had just won a tough pennant race against a damned good Cardinal team. Furthermore, Pete Reiser had taken the National League batting crown with a .343 average, and Brooklyn had two twenty-two-game winners in Kirby Higbe and Whit Wyatt. The winningest pitcher on the Yankees was Red Ruffing, whose record was a mere fifteen and six.

"But look, Alex," Harry said after his brother had articulated all the arguments on the Brooklyn side, "if you go down the two lineups man by man, the only position where the Dodgers have the edge is at first base. I'll give you Camilli over Sturm hands down, but after that forget it."

"Come on, Harry, get off your high horse. The Yanks aren't supermen."

"Oh no? How come they've won their last nine World Series games in a row?"

Alex didn't try to answer that one.

Joe McCarthy picked Red Ruffing to start the Series opener, but Leo Durocher refused to name his man until fifteen minutes before game time. His choice surprised everyone in Yankee Stadium, including Harry, Alex, and Damon, who were seated together in the upper deck out in right field.

Durocher decided to go with Curt Davis. Curt had been a big help to the club during the pennant drive, and he was a low-ball pitcher. Leo figured the Yanks wouldn't get many homers off Davis, and if the Dodgers could squeak out a victory they'd be one game up, and they'd still have their two aces—Wyatt and Higbe—rested and rarin' to go.

Alex thought the strategy was a bit peculiar, but Harry couldn't help admiring Durocher for taking a well-calculated gamble. The Yankees drew first blood in the bottom of the second when Joe Gordon blasted a homer into the left-field seats. In the fourth Ducky Medwick made a sensational catch to rob Joe DiMaggio of a home run, but then Charlie Keller walked and Bill Dickey doubled him home with the second New York run of the day.

In the fifth Pee Wee Reese singled and Mickey Owen hit a liner that went between Keller and DiMaggio for a triple, bringing Pee Wee in with the first Dodger run. Then, in the bottom of the sixth, the Yankees scored their third run when Keller walked, moved to third on a single by Dickey, and came home on a single by Gordon. At this point Leo brought in Hugh Casey, who put an end to the Yankee scoring.

Then came the weird Dodger half of the seventh. Lavagetto, the lead-off batter, hit a grounder to Rizzuto that should have been an easy out. But Johnny Sturm failed to hold onto Rizzuto's peg, and Cookie was safe. "Yea, Cookie!" Damon shouted from his right-field perch. Reese then singled up the middle. Lew Riggs, sent in to bat for Owen, singled to shallow center, enabling Cookie to reach home a split second ahead of DiMaggio's throw. Now Brooklyn had men on second and first, they needed only one run to tie, and there was still no one out.

Jimmy Wasdell came up to pinch-hit for Casey. This situation calls for a bunt 100 times out of 100, and the bunt was definitely on. But Wasdell either didn't pick up the sign or was daydreaming. He hit a high foul near the Yankee dugout that Red Rolfe was able to snag. As Rolfe caught the ball Pee Wee, in another bad move, took off for third.

The Yankees in the dugout yelled to their third baseman to get rid of the ball. Rizzuto covered third, took the peg from Rolfe, and tagged Reese out to end the Dodger threat. That closed out the scoring. Brooklyn had handed New York a 3–2 victory on a silver platter.

"Jesus, we should have won that game," Alex moaned as he, Damon, and Harry filed out of the stadium.

"Do you think so?" Harry asked. "Maybe, but let's see what happens tomorrow. Brooklyn's going to have to do a hell of a lot better against Chandler than they did against Ruffing. I'll bet Ol' Red didn't throw more than one or two curves all day. He kept the Dodgers guessing with his change of pace."

During the first four innings of game two Spud Chandler mowed down twelve Dodgers in a row while his opponent, Whit Wyatt, struggled along, giving up a run in the second and another in the third. In the bottom of the fourth Chandler, after reaching first on a force out, tried to leg it all the way to third on a pop single by Johnny Sturm. Medwick threw Chandler out by a mile, and when the winded pitcher took to the mound in the fifth, he'd lost his stuff. Brooklyn quickly tied up the game at 2–2.

In the next inning the Dodgers threatened to go ahead for the first time in the Series after Dixie Walker reached first on an error and then made it around to third when Billy Herman, on a hit-and-run play, pulled the ball into left field for a clean single.

Joe McCarthy pulled his dejected pitcher out of the ball game, replacing him with Johnny Murphy. The Yankee fireman fanned Pete Reiser, but then Dolf Camilli singled to put the Dodgers out in front, 3–2. Wyatt held the Yanks the rest of the way, and the Series moved over to Ebbets Field tied at a game apiece. As far as Alex and Damon were concerned, the Dodgers should have been two games up.

The third game of the Series was delayed a day by rain. The action resumed with Marius Russo on the mound for New York against ancient Freddie Fitzsimmons for Brooklyn. Freddie still had it in him to have a good day, and that afternoon he pitched beautiful baseball. All his pitches were working for him, and for six innings he had the Yankees completely fooled. But Russo also pitched brilliantly. When the Yanks came to bat in the top of the seventh, the game was still scoreless. With one down Joe Gordon walked and then advanced to second on an infield out.

Up came Russo, a good hitting pitcher. He drilled the ball right back at Fitzsimmons; it was such a wicked shot that Freddie had no chance to get out of the way. The ball smashed off his left kneecap and sailed into the air without ever touching the ground. Reese came over to catch it for the final out of the inning. The Yankees hadn't scored, but they had literally knocked Brooklyn's starter out of the box. Ol' Fitz was carried off on a stretcher. Hugh Casey, who'd been keeping warm in the bullpen, would take over in the eighth.

"God damn it! I don't believe it!" Alex screamed from the roof of his brother's apartment house. Damon just stood in silence, hoping against hope that Casey could pick up where Fitz had left off.

The Dodgers failed to score in their half of the seventh, and when Casey came in the Yanks were waiting for him. With two quick runs they sent the Dodger reliever to the showers. Larry French came in to end the rally, but the damage had been done. Brooklyn came back gamely with a run in their half of the inning, but Russo quickly closed the door again and went on to win, 2–1.

"Can you believe this hard luck?" Alex screamed. He made a few gestures with his feet as if to kick in the old Crosley, but then pulled himself together. The other spectators on the roof had no trouble sympathizing with their fellow Brooklynite.

The beauty of baseball is in its unpredictability. No doubt about it. But therein lies the agony of the game as well. Alex and Damon watched game four from the left-field grandstand, while Harry was across the street in his living room smugly listening to Red Barber's account of the action. Atley Donald started for the Yanks, and Kirby Higbe for the Dodgers. New York scored once in the first and twice more in the fourth, knocking Higbe out of the game. In the bottom of the fourth Brooklyn came back with two runs, and then, in the fifth, with Dixie Walker on second, Pete Reiser lofted a homer over the scoreboard clock into Bedford Avenue to put the Dodgers ahead, 4–3.

The crowd was delirious. Surely this was going to be Brooklyn's day. The game went into the ninth with the score intact, and with Hugh Casey—the fourth Brooklyn hurler of the day—looking good enough to put the Yankees down one, two, three. Which is what he did.

He retired Johnny Sturm and Red Rolfe, leaving only Tommy Henrich standing in the way of victory. The count went to three and two. Many fans believe to this day that Casey loaded up and delivered a low spitter. Henrich was completely fooled by the pitch. He swung and missed, but the ball got away from Mickey Owen, who was also baffled.

As the Dodger catcher ran back to the screen to retrieve the ball, Henrich dashed up the line and reached first safely. In a few terrible seconds the Yankees had come back from the dead. Joe DiMaggio then singled, and Charlie Keller doubled off the right-field screen to put New York ahead, 5–4. Two more runs crossed the plate before that disastrous inning ended. The Dodgers went down in order in the ninth, losing the game, 7–4, and fell behind in the Series three games to one.

Until that moment Damon had never seen his father cry. But there, in the slowly emptying grandstand, Alex was crushing a pack of cigarettes in one hand while he used the other to try to cover the fact that he was bawling like a baby.

"Come on, Pop, let's go over to Uncle Harry's," Damon said.

"No, son, I think we better go home."

The next day the Yankees, behind Ernie Bonham, defeated Whit Wyatt and the Dodgers, 3–1. Brooklyn had lost the Series in five games. On paper, it appeared that the Dodgers got creamed, when in fact they gave the almighty Yankees the battle of their lives. The Flatbush Faithful had plenty to be proud about.

Two months later the Japanese attacked Pearl Harbor. Life suddenly became very different—for baseball, for the Rice family, and for all Americans.

BOOK THREE
Damon

They came to root, and they never gave
up. It was Brooklyn against the world.
They were not only complete fanatics,
but they *knew* baseball like the fans of
no other city. It was exciting to play
there. It was a treat. I walked into that
crummy, flyblown park, as Brooklyn
manager, for nine years, and every time I
entered, my pulse quickened and my
spirits soared.

Leo Durocher, *Nice Guys Finish Last*

I'll tell you one thing—there wasn't nothing in baseball DiMaggio couldn't do
with his head or body. He was rather
splendid in his line of work.

Casey Stengel

8

"Damon, m'boy, how about you and me takin' in a ball game this afternoon?" my father would ask.

"Your treat, Pop?"

"My treat," he would almost always reply, meaning I wouldn't have
to blow my whole allowance on the price of admission.

My father and I must have gone to forty or fifty ball games together
during the early forties. Those games were, of course, played on every
conceivable kind of day—cold, windy, gray, and scorching. Some of them
were played at night. But my recollections of going out to the ball park
with Alex have merged into a single memory, which plays itself out like
a dream. Every so often it pops into my thoughts and stays there until
I've gone through every step of it.

It begins on an ancient subway car, the kind with wicker seats. My
father and I are sitting together; he is reading the *Herald Tribune*, I the
Daily News. Suddenly the train rushes out of the tunnel and pulls into
the Prospect Park station—the first stop above ground. It is a cloudless,
sunny day. Pop and I step off and walk to the end of the platform, up
a flight of stairs, through the old station house, and out onto Flatbush
Avenue. The first thing we see is the clock tower of the Bond Bakery
building. We cross Flatbush Avenue in the middle of the block, weav-
ing our way through honking autos, walk up to Empire Boulevard, and
turn right. Across the street is the Botanical Garden, and up ahead, in
the distance, is Ebbets Field. We march quickly up Sullivan Street,
stopping at the hot dog stand just across the street from the rotunda to
pick up a Stahl-Meyer frankfurter and a Coke.

Then we make our way past the souvenir hawkers and converging fans, through the turnstiles, and into the ball park, where we climb up a maze of ramps and finally step out of a tunnel into the bright sunlight. Below is the playing field, which strikes me as being much smaller than I remember from the last time I was here. The grass is remarkably green. The batting cage is in place, and the Dodgers are taking their practice swings. My hero, Cookie Lavagetto, is waiting for his turn. By the time Pop and I have found our seats Cookie has come up to the plate. He swings late on the first pitch but still manages to drill the ball off the right-field screen. My memory begins to fail here. Gladys Goodding is playing the organ, but I can't remember the tune. As the game draws nearer, the picture fades away.

Unless you're an old Brooklyn fan, it probably amazes you that I should cling to such a trivial recollection. I am not alone. One night last fall I was sitting with a friend at a table in a Manhattan saloon talking about how Walter O'Malley sold Brooklyn down the river. A guy at the next table overheard us, joined the discussion, and ignored his date for almost an hour. Two other fellows standing at the bar also got into the act. There we were, strangers, all old Dodger fans, heatedly discussing a baseball team that ceased to exist twenty years ago.

Why? Who knows. I'm sure there are thousands who still can't get the old days out of their systems. Maybe Red Barber had the answer. As he saw it, the fanaticism that pervaded Ebbets Field was a symptom of a borough-wide inferiority complex. He once wrote:

> Brooklyn's resentment at being treated like a poor relative was real. It had the bridge, but Manhattan had the skyscrapers, the theater, Wall Street, the landmarks. The great ocean liners docked in Manhattan; Brooklyn got the cargo ships. Broadway was a glamorous name; Flatbush Avenue sounded funny. Brooklyn became a joke; the laughingstock of comedians. Say "Brooklyn" and you got an automatic laugh.

Whatever the reasons for the fans' devotion to the Dodgers, they made Ebbets Field a great adventure. The atmosphere in that old bandbox crackled with electricity. You always hear that Ebbets Field was "intimate." Well it was. A seat in the center-field bleachers was better than 85 percent of the seats in Shea Stadium today. So you had an intimate ball park plus highly knowledgeable, fanatical fans. What a combination!

Actually, when it comes to the legend of the Dodger fan, Robert Joyce and Frank Germano were Johnnies-come-lately. My father alone had a million stories about the Flatbush Faithful, some of them going back to the turn of the century.

Alex's favorite Dodger fan of all time was a gnarled, Runyonesque old lady known as Apple Annie. She first appeared in the upper tier above third base sometime before 1920 and yelled her mind for more than a decade. One day in 1924 Annie read a caustic item about the Dodgers in the *Daily News*. She was livid.

That afternoon at the ball park she appeared at the pressbox, which was not enclosed in those days, and politely asked to speak to the *News* man. "Here I am," piped up tiny Jack Farrell. Annie sauntered over to him and suddenly began beating the poor reporter over the head with her umbrella. Unfortunately, Jack was not the guilty party. Paul Gallico, another writer on the *News*, who was 6 foot, 3 inches, had authored the column that sent Apple Annie on the warpath.

According to Alex, Annie disappeared from Ebbets Field at the end of the 1930 season. I guess she gave up when Uncle Robbie's boys collapsed during the wild pennant drive that year.

Another story Alex liked to tell was the one about the fan from "Greenpernt" who made a habit of yelling at every Dodger who came to the plate, "Come on, you bum, let's get something started!" One afternoon the fan had just finished calling Dolf Camilli a bum when a patron sitting behind him tapped him on the shoulder and asked, "Do you know Mr. Camilli?" The fan shook his head and the stranger went on, "Well, Dolf is one hell of a nice guy. And he comes from a fine family."

"Are you sayin' he's a friend of yours?" the Greenpointer asked. The stranger nodded. "Well, in that case, I'll lay off."

But then, when Cookie Lavagetto came to bat, the fan once again stood up, cupped his hands around his mouth, and yelled, "O.K., Cookie! Let's go, you bum! Show 'em what you can do!" When the fan sat down he received another sharp tap on the shoulder. "This guy a friend of yours too?" he asked. The stranger nodded again. The fan stood up, picked up his beer, and began to look for another seat. "I'm gettin' outa here. You ain't gonna ruin my afternoon."

Toots Shor was supposed to be the stranger who spoiled the Greenpointer's fun. I don't believe it. Toots, though a Giant fan, knew Brooklyn well enough to understand the rules that prevailed in Ebbets Field. Every time a Dodger came up to bat he had to show us that he *wasn't* a bum. Because in Brooklyn we were all bums until we proved otherwise. The only way to prove otherwise—for fans and players alike—was to win the pennant and then go on to cream the Yankees in the World Series.

If you were to ask me when I became a fanatic about the Dodgers, I would say during the summer of 1940. I was twelve then, an age when taking things seriously comes naturally. I couldn't believe it. Out of nowhere Brooklyn suddenly became a contender. For the first time in my memory a pennant was a possibility, not just a dream. By 1941 the Dodgers were a matter of life and death.

The Giants in those days were not my mortal enemies. My father hated them, of course, but I was too young to remember the days when

John McGraw dominated the National League while Uncle Robbie's daffiness boys were good for laughs but not much else. To me the Giants were too pathetic to worry about. The team that scared me to death was the Cardinals. So I was only mildly interested when, shortly before Pearl Harbor, Horace Stoneham named Mel Ott as his new manager. To make room for Master Melvin, Stoneham made Bill Terry director of the Giants' farm system.

I *was* impressed, however, when the Giants announced the first major trade of Ott's regime. New York acquired slugging Johnny Mize from the Cardinals. Branch Rickey, who made a habit of trading away players a year or two before they went over the hill, miscalculated a bit with Big Jawn. He was destined to put in nine more highly productive seasons with the Giants and the Yankees before calling it a career.

In January of 1942 Landis picked up a pencil and scribbled out, in his almost indecipherable scrawl, a note to President Roosevelt. The substance was:

> Baseball is about to adopt schedules, sign players, make vast commitments, go to training camps. What do you want it to do? If you believe we ought to close down for the duration of the war, we are ready to do so immediately. If you feel we ought to continue, we would be delighted to do so. We await your order.

FDR's reply, which came by return mail, said, in part:

> I honestly feel that it would be best for the country to keep baseball going. There will be fewer people unemployed, and everybody will work longer hours and harder than ever before.
> And that means that they ought to have a chance for recreation and for taking their minds off their work even more than before. . . .
> As to the players themselves, I know you agree with me that individual players who are of active military or naval age should go, without question, into the services. Even if the actual quality of the teams is lowered by the greater use of older players, this will not dampen the popularity of the sport.

So our great American pastime went on, doing its bit for morale.

As the 1942 season got under way, Pop and I firmly believed we were about to enjoy another year of glory in Brooklyn. As we figured it, the Dodgers would win the pennant going away, even though five of the Lip's regulars—Walker, Camilli, Medwick, Herman, and Vaughan— were over thirty.

The Dodgers began by playing great baseball. By the time the campaign was half over it looked as if they were going to laugh their way to the pennant. On August 5 Brooklyn was in first place by ten games. "We've got great spirit on this club," Durocher boasted to MacPhail.

"That's the trouble," Larry replied. "You're all fat and happy. This time I don't think you'll win."

MacPhail knew the Cardinals were a great finishing team. Back in 1930 they had come on to steal the flag from Uncle Robbie, and in 1934, with a little help from Brooklyn, they'd snatched the pennant right out of Bill Terry's clutches. In 1941 the Redbirds gave Leo fits before finally dropping out of the race during the last week of the season.

MacPhail could also see that Pete Reiser, the key to the Dodger attack, was not his old self. On July 19, in the eleventh inning of the second game of a doubleheader in St. Louis, Pete crashed into the bleacher wall going after a drive hit by Enos "Country" Slaughter. Reiser managed to catch up with the ball, but when he hit the wall it squirted loose, allowing Slaughter to get all the way around the bases for an inside-the-park homer that won the game and gave the Cardinals a sweep of the twin bill. Reiser's accident kept him out of action less than a week, but for the rest of the campaign he was never quite the same.

Every team in the league was laying for the Dodgers that year. During a midseason road trip Dick McCann of the *Daily News* observed that "your Brooks are fast becoming the most hated club in the game. Every club—especially a pennant winner—develops a feud each year with some other outfit. But the NL champs have set a new record. If there was a priority on hate, the Dodgers would be arrested right now for hoarding. They have stirred up more feuds than the West Virginia hills ever had. Everywhere you go, you find white-hot anger against them."

As late as August 16 Brooklyn was still nine and a half games in front, but then St. Louis made its move. While the Dodgers fell into a mild slump, losing eighteen of thirty-five, the Cardinals went on a tear. They forgot how to lose. Every day, it seemed, they gobbled up another game or half game of the Dodgers' lead.

The most devastating blows came over the second weekend in September. The Cardinals arrived in Brooklyn on Friday, September 11, for a two-game series. Oh, the pains I get just thinking about that weekend. The Dodgers' lead was down to a measly two games. They had to get at least a split. They didn't. They lost the opener, 3–0, and then dropped the Saturday contest, 2–1. The race was all tied up. On Sunday the Reds invaded Ebbets Field for a doubleheader. Brooklyn lost both games, while the Cardinals split a pair with the Phillies to take sole possession of first place. You have to hand it to the Dodgers, though: They didn't roll over and die. The race went down to the last day of the season. Brooklyn, a game and a half off the pace, still had a chance to squeak out a tie for first. All they had to do was beat the Phils while the Cards lost a doubleheader to the Cubs. Fat chance. Brooklyn won its game all right, to finish the season with an eight-game winning streak, but the

Cardinals creamed Chicago, 9–2 and 4–1, to end the year two full games ahead of the Dodgers. Brooklyn won 104 games in a losing cause.

"Jesus, do you believe it?" Alex asked his brother. "How the hell can you win a hundred four games and still come in second?"

"Easy. Back in 1909 the Cubs won a hundred four and wound up six and a half behind the Pirates," Harry explained.

"It can't be all *that* easy if it hasn't happened in thirty-three years," I said bitterly.

My summer wasn't made any more pleasant by the fact that over in the American League the Yankees were ho-humming their way to another pennant.

During that summer almost all the major league teams staged various special programs, the proceeds going to help the war effort. The Yankees got into the act in August by holding a field day between games of a doubleheader with Washington. Members of each team were going to compete in sprints, relay races, fungo hitting, and throwing contests. But there was a bigger attraction—Walter Johnson was going to pitch to Babe Ruth. Uncle Harry announced early in the month that he was going to treat Alex and me to the spectacle. Both Pop and I had mixed feelings because the Dodgers were playing a twin bill against the Giants on that same Sunday, August 23.

In the end Harry convinced us that the Dodgers and Giants would always be around, whereas the Babe and Big Train wouldn't.

It was a hot, muggy day, and nearly seventy thousand people crowded into Yankee Stadium to see the two legends. Fans were shoulder to shoulder on the ramps and walkways. The Babe, pushing fifty, stepped into the box. Johnson, already in his mid-fifties, tossed a few warmups to Benny Bengough, now a Senators coach. When Johnson signaled he was ready, old Billy Evans, out of retirement to call balls and strikes, stepped into place. Johnson delivered with a big, fluid motion, and Evans called a ball. Ruth took the next pitch for a strike. "Oh my God," I thought, "the old man's afraid to swing." Even though the rest of the crowd was cheering and yelling encouragement, they seemed to share my fear. There was an underlying tension. The whole scene seemed very strange to me, the more so because for the past several weeks *The Pride of the Yankees*, Lou Gehrig's life story, starring Gary Cooper and Teresa Wright, had been breaking records at the Astor Theater on Broadway. The Iron Man was gone, and here was his teammate, the Bambino, looking paunchy and wan and tired. I looked over at Alex. He had his fingers crossed.

Ruth cut at the next pitch and sent a weak fly to the outfield. Cheers and polite applause. Evans called the next pitch a ball. Johnson delivered again, and there it was. A sharp crack, the ball lofting out toward the right-field stands and disappearing into Ruthville near the 344-foot sign. The crowd went crazy. Uncle Harry was on his feet, but Pop was standing on his seat, yelling himself hoarse. The tension had been replaced by jubilation.

On the twentieth pitch, the Babe sent another shot into the right-field stands. It curved foul at the last moment, but it didn't matter. Ruth minced stiffly around the bases holding his cap aloft, a big grin on his moon face. Alex was standing on his seat again, and this time there were tears streaming down his face. The next time I glanced over, Alex was gone.

When I reached home, Alex had polished off half a bottle and was snoring, fully clothed, on the bed. I removed his shoes and closed the door. Seeing Ruth had obviously touched him. Funny. I would never have thought that Pop could love a Yankee.

The Yankees clinched the pennant on September 14 and coasted the last two weeks of the season. There was no doubt in anyone's mind that they would make quick work of the upstart Cards. By the time the first game of the Series was played, on September 30, Alex had forgotten any feelings of affection he might have had for the Yanks. We listened to the game on WOR and rooted for the Cardinals.

In that first game Red Ruffing set two Series records. He held the Cardinals hitless for seven and two-thirds innings, beating by one out the record held jointly by two other Yankees, Monte Pearson and Herb Pennock. And, when he eventually won the game, he became the first pitcher to notch seven World Series victories. That victory, however, very nearly eluded him. Going into the last of the ninth, the Yankees held a 7–0 lead. But suddenly the Cards came alive. They whacked Ruffing and his replacement, Spud Chandler, for six hits and four runs—and the bases were loaded when Chandler finally got the last out.

That explosive ninth inning was a sign of things to come. The next day the Cards beat the Yankees, 4–3, on Stan Musial's first hit of the Series, a single. Both teams boarded the same train to head for New York.

The Yankees played well for the rest of the Series, but St. Louis played better. The Cards swept all three games in New York to win the Series, four games to one.

"See how the mighty have fallen," Alex chortled gleefully, rubbing his hands together. And indeed, the mighty had fallen. The Yankees hadn't lost a Series in sixteen years. It was McCarthy's first—and only—World Series loss. Uncle Harry didn't show his face for two weeks.

A week before the close of the 1942 season Larry MacPhail tore up his contract with the Dodgers for a commission as a lieutenant colonel in the army. Larry had accomplished what he'd set out to do—he'd brought Brooklyn a pennant and he'd gotten the club out of hock.

It was now apparent that the team was in need of another overhauling, with someone a bit more conservative to do the job. Now that Mac-Phail was gone, the Dodger owners knew whom they wanted—Branch

Rickey, the man who had made the Cardinals the most powerful organization in the National League. Rickey's five-year pact was coming to an end that year. But would he be available? Would he suddenly pull up stakes and move halfway across the country to begin a brand-new baseball career at the age of sixty-one?

The answer was yes, for a number of reasons. For one thing, the uncertainties of the war made Sam Breadon in St. Louis reluctant to offer Branch another long-term contract. For another, Breadon and Rickey had, in recent years, been somewhat cool to each other. Rickey, a deeply religious man, refused to attend ball games on Sunday. He was also an avowed teetotaler who favored a return to Prohibition.

Breadon had no sympathy for either position. His ball club (not to mention Rickey's salary) depended heavily on Sunday games. And if a guy wanted to take a drink, well, that was his business, not the government's. When Rickey tendered his resignation Breadon accepted it without a whimper.

Rickey's appointment to a five-year term as president of the Dodgers was announced on October 29, 1942. His salary was estimated at $75,000 a year. Signing him was a brilliant move. The baseball writers were all quick to point out that the new Brooklyn chief was the antithesis of his predecessor. Rickey didn't wear loud clothes, didn't throw tantrums, didn't drink—and didn't go to the ball park on Sundays.

There was widespread speculation that Branch would drop Leo Durocher, possibly in favor of Burt Shotton, a coach with the Cleveland Indians whom Rickey had once described as "the greatest manager since John McGraw." Branch had his doubts about Durocher, and with good reason.

Many of the Dodgers took part in an ongoing high stakes poker game, and Leo was always right in the thick of the action. Some critics blamed the Dodgers' downfall in 1942 on the gambling in the clubhouse.

Rickey also knew that Durocher was slated to be drafted; if Branch stayed with Leo he might find himself without a skipper in the middle of the 1943 campaign. But above all else Rickey knew that Lippy was the darling of the Brooklyn fans. To fire him would bring down the wrath of Flatbush.

At the time Durocher lived in St. Louis, and one morning his new boss summoned him for breakfast and a little chat. After extracting a pledge from Leo that the gambling would come to an end, Rickey offered him a new contract that tied his earnings to the Dodgers' home attendance. If the team drew over a million, almost a shoo-in, Leo would get $50,000. Before the meeting was over Branch recited the parable of the Prodigal Son, supposedly in a reference to a minor league pitcher who was known as quite a carouser.

So Leo Durocher kept his job. That summer he flunked his induction physical because of a punctured ear drum. He had every reason to expect a long, happy tenure as pilot of the Dodgers.

In the fall of 1942 I entered high school. While baseball remained of great importance to me, I did have a few other interests—the war and girls, to name just two. The war was always the number one topic of the day. At the drop of a hat everyone, from the neighborhood grocery clerk to the usher at the local movie house, would snarl and ask, "Hey, don't you know there's a war on?" We knew it, all right. Why else would we be singing "Don't Sit Under the Apple Tree with Anyone Else but Me," or "Praise the Lord and Pass the Ammunition," or that real howler, "Der Fuehrer's Face."

My home room teacher, a kind old lady named Miss Martinelli, told us she prayed every night that the war would be over before her freshman boys became old enough to fight. We didn't like to hear that. God, how I wanted to join up. As I read about the exploits of the Marines on exotic islands such as Guadalcanal, Tulagi, and Gavutu, I lamented the unhappy fact that I was still only fourteen.

I fell in love that autumn with a very pretty Norwegian girl with blue eyes and long blonde hair. Her name was Karen Holmquist. Her father was the superintendent of an apartment house down the block from where I lived. My most cherished memory of Karen is the night I took her to our high school's Halloween dance.

That evening, after we necked for more than an hour in the back seat of her father's 1937 Chevrolet, I knew I was in love for life. I'm sorry to have to report that by Christmas she had thrown me over for some big wheel in the junior class. The following spring Karen's father entered my life in a different way. He organized a victory garden in a huge vacant lot down the street from the Web Café.

Alex decided to do his part in the war effort by taking a plot in the garden, and he recruited yours truly to help him rake out the stones and weeds on the piece of land Mr. Holmquist assigned to him. Right in the middle of my father's plot was a huge boulder. Even after two days of grunting and digging and heaving, Pop and I were unable to budge it.

We finally enlisted the assistance of Mr. Holmquist. He tied a rope around the big rock, hitched the line to the bumper of his car, and dragged it away. I can't tell you what a warm spot I had in my heart for Mr. Holmquist's Chevy. Because of the war, he had no choice but to hold onto it for several more years. Whenever I walked by it parked on my block I always thought back to the night when I made out like a bandit with his daughter.

Every morning, before opening the bar, Alex tended his garden. He planted a few radishes, lettuce, carrots, and lots of tomatoes. It became the most important thing in his life. He nursed his vegetables along with all the love he could muster. I don't know whether his garden had anything to do with the Allied victory, but it contained the most delicious tomatoes I've ever eaten.

Uncle Harry was too busy to worry about radishes and tomatoes. For the second time in his life he had left the security of Kaplan, Cohen and Cohan to embark on a hazardous course. He was now an entrepreneur, quite by accident.

During the late 1930s, Harry's firm assigned him to handle the books of a down-and-out concern in Long Island City called the Gowanus Workshirt Company. I guess it had fallen on tough times because with so many people out of work there wasn't much call for its product. Harry became a good friend of the owner, a gentle old guy by the name of Sam Berns. Through imaginative accounting and his connections at the banks, Harry succeeded in keeping the factory going. By 1939, however, he had run out of ideas.

Whether out of friendship for Sam or to satisfy that old gambling urge, Harry offered to put up enough cash to see the company through the next year. Once he was involved, there was no turning back. By the time of Pearl Harbor, Harry owned half the company and felt obliged to join the firm to protect his investment. Sam, well aware of his own administrative shortcomings, was happy to turn over the president's chair to his new partner. Harry's first task was to drum up some new business. The war was tailor-made for Gowanus Workshirt.

As the war progressed, America began to strain its manpower supply. The government began to look upon the country's women as a largely untapped reservoir of workers. My mother wanted to do her part, of course, but she was also fed up with living on the borderline of poverty. She was forty years old; she hadn't held down a job in the six years since she'd left the tea room, but she was ready and willing to go to work.

During the spring of 1943, Sally joined Sperry Gyroscope in Brooklyn, where she trained to work on an assembly line. Her starting pay was $22.50 a week, enough to improve radically our family's standard of living.

A few weeks after Mom started her new job, Uncle Harry and Aunt Ellen came to Bay Ridge for Sunday dinner with some rather surprising news. They were about to leave Flatbush and move to Manhattan, where they had taken an apartment on Fifth Avenue in the Sixties.

"What bullshit!" Alex said after they had left. "After fifty-four years, Brooklyn isn't good enough for my big-shot brother."

In February of 1943 Joe DiMaggio made headlines by volunteering for the draft, thereby swapping forty thousand a year for fifty bucks a month as an army private. The exodus of players was by then well under way. The Yankees had also lost Phil Rizzuto, Red Ruffing, Tommy Henrich, and George Selkirk. The Giants had said goodby to Johnny Mize, Willard Marshall, Harry Danning, and Babe Young. And in Brooklyn Pete Reiser, Pee Wee Reese, and Hugh Casey had followed Cookie Lavagetto into the service.

Baseball was left in a sad state indeed. To make matters worse, a curb on wartime travel forced the major league clubs to hold spring training in the North. The Dodgers pitched their camp at Bear Mountain, New York. On inclement days they drilled in the field house at West Point. The Yankee camp that year was at Asbury Park, New Jersey, and the Giants returned to Lakewood, New Jersey, where they had last trained way back in 1897 and 1898.

As the campaign drew near, I scratched my head in bewilderment as I tried to guess how the two pennant races would turn out. Even Uncle Harry, usually the confident Yankee rooter, was unwilling to predict that Joe McCarthy would win the flag with his usual efficiency. "The Cardinals are definitely my choice in the Senior Circuit," Harry remarked, "but I'll be damned if I can figure out the American League. Christ, for all I know the Browns will win it." That would have been a laugh. The Browns were the only team in either league that had never won a pennant. Dan Daniel, writing in the *Sporting News,* summed up the situation well when he wrote, "because of calls to war, an effort to foretell what is likely to happen in the two races seems downright foolhardy." Nonetheless, Daniel went out on a limb and predicted that the Cardinals and Yankees would repeat.

He turned out to be right. The Cardinals made a joke out of the National League race, finishing eighteen games up on the second-place Reds. Brooklyn came in a weak third, twenty-three and a half games back. Uncle Harry wasn't really surprised when the Yanks won the pennant in the American League, but he was amazed at the margin of victory—thirteen and a half games over the Senators.

The large margin of victory was a source of satisfaction to Joe McCarthy, who had been more than a little upset with the reaction of the press and public to the Yanks' World Series loss in 1942.

It was a ragtag bunch that McCarthy had convened that spring. The young, patchwork team proceeded to have a disastrous exhibition season, but magically the team jelled just about the time the regular season opened. The season was a laugher, as Marse Joe pulled the strings and called the shots.

If McCarthy was happy about his margin of victory over Ossie Bluege's Senators, he was ecstatic about the outcome of the Series with Billy Southworth's Cardinals. The Yanks won the opener behind Spud Chandler, who was 20–4 on the regular season and the American League's most valuable player. St. Louis squeezed out a one-run victory in the second game, but the Yankees then reeled off three consecutive wins to wrap up the Series.

One Saturday shortly after the World Series, I was in Manhattan for a movie. I decided to give Uncle Harry a call, and he invited me up to his new place. When I arrived at the building, I knew my uncle had struck it rich. A doorman in a fancy uniform glowered as I approached the entrance and eyed me suspiciously while he called upstairs.

The apartment was even more impressive than the building's façade. It had a wide foyer that opened onto a living room with six large windows looking out on Central Park. The living room alone must have been twice the size of the flat in Brooklyn where we'd all lived together. Rooms went off in all directions.

Greeting me warmly, Harry asked, "How's your old man? You know, I've been after him for weeks to come over and see the new place."

"To tell you the truth, Pop's been staying home the last couple months. His stomach's been acting up."

"Oh, really? It must have killed him to miss going out to the ball game."

It was true that Pop was feeling out of sorts, but I couldn't tell Uncle Harry that Alex had still managed to spend as much time as ever at Ebbets field.

At the time there was no way I could comprehend how wealthy my uncle had become. Gowanus Workshirt had landed several large government contracts for army fatigues. Eighteen months earlier, the factory had twenty employees; now it had almost two hundred, working eight-hour shifts around the clock. Harry Rice, the firm's president, would soon become a millionaire for the second time in his life.

By 1944 the quality of major league baseball had deteriorated to the point of absurdity. For Dodger fans the season was a disaster. Personally, it was the worst year of my career as a Brooklyn fan.

Leo Durocher characterized his team this way: "We had about a dozen humpty-dumpties, and it didn't matter much which of them played. Most of the lads were just props, so to speak, for a few promising kids we thought we could see a year, or two, or three ahead." The team had zero pitching. Players came and left as if through a revolving door.

It was nobody's fault, of course, that things had gotten so bad. The minor leagues were a shambles, and in the majors only 40 percent of the players who had started the 1941 season were still around. The Dodgers, who in July broke a club record by losing fifteen straight, plummeted into seventh place, forty-two games out of first and only a game and a half out of the cellar, which was occupied by Philadelphia, the National League's perennial doormat in those days.

The Dodgers' only bright spot was Dixie Walker, who hit .357 against wartime pitching to capture the batting crown. The saddest thing to watch was poor Whit Wyatt, his arm completely gone. Looking more like a shot putter than a pitcher, he won two, lost six, and compiled an ERA of 7.17. The Giants were a mild surprise that year; Mel Ott boosted his club up to fifth. The Cardinals, however, were no surprise at all. They won the pennant by fourteen and a half games over the Pirates. Only two players on the Cardinal roster—Danny Litwhiler and Debs Garms—had come to St. Louis through trades. Everyone else had come up through Branch Rickey's farm system.

Branch was in Brooklyn now, running a club that appeared to be going nowhere. The Dodger farm system, built up to thirteen teams by MacPhail, was down to a pathetic four. It was a sorry situation all right, but no sorrier than the plight of most of the other clubs in the majors. While his rival club owners were preoccupied with the day-to-day problems of fielding their teams under nearly impossible circumstances, the Mahatma had a squad of scouts searching for young talent. He was turning up kids such as Gil Hodges, Ralph Branca, Duke Snider, Clem Labine, and a pitcher by the name of Rex Barney who had a fastball the likes of which had not been seen in Brooklyn since Van Mungo.

Rickey, looking into his crystal ball, knew that the only way to make room for his future stars was to weed out the players who could not help him in the long run. He had caused a furor in Brooklyn in August 1943, when he traded Dolf Camilli to the Giants.

I'll never forget my father's reaction to the trade. "Rickey's no baseball man. He's nothing but a goddamn flesh peddler," Alex had said bitterly. I'm sorry, but my father was wrong and Rickey was right. Camilli refused to report to New York and admitted publicly that he was washed up, but the Brooklyn fans were still furious with Rickey. That was O.K. The time would come when the Flatbush Faithful would understand.

To realize how bizarre major league ball had become in 1944, all you have to do is take a look at the American League race. From the beginning of June until Labor Day the St. Louis Browns were in first place. It was especially weird, because the statistics showed them to be sixth in the league in hitting and fielding.

Even Luke Sewell, the St. Louis manager, was baffled by his club's surprising performance. So was my Uncle Harry. "What's keeping them up?" every fan was asking himself. The Brownies were defying the laws of gravity. In September both the Yanks and the Tigers made a dash for the pennant, and it began to look as if the Browns were finally going to be brought down to earth. In mid-September, each of the three teams held the league lead in as many days. On September 27 the Tigers nosed by the Browns and took a one-game lead, leaving the Yankees in third, three games off the pace.

Two days later the Yankees traveled to St. Louis for a four-game, season-ending series with the Browns. Detroit, meanwhile, was locking horns with the cellar-dwelling Senators in a similar series.

On October 1, the Browns sent Sig Jakucki, a pitcher who had come out of a five-year retirement sporting a lifetime major league record of 0–3, to the mound. The Yankees played hard and well, but in the end they succumbed to what had to be destiny. Jakucki notched his thirteenth win of the season, and the Browns had their first flag ever.

Joe McCarthy, who had missed a month early in the season because of illness, had reason to be proud. Ed Barrow issued a statement praising Joe and calling the season McCarthy's best ever. A number of sportswriters seconded the motion, unofficially nominating Joe as the best manager in baseball, perhaps of all time. The Yankee skipper, maligned as a "pushbutton" manager who always had the best available talent, had shown that he could take a second-division team, a bunch of rejects, leftovers, and greenhorns, and turn them into winners.

Uncle Harry was not pleased. "When the Yankees come in third," he said, "and McCarthy still gets good press, then the Yankees are no longer the Yankees."

So baseball had its first one-stadium World Series since the Giants had played the Yankees in the Polo Grounds in 1922. The 1944 Classic was billed as a "streetcar series." When the Browns won the first game, defeating Mort Cooper, 2–1, even though the Cardinal ace gave up only two hits, I began to think that maybe God had decided to let the Brownies go all the way. They lost game two, came back to win game three, and then collapsed as the Cards won three straight and took the Series, four games to two. I suddenly realized that for the first time in my life I'd rooted for an American League team in the World Series.

When I think of 1944 I don't automatically go back to the baseball season. I think of D-Day and of FDR running against Dewey for a fourth term. I remember that during that summer Detroit ran out of new automobiles and wouldn't begin making them again until the end of the war.

I can still see myself walking to school that year, humming, "Mairzy doats and dozy doats and liddle lamzy divy." In the fall I made a bad mistake and went out for football. I never could hit a baseball, so I figured maybe I'd have better luck on the gridiron. I tried out for fullback. During my very first scrimmage I got my two front teeth knocked out. My mother begged me to quit. That was just fine with me.

In the fall of 1944 Branch Rickey planted his roots firmly in Brooklyn by buying into the ball club. At the time the ownership of the Dodgers was still divided evenly between the descendants of Charles Ebbets and those of the McKeever brothers: 50 percent of the stock was held in trust for the fifteen Ebbets heirs by the Brooklyn Trust Company, 25 percent was owned by the heirs of Ed McKeever, and 25 percent was held by Dearie Mulvey, the daughter of Steve McKeever.

Rickey and a lawyer named Walter O'Malley purchased the Ed McKeever stock. O'Malley was the club's attorney. George McLaughlin had brought him in to handle the Dodgers' legal affairs after Larry Mac-Phail departed in 1942.

In the spring of 1945 it came out that the buyers had a third partner—John L. Smith, executive vice-president of the Charles F. Pfizer Company, the well-known pharmaceutical house. Before the end of the 1945 season Rickey, O'Malley, and Smith made a deal to acquire all the Ebbets shares for $750,000. At long last the Ebbets–McKeever deadlock, which had its origins way back in 1912 when Charlie Ebbets sold half the club to build his ball park, had come to an end. Branch Rickey was firmly in the driver's seat.

Whatever Alex's reason for not wanting to visit his brother's Manhattan apartment, in November 1944 he received an invitation he could not turn down. Harry invited us over to celebrate Pop's fifty-second birthday.

As we stepped into the foyer of Harry's apartment, we were surprised to discover that we were not the only guests. Uncle Harry had invited about fifteen other people—business associates and friends from a world as foreign to Alex as the Belgian Congo.

Sally seemed tense as Harry led her and Alex around to meet the other guests. But Pop, who'd been grouchy all day, suddenly rose to the occasion. He smiled and chatted freely with men and women who were obviously above him in station, and I saw for the first and only time in my life the Alex Rice who had moved with ease through the sophisticated New York of the twenties.

A maid circulated serving goblets of champagne punch. When she came to Alex, he peered at the tray disdainfully and said, "No thanks, make mine whisky."

And several whiskies it was. Nonetheless, Pop remained charming and collected. When dinnertime came, his brother escorted a smiling Alex to the seat of honor.

As I took my place, I was confused by the display of silverware that surrounded my plate. There was a variety of knives and spoons, forks of every size and shape, and a few implements that were a mystery to me.

The first course was *escargots*. It was the only time in my life I was ever forced to eat snails.

I was surprised at how well Alex was keeping his composure. The pretentious chit-chat around the table was certainly more than I could stomach.

The meal dragged on, as did the conversation. After snails, poached trout, *tournedos béarnaise*, a green salad, and crêpes suzette—each served with the proper wine—I'd completely lost my appetite for the good life.

By the time Harry began tinkling his wine glass with his dessert fork, I knew I'd be a candidate for the nuthouse if we didn't get out of there pretty soon.

". . . and so, I give you my brother, the birthday boy—Alexander Rice!"

Polite applause.

Pop, who'd been staring into his coffee cup, rose and slowly looked from grinning face to grinning face.

"As I look around this elegantly appointed table and see all you elegantly appointed guests . . ."

"Hear! Hear!" interrupted a stout man smoking a cigar.

". . . I have but one question." Alex cleared his throat. "How come I don't see any horses, when I'm surrounded by so many horses' asses?"

On November 25, 1944, five days after his seventy-eighth birthday, Kenesaw Mountain Landis died. At his request, he was cremated without fanfare: no flowers, no funeral, no memorial. As Landis's ashes were being interred, thousands of stories concerning "The Squire" were being exhumed.

He was remembered not only as the man who fined Standard Oil and saved baseball, but also as the man who had wanted to try Kaiser Wilhelm for the murder of a Chicagoan who died in the sinking of the *Lusitania*. He finally gave up when government officials pointed out that certain existing treaties might make it difficult to extradite the Kaiser.

He was remembered as the man who released scot free a messenger boy who had absconded with bonds worth $750,000, the man who was late for his original installation as commissioner because he was watching some boys play baseball in a cow pasture, the man whom Indians near his Wisconsin fishing cottage called Sago-Ye-Wat-Ha, "He Who Keeps 'Em Awake," a reference to the fact that no jury member ever dared nod out in Landis's courtroom.

Baseball fans experienced a feeling of loss. No one I knew had much affection for the old man, but he was a fixture, a deity. It seemed he would always be commissioner. It never occurred to most of us that someday he would be gone.

That year, for the first time, I did not spend Christmas Eve with Uncle Harry and Aunt Ellen. Pop and his brother weren't on speaking terms. They differed over the definition of a horse's ass. For a while, I thought the whole silly thing would blow over, but as the months went by reconciliation became less and less likely.

Sorrow over Landis's death had kept no one from voicing an opinion as to who should replace him. There were those who thought the new commissioner should come from big business; after all, nearly $27 million—revenues from World Series, All-Star games, and city series—had passed through the commissioner's office since 1921. There were those who thought the new man should be from inside the game, someone conversant with the needs of the owners. And there were those who thought the man should be from outside the game, someone who could maintain public confidence in baseball. The names bandied about included FBI director J. Edgar Hoover, former Postmaster General James Farley, General George C. Marshall, former New York mayor Jimmy Walker, and baseball men Ford Frick, Branch Rickey, and Larry MacPhail.

After nearly six months of bickering and politicking, the owners finally decided that in those uncertain times it was best to have some influence in Washington. They named Senator Albert Benjamin "Happy" Chandler of Kentucky to the post. Shortly after Chandler, also a former governor of Kentucky, became commissioner, he received his first protest. It was from none other than Lippy Durocher:

> Nieman hit ninth-inning homer to beat me here today. Hereby file first protest. What do you intend to do about it?

Chandler, using the middle name that Durocher despised, responded quickly:

> Dear Ernest:
> Nieman's hit stands and I hereby award Philadelphia the game— and what are you going to do about it?

Shortly before Chandler's appointment, a second large financial transaction, larger even than Rickey's, took place in New York baseball. Larry MacPhail and two millionaire associates, Del Webb and Dan Topping, purchased the Yankee empire, generally regarded as the most valuable in baseball, for the bargain-basement price of $2.8 million. The empire included some four hundred ballplayers and three ball parks, including one in Newark and one in Kansas City. Yankee Stadium alone was worth nearly as much as the purchase price.

Barrow was opposed to the sale. After all, MacPhail not only did not fit the Yankee image, but he was also the creator of night baseball, an innovation Barrow detested.

And there was another reason. Topping, husband of Olympic and Hollywood star Sonja Henie, was owner of the Brooklyn Football Dodgers; rumor had it that he was bent on moving his team to the Bronx as the New York entry in the new All-America Conference. Financial considerations aside—as early as 1944, Branch Rickey, the resident prophet of baseball, had said, "Football is a wolf at our door"—Barrow could not abide the thought of cleated hordes tearing up the outfield of his beloved stadium.

But Barrow was seventy-six years old and in poor health. The three women, Ruppert's heirs, who owned the Yankees had inheritance taxes to pay, and they had no interest in the game. Cousin Ed, whose share of the sale price was $300,000, had little choice.

MacPhail promised to remain in the background, leaving the running of the club to Barrow, Weiss, and McCarthy, but no one really believed him. The controversial Larry was sure to make things happen. Exactly what things remained to be seen. As one reporter put it, "He can make a morning frock coat exciting."

By the spring of 1945 it was clear that the war would soon be over. Before long the players would be coming home, and baseball would begin returning to normal. As Branch Rickey contemplated the future, he could see that the Dodgers had all the makings of a dynasty similar to the one he had built in St. Louis.

He had a whole army of potential stars under contract to Brooklyn. Yet no baseball club ever has more talent than it can use. The skills that go into playing the game are transitory, injuries are a never-ending problem, and the need to make trades is always present.

For years Rickey had been looking ahead to the day when Organized Baseball would begin to tap a reservoir of outstanding talent that was there, ready to be used, but completely ignored. It is almost impossible to believe that as recently as the 1940s major league baseball was for whites only. Blacks had their own leagues, where living and traveling conditions were abysmal and where the pay, except in the case of a few superstars, didn't compare to the money white players could earn.

White America was fighting a war against tyranny in Europe and Asia while condoning its own brand at home. During the war years, however slowly, our country was beginning to develop a social conscience.

But social change, if left to its own timetable, moves at a snail's pace. Branch Rickey knew that if baseball were to be desegregated with any semblance of deliberate speed, someone would have to stick his neck out and make it happen. He appointed himself to the job. After all, the man who made the first move would have his pick of the best talent.

Before you can sign players, however, you first have to scout them. It was unthinkable in 1945 to send scouts out to the Negro leagues with the open intention of looking for major league talent. Rickey needed a cover, so on May 7, 1945, he announced the formation of the United States Negro Baseball League—a six-team circuit that would play in major league ball parks.

The Ebbets Field entry in the league would be known as the Brown Dodgers. The new circuit actually played a schedule that year. The Brown Dodgers began their home season in a night game at Ebbets Field on May 24. They beat the Philadelphia Hilldales, 3–2, before a crowd of two thousand.

Rickey was now free to scout black talent without raising any suspicions. In fact, when he unveiled the new circuit he was careful to insist, "It is not my intention to discuss today Negro players becoming members of clubs in our present organized baseball league." He did express the hope that in time players in the new league would be drafted into the majors, but most people thought he was merely paying lip service to an idea whose time would not come for many years.

Ironically, there were those who thought Rickey's real intention was to bring Negro baseball under white control—to make money off the black man while keeping him in his place. Clark Griffith, for one, accused Rickey of setting himself up as "the dictator of Negroes in baseball." The Mahatma didn't have time to pay attention to such charges. Before his plan could work he first had to find a black man who not only had enough talent to make it in the big leagues but also had enough character to weather unrelenting abuse.

If the 1944 baseball season was a laugh, the 1945 campaign was enough to make strong men cry. The players who were still around were either kids with peach fuzz on their cheeks or veterans who'd have been long gone had it not been for the war. Branch Rickey even offered Leo Durocher—now thirty-nine—a $1,000 bonus to start the season at second base. After two games Leo, who managed to get one single in five at bats, told the Mahatma to forget it.

At the other end of the age spectrum was Tommy Brown, a shortstop who'd come up to the Dodgers the year before at the ripe old age of sixteen. The Dodgers' radio sponsor was Old Gold cigarettes; homers were nicknamed Old Goldies, and when a ball was hit out of Ebbets Field Red Barber would reward the batter by tossing a carton of Old Golds out of the booth and down the screen behind home plate. After Tommy hit his first homer Leo Durocher confiscated the cigarettes. His shortstop was too young to smoke.

To the delight of Brooklyn fans, the Dodger roster that year included none other than Babe Herman. He was forty-two but was still in fine shape because he had been playing for Hollywood in the Pacific Coast League. Brought up to do some pinch-hitting, the old Flatbush favorite did fine; he went nine for thirty-four for a .265 batting average, and his presence on the roster did wonders for attendance. More than thirty-six thousand fans were in Ebbets Field on Sunday, July 9, when Babe made his first appearance at the plate. He came up to bat for Eddie Stanky in the first game of a twin bill against the Cards. There was a runner on third at the time. As Babe strolled up to take his turn, the crowd went wild. "Come on, Hoimen, you kin do it," shouted the Flatbush Faithful.

He had scarcely changed. He dug in his spikes the same way he used to, and he still had that huge chaw of tobacco lodged high in his left cheek. A chill went up Alex's spine as he watched Babe get ready for the first pitch. It was as though time had suddenly bent backward fifteen years.

After breaking a bat on the first delivery, Babe thrilled the crowd by drilling a clean single to right to drive in a run. But when he arrived at first he overran the bag, stumbled and fell down, and dived back just in time to escape being tagged out. "Same old Babe," Alex said with a laugh. Leo wasted no time pulling him out for a pinch runner.

In 1945 Brooklyn was not the only team that was forced to desperate measures to fill out its roster. Over at the Polo Grounds the ace of the Giant mound staff was, of all people, Van Lingle Mungo. As a reliever with the Giants in 1944 Van had been a total bust. So what did Mel Ott do? He turned him back into a starter.

But of all the curious players who made it to the majors that year, not one could hold a candle to Pete Gray, the one-armed outfielder with the St. Louis Browns. Pete had lost his right arm when he was a kid but had learned to bat and field remarkably well with the arm he had left. He got his start with the Bushwicks, the famous semipro team that played at Dexter Park in Brooklyn. By 1944 he was with Memphis in the Southern Association, where he batted .333, drove in sixty runs, and was named most valuable player of the league.

In 1945 he was brought up to the Browns. One afternoon Uncle Harry and I went up to Yankee Stadium to see him play. Watching him relay the ball in from the outfield was an unforgettable experience. As soon as he caught a fly he would tuck his glove under the little stump that was left of his right arm. Then, quick as a flash, he'd pull the ball out of the glove and fire it in. Pete batted only .218 for his one year in the majors, but one afternoon in St. Louis, in a doubleheader against the Yankees, he put on an amazing exhibition—he got four hits and a walk, drove in two runs, and scored two more himself.

By 1946 the players were home from the war. There were no jobs left for an outfielder with only one arm.

Even the mighty Cardinals were badly hurt by the draft in 1945. The entire outfield—Stan Musial, Johnny Hopp, and Danny Litwhiler—had gone into the service, and so had Walker Cooper, their catcher. The National League pennant was completely up for grabs, and the first team to make a bid for it was the Giants, who jumped into the lead by winning twenty-one out of their first twenty-six contests. Mel Ott, in his twentieth season with the club, was hitting the ball well and providing his boys with plenty of inspiration (he would finish the year with a .308 batting average). Unfortunately, inspiration can take a mediocre team only so far; by the middle of June the Giants had slipped out of first place, and the Dodgers, of all people, had put together an eight-game winning streak to take over the lead.

As I looked over the Dodger roster I said to myself there was *no way* the team could stay on top. Not with the likes of Frenchy Bordagaray, Eddie Basinski, Clyde Sukeforth, Goody Rosen, and Howie Schultz.

Frenchy, a clown from the daffy days, had been with the Flock back in 1934 and 1935. He once spat in an umpire's eye and, when he was fined for it, remarked, "The penalty was more than I expectorated." Clyde Sukeforth, a bullpen catcher, hadn't played in a regular season game since 1934. Eddie Basinski was a violinist with the Buffalo Philharmonic. Goody Rosen looked good on the surface, but he didn't hustle—he got to fly balls barely in time to catch them, and he didn't get away from the plate with the speed it takes to turn a single into a double.

And Howie Schultz, whom Rickey had purchased for the ridiculous price of $52,000, was strictly a wartime player. He'd be out of the starting lineup when the regulars came home. Of course, the Bums did have Dixie Walker, whom Alex described as "a tough man to fool when the ducks were on the pond." Dixie would lead the league in RBIs with 124. Then there were Eddie Stanky, who couldn't hit worth a damn but somehow always managed to get on base so that Dixie could knock him in, and Augie Galan, a player I always liked though I'm not sure why. Maybe it was because he was great at drawing walks; for two years he led the league in that department, and then Eddie Stanky came along. Eddie drew 148 walks in 1945 to Augie's piddling (but second in the league) 114. In the pitching department Leo got great work out of Hal Gregg, who would win eighteen and lose thirteen for the best performance of his career, but that was about it. No, the Dodgers didn't figure to stay in the race, but I sure as hell wasn't going to give up on them as long as they were playing over their heads.

During that spring a noisy, abusive fan sat every day in the mezzanine behind third base near the pressbox, just waiting for Durocher to appear on the field. The fan, whose name was John Christian, professed to be an avid Dodger fan; but, for whatever reason, he despised the Dodgers' manager.

On Saturday night, June 9, during a game against the Phillies, Christian went on a verbal rampage that not only angered Leo but annoyed the fans around him as well. After the sixth inning, Joseph Moore, a special patrolman who'd worked at Ebbets Field for more than twenty years, stepped up to Christian and said, "Mac, you're wanted in the office." Reluctantly, the heckler followed the cop out of the stands to the dirt runway that led from the dugout to the clubhouse. Waiting for him was Leo himself, who greeted Christian with the words, "How would you like someone calling *your* mother names?"

Christian emerged from the encounter with a broken jaw. The next day he reported the incident to the police, claiming that Moore and Durocher had taken turns pounding him with a "blunt instrument." The Dodger manager and the special cop were arrested and charged with felonious assault.

On Monday morning the story was splashed all over the papers, complete with pictures of the injured veteran in a bed in Kings County Hospital, his face so swollen it looked like a watermelon. After receiving a $6,750 payoff Christian dropped the civil charges, but the authorities pressed the matter in criminal court until, on April 25, 1946, Moore and Durocher were finally acquitted.

Leo was gaining a reputation off the field that was beginning to overshadow his image on the diamond. He was now a radio celebrity, appearing regularly on shows with personalities such as Milton Berle and Fred Allen. And he had become a good friend of actor George Raft, who was thought to have connections with the underworld. Branch Rickey was not happy with his manager's rising notoriety. The prodigal son seemed to be asking for big trouble.

In July 1945 the Chicago Cubs suddenly got hot; they won twenty-six while losing only five and ended the month solidly in first place, six games up on the second-place Dodgers. To get some extra pennant insurance the Cubs, in a move that caused quite an uproar, picked up pitcher Hank Borowy from the Yankees for $100,000 plus a few lesser players. Borowy was an excellent hurler, but MacPhail was willing to part with him for the right price. Larry knew the Cubs were ready to pay plenty for Hank, but the interleague trading deadline had long since passed.

The Yankees could make a deal with the Cubs only if the other American League clubs all passed up the chance to pick up Borowy on waivers. Larry put his pitcher on the waiver list, it went out to the other owners, and—lo and behold—no one claimed him.

As soon as Hank had been passed up by the American League, MacPhail was free to make a deal with the Cubs. When the news got out, several of the American League owners, and some in the National League as well, did a lot of wailing and moaning. But Happy Chandler ruled that MacPhail had followed the established procedures to the letter.

Borowy probably won the pennant for the Cubs; after joining them he won eleven games and lost only two. With him, the Yankees might have won the pennant. Bill Bevens, 13–9, finished the season with the best record among Yankee hurlers. Second-best was Borowy's 10–5 record acquired before his inexplicable trade. One thing was for certain—Borowy's presence would have brought the Yanks in higher than fourth and prevented McCarthy's lowest finish ever as Yankee manager.

As the 1945 season progressed, there was a trickle of stars from the armed services back to the game. Hank Greenberg, back after a four-year stint, made his presence felt more than any other returnee. He blasted a dramatic grand-slam home run to win the American League pennant for the Detroit Tigers, who went on to beat the Cubs in a seven-game World Series that was marred or enlivened, depending on your point of view, by a total of eleven errors.

For me, the best thing about 1945, aside from the end of the war, was that the Dodgers had started to climb back toward the top. And, unknown to me and everyone else, the leader of the Dodgers was about to make a move that would make Brooklyn baseball even more exciting and interesting.

While the 1945 baseball campaign was winding its way to a conclusion, Branch Rickey was making his final preparations to break the color barrier. Soon after he formed the Brown Dodgers, the Mahatma sent his ace scouts—Tom Greenwade, George Sisler, and Clyde Sukeforth—out to the Negro Leagues to search for talent.

All three reported back that the top black prospect was Jack Roosevelt Robinson, shortstop with the Kansas City Monarchs in the Negro American League. Robinson, a product of Southern California, had attended Pasadena Junior College and then moved on to UCLA, where he gained a reputation as one of the finest college athletes on the Coast, winning varsity letters in football, basketball, baseball, and track.

Jackie had entered the army shortly after Pearl Harbor, received a commission as a lieutenant, and remained in the service until his discharge in November 1944. The following spring he joined the Monarchs for a salary of $400 a month. There was no doubt that Robinson's playing abilities made him an excellent prospect; he appeared in forty-one games in 1945, batted .345, and was the shortstop for the West team in the NAL's annual East–West game.

He was a promising player, all right, but would he have the grit to stick with the almost impossible assignment Rickey had in mind for him? Before approaching Robinson, Rickey thoroughly investigated his prospect's background and came to the conclusion that Jackie had the necessary character, as well as the competitiveness, to do the job. In August 1945 the Mahatma sent Clyde Sukeforth to Comiskey Park in Chicago—where the Monarchs were playing the Chicago American Giants—to invite Robinson to Brooklyn, ostensibly to talk to Mr. Rickey about playing for the Brown Dodgers. Jackie, who at the time was sidelined with a shoulder injury, figured he had nothing to lose, so he agreed to make the trip.

On August 28 Jackie appeared at 215 Montague Street for his interview with Branch Rickey. "The truth is I'm not considering you for the Brown Dodgers," the Mahatma confessed in his booming voice. "I've brought you here because I'm interested in you for the Brooklyn National League Club. We think you can make it in the majors. What do *you* think?"

Robinson sat glued to his chair, speechless, unable to assemble his thoughts and come up with an answer.

"My idea is to assign you to Montreal, as a start," Rickey went on. "Do you think you can play for the Royals?"

"Yes," replied Robinson, who finally had regained his composure. As anyone vaguely familiar with baseball knew, the Montreal Royals were Brooklyn's AAA farm club in the International League. If Jackie could make it on the Royals, the best club in the minors, he would have an excellent shot at moving up to the Dodgers.

For more than three hours the two men discussed the ramifications of the course they were embarking upon. Actually Rickey, the philosopher and lecturer, did most of the talking. He described, in graphic detail, how miserable Jackie's life would be as the lone black man in a lily-white world. Before the meeting was over Rickey made Jackie vow that he would not lose his self-control. He was to keep his dignity no matter what the bigots threw at him.

Robinson didn't know how he was going to be able to turn the other cheek, but he promised himself he would do it at all costs. Sworn to secrecy, Jackie left Brooklyn with a verbal agreement to sign with the Royals for a $3,500 bonus and $600-a-month salary. Rickey promised to put it in writing no later than the first of November.

While Branch Rickey was working toward the integration of baseball in secret, other pressures to get the major leagues off the dime were building out in the open. New York Mayor Fiorello LaGuardia had recently established a program to improve racial relations in the community. This program was administered by a group known as the Mayor's Committee on Unity of New York City.

During the summer of 1945 the leadership of the Committee on Unity persuaded the mayor to appoint another special committee to "study the color line in baseball." LaGuardia agreed, and on August 11—only two weeks before the Mahatma was to summon Jackie Robinson to Brooklyn—the new committee, comprised of ten prominent citizens, including Branch Rickey and Larry MacPhail, came into being. The mayor asked the group "to give this one subject thorough study and make specific recommendations to the Major Leagues. Any plan accepted by the Major Leagues would automatically revert to the Minor Leagues."

On October 23, a week before the Mayor's Committee on Baseball was scheduled to make its report, the Mahatma set off his bombshell. In Montreal, Branch Rickey, Jr., head of the Brooklyn farm system, and Hector Racine, president of the Royals, announced that Jackie Robinson had signed to play with the Royals in 1946.

The reaction to the news was generally favorable. Tommy Holmes, writing in the *Eagle*, observed, "The three Dodger ivory hunters who scouted him rate him A-1 as a shortstop prospect. Granting that their estimate is correct, Robinson represents for his race an ideal candidate to crash through the invisible color line in what, from time to time, has been called our national pastime." Al Laney of the *Herald Tribune* got wind that Robinson had come to New York from Montreal and was visiting friends in Harlem. Laney rushed uptown to interview Jackie and came away with this impression: "If there are baseball players who will refuse to play with or against this personable, intelligent and sensitive man, they must indeed be blinded by prejudice."

The black world was delighted with the news. Satchel Paige, Robinson's teammate on the Monarchs and already a living legend, remarked, "They didn't make a mistake in signing Robinson. He's a number one professional player. They couldn't have picked a better man." Adam Clayton Powell, congressman from Harlem, called it "a step that will cheer all Americans, a definite step toward winning the peace."

There were, of course, the nay-sayers. Reached in Birmingham, Dixie Walker said, "As long as he isn't with the Dodgers, I'm not worried." And Jimmy Powers, in his column in the *Daily News*, declared: "We would like to see him make good, but it is unfair to build high hopes and then dash them. Mark it down now. Robinson is a 1,000–1 shot to make the grade. And this talk of 'raiding' Negro leagues for more players is silly."

One of the ironies of the situation was that the Kansas City Monarchs were threatening to protest the signing of Robinson to Commissioner Chandler. Rickey scoffed at the suggestion that Jackie had violated any legal agreement, written or otherwise. He simply had no contract. "I have investigated Negro organizations," Rickey explained, "and I've found that they are not leagues—not even organizations." Before long the Monarchs decided to drop the matter.

And what about Robinson himself? When asked to comment on his chances Jackie said, "I think I am the right man for this test. There is no possible chance that I will flunk it or quit before the end for any other reason than that I'm not a good enough ballplayer. That is the only thing I could be mistaken about. The other things I know."

As for myself, my father, and Uncle Harry, we all felt positive about the signing of Jackie Robinson. As Pop put it, "Who cares if he's purple if he can knock in some runs?" Uncle Harry, who had in his time taken in a few Negro league games, told me over the phone that Robinson would have to work hard to adjust to major league pitching.

"But he should make it," Harry said. "If he's one of the best in the colored leagues you can damn well be sure he's plenty good enough to help the Dodgers, or any other National League team for that matter."

"My only worry, Uncle Harry, is that Robinson might take a job away from Pee Wee Reese or Eddie Stanky." Reese and Stanky were two of my favorites. But being from Brooklyn, I knew what it meant to be an underdog. No, I wouldn't have any trouble getting behind Jackie—as long as he did his job.

I had a feeling Uncle Harry hadn't called to talk about Jackie Robinson. We hadn't seen each other since his great falling out with Pop, but every once in a while he'd phone to see how I was doing.

"Damon, have you thought at all about going to college next fall?" Uncle Harry asked, finally coming to the point.

"It's crossed my mind, but I really haven't thought about it seriously."

"Well, if you decide to go, I'd be hurt if you didn't let me help."

The coming of 1946 brought with it a host of signs that baseball was at last returning to normal. For the first time in four years the clubs were free to train in the South. The Yankees went way down to the Canal Zone, the Giants traveled to Miami, and the Dodgers pitched camp in Daytona Beach. The great stars of the game—players such as Joe DiMaggio, Ted Williams, Enos Slaughter, and Johnny Mize—were all ready to pick up where they left off before the war, and it didn't take them long to prove that they still knew how to play the game.

As I devoured the reports from spring training in the papers, I convinced myself that Leo had the makings of a great team. He had most of his prewar reliables back, including Cookie Lavagetto, Pee Wee Reese, Kirby Higbe, Hugh Casey, and Pete Reiser. The Dodgers also had a crop of talented newcomers, including Gene Hermanski, an outfielder everyone thought was destined to be a superstar, and Carl Furillo, another outfielder who had a rifle for an arm. And then, of course, there were the wartime standbys—Eddie Stanky, Dixie Walker, and Billy Herman. I was a little worried about the pitching, but something told me the Dodgers were going to kick up more than a few waves around the National League before the campaign was over.

That spring baseball encountered a problem that threatened to put a real damper on the first postwar season. A Mexican industrialist by the name of Don Jorge Pasqual decided the time had come to upgrade the Mexican League to the level of the two established major circuits. To accomplish his goal Pasqual unfolded an enormous bankroll and began offering players in the majors huge salaries to come down and play ball in the Tamale Circuit.

When the big league owners began to squawk, Pasqual laughed and remarked, "Organized Ball is getting a dose of its own medicine. For many years, while our Mexican League was struggling to get along, major league scouts visited our cities and, right under our noses and over our protests, stole our players who were signed to Mexican League contracts."

Several players swallowed Pasqual's bait. Luis Olmo signed for $40,000 and left Brooklyn for Vera Cruz. Mickey Owen was another Dodger who headed south of the border. The Giants lost Danny Gardella, George Hausmann, Roy Zimmerman, and a pitcher named Sal Maglie.

Most of those who went down to Mexico quickly regretted it. The playing fields, the clubhouses, and the living accommodations were all wretched. Unfortunately for the deserters, they were no longer welcome back home. Happy Chandler banned them for five years. His action, along with the reports of the terrible conditions, kept the revolt from spreading out of control.

Now that the war was over, Americans, including my mother and father, were expected to return to "normal" living. Sally, much to her displeasure, lost her job with Sperry Gyroscope and returned to her housework. She talked a lot about taking a course—going to secretarial school or something—but slowly she was drawn back to her daily chores.

Early in May, Alex got a severe jolt when he showed up at Mr. Holmquist's victory garden for spring planting. The gates were padlocked, and there was no sign of activity.

Pop went over to Holmquist's building, where he found the super at work in the boiler room. "Well," Alex said proudly, "it looks like I'm the first farmer out this spring."

The old Norwegian snorted. "What the hell are you talking about? Don't you know the war's over?"

"So what if it is?"

"No more victory gardens—not here, anyway. They're gonna put up a new apartment house over there."

A few weeks later Alex, still despondent over the loss of his tomato patch, walked over to take another look at the plot where he'd whiled away so many pleasant hours. Steam shovels had already taken it away.

The first postwar baseball season began. As I expected, the Cardinals and Dodgers jockeyed for position in the early going, but then, in the last week of June, Brooklyn won six out of seven while St. Louis dropped three out of five, and suddenly the Flock had opened up a five-and-a-half-game lead. By the Fourth of July Durocher's men were seven games in front.

That afternoon Pop and I journeyed up to the Polo Grounds to take in a holiday twin bill between the Dodgers and the Giants. New York won the opener, 7–5, and Brooklyn took the nightcap, 8–5. What impressed both Alex and me about the Giants was the awesome power Mel Ott had in his lineup. New York hit five home runs that day; they came off the bats of Johnny Mize, Buddy Blattner, Willard Marshall, and Ernie Lombardi, who hit one in each game.

Despite all their muscle New York was in last place, with no hope at all of moving very far up in the standings. In fact, they would end the year in the cellar, even though they would lead the league in homers.

The next evening Brooklyn returned to the Polo Grounds for a night game. While the Dodgers were taking batting practice, Red Barber came into the dugout to have a chat with the Lip. "How about all those homers the Giants hit yesterday?" Red asked, putting the needle to Durocher.

"Home runs?" Leo replied. "Some home runs. Line drives and pop flies that would have been caught anywhere else in the league."

"Come on, Leo, why don't you admit they were real homers?" Red asked. "Why don't you be a nice guy for a change?"

"A nice guy!" shouted the Lip. "I never saw a nice guy who was any good when you needed him. Go up to one of those nice guys some time when you need a hundred to get you out of a jam. Ya know what that nice guy's gonna say? He's gonna say, 'Sorry Pal, I'd like to help, but things aren't going so good back at the ranch.'"

Leo paused, snickered, and put his hands on his hips. "I'll take the guys who ain't nice," he continued. "The guys who would put you in a cement mixer if they felt like it. But just you get in a bind. You don't have to come to them. They'll come looking for you and ask, 'How much do you need?'"

Durocher strutted up and down the dugout, then spun around and pointed to the Giant bench. "Look over there. Do you know a nicer guy than Mel Ott?" Leo asked. "Or any of the other Giants? Why they're the nicest guys in the world. And where are they? In last place!"

At the moment Eddie Stanky was taking his final practice swings. "Look at that little bastard," Leo said. "Think he's a nice guy? The hell he is. He'll knock you down and pick you up and say, 'I'm sorry.' That's the kind of guys I want on my club. He can't run, he can't hit, he can't do nothing. But what a ballplayer. I wouldn't trade him for any two second basemen in the league!"

Frank Graham of the *Journal American* was in earshot. The next day in his column Frank printed the remarks, and the Lip became known as the guy who believed that "nice guys finish last." Taken out of context the slogan is tinged with arrogance, no doubt about it. I'm sure Happy Chandler, who was paid a bundle of dough every year to sell the idea that baseball is pure as the driven snow and the players all live and breathe good sportsmanship, was less than happy when he heard about the Lip's little speech.

The Dodgers were taking on a new look. Slowly but deliberately, they were becoming a brand-new ball club. Earlier in the season Rickey had traded Goody Rosen to the Giants and Billy Herman to the Braves. Then he brought up catcher Bruce Edwards from Mobile. But the Mahatma took a slight step backward when he let Leo talk him into bringing back Joe Medwick. As Brooklyn entered the second half of the season, the Flatbush Faithful were filled with an optimism that was only slightly marred by the knowledge that the Cardinals were always a threat to gum up the works.

After the All-Star Game, in which the American League creamed the Nationals, 12–0, Brooklyn began to struggle. The Cards fought their way into first place by a half game on July 18, but the Dodgers quickly regained the lead and held it until the last week in August, when St. Louis again took over.

An important date in the Cardinals surge was August 29; they took a doubleheader from the Giants that day, while the Dodgers were losing a single game to the Cubs on a ninth-inning Chicago rally. St. Louis was one and a half games in front, and as far as I was concerned the season could have ended right there. But it went right on.

On September 16, still trailing the Cards by one and a half games, Leo sent Ralph Branca in as a decoy in the last game of a three-game series with St. Louis. The plan was to force Eddie Dyer, the Cardinal manager, to start his left-handed hitters; after hurling to one or two batters Ralph would be pulled for Vic Lombardi, a southpaw. As Branca went to the mound the stands buzzed, "Hey, what gives here?" Everyone was expecting to see Lombardi. After looking over Branca's first few pitches the Lip turned to coach Charlie Dressen and asked, "Is that ball jumping, or are my eyes playing tricks on me?" When Dressen assured his boss that his eyes were fine, Durocher decided to stay with Ralph, who rewarded Leo by shutting out the Cardinals, 5–0, moving Brooklyn up to just a half game out of first place.

Despite the Dodgers' determination the Cards clung to the lead, and time was running out. On Wednesday, September 25, the Reverend Benny J. F. Benson, pastor of the Brooklyn Dutch Reformed Church, decided to enlist the aid of God in the Dodgers' cause. On the steps of Borough Hall, in front of two hundred amused onlookers, the good reverend offered this prayer to the Almighty: "We're praying for the Dodgers. Their chances don't look so good right now, but everyone is praying for the Bums to win. We ask You not to give the Anheusers out there in St. Louis any better break than You give us, and we ask this in all sincerity."

Maybe the prayer worked. On Friday, September 27, while the Dodgers were idle, the Cubs beat the Cards, 7–2; with only two days left in the season Brooklyn and St. Louis were in a dead tie for the league lead.

The next day the Boston Braves came to Ebbets Field for the final two games of the year. That afternoon the Dodgers, with Joe Hatten, beat the Braves, 7–4. But that night, out in St. Louis, the Cardinals polished off the Cubs, 4–1, to hold their share of first place.

Pop and I arrived at Ebbets Field early that Sunday. Any hope I might have had for a Brooklyn victory went out the window in the top of the third inning, when Billy Herman got sweet revenge for being traded by doubling home the first run of the game.

"God damn that Rickey," Alex moaned. He'd been griping about the Herman deal all summer, and now his feelings had been vindicated. "That should have been our run, not Boston's."

The score remained 1–0 until the ninth. Vic Lombardi, the Brooklyn starter, had gone out for a pinch hitter in the previous inning; Higbe and Casey then threw the game away, giving up three runs between them in the top of the ninth. But, while the Dodgers were falling apart in Brooklyn, the Cardinals were having troubles of their own in St. Louis. The Ebbets Field scoreboard had shown the Cards to be ahead of the Cubs, 2–0, in the bottom of the third; then Chicago scored a single run in the fourth and five more in the fifth. The weird thing about the Cubs' rally was that it was going on while the Braves were scoring their runs. As the portable-radio grapevine at Ebbets Field spread the word of the goings on at Sportsman's Park, the fans in Brooklyn gave up one wild cheer after another even while the Braves were rounding the bases. When the Brooklyn game was finally over the score was, 4–0; Mort Cooper had held the Dodgers to four puny hits.

The fans in Ebbets Field were invited to stay in the park until the final results of the game in St. Louis had gone up on the scoreboard. Hardly anyone left. Pop and I both gave out heavy sighs of relief when the final was posted. Chicago won, 4–3, forcing the Dodgers and Cardinals into the first playoff in history. The pennant would go to the first team to win two games.

Tuesday, October 1, the Cardinals played host to the Dodgers in game one of the playoff. As I listened to Red Barber go over the lineups on the radio, I tried to convince myself Brooklyn could do it. My biggest concern was that Pete Reiser was out of action; he had broken his leg during the last week of the season, leaving left field to be played by aging Ducky Medwick.

The starting pitchers were Howie Pollet and Ralph Branca. Unfortunately, young Ralph was not up to the job. He loaded the bases in the top of the first and then gave up the first run of the afternoon when Joe Garagiola hit a slow bounder to short that went for an infield single, making the score 1–0.

Brooklyn tied up the game in the third on a homer by Howie Schultz, but the Cards came right back with two big runs in the bottom half of the inning to knock Branca out of the box. The Dodgers scored once in the top of the seventh, but the Cards immediately got the run back when Stan Musial tripled and was singled home by Garagiola. That ended the scoring; the Dodgers lost the game, 4–2, and returned to Brooklyn on the brink of elimination.

In his *Brooklyn Eagle* column, at least, Durocher wasn't worried. He wrote: "Things will not be that way when we get home to dear old Ebbets Field. They will not out-luck us there. Why, our Dodger fans wouldn't stand for it."

More than thirty-one thousand fans squeezed into Ebbets Field for game two. The Dodgers drew first blood in the bottom of the first when Ed Stevens singled home Augie Galan from second. "It looks like tomorrow will tell the story," I told myself. But in the second the Cardinals shook up Joe Hatten, the Dodger starter, for two runs.

In the fifth St. Louis scored three more times, sending Hatten to the showers and bringing on a parade of Brooklyn pitchers that included Behrman, Lombardi, Higbe, and Melton. Going into the last half of the ninth the Cards were ahead, 8–1, and many fans had left the park to escape the agony of the final out. Augie Galan led off the Dodger ninth with a booming double up the alley in right center. Dixie Walker flied out to empty a few more seats. Ed Stevens then tripled to score the second Dodger run of the day. It was apparent that Murry Dickson, the Cardinal starter, was beginning to tire. Carl Furillo then came up and quickly singled to center, adding another run.

Ebbets Field came back alive. Pop and I, along with every one of the remaining Faithful, begged Pee Wee Reese to knock in one more. Pee Wee came through with a walk, and Eddie Dyer, the Cardinal pilot, strode to the mound, patted Dickson on the back, and called for his ace southpaw—Harry "the Cat" Brecheen.

Bruce Edwards promptly singled home the fourth Dodger run, and Cookie Lavagetto walked to load the bases. The tying run came to the plate in the person of Eddie Stanky. Eddie, the great walk-drawer, struck out trying to coax a pass, and a pitiful groan emanated from the stands. The ball game was now in the hands of Howie Schultz, whom Leo sent in to bat for Dick Whitman, a lefty.

The crowd, remembering that Howie had homered in the opening game of the playoff, gave him a wild ovation. But Howie fanned, and the pennant belonged to St. Louis. The next day in his column Durocher predicted, "This is the last time the St. Louis ball club will be that close to us. I told our boys yesterday they have some big years ahead of them. We will all be riding high with the players already here, plus the sensational kids Branch Rickey has been getting ready at Montreal, Fort Worth, and Mobile."

Prior to the 1946 season, and much to Ed Barrow's disgust, Larry MacPhail announced that lights would go up over Yankee Stadium. He also announced that the team would fly to the Panama Canal Zone to take early spring training. When a bronzed and healthy-looking group, including returned servicemen DiMaggio, Rizzuto, Henrich, and Keller, among others, moved north to Florida in March, it looked as though the rest of the league might just as well take the season off.

The Bombers dumped on everybody they played in preseason and continued their explosive ways into the first several weeks of the regular season. But at the end of April the Yankees took their last look at first place and began a long, slow fade.

Joe McCarthy was in middling health and was exacerbating the problem with liquor. But the biggest exacerbation was the redhead in the front office. MacPhail and McCarthy saw eye-to-eye on virtually nothing. In late spring they finally agreed on something—McCarthy went home, and Bill Dickey, in his last season as a player, became the Yankee manager.

Dickey experienced difficulties similar to those of Sailor Bob Shawkey in a long-past season. The Yankees, accustomed to being chums and teammates with Dickey, were not disposed to accept his newly bestowed authority. Disharmony grew. In early September Yankee coach Johnny Neun became the new Yankee skipper. The Yankees walked through what was left of one of their most disappointing seasons, finishing third, seventeen games out. The American League flag was captured by the Red Sox, who lost the Series to the Cards, four games to three.

I began my freshman year at Columbia in September of 1946. I can't remember all the reasons I decided to go to college, but Uncle Harry's offer to foot the bills wasn't the least of them.

When I went over to Harry's place to pick up my check for fall tuition, my uncle appeared worried. "Does your father know about this?" he asked.

"He knows. Only he won't admit it. He's telling himself and all his drinking buddies that I got a scholarship."

"Jesus, I wish we could stop this stupid feud. If he'll give an inch, I'll give an inch," Harry said. "Can't you persuade him to come to his senses?"

"I'll try, Uncle Harry," I replied. But I knew it was no use.

Not long after the end of the 1946 season Westbrook Pegler, the Hearst columnist, began a smear campaign against Leo Durocher. Pegler dredged up an incident that had occurred back in March 1944 and began playing it for all it was worth. While Leo was up at Bear Mountain that year for spring training, George Raft had borrowed the Lip's Manhattan apartment.

Raft had supposedly held a crooked crap game in Durocher's pad, and one of the actor's guests, a fellow by the name of Martin Shurin, Jr., had later complained to the New York District Attorney that he'd been cheated out of $18,500.

More than two years later, Pegler decided to give Durocher the business. He began his campaign in his column of October 26, 1946, by asking this circumlocutory question:

> How tough is Raft, the great Hollywood actor and celebrity, I want to know, and is he really a gangster, and if so, how about some details? And if Durocher is so chummy with Hollywood characters—jerks one sport writer called them recently—that a baseball

writer can't get into his dressing room during the season, and he hangs around places frequented by gamblers and lends his apartment to Raft for a dicing party in which a chump is taken for $18,500 on 13 straight passes, all fours and tens, why not give us a tell?

It was a classic example of guilt by association. Pegler went several steps further in his column of October 29, in which, for no logical reason, he recalled the Black Sox scandal:

> After the exposé in 1920, when one of the poor, humiliated crooks came out of the Grand Jury room, a Chicago kid was said to have cried from his heart, "Say it isn't true, Joe; say it isn't true."
> But times and morals change and the Brooklyn kid of today might pluck Durocher's sleeve and ask to be introduced to his friend George Raft, as a hero who made 13 consecutive fours and tens, most of them the hard way. There would be a hero to emulate.

The next day Pegler took his cheapest shot of all. It was aimed squarely at the jugular:

> Durocher's choice of companions has been a matter of deep concern to Branch Rickey, the business manager of the Dodgers. The old practice of "whispering out" players and managers "for the good of the game" could be revived. . . . Rickey has pleaded with Durocher to change his associations lest a scandal occur which could end his career. . . . The moral "climate" of Durocher's circle and Raft's is ominously similar to that in which the corruption of 1919 occurred.

Not long after his public attack against Durocher, Pegler telephoned Branch Rickey to demand that this "moral delinquent" be fired. Pegler named several unsavory characters who were supposedly friends of Leo's, and he reported that at that very moment Durocher was a guest in George Raft's house out in Hollywood.

Rickey refused to knuckle under to Pegler, but after the conversation the Mahatma decided the time had come to straighten out his prodigal son. Leo hadn't broken any laws, but he had certainly behaved thoughtlessly. Living under Raft's roof, after all that bad publicity, was asking for trouble. A few days after his conversation with Pegler, Rickey dispatched his assistant, Arthur Mann, to Happy Chandler's office in Cincinnati. Mann's mission was to ask the commissioner to pressure Durocher into breaking off all ties with "people regarded as undesirable by baseball—gangsters, known gamblers, companions of known gamblers and racketeers." Leo wasn't to know that Chandler had been prodded by Rickey. In Mann's presence the commissioner immediately put in a call to George Raft's house. Leo wasn't there; he was at the NBC radio studios rehearsing for that evening's Jack Benny program.

When Chandler finally got through to Durocher at NBC, he ordered Leo to meet him at the Claremont Country Club in Berkeley, California, the following Friday. The Lip protested that he had personal business in Texas that day and couldn't possibly make it. "You'll be there, boy," Chandler boomed. "I know you won't disappoint me."

And so a perplexed and worried Leo Durocher traveled to Northern California. A cold rain was falling as the two men walked out onto the Claremont golf course to have their little chat. The commissioner began by pulling a slip of paper out of his pocket and reading off several names —all people Durocher was, from then on, forbidden to associate with.

The list included underworld figures such as Joe Adonis and Bugsy Siegel—men it would be easy enough to ignore since Leo didn't number them among his friends. There were, however, two people on Chandler's list who were pals of the Dodger manager. One was Memphis Engelberg, a tout who sometimes joined Durocher at the races; the other was Connie Immerman, manager of a casino in Havana. Leo didn't like it, but he agreed to stay clear of both Engelberg and Immerman. Finally, Chandler ordered Durocher to move out of Raft's house at once.

The plot thickens. On November 5 Larry MacPail had announced that Bucky Harris would be the new Yankee manager, and Charlie Dressen, who had mysteriously quit the Dodgers a few weeks earlier, would be the Yankees' number one coach. The loss of Dressen galled Rickey and Durocher for two very good reasons. First, Dressen was beyond a doubt one of the most talented men in baseball, and second, he had a verbal contract to remain in Brooklyn for two more seasons.

Rickey and Dressen had agreed that Charlie could get out of the commitment only if he were offered a job as manager elsewhere in the majors. As far as Branch and Leo were concerned, MacPhail had tampered with a member of the Dodger organization.

To aggravate the hard feelings, MacPhail claimed, at the press conference announcing the signing of Harris and Dressen, that Durocher had actively sought to become the new Yankee manager. "I didn't seek him out," MacPhail bragged, "he came to me. I didn't think Leo was exactly the man to lead the Yankees, although I do think he's a great manager and he did a wonderful job in Brooklyn last year."

It's pretty easy to understand why Durocher was sore at his old buddy MacPhail. On November 25 Leo came back to Brooklyn to sign his 1947 contract. Inevitably, the reporters on hand asked him if he had indeed applied to Larry for the Yankee manager's job. Leo explained that it was not he who had gone to MacPhail, but MacPhail who had come to him, four or five times in fact, with an offer of "more money than I am making in Brooklyn."

Leo said he had turned Larry down because "I want to remain in Brooklyn till the day I die." Now the feud was really getting hot. Mac-

Phail made the next move. He stole Red Corriden, another of Leo's coaches, away from the Dodgers.

In the middle of December, Pegler went back on the attack. In two separate columns, on December 12 and 13, he once again dragged out the story of the crooked dice game, and he accused George Raft of being a buddy of Bugsy Siegel, Joe Adonis, and Longie Zwillman, whom the columnist described as another "bootlegger, hoodlum, gambler and gangster."

Pegler also charged that Durocher was, against the express wishes of Branch Rickey, continuing to live in George Raft's house. Then Pegler swung his guns around and aimed them squarely at Happy Chandler. He described the commissioner as a "machine politician from a political environment in Louisville that includes professional underworld types that Fiorello LaGuardia used to call tin-horns and punks." Pegler concluded that "there has been a change of atmosphere in baseball since Judge Landis died. Your nose knows."

In Cincinnati Happy Chandler was squirming like a worm on a fish hook. Pegler was not the only journalist who accused him of being a do-nothing commissioner. If this goddamned Durocher problem wouldn't go away by itself, why then Happy would just have to do something to *make* it go away.

As if Durocher's life were not complicated enough, he was spending his winter in California wooing and winning actress Laraine Day. Miss Day, cool and beautiful, was desired by a million red-blooded American boys.

And here was old Leo, the pugnacious loudmouth, actually living out all our fantasies by having a love affair with an actress famous for her roles in syrupy pictures, such as those in the Dr. Kildare series. Laraine, a devout Mormon who neither drank nor smoked, didn't appear on the surface to be Leo's type. But they were drawn together by a chemistry that was bigger than both of them.

At the time they began seeing each other Laraine was still married, but she had already filed for divorce. The tabloids had a field day. Had the object of her affections been anyone other than Lippy Durocher, there wouldn't have been any scandal at all. Laraine's husband was Ray Hendricks, who managed an airport owned by Edgar Bergen. On December 4, Hendricks replied to the divorce petition by accusing Leo of posing as a friend of the family while "clandestinely wooing my wife in my home and under my very eyes."

"LARAINE DAY'S HUBBY HAS WORD FOR LIPPY: SNAKE IN THE GRASS," blared the *Daily News*.

On January 20, 1947, Miss Day was granted an interlocutory divorce by Superior Court Judge George A. Dockweiler. Under the terms of the decree she would not be permitted to remarry in California for one year.

337

As soon as the divorce was granted Leo and Laraine flew to Juarez, Mexico, where the actress obtained a second, "quickie" divorce. The couple then crossed the border to El Paso, Texas, where they were married by a justice of the peace.

Shortly after the ceremony they flew back to Los Angeles. They saw nothing wrong with being married as long as they didn't live as man and wife in California. And they had every intention of spending their nights apart until Leo left the Coast to begin spring training.

When Judge Dockweiler learned that the couple had jumped right into matrimony he was furious. The newlyweds appeared before him on January 22; after discussing the situation with them in his chambers for more than an hour, the judge ordered Laraine to show cause why the California divorce decree should not be set aside. Later, while discussing the case with reporters, Judge Dockweiler remarked that Durocher "wants to have his cake and eat it too."

Leo was burned up over the way the judge was administering justice. His Honor had apparently told the couple in his chambers that he didn't really care whether or not they lived in sin—that was something that couldn't be policed. What really bugged him was that Laraine had gone outside his jurisdiction to get around the divorce degree.

Lippy restrained himself for a week, but then, pop-off artist that he was, he issued a statement calling Dockweiler "a most unethical and publicity-conscious servant of the people." Leo went on to say that "it is a disgraceful situation when a supposedly holier-than-thou jurist can suggest—as he did, to my wife and myself—that we annul our marriage and her Juarez divorce, and that the court would overlook our living in sin until her interlocutory decree becomes final." Dockweiler responded to the charges by naming a panel of three prominent lawyers to determine whether Durocher should be cited for contempt of court.

Eventually the Durochers' problems on the Coast blew over. Laraine's divorce was not overturned and Leo was not punished for his outspokenness. But 3,000 miles away in Brooklyn, the case was taking another weird turn. The Dodgers sponsored a youth organization called the Knot-Hole Club, whose one hundred twenty thousand members, all kids between the ages of thirteen and fifteen, were entitled to attend three free games at Ebbets Field every summer.

One of the groups that passed out Knot-Hole tickets was the Catholic Youth Organization. Durocher's "bigamous" marriage was the last straw for the leaders of the CYO.

On February 28 the Reverend Vincent J. Powell, director of the CYO's Brooklyn diocese, withdrew his organization from the Knot-Hole Club because, as he put it in his letter to the Dodger management, "the present manager of the Brooklyn baseball team is not the kind of leader we want our youth to idealize and imitate."

The letter further explained that the CYO could not continue to be "officially associated with a man who presents an example in complete contradiction to our moral teachings." No matter which way he turned, Leo kept drawing fire.

The CYO pull-out took place shortly after the Dodgers departed for Havana, where they and the Montreal Royals trained for the 1947 season. Branch Rickey chose Cuba for the training site for a very good reason. The year before the Royals, while conditioning in Florida, had run into all kinds of hassles because they had a black man on their roster.

The Mahatma wanted to take a good look at Robinson before deciding whether to bring him up; the best way to do that was to have the Dodgers and Royals train in the same place. To avoid the problems that would come along with setting up camp in the South, Rickey took the two clubs to Havana. At the time it struck me—and most other Brooklyn fans—that the Mahatma was being overly cautious about Robinson. He had, after all, proved he was the best batter in the International League, hitting .349 the previous year. It was true enough that the Dodgers had the middle of their infield well covered with Reese and Stanky, but there had to be room somewhere on the roster for a player as talented as Jackie.

A few days after Leo arrived in Havana, he banned all card playing in the Dodger clubhouse. He spent most of his time off the playing field in his hotel room, avoiding any chance of bumping into anyone who might be considered an unsavory character. It appeared that he was determined to be a good boy, whatever the price. But on March 3, while the Dodgers were in Caracas, Venezuela, for an exhibition series with the Yankees, Harold Parrott, the Dodger road secretary and Lippy's ghostwriter, decided to spice up the "Durocher Says" column in the *Eagle* by taking some fresh swipes at MacPhail and Dressen. He wrote these words in Leo's behalf:

> This is a declaration of war. I want to beat the Yankees as badly as I do any team in the National League. And that is certainly saying plenty. I want to wallop them because of MacPhail and Dressen. John Corriden might be included in that group by some, but he is just a nice old guy nobody can get mad at. I want to beat the Yankees because MacPhail knows in his heart that I love Brooklyn, always want to manage there and regard Branch Rickey as my father.

Larry MacPhail blew his top when he learned that Harold Parrott and Leo were using the column to take potshots at him and Dressen. Just before the second game in Caracas (the Yanks had slaughtered the Dodgers, 17–6, in the opener), Larry told a group of reporters that without Pistol Pete Reiser Brooklyn was a third-rate ball club that wouldn't have a prayer of reaching the first division.

When the writers ran back to Durocher to get his reaction to Larry's jibe, the Lip said, "Well, I think more of the Yankees than that. I'd say they'd float right up to the top of the American League if they didn't have MacPhail as ballast." That afternoon the Dodgers, who were all pretty steamed about MacPhail's slur, rallied for five runs in the ninth inning to beat New York, 7–3.

The next day Leo's column carried the feud a step further. It charged that "MacPhail, knowing he has a weak ball club and seeing that it will bring him so few of the personal headlines that are his bread and butter, has started knocking whoever happens to be near him." While the readers of the *Eagle* were enjoying the backbiting in Brooklyn, the Yanks were taking the final game in Caracas by a score of 4–0.

On Saturday, March 8, the Dodger–Yankee exhibition series resumed in Havana, and Durocher's pitchers—Higbe, Hatten, and Melton—hurled nine innings of no-hit ball to beat New York in the tenth, 1–0. After the game two reporters looking for a story bumped into Branch Rickey in the lobby of the Nacional Hotel and were stunned when the Mahatma suddenly launched into a show of temper that was completely out of character for a person who had a reputation for maintaining his dignity at all times. "Did you see those two men out there today?" Rickey screamed. "Those gamblers sitting in MacPhail's box?"

One of the writers admitted that he had indeed seen them. The men in question were none other than Memphis Engelberg and Connie Immerman—two of the "undesirables" Chandler had expressly forbidden Leo Durocher to associate with.

"You can imagine what would happen if those two men were seated in the Dodgers' box," Rickey went on, still fuming. "Why my own manager can't even say hello to George what's-his-name. He won't have anything to do with gamblers, but apparently there are rules for Durocher and other rules for the rest of baseball."

The following afternoon the members of the press were less interested in the outcome of the rubber game in the exhibition series than they were in the next battle in the war between Brooklyn and the Bronx. After all, Rickey's outburst had provided some mighty juicy copy. When, right before the game, Engelberg and Immerman once again appeared in MacPhail's box, Dick Young of the *Daily News* ran down to the Dodger dugout to get Leo's reaction. The Lip, pacing up and down the dugout in anger, howled, "Where does MacPhail come off flaunting his company with known gamblers right in the players' faces? If I even said hello to one of those guys, I'd be called up before Commissioner Chandler and probably be barred."

The Yankees won that afternoon, 4–1, but back in New York the next day the papers devoted most of their space to the bitter remarks made by Rickey and Durocher and, of course, MacPhail's reply. Larry reacted to the charges by saying, "In the first place, it's none of Durocher's business who I have in my box. In the second place, if Durocher was quoted correctly, he is a liar. I understand that in the box next to me were two gentlemen later identified as alleged gamblers. I had nothing to do with their being there. And you can quote me as saying it's none of Durocher's business."

The Dodgers and Yankees went their separate ways. As far as Leo and the Mahatma were concerned, the incident was over. However, on March 13 in St. Petersburg, MacPhail and Will Harridge, president of the American League, collared Happy Chandler and issued a complaint against Durocher and the Dodgers. They asked the commissioner to investigate certain statements that had appeared in the press and were allegedly made by Rickey and Durocher. MacPhail also petitioned Chandler to determine whether articles appearing in the *Brooklyn Eagle* under the byline of Leo Durocher were authentic, whether Mr. Rickey and the Brooklyn club might be responsible, and if so whether their publication might be detrimental to baseball. The written charges reached the commissioner at his hotel in Sarasota on March 15. That afternoon Walter Mulbry, Chandler's assistant, telephoned Branch Rickey to apprise him of the situation. The Mahatma, in Pensacola at the time, was about to depart by private plane to the Canal Zone, where the Dodgers and Royals were playing an exhibition series. He took a quick detour to Sarasota, where Mulbry gave him a copy of MacPhail's complaint. Several days later Rickey and Durocher were told to appear in Sarasota for a hearing before the commissioner on Monday, March 24.

Meanwhile, Branch Rickey was tackling a problem that at the time seemed far more important than MacPhail's crybaby act. Ever since spring training began the Dodger players were wondering whether or not Jackie Robinson would be brought up. All the evidence suggested that he would make the team. The one infield position where Brooklyn was weak was first base. Both Ed Stevens and Howie Schultz—the two men who'd played that position the year before—left a lot to be desired. Rickey had instructed Clay Hopper, the Royals' manager, to play Robinson at first during spring training even though Lou Ruchser, Montreal's regular first baseman, needed practice at the position. As Durocher himself explained the situation, "Stanky is set at second, Reese is our shortstop, and we've got Vaughan at third. So we've got to play Robinson at first or nowhere."

Several of the Dodger players, fearful that this black man was about to become their teammate, decided to start a petition declaring that they would not play if Robinson were on the club. Kirby Higbe, though a Southerner, couldn't bring himself to go along with the plot.

He told Harold Parrott what was going on, and Rickey got the story as soon as he arrived in Panama. One by one the Mahatma called the ringleaders—Hugh Casey, Bobby Bragan, Dixie Walker, and Carl Furillo—into his hotel suite. He gave them each a chewing out, booming that if they didn't like the idea of playing with a Negro, they were perfectly free to quit baseball. The revolt was quickly quashed.

On March 18, in the Canal Zone, the Royals and Dodgers played their first exhibition game of the season against each other. Robinson played first base for Montreal. He had an excellent day, going two for four. During seven games between the Royals and Dodgers Jackie would bat .625 and steal seven bases. And still there would be no sign from Rickey when, if ever, he would be brought up. There was, however, convincing proof that it was only a matter of time. Three other black players—catcher Roy Campanella and pitchers Don Newcombe and Roy Partlow—were assigned to Montreal that spring.

Two days before Happy Chandler's hearing, Branch Rickey learned that his brother-in-law, who lived in Ohio, had passed away. Branch requested that the hearing be postponed while he attended the funeral, but Chandler insisted on going ahead, even without the Dodger president. On the afternoon of March 24, Walter O'Malley, Branch Rickey, Jr., Arthur Mann, and Senator George Williams, Rickey's friend and legal counselor from St. Louis, entered the roof garden of the Sarasota Terrace Hotel to represent the Dodgers in proceedings that were closed to the press.

Larry MacPhail and Dan Topping were there on behalf of the Yankees. Leo Durocher and Harold Parrott sat outside the hearing room waiting to be called as witnesses. After several witnesses whose testimony was for the most part irrelevant, Parrott was brought in. The Dodger road secretary admitted to having written the "Durocher Says" column that had vexed MacPhail. Chandler ordered Harold to take his choice—he could either be a baseball executive or a journalist, but not both. Parrott assured the commissioner that from then on he would stick to baseball. Charlie Dressen was the next witness. The gist of his testimony was that he had indeed violated an agreement with Rickey when he signed with the Yankees.

Durocher was then called in. He was asked about the column in which he "declared war" against the Yankees. Leo took full responsibility for the piece even though he hadn't written it, and then he turned to Mac-Phail and apologized for hurting his feelings. MacPhail accepted the apology, but then Chandler began interrogating the Lip about gambling in the Dodger clubhouse. He asked if there had been any high-stakes card playing going on. Leo admitted that in the past he had played a little gin rummy with Kirby Higbe. The pitcher, a terrible card player, always seemed to be $600 to $800 in debt to Leo. "I'd take his money in card games and give it back to him as a bonus when he pitched well," Durocher explained.

Then Chandler got to the question of the two gamblers who had supposedly occupied MacPhail's box in Havana. Leo had no qualms about confessing that he had expressed his indignation loudly and openly. And why shouldn't he? Hadn't the men in question been labeled undesirables by Chandler himself when he and Lippy met in Berkeley?

The commissioner didn't seem to comprehend what Leo was trying to say. Happy turned to MacPhail and asked him whether or not he had tried to hire Durocher away from the Dodgers. After giving the floor to Dan Topping for some vague introductory remarks, Larry, as Leo later described it, "gave a long, rambling talk in which he consistently avoided making any flat statement about offering me the job, one way or the other." Surprisingly, Chandler never probed to get a definite yes or no from MacPhail, nor did he ask Leo for his side of the story.

Instead, Happy turned to Durocher and said, "You are hereby dismissed." With Leo out of the room MacPhail complained to the commissioner that the hearing had not yet accomplished its purpose. He would not be satisfied until Branch Rickey had either affirmed or denied the statement allegedly made in Havana charging that "apparently there are rules for Durocher and other rules for the rest of baseball." The hearing was then adjourned until the Mahatma could be present. The proceedings would resume on March 28 in St. Petersburg.

At that hearing, Rickey readily admitted he had openly expressed displeasure to the press over the presence of well-known gamblers in MacPhail's box. He went on to say that he had no intention of retracting his remarks.

After Rickey finished his testimony Chandler called in Arthur Patterson, the Yankees' public relations man. The commissioner brought up the question of how Immerman and Engelberg happened to get their tickets to the Havana ball games. When Chandler finally asked Patterson point-blank if the tickets had come from him, the reply was, "I can't recall." Upon further questioning by Walter Mulbry, Patterson admitted that it was indeed conceivable that he had provided the gamblers with the tickets.

At this point Rickey, still fuming with indignation, figured his point had been made. After dismissing Patterson, Chandler then cleared the room of everyone except Rickey, O'Malley, and Mann—the three Dodger executives. Much to the astonishment of the Brooklyn contingent, the commissioner then asked, "How much would it hurt you folks to have your fellow out of baseball?"

Nothing—absolutely nothing—that had taken place during the two hearings had anything to do with Durocher's fitness to manage a major league ball club. It was beginning to look as if Chandler's only reason for holding hearings on MacPhail's charges was to provide a platform for drumming Leo Durocher out of baseball. "Happy, what on earth is the matter with you?" Rickey asked.

Chandler explained that at least one "big man in Washington" was pressuring him to toss Durocher out of the game. After listening to a heated protest from Rickey and his associates, Happy said he was merely sounding them out on the idea, and that they shouldn't worry. Everything would turn out all right. The Mahatma didn't believe that for a minute. He left the hearing room perplexed and worried. Enough time had been wasted on this farce. Whatever the final outcome, he now had to concentrate on running his ball club. The time for a decision on Robinson was drawing near.

Two weeks later, on the morning of April 9, the top Dodger executives were meeting to decide on the final roster for the new season, now less than a week away. The discussion centered on how and when to call up Jackie Robinson.

Rickey's private phone rang. As the Mahatma spoke, those present could see the agitation swelling up inside their boss. The caller was obviously Chandler. Rickey finally hung up the phone.

"Harold," he said turning to Parrott, "you've been fined five hundred dollars." Parrott, a family man, was paying a heavy price indeed for being the Lip's mouthpiece. Charlie Dressen had also been punished. For breaking a verbal agreement with the Dodgers, he was suspended for thirty days.

"And the Dodgers and Yankees have each been fined two thousand dollars," Rickey went on.

"But what happened to me?" Lippy asked, knowing damn well he couldn't possibly have come out unscathed.

"Leo, you've been suspended from baseball for one year."

"For *what?*" Leo implored.

For what indeed? If Durocher couldn't figure out why he'd been given the ax, your typical Dodger fan was completely baffled. The news spread through Brooklyn with amazing speed. By noon just about everyone in the borough was expressing an opinion about the case.

"We wuz robbed," was the most common reaction. As far as I was concerned, the suspension was a disaster. Durocher had made something out of the Dodgers—he'd given the team pizzazz, and in the process he'd given every loyal Brooklynite something to be proud of. How could the Bums possibly win without him?

That afternoon I dropped by the Web to have a beer with Alex. "The way I see it," my father said as he poured me a glass of Schaefer, "Chandler must have something on Leo that's so bad he's keeping it a secret."

The next day, just before an exhibition game with the Royals, Leo met with the Dodger players in the Ebbets Field clubhouse. "Put your faith in Mr. Rickey," Lippy told his boys. "There's never been a thing Mr. Rickey won't do for you if you ask him. You'll find that he'll bring you through."

And then, with Laraine at his side, Leo left Ebbets Field for a year. He would spend his period of exile in California.

That afternoon, when Brooklyn and Montreal took the field, Jackie

344

Robinson was still wearing a Royals uniform. The crowd gave Jackie a generous ovation every time he came to bat, but unfortunately he failed to get a hit. In the fifth inning a release was passed around the pressbox. It read, simply: "The Brooklyn Dodgers today purchased the contract of Jackie Roosevelt Robinson from the Montreal Royals." Crafty old Branch Rickey, making the announcement at the height of the Durocher controversy, diminished the impact of the historic move.

Five days later, on April 15, in the opening day contest against the Braves, Jackie became the first black player to appear in a major league game in this century. His debut was a mild disappointment. He went 0 for 3, but he did manage to score the winning run.

Branch Rickey still had a slight problem. He didn't have a manager. First he thought of Joe McCarthy. That would have been ironic—hiring a man who had left the Yankees because he hated MacPhail's guts. Unfortunately, McCarthy wasn't interested.

The papers issued reports that Bill Terry was the next choice. Think of that! Memphis Bill as the Dodger manager. Talk about irony. But the man the Mahatma finally settled on was his old friend Burt Shotton. Shotton, sixty-two, lived in Bartow, Florida, in semiretirement and assisted Rickey by scouting.

He had managed the Phillies from 1928 to 1933, never finishing higher than fourth. On April 17, Rickey wired Shotton to come at once to New York without saying a word to anyone. The next morning the Mahatma was waiting at LaGuardia Airport to tell Burt that he was the new pilot of the Dodgers. Rickey then dispatched his new manager to the Polo Grounds, where Brooklyn was opening a two-game series with the Giants. Burt entered the dugout in his street clothes. Like Connie Mack, he would not suit up, preferring to run the team completely from the bench. That afternoon the new Brooklyn manager watched his ball club get creamed by New York, 10–4. The following afternoon, the Giants won again, this time by a score of 4–3.

The rumor around baseball circles was that, if Mel Ott didn't produce in 1947, he would be out. He certainly had some promising players—Mize, of course, and Walker Cooper, whom many regarded as the best backstop in the game. In the outfield New York had Willard Marshall, Sid Gordon, and a good-looking newcomer by the name of Bobby Thomson. Another outfielder with plenty of potential was Whitey Lockman, who'd broken his ankle in spring training and would have to wait a year before getting into the lineup as a regular.

The infield was only fair. In addition to Mize at first, New York had Bill Rigney at second, Buddy Kerr at short, and Lucky Lohrke at third.

The weakest part of the club was the pitching staff. In Larry Jansen the Giants had their best hurling prospect in a decade, and then there was Dave Koslo, but after that, forget it.

Robinson was now a major leaguer, but his battle for acceptance had barely begun. The hatred he was subjected to during the opening weeks of his first season in the majors would have broken a lesser man. On April 22 the Phillies came to Ebbets Field for a three-game series. If ever there was a first-class redneck it was Ben Chapman, the Philadelphia manager. He instructed his players to give the "nigger" the works, and they happily obliged him. As Robinson came to bat in the first inning of the opening game, taunts issued forth from the Philadelphia dugout:

"Hey, nigger, why don't you go back to the cotton fields?"

"Get lost, jungle bunny."

"Send that coon back to the plantation."

Robbie couldn't believe this was happening. He later confessed he came within a hair's breadth of throwing away his career to get back at his tormentors. He somehow managed to hold back an urge to throw down his bat and "stride over to that Phillies dugout, grab one of those white sons of bitches and smash his teeth in with my despised black fist."

After seven innings the game was still scoreless. With the abuse still flowing Robinson led off the bottom of the eighth with a single to center. Then, when Reiser fanned on a hit-and-run, Jackie moved all the way to third as catcher Andy Seminick first mishandled the pitch and then threw the ball into center field. Gene Hermanski then singled home Jackie with the only run of the ball game. Brooklyn took all three games of the series.

The St. Louis Cardinals were scheduled to play their first series in Brooklyn on Tuesday, May 6. Three men on the team didn't fancy the idea of going out on the same field with a black man. They began persuading their teammates to go on strike the day of the first game at Ebbets Field.

Then one of the ringleaders came up with an even better idea—to get every club in the league to strike on a certain date. Sam Breadon, learning of the plot, rushed to New York, where he brought the matter to the attention of Ford Frick. The National League president and the Cardinal owner went over to the hotel where the club was staying to get to the bottom of the situation.

After lengthy discussions with the ringleaders Frick gave Breadon this statement to pass on to the players: "If you do this you will be suspended from the league. You will find that the friends you think you have in the pressbox will not support you, that you will be outcasts. I do not care if half the league strikes. Those who do it will encounter quick retribution. All will be suspended, and I don't care if it wrecks the National League for five years. This is the United States of America, and one citizen has as much right to play as another."

The rapid, decisive action by Breadon and Frick defused a highly explosive situation. Jackie Robinson continued to get plenty of abuse.

Hate mail included threats against him, his wife, and even his infant son. The vicious heckling from the opposing benches kept coming.

In Philadelphia, the cradle of liberty, he was refused accommodations at the Benjamin Franklin Hotel. But the initial shock of Jackie's arrival in the majors passed. As the season progressed he would win the admiration of the press, the Brooklyn fans, and even his teammates.

In May, while the teams in the National League were jockeying for position, Branch Rickey pulled off another of his famous deals. He sent pitchers Kirby Higbe, Cal McLish, and Hank Behrman, along with infielder Gene Mauch and catcher Dixie Howell, to the Pirates for $250,000 and an undistinguished outfielder named Al Gionfriddo.

The Bucs gave Behrman a quick look and sent him back to the Dodgers. The departure of Higbe, who'd played such an important role in the rebirth of the Dodgers, saddened both me and Alex. It was hard to figure out why Rickey had bothered to pick up Gionfriddo. The joke around Flatbush was that "they threw little Al into the deal because they needed someone to haul all that money to Brooklyn." As it later turned out, Gionfriddo had a rendezvous with immortality.

As the pennant race began to take shape, it became clear that the Giants were the most improved team in the league. New York was in first place at the start of June but then began to fade as their pitching gave out. Still, they wound up the season in fourth—a big jump upward from their last-place finish of the year before. Larry Jansen had a sensational rookie season, winning twenty-one and losing only five for a league-leading winning percentage of .808. And Big Jawn Mize tied Ralph Kiner of the Pirates for the home-run championship of the majors: Each hit fifty-one.

After the All-Star break the Dodgers began to roll. By August they had broken away to a ten-game lead. Alex and I got cocky. This time the pennant was in the bag. A week later the margin had been cut to four lengths, the Cardinals were in second place, and suddenly we were frightened to death.

But the Bums did not fold; they clung to first place all through August and September. They arrived in St. Louis for a three-game series on September 11, four and a half games in front. "All we have to do is win one. Just one," I told Pop. If the Dodgers could get out of Sportsman's Park three and a half games up, they'd be home free.

The Brooklyn pitcher in game one was Ralph Branca, who, with nineteen victories already notched, was having an excellent year. Harry Brecheen went to the mound for the Cards. Listening to the game on the radio, Pop and I each had a mild stroke when the Cards scored two runs in the second inning. I wasn't sure I could stand it if St. Louis humiliated Brooklyn once again.

But the Flock came back with two in the fifth, scored another run in the top of the sixth, and then allowed the Redbirds to score once and

347

tie the ball game at 3–3 in their half of the sixth. In the Dodger eighth Cookie Lavagetto hit a pinch-hit single with the bases loaded to drive in the go-ahead run. Brooklyn held on to win the game, 4–3, and Ralph Branca became the club's first twenty-game winner since 1941.

The next day the Cards scored two runs in the bottom of the ninth to pull out an 8–7 victory, but in the final game of the series the Bums managed to stomp out another ninth-inning rally to win by the same score, 8–7. Brooklyn coasted through the final weeks of the season, winning the flag by five games.

Just before the close of the campaign the *Sporting News* named Jackie Robinson the National League Rookie of the Year. Jackie certainly deserved the honor. He led the league in stolen bases with twenty-nine. He batted .297, and his drive and hustle were an inspiration to his teammates.

Shortly after the 1946 campaign, the Yankees had released Johnny Neun as manager. At about the time Neun began his short tenure, MacPhail had hired Stanley "Bucky" Harris. Exactly what the duties of Harris were to be, no one knew, including Harris. It was a good bet, however, that MacPhail was planning to oust George Weiss, who along with Topping and Webb was a vice-president of the club, and replace him with Harris.

The speculation about Durocher, Dressen, and Frankie Frisch was quelled by the appointment of Harris as new manager of the Yanks. Harris, the Boy Wonder of the 1924 Senators, was now an old boy wonder of fifty and had more major league managerial experience than anyone except Connie Mack.

"Did you know," Uncle Harry said, the computer between his ears whirring, "that Bucky Harris equaled an American League record by being hit with twenty-one pitched balls in the 1920 season?" Harry liked the choice, though he sorely missed Joe McCarthy.

Undoubtedly, Ed Barrow did too. In January of 1947 he resigned as chairman of the board of the Yankees, a nominal position he had held since the coming of MacPhail.

The team got off to a mediocre start, and MacPhail's meddling wasn't helping matters any. One day in late spring, the team threatened to go on strike, leaving fifty thousand spectators to contemplate the empty expanse of Yankee Stadium. DiMaggio, always the leader, convinced his teammates they'd be hurting themselves more than MacPhail, and the game was played. In spite of the turbulence throughout the organization, by mid-July, ending a nineteen-game winning streak, the Yankees had a firm hold on first place. They clinched in early September and went on to win by twelve over Detroit.

In the first game of the Series, played in Yankee Stadium, the Dodgers sent Ralph Branca against Spec Shea. For four innings Branca pitched nearly flawless ball. But the Yankees were specialists in the big inning, and the Dodgers had some experience in the same department—on the defensive end. When the fifth was over, the Yanks had scored five. Branca was in the clubhouse, Shea had been removed for a pinch hitter, and ace reliever Joe Page, a happier man under the live-and-let-live Harris than under the strict McCarthy, was blowing smoke past the Brooklyn batters. The final was 5–3, Yankees.

The next day Allie Reynolds, acquired the year before from the Indians in return for Joe Gordon, faced Brooklyn left-hander Vic Lombardi. The Yanks not only specialized in the big inning, they also specialized in the big game. They walloped the Bums, 10–3.

There was no joy in Brooklyn, where the teams headed for game three. Then the tide turned—or at least was stemmed. The Dodgers whacked Bobo Newsom for six runs in the second inning, putting the game seemingly out of reach. But the Yankees kept nibbling away at Joe Hatten, Branca, and Hugh Casey. It wasn't until Casey had notched the third out in the ninth that the denizens of Ebbets could celebrate. It was an electric, exciting game, and the Dodgers had come away with a 9–8 win. Along the way a stocky young outfielder–catcher named Yogi Berra hit the first pinch-hit homer in the history of the Series.

That year the World Series was televised for the first time. Uncle Harry invited me up to his place to watch game four on his brand-new ten-inch Dumont TV set. We closed the blinds, turned off the lights, and fussed endlessly with the control panel. Harry was very proud of his new toy. The cabinet was about twenty times the size of the little screen; but the reception was surprisingly good, and it didn't take much concentration to get lost in the game.

Ellen brought out pretzels and beer, and the action began. I prayed that the Dodgers wouldn't make me look like a fool in front of my-uncle-the-Yankee-fan.

Today, Red Barber remembers this game as "the most exciting baseball game ever." Many fans would agree. Yankee hurler Bill Bevens was pitching wildly—he would walk ten before the game was over—but with luck. The luck consisted mainly of an exceptional Yankee defense. Even though the Dodgers had scored a run in the fifth with two walks, a sacrifice, and an infield out, Bevens went into the last of the ninth with more than a 2–1 lead. He also had a no-hitter going.

With the pretzels gone, I took to chewing my fingernails. Uncle Harry's teeth clamped down hard on his pipe stem.

Bruce Edwards led off with a smash to left, but Johnny Lindell was there, as the Yankee outfielders had been all day, to make a good catch. Furillo wangled walk number nine out of Bevens. After Spider Jorgensen fouled out, Furillo was replaced on the basepaths by the speedy Al Gionfriddo. Pete Reiser pinch-hit for Casey. While Reiser was working the count to 3–2, Gionfriddo stole second. At that point, Bucky Harris ordered Bevens to put Reiser on.

"Oh no," Harry groaned. "You can't *do* that. Nobody puts the winning run on base!"

The batter who strode to the plate was Cookie Lavagetto. The end was in sight for Cookie, but he was still my boy. He cut at the first pitch and missed. The second delivery came in high and fast. Lavagetto connected; as the ball sailed out to right field, Tommy Henrich helplessly tried to position himself to make a play. It caromed off the wall for extra bases, sending home first the tying run and then the winning run. Bevens's no-hitter had gone up in smoke, and so had the ball game. By winning, 3–2, Brooklyn had evened the Series at two games apiece.

"Tomorrow's another day," Uncle Harry said, displaying not a care in the world.

Of course he was right. But for today at least, those goddamned Yankees had gotten a healthy dose of their own medicine.

In game five Shotton used eighteen players to try to wrest another win from the Yanks, but to no avail. Spec Shea held the Dodgers to four hits. On a homer by DiMaggio, the Yanks won it, 2–1.

The sixth game, back at Yankee Stadium, was a slugfest. Nearly seventy-five thousand watched as a total of thirty-eight players divided up twenty-seven hits. When DiMaggio came to bat in the sixth with two out and two on, the seventh pitcher—three for the Dodgers, four for the Yanks—had already entered the game. The Dodgers were leading, 8–5. Amid the deluge of substitutions, Shotton had made one that was to prove fateful; he inserted Al Gionfriddo in left field in place of Hermanski. DiMadge picked his pitch and cracked a game-tying homer—at least, nearly everyone in the park thought it was a homer. Gionfriddo blazed toward the bullpen fence and somehow, miraculously, snagged the ball as it arched over the railing. It was one of the most spectacular plays in history. Gionfriddo had indeed proved to be a bag man. DiMaggio was loping into second when the gasp and roar came from the crowd. He kicked the dirt in disgust, possibly the only public display of emotion ever made by the Yankee Clipper. The Dodgers won the game, 8–6, making it a one-game, sudden-death Series.

And it was the Dodgers who suddenly died. The Yankees, behind brilliant relief pitching by Joe Page, won the game, 5–2. The Yankees had won another Series. The Dodgers had lost another. Would I never get the last laugh on Uncle Harry?

The Series had been a grudge match between MacPhail and Rickey, and MacPhail rubbed salt in the wounds by saying to the press after the final game, "Don't congratulate *me*. I built the losers!" Later, MacPhail had something more to say: "I retire." He would have preferred to retire George Weiss and install his son Lee in Weiss's spot. Instead, MacPhail was gone and Weiss was the new general manager. Topping and Webb bought out MacPhail, who left the Bronx with more than two million bucks in his pockets.

The big question during the fall of 1947 was: Will Leo get his job back? Had Rickey decided not to open his arms to his problem child, he surely would have escaped without much criticism. After all, Burt Shotton had won the pennant and almost won the Series too. Nonetheless the Mahatma announced in December that the Lip would be his man in 1948. At a press conference during the first week of January Leo remarked, "What happened in 1947 is history. The Dodgers won the pennant and Burt Shotton did a wonderful job." When asked by reporters how he would treat umpires in the coming season, Leo said, "Any time I see them making any glaring mistakes you can bet I'll be right out there calling their attention to them."

The upcoming campaign was filled with question marks for the Dodgers. Rickey was hard at work juggling his roster. Over the winter he had sent Dixie Walker to the Pirates in a trade that brought pitcher Preacher Roe and third baseman Billy Cox to Brooklyn. During spring training, against Leo's vehement opposition, the Mahatma sold Eddie Stanky to the Boston Braves.

Eddie was terribly bitter over the trade and accused Leo of "knifing me in the back." But it was Rickey who had scuttled Stanky to make room at second for Robinson, who was clearly not a first baseman.

There was, however, a hitch to the plan. Robbie had come to camp after a winter on the rubber-chicken circuit tipping the scales at 230 pounds, 35 over his normal playing weight! There was no way he could play second decently, let alone steal bases, beat out bunts, or do any of the other things that had made him Rookie of the Year in 1947. Durocher, hoping to shame Robbie into getting into shape, rode him without mercy throughout the spring. But he was so far gone that he didn't reach peak condition until the season was half over.

The great Dodger team of the fifties began to take shape in 1948. Preacher Roe, a crafty spitball artist, would become a household name in Flatbush. Billy Cox was destined to prove himself as one of the best fielding third basemen anywhere. But they were only the beginning.

Duke Snider, an outfielder Rickey had already sent back to the minors once before because of his "appalling unfamiliarity with the strike zone," was brought up for another look. Roy Campanella, called up from the Royals at the start of the season, was sent down to St. Paul mainly to break the color line in the American Association.

But when Bruce Edwards developed arm trouble, Campy came back to Brooklyn and took over as the regular catcher. That same year Leo converted Gil Hodges from a backstop to a first baseman, solving the Dodgers' first base problems for many years to come. And later on in the season Carl Erskine, a right-handed hurler, was brought up from Fort Worth and quickly displayed a lot of promise. "Oisk" would go back down for more seasoning during part of 1949, and then he would become a Flatbush legend.

With such an array of talent you'd think the Dodgers would have waltzed to the pennant. But this was 1948, not 1952. The team was, for the most part, young and inexperienced. It got off to a terrible start. The Bums lost eight straight from May 15 to May 23 and for one whole day suffered the disgrace of residing in the cellar.

Leo, who coached at first base in those days, got heckled every time he appeared in the coach's box. "Hey, Hollywood, why don't ya go back to your flower garden?" the fans would holler.

In the Web Café, where Dodger home games were now available for the price of a beer on a Philco TV set, the consensus was that the club wasn't running right because Rickey had pulled out all the sparkplugs. The fans were especially galled by the Stanky deal. There were those who also blamed Durocher, but for most diehards the real villain was the Mahatma.

To make matters worse, it looked for a while as if the Giants might make a run for the pennant. They were in first place at the start of June but then gave way to the Braves, the team Uncle Harry had picked to win that year. "It will be an all Boston Series," he had informed me in April. "Ol' Joe McCarthy has come back to run the Red Sox, and he's gotta be the greatest pilot in the game today. Besides, he's got a team that's loaded with talent. No, there's no question about it. The Braves and the Red Sox will go all the way."

Whatever the Braves' chances, the Dodgers didn't appear to be going anywhere. On July 4, after Lippy had been tossed out of a game against the Giants, Harold Parrott came to him in the locker room and said, "I hate to tell you this, Leo, but the boss wants you to resign."

"Tell Mr. Rickey to go to hell," Durocher answered. "If he wants me out, he's going to have to fire me, and he's going to have to do it man to man. Get him on the phone and let's have him do it like a man."

Rickey kept Leo on the job, at least for the time being.

By the beginning of July the Giants, riddled by injuries and stymied by lousy pitching, were fading. Horace Stoneham decided the time had come to get rid of Mel Ott. He asked Branch Rickey if it would be all right to talk to Burt Shotton about managing the Giants. Rickey surprised Stoneham by saying, "Sure. You can talk to Shotton. If you'd like, you can also talk to Durocher. You can have either one."

"If I can have my choice, Leo is the man I want," Horace replied.

On Thursday, July 15, the Mahatma summoned Leo off the road. Durocher arrived at 215 Montague Street just before nine o'clock in the evening and was told by Branch that the Giants were interested in him. If Leo wanted the job he could call Stoneham then and there.

Without much hesitation Durocher phoned the Giant owner and arranged to meet him that very evening. The next morning a shock jolted Brooklyn. Lippy Durocher, the idol of Flatbush, had gone over to the Giants. It was one of the most bizarre stories in the history of sports.

"Imagine Durocher turning his back on Brooklyn, after all Brooklyn's done for him. What a crumb," Alex said. I agreed. How could Leo have done it? Did I hate the Giants after that! Stoneham was nobody's fool. He knew that hiring Leo would reheat a rivalry that had cooled down since New York had fallen on bad times and St. Louis had become the Dodgers' most hated opponent.

There was only one hitch. Every Giant fan worth two cents hated the Lip with a passion. He was despised as much at the Polo Grounds as he had been loved at Ebbets Field. It would be two years before Leo would gain acceptance, let alone affection, from the denizens of Coogan's Bluff.

Leo wasn't going to let that stop him. He vowed that "like me or not, I was going to give them a ball club so exciting to watch that they'd come out in spite of me and in spite of themselves."

Leo's first appearance as a Giant at Ebbets Field was at a night game on Monday, July 26. Thousands of fans, expecting the unexpected, were turned away. Just before the game, Durocher walked out onto the field to shake hands with Burt Shotton, who'd been called back once again to run the Dodgers. The ovation was mixed, with Durocher getting almost as many cheers as boos. The Giants mauled the Bums that night, 13–4.

As the season progressed it became clear that the Braves were hell-bent to make their half of Uncle Harry's prediction come true. They held onto first place through July and well into August. Then, quite by surprise, the Flock made a move and jumped into the lead. On Friday, September 4, just as things appeared to be going Brooklyn's way, the Dodgers collided with Leo's Giants. New York took both ends of a doubleheader that day and then came back the following afternoon to shut out the Bums, 3–0. Brooklyn managed to salvage the final game of the series, but it took a double by George "Shotgun" Shuba with two outs and the bases loaded in the twelfth inning to do it.

The Dodgers were suddenly two games back. On Labor Day the Braves swept a twin bill. That put the kibosh on the Dodgers' pennant hopes. They wound up the year in third place, a game behind the runner-up Cards and seven and a half in back of the Braves. I couldn't help but notice that in Boston Eddie Stanky had hit .320—the highest average of his career!

For the Yankees and Bucky Harris, 1948 was another disappointing year. Even though DiMaggio, playing in pain as usual, had what would prove to be his last great season, the flag fluttered from the Yanks' grasp. For a while it looked as though they would latch onto it down the stretch, but in the end they had to settle for a third-place finish, two and a half games back.

The pennant wasn't the only thing New York fans—and the entire world—lost. On August 16, Babe Ruth died. Not since President Roosevelt's death had the nation been so moved. Uncle Harry and I—Alex of course refused to come along—joined the thousands who traveled to Yankee Stadium to view the Babe's remains. I turned away from the catafalque and stared at the empty infield, where I had once been lucky enough to see Ruth, hat doffed, touring the basepaths.

Shortly after Cleveland defeated Boston in the first-ever playoff for the American League pennant, the Yankees fired Bucky Harris. "What the hell do they expect from the guy?" was the general reaction. But the Yankee brass contended Bucky was too easygoing, that instead of leading the team he followed it.

A few days later the Yankees announced their new manager. It was none other than Casey Stengel. He had sat out a year after leaving the Dodgers, had managed the Boston Braves for six years with meager luck, and had managed several minor league teams with somewhat better success.

During his lean years with the Braves—who were in the process of losing the World Series to the Indians even as Case was signing his Yankee contract—Stengel was struck by a car, breaking his leg and nearly crippling him. A Boston sportswriter nominated the driver as "the man who did the most for the Braves in 1943."

"Not only that," Casey said with a wink, "they said he could manage better'n me."

The baseball world had just lost a legendary figure in Ruth. Over the next twenty-seven years, Casey Stengel would gradually fill the vacant slot.

At the start of 1949, the Baseball Writers Association consensus picked the Red Sox and the Dodgers. Loyal Giant rooters, however, felt they had pretty good reason to believe that this was going to be New York's year.

The Giants appeared, at long last, to be developing a pitching staff. In addition to Jansen and Koslo they had a promising third starter in Sheldon "Available" Jones, who'd won sixteen and lost only eight. Now if only Monte Kennedy or Clint Hartung could come through. With decent pitching—so the argument went—the musclemen from Coogan's Bluff were bound to make a run for the money. Maybe, but maybe not.

As far as Durocher was concerned it just wasn't his kind of team. He'd already fired Ott's coaches—Travis Jackson and Hank Gowdy—and replaced them with two able practitioners of inside baseball—Freddie Fitzsimmons and Frankie Frisch. As the season got going, Leo, to the anguish of many Giant rooters (especially the Durocher haters), began fooling around with his lineup. He simply wasn't the kind of manager who could sit back and wait for home runs.

When, after a brief stay in first place in May, the Giants went into their annual June slide and fell into fifth place, Leo benched Mize, Buddy Kerr, Rigney, and Lockman. Walker Cooper was traded to the Reds, causing the veteran catcher to remark bitterly, "I've always felt Durocher would ruin any good ball club." To replace Cooper, the Giants called up Wes Westrum from Jersey City.

Later in the season the Giants got waivers on Mize and shipped him off to the Yankees. The Lip had no use at all for men who couldn't play the inside game.

Unfortunately, he didn't have very many hustlers or "bad guys" around to do the job. Fans looking to the future had their eyes on Monte Irvin and Hank Thompson, two black players who, it was hoped, would become the Giants' answer to Jackie Robinson and Roy Campanella.

But they were still unknown quantities. It was clear that if New York—which finished 1949 in fifth place, twenty-four games out—was to go after the pennant anytime soon, the club would have to trade for men who played the game in the Durocher style.

The most unbelievable thing about Leo in those days was that he was able to hold his job. Early in the 1949 season he got into another of his famous scrapes—this time with a Dodger fan named Fred Boysen, who accused the Lip of assaulting him.

The incident took place after a Giant–Dodger game at the Polo Grounds. The Giants were terrible that day—they lost, 15–2—and all afternoon Boysen heckled Durocher without mercy. As the game ended the teams began their long walk back to the clubhouse, and, as was customary in those days, the fans rushed out onto the field.

Boysen claimed to have been running out to shake Jackie Robinson's hand when Leo allegedly intercepted him and knocked him off his feet. When Happy Chandler heard the story he leaped into action like a goosed gazelle. He figured this was his chance to get rid of Durocher once and for all. Unfortunately for Happy, he couldn't find anyone to corroborate Boysen's story and was forced to drop the matter.

Still, it's amazing that Horace Stoneham stuck with Durocher. Leo was hardly the darling of the Giant fans, and here he was going through his Peck's Bad Boy act all over again. Perhaps Horace sensed that Leo was destined to bring the Giants to their greatest moment since the days of John McGraw.

Burt Shotton, meanwhile, was having problems of his own. One of the biggest sources of concern was the erratic pitching of Rex Barney. The year before, Rex, a fireballer who'd become famous for his wildness, appeared to have licked his control problem.

On September 9, 1948, he'd flirted with greatness by twirling a no-hitter against the Giants. But now Rex was slipping, and the strike zone was moving around on him like a duck in a shooting gallery. In May, to beef up his pitching staff, Shotton called up Don Newcombe from

Montreal. Newk, who with Campy formed the first black battery in the majors, worked wonders for the club. By the close of the season he would win seventeen and lose only eight.

The big trouble with the Bums that year was that one day they were great, the next day horrible. Still they managed to knock the Braves out of first place early in June, and they held onto the lead, however slimly, well into July. During the early going Brooklyn's old nemesis St. Louis appeared to be going nowhere. On May 23 the Redbirds were five games under .500, but then they began playing at a .700 clip, and by the start of August they'd overtaken the Bums. Speaking of the Cardinals, on July 24 Alex and I witnessed one of the most remarkable feats ever performed on a baseball diamond. Stan Musial hit for the cycle—he tripled, flied out, singled, homered, doubled, and walked in that order. The Redbirds won that ball game, 14–1.

In September, as I watched Brooklyn hang onto St. Louis's tail for dear life, I got this sudden *déjà vu* feeling. And then it hit me. The Cardinals and Dodgers were playing out the 1946 stretch drive all over again! The Redbirds held the lead from one day to the next, but they just couldn't manage to squirm out of the Dodgers' reach. The Flock was right there behind them, never more than two and a half lengths back.

All the other clubs were out of it. The two contenders were on a collision course. They were scheduled to meet in St. Louis on September 21 in a day-night doubleheader, and the next day they would play their final contest of the season against each other. The sportswriters, as they were wont to do, dubbed the three-game set the "little world series." The Cards were only one and a half games in front when the Dodgers arrived at Sportsman's Park.

I listened to Red Barber's description of the opening game with my father in the Web Café. Alex was helping himself to an occasional beer from behind the bar when the contest began. The opposing pitchers were Don Newcombe and Max Lanier, who, along with several other Tamale-Circuit jumpers, had recently received amnesty from Happy Chandler. For eight innings the two starters pitched flawlessly. When the Dodgers came to bat in the top of the ninth the game was still scoreless. By then Alex, who had taken to pouring himself shots of whisky around the sixth inning, was getting thoroughly skunked.

When Brooklyn failed to score in the top of the ninth, Pop poured himself a double. Enos Slaughter led off the Cardinal ninth. Big Don fired over two quick strikes, and his next pitch just nicked the edge of the strike zone. "Ball one," cried umpire Bill Stewart.

Newk grumbled in disgust. That ball had been in there. Slaughter then sliced the next pitch down the left-field line for a two-bagger. As the Dodger infield gathered around the mound, Jackie Robinson peered over to Stewart and gave him the "choke" sign, running his hand up and down his neck. When play resumed Newcombe gave Ron Northey an intentional pass. Bill Howerton then bunted down the third base line. The ball was on a foul trajectory when suddenly, as if possessed, it changed directions and rolled to a halt in fair territory.

Howerton had a single, and the bases were loaded. Again the Brooklyn infielders came to the mound, and again Robbie gave the ump the choke sign. This time Jackie was thrown out of the game and left the field to the accompaniment of raucous laughter and heckling from the St. Louis bench. Joe Garagiola then singled to end the ball game.

"Oh, shit," Alex grunted, slumping to the floor behind the bar. Luckily there were no customers in the place. I threw a glass of water in Pop's face, pulled him up on his feet, dragged him home, and put him to bed. It took me the better part of a half hour. When I got back to the Web there were three or four customers around wondering where the hell the bartender was. I took over behind the bar, served up beers on the house all around, and did my father's job until eight o'clock, when Willy, the night man, came in.

I stayed around to listen to the night game, which Brooklyn won on a dandy two-hitter by Preacher Roe. The next day, with Joe Hatten doing the hurling, the Bums won a laugher, 19–6. The Dodgers said goodby to the Cards for the season a mere half game out of first.

For the rest of September, I was on pins and needles and Alex was on the bottle. The Cardinals just wouldn't budge, but neither would they pull away and take us out of our misery. September 29 began with St. Louis a full game ahead of Brooklyn.

Up in Boston the Dodgers, going with Preach and Newk, took two easy games from the Braves, 9–2 and 8–0. The Redbirds, meanwhile, were in Pittsburgh, where they lost to the Bucs, 7–2, and dropped into second by a half game.

The next afternoon, while the Bums had an off day, the Cardinals lost to the Cubs, 6–5, to move a full game back. On October 1, both Brooklyn and St. Louis lost, assuring the Dodgers of a tie. On October 2, the last day of the season, the Cardinals snapped their four-game losing streak by walloping the Cubs, 13–5. In Philadelphia the Dodgers didn't have quite as easy a task. After nine innings the score was tied, 7–7. In the top of the tenth Reese singled, Eddie Miksis sacrificed him along, and Snider singled up the middle to drive in the go-ahead run. Robinson, the new batting champ of the National League, got a free ticket to first. Louis Olmo, another returnee from the Mexican League, then knocked in the Duke with a single to make the score 9–7. Carl Furillo hit into a double play to end the rally. Brooklyn held the Phils in check in the bottom of the ninth to give Burt Shotton his second pennant in three seasons.

All Brooklyn went wild. There was dancing in the streets. Flatbush Avenue, from the Long Island Railroad Station to the Brooklyn Paramount, was one long conga line. Pop and I went downtown to join in the fun. We hit at least a dozen saloons. At the Dodger Tavern on De-Kalb Avenue a curvaceous lass named Maura, who had long red hair and a mild case of buck teeth, gave me a warm, happy hug and invited me to take her home. I had to pass it up. I couldn't leave Alex alone.

My fears turned out to be well founded. On the way into the subway he fell down the stairs, spraining his ankle and busting his nose. When we got home Mom was beside herself. She didn't know whether to treat her drunken, battered husband with pity or anger. She dressed his wounds and cried herself to sleep.

In the spring of 1949, Casey Stengel had surprised his new charges by greeting them with the announcement that he would spend the year observing and learning the American League. He wouldn't, Casey vowed, even give signals; the team was on its own.

Stengel may not have known the American League, but there was one thing he did know—fundamentals. His well-organized training camp focused on these. While Casey was drilling the team in base running, cutoff plays, and other basics, coach Bill Dickey was trying to make Yogi Berra into a catcher—"learning me his experiences," as Berra later put it.

Berra was a notorious bad-ball hitter. Bobby Brown said of him, "Yogi has the biggest strike zone in the U.S. It goes from his ankles to his nose, and from his breastbone as far out as he can reach." In spite of his lack of selectivity, Berra was already an established slugger. But there were few who thought he would ever make the grade behind the plate.

As the regular season approached, the team suffered a serious setback. DiMaggio, who'd made history by signing baseball's first $100,000-a-year contract, was to go under the knife. There had been an off-season operation on the bone spur that had been troubling him, but the incision hadn't healed properly. Joe was in more pain than ever. With only days remaining in the preseason, DiMaggio checked into John Hopkins.

Shortly after the campaign opener, George Stirnweiss was injured. Stengel put rookie Jerry Coleman at second and received a pleasant surprise when Coleman proved to be a natural, a perfect match for virtuoso Phil Rizzuto at short. Suddenly the Yankees had one of the best double-play combinations in baseball.

The team jumped to an early lead behind the slugging of Tommy Henrich, who had assumed the leadership role in DiMaggio's absence. But the Red Sox stayed right with them, as they would throughout the year.

In late June the teams squared off for a three-game series in Fenway. Besides being a crucial series between two great rivals, there was something else special about the event—DiMaggio was back. The Yankee Clipper, out of shape but relatively pain-free for the first time, won over

358

even the Boston fans as he hit four home runs, scored five, and drove in nine. The Yanks swept the series.

The Red Sox did not toss in the towel. In August they surged, and by the time the season was down to the final two contests they held a one-game lead. Those two final games were between the Yankees and the Red Sox.

In a similar series the year before, the Sox had knocked the Yanks out of the race. This time the Yankees had the home-field advantage. But it also looked as though they would be playing without DiMaggio, who had been in the hospital with pneumonia.

When, on that cool Saturday in September, Allie Reynolds threw his first pitch, Joe D. was in center field. Thin and pale, his mere presence was an uplift to the team. Behind brilliant relief pitching by Joe Page and a homer by Johnny Lindell, the Yankees won the game, 5–4. The next day Vic Raschi survived a three-run ninth inning for a 5–3 victory. Casey Stengel, in his first year with the Yanks, had surprised everybody by winning the pennant.

Alex, in bed with two black eyes, his nose stuffed with cotton, was sure the Bums would win it all. "Remember those exhibition games right before the season?" he asked me. "We beat the stuffing out of 'em three times in a row. Robinson'll steal their jock straps. They can't touch us."

Uncle Harry had a different view when I, unknown to Pop, went to the first game with him. "Pitching," he said, "it'll all come down to pitching."

Grudgingly, I had to admit he was probably right. Two months before the end of the season someone had asked Shotton who would be his first three World Series pitchers should the Dodgers win the pennant. "Newcombe . . . er, Newcombe, and, er, did I mention Newcombe?"

Sure enough, Don Newcombe faced Allie Reynolds in the opener. It was a muggy afternoon, and the crowd was unbelievably quiet. They sat under the threatening sky and watched in near silence as the two hurlers pitched scoreless ball for almost two and a half hours.

Old Reliable Tommy Henrich led off the last of the ninth. He looked at two balls and then parked a low curve into the right-field stands. Newcombe was nearly to the dugout when the ball disappeared into the crowd. He had never looked after Henrich's swing.

"Don't tell your old man I said so, Damon," Uncle Harry said as we made our way out of the park, "but we've got you where we want you. Stengel got something he didn't expect—a full game out of Reynolds. We've got Page rested, and we've got Raschi rested and ready to go tomorrow. We just beat your best man. You'll never beat ours."

I gritted my teeth. "Wait'll we get you in Flatbush," I said, trying to sound confident.

The next day the weather was better, and so was the Dodgers' luck.

Preacher Roe, whom Red Smith of the *Herald Tribune* described as an "angular, drawling splinter of gristle," beat Vic Raschi in a brilliant pitching battle, 1–0. It was the first time the Yankees had been shut out in Yankee Stadium in 156 games.

In the third game Yank pitcher Tommy Byrne nailed Pee Wee Reese in the leg with his first pitch. Pee Wee responded by belting a homer in the fourth to tie the game at 1–1. It stayed that way to the ninth, at which point rain began to fall and the Yankees began to fill the bases. With two out and the bases full, Stengel sent Big Jawn Mize up as a pinch hitter. With the count 2–1, Mize hit a drive off the right-field screen; Furrillo caught the rebound and rifled it in, but two runs scored. Coleman followed with a single, and the score was 4–1, Yankees.

In the Dodger ninth, Olmo and Campanella homered off Page, who up till then had been untouchable in relief of Byrne. But Page rared back and hummed his fastball through the raindrops to strike out Bruce Edwards and win the game. Dodger starter Ralph Branca had walked a total of four; three of them scored.

Trailing in the Series, 2–1, Shotton sent out Newcombe with only two days' rest. But Newk could go no farther than the fourth, and when the Dodgers came up with four runs in the sixth it was too late. The final score was 6–4, and the Dodgers were in big trouble.

The fifth and last game of the Series was finished under the arclights of Ebbets Field, a World Series first. The Flatbush Faithful would have preferred darkness. From the time Rex Barney needed thirty-seven pitches to get out of the first inning, they had little to cheer about. The Yankees went through six Dodger pitchers en route to a 10–4 victory.

That same fall I entered New York University law school. I had, by taking extra credits and attending summer school, finished college a year early. Even though I had appreciated Uncle Harry's generosity, I was eager to stand on my own feet. Rather than ask for any further subsidies, I took a job as a part-time night clerk in a Times Square hotel.

During the spring of 1950 Harry Grayson, a writer for Newspaper Enterprise Association, toured the Grapefruit Circuit to file stories on each of the major league teams. At the Phillies' camp Harry was impressed by the hustle and spirit displayed by a squad that included Eddie Waitkus, Granny Hamner, Del Ennis, Richie Ashburn, Dick Sisler, Andy Seminick, Robin Roberts, and Curt Simmons. In his writeup Grayson dubbed them the Whiz Kids—a nickname that began to stick when the club surprised everyone by making a serious bid for the National League flag.

By the All-Star break the Phillies were in the thick of a race that also included the Braves, the Cards, and the Dodgers. Philadelphia's success was the result of superb pitching. In addition to Roberts and Simmons the club had a dependable third starter in Bob Miller. It also had the National League's most sensational reliever in many a season—a bespectacled fellow named Jim Konstanty. At the midway point of the race Jim had already appeared in thirty-three games. He would, by the end of the year, go to the mound seventy-four times, win sixteen while losing seven, rack up twenty-two saves, and compile an ERA of 2.66. Everyone called him a junk pitcher, a charge that Konstanty himself would not deny.

If pitching was the strength of the Phils, it was surely the Dodgers' biggest weakness. Roe and Newcombe were pretty much it. Carl Erskine had still not come into his own, and neither had Clem Labine, a reliever who had appeared in sixty-three games at St. Paul in 1949, setting an American Association record.

The Giants were another story. Over the winter, in a trade that enraged many New York fans, Durocher had sent Buddy Kerr, Sid Gordon, Willard Marshall, and a mediocre pitcher named Sam Webb to the Braves. In return the Giants got Eddie Stanky and Alvin Dark for second and short.

Leo had the kind of team he'd been looking for. As he later put it, "from that time on we had a tight infield—which improved our pitching one hundred percent—and we had two guys who could do things with a bat, could run the bases and who came to kill you." The Giants also got back Sal Maglie from the Mexican League that year. By July "The Barber" had worked his way into the starting rotation.

During the early months of the season the club looked like anything but a contender, but in the closing weeks, when all of Leo's new pieces began fitting together, the wisdom of his reconstruction program became obvious.

Looking back on the 1950 campaign, I find it impossible to separate it from the season that followed. It sticks in my mind as a kind of prelude to the disaster of 1951. I'm sure part of it has to do with my own state of mind at the time—those two years were a particularly depressing period in my own life. In June of 1950 I flunked out of law school. So many years have passed that it's hard to remember exactly why I failed. I can remember studying at the kitchen table for hours and hours. Mother, before going to bed, would brew me a fresh pot of coffee. But despite these efforts my performance in the classroom was abysmal, and when my first year was over I received my walking papers.

If you were able to ask my mother she would tell you the reason for my failure was Marilyn. I had the misfortune of being in law school and in love at the same time. I met her at a New Year's party in Brooklyn Heights. The host was a friend of a friend; by midnight the people I'd come with had disappeared, leaving me to ring out the forties and ring in the fifties alone, in an apartment full of strangers. Suddenly, a few seconds after midnight, I found myself kissing a beautiful, dark-haired girl two inches taller than I.

"My date just up-chucked all over the kitchen floor," she told me when our lips parted. "What a pig. Hi, my name's Marilyn. What's yours?"

She, too, lived in Bay Ridge, but several blocks from my house. I can't tell you how stunning she was. Her father was Lithuanian and her mother Swedish. It was a striking combination. She was eighteen, a freshman at Brooklyn College. We danced to three or four records, and then I offered to take her home.

She was delighted to get out of there. When we got to her neighborhood I took her into Oscar's, a cavernous bar where a Dixieland band was playing the "Basin Street Blues." We didn't say much; we spoke with our eyes. By the time I pecked her on the cheek and said goodnight I was hopelessly in love.

I don't remember spending an extraordinary amount of time with Marilyn that spring, but even when we weren't together she occupied most of my thoughts. A few weeks after NYU Law and I parted company Marilyn and a girl friend drove out to California for the summer. I never saw her again.

What a miserable summer! I spent most of my afternoons moping around the Web drinking beer with Alex and watching the Dodgers on TV. By August I'd gained twenty pounds and lost all interest in baseball. The Phillies appeared to have everything going for them, while the Dodgers, though in second place, were playing lackluster ball. Branch Rickey publicly accused his players of "satiety and complacency." I went through the motions of following the season to its conclusion, but my heart wasn't in it.

Despite the Dodgers' listlessness, there were a few remarkable personal efforts. On August 31 Gil Hodges hit four straight home runs in a nine-inning game against the Braves. On September 6 Don Newcombe beat the Phils, 2–0, in the opening game of a doubleheader, and then came right back to pitch seven innings of the nightcap. He was taken out for a pinch hitter with the score 2–0 in favor of Philadelphia. The Dodgers went on to win, 3–2. It's a shame Newk wasn't able to hang in there. He might have become the first pitcher in a quarter-century to win both ends of a twin bill singlehandedly.

By September 19 Brooklyn had dropped into third place, nine games back and only a half-game ahead of the red hot Giants. I was more worried about falling below Durocher's men in the standings than I was about not winning the pennant. With only seventeen games to play, Brooklyn didn't have a chance of catching Philadelphia. That day the Flock took a pair from the Pirates while the Phillies lost to the Cubs, cutting their lead to seven and a half games. That was all very nice, but it didn't do much to raise my already faded hopes.

On September 23 Branch Rickey announced he was selling his 25 percent of the Dodger stock to real-estate tycoon William Zeckendorf. Rumor had it the Mahatma would be moving on to the Pirates.

The next day Brooklyn pitcher Erv Palica hit a grand-slam home run and hurled a two-hitter to beat the Phillies, 11–0. The Dodgers were now five games out.

On September 27 the Bums split a twin bill with Boston while the Giants took two from the Whiz Kids, reducing Philadelphia's advantage to four. The next day the same thing happened—the Dodgers and Braves split, while the Phils bowed twice to New York. Now the margin was only three, but time was running out. With three days to go the standings looked like this:

	W	L	Pct	GB
Philadelphia	90	62	.592	—
Brooklyn	86	64	.573	3
New York	84	68	.553	6

As Dick Young of the *News* put it, "All that stands between the Brooks and the stigma of 'ex-champs' is any combination of 1." But that afternoon in Brooklyn, while the Phils were idle, the Dodgers took two from the Braves, closing the gap to two games. The next afternoon the Whiz Kids moved into Ebbets Field for the final weekend of the year. The Dodgers won the Saturday game, 7–3. If they could repeat on Sunday they'd force Philadelphia into a playoff.

Alex and I had seats in back of the screen behind home plate for that ball game. We hadn't been to Ebbets Field together for some time and wouldn't have gone that day had we not followed every step of the Dodgers' amazing comeback listening to the radio and watching TV together in the Web Café.

During batting practice I looked over at my father. I couldn't help but remember how tall and proud and handsome he'd been when, fifteen years earlier, he'd taken me to this nutty old ball park for the first time. Alex was approaching sixty. His spirit had started to leave him long ago. But he still could get excited over a hot pennant race, and this one hadn't required much energy at all. Only two days ago the Dodgers had been dead ducks; now they were on the verge of one of the most amazing comebacks in baseball history. "If Brooklyn wins, there won't be a comeback to match this one for years," I told Alex confidently.

The opposing pitchers were Newcombe and Roberts. Both had excellent stuff; they mowed down the opposition with popping fastballs, and after five innings there was still no score. The Phils got on the board first with a run in the top of the sixth. In the bottom half of the same inning Pee Wee Reese sliced the ball into right field; it hit the screen about five feet inside the foul line, dropped down to the top of the wall above the Esquire Boot Polish sign, and stayed there. The ball was still in play, so Pee Wee laughed his way around the bases for a weird inside-the-park home run to tie the game. The proceedings were suddenly halted when a young boy, to the great amusement of the crowd, edged his way out onto the wall and retrieved the ball.

The score was still tied going into the Dodger half of the ninth. Cal Abrams, who had made a great catch to rob Puddin' Head Jones of an extra-base hit in the Phillies' half of the inning, led off with a walk. Then Reese singled to center, moving Cal to second.

Abrams was a pretty fast man. The Phils were expecting a bunt, but Snider, the next batter, singled to shallow center. Milt Stock, the third base coach, gave Abrams the green light. He rounded third as Ashburn wheeled and threw to the plate. Cal was out by a mile.

"Jeezus," Alex moaned. "Stock should *never* have brought him in. We'da had Robinson coming up with the bases loaded, no place to put him. Now he gets an intentional pass." Which is exactly what he got. Furillo then fouled out on the first pitch and Hodges sent a fly to right that Ennis caught up with a few steps in front of the scoreboard.

In the tenth Dick Sisler hit a towering home run into the left-field seats with two men aboard to win the game and give the Phillies their first pennant in thirty-five years. And Robin Roberts, by defeating New-combe, became the Phils' first twenty-game winner since Grover Cleveland Alexander won thirty-one in 1917.

Pop and I could afford to be philosophical. After all, the Dodgers' shot at the pennant really had come out of the blue.

"Too bad we had to lose this one," Pop said to me as we walked through Charlie Ebbets's rotunda, "but what the hell—next year, with a little extra pitching, we'll win by at least ten games."

It would be the Yankees against the Phils in the World Series. From the beginning of the season, when the Yanks were given little chance to repeat, Stengel had made it clear that his apprenticeship was over and that he planned to take firm hold of the reins.

He had three promising youngsters in Billy Martin, Joe Collins, and Jackie Jensen—and it was youth that Casey's plans revolved around. Old Reliable Tommy Henrich's knees forced him to retire during the season, and before the campaign was through Casey would trade away veterans Johnny Lindell and Snuffy Stirnweiss.

On opening day the Yankees proved they had the bats. Trailing the Red Sox, 9–0, they stormed back to win it, 15–10. And by midsummer, when a rookie left-hander Ed "Whitey" Ford joined Raschi, Lopat, Reynolds, and Byrne on the mound staff, it was evident that the Yanks had the pitching to go with the bats.

In the World Series it was the pitching that was dominant. Raschi,

Reynolds, Lopat, and Ford required fewer than two innings' worth of relief help as they held the opposing batters to a total of six runs. The Yanks whizzed by the Whiz Kids in four straight.

On October 24, 1950, Walter O'Malley announced that he and Mrs. John L. Smith (who'd been widowed the previous July) had arranged to purchase the Dodger stock that Branch Rickey had offered to William Zeckendorf. When John Smith, Rickey, and O'Malley had combined forces to buy out the Ebbets heirs, they agreed that if one of them later wanted to sell his stock, the other two had the right to match any outside offer.

Rickey, who'd paid $350,000 for his shares back in 1945, wanted a cool million now. Zeckendorf had agreed to pay the price. O'Malley, who'd come to resent Rickey for a variety of reasons, hit the roof when he learned that Branch had found a buyer willing to pay such a huge sum. The last thing Walter wanted was for an outsider to come in and once again split the Dodger ownership into two equal factions. So he swallowed his pride and arranged to meet Rickey's price. The Mahatma's money would be paid to him over ten years, and O'Malley, with Mrs. Smith's consent, would have absolute control over the club.

Two days later, at a press conference at the Hotel Bossert in Brooklyn, Branch Rickey announced his "resignation." He then introduced O'Malley as the new Dodger president. Rickey would indeed be moving on to Pittsburgh, where his old friend John Galbreath, owner of the Pirates, had invited him to try to work his magic with the worst ball club in the National League.

A month later the new Dodger president announced that Burt Shotton, a Rickey man if there ever was one, had been replaced by none other than Charles Dressen. Clearly, the Dodgers were on the eve of a new era.

The Dodgers were not the only New York team embarking on a new path in 1951. On opening day, when number 5 trotted out to center field, DiMadge could look over toward right and see twenty-four-year-old Jackie Jensen. On his other side was another kid, a nineteen-year-old rookie named Mickey Mantle.

Mantle had come through Casey Stengel's first "instructural" school, as had two other members of that day's lineup—infielder Gil McDougald and pitcher Tom Morgan. Because of his blazing speed and awesome ability to hit the ball out of sight from either side of the plate, Yankee fans were already expecting miracles from the kid.

It was DiMaggio's last year. After the Yankees had clinched the pennant with Big Chief Allie Reynolds's second no-hitter of the season, after they had won yet another world championship, the Yankee Clipper would announce his retirement. When asked why, he would say, "Because I no longer have it."

I had this queasy feeling all through the summer of 1951. That final game of 1950 kept haunting me—reinforcing my belief that the Bums were choke artists. I ignored the fact that had it not been for a minor miracle Brooklyn would never have been in a position to tie the Whiz Kids in the first place. So now, even when the Dodgers began building up what appeared to be an insurmountable lead, I wasn't able to feel confident.

The story of the Giants' amazing surge is the most famous of all baseball legends. It need not be belabored here. In any case, I don't have the stomach for every painful detail. Most fans who remember that season would agree that New York would never have caught Brooklyn had it not been for Leo's artful juggling of the Giant lineup and his timely call-up of Willie Mays.

In May, after a terrible start that included an eleven-game losing streak, Lippy brought Whitey Lockman out of the outfield and put him on first. Monte Irvin, who'd been playing first poorly and whose batting had suffered accordingly, was sent into the outfield where he belonged. Shortly after the Lockman-Irvin shift Durocher got Horace Stoneham's permission to bring up Mays from Minneapolis, where he was batting .477. Willie was immediately installed in center field.

At first, he had a bad time adjusting to major league pitching. On June 2 he was batting .038. But Leo knew his rookie outfielder was a natural and stuck with him. Three weeks later his average was up to .316. He would end up the year batting .274, and would drive in sixty-eight runs and hit twenty homers.

The Dodgers also had a trick or two up their sleeve. On June 15 they announced one of the most sensational trades in recent years. They acquired Andy Pafko, one of the big stars in the league, from the Cubs in a trade that sent Joe Hatten, Bruce Edwards, Eddie Miksis, and Gene Hermanski to Chicago and brought Pafko, pitcher Johnny Schmitz, catcher Al "Rube" Walker, and infielder Wayne Terwilliger to Brooklyn. Andy, a center fielder with the Cubs, was put in left by Charlie Dressen. The Dodgers, with Pafko, Snider, and Furillo, now had the best outfield in the majors.

Dressen had finally filled a position that had been a problem since the departure of Pete Reiser. At the time I figured the Cubs must have had a few screws loose, giving up one of their best for a bunch of benchwarmers. Only later, when the bottom fell out, did I decide that the trade had been of dubious value. To get Pafko, who batted only .249 that year in Brooklyn, the Dodgers had seriously weakened their bench. Had Dressen kept right on platooning Abrams and Hermanski in left, Brooklyn might just have picked up the one extra win that would have given them the flag.

On July 4 Brooklyn took both ends of the traditional holiday double-header with New York. After the second game Charlie Dressen boasted, "The Giants are through. Those two beatings we gave them knocked them out of it. They'll never recover. They'll never bother us again."

"We'll show 'em yet," Durocher proclaimed, as he did some more juggling. Hank Thompson was sent down temporarily to Ottawa, leaving a gap at third base. Leo installed Bobby Thomson at the hot corner, and the former outfielder's slumping bat suddenly came alive.

Meanwhile, the Giant pitching staff was coming into its own. Durocher had three superb starters in Maglie, Jansen, and Jim Hearn. Dave Koslo and Sheldon Jones were backup starters who also pulled relief duty, and George Spencer was the mainstay of the bullpen. As I observed Leo's manipulations I was forced to admit New York had a fine ball club. Its pitching was probably better than Brooklyn's, even if the Dodgers were far superior in fielding and hitting. The large gap Brooklyn was opening up in the standings was out of all proportion to reality.

The Giants bottomed out on August 11. At the Polo Grounds they lost to the Phillies, 4–0, while over at Ebbets Field the Dodgers took the first game of a doubleheader, 8–1. The Bums' lead was briefly thirteen and a half games, but they lost the nightcap, 8–4. The next morning the standings of the first division looked like this:

	W	L	Pct	GB
Brooklyn	70	36	.660	—
New York	59	51	.536	13
Philadelphia	57	52	.523	14½
St. Louis	51	52	.495	17½

"It looks like we're in," Alex told me over breakfast that Sunday morning. "If the Brooks play five-hundred ball the rest of the way, they'll win ninety-four games—three more than the Phils won last year. The way everybody else is going, the pennant would be in the bag."

The Bums would do better than that. Their winning percentage for the remainder of the season would be .522.

The night of August 13 was one of the zaniest in the history of Ebbets Field. Walter O'Malley dubbed the evening "Music Appreciation Night." Every fan appearing with a musical instrument was admitted free. More than two thousand "musicians" showed up with instruments ranging from cymbals and drums to violins and zithers. I made a sad mistake that evening—I dragged Pop out to the ball park. From a friend I borrowed a trombone for myself and a guitar for Alex. Along with the rest of the instrument-bearers we were given seats in the upper deck in left field.

I can't tell you how nerve shattering it was. To our left was a Dixieland band playing "The Darktown Strutters Ball." To the right was a Boy Scout troop blaring out classy numbers such as "Reveille" and

"Come 'n Get Your Beans, Boys." Everywhere there was banging and blowing and discordant strumming. When the players took the field they were white with horror. By the second inning Alex had had enough. "Let's go home," he shouted over the cacophony, "if I don't get outa here I'm gonna be cold stone deaf in the market."

So we left. The Dodgers beat the Braves that night, 7–6.

The Dodgers' demise commenced the following night. They invaded the Polo Grounds for three games and lost the opener, 4–2. The next afternoon Alex and I, who watched the second game of the series on TV, saw one of the most unbelievable plays of all time.

The score was tied, 1–1, in the top of the eighth. One man was out. Billy Cox was on third and Ralph Branca was at first. Batting against Jim Hearn was Carl Furillo. Carl sent a drive to deep right center that Willie Mays dashed after and hauled in going away to rob Furillo of extra bases.

As Cox tagged up and darted homeward, Willie, in one sleek motion, spun around and fired off balance toward the plate. Whitey Lockman, the cutoff man, ducked out of the way of the ball, which arrived in Wes Westrum's mitt in plenty of time to tag out a bewildered Billy Cox.

"Jesus," I groaned. "All the Giant fans ever talk about these days is Willie Mays. Now I know why."

Willie singled to lead off the bottom of the inning, and then Wes Westrum homered. The Giants held on to win the ball game, 3–1.

The next afternoon Brooklyn lost to New York again, 2–1. In five days the Bums' lead had been shaved to nine and a half games. Rud Rennie, writing in the *Herald Tribune*, observed, "Now the Dodgers' lead is even less than it was in 1942 at this time. That was one of the years they did not win the pennant. It could be they are getting ready to blow another one on the final day of the season."

That summer I was preoccupied not only with the fortunes of the Dodgers but with my own rather bleak fortunes as well. I'd been bumming around for more than a year, and I was completely disgusted. Now that I was no longer a student, I was subject to the draft. If called, I would more than likely be sent off to fight in the Korean War.

In August I was ordered to report to the Army Induction Center on Whitehall Street for my physical. It didn't exactly come as a surprise when I was classified 1–A. Before long I received my draft notice. My two years of active duty would begin on Monday, October 8, 1951.

Over the next two weeks the Giants extended their winning streak to sixteen while chopping the Bums' lead down to five games. Alex and I were both scared stiff.

During the early part of September things settled down. The Giants were still playing way over their heads, but the Dodgers, back on the winning track, managed to keep their five-game advantage intact.

Then, in the next-to-last week of the campaign, New York chipped two more games off Brooklyn's lead. I went into a panic. I couldn't sleep, I couldn't eat, I couldn't think. All I could do was sit around wiping my palms.

The Dodgers were in a panic too. As Roy Campanella later described the situation, "We were playing tight and nervous baseball, looking over our shoulder and watching the scoreboard to see how the Giants were doing."

Tuesday, September 25, was the day Brooklyn blew its last chance to wrap up the flag. The Dodgers lost two to the Braves, while New York defeated the Phils in a single contest. The Giants were now only one game behind.

On Thursday, while the Giants had an off day, the Bums played their getaway game in Boston. It was tied, 3–3, in the bottom of the eighth when, with Bob Addis on third and Sam Jethroe at first, Earl Torgeson grounded to Robinson. Jackie fired to Campanella. To this day Campy swears he put the tag on Addis, who came rushing in from third on the play.

"Safe!" yelled plate umpire Frank Dascoli.

Campy went berserk. His protest was so violent that Dascoli thumbed him out of the game. Then he cleared the entire Dodger bench except for Charlie Dressen and coach Jake Pitler. The run cost Brooklyn the ball game. Later, in the clubhouse, several of the Dodgers kicked the door of the umpires' dressing room and cursed Dascoli. For their part in the incident Robinson and Campanella were fined $100 each and Preacher Roe was penalized $50. Even worse, the Dodgers' lead was now only a half game.

The following afternoon in Philadelphia the Bums lost their second 4–3 game in two days. Once again the Giants were idle. The race was all tied up. New York and Brooklyn each had two games left to play. How much more of this could I be expected to take?

The next day both teams won. The race was down to the final afternoon of the season. Alex, unable to bear up under the strain, drank himself into a stupor that morning to escape the agony. He knew in his heart the Bums were going to lose.

In Boston Larry Jansen snuffed out a ninth-inning rally to win, 3–2, and ensure the Giants no less than a tie.

Meanwhile, Connie Desmond's and Red Barber's radio account of the game in Shibe Park went from bad to worse as the afternoon wore on. Neither Preacher Roe, nor Ralph Branca, nor Clyde King could contain the Phils. Going into the eighth Philadelphia was ahead, 8–5, and I knew the long season was finally over. In a way I was relieved to be out of my misery.

Miraculously, Brooklyn came back with three runs in the eighth. I pulled myself back together and forced myself to hope for the impossible. Don Newcombe, always called upon in Brooklyn's most trying moments, was brought in to save the day. The game went into extra innings.

In the twelfth the Phils loaded the bases with two out. I stood up and began pacing the living room floor. More than once I was tempted to turn off the radio. Eddie Waitkus came to the plate and ran the count to 3 and 2; then he drilled Newk's pitch toward center. The game should have been over. But then, as if lifted to the spot where the ball was destined to hit the ground, Jackie Robinson made a diving catch to end the inning and save the Dodgers' ass. I groaned with relief.

Two innings later Robinson, batting against Robin Roberts, powered the ball into the left-field stands to give Brooklyn a one-run advantage. I held my breath while Bud Podbielan put away the Phillies in the bottom of the fourteenth to ensure the Dodger victory. I went to the kitchen and took a swig of Pop's whisky. Then I woke Alex up and told him the news. He went out and got drunk all over again.

It was all very weird. In one month the Dodgers had been transformed from swaggering favorites into cowering underdogs. Now they faced the formidable task of reversing the Giants' supernatural momentum in a three-game playoff series. Alex and I didn't believe they could do it.

Rather than witness the Bums' demise in the flesh, we decided to watch the first two games of the playoff on TV. When Brooklyn lost the opening contest, 3–1, at Ebbets Field, we once again pronounced our boys dead. But the next afternoon Clem Labine started for the Dodgers and pitched beautifully. The Flock gave Durocher's men a 10–0 shellacking and tied up the series at a game apiece.

Was there now reason to hope? Pop and I weren't sure, but when we woke up the next morning—October 3, 1951—we knew that, despite the gloomy skies overhead, we had an appointment at Coogan's Bluff. Anticipating a turnaway crowd, we arrived at the Polo Grounds three hours before game time. Surprisingly, there were fifteen thousand empty seats when Sal Maglie threw his first pitch to leadoff batter Carl Furillo. Only 34,320 fans were on hand for the most unbelievable baseball game ever played.

Two things had me worried. First, Roy Campanella was out of action with a charley horse. Rube Walker, the second-string catcher, was a competent man, but he was no Campy. The day before Rube had contributed to the 10–0 rout with three hits. His luck had to be running out.

The other big question mark was Don Newcombe. Over the previous weekend Newk had started on Saturday night and then come back the next afternoon to hurl six innings in relief. Working now with only two days' rest, Big Don had to be tired. I didn't see how he possibly could go nine innings.

In the first inning Maglie, after retiring Furillo, walked Reese and Snider. Robinson then cracked a single to left to bring in Pee Wee with the first run of the day. The Giants might have tied it up in the second had it not been for a bonehead maneuver by one Bobby Thomson. With one out Whitey Lockman singled to right. Up came Thomson, who drilled the ball off the left-field wall. Certain his hit was good for extra bases, Bobby put down his head, barreled around first, and headed for second. It wasn't until he was almost there that he looked up to discover that Lockman still occupied the bag. Thomson was tagged out trying to scamper back to first, and the Dodgers got out of the inning unscathed.

At 2:04, just before the start of the third inning, the sky became so dark that the lights were turned on. Under the burning arcs Maglie and Newcombe pitched four more innings of scoreless baseball. Then, in the bottom of the seventh, New York got even when Monte Irvin doubled, reached third on a bunt by Lockman, and came home on a towering sacrifice fly to center off Thomson's bat. It was the first run off Newcombe in twenty-one and two-thirds innings.

The Dodgers quickly dispelled their fans' anxiety. In the top of the eighth, after Furillo struck out, Reese and Snider got back-to-back singles. Up came Jackie Robinson with runners at first and third. Maglie, desperately trying to prevent Robbie from pulling the ball, dished up a succession of breaking balls. Finally one of them broke into the dirt and rolled back to the screen, allowing Reese to dash in with the tie-breaking run. On the play the Duke raced all the way to third.

Leo then ordered Maglie to put Robinson on. The Giants were hoping to get the next batter, Andy Pafko, to hit into a double play. Instead Andy hit a grounder down the third base line that Thomson knocked down but could not retrieve in time to make a put out. Snider came home with the second run of the inning, and Pafko was credited with a single. The Dodger fans in the crowd were in a frenzy.

"We've got those bastards now!" Alex screamed as a vendor sold him another can of beer.

Gil Hodges, who couldn't get a hit off Maglie if his life depended on it, followed with a pop-up for out number two. But the next hitter, Billy Cox, drilled the ball sharply toward third. Thomson lunged helplessly and watched it go by him into left as Robinson came in with the third and final tally of the inning.

The Giants went down one-two-three in the bottom of the eighth. For the first time in over a month I began to relax, savoring Brooklyn's forthcoming victory. Beside me Alex wore a carefree, confident smile. We were in. We couldn't have cared less when Larry Jansen came in in the ninth and put the Dodgers down in order. We had a 4–1 lead with only three outs to go.

New York's first batter in the ninth was Al Dark, who singled to right. Then Hodges mysteriously held Dark close to the bag, as if one more Giant run really mattered. Gil's strange tactic allowed Don Mueller to smash another single through the gap that he should have been covering.

Now there were runners at first and third. While Charlie Dressen was cursing himself for not positioning his first baseman properly, the Giant fans were on their feet screaming for a miracle. My heart, and Alex's too, began thumping madly all over again. Shit. Monte Irvin, who was making his way to the plate, represented the tying run.

As Leo yelled encouragement to Irvin, Dressen went to the mound to talk to Big Don. Charlie had Branca and Labine working in the bullpen, but if at all possible he wanted to stay with his best. So after a short pep talk Dressen returned to the dugout and crossed his fingers as Newk got ready to pitch. Alex gave out a contented belch when Irvin fouled out to Hodges. Leo's hopes to get the tying run on now rested upon the shoulders of Whitey Lockman.

Whitey jumped on the exhausted Newcombe and doubled to left, bringing in Dark with the Giants' second run of the afternoon. Now the score was 4–2. Mueller, sliding awkwardly into third, twisted his ankle and had to be removed for a pinch runner.

The air in the Polo Grounds pulsated with tension. Dressen called in Ralph Branca to get the final two outs. Leo sent Clint Hartung in to run for Mueller at third. Then we all waited while Ralph took his final warmup pitches and the stretcher-bearers carried Mueller to the clubhouse in center field. Alex and I didn't say a word as we sat through an eternity waiting for Thomson, the next batter, to move up to the plate.

The thought of Branca coming in to save the day didn't exactly bowl me over with confidence. Precisely five years earlier Ralph had lost the opening game of the Dodgers' disastrous 1946 playoff with the Cardinals. Two days ago he'd lost the first game of this playoff.

I tried to second-guess Charlie Dressen. How should he pitch to Thomson? First base was open. Bobby was the leading home-run slugger on the Giants. He'd already tagged Branca for a four-bagger in game one of the playoff series. Maybe the way to play it was to put him on and pitch to Willie Mays. Young Willie hadn't had a hit all day. There was a fair chance he'd choke, coming to bat in the ninth with the weight of the world on his shoulders. Then I realized Charlie wasn't about to put the winning run on. Bucky Harris had done that in the 1947 Series and would never live it down.

As Thomson came to bat he was sulking about his horrible afternoon. He saw himself as the "guy who flubbed for the old man." If it hadn't been for his lousy baserunning in the second and his lackluster fielding in the eighth, he might not be in this situation now. The Giants might already have won it.

Branca's first delivery was a sharp curve that broke down and inside for a called strike.

Later that day Bobby remembered the next pitch as "a bad ball, high and inside." As the ball left Thomson's bat I said to Alex, "Oh *no!* Extra innings." From our vantage point in the upper deck behind first base Alex and I both thought the ball was going to carom off the left-field wall. Instead it gained altitude as it went and sailed into the lower grandstand with only five inches to spare.

Silence.

It took several seconds for the crowd—Giant rooters and Flatbush Faithful alike—to comprehend what had happened.

A tremendous roar came out of the Polo Grounds. It shook the foundations of Yankee Stadium on the opposite bank of the Harlem River. Alex and I were thrown into shock. We couldn't pull ourselves out of our seats. Delirious Giant fans swarmed onto the field below, creating a panorama of jubilation. The Dodgers had all disappeared.

Half an hour later the ball park was still a madhouse. I finally summoned enough energy to pull my father up and lead him out. Alex wouldn't be able to talk about what had happened that day until long after the World Series was over.

The Dodgers of 1953—not the pitching
staff but the eight men in the field—can
be put forth as the most gifted baseball
team that has yet played in the tide of
times.

Roger Kahn, *The Boys of Summer*

To Dodger rooters, 1955 is the year of
destiny.

Time, August 8, 1955

It was a crime against a community of
3,000,000 people to move the Dodgers.

Branch Rickey, *The American Diamond*

9

The 1951 World Series is a bit of a blur. I distinctly remember rooting
for the Giants, though, even after what had just happened. No amount
of torture could have persuaded me to cheer for the Yankees. By now
we had our own TV set, so I was able to watch the Series at home. Alex,
for the first time in memory, took no interest.

He'd watch an inning or two and then stand up, walk out of the living
room, and drift down to the Web, where he could take a drink out of
range of his wife's reproachful glances.

The first game of the Series was played on a cold, breezy day in Yankee Stadium. I remember Mel Allen, broadcasting along with Jim Britt
over WOR-TV, commenting that the rooftops of the buildings beyond
the center-field fence were nearly empty. In years past they had been
packed to overflowing. The people had been replaced by row after row of
television aerials.

The opposing pitchers were the Giants' little Dave Koslo and Allie
Reynolds for the Yankees. The three-game playoff had upset Durocher's
pitching rotation. Koslo, a junk artist used mainly in relief, had pitched
only five complete games all year. The Yankees, many of whom had
lolled about behind the temporary press section in the Polo Grounds
during the playoff, were fresh. Reynolds had rested the six days since he
had thrown his no-hitter to clinch the pennant. He was not only fresh,
he was riding a string of eleven and a third consecutive no-hit innings
and fourteen scoreless ones.

In the spring of 1951, Happy Chandler had been ousted as commissioner by the owners. In the grandstand was Ford Frick, president of the

National League and commissioner-elect. He motioned Yogi Berra closer to the stands and tossed out the first ball.

In the first inning Reynolds easily retired Stanky and Dark. But then he walked Hank Thompson, playing for the injured Meuller. Monte Irvin followed with a single to right, the first of four consecutive hits he would have that day. When Whitey Lockman bounced one into the left-field stands, both runners crossed the plate, but Irvin was forced to return to third on the ground rule. He didn't stay there long. As Reynolds went into his motion, Irvin broke for home. The Chief's hurried delivery arrived high and wide. Berra snagged the ball and lunged at the runner. Too late. Irvin had stolen home to make the score 2–0, Giants.

In the Yankee second rookie Gil McDougald, the Yankees' only .300 hitter, doubled to left and scored on Jerry Coleman's single. The score remained 2–1 until the fifth. After Willie Mays flied out for the third time, Wes Westrum singled, Koslo sacrificed, and Stanky walked. With runners on first and second and two down, Alvin Dark lofted a 3–1 pitch into the left-field stands. Koslo, throwing mainly sinkers after the third inning, blanked the Yanks the rest of the way for a 5–1 win.

In game two the Giants sent Larry Jansen against the Yanks' own junkman, pudgy, blond Eddie Lopat, famed for his three delivery speeds— slow, slower, and slowest.

The Yankee batters were determined to be as tricky as their pitcher. Mantle led off the Yank first with a surprise bunt and blazed down to first ahead of the throw. Rizzuto laid down another bunt. The Scooter was safe at first, and Mantle took third on a bad throw by Lockman. MacDougald followed with a slice down the right-field line that gave the Yankees a 1–0 lead. They added another run in the second, and that was all they would need. Lopat pitched nine strong innings, allowing the Giants only five hits and one run. The final was Yankees 3, Giants 1.

The game was generally ho-hum, except for a strange incident in the fifth. Mays, fighting a tough slump, sent a lazy fly to right center. As DiMaggio glided under it, Mantle charged over from right. When he was about ten feet from DiMaggio, Mantle suddenly collapsed. The Clipper, who'd seen plenty of outfielders bail out to avoid a collision, thought nothing of it. He made the routine catch and returned the ball to the infield. Then he noticed that Mantle hadn't moved. He spoke to the kid. No answer.

"I wasn't hurt," Mantle said later. "At least I wasn't in pain. But I was scared shitless. I couldn't move, and I couldn't answer Joe."

The injury was diagnosed as a "fresh knee sprain." Mantle would be out for the rest of the Series; with rest, the doctor said, he would be as good as new.

The teams moved to the Polo Grounds for game three. In the Giant fifth, with the Giants leading, 1–0, Stanky walked and then tried to steal second. Berra's throw was on the money, but clever Eddie, Durocher's favorite un-nice guy, kicked the ball out of Rizzuto's glove and into center field. Then he jumped up and dashed safely to third. The Giants went on to score five unearned runs in that inning. They eventually took the game, 6–2.

"They come up with a five-point field goal and beat us," grumbled Stengel.

I watched that game with Pop at the Web Café. Across the river, in Times Square, taverns with TV sets had jumped the price of a bottle of beer to thirty-five cents—and it was best not to dawdle too long over one bottle. Alex was still dazed by the outcome of the playoff. The fate of Willie Moretti, avidly discussed in the Web, should have made him feel better by comparison, but it didn't.

Moretti, a big-time gambler, had bet $125,000 on the Bums to win the playoff. When the playoff ended and payoff time arrived, Willie couldn't come up with the scratch. So he was scratched. They found him slumped over a table in a restaurant in Cliffside Park, New Jersey, full of bullets.

On the morning of October 8, the day of game four, I reported to Whitehall Street for induction into the army. By game time I was in a bus headed for Fort Dix, New Jersey—the garden spot of the Garden State. The guy in front of me had a portable radio, so I was able to follow the action as Allie Reynolds threw an eight-hitter and the Yankees turned the tables on the Giants, beating them, 6–2. DiMaggio, who had gone 0 for 12, broke out of his slump with a single and a homer. Willie Mays, still fighting his own slump, hit into three double plays.

It took several days for the army to get me through the tests and exams required before I could be shipped off to basic training. I caught games five and six in bits and pieces. An instant grapevine sprung up on the post, and as those soldiers lucky enough to be near a radio heard a new development, they would pass along the word. So through those afternoons, between inoculations and tests to see whether I knew a hawk from a handsaw, I was able to keep on top of what was going on.

In the fifth game the Yankees reestablished themselves as the Bombers. They routed the Giants as Gil MacDougald blasted a grand-slam homer and Eddie Lopat delivered another strong, complete-game victory. They then went on to scratch out a 4–3 win in the sixth game, behind Hank Bauer's three-run triple and his brilliant, game-ending catch. The Series was over. The Yankees had done in the Giants with the same precision they had so often shown in destroying the Bums.

After basic and advanced infantry training at Fort Benning, Georgia, I was fully prepared to become cannon fodder in Korea. When I came home for my final leave, Mom commented on how handsome I'd become with my crew cut and my new physique. The army had relieved me of twenty-five pounds.

I was as trim as a high school freshman—all ready to go out and incur the wrath of some Red Chinese. I spent every night of that furlough making the rounds of the Bay Ridge bars—places like Hartman's, Kelly's, and McQuire's—with a few of my old high school chums. On every juke box Johnny Ray was singing "The Little White Cloud that Cried."

By the time I got to Korea, in April of 1952, the war there was no longer on the front pages. The armistice talks were droning on, and on the battlefield the two sides were engaged in a holding action. My unit was part of a city of Quonset huts about thirty miles south of Seoul.

I spent my entire tour of duty going from one chickenshit detail to another. Korea in 1952 and 1953 wasn't exactly what you'd call paradise. In the summer the stench of night soil off the rice paddies made you gag on your food. The winter nights were so cold that I sent icicles out of my fly whenever I went to the latrine.

I followed baseball in *Stars and Stripes* and the *Sporting News*. Alex bought me a subscription to the latter, which always arrived two months after publication. That was all right. Time was no longer of the essence.

Not only had Sally Rice lost her son to the army in 1952; the Dodgers had lost Don Newcombe, and the Giants had been forced to part with Willie Mays. Most of the experts believed that Brooklyn, despite its weakened pitching staff, had enough power in its lineup to take the National League flag. There had been reports during spring training that a nineteen-year-old kid named Johnny Podres was going to fill Big Don's shoes. But when the season began Podres was in Montreal.

On June 19, 1952, Carl Erskine pitched a no-hitter against the Cubs. Had it not been for a walk to opposing pitcher Willie Ramsdell, Carl would have hurled a perfect game. Ersk had finally come into his own.

But Charlie Dressen still didn't have a cohesive pitching staff. He had a couple of hopeful starters in Chris Van Cuyk and Ben Wade, but neither was destined to achieve greatness. And then there was Billy Loes, a $21,000 bonus baby who had flashes of brilliance, but who never would fulfill his promise.

That year Clem Labine's record was eight and four, but his ERA sky-rocketed from 2.20 to 5.14. Preacher Roe was winning, but he wasn't completing many ball games and he was dishing up far too many home-run balls. Ralph Branca was fast becoming a has-been.

Suddenly, as if on a white horse, Joe Black came to the rescue. Over-night he became the most celebrated relief artist in baseball, and Brook-lyn's first genuine bullpen hero since Hugh Casey. What made Joe especially interesting was that, unlike most relievers, he didn't throw any junk at all. His primary weapon was a dynamite fastball.

If Charlie Dressen had pitching problems, Leo Durocher had them in spades. His two aces—Larry Jansen and Sal Maglie—both developed back trouble as the season wore on, and Max Lanier, brought over from the Cards, arrived in New York without his stuff. In the early going the

Giants' hopes were brightened by Dusty Rhodes, a rookie outfielder who began his career in the Polo Grounds by hitting home runs as if there were no tomorrow. When tomorrow came, Dusty fizzled.

Leo's most valuable newcomer that year was reliever Hoyt Wilhelm, destined to become the greatest knuckleballer of all time.

Everyone expected the race to be another bitter struggle between Brooklyn and New York, and that's exactly how it turned out. The Giants held the lead by a slim margin during the latter part of May, but on June 1 the Dodgers captured the lead and held onto it with grim determination.

A Brooklyn slump in late July, combined with a sudden Giant hot streak, prompted the pundits to predict a second "miracle of Coogan's Bluff." But the Dodgers pulled out of it and stayed in front. The final showdown between the two clubs began at the Polo Grounds on Saturday, September 6, when they played the first two of five straight games. Brooklyn went into the series six games up on its archenemy.

The Giants won both ends of the Saturday doubleheader, 6–4 and 7–3, slicing the Dodgers' lead to four games and reinforcing Durocher's dream that 1952 could become a playback of 1951. The next afternoon, however, Preacher Roe, looking the way he did in 1949, hurled a stunning three-hitter to stop the Giants, 4–1, and bring Brooklyn's advantage back to five games.

On Monday the teams faced each other for the last time. They played a day-night doubleheader with two separate admissions. The matinee was one hell of a brawl. Alex, in one of his infrequent letters to me, described it as "the most vicious ball game I've ever seen. In the old days it was the fans who caused all the trouble. Now it's the players."

The trouble started in the fifth inning. The score was 5–0 in favor of Brooklyn. Hoyt Wilhelm let a pitch get away from him and it hit Gil Hodges. To retaliate, Gil, on a double-play ball by Furillo, came into second with his spikes high and opened up a three-inch gash in Bill Rigney's leg. For the rest of the afternoon the beanballs kept coming. In the seventh, after Giant hurler Monte Kennedy threw two pitches in a row right at Joe Black's head, the umpires called both Dressen and Durocher to the mound and warned them to cut it out.

With two gone in the ninth Larry Jansen kept up the feud by landing a fastball on Billy Cox's behind. Umpire Lee Ballanfant immediately threw Larry out of the ball game. When the ruckus was finally over the Dodgers had won, 10–2, and Joe Black had turned in another great relief performance, pitching seven and two-thirds scoreless innings after coming in to bail out Ken Lehman in the second.

Durocher's men won the night game, 3–2. The Giants had taken the season series, fourteen games to eight, but the Dodgers were still five games in first place.

In an article that appeared in the *Saturday Evening Post* the following week, Charlie Dressen predicted, "The Dodgers will nail the pennant they missed last year. I'm safe in going out on a limb. I've got the ball club to support me—and the percentages are all against lightning striking in the same tree twice."

The tree that grows in Brooklyn was indeed safe. The Dodgers won the pennant by four and a half games. Now, if only the lightning would stay clear of Yankee Stadium.

When Casey Stengel assembled the 1952 Yankees, he had been faced with a problem: replacing Joe DiMaggio. The Yankee Clipper was gone. To add to Casey's woes, a good many of the remaining Bombers belonged in a hospital ward. Billy Martin was injured, 1951 MVP Yogi Berra was injured, Joe Collins was injured, and Mickey Mantle, coming back from off-season surgery on the knee he'd torn up in the World Series, was still not able to play.

While his stars were knitting and mending, Casey tried gigantic Bob Cerv in center. Big Bob had the firepower at bat, but he couldn't close in on airborne balls fast enough to suit the Ol' Perfessor. Stengel pulled Cerv and tried Jackie Jensen, who had great ability but was inexperienced. Early in the season, Case traded Jensen and pitcher Frank Shea to the Senators for Irv Noren. The first week in May, Stengel pulled Noren and inserted Mantle. Mickey had never played center, and his knee was less than perfect, but he was there to stay.

By early June, Berra was back, playing solid defense and slugging any pitch that came close to crossing the plate. Feisty Billy Martin was also back, playing his dogged second base and slugging any opposing ballplayer who came close to crossing him. And Mantle had already become one of the most celebrated players in baseball, awing observers with his tape-measure shots from both sides of the plate. Not surprisingly, the Yankees were in first place.

They stayed there until late August, when the Cleveland Indians—sporting such names as Bob Lemon, Early Wynn, Mike Garcia, Luke Easter, Bobby Avila, Al Rosen, and Larry Doby—came on with a surge. Manager Al Lopez announced he would go with a three-man rotation down the stretch. His three aces would not only start all the games, they would also do all the relief work.

"Well, yes, I see where he's doing that," said Stengel. "They say you can never do that, but he is, and it's a good idea but sometimes it doesn't always work."

It didn't. The Yankees cruised to their fourth straight pennant, two games ahead of the runner-up Indians.

So once again it would be the Bums and the Bombers. Much of the world began matching the teams position by position, pitcher by pitcher. Red Smith cut through the confusion. "The simplest argument to support a belief that the Yankees will win," he said, "is to point out that they always do."

Fatalism aside, it seemed to come down, as usual, to the pitching. There seemed to be no way that Erskine, Roe, and Loes could match Reynolds, Raschi, and Lopat.

But Dressen had a surprise up his sleeve. He named Joe Black to start the first game. The Dodger bullpen ace proved more than equal to the task. He outpitched Allie Reynolds to beat the Yankees, 4–2. All the Brooklyn runs came on homers—one by Furillo and two by Reese, the first Dodger ever to do it in a single Series game. It was also the first time in history that the Flock had won the opener.

But the Bombers quickly struck back in game two, drubbing the Dodgers, 7–1, with Mantle and Martin pacing a ten-hit attack and Vic Raschi hurling a three-hitter. Game three was a battle of junkmen, Preacher Roe versus Eddie Lopat. Going into the ninth, the Dodgers were clutching a 3–2 lead. With one out, Reese singled to right, and Robinson followed with a single to center. That was the end for slow Eddie; Stengel pulled Lopat and replaced him with Tom Gorman. While the rookie right-hander was concentrating on Campanella, the batter, Reese and Robinson pulled a double steal. Campy then popped to Rizzuto. Gorman blew two strikes past the next batter, Andy Pafko.

Yogi Berra, who always caught with his left index finger outside his mitt, signaled for a fastball. Gorman delivered it. Somehow the pitch struck Berra's exposed finger, splitting it, and then rolled seventy-five feet to the stands. Yogi, in pain, had trouble finding the ball. By the time he did, Reese and Robinson had crossed the plate.

Johnny Mize delivered the second pinch-hit homer in Series history to no avail in the Yankee ninth, and the Dodgers won the game, 5–3.

Game four was a repeat of the first game matchup—Black against Reynolds. Black again had his stuff, but this time so did Reynolds. Mize, who had replaced the slumping Joe Collins at first base, homered in the fourth. It was the only run the Chief needed; he notched a 2–0 shutout, evening the Series at two games each.

Carl Erskine went to the mound for the Dodgers in game five. Ersk began the game beautifully, and going to the last of the fifth he'd yielded only one hit and two walks. But the Yankees reached into their big-inning bag and pulled out five runs, three of them coming on Big Jawn's third homer of the Series.

The Dodgers scored once in the seventh to tie the game at 5–5. And then the tension really set in. Johnny Sain was pitching well in relief of Yank starter Ewell Blackwell, and Erskine was hanging tough. In the top of the eleventh, Duke Snider, who'd homered in the fifth, blasted a double off the railing in front of the Yankee bullpen, and Billy Cox came in with the go-ahead run. It took a spectacular catch by Carl Furillo, robbing Mize of yet another homer, to preserve the 6–5 Dodger victory.

Back in Ebbets Field for game six, with the Dodgers only one win away from victory, Raschi and Reynolds combined to defeat Loes and Roe. Homers by Mantle and Berra offset two by Snider. Another Yankee run scored as a result of a fluke that could only happen in Flatbush.

In the seventh, Gene Woodling was on first with none out. Loes, pitching to Irv Noren, had thrown a ball and a strike. As he went into his motion to deliver the next pitch, the ball suddenly squirted up and landed several feet behind the mound. Woodling moved to second on the balk. Billy collected himself and fanned Noren, but Raschi followed with a vicious one-hopper that struck Loes on the knee and skittered out of Hodges's reach into right field. Woodling scored easily. The 3–2 Yankee win evened the Series at three-all.

At the start of the deciding game of the Series, it was Lopat versus Black. Both would yield early to a parade of relievers as Dressen and Stengel pulled all their stops. At the end of four it was 1–1. At the end of five it was 2–2. But at the end of nine it was 4–2. Casey Stengel had won his fourth consecutive championship. For the Yankees, it was the fifteenth time they had won it all.

In March of 1953 I was stunned by the news that the Boston Braves were no more. They were on their way to Milwaukee. It was an extremely disquieting development. Why, Boston was one of the original franchises in the National League, going all the way back, without interruption, to William Hulbert's organizational meeting in 1876. The only other club with that claim was the Chicago Cubs.

Why was I so dismayed? Perhaps I just couldn't conceive of a National League without the eight cities that had made up the circuit since the turn of the century. The major league map hadn't changed since 1903, when the Baltimore Orioles folded and were replaced by the New York Highlanders. This was definitely going to take some time getting used to. The *Milwaukee* Braves? It sounded ridiculous.

Sentimentality aside, the Braves appeared to have no choice but to move. The year before they'd drawn only 281,278 fans to Braves Field and had lost $600,000. On March 18, 1953, the other owners gave Lou Perini permission to shift his franchise. The motion to allow the transfer was made by Walter O'Malley and seconded by Horace Stoneham.

The news was a shock not only to many fans but also to the players on the Braves and the reporters who covered the team. The club was already in spring training, and its progress was being followed by sportswriters from seven Boston papers. As soon as the writers wrapped up their stories on the move they headed North, leaving the players to grapple with their identity crisis all by themselves.

As it turned out, the move did wonders for the ball team. The Braves, who packed County Stadium for every home game, were miraculously transformed from a seventh-place club to a pennant contender. They took over first place from Philadelphia late in May and held it until the end of June. That's when the greatest Dodger team of all time finally got in gear and began to roll.

One of my biggest regrets in life is that I was in Korea instead of Brooklyn during the summer of 1953. Old Dodger fans still talk about that season, when their heroes were a joy to behold.

Carl Furillo came back from a lousy year in 1952 to bat .344. Gil Hodges batted .302 and blasted thirty-two balls out of the park. Jackie Robinson gracefully relinquished second base to newcomer Junior Gilliam, and then Robbie turned in a sensational year at third base and in left field, hitting .329.

The Duke also had an outstanding season, batting .336, hitting forty-two homers, and leading the league in runs scored by crossing the plate 132 times. Cox, Reese, and Gilliam were like vacuum cleaners around the infield. And Campy—well he was just plain sensational. On his way to winning the MVP award for the second time in three years he became the only catcher ever to lead the league in homers and RBIs. In the process he set two new marks for backstops.

He broke Gabby Hartnett's old mark of thirty-seven homers in a season by clouting forty-two, and he canceled out Walker Cooper's RBI mark of 122 by sending home 142 runners. Campanella himself later looked back on that season and called it "the best year I ever had in baseball. Free of injuries for the first time in several years, I hit everybody and everything."

It didn't matter that the Dodgers were still having problems with their pitchers. Through most of those golden years of the fifties Brooklyn searched in vain for a fourth, and sometimes even a third, front-line starter. In 1953 the mainstay of the staff was Carl Erskine. Ersk won twenty games and lost only six, but his ERA of 3.54 showed that he needed lots of help from the Dodgers' awesome batters.

Billy Loes got off to a fine start that year; by July 8 he was eleven and five, but then he sputtered and died. His final record was fourteen and eight. Preacher Roe, though still able to pitch, was, at thirty-eight, near the end of the line. And then there was Russ Meyer, a journeyman hurler brought over from the Phillies, who managed to pitch his way through several ball games. Russ's record for the year was fifteen and five, but his ERA was a pallid 4.56.

The man Dressen relied on as much as anybody in 1953 was Clem Labine. He became the workhorse of the bullpen, winning ten and losing only four in relief.

It was lucky Clem came through, because Dressen's biggest pitching hope, Joe Black, became a has-been overnight. As writer Roger Kahn tells the story, "The saddest spectacle of the 1953 season was watching Joe Black recede. The outward mansion never changed. The man remained warm, perceptive, and fiercely determined to do well. But now his fastballs moved to the center of the plate and became high doubles, and the small, sharp curve, breaking at belt level, was driven on a long, low line." Joe's record on the year was six and three, his ERA 5.33.

The Giants that season suffered as disastrous a collapse as Joe Black. Leo had begun the year with high hopes, largely because Monte Irvin, who'd missed most of the 1952 season because of a broken ankle, was back and in fine form. The trouble was the rest of the Giants. Maglie, Jansen, and Jim Hearn all became losers. Ruben Gomez, a Puerto Rican picked up as a free agent over the winter, was the only regular starter who finished the year with a winning record. He won thirteen and lost eleven.

At the season's halfway point New York was in fifth place, nine and a half games back. Leo thought he'd solved his problems when, after he brought up pitcher Al Worthington from Minneapolis, his rookie's first two starts were shutouts. Al was, unfortunately, destined to finish the year with a record of four and eight.

Early in August Charlie Dressen proclaimed, "The Giants is dead." He was right, and the fans at the Polo Grounds knew it. They screamed for Leo's hide. They pointed over to Yankee Stadium, where Johnny Mize was still hitting homers and winning ball games, and asked, "What kind of team did Durocher have in mind when he couldn't find a spot for a great hitter like Big Jawn?"

Speculating that he might be all washed up, Leo told the press, "When I'm through with the Giants, I'm through with baseball. This is my last job." But then Horace Stoneham turned around and offered him a brand-new two-year contract.

On September 6, in the second inning of a meaningless game at the Polo Grounds between the Dodgers and the Giants, Ruben Gomez threw to batter Carl Furillo and hit him in the right wrist. Slowly, Carl tossed away his bat and then headed for the mound. Both dugouts emptied in a hurry. Before any damage could be done Carl was intercepted and persuaded to go over to first base where he belonged.

As Furillo got ready to take his lead he could hear the Lip heckling him. Carl glanced over to the Giant bench, where he thought he saw Durocher beckoning him to "come on over."

He accepted the invitation. He ran toward the New York dugout, and Leo came out to meet him. Both were swinging as they came together and wrestled each other to the ground. The Giants rushed out of their dugout, and several of them piled on. In the scuffle someone stepped on Furillo's hand, fracturing his palm and breaking the little finger while knocking it out of joint.

Before Carl could get in a good punch the fight had been broken up. But Furillo, convinced that Leo had ordered the beanball, swore he wasn't finished with Durocher. "I'll get him," he vowed, "on the field or the street or anywhere else. He has crossed me once too often."

Carl was the league's leading hitter at the time of the incident. He was out for the remainder of the campaign, but his hand did heal well enough to enable him to play in the Series. His .344 average held up the rest of the way, giving him the batting crown.

Brooklyn finished the year thirty-five games ahead of the fifth-place Giants and thirteen lengths up on the runner-up Braves. Lou Perini, however, had no difficulty consoling himself. Milwaukee drew 1,826,397 fans into County Stadium to set a National League record. Walter O'Malley watched jealously as the erstwhile Bostonians rang up 650,000 more customers than his victorious Brooklynites.

By taking their second pennant in a row, the Dodgers laid to rest an old jinx. The club hadn't won back-to-back pennants since Ned Hanlon turned the trick in 1899 and 1900. Now, with a brand-new World Series to play, Brooklyn once again faced the most tenacious jinx of all.

And if the jinx weren't enough, there to help, once again, would be the Yankees. Stengel's men had thundered to their fifth straight pennant with all the subtlety of a runaway freight.

After dropping the season opener, the Yanks won nine straight to jump into first place. In May and June, when they put together an eighteen-game winning streak, it was obvious no one would catch them. The Yankees rolled to an eight-and-a-half-game margin of victory over the second-place Indians.

My tour of duty came to an end in September 1953. A week before I was scheduled to begin the long sea journey home, I received this letter from my mother:

8/27/53

Dear Son,

I'm so glad you'll be home soon—not only because your father and I miss you, but because you are needed here.

Your father is not a well man. I feel I must tell you before you get back that he had a stroke last June. When he left the hospital the doctors told him to quit drinking and to rest a lot. Instead, he's going at it worse than ever.

I can't understand how he manages to hold onto his job. One of these days he's going to be fired for sure—which might not be so bad. There are too many temptations in that barroom. I've started taking courses in typing and shorthand, and for an old lady, I'm doing pretty well. I hope to have a job of my own by the end of the year.

It will be so nice to see you again. I hope the news about your father doesn't depress you. I felt I had to let you know, so it wouldn't come as a complete shock.

Love
Mother

The World Series of 1953 was one of the most exciting ever played. Eighty-six-year-old Cy Young, who had pitched the first game of the first World Series fifty years earlier, threw out the first ball. Then two younger pitchers, Carl Erskine and Allie Reynolds, took over. It was not a pitcher's day. When the bats were finally racked, there had been five home runs, two triples, three doubles, and fourteen singles.

Right from the start, Erskine had trouble finding the plate. After retiring MacDougald on a pop fly, he gave Joe Collins a free pass on four straight pitches. Hank Bauer sliced one into the gap in right center for a triple, giving the Yanks a 1–0 lead. After Berra struck out, Mantle worked out a walk. Woodling stepped in, looked at four wide throws in a row, and trotted down to first. There was furious activity in the Dodger bullpen, but Dressen decided to stick with Erskine. Carl worked Billy Martin to a 1–1 count but then hung a curve. Martin pounced on it and slashed it into left center between Snider and Robinson. Billy, always a slugger in the money games, went all the way to third, and the Yankees were leading, 4–0.

In the Dodger fifth, Junior Gilliam, playing in his first Series, drilled a home run. In the Yankee fifth, Berra matched it. And then Gil Hodges, who had gone 0 for 25 in Series play since 1949, opened the first of the sixth by drilling one into the left-field stands. After Furillo flied out and Cox singled, Shotgun Shuba pinch-hit for the pitcher and poled one into the right-field seats. There had now been three pinch-hit homers in Series history, and the three men who hit them—Berra, Mize, and Shuba—were all present. Johnny Sain came out of the bullpen to retire the side and hold the Yankee lead at 5–4.

Clem Labine came on to blank the Yankees in their half of the inning. When the Dodgers came to bat in the seventh, they were still steamed up. Campanella led off with a single to center. Hodges followed with a single just beyond Rizzuto's reach. And then Furillo smacked another single to center. Campy came across the plate with the tying run.

With runners on first and second and nobody out, Dressen gave the second-guessers food for thought. He ordered Billy Cox, who already had a single and a double, to bunt. Cox dropped a beauty down the third base line. Berra, forever surprising with his quickness and agility, sprang from behind the plate, grabbed the ball, and fired to MacDougald at third. Hodges was out by a heartbeat. Dressen staggered about in the coach's box as though his own heart had stopped. When he recovered, he ordered Clem Labine to bunt. Clem dutifully laid it down, and Berra provided an instant replay. This time it wasn't even close. Gilliam fouled out to end the inning. Berra had already ended the rally.

In the Yankee half of the seventh, Joe Collins, still smarting because he had been benched in favor of Mize in last year's Series, drove the ball deep into the right-field stands. The Yanks added three insurance runs in the eighth to ice a 9–5 win.

When the game was over, it was time to take stock of the walking wounded. Furillo, playing with a bandaged hand and a sponge taped to his bat, had almost recovered from his scuffle with the Lip. Campanella had been struck on the hand by a pitched ball and was in dubious condition. But Campy refused to have the hand x-rayed and insisted he would play the next day. Although it didn't appear so at the time, the most serious injury of all was to the Superchief, Allie Reynolds. In mid-season, the Yankee team bus had been involved in an accident. Although no one had been seriously hurt, Reynolds's back had been injured. In the third inning of this game he had felt it pop. In the fifth he wrenched it again. By the middle of the sixth he was in the showers, wondering whether he would be able to pitch again in the Series. He would make two more brief appearances in the Series, agonize through one more season, and then be forced to retire.

The second game of the Series was the second annual match-up of the junkmen—Roe and Lopat. Going into the seventh, Roe was pitching a two-hitter and was ahead, 2–1. But little Billy Martin took a 2–2 pitch to left. The ball arched through the bright sunlight, skimmed Robinson's glove, and settled into the left-field stands. The next inning, after Bauer's single, Mantle cracked one into the same vicinity. If Martin's homer was a cheap shot, Mantle's was pure Tiffany's. The Yankees won it, 4–2.

On the morning of October 2, the day of game three, I arrived home from Korea. Mom greeted me tearfully at the door. Alex had taken the day off from work, but he'd gone out for a walk. Before I had a chance to question Mom about him, he returned and gave me a pleasant surprise. He was thinner and looked older and frailer, but he seemed generally alert and happy. Pop was anxious to hear all about Korea, but he kept interrupting me with tales of his own exploits in France during World War I.

After Pop and I had run through our best stories and I had unpacked my duffle bag, we warmed up the Philco and settled in to watch the game. After each inning, Pop would dash to the kitchen to get a refill of his glass of icewater.

The pitchers were Carl Erskine for the Dodgers and Vic Raschi for the Yankees. "I don't know about Ersk," Pop said. "Last Wednesday he couldn't have hit the ground from an airplane."

Erskine immediately dispelled Pop's doubts. His fastball was smoking, and his big overhand curve was breaking almost straight down. And all his pitches went right where he wanted them. Going to the top of the fifth, he was throwing a no-hitter.

Raschi was also overpowering. The score was 0–0 when Billy Martin led off the fifth with an infield single. Rizzuto followed with a single through the box, and Raschi moved the runners with a sacrifice bunt. Gil MacDougald, 0 for 12 in the Series, stepped in and hit a line shot down the third base line. It looked like extra bases for sure, but Billy Cox made a desperation dive and knocked the ball down, allowing Erskine to get out of the inning only one run behind.

After Furillo flied to Mantle to open the Dodger fifth, Jackie Robinson doubled off the right-field screen. Raschi balked him to third, and Robbie scored standing up on Cox's squeeze bunt.

Erskine resumed his stingy ways in the sixth, and the game was still 1–1 as the Bums came to bat. The Duke of Flatbush singled through the right side to open the inning. Hodges walked. Campanella, who had stubbornly played the second game and gone hitless, had been a doubtful starter for this contest. But here he was, with Snider on second, Hodges on first, and no outs, swinging away—and missing badly. On the next pitch he shortened up and tried to bunt. The result was a pop-up that Raschi caught near the third base line for the first out. Furillo looked at a third strike. Just as the rally appeared to be dying, Robinson cracked a sharp single to left, and the Dodgers had a 2–1 lead.

The score remained unchanged until the eighth. Collins led off for the Yankees and struck out. After Bauer poked a base hit through the middle, Erskine hit Berra with a pitch for the second time in the game. It was a terrible time for Mickey Mantle to come to bat. Mickey looked at two curves that broke into the dirt for called strikes. Stengel bounced angrily out of the dugout and pantomimed a swing with an invisible bat. Mick's bat might as well have been invisible too. He cut at the air and trudged slowly, head down, to the dugout. Gene Woodling followed with a single, and the score was tied, 2–2.

In the Dodger half of the inning, there were groans from Dodger rooters as Roy Campanella strode to the plate with one away. Campy was playing well defensively, but with his injured hand he'd become an automatic out. Raschi confidently sent his fastball down the pipe. Campy rippled his hulking shoulders and turned the groans to cheers by planting the ball deep into the lower deck in left. The score was 3–2, Dodgers.

Erskine made the score stand by striking out pinch hitters Don Bollweg and Mize and getting Collins on a lazy bouncer. Carl had fanned Collins and Mantle four times each and had struck out a total of fourteen, one better than the all-time Series record.

Alex, who'd alternated between sipping his icewater and pacing the living room floor, let out a whoop when the last out was recorded. He went to the kitchen, fished a bottle of bourbon out from under the sink, and poured himself a double.

"To Ersk," he said, draining the glass. "The doc said it'd kill me," he added with a wink, "but he didn't say when."

The opposing pitchers for the fourth game of the Series were two youngsters who'd grown up within ten blocks of each other in Queens: Billy Loes for the Dodgers and Whitey Ford for the Yankees.

After Loes put down the first three Yank batters, Jim Gilliam led off the bottom of the first and started a wild, whacky, and—for the Dodgers—wonderful afternoon. He hit a huge skyrocket of a fly ball down the right-field line. Hank Bauer positioned himself in foul territory in front of the Dodgers' bullpen and waited patiently for the ball to come down. As he reached up to haul it in, the ball suddenly hooked left and landed three feet inside the foul line. The confused Bauer lunged frantically, but the ball wasn't finished playing tricks. It bounced sharply back to the right, whizzed past him, and disappeared into the stands for a ground-rule double.

After Gilliam moved to third on Reese's groundout, Robinson slapped a solid single to center, and Gilliam romped home with the first run of the game. Campanella was the next batter; with the count 2 and 0, Ford lost the handle on his next delivery, and the ball shot past Berra. Robbie moved to second on the wild pitch. With first base open and the count 3 and 0, Stengel ordered an intentional pass.

Duke Snider stepped in and lifted a mile-high fly to right. The ball flashed through the autumn sunlight, struck the screen—and stayed there, tangled momentarily in some strips of bunting. By the time it dropped into the bedeviled Bauer's hands, the Duke was standing on second and two more runs had come in.

For once the gremlins were tormenting someone other than the Dodgers. The Flock went on to win the game, 7–3, and even up the Series at two games apiece.

Alex was buoyant after the game. "Stengel's gonna have to pitch the next game himself," he chuckled. "He's got no one left!" I agreed, but I also felt obliged to point out that Dressen was in a similar predicament.

"Don't worry about it," Pop told me. "He'll probably go with Podres. He's just a kid, but he's got the Yankees' number." Johnny Podres, a rookie who'd pitched three complete games all season, had faced the Yanks twice: once in a preseason game and once in the midsummer Mayor's Trophy Game. For a total of thirteen innings, he'd held the Yankees scoreless.

Dressen did indeed name Podres to start the fifth game. Stengel came up with Jim McDonald, a righty who'd been the Yanks' batting practice pitcher during the previous year's Series.

Podres's perfect record against the Yanks extended four pitches into the first inning. Lead-off batter Gene Woodling skimmed the ball inches over Snider's glove and the center-field railing to give the Yankees a 1–0 lead. In the Dodger bullpen, Russ Meyer had been warming up since before the game started. Even though Dressen obviously lacked confidence in his young starter, he decided to stay with him. Podres managed to get out of the inning with no further damage.

In the Dodger second the Bums tied the game on singles by Campanella and Hodges and a muffed double play by the Yankee infield.

Phil Rizzuto led off the Yankee half of the third with a walk. Mc-Donald sacrificed him to second. Woodling, the next batter, hit a hard shot back to the mound that tore the glove right off Podres's hand. Even though he retrieved his glove first and the ball second, Podres still managed to nip Woodling at first. With two out and Rizzuto on third, the batter was Joe Collins. He hit a wicked shot off Hodges's glove, scored as an error, to give the Yankees back the lead.

Podres became rattled. He hit Bauer on the arm and walked Berra to load the bases. Dressen called in Russ Meyer, who by this time had probably thrown as many pitches as Podres, to face Mickey Mantle.

Mantle, batting from the left side, hit Meyer's first pitch into the upper stands in left center. It was the fourth grand slam in Series history; three had been by Yankees—Lazzeri, McDougald, and Mantle.

"Nuts," said Alex. "He didn't warm up long enough."

The Yankees scored three in the seventh and one in the eighth. Going to the bottom of the eighth, they led, 10–2, but the Dodgers stormed back with four runs, three of them coming on a Billy Cox homer that finished McDonald for the day. Bob Kuzava came on to fan pinch hitter Dick Williams and end the inning.

The Yanks added another tally in the ninth on McDougald's home run. In the Dodger half of the ninth, with one out, one run already in, and Snider on first, Stengel called in the injured Allie Reynolds to pitch to Robinson.

The Chief strode grimly to the mound. Although the sun was still shining, the lights had been turned on. Even hurt, Reynolds still had velocity. Robinson teed off on his fourth delivery and cracked a hard grounder to the right of second, a sure base hit. But Billy Martin, who already had ten hits in the Series and was fast becoming the most hated man in Flatbush, streaked to his right, stabbed the ball, and flipped to Rizzuto. In one smooth, effortless motion, the Scooter turned the double play, and the game was over. The Yankees had won the slugfest, 11–7.

On Monday, the day of game six, Alex had to return to work at the Web. I told him I might drop by to watch the game. What I couldn't tell him was that, when I had called Uncle Harry to let him know I was back, he'd invited me to join him at Yankee Stadium.

"I've got a couple extra spots in the company box for game six," he'd said. "You're welcome to come—if the Brooks last that long." As I rode over to Manhattan, I prayed there would be a game seven as well.

While I had been in Korea, the caterpillar that was Gowanus Workshirt had become a butterfly known as Go! Sportswear, Inc. The Long Island City operation had been phased out. Harry's executive offices were now in Manhattan, and he had factories in North Carolina and Maine.

Harry had put on a few pounds, and his hair was now a solid silver. He'd given up his pipe for handmade Havana cigars. He was beautifully groomed, perfectly tailored—a winner if there ever was one.

Earlier in the Series, an actor named Jimmy Little had been quoted as asking, "How can you root for the Yankees? It's like rooting for U.S. Steel." When I mentioned the line, Harry shrugged.

"Contrary to what you might think, Damon," he said, as we settled into his front-row box behind first base, "it's not un-American to root for a winner."

"That's good," I said, returning his grin, "because when this Series is over and the Bums have won it, I don't want you calling me a Commie."

Brave words, but I was worried. The Yankees were going with Whitey Ford, who'd pitched fewer than two innings two days earlier. Brooklyn's hopes were pinned on Carl Erskine, who'd thrown a complete game just three days ago.

My fears were heightened when Ersk walked leadoff batter Woodling and then proceeded to give up two runs on a single by Bauer, a double by Berra, and some sloppy work by the Brooklyn infield.

The Yankees scored another run in the second on singles by Rizzuto and Ford and a sacrifice fly by Woodling. The Yanks would have scored again except for some strange baserunning by Ford. With the bases loaded and one out, Berra whacked a long fly to center. Ford tagged at third and started home. Snider, conceding the run, threw to second. Halfway to the plate, Ford suddenly changed directions and headed back. When he saw Joe Collins steaming into third, he reversed directions again. In the meantime, Gilliam had relayed the ball to Campy, and Ford was out.

"He tagged before Snider caught it," Harry said, shaking his head, "and halfway home his conscience got the better of him."

In the fifth Robinson doubled, stole third, and scored on an infield out to make the score 3–1. Erskine, who'd been having trouble finding the plate and was obviously tired, stayed in the dugout when the Dodgers took the field. His replacement, Bob Milliken, staved off the Yanks until he himself was replaced in the seventh by Clem Labine.

For the Yankees, Ford had been throwing well. But as the game progressed, the fly balls were getting deeper and deeper. When pinch hitter Bobby Morgan backed Bauer against the wall for the final out in the seventh, Stengel decided it was time for a change. Allie Reynolds took the mound in the eighth and held the Bums scoreless.

But in the ninth, after Mantle had made a sparkling catch to retire leadoff batter Gil Hodges, the Chief ran into problems. With the count two and two on Snider, Reynolds rared back and blew his fastball down the middle. At least the Chief thought it was down the middle. The umpire disagreed. Annoyed, Reynolds threw another pitch that was undeniably wide, and the Duke took first.

The batter was Furillo. Carl worked the count to three and two. The Brooklyn contingent, comprising more than half the Yankee Stadium crowd, knew it was now or never. Reynolds delivered.

It was now. Furillo connected for a two-run homer. Reynolds fanned the next two batters, Cox and Labine, and going to the bottom of the ninth it was a 3–3 tie.

Bauer drew a leadoff walk, but then Berra lined out to Furillo. The next batter, Mickey Mantle, hit a check-swing dribbler between first and third, sending Labine and Cox into an "after you, Alphonse" routine. Cox finally fielded the ball, but Mantle beat the throw.

Billy Martin stepped in, looking for his twelfth hit to tie a Series record. He got it. He knocked the second pitch up the middle for a single. Snider fielded the ball but didn't bother to make a throw. The Series was over.

It was the fiftieth anniversary of the World Series. The Dodgers played in seven and lost them all, five of them to the Yankees.

It seemed always to be the Yankees. I hated them then, as did most of the baseball fans in America. Even in their own park, the Yankees were often subjected to boos and jeers. They were one of the few teams in the history of sports that fans turned out to root *against*. The Yankees were symbolic of something most Americans instinctively disliked. They won consistently and so were considered inhuman, cold, smug. They won relentlessly, and few could forgive them for it.

But time dulls the edges of pain, and over the years hatred turned to respect and even a little affection. When I think of the Yankees, I tend to picture the 1953 team, and I miss them: The comical but deadly Berra behind the plate; Joe Collins at first; at second, tough little Billy Martin, "the most combative Yankee since William Tecumseh Sherman," according to Red Smith.

In my mind, the incomparable Phil Rizzuto will always be the Yankees' shortstop. Casey Stengel once said, "If I were a retired gentleman I would follow the Yankees around just to see Rizzuto work those miracles every day." Rounding out the infield was Gil McDougald, tough, versatile, and deadly as a hired gunman at the plate. The core of the pitching staff was Ford, Lopat, Raschi, and Reynolds; each was overpowering in his own way. And the outfielders, all frightening to opposing fans, were Bauer, Woodling, Noren, and Mantle.

And when I think of Mantle, I always think of the front-page photo that appeared during the 1951 Series. There was Joe DiMaggio, lining up Willie Mays's fly ball, and near him was Mantle, lying in a crumpled heap. The Yankee Clipper was several games from retirement; Mantle was just beginning. For me, the picture symbolized more than just the changing of the guard. It symbolized the legacy of the Yankees' center field, a legacy of pain and greatness.

Like DiMadge, the Mick had almost superhuman talents, and like Di-

Madge, he would play most of his career in excruciating pain. Birdie Tebbetts, in a 1964 scouting report for the Cleveland Indians, said it as well as it can be said:

JULY:
A very crippled athlete.

7/14
Bad legs.

FINAL:
He is a great leader
with great talent
with big physical problems
with big courage.
On one leg he is still the top talent in our game.

But as Harry and I made our way out of Go! Sportswear's box and headed to the Stadium Club for a drink, I was feeling no affection for the Yankees. I was sick. Harry, a practiced Brooklyn baiter, for once was kind enough not to rub it in.

When we'd found a spot in the crowded room and ordered drinks, Harry motioned at the huge photo blowups of Yankee greats of bygone days.

"Fletcher knew 'em all," he said. Then he shook his head sadly. "He'd be very upset if he knew his sons weren't on speaking terms."

"Maybe you should give Pop a call," I suggested. "It's been a long time."

"Like hell I will. It's up to *him* now. I called him last year about disinterring Fletcher, and the son of a bitch wouldn't even talk to me."

"You called him about *what?*"

The story that Harry told me was, to put it mildly, surprising. In the course of revising his will, Harry's lawyer had suggested he provide for his and his family's afterlife. Harry looked for a plot near Fletcher, but there were no vacancies. When the salesman showed him a large plot on the other side of Greenwood, Harry had a brilliant idea. He would build something "lasting," a monument to the Rice family. When the mausoleum was completed—"The marble came all the way from Greece"—Harry decided Fletcher should be with the rest of the family. He had Fletcher's remains disinterred and sealed in the first vault.

"And Alex doesn't know?" I asked.

"How could I tell him? The son of a bitch wouldn't talk to me!"

After the Series, I spent most of my time reading newspapers and magazines and watching television, trying to catch up on what I'd missed. I'd been away a long time and was suffering from a mild form of culture shock. Everything about New York City, and America, seemed large and fast—and slightly unreal.

Sharp-tongued Harry Truman had been replaced by grandfatherly Dwight Eisenhower. The benign Ike had recently appointed Earl Warren to be Chief Justice of the United States, much to the joy of Warren's fellow Californian, Richard Nixon. On the cover of the current issue of *Newsweek* was a photo of the pudgy-faced vice-president. The caption read: "Richard Nixon: Going Places." Inside there was an article about West Germany's desire to trade with the United States. Accompanying the article was a photo of a strange little car called the Volkswagen.

The United States had just announced a huge monetary aid program to France to destroy the communist threat in Indochina and bring about a speedy end to the eight-year-old war there. Senator Joseph McCarthy was still leading his witch hunt. Eisenhower said he agreed with McCarthy's intentions but not his methods. "Still," Ike said, "a Red is a Red."

At the United Nations, an Egyptian spokesman was claiming that Israeli troops were guilty of border violations in the Gaza Strip. And Mrs. Oswald B. Lord, U.S. delegate to the Social Assembly of the U.N., answered a Soviet charge that women's rights were severely restricted in America by pointing out that almost as many women as men had voted in the last election.

Across the country there was a continuing controversy about women's wearing trousers. On the more traditional side of femininity, the current issue of *Collier's*, with a cover shot of a new television comedian named Red Buttons, featured a picture story on Marilyn Monroe, complete with the first exclusive, full-color shots of Marilyn and Joe DiMaggio, the "will-they or won't-they couple."

The Russians had just exploded a hydrogen bomb, and there was a lot of talk about bomb shelters and the end of the world. But there was plenty of entertainment to take the public's thoughts away from nuclear holocausts. In movies, 3-D was the rage. The first movie ever filmed in a new process called Cinemascope, *The Robe*, was packing them in at the Roxy. Cinerama was a year old. *Mogambo*, a conventional film with Clark Gable, Ava Gardner, and Grace Kelly, had just opened at Radio City Music Hall. A bumper crop of musicals on Broadway included *Can Can*, *South Pacific*, and *Guys and Dolls*. *Tea and Sympathy* had just opened to mixed reviews. *Oklahoma!* had just closed.

A week after the World Series was over, Walter O'Malley called a press conference to announce that Charlie Dressen would not be back as manager of the Dodgers in 1954. O'Malley explained, with Dressen at his side, that Charlie had demanded a three-year contract. Citing the fact that "the Brooklyn club has paid more managers not to manage than any other club," the Dodger boss declared a pact for more than one year was out of the question.

"The door is still open for Charlie," O'Malley hastened to add. "All he has to do is say the word, and I'll pull a contract out of the drawer here and sign him to it. . . . It'll have to be a one-year contract, however."

Dressen did not accept O'Malley's invitation, at least not then. A few days later Charlie tried to reopen negotiations, but Walter would have none of it. The man who had just led Brooklyn to two straight pennants was out.

Pop and I, along with most Dodger fans, wanted to see Pee Wee Reese get the job. The team captain was not only a Flatbush favorite, but he appeared to have what it takes to be a good field boss. O'Malley apparently agreed. He offered his shortstop a chance to be the team's player-manager, but Reese turned him down. Even though he was thirty-five, Pee Wee felt he had a few good playing years left. Rather than try to put on two hats, he decided to wear the one he was more comfortable with.

O'Malley's second choice was Fresco Thompson, his vice-president in charge of minor league operations. When Fresco also refused, Walter dug down into his farm system and came up with forty-two-year-old Walter "Smokey" Alston, pilot of the Montreal Royals. Unknown to most Brooklyn fans, Alston was a career manager in the Dodger organization, having worked his way up from the lower bushes to Brooklyn's top minor league post.

"Alston? Who's he?" was the way most Brooklynites reacted to the appointment. They felt O'Malley had hired a bush league manager mainly to save money. "It's cheap gas, but maybe we'll get some mileage out of it," was Alex's comment.

Many fans believed Alston was an interim manager—hired to run the club until Pee Wee was ready to hang up his spikes. At the news conference announcing Walt's appointment, O'Malley denied the charge vehemently. "I want to assure the new manager there's no one breathing down his neck," he said. "It's your job, Walter. I hope you can manage for ten years under a series of one-year contracts."

I had been sorry to see Charlie Dressen go. He was an exciting manager—a solid baseball man who'd been an obvious asset to the ball club. But I'd been away for two of Charlie's three seasons in Brooklyn, so his departure wasn't much of a shock. It had been quite another matter five years earlier when Leo had kissed Brooklyn goodby.

The biggest shock old Dodger fans received that autumn was the news that Red Barber, fifteen years behind the microphone at Ebbets Field, was moving over to the Yankees. In recent years there'd been no love lost between Red and O'Malley, who still looked upon his veteran broadcaster as a "Rickey man." When Red's contract expired at the end of the 1953 season, he did not ask for a renewal, choosing instead to seek work elsewhere. The Yankees were delighted to add him to their broadcasting team.

As Autumn wore on, it became difficult to shrug off the question mother and all my friends kept asking, namely, "What in the world are you going to do with your life?"

Pop wasn't at all worried about my destiny. He was happy to have me around the Web, where I found myself covering for him more and more. His drinking went in spurts. He would stay sober for a week or two and then go off the deep end. More than once one of his cronies had to call me up to ask me to come over to one saloon or another to drag him home.

Mom wanted me to go back to law school. After all, I had the GI bill now, so wasn't it worth another try? Sally couldn't believe I didn't have it in me to be my generation's Clarence Darrow.

Two years in the army had helped me forget how much I'd hated that year at NYU, so I found myself believing Mom's argument that I was now more mature, more capable of handling the work load. Despite a nagging worry that I was flirting with disaster, I transferred my credits to Long Island University, and in February 1954 I took another crack at the law.

About the same time, Sally finished secretarial school and found a job in a Wall Street brokerage firm. I was proud of my mother. Past fifty, she had the gumption to tackle a new career.

One morning in March, when I should have been attending a lecture on jurisprudence, I was awakened by a phone call from the Web asking why Alex hadn't come to work. He wasn't at home, so I assumed he'd been sidetracked into some other gin mill. I got dressed and began to make the rounds.

He was in none of his regular haunts. I gave up the search just before dinner time and arrived home a few minutes after Sally.

It was past ten before we decided to call the police. Before I could pick up the phone, it rang. It was Western Union with a collect telegram from Richmond, Virginia:

HEADING DOWN TO VERO TO CATCH
SPRING TRAINING. BACK SOON. ALEX

On his way to work that morning, Pop had run into Poopsy Sullivan, a truck driver who was a regular at the Web. He was on his way to pick up his rig and head for Jacksonville. The conversation between the two old Dodger fans took three quick quantum leaps—from Florida, to baseball, to an offer from Poopsy to lend Alex a hundred bucks. In less than an hour they were highballing south.

Sally took the news of Alex's latest defection with typical stoicism.

"Do you want me to go down there and bring him back?" I asked.

"No, Damon. He'll come home when he's ready—if he doesn't kill himself first. You just attend to your studies."

I couldn't tell her that Alex had a better chance of signing as a free agent than I had of becoming a lawyer.

Alex arrived home at the end of the month with a great tan, a horrendous Hawaiian sportshirt, and a baseball autographed by all the Dodgers. He had crashed a St. Patrick's Day party at a tourist attraction in Vero Beach called McKee's Jungle Gardens. The host was Walter O'Malley, who had plied his guests with green whisky and green beer. Alex had come away with one of the ladies' party favors—a green apron—which he now produced from a shopping bag that had obviously been with him the entire journey.

"Someday that'll be worth plenty," Alex said, handing it to his bewildered wife. "I got it from Gil. Now there's a hell of a nice guy. In fact, all the boys are O.K. in my book."

Alex wasn't quite such a big shot the next morning, when he discovered he was out of a job. The owner of the Web was still willing to use Alex as a fill-in man, but he'd found someone more reliable to work the regular shifts.

When opening day arrived Red Barber's replacement in the Ebbets Field radio-TV booth was Andre Baruch, who had to be the worst play-by-play man ever to call games for a major league team. Baruch had two claims to fame—he was the announcer on Lucky Strike's "Your Hit Parade," and he was married to Bea Wain, the glamorous singer. His baseball knowledge, however, was so meager as to insult his sophisticated audience.

No one in Brooklyn could figure out why in God's name O'Malley had hired him. Maybe Walter was impressed by the fact that Baruch, and especially his wife, were show biz personalities.

Luckily the Dodger broadcasting team still included Connie Desmond, who'd been Red Barber's sidekick for ten years, and young Vince Scully, whom Red had hired in 1951. Anyone who listened to Vince once knew he was a man with a future.

Who will ever forget the campaign of 1954? It was a wild, wonderful baseball season for National League fans in New York. As the race got under way, I, like most of the Faithful, was certain Brooklyn would coast to its third pennant in a row. With Don Newcombe back from the army, who could stop us? Willie Mays, that's who.

Willie also returned from the service, and that summer he owned New York City. With his basket catch he made playing center field out in the vast regions of the Polo Grounds look ridiculously easy. Routinely, he made fielding plays that astounded veteran Giant fans. After a so-so start at the plate his bat suddenly caught fire. At one point he was ten games ahead of the home-run pace set by Babe Ruth the year the Bambino walloped sixty. Every time Willie came to bat the denizens of Coogan's Bluff rose to cheer him on.

He became the talk of the town. Even Yankee fans, usually aloof from the paltry concerns of New York's two other teams, began commenting on the exploits of the Giants' twenty-three-year-old superstar. Willie's ingenuous charm endeared him to everyone. He had difficulty remembering names, so when he wanted to get another player's attention he'd simply holler, "Say, hey!"

That summer a rhythm and blues group named the Treniers came out with a record called just that: "Say Hey." When the singers ended their number by asking the musical question, "Whaddya say?" Willie himself chimed in with the only posible answer: "Say hey!"

Willie not only put New York in seventh heaven, he put Leo there as well. The Lip retreated from his position coaching at third base and sat in the dugout quietly making his moves, staying out of rhubarbs. It was that kind of summer—the summer of Willie Mays.

Over in Brooklyn we liked to think that *our* center fielder was the best in baseball. Was this upstart really a match for the Duke? Our boy had been around long enough to prove he was no flash in the pan. Snider's awesome power was never questioned, not even by the least charitable Giant fans, but people sometimes forgot that he was also a stupendous fielder.

On May 31, 1954, he saved a ball game against the Phillies by making what had to be one of the most dramatic catches of all time. The score was 5–4, Brooklyn ahead, in the bottom of the twelfth. Two men were on base. Willie Jones jumped on Clem Labine's pitch and blasted it to the outfield. Harold Rosenthal of the *Herald Tribune* described the play this way: "First it looked like the seats in left center, then it looked like a rebound off the wall which would have been good for a double and two runs. But Duke Snider somehow got to it, made a climbing catch and held the ball. It was a positive sparkler by a center fielder to whom fine plays are routine."

Many a beer drawn in the Web that summer fueled the debate over who was better—the Duke of Flatbush or the Say Hey Kid. Snider had the poise and savvy of a veteran; he had, through several long seasons, worked on his swing and timing to overcome an inbred inclination to lunge after bad pitches. Mays, still inexperienced, had the kind of natural ability that's reserved for only a few players in a single generation.

My vote went for the Duke. Most of my fellow beer drinkers were with me, but there were a few guys around the Web—men whose knowledge of baseball could not be taken lightly—who told me I was nuts.

The morning after Snider made that sensational catch the Milwaukee Braves were in first place; the Dodgers were second, one game behind, and the Giants were third, one and a half games off the pace. Two days later the Dodgers took over the lead. I fully expected them to remain there for the rest of the season.

But Brooklyn was at the time in the middle of a ten-game winning streak. Less than a week after the string was broken I watched in disbelief as Durocher and his Giants shoved their way into first.

Willie Mays was, of course, the most important factor in the Giants' remarkable turnaround from the year before. His presence in the lineup transformed a fair attack into a powerful one. He would finish the year with forty-one homers and a league-leading .345 batting average. He was the league's most valuable player, hands down. Even so, he was not the only reason for New York's sudden success.

Don Mueller, swinging for average instead of the fences, led the league in hits with 212 and batted .342. Leo's most important acquisition that year was pitcher Johnny Antonelli, who came to the Giants in a trade that sent Bobby Thomson to Milwaukee. Johnny put in a tremendous season, winning twenty-one, losing only seven, and posting a 2.30 ERA, best in the league. Another important addition to the pitching staff was Marv Grissom, who'd come over from the Red Sox during the previous season and became the ace of the bullpen in 1954. Ruben Gomez enjoyed another excellent year, and to make the picture even brighter Sal Maglie rebounded from his poor showing in 1953 to win fourteen while losing only six.

And to prove that Leo's fairy godmother was watching, Dusty Rhodes, swigging bourbon as if the world were about to run out of charcoal, had a sensational season at the plate, batting .341. Leo later described the phenomenon this way: "He thought he was the greatest hitter in the whole world and for that one year I never saw a better one. The best pinch hitter, no contest, I ever looked at."

The Bums, meanwhile, were having nothing but woes. Walt Alston made only one important personnel shift—he benched Billy Cox and installed Don Hoak at third. The Dodgers had essentially the same lineup that had brought them their recent glories, but unfortunately the players were not themselves.

Robbie, after getting off to a fine start, suffered a series of injuries that had him in and out of action during the second half of the campaign. Don Thompson, his replacement in left field, was a good fielder but a meager hitter. To make matters worse, Campy was suffering from a nasty hand injury he'd received in a spring exhibition game against the Yankees. In May he was operated on to remove a bone chip from his left wrist. Even when he returned to the lineup, he still wasn't right; 1954 was Campanella's worst year. He appeared in only 111 games and batted .207.

Brooklyn also had plenty of pitching problems. Carl Erskine was brilliant one day, terrible the next. Johnny Podres started the season with a flourish but then was knocked out of action by an appendectomy. The biggest problem of all was Don Newcombe. Bothered by a stiff right shoulder, he bore no resemblance to the Newk of old. His stuff gone, he won only nine games, lost eight, and compiled a 4.55 ERA.

Despite the Giants' highs and the Dodgers' lows, the fans were treated to an exciting pennant race. Just when it began to look as if Leo's boys were going to run away with it, they'd go into a slump and Brooklyn would close in. In July, after leading by six and a half, New York dropped six in a row and watched its margin dwindle to two games. The Giants resumed their winning ways until the middle of August, when they came to Ebbets Field for a three-game series that was almost their undoing.

When the series began on August 13, the Jints were three and a half up on the Flock. Brooklyn took the first game, 3–2, and won the second, 6–5. The Lip had lost two ball games by one run and had watched his lead chopped to a game and a half. Oh, how sweet it was!

The third contest was ridiculous. Billy Loes served up four home-run balls—to Al Dark, Hank Thompson, Willie Mays, and Ray Katt—but Brooklyn won anyhow, 9 4. Now we were only a half game behind. Alex and I just knew the Flock was about to fly in the face of New York.

Guess again. In two days the Giants built their lead back up to two games. Still, the Dodgers stayed right on their tail until Labor Day weekend. On Friday night, September 3, New York beat Brooklyn at the Polo Grounds, 7–4. The next afternoon the Giants murdered the Bums, 13–4. On Sunday the Dodgers salvaged a 7–4 win over their archenemies, but the following day they dropped both ends of a twin bill with Pittsburgh. The Pirates, still the sorriest team in the league, snapped a ten-game losing streak by winning the opening game.

The Bums were now five games back, and that's precisely where they were when the season ended. Many Flatbush fanatics succumbed to the temptation to blame Walt Alston for Brooklyn's demise. I did not. It was obvious to me that the Dodgers' miseries, coupled with the Giants' serendipity, were part of a larger design. They were basic elements in the summer of Willie Mays.

That September I began working toward a Ph.D. in English. Months earlier, I'd realized I was wasting my time with law and had applied to NYU graduate school. After being accepted, I took an apartment on Christopher Street and moved into Manhattan. I had some doubts about leaving Alex and Sally alone, but it was time to be on my own. With the GI Bill and income from a part-time job at Go! Sportswear, I had few financial worries.

For the first time since Casey Stengel became manager, the Yankees would not be in the World Series. At the beginning of the season, Casey had been faced with a number of holes to fill. The army had reclaimed Billy Martin. Johnny Mize had retired. And, in a move designed to shake up the Yankee "fat cats," George Weiss had sold Vic Raschi to the Cardinals. To add to Casey's problems, Mantle had undergone knee surgery twice in the off-season and reported wearing a heavy brace. It would be several months before he could hit, run, and field with his usual efficiency.

On the brighter side, Stengel had three good-looking rookies: Bill "Moose" Skowron, a power-hitting first baseman; Bob Grim, a right-handed pitcher; and Andy Carey, a third baseman.

But no amount of young blood would help the Yankees in 1954. What Casey didn't know as the season started was that his real problem was a team from the shores of Lake Erie. No matter how well the Yanks played that summer, no matter how many games they won, the Indians always played a little better and won a few more.

The Yanks finished with a record of 103–51—their best season ever under Stengel—for a winning percentage of nearly .700. But the Indians, with Bob Lemon, Early Wynn, Mike Garcia, Bob Feller, Bobby Avila, Al Rosen, and Larry Doby, tore off an amazing 111 victories to set an American League record and outdistance the second-place Yanks by eight lengths. After five straight world championships, the Yankees could afford to be philosophical.

On September 29, twelve days after Rocky Marciano knocked out Ezzard Charles in the eighth round at Yankee Stadium to retain his heavyweight title, the Series between the Indians and the Giants began at the Polo Grounds. Out in Colorado, President Eisenhower interrupted his golf game to watch the game on television.

After Perry Como crooned the National Anthem, the shirtsleeved crowd settled back to watch this strangely Yankee-free Series opener. Sal Maglie was opposing Bob Lemon. The Barber took the mound and almost immediately gave Giant fans reason to believe the oddsmakers were right to favor the Tribe. After missing the strike zone with his first three pitches, Maglie hit leadoff batter Al Smith with his fourth.

Bobby Avila, the American League batting champ, followed with a single over the head of Davey Williams. When Don Mueller bobbled the ball, Avila scooted on to second, and Smith took third. After Larry Doby and Al Rosen flied out, Vic Wertz, the Indians' muscular first baseman, began one of his most productive and frustrating days in baseball. The big former Tiger and Oriole laced one of Maglie's deliveries off the right-field wall for a triple, giving the Indians a two-run lead.

In the Giant third Whitey Lockman led off with a sharp single to right, and Alvin Dark followed with a single through the box, moving Lockman to third. Mueller then forced Dark at second, but Lockman crossed the plate on the play, making it a 2–1 game. After Willie Mays walked, Hank Thompson slashed yet another single to score Mueller and tie the score. With one out, runners on first and third, the Giants had a chance to move into the lead. But Lemon bore down. He fanned Monte Irvin and got Davey Williams on an easy groundout to George Strickland.

From the moment the Giants tied the game, Lemon began to get tougher with every pitch. Maglie, meanwhile, was having his problems. He pitched out of trouble in the fourth, fifth, and sixth. The Indians were getting plenty of baserunners, but they couldn't bring them home.

Going to the top of the eighth, it was still a 2–2 tie. Doby worked out a leadoff walk, and then Rosen cracked a sharp grounder to Dark's right. Al managed to barehand the ball, but it was too late to make a play. There were runners on first and second, no outs, and the batter was Vic Wertz, who already had a triple and two singles. Durocher pulled Maglie and replaced him with Don Liddle, a left-hander.

Wertz swung at Liddle's first delivery and drilled the ball toward center field. Willie Mays turned and began to sprint toward the bleachers. The ball arched through the steamy afternoon air, and Willie kept running. As he reached the warning track and neared the green wall, he extended both hands. The ball streaked almost directly over his head and settled into his glove. The runners tagged. Willie whirled, his hat flying off, whipped the ball toward the infield with every ounce of strength, and sprawled to the ground. Davey Williams took the throw behind second. Doby was able to advance no farther than third; Rosen had to hold at first.

After Mays's stupendous catch, Cleveland manager Al Lopez and Durocher played the old lefty-righty-lefty game. Lopez sent righty Hank Majeski up to bat for Dave Philley. Leo replaced Liddle with right-handed Marv Grissom. Lopez called Majeski back in favor of lefty Dale Mitchell.

Grissom worked carefully to Mitchell and wound up walking him. But he then got pinch hitter Dave Pope on a called third strike and retired catcher Jim Hegan on a long near home run to left.

Grissom was again in trouble in the ninth when, with two outs, an error and an intentional pass put runners on first and second. He escaped unscathed by getting Rosen to loft a fly to Irvin. The troubles that had beset Giant hurlers throughout the afternoon continued right on as the deadlocked game moved into extra innings.

In the top of the tenth, Wertz blasted a double up the power alley in left center. It took another outstanding play by Mays to keep the shot from becoming an inside-the-park home run. Rudy Regalado came on as a pinch runner, and as Wertz—four for five and a 460-foot out on the day—trotted to the dugout, the Polo Grounds crowd gave him an ovation.

With no outs and a runner in scoring position, Grissom had his work cut out. After Sam Dente sacrificed Regalado to third, Bill Glynn batted for Hegan and struck out. Lemon ended the inning with a line drive that Lockman caught just above his shoe tops.

Lemon, who'd given up only one hit in the past five innings, started the bottom of the tenth by fanning Mueller. But the next batter, Mays, worked him for a walk. As Hank Thompson stepped into the batter's box, wheels were turning in Durocher's head. Hegan, the Indians' agile, strong-armed catcher, was on the bench. Leo flashed the steal sign to Willie. Mickey Grasso, Hegan's replacement, threw into the dirt in front of second and Mays was safe. With first base unoccupied, Lemon intentionally walked Thompson.

Durocher sent out his first pinch hitter of the day—Dusty Rhodes. The left-handed Rhodes cut at Lemon's first pitch and sent a fly ball along the right-field line. Dave Pope went to the wall and leaped high. The ball skimmed his glove, skimmed the railing on the wall, hit a fan in the chest, and bounced back onto the field. The crowd was hushed. No one was sure what had happened. Suddenly right-field umpire Larry Napp began waving his arm in circles. Dusty's hit had traveled only 258 feet, but in the Polo Grounds that was enough.

Willie Mays had taken two steps off second and then watched the flight of the ball intently. When he saw Napp's signal, he jumped up and down. While Willie was celebrating, Thompson and Rhodes were closing in on him. As Willie bounded into third, he turned and waved at the other runners to slow down. He stomped firmly on the bag and rounded the corner. After a few steps, he turned and pointed at the bag to be sure that Thompson touched it. A moment later, he did the same for Rhodes. The three men crossed the plate in a tight pack, one after the other, and fell into the arms of their waiting teammates.

Rhodes's homer may not have been spectacular, but it did the job. As Red Smith put it, the clout "was as oriental as a geisha girl eating chow mein in Shanghai. It was struck with a chopstick on a tall, flabby arc. . . . Laundry tickets fluttered in all directions, but it was official."

The Giants would go on to sweep the Indians in four straight, and Dusty Rhodes's name would become a household word.

The next year, 1955, was the most complicated year of my life. It had its unexpected joys, but I remember it now mostly as a year of confusion and sadness.

I began the year with the unhappy discovery that English literature was no more my forte than the law. Only after facing up to an enormous amount of guilt was I able to admit to myself that I did not enjoy plowing through Wyatt and Surrey, or even Spenser and Milton. I had my moments with Shakespeare and Donne, but for the most part graduate school was a dreary affair. Unwilling to own up to yet another personal defeat, I struggled through my finals, got passing grades, and went right into another semester.

The same week that I completed my first-semester finals, the *Brooklyn Eagle* closed its doors forever, after 114 years of publication. Alex and I thought at first that the paper, struck by the Newspaper Guild of New York, would be back on the stands in a matter of weeks. We didn't take seriously publisher Frank D. Schroth's "parting word" in a front-page column of the *Eagle*'s final edition of January 28, 1955:

> Again Brooklyn falls victim to the Manhattan pattern. It has been that way since Brooklyn became a part of New York City. The borough has been a stepchild in government services, charity, social activities, and indeed in every phase of community life. The Manhattan pattern now closes . . . the last voice that is purely Brooklyn. All the other Brooklyn newspapers fell by the wayside years ago. This borough seems doomed to be cast in Manhattan's shadow.

"Who ever heard of such a thing—Brooklyn without the *Eagle?*" Alex asked.

I had no answer. As the weeks passed, hope for the grand old newspaper faded. By March the *Eagle* was dead.

Alex and I had our doubts about the Dodgers. We wondered, after the team's problems in 1954, whether it would show much in 1955. Our heroes were getting old.

Imagine our surprise when the Bums set a modern record for victories at the start of a season by winning their first ten ball games. The game that established the new mark was especially satisfying. On April 21 the Dodgers clobbered Robin Roberts, the ace of the league, knocking in ten runs in the first four innings. We won that game with the Phillies, 14–4.

The following night the Giants came to Ebbets Field for what proved to be the most exciting game of the season. It was played under a blanket of fog and drizzle. Brooklyn's starter was Johnny Podres; going into the eighth he was coasting along with a 3–0 lead. When the Giant half of the inning was over Johnny was taking a shower and New York was ahead, 5–3.

In the bottom of the eighth, Brooklyn, batting against reliever Marv Grissom, quickly loaded the bases when Campy singled, Don Zimmer was hit by a pitch, and Don Hoak reached first on an error by Whitey Lockman. Junior Gilliam forced Hoak at second, bringing Campy home. Now there were runners at first and third, and Jackie Robinson was the batter.

The squeeze was on, and everyone in Flatbush knew it. Lockman, lunging in to field Robbie's bunt, flipped to Wes Westrum. Zimmer, attempting a fadeaway slide, was called out by umpire Babe Pinelli. Don got into a furious debate over the call. Walt Alston raced in from the third base coach's box to join the rhubarb. Displaying out-of-character ferocity, Walt was thumbed out of the ball game for the first time in his managerial career.

In the ninth Willie Mays made a beautiful shoestring catch of a bloop fly by Carl Furillo to end the game and the streak.

The Dodgers and Giants split the remaining two games of the series, and then Brooklyn went back on the rampage. They won eleven more in a row. On May 11, the day the Cubs finally put an end to the second streak, the Flock was eight and a half games in first place. No one had a prayer of catching them.

At 6:03 P.M. on May 12 the last train of the Third Avenue El, a Manhattan institution for seventy-seven years, left Chatham Square for One Hundred Forty-ninth Street. Eight hundred persons jammed into the five cars; along the way dwellers in the tenements lining Third Avenue waived a final salute to the noisy conveyance whose end had finally come.

I paid only passing attention to the demise of the El. I was too wrapped up in the amazing Dodgers. The Bums were winning because they were, for an aging team, in remarkably good form. Don Newcombe, completely rejuvenated, was having a sensational season. He won his first ten starts, went on to a record of twenty and five for the year, and helped his cause by batting .359, positively inhuman for a pitcher. Campanella was his old self too—so much so that in August he would be the subject of a cover story in *Time*. Roy would have a .318 batting average and thirty-two homers at the end of the campaign.

Aside from Newk, Brooklyn continued to have pitching problems. Erskine, Podres, and Spooner all struggled at times during the season. But three newcomers—Don Bessent, Roger Craig, and a wild but fast bonus baby named Sandy Koufax—helped take up some of the slack.

The attack, however, was fearsome. Paced by Snider, Campanella, Hodges, and Furillo, the club hit more than eighty homers in the first eight weeks of the season. On the night of June 1 alone, the Dodgers walloped six circuit clouts off Milwaukee, including three by the Duke. Leo Durocher, who happened to be watching the game on TV, gave most of the credit to Ebbets Field. "I was just plain disgusted by those fly ball homers," Leo whined. "With the exception of Snider's second one, all were fly balls."

Twenty years later, looking back on his career, the Lip would write, "A Chinese home run? What are you talking about? A Chinese home run is a pop fly hit by the *other* team."

Leo had good reason to moan. His days of glory at the Polo Grounds were over. The veterans who had played such an important part in the miracles of 1951 and 1954 were fading. The shape of things to come became painfully clear when Horace Stoneham sold Sal Maglie on waivers to the Indians for a paltry $10,000. Oh sure, the Giants were still a decent club. But they were no match for either the Dodgers or the rising Milwaukee Braves.

While the Dodgers were winning ball games at an unprecedented pace, the Brooklyn front office appeared eager to lose fans at about the same rate. Unbelievably, Andre Baruch was hired back for a second season behind the microphone, forcing the Faithful to endure another year of "He slides into second base with a stand-up double" and "There go the Cardinals in their cerulean red uniforms." There were times when poor old Andre got so confused Vince Scully had to jump in to clarify exactly what had just happened on the field. Also on the broadcast team that year was Al Helfer, who was so slow gathering his wits that he wasn't able to tell you what was going on till after the noise of the crowd had died down.

If it was hard following a game on TV or radio, it was equally difficult getting seats at the ball park—even though Walter O'Malley was crying the blues about lousy attendance. Whenever I tried calling up the ticket office for information, the phone would ring forever. Going down to Montague Street wasn't much better. The ticket sellers would give you "the best seats left" for the game in question and move you along. It wasn't uncommon to get to the game and discover whole sections of better seats had gone begging.

On days of big games the club would often sell more general admission tickets than there were seats. People would clog the aisles looking for places that simply didn't exist, getting angrier by the minute. Many swore, "This is the last time you'll ever see *me* at Ebbets Field."

Pop and I, incurable diehards, would sheepishly take our places in the enormous line leading to the two exchange windows. We'd wait forty-five minutes for the privilege of buying whatever seats happened to be left. That usually meant paying $2.50 to sit in a center-field box that wasn't nearly as good as the seventy-five-cent bleacher seats overhead.

It simply didn't make any sense. When O'Malley took over the Dodgers he'd given an extraordinary amount of lip service to the notion that the fans must be kept happy at all costs. Now he appeared to be doing everything in his power to destroy public relations. I couldn't help but suspect that there might be a method to his madness.

August came, and with it the hurricane season. A violent hurricane called Diane, a black fury with 115-mile-an-hour winds, was heading toward the coast of South Carolina on August 16. As Diane made ready to strike an innocent populace, Walter O'Malley made an ominous announcement in Brooklyn. He informed the press that in 1956 the Dodgers would play seven games—one with each of the other clubs in the league—in Roosevelt Stadium in Jersey City. This was the age of the automobile, and Roosevelt Stadium—the old home of the Jersey City Giants in the International League—had four thousand parking spaces as compared to Ebbets Field's seven hundred.

Giving declining attendance as the sole reason for his experiment, O'Malley explained that the time had come to prepare "for the day when Ebbets Field would have to be sold." Blaming the loss of patrons on the antiquated park, the Dodger boss declared that if the ball club were to remain in Brooklyn it would require a new stadium—one with good parking, clear sight lines, convenient restrooms, and every other modern comfort.

"We intend to play almost all our home games at Ebbets Field in 1956 and 1957. But we'll have to have a new stadium built shortly thereafter," warned O'Malley.

Asked by the press to elaborate further on this startling development, O'Malley said with a chuckle, "If you wish, you may call it Hurricane Dodger. And the core of the hurricane is now passing over Brooklyn."

Dodger fans everywhere were outraged. There was some talk of holding a demonstration, but nothing came of it. "Jersey City? What the hell do they have in Jersey City?" Alex asked me after he'd learned the disquieting news.

"Nothing. A two-bit intersection called Journal Square—period," I replied disdainfully. But it was hard not to feel more than a tinge of uncertainty, and fear, over the disclosure that the Dodgers would be deserting Ebbets Field next year, if only for seven games.

Arthur Daley, in his column in the *Times*, defined our uncertainty in terms more vivid than we were prepared to accept. He wrote, "If O'Malley can't resettle in Brooklyn, he'll move to Queens, or Long Island or—who knows?—California. Hence this becomes a civic matter after all. That's why he sent up his trial balloon into the heart of Hurricane Dodger, a creature of his own making."

Three days later O'Malley went to Gracie Mansion with Brooklyn Borough President John Cashmore to present an imaginative plan to Mayor Wagner and Robert Moses, the czar of several New York agencies, including the Triborough Bridge and Tunnel Authority. O'Malley's idea was for the city to condemn several blocks in a run-down section of Brooklyn and to construct a municipal stadium on the site. The area in question, at the intersection of Flatbush and Atlantic avenues, was then and still is partly occupied by the decrepit passenger terminal of the Long Island Railroad. The stadium plan, if approved, would become part of a larger urban renewal project that would include a complete renovation of the train station.

O'Malley claimed the Dodgers were willing to invest $6 million in the project. The plan was not without precedent. The New York Coliseum, a convention center then under construction, had been financed by the Triborough Bridge and Tunnel Authority. Robert Moses, however, had absolutely no enthusiasm for O'Malley's proposal. Claiming there were "very serious limitations" on the purpose for which condemned land could be used, Moses dismissed the possibility of building a ball park on the desired property.

"Then, if you don't get this particular site you'll pick up your marbles and leave town?" Moses asked.

"I didn't say that. I don't want to even consider leaving Brooklyn," was O'Malley's reply.

A week later an innocuous item appeared in the second section of the *Times*. It reported that the Los Angeles City Council had sanctioned "official reconnaissance into the matter of bringing big league baseball here." One of the council's first moves would be to invite Walter O'Malley and Horace Stoneham to L.A. to discuss the situation.

I wasn't prepared even to think about the possibility that the Dodgers would move away. Hurricane Dodger began to subside, allowing me to turn my attention back to the pennant race, which was all but over.

In Milwaukee on September 8 the Dodgers murdered the second-place Braves, 10–2, clinching the pennant earlier than ever before in the history of the National League. Brooklyn ended the year thirteen and a half games ahead of Milwaukee, and the Giants came in third, eighteen and a half games out of first.

At high noon on September 24 Leo Durocher, plagued by rumors that he was about to be ousted to make way for Bill Rigney, stepped into Horace Stoneham's office and proclaimed, "I'm retiring from the game." The announcement may have been somewhat premature, but it did mark the end of the Lip's twenty-year love-hate affair with New York City. Stoneham was happy to "accept Durocher's decision with deep personal regret." Horace did indeed have Rigney, now manager of the Minneapolis club, waiting in the wings.

In the American League it was again a battle between the Indians and the Yankees, with the White Sox standing by in case either faltered. But the Tribe, even with rookie fireballer Herb Score, couldn't produce the quantity and quality of pitching that had made the 1954 season a runaway.

The Yankees, meanwhile, with off-season trades, had turned one of the oldest pitching staffs in the game into one of the youngest. In a huge swap with the Baltimore Orioles, the Yanks had given up Gene Woodling and a number of other players to get two young righties, Bob Turley and Don Larsen. From the minors Casey called up rookie Johnny Kucks, another right-hander, and a rejuvenated Tommy Byrne.

Stengel added some power to his bench by bringing up outfielder and backup catcher Elston Howard, the first black ever to make the Yankees. Shortstop Billy Hunter had come along in the Baltimore trade to spell Rizzuto, but it wasn't till Billy Martin returned from the army late in the season that the infield jelled.

In mid-September the Yankees nosed into first place for good. They held on to nip the Indians by three, the White Sox by five.

The World Series of 1955 was the first to be played on Daylight Savings Time; the autumn shadows that often bothered batters were expected to be no factor. It was also the first Series to be televised in color, though the harshness of the picture and the continuous variation of hues left a lot to be desired.

Alex was certain it was the Dodgers' year. No pitcher on the Yanks' staff had ever beaten the Flock in a Series game. What was more, Stengel's hurlers for the first two games—Ford and Byrne—were both lefties. It was axiomatic that no southpaw could stand up to the Bums for nine innings, even in Yankee Stadium.

As the clubs took the field for the opener, only two players remained who'd participated in the 1941 Brooklyn–Yankee matchup: Pee Wee Reese and Phil Rizzuto. It was the thirty-first time the two mighty mites had been opposing shortstops in a World Series game.

The Dodgers pecked away at Ford throughout the game, but they couldn't rout him. Furillo, who'd homered his last time up in the 1953 Series, made it two in a row by connecting his first time up. Duke Snider blasted his sixth Series homer, adding to his National league record, and Jackie Robinson brought the crowd to its feet by successfully stealing home.

But Don Newcombe, weakened by a virus and suffering from a sore back and shoulder, was ineffective. Ellie Howard, in his first Series at bat, homered. Joe Collins borrowed a bat from Mickey Mantle, benched with a pulled hamstring, and blasted two circuit clouts.

Bob Grim relieved Ford in the top of the ninth and blanked the Dodgers. The final was 6–5, Yankees.

Back in 1951, when the Yankees sent him down, Tommy Byrne had been an aging fastball pitcher with poor control. In the minors Byrne developed control, a slider, and guile; he changed vocations from speed merchant to garbage man.

In the second game of the Series, Byrne pitched a complete game, allowing the Dodgers only five hits and driving in the winning runs in a 4–2 Yankee victory. The thirty-five-year-old lefty had handcuffed the Bums with what they themselves called "a helluva assortment of curves at different speeds."

But the day had a negative side for the Yankees. In the first inning Hank Bauer ripped a thigh muscle trying to steal second and had to join the already injured Mantle on the bench. For the rest of the Series, Stengel would play musical outfielders.

In Brooklyn gloom was abundant. Even Alex had to admit that things looked bad. The Dodgers had lost twice in a row to left-handers. Stengel had his righties rested and ready for duty at Ebbets. In every bar in Brooklyn you could hear the same sad refrain: No team had lost the first two and come back to win since McGraw's Giants in 1921, and that had been a five-of-nine Series. No one had ever done it in a seven-game Series.

Shortly after the second game, I received a phone call from an excited Alex. Through the dock foreman at Poopsy Sullivan's trucking company, Alex had managed to get two box seats for game three at Ebbets Field.

The seats turned out to be exceptionally good ones—several rows from the railing and directly opposite third base. Pop finished off his frankfurter, wiped a trace of mustard off his fingers, and squinted toward the bullpen.

"Yep," he said, "Alston's gonna start Podres. What is he, crazy? When's he gonna start Ersk? How are you gonna start a kid lefty in Ebbets Field when you got the best right-hander in the business?"

I didn't bother to point out to Alex that Carl had been only 11–8 that year. He would have just pointed out that Podres was 9–10.

Alston had juggled his lineup somewhat. Wanting another right-handed hitter, he'd benched Don Zimmer, moved Gilliam to second, and put little Sandy Amoros in left. Stengel, platooning as usual, had inserted Bill Skowron in place of Collins. And to everybody's surprise, Mantle was in center. After the first inning, when Mickey hobbled painfully after a fly ball, Casey would move him to right.

As the Dodgers came out on the field for the top of the first, Jackie Robinson took his place at third base. It was the fourth position for Robbie in Series play. When he removed his cap to wipe his brow, Alex and I could see a lot of gray hair on his thirty-six-year-old head. But the minute he replaced the cap and began to chatter encouragement to the kid on the mound, he was the Robbie of old.

It was Johnny Podres's twenty-third birthday. He began the celebration well by easily disposing of the Yanks in the first inning.

Bob Turley, the Yankee pitcher, could throw an awesome fastball, but he wasn't noted for his consistency. With one away, he walked Reese and then fanned Snider. Roy Campanella, 0 for 8, stepped in and lined the second pitch into the left center stands to give the Bums a 2–0 lead.

But Mantle led off the Yankee second with a 400-foot shot to center. Skowron followed with a double to left. After Howard grounded out and Billy Martin struck out, Rizzuto cracked a single to left. Sandy Amoros ran the ball down and let fly a perfect throw to the plate.

Skowron rounded third and thundered homeward. The throw was well ahead of him. But Moose, a former star halfback at Purdue, didn't bother to slide. As Campy reached out to tag him, he twisted down and away. Skowron's shoulder slammed into Roy's hand. The ball popped free and rolled toward the dugout. Rizzuto also crossed the plate before Campy could retrieve the ball, but because it had dropped into the dugout Phil was ruled back to third. Podres then retired Turley to end the inning.

The Dodgers broke the tie almost immediately. With one away, Robinson singled. Turley hit Amoros with a pitch, and then Podres, attempting to sacrifice, came up with a bunt single to load the bases. When Turley walked Gilliam to force in a run, Stengel had seen enough. He called in Tom Morgan, a tall right-hander. Morgan managed to retire the side, but not before he had walked Reese to give the Dodgers a 4–2 lead.

Podres allowed the Yankees only one more run, while the Dodgers collected four more. Going to the top of the ninth, it was 8–3. And that was the way it stood when Hodges gloved Rizzuto's pop-up for the final out. Organist Gladys Goodding broke into "Happy Birthday to You," and most of the crowd joined in.

Alex was impressed with Podres, but he couldn't stop talking about Jackie Robinson. "Just goes to show you," he said, "that us older guys can still cut the mustard."

Robbie had played a great game at bat, on the basepaths, and at third, where he'd handled several tough chances with ease. But the high spot of his performance came in the seventh when he doubled to left. As Howard was fielding the ball, Robbie made a seductively wide turn at second. Howard, who'd thrown out runners in similar situations during the season, fired to second. But Robbie had a surprise for the youngster. He broke for third and made it easily. Alex yelled himself hoarse. For one brief moment, I had a glimpse of not only the Robbie of old but the Alex of old as well.

Game four was played on a bleak, gray day. Alston was finally giving Carl Erskine a start. The day became even more somber for Dodger fans when Ersk, after striking out leadoff batter Irv Noren, grooved a fastball to Gil McDougald. Gil drove it into the lower stands in left center field for a 1–0 Yank lead.

The carefree Don Larsen held the Dodgers in check in their half of the first. In the second the Bombers scored again on a walk by Collins, a sacrifice by Howard, and a single by Rizzuto. But in the third the Dodgers narrowed the gap to one run when the speedy Sandy Amoros, after walking, scored all the way from first on a Junior Gilliam double.

But the Yankees continued to be pesky. In the fourth Berra singled and Collins followed with a walk. That was all for Erskine. He was replaced by Don Bessent, who came off the mound quickly to field Howard's sacrifice attempt and force Berra at third. But then the youngster made a mistake. He allowed Collins to get a jump on him and then delivered the ball in the dirt. Campy made a fine stop, but Collins was safe at third with his first stolen base of the season. Billy Martin followed with a blooper to shallow right, and the Yankees were again up by two, 3–1.

In the fourth, the Dodgers launched a blitzkrieg. Campanella led off the inning and parked one in the left-field seats; Furillo got an infield single; and Gil Hodges blasted one over the right-field scoreboard. In a matter of minutes, the Flock had a 4–3 lead. Larsen settled down and retired the next three batters.

In the top of the fifth the Yankees filled the bases on singles by Noren and Mantle and a walk to Berra. With two away the batter was Joe Collins. Clem Labine came out of the bullpen to face him. He got Collins to hit into a force-out, and Ebbets Field was bedlam.

After Larsen had walked Gilliam in the bottom of the fifth, Stengel brought on Johnny Kucks. Reese singled, and then the Duke caught one on the fat part of the bat. It was still climbing when it disappeared over the right-field screen. It finally came down in the used car lot on the other side of Bedford Avenue. Snider had again added to his National League record, now seven. In the American League three men had hit more World Series homers: Ruth, fifteen; Gehrig, ten; and DiMaggio, eight.

The Yankees scratched out two more runs in the sixth, and the Dodgers added a tally with three consecutive singles in the seventh. The final was 8–3, and the Bums had evened the Series at two apiece.

With his two aces, Newcombe and Erskine, in poor condition, Alston was hard pressed to find a pitcher for game number five. He decided to gamble with Roger Craig, a 6 foot, 4 inch youngster who'd been five and three on the season.

Stengel, meanwhile, was hard pressed for outfielders. He moved Collins to right, inserted Eddie Robinson at first, and played Howard and Noren in left and center. Bob Grim was on the mound for the Yanks.

After a scoreless first, Craig walked the first two batters he faced in the second. It looked at though the pressure was going to get to him, but he pulled himself together and retired the next three batters on easy infield outs.

Furillo opened the Dodger second by lining to McDougald. Hodges followed with a bloop single. Jackie Robinson stepped in and cracked a sharp drive down the right-field line. The crowd was pulled to its feet. The ball was foul by inches. Robbie then lined to Rizzuto for the second out. The next batter was Amoros. Joe Collins watched helplessly as Sandy's lazy fly to right plummeted in an almost straight line. It cleared the screen by inches, and the Bums had a 2–0 lead.

Snider made it 3–0 leading off the next inning when he hit a fly that was a replay of Amoros's homer.

Craig, meanwhile, had been doing a surprisingly good job holding the Yankees at bay. But they finally got to him for a run in the fourth, when Berra singled, Eddie Robinson walked, and Martin singled Berra home.

It was still a 3–1 ball game in the fifth when the Duke, with one away and the count three and two, clouted a huge, no-contest homer over the barrier in right center field.

In the seventh big Bob Cerv, batting for Grim, closed the gap again.

Craig offered him a high, hanging curve, and Cerv slapped it into the lower tier in left. After Howard walked, Clem Labine came on for his fourth appearance in the five games. Labine delivered his best pitch, a sinking fastball, and Noren promptly hit into a double play. McDougald grounded back to the pitcher to end the inning. The crowd had given Craig a rousing hand when he left the game. Now they roared their approval of Labine.

When Labine threw his fastball low, it sank sharply, and a batter was hard put to do anything but hit it on the ground. But when Clem threw his fastball high, it tended to stay flat. Beginning the eighth, he threw a high fast one to Yogi Berra, and the score was suddenly 4–3.

The Dodgers got the run back in the eighth on a single, a sacrifice, and a single. Labine put down the Yanks easily in the ninth, and the Dodgers had a 5–3 victory. Miraculously, they were now ahead in the Series, three games to two.

The refrain in Brooklyn's taverns had changed. Sure, no team had ever dropped the first two and come back—but the Bums could. Sure, the Series was going back to Yankee Stadium where Ford and Byrne had stymied the Flock. But the two lefties couldn't do it again. The Bums were hitting now. In the three games in Flatbush, the Dodgers had produced thirty-four hits, including six doubles and seven home runs.

But the Faithful weren't counting on the competitive spirit and remarkable ability of Whitey Ford. Throughout his career, Ford had been spotted against the toughest teams, always pitching the "must" games. Yet he had the highest winning percentage, .735, of all active major league pitchers.

The Yankees gave Whitey a five-run lead in the first inning, far more than he needed. He allowed only four hits and one run. At times he seemed to be toying with the Dodger batters. He was in complete control of the game, and there was never any doubt of its outcome.

Harry had called to offer me a seat in his company box for games six and seven, but I'd politely turned him down. If the Dodgers blew it, I didn't want to be in the Stadium. If they won, if the miracle happened, I wanted to be in Brooklyn.

But as Pop and I walked to the Web to watch game seven, I had to admit that chances were slim. The pitchers would be Podres and Byrne. Podres was young, had had shoulder trouble, and prior to his birthday victory hadn't pitched a complete game since the middle of the season. Byrne was a veteran and seemed to be in fine shape. Chances were he'd be even tougher on the second go-around.

To make matters worse, the Duke had popped something in his knee early in game six and had left the game. He was a doubtful starter. Robbie, who'd been a ball of fire in the three Ebbets Field wins, was definitely out with a strained Achilles' tendon.

The mood at the Web was one of cautious optimism. After the first scoreless inning, the men in the crowded bar grew even more subdued. The game took on a fragile, brittle quality. It was ready to shatter at any moment. Plays were acknowledged with gasps or mutters. Between innings, drinks were ordered in quiet voices.

A ground-rule double by Skowron in the second came to nothing. But in the third the delicately balanced contest began to teeter. With two away, Rizzuto walked. Martin cracked a single to short right, and Rizzuto held at second. McDougald was the batter. He hit a vicious chopper down the third base line. Had Don Hoak, playing in place of Robbie, been able to reach the ball, the bases would have been loaded. But Hoak was playing back, and Rizzuto slid in front of him. Just before the Scooter's foot touched the bag, the bounding ball struck him. Rizzuto was out and the inning was over.

In the Dodger fourth, after Snider, playing despite his injured knee, struck out, Campanella smashed a hard double to left. Furillo followed with an infield out, moving Campy to third. And then Gil Hodges singled over Rizzuto's head. The Brooks had a 1–0 toehold.

Leading off the bottom of the fifth, Berra lofted one to left center. As Snider moved over, Gilliam charged from left field. The Duke saw Junior out of the corner of his eye and shied away. Gilliam shouted, "Take it!" It was too late. The ball dropped, and Berra had a double. But Podres retired the next three batters.

Byrne was also pitching a strong game. Reese's leadoff single in the top of the sixth was only the third Dodger hit. Snider emphasized the tightness of the game by laying down a bunt. Byrne fielded the ball and threw to Skowron, who made the mistake of trying to tag the Duke. The ball came free and skittered away. There were runners on first and second, no outs. Campanella stepped in. Would he swing away? Campy answered the question by dropping a perfect sacrifice bunt, advancing both runners.

While Bob Grim finished his warmups in the bullpen, Byrne issued an intentional pass to Furillo. With the bases loaded, one away, Grim came on to pitch to Hodges. Gil hit a long fly to center, Reese tagged and scored, and it was 2–0. After throwing a wild pitch, Grim walked Hoak purposely, and the bases were loaded again. Shotgun Shuba came on to bat for Don Zimmer and hit an easy grounder to Skowron to end the inning.

With Zimmer out of the game, Alston had to do some juggling. He moved Gilliam to second base and inserted Sandy Amoros in left field.

Martin led off the Yankee sixth with a walk. McDougald beat out a bunt. No outs, two on, and the batter was Berra. Yogi was a dangerous batter anywhere, but as a left-handed, dead pull hitter, he was especially dangerous in the stadium that had been custom-tailored for the left-handed Ruth. Alston shifted the outfield toward right.

Podres didn't want to give Berra anything he could pull. He delivered outside. Berra reached out and slapped the ball down the left-field line. Amoros, playing in left center, seemed to have no chance. McDougald, aware he represented the tying run, was off at the crack of the bat, intent on scoring all the way from first.

But little Sandy was flying across the outfield. As he neared the foul line—and the wall that jutted out—he stretched and extended his glove hand. And caught the ball. Inches from the barrier, Amoros whirled and fired a perfect throw to Reese, who made a perfect relay to Hodges. McDougald was doubled up, and the rally was nipped in the bud. The crowd went wild. In the Web, there was a tremendous sigh of relief. Something delicate and priceless had swayed on the edge; at the last moment, a sure hand—a gloved right hand—had saved it from destruction.

Alston's offensive move, substituting Shuba for Zimmer, turned out to be a stroke of defensive genius. Had Gilliam, with his glove on his left hand, been in left field, chances were he would have missed the ball.

But the Yankees weren't finished. In the eighth Phil Rizzuto, playing in his fifty-second Series game, led off with a single. After Martin flied out, McDougald smashed another hopper down the third base line. The ball caromed off Hoak's shoulder for a single. But Podres retired Berra on a pop to Furillo and then struck out Bauer. The Stadium crowd roared. In the Web, tension was beginning to ease. There was more movement, and excitement was creeping into the voices.

Bob Turley, who'd come on in the eighth, set the Dodgers down in the bottom of the ninth. And then the Yankees came to bat. Podres was still on the mound.

Skowron grounded to Podres. Cerv flied to Amoros. Howard stepped in. The count went to 2 and 2. Podres shook off a sign. Then another. Then he delivered an offspeed floater. Howard stroked a slow roller to Reese. Pee Wee came up with the ball and threw to first. The throw was low and wide, but Hodges stretched and dug it out. The Dodgers were world champions.

The crowd in the Web went crazy. There was shouting, back-slapping, hugging, kissing. The owner was lining the bar with free drinks, and Alex was behind the bar, laughing hysterically with tears streaming down his face, filling steins with beer and handing them out.

Even in Manhattan there was celebrating. On Wall Street, where business had slowed to a trickle at game time, confetti and ticker tape cascaded from the office building windows. Official forms and documents swirled in the air around the Municipal Building. On the east side of Manhattan, telephone service was interrupted by the biggest flood of calls since V-J Day.

But the party belonged to Brooklyn. From the Court Street skyscrapers flew a blizzard of newspapers, torn telephone books, ticker tape, confetti. Motorcades, horns screaming, raced along Flatbush Avenue and Montague, Fulton, Joralemon, Remsen, and Court streets. Factory whistles blew. On front stoops throughout the borough, there were people banging on pots and pans. Everywhere were signs: "Supermen of the World," "We Doo'd It!" At the *Daily News*, they were composing tomorrow's headline: THIS IS NEXT YEAR!

Whenever I think back on those delirious hours that followed Brooklyn's first and only world championship, I am struck by two thoughts. First, I remember how great it was to be freed from a lifetime of frustration. But then, before I can savor that long ago happiness, I recall the tragic weeks that followed.

All summer long Sally had been suffering from flashing pains. She'd kept her miseries to herself, until finally one day in October she collapsed at the breakfast table. Alex put her to bed and called Dr. Mandel, our family physician.

The doctor didn't arrive until late that afternoon. He found Mom in such severe pain that he gave her an injection of morphine and called an ambulance.

By the time I arrived at the hospital, she was feeling much better. After two weeks of tests and medication, she was strong enough to go home, but she was ordered to report back twice a week for radiation treatments. At first she seemed to respond to the therapy, but the pain soon returned.

The graveness of my mother's condition completely escaped me. I was teaching a section of freshman English and had taken up with one of my students. Her name was Jennifer; she found me irresistibly erudite and articulate. Alex never called, so I assumed all was well.

When I came home for Thanksgiving I was shocked by what I saw. Mother had lost fifteen pounds. She insisted on preparing dinner, but she'd become so frail that the task she always enjoyed in years past was a struggle.

She barely touched her food. As soon as we finished our coffee, she excused herself and went to bed. Alex and I went to the kitchen and stood together over the sink doing the dishes. Neither of us was willing to say what was on our minds.

The next day I called Dr. Mandel, who confirmed my suspicions. Then I phoned Uncle Harry and told him what to expect. He wanted to go right over to Brooklyn to see his brother, but I talked him out of it. I didn't feel Alex was ready to face up to what was happening.

On December 10 Sally returned to the hospital. At first Alex visited her twice a day, but before long he found it impossible to stay with her. Withering to the point that she was more bone than flesh, she looked like a ghost. Except for brief visits in the early mornings, Alex kept his distance.

Harry and Ellen began making daily afternoon visits to Sally's bedside.

Weak as she was, she was happy to see her old friends. She told them the saddest thing about her life these past years was that the family had been torn apart. Sally died the day after Christmas.

Alex took the news quietly. His face reddened as if he were about to cry, but the tears never came. He and I spent most of that night drinking beer at the kitchen table. We talked about many things—Fletcher's grand old house in Park Slope, the Actors Club and the Epicure, Uncle Robbie and the Daffiness Boys. But Alex kept returning to a scene he now remembered in every detail—the day he first met Sally on the boardwalk of a Coney Island that no longer existed.

Before going off to bed I raised a subject I'd been putting off all night. I told Alex something had to be done about making funeral arrangements.

"Damon, whatever you decide is all right with me."

"Harry wants to help—if you'll let him."

"It's up to you."

I was surprised that Alex gave in so easily. But there really wasn't much choice. If Harry didn't take care of the funeral, who would?

Sally was laid to rest the following Thursday. On the way from the funeral home to Greenwood, Alex said a few words to Ellen and me but spent most of the trip looking out the window of the limousine. Several times Harry took a breath as if preparing to say something, but nothing came out.

As the car entered the cemetery, Alex turned to his brother and said, "Harry, I want you to know I appreciate your taking care of all the details."

"Don't worry about it," Harry said. "Look, Alex, we have a lot to talk about. I hope we'll get the chance."

Alex nodded. I could see a look of relief on Harry's face. The car stopped; we all got out and followed the pallbearers up the hill.

Ahead and to the left was a miniature Greek temple, its huge iron door set between two Corinthian columns. When the pallbearers unexpectedly turned and disappeared into the marble edifice, Alex stopped in his tracks and looked aghast at the frieze. There, emblazoned for posterity, was the word "RICE."

I took Alex by the arm and led him into the mausoleum. He was trembling as we took our places. The interment lasted only a few minutes, as Sally was put to rest alongside her father-in-law. Throughout the ceremony, Alex's eyes were fixed upon the stone that read "Fletcher Rice, 1846–1920."

As the ceremony ended, Alex turned and hurried out. By the time the rest of us emerged, he was off in the distance, walking fast along an unending row of headstones. I shouted out to him, but he continued on his way.

"Don't worry about him," Harry said, patting me on the shoulder. "Alex has spent his whole life running off to nowhere."

I found my father that night in the Web Café. He was sitting in a booth in the back room, drinking his whisky with beer chasers. The juke box was playing a medley of Christmas carols. I got a pitcher of beer at the bar and sat down across the table from him.

"It was bad enough he had to put poor old Sally in that fun house," Alex said, shaking his head. "But I still can't believe that phony son of a bitch had the nerve to dig up my old man."

In the early months of 1956, Dodger fans were given reason to hope that Walter O'Malley might just get his stadium in downtown Brooklyn. In February Mayor Wagner sent to the state legislature a bill that would give him the power to create a Brooklyn Sports Center Authority. The authority, to comprise three prominent citizens serving without pay, would be empowered to issue $30 million in bonds to redevelop five-hundred acres surrounding the Long Island Railroad terminal into a stadium complex. O'Malley quickly backed the plan, announcing that the Dodgers were ready to invest $4 million in the bonds.

On April 21, just two days after the Dodgers played their first game in Jersey City, Governor Averell Harriman traveled from Albany to Brooklyn to sign the bill into law. The next day an editorial in the *Times* observed, "there is happiness and relief in Brooklyn," but also warned, "the hardest work is still ahead."

Indeed it was. The bill may have been signed, but Mayor Wagner, facing strong opposition to the project from within his own city government, stressed he would not create the authority until an engineering survey of the site was completed. The $100,000 survey had been approved by the Board of Estimate shortly after O'Malley began his threats. The engineers assigned to the job had submitted a preliminary report during the recent session of legislature. The initial finding was that construction of the stadium would be an "appropriate use" for part of the five-hundred-acre site.

Mayor Wagner didn't get around to appointing the Brooklyn Sports Center Authority until July 24, when he named Charles J. Mylod, a Brooklyn real estate man, to head the panel. In the twelve months since Walter O'Malley first announced he intended to abandon Ebbets Field, the search for a new home for the Dodgers had gotten almost nowhere.

While O'Malley continued to threaten the city, Horace Stoneham said almost nothing. But the Giants, whose attendance had dropped from 1,115,067 in 1954 to 824,112 in 1955, were headed for disaster if something wasn't done to bring their fans back out to the ball park. To add to the club's difficulties, the football Giants had decided to move from the Polo Grounds to Yankee Stadium, depriving Stoneham of an annual rental of $75,000.

The Giants' farm club in Minneapolis would soon have an ultra-modern stadium, financed with public funds. This gave credence to rumors that Stoneham was considering moving to Minnesota. Horace denied it emphatically, saying, "The future of the Giants is in New York. In the Polo Grounds, perhaps in Yankee Stadium at some time, but in New York."

If a new ball park would cure the Dodgers' ills, it would do the same for the Giants. So reasoned Manhattan President Hulan E. Jack when, in March 1956, he unveiled a proposal for a new Giant stadium. I must say the scheme taxed my own imagination to its very limits. Jack's idea was to build a 110,000-seat ball park on stilts over the tracks of the New York Central Railroad on the West Side of Manhattan, between Sixtieth and Seventy-second streets. In May, Mayor Wagner met with Stoneham and Jack to look over architects' drawings for the project. The mayor came away calling the plan "interesting and ambitious."

While old Horace was nibbling away on Hulan Jack's pie in the sky, his baseball team was sliding into the depths of the National League. Giant fans got solid evidence that their team was washed up when it lost four of its first five games with the Dodgers. Lockman and Dark had been traded away, and Don Mueller was getting old before his time. The club was almost without an offense, except for Willie Mays.

In a desperate attempt to find a winning combination, Bill Rigney began shuffling his players like a Las Vegas blackjack dealer. By June 16 the only man in the lineup who'd been there on opening day was Mays. Unfortunately, men such as George Wilson, Ed Bressoud, Jackie Brandt, Jim Mangan, and Foster Castleman couldn't quite fill the shoes of Don Mueller, Alvin Dark, Whitey Lockman, Wes Westrum, and Hank Thompson.

The Giants occupied the cellar from June till late August, before finally rising up to sixth place. They finished the year twenty-six games back. The club's terrible performance sent its season attendance plummeting to 629,267, a disastrous level. And two hundred fifty thousand of those customers attended New York's eleven home games with Brooklyn. The Flatbush Faithful were giving the Giants almost as much support at the gate as their own fans.

The team to beat that summer was the Milwaukee Braves. Manager Fred Haney appeared to have everything. In Warren Spahn and Lew Burdette he had the best one-two hurling punch in the league. He also had righty Bob Buhl, who mesmerized the Dodgers every time he faced them. Then there were sluggers such as Eddie Mathews and Joe Adcock, not to mention young Hank Aaron, destined to win the 1956 batting title with a .328 average. I honestly figured it would be only a matter of time before the Braves began running away from the rest of the league.

Aside from fearing the Braves, I was also losing faith in the Dodgers. Brooklyn got off to a fair start in 1956, but nothing like its great performance during the opening weeks of the year before. The average age of the Dodger lineup, not counting pitchers, was almost thirty-two. It was hard not to believe that the Bums were playing on borrowed time.

On April 19 the Dodgers initiated New Jersey into the major leagues. It was an icy, windy day, and the Bums defeated the Phils, 5–4. The Jersey City crowd of 12,214, made up largely of Giant fans, gave the Dodgers many more jeers than cheers. None of the players was particularly thrilled over having to endure seven "home" games on foreign soil.

At the start of the second month of the campaign Brooklyn was in fourth place, two games behind the league-leading Braves, and no one on the Dodgers was batting over .300. It was beginning to look as if Walt Alston would have to pin his hopes for a pennant on his mound corps. He had lost Johnny Podres to the army, but Don Newcombe was going great, winning five of his first six starts. Roger Craig's solid hurling had won him a spot in the starting rotation, and Clem Labine's almost daily relief appearances supported his credentials as the best fireman in the majors. Carl Erskine, after starting the campaign with arm trouble, became the first Dodger ever to pitch two no-hitters when, on May 12, he held the Giants to two walks and zero hits. In addition to his regular starters Alston still had Sandy Koufax and another promising kid, Don Drysdale. The batters were having problems, but the pitchers were keeping the Dodgers in the race.

In May the Dodgers sold Billy Loes, whom they'd carried long enough, to the Baltimore Orioles. To replace Billy they picked up none other than Sal Maglie from the Indians. The Barber, whose lifetime record against Brooklyn was twenty-three and eleven, had scared the daylights out of me and everyone else in Flatbush whenever he faced the Bums. Glowering down from the mound, his face blackened by a five o'clock shadow, he was the very definition of intimidation. The press liked to call him saturnine—a most appropriate adjective. I was delighted when he left New York for Cleveland, and I was just as happy to see him come to Brooklyn.

"Even though he's thirty-nine, he might just help us," Alex remarked. "If he does, he won't be the first Giant castoff to give Brooklyn a hand. Rube Marquard was no slouch at Ebbets Field, and neither was Freddie Fitzsimmons."

The pennant race developed into a three-team struggle among Milwaukee, Brooklyn, and a surprising Cincinnati ball club. During the last half of July the Dodgers appeared to be folding, as they dropped back to six games behind the Braves. But just as I was getting ready to count the Bums out, they put together a string of eight victories—including two each by Newcombe, Erskine, and Maglie—to pull back within two games of Milwaukee.

On August 23 President Eisenhower accepted his party's nomination for a second term. That same night Don Newcombe won his twentieth game of the year, beating the Reds, 6–5. The Dodgers defeated Cincinnati the following day, 6–4, but lost the getaway game, 5–2. The loss, Carl Erskine's first setback after nine straight wins, sent the Dodgers to Milwaukee two games behind the front-running Braves.

In the first of the two games at County Stadium, Bob Buhl defeated Roger Craig, 6–2. It was Buhl's seventh win that year over the Bums. The Brooks bounced back to beat the Braves, 6–3, and left Wisconsin still only two games out.

So it went into September, with the Braves clinging to a small lead, the Dodgers holding onto second place, and the Reds right behind. It was a good, old-fashioned pennant race, as exciting as those between the Dodgers and Cardinals in the forties.

The lowly Giants put a real scare into the Dodgers by beating them twice the day before Labor Day and dropping them three games behind Milwaukee. But a week later, aided by a five-game losing streak by the Braves, Brooklyn was right back in the fight.

On the night of September 11 the Braves came into Ebbets Field one game up on Brooklyn. Not surprisingly, Fred Haney sent Buhl, his ace Dodger killer, out to face Maglie. The evening belonged to Sal. Aside from giving up two homers—one to Eddie Mathews and the other to Joe Adcock—the Barber baffled the Braves with his amazing assortment of inside and outside curves.

To aid his own cause, Sal drove in two runs with a bases-loaded single in the fourth. The Dodgers scored twice again in the eighth. Jackie Robinson dashed home from second after relief pitcher Ernie Johnson, trying to pick off Robbie, threw the ball into center field. A minute later Gil Hodges knocked one into the left-field seats.

Brooklyn was now tied for first place. It was the first time the Flock had seen the top of the standings since April 28.

The next day the Dodgers sent Lew Burdette to the showers in the first inning, and then the Braves knocked Newcombe out of the box in the second. Milwaukee went on to win the poorly pitched game, 8–7. The winning pitcher, surprisingly enough, was Buhl. His relief victory made him the first hurler in National League history to beat one club eight times in a single season. By taking the final game of the year between the two contenders, the Braves once again took sole possession of first place.

On September 15 Newcombe spun a three-hit shutout to beat the Cubs, 3–0. The Braves, meanwhile, lost to the Phils and relinquished the league lead for the first time in two months.

The Dodgers clung to a paper-thin lead until September 23, when the Braves beat the Cubs while a game between the Dodgers and the Giants was halted in the ninth inning by the Pennsylvania curfew law, with

Brooklyn ahead, 8–3. The Dodgers won the suspended game the next night, but then lost the regularly scheduled contest with the Bucs, 6–5. Milwaukee was back in front by a half game.

The season was running out. The Dodgers had only five games to play as they returned to Ebbets Field to wind up the campaign.

The opener against the Phillies was Brooklyn's most thrilling game of the year. Maglie pitched inning after inning of hitless ball. Going into the ninth the Dodgers were ahead, 5–0, and Maglie had given Philadelphia nothing but a pair of walks. The Faithful were on their feet, urging the Barber on with every pitch.

Frankie Baumholtz led off the inning with a foul pop that Campy pulled in on the steps of the Brooklyn dugout. Then Harvey Haddix struck out on three pitches. The crowd groaned when Richie Ashburn, the next batter, was hit on the foot and awarded first. But Sal got Marv Blaylock to ground out to Jim Gilliam, ending the game and giving him the first no-hitter of his career.

The next day, the jubilation over Maglie's masterpiece gave way to despair, as the Dodgers lost to the Phils, 7–3, and dropped a full game behind the idle Braves.

The final weekend of the season began with a rainout of the Dodgers' Friday night contest with the Pirates. The Braves, playing in St. Louis, lost to the Cardinals, 5–4, narrowing the race to a half game. To make up the washout, Brooklyn scheduled a doubleheader for the following afternoon.

In the first game Saturday, Maglie faced another old Dodger nemesis, Bob Friend. After giving up a two-run homer to Frank Thomas in the first, the Barber became razor sharp. He held the Pirates scoreless for eight innings, while Amoros, Furillo, and Hodges all socked homers to contribute to a 6–2 Dodger victory.

Walt Alston pulled Clem Labine out of the bullpen to start the nightcap. It was a wild affair, with the Faithful almost causing a forfeit. In the fifth, with Brooklyn ahead, 1–0, Campanella reached first on a scratch single. Labine bunted in front of the plate, and catcher Hank Foiles threw to second hoping for the force. The high peg pulled shortstop Dick Groat off the bag, and before he came down Campy had slid in. Umpire Vic Delmore, to the astonishment of everyone in the park, called Campy out.

The crowd continued to protest the call long after Alston and Campanella had given up the ghost. White handkerchiefs fluttered in every corner of the old ball park. Scraps of paper were thrown on the field as the crowd booed and hissed and jeered into the next inning.

Finally Jocko Conlan, the chief of the umpiring crew, walked in and ordered Tex Rickard, the public address announcer, to warn the fans to quiet down, "lest the game might be forfeited."

The crowd didn't stop grumbling about the lousy call until the bottom of the sixth, when Gil Hodges tripled home two runs to put the game on ice. Clem Labine went all the way to register his first complete game in more than a year.

That evening the Cards beat the Braves, 2–1, in twelve innings, giving Brooklyn at least a tie for the pennant.

As usual, Newcombe was called upon to pitch the game that would seal Brooklyn's fate. A crowd of 31,893, myself included, was on hand to watch a contest that could, at the very least, send the Dodgers into a playoff with Milwaukee. Brooklyn's two victories the day before had eliminated the Reds, leaving only the Braves to be disposed of.

Vern Law, the Pirate starter, was bounced from the rubber in the very first inning when Duke Snider homered into the center-field seats with Gilliam and Reese aboard. In the third, however, Roberto Clemente singled home two runners to narrow the gap to only one run.

Everyone in Ebbets Field began to breathe easy when Robbie homered in the bottom of the third, and we all became downright carefree in the fifth, when Newcombe scored from third on a sacrifice fly by Reese, and then the Duke sent his second homer of the day into Bedford Avenue. Sandy Amoros homered in the seventh to make the score 7–2, a positive laugher.

Our grins turned to groans in the seventh, when Bill Virdon doubled with the bases loaded to drive in three runs.

After getting one man out in the eighth, Newk served Lee Walls a home-run pitch that narrowed our lead to only one run. Alston then yanked Big Don and brought in Don Bessent, who got into an immediate jam when Groat singled and Robbie bungled a double-play ball. But then Bessent settled down and got the two outs he needed. In the bottom of the eighth Sandy Amoros became the second Dodger to hit two homers, and Brooklyn had an 8–6 lead.

Anyone who might have been thinking about heading for the exits in the top of the ninth quickly settled back down when Clemente led off with a clean single. But then Virdon hit a bullet right at Gilliam, and Jim converted it into a double play. Finally, Foiles struck out swinging to give the Dodgers the flag.

It had been a gratifying season for Dodger fans. Instead of choking, the Bums had put on a remarkable team effort in the homestretch. Bessent's fine relief job in the last game gave Don Newcombe his twenty-seventh win against only seven losses.

Attendance in Brooklyn that year defied Walter O'Malley's logic. It rose from 1,033,589 in 1955 to 1,199,775 in 1956. Even though every home game was on TV, the Faithful braved inadequate parking facilities, the same terrible ticket situation, surly and indifferent ushers, and all the other discomforts of Ebbets Field because their Dodgers were in the middle of an exciting pennant race. Despite the small capacity, the

Brooklyn club netted more money in broadcasting rights, concessions, and admissions than every other team in the majors except the Yankees and the Braves.

Dodger fans had good reason to believe their heroes would make it two World Series in a row over the Yankees. Games one and two, and six and seven if needed, would be played in Ebbets Field, where left-handed pitchers invariably got murdered. There was no way Casey Stengel could wait until the third game to use Whitey Ford. If the Dodgers could knock over the Yanks' ace southpaw on their own turf, they'd be well on their way to victory.

Even though the Bums had the home field advantage, the Yankees, as always, could not be taken lightly. Mantle had put together a tremendous season, leading both leagues in home runs with fifty-two, RBIs with 130, and batting average with .353. He was now baseball's premier star and would remain so for a decade. Berra had been the league's MVP the two previous years.

Phil Rizzuto was gone, released in late August, on Old Timers' Day. But Gil McDougald, shifted from third to short, had earned himself a spot on the All-Star roster. It was the third position he had started in that game.

In spite of numerous injuries, the Yankees had leaped into first place in May and had never been headed. They coasted to the pennant with a nine-game margin over second-place Cleveland.

Stengel went ahead and named Ford, who'd won ten of his last eleven starts and had beaten the Dodgers twice in the previous Series, to start the opener against Sal Maglie. The Barber gave up a two-run homer to Mantle in the first inning but went on to pitch a strong complete game. The Dodgers routed Ford after three and went on to win it, 6–3, sparked by home runs from Jackie Robinson and Gil Hodges.

In the second game Don Newcombe went against Don Larsen. It was a slugfest, and both pitchers were in the clubhouse early. With the help of Berra's grand-slam homer, the Yankees put together a five-run second inning to lead, 6–0. But in the Dodger half of the inning Duke Snider matched Berra's feat, as the Bums scored six runs to even the score. Don Bessent came on for the Dodgers in the third and was eventually credited with the 13–8 win.

Because there had been a one-day rain delay between the first and second games and because Ford had pitched only three innings in his first start, Stengel decided to go again with his ace in the third game. This time Whitey, back on his home ground, pitched a complete game and beat the Dodgers, 5–3.

The following day, Tom Sturdivant delivered another complete game, and the Yankees evened the Series by defeating Carl Erskine, 6–2.

October 8, 1956, was a bright, clear day. On the mound for the Yankees was Don Larsen, "that misbehavin' fella," according to Stengel. The Dodger pitcher was Maglie.

From the start the game was a defensive masterpiece. Twenty-three batters came to the plate before the first hit was recorded. The twenty-fourth batter, Mantle, drove a home run into the right-field stands to make it a 1–0 game.

It was 2–0 when Jackie Robinson, playing in his last Series, led off the eighth with an easy grounder back to Larsen. The tremendous roar that greeted this mundane play was the first overt indication that something special was happening. One by one the dangerous Dodger batters had come to the plate, and one by one they'd each returned to the dugout. No Dodger had yet reached first base.

Larsen, who had been helped by spectacular defensive plays by Mc-Dougald, Mantle, and Andy Carey, received a standing ovation when he led off the bottom of the eighth. At the end of the inning, Maglie, who'd pitched a fine game himself, received a similar tribute as he walked to the dugout.

A tense silence fell over Yankee Stadium as the ninth inning began. Furillo led off. Larsen, who had been throwing without a windup and working quickly, began to take his time. The tension grew as Furillo fouled off one pitch after another. Finally he lofted a fly to Bauer for the first out. Campanella was the next batter. After electrifying the crowd with a drive that curved foul at the last moment, Campy bounced out. Dale Mitchell batted for Maglie.

Larsen had seemed cool and composed throughout the game. Now he felt ready to faint. "My legs were rubbery, and my fingers didn't feel like they were on my hand. I said to myself, 'Please help me out, somebody.'"

The first pitch to Mitchell was ball one. The crowd groaned. Larsen fiddled with the resin bag, stared at the outfield, and threw a slider for a called strike. Then he came in with a fastball. Mitchell swung and missed. The crowd screamed, then fell silent. Mitchell fouled off the next pitch. Berra called for a third fastball in a row, and Larsen delivered it. Mitchell checked his swing. Babe Pinelli, the home-plate umpire, shot his right arm into the air. Before Mitchell could protest, Berra had raced to leap into Larsen's arms, and pandemonium had broken loose. Don Larsen, who'd pitched only five complete games all season, had just pitched the only perfect game in the history of the World Series.

Larsen's perfect game signaled the end of the powerhouse Dodgers of the fifties. Even though Clem Labine outdueled Bob Turley for an extra-inning 1–0 win in the sixth game, the Yankees won the Series by walloping the Dodgers, 9–0, in game seven behind Johnny Kucks. Over the last three games, a total of twenty-nine innings, the Dodgers had managed only one run and seven hits.

The Series had been a mirror image of the previous year's. Just as the

Bums had done in 1955, the Yanks had dropped the first two, won the next three, lost the sixth game, and won it all in the seventh.

The year ended on several sour notes. In late October Walter O'Malley sold Ebbets Field for $3 million to Marvin Kratter, a real estate developer. Kratter announced he planned to use the property to build a "middle income residential community." The Dodgers took a three-year lease on the park, with an option to renew for an additional two years. So O'Malley could, if he wanted, stay in Ebbets Field until 1961. Not even the most optimistic Dodger fans believed the old ball park would survive that long.

In December the New York City Board of Estimate granted the Brooklyn Sports Center Authority a measly $25,000 for another "engineering and economic" survey of the proposed stadium site. The members of the authority were shocked. Having expected $278,000 to begin the preliminary phases of the project, they accused the city of failing "to go forward with the program as originally contemplated."

O'Malley responded to this further foot-dragging by issuing a stern warning. He said there was only "a short time" left before he might begin taking steps to "commit the Dodgers elsewhere."

On December 13, Brooklyn got its rudest shock since Leo Durocher left Flatbush for Coogan's Bluff. Jackie Robinson was traded to the Giants for Dick Littlefield, a left-handed pitcher, and $30,000.

Dodger fans were outraged. The Montague Street switchboard was overloaded all day, as fans called in first to verify the awful news and then express their indignation.

"I just can't believe it," Alex said. "I'd be happier if they'd sold the Brooklyn Bridge."

Jackie took the news gracefully. "It's the end of ten wonderful years," he said, "but it's not the end of the world."

The world may not have been ending, but it was certainly changing. Who could envision Jackie Robinson, with his daring baserunning, his fire and dash, his indomitable spirit, playing for the Giants? He was the essence of Brooklyn. Such considerations didn't matter to Walter O'Malley.

In January, Robbie announced he was quitting baseball to take a job as vice-president of personnel relations with the Chock Full O' Nuts fast-food chain.

"I'm not going to be shoved around from pillar to post," Jackie explained. "It's a good thing I've gotten out now. This is what I was afraid would happen. Baseball may be a sport to some, but it's really a great big business to me."

The week Robinson quit baseball, Walter O'Malley was in Los Angeles. While there he visited a 257-acre site near the heart of the city called Chavez Ravine. There was talk of building a stadium there, if and when big league ball came to L.A.

"We were just window shopping," grinned O'Malley when asked to explain his mission. "Ostensibly we were in the West to accept a new forty-four passenger Convair plane for the Dodgers. We just happened to be driving past Chavez Ravine, so we thought we'd have a look."

Late in January, O'Malley, always full of surprises, announced that Emmett Kelly, formerly a clown with the Ringling Brothers and Barnum & Bailey Circus, had been hired to entertain the fans at Ebbets Field for the 1957 season. Kelly's role as the forlorn tramp had made him the most famous clown in America. As it happened, he bore a remarkable resemblance to cartoonist Willard Mullin's equally famous Brooklyn Bum, long the unofficial symbol of "Dem Bums" in the sports pages of the New York *World Telegram*. When asked why he'd retained Kelly, O'Malley replied, "Oh, just to ease the tension at Ebbets Field."

If O'Malley was out to ease the tension of loyal Dodger fans, he was going about it in a bizarre manner. On February 21 he set off a new wave of fear that the team would soon leave Brooklyn by announcing he had purchased the Los Angeles Angels' franchise in the Pacific Coast League from the Chicago Cubs. The deal gave the Dodgers Wrigley Field, a twenty-thousand-seat ball park four miles from downtown L.A. The park, which was not easily accessible by public transportation and had poor parking facilities, was hardly an improvement over Ebbets Field.

It was difficult to believe O'Malley actually planned to transplant the Dodgers to Wrigley Field in Los Angeles. The purchase was portentous because it gave Brooklyn territorial rights over the country's largest city without big league ball. Everyone in baseball knew it was only a matter of time before the majors invaded California. In fact, the Washington Senators had been eying Los Angeles for some time. Any other clubs coveting the biggest prize on the West Coast would now have to wait until O'Malley played out his hand with the City of New York.

Horace Stoneham's reaction to the news gave New York another jolt. "If the Dodgers should move to Los Angeles our rivalry with them will suffer considerably, even though we should still be in the same league," he said. "In that case we would have to decide whether it would be better for us to move too."

Los Angeles Mayor Norris Poulson was as surprised as anyone by the rapid course of events. Two weeks later he and other city officials flew to Vero Beach to begin enticing the Dodgers to L.A. After the meeting O'Malley said, "Today's meeting was important. We got to know each other. But the Dodgers are still in Brooklyn and Jersey City."

While Los Angeles was making its overtures, New York was fiddling around, watching its last chance to save the Dodgers go up in smoke. City officials simply couldn't agree where in Brooklyn the new stadium should be built or how much money should be spent to get the project moving.

O'Malley had four meetings with Mayor Poulson that spring. The mayor repeatedly assured Walter the Chavez Ravine stadium would become a reality. In the meantime the Dodgers could play in Wrigley Field, or, possibly, the Los Angeles Coliseum. By the final meeting on Friday, May 3, O'Malley had agreed to move the Dodgers to California in 1958.

That meeting not only sealed the fate of the Brooklyn Dodgers, it was also the beginning of the end for the New York Giants. Mayor Poulson had secretly brought George Christopher, San Francisco's mayor, to the Beverly Hilton Hotel to join the discussions.

After his business with the Los Angeles crowd had been completed, O'Malley turned to Christopher and said, "O.K., it's your turn next. Some day we'll have to get together and see what we can do for San Francisco."

"Well," Christopher said, "Los Angeles and San Francisco have always been natural rivals—just like the Dodgers and Giants. I understand the Giants' attendance has been getting worse every season. Why not bring *them* out?"

"By God, that's it!" O'Malley exclaimed, slapping his thigh. "Of course. The Giants should be out here too!"

On Monday, O'Malley telephoned Christopher from Brooklyn and told him to come east at once. Horace Stoneham was eager to hear what the mayor had to say. By Friday, Christopher was in New York selling the Giant owner on the wonders of the Bay Area. Walter O'Malley wasn't satisfied killing only one of New York's great National League traditions. He was out to destroy them both.

Red Barber once wrote, "O'Malley is a devious man, about the most devious man I ever met." Never was the owner of the Dodgers more devious, or cold-blooded, than during the summer of 1957. He had already made up his mind to move to Los Angeles but continued to deceive the City of New York and the people of Brooklyn. He told us there was still a chance the Dodgers would stay long after that chance was gone.

All he cared about now was squeezing the last nickel out of the Faithful. After all, over the five previous seasons the Dodgers had been the most profitable franchise in baseball. The club's net profit after taxes from 1952 to 1956 was $1,860,744. Playing in their so-called bandbox the Dodgers had earned $400,000 more than the mighty Yankees over the same period. O'Malley had no intention of coming clean with the suckers who'd lined his pockets until he had finished taking them.

Meanwhile, those suckers, still believing they had a chance, had formed a "Keep the Dodgers in Brooklyn" Committee, with headquarters in the Hotel Bossert. The committee's workers, mostly kids, had distributed ten thousand buttons and collected twenty-five thousand signatures.

Life carried a story on O'Malley's May visit to Los Angeles. It showed Walter flying over Chavez Ravine in a helicopter provided by the Los Angeles County Sheriff. The magazine predicted: "The Brooklyn Dodgers as the world knows them will soon cease to be—barring an unexpected rescue."

All spring I had clung to the hope that a *deus ex machina* was still possible. I'd worn my "Keep the Dodgers in Brooklyn" button religiously. But what did that matter? Walter O'Malley was wearing one too.

My own last hope for Brooklyn disappeared on May 28. On that day the National League owners, meeting in Chicago, granted the Dodgers and Giants permission to move to the Coast. As Warren Giles, the league president, explained the action, "If New York and Brooklyn request consent before October 1 to relocate their franchises in San Francisco and Los Angeles respectively, the league president is authorized to grant it."

When I heard the news I called Alex. He had just moved into a furnished room. The house on Shore Road where we'd lived all those years was being torn down to make way for an apartment house.

"Well, there's nothing stopping O'Malley now. He's selling us right down the Hudson River," I moaned.

"Don't you believe it," Alex said. "It's all a big bluff. The Dodgers *can't* leave Brooklyn. They wouldn't belong anywhere else."

Alex's life was being pulled out from under him piece by piece. I couldn't blame him for not facing up to another bitter truth.

That summer I was in a continuous malaise. A nagging unpleasantness was almost always with me, its source often difficult to locate. A lot of the time I was brooding about the Dodgers. But I had other worries too. For one thing, I'd begun drifting out of graduate school, ostensibly to get started on my thesis. To get myself in the proper frame of mind I quit my part-time job with Go! Sportswear and went to work two afternoons a week in a bookstore on Eighth Street. Every morning I told myself this was the day I would get down to work on my dissertation. By noon I'd put it off till tomorrow.

I was coming around to the belief that getting a Ph.D. was a big fat waste of time. College professors wore gray flannel suits like everybody else. Most of my friends agreed with me. Jennifer and I had drifted into a Greenwich Village scene that was seeking truth, however stark or cruel it might be.

Outsiders went to great lengths to analyze my generation. They called us neo-dadaists, or neo-surrealists, or neo-romantics. Better to be a neo-somebody, I thought, than an old, tired nobody.

I must confess I wore sandals. And Jennifer and I slept together, though she drew the line on moving in. We even experimented with marijuana. We called it tea in those days. I took Jennifer to poetry readings at the Artists Studio and the Seven Arts Coffee Shop. I read Sartre and Camus, of course, and magazines such as *Neurotica* and *Exodus*. Ginsberg and Ferlinghetti could both get to me, but I also had a warm spot in my heart for James Broughton, who wrote such devastating lines as these:

> I am damp, I am dwindling in the hampers of the lame.
> They would launder me away with the fogs of dread.

I wonder now whether my despair didn't have something to do with the fact that on my next birthday I would be thirty. I knew that, if Mother had still been alive, she would have accused me of frittering away my life.

Despite my new preoccupations, I could not ignore Brooklyn's last baseball season. I bought a secondhand TV, even though I knew my friends would ridicule me for owning an idiot box. I was praying the Dodgers would leave town in a shower of glory, winning the pennant and then bowling over the Yankees four straight in the World Series.

There were those who believed Brooklyn as a team, as well as a town, was finished. Before the season began, Warren Spahn had voiced a widespread opinion when he said, "I can't see how the Dodgers can hold up for another year. They won't be the same club without Jackie Robinson, and outside of Duke Snider they're all getting pretty old. I honestly think the Dodgers will be lucky to finish fourth."

Spahn had a strong argument. But Brooklyn did have some young, talented pitchers. Don Drysdale was coming into his own, and so was Sandy Koufax. Johnny Podres was back from the service, and a rookie named Danny McDevitt appeared to have good stuff.

From the start of the season to well past the halfway mark the National League race was a mad scramble, with five teams pushing and shoving for the lead. The Braves, Reds, Phillies, Cardinals, and Dodgers were all together in a tight pack. In sixth place, far behind, were the Giants. Not surprisingly, the Polo Grounders were suffering another terrible year at the turnstiles.

On July 19 Horace Stoneham threw in the towel. He announced that his board of directors had voted to leave New York for San Francisco at the end of the season. The inducements to move were too great. Stoneham was not willing to turn down Mayor Christopher's offer of a new forty-five-thousand-seat municipal stadium with parking for ten thousand cars, plus the right to operate all concessions.

"We have no chance to survive here," Horace explained.

Mrs. John McGraw was asked to comment on the unhappy situation. "I guess all I have left now are my memories," she said.

The Dodgers were kept alive by their hurlers until August, when the

429

Cardinals completed a nine-game winning streak that knocked every team except the Braves out of the race. Then St. Louis collapsed, dropping nine straight while Milwaukee won ten in a row. The Braves would coast home in September to win the flag by eight games over the Cardinals.

Brooklyn was destined to come in third, eleven games out. Snider would hit forty homers and Hodges would hit twenty-seven, but three teams in the league would score more runs than the Bums. Now that the Dodger attack had gone soft, games that once took three hours were over in two hours or two and a half.

"The pitchers used to drag out the games because they used to have to be so careful with our lineup," Pee Wee Reese explained. "They'd pitch ball one, ball two, maybe ball three, always trying not to give us anything too good. Now they lay their first pitch right in there and get us out in two hours. We don't scare them anymore."

In September, Walter O'Malley gave the fans of Brooklyn a cruel and needless parting blow. He cynically encouraged Nelson Rockefeller's last-ditch effort to save the Dodgers. Rockefeller, a philanthropist with a deep love for New York City, came forward with an offer to help finance the new stadium. If the city would agree to condemn the land in downtown Brooklyn that O'Malley wanted, a Rockefeller corporation would purchase the property for $2 million and lease it to the Dodgers rent-free for twenty years. The Dodgers could then build their new ball park, and they would have an option to buy the land at any time for $2 million plus interest compounded at 2½ percent.

The difficulty with Rockefeller's proposal was that it would cost the city $8 million to acquire the land by condemnation. As most members of the Board of Estimate viewed it, the plan called for a "giveaway" of $6 million of the taxpayers' money to aid a private business. When Rockefeller then upped his buying price to $3 million, O'Malley quickly backed off, claiming the Dodgers had been "priced out."

O'Malley still wasn't willing to come out and say the Dodgers were definitely moving to California. He wouldn't make that announcement until a week after Brooklyn's long final season was over.

On the morning of Sunday, September 8, I received an unexpected phone call from Alex. I hadn't spoken to him since May.

"Damon m'boy, how about going up to the Polo Grounds with me this afternoon to watch the Bums play the Giants?" he asked. There was nothing in his tone to suggest there was anything unusual about today's game. But I knew he had finally faced up to the sad truth.

"Sure, Pop, I'll meet you at one o'clock in front of the ticket booths near the Eighth Avenue subway." I said. I hadn't really wanted to go to the final game ever between the Brooklyn Dodgers and the New York Giants. Jennifer and I had planned to spend the day as we did most Sundays—strolling through the Village checking out the bars and coffee houses, taking time at some point in the afternoon to mingle with all the weirdos who congregated on Sundays at Washington Square Park. The folksingers, pushers, queens, bongo drummers, guitar strummers, voyeurs, Reds, and nymphets would have to live without me today. I was going to the ball game with my old man.

Alex and I went through all the normal motions. We had hot dogs and beer and two or three bags of peanuts. Neither he nor I wanted to dwell on the significance of the occasion. We settled down and watched a hell of a good ball game.

Don Drysdale pitched against Curt Barclay. The Flock loaded the bases in the first with only one out, but Curt pitched his way out of the jam. But in the second Jim Gilliam put Brooklyn on the scoreboard first with a two-run homer.

In the fourth Mays singled and then raced home when Ray Jablonski punched a hanging curve off the right-field wall for a triple. Hank Sauer then homered off the left-field scoreboard to put the Giants ahead, 3–2.

That was all the scoring. Willie Mays got the last hit in the history of the Brooklyn-New York rivalry when he tripled in the eighth, but he died on third when reliever Ed Roebuck fanned Jablonski. At 3:55 P.M. Marv Grissom, who'd come in to bail out Barclay in the seventh, threw to Sandy Amoros, who sent an easy grounder to second baseman Danny O'Connell. The flip to Whitey Lockman was in plenty of time, and the most glorious rivalry in the history of sports was over.

There would be other sad endings before that September ran its course. The Dodgers would represent Brooklyn for the last time on Sunday, September 30, in Philadelphia. The Giants would say goodby to the Polo Grounds that same day. A group of diehard Giant fans would implore their heroes with a huge banner reading, "STAY TEAM STAY." Pittsburgh would maul New York, 9–0, and at the end of the game the forsaken denizens of Coogan's Bluff would mob the field, engulf the players, and escape with second base, home plate, and clumps of Polo Grounds turf.

But Alex and I had only one sad ending left to endure. We agreed to meet in Flatbush on Tuesday, September 24, to bid adieu to Ebbets Field.

The day before, the Braves had clinched the pennant and so had the Yankees. I couldn't imagine a World Series played in Milwaukee. Maybe I wouldn't even watch.

I found Pop waiting for me in the rotunda. We took a box not far from the seats where we had watched my very first ball game. It was a cool September night. The atmosphere was made especially chilly by rows of empty seats. Only 6,702 fans had come out to take part in Brooklyn's last hours in the majors.

I didn't pay much attention to the game, which was just as well. It was a listless affair, with the Dodgers beating the Pirates, 2–0. All during

Brooklyn's final innings my eyes wandered over every corner of the old park, straining to fix in my memory pictures I would never see again. I wondered why the whole world felt obliged to ridicule Ebbets Field—to call it moth-eaten, or rattletrap, or flyblown. What was so goddamn wrong with it? Only that it represented the past. Nowadays people saved all their respect for the future.

Gladys Goodding was as sad as anyone in Ebbets Field that night. She'd been playing the organ there for sixteen years. She accompanied the passing innings with such melodies as "Thanks for the Memory," "Am I Blue," "After You've Gone," "When the Blue of the Night Meets the Gold of the Day," and "Que Sera, Sera."

Alex sat red-faced through it all, drinking a fresh can of beer every inning, feverishly recording every play on his scorecard.

At last Pirate first baseman Dee Fondy grounded out, giving Gil Hodges the final putout in the history of Brooklyn. As the Dodgers headed for their dugout, Tex Rickard announced, as he always did, "Please do not go on the playing field at the end of the game. Use any exit that leads to the street."

Didn't Tex know his little speech didn't matter anymore? Or was this all a bad dream? Someone put on the record "Follow the Dodgers," another sign that all was normal. But the silly tune was abruptly stopped, as Miss Goodding began to play "Auld Lang Syne."

Those tears Alex had been holding in so long began flowing out of control. Down on the diamond the ground crew was raking the infield and putting tarps over the mound and home plate.

I had to keep telling myself there wouldn't be a tomorrow.

Epilogue

It was February 23, 1960. I arrived late for work that cold Tuesday morning. Peg, my secretary, handed me several messages, including two marked "Urgent." One was from my wife, the other was from Alex's nursing home. I quickly called Jennifer.

"The nursing home just phoned," she began.

"What happened?" I interrupted, expecting the worst.

"Alex has run off somewhere. After breakfast he got dressed and disappeared."

Alex had slipped out of the home several times before, but this was his first escape since last summer, when he'd begun deteriorating rapidly. I cut short the conversation, got up from the desk, and crossed the hall to Harry's office. At seventy, my uncle was still as fit and energetic as ever—a striking contrast to his brother, who was three years younger.

"Good morning, Damon," Harry said, looking up from his work. "How soon can you pack? I'd like you to fly down to North Carolina this afternoon."

"Can it wait till tomorrow?"

"I suppose. But why? Don't tell me you're going out to Ebbets Field?"

"Ebbets Field?"

"Sure. To attend the ceremony. Today's the day they begin tearing it down."

Out of nowhere I remembered Pop once boasting to me about how he'd ragged Charlie Ebbets the day they broke ground for Ebbets Field. If Alex, with his great sense of history, had been there the day it all began, surely he would try to get there today.

"As a matter of fact, that's exactly where I'm going," I said. And then I told Uncle Harry about Alex's disappearance, and about my hunch.

"I'm going with you," Harry said.

Within minutes we were in the back seat of my uncle's Cadillac, crossing the Brooklyn Bridge. We arrived at Ebbets Field sometime after 11:00 A.M. The park's gates, locked for almost three years, had been thrown open. Anyone who wanted to pay his last respects was welcome.

We hurried inside. About two hundred people were in the boxes and on the field around home plate. Along the third base line was a giant crane, its cast-iron wrecking ball painted to look like a baseball. On the pole in center field, the flag fluttered upside down. The turf was scarred and ragged, the billboards faded. In the outfield there were still printed reminders that baseball had been played here—the distance markers and the words "AT BAT" and "UMPIRES" and "BATTING ORDER."

On hand for the occasion were, among other dignitaries, Carl Erskine, Ralph Branca, Roy Campanella in his wheelchair, and Otto Miller, who'd caught the first game here in 1913—a game Harry and Alex had attended.

It didn't take long to spot my father. He was standing in a box behind the Dodger dugout, huddled over to protect himself from the cold. The sound of a brass band echoed through the empty stands as Harry and I approached Pop.

He was engrossed in the ceremonies. On the field Campy was being presented with his old locker, his number 39 uniform, and an urn containing earth from behind home plate.

We stopped a few rows away from Alex. As Harry caught his brother's profile, he was taken aback by how frail he had become. He was obviously gravely ill. We drew closer, and then Harry called out, "Dig up a couple of new players, Charlie!"

Alex turned. As he recognized Harry his sad, drawn face lit up. He smiled for a few seconds and then said, "Son of a bitch, Harry, those were wonderful days, weren't they?"

The two brothers embraced. At last my father had shaken off the furies that had plagued him so many years.

The ceremonies ended and the crowd was moved back into the stands. The crane made its way over to the visitors' dugout, and the wrecking ball began to rise.

Not far from where Harry, Pop, and I were standing, Carl Erskine was glumly watching the proceedings. Ersk turned to the man next to him and said, "You know, when I look at the field now I see the past. I think of things that happened in this nook and that cranny. I'm remembering bad pitches I made from out there and great days we had. That dugout's empty, but when I look at it I can see all the men that used to be there."

The ball fell. As it crashed through the dugout roof, it knocked away the bullpen telephone.

"I see things as they were, as they used to be. I don't see—this," Erskine said.

434

The crane turned and wheeled onto the remains of the diamond. It kept right on going until it reached the 376-foot marker in straightaway center field. The iron ball was thrown up against the wall, opening a large hole. I couldn't hold in a pained laugh. All I could think of was Red Barber exclaiming, "It's off the wall for extra bases!"

We turned and walked to a nearby exit ramp. Harry took off his greatcoat and wrapped it around his shivering brother. As we left, I looked around for familiar shadows. There were none. Long before the summer sun would arrive, this place would be gone.

Acknowledgments

My greatest debt is to Harry Rice, who, at eighty-seven, is still active and still loves baseball. His remarkable memory is the source of much that is recorded in these pages. My original editor, Léon King, deserves special thanks for encouraging me to embark on a project that was as rewarding as it was challenging. I am also indebted to Harold Rosenthal, who reviewed and edited the final manuscript. A distinguished journalist who covered the Brooklyn Dodgers for the *New York Herald Tribune*, Harold cut away yards of excess wordage, sharpened my prose, and made this a far better book than it might have been. Another former *Trib* staffer who provided valuable assistance was Jack Redding, librarian at the Baseball Hall of Fame, who gave me a warm welcome on three separate trips to Cooperstown. Jack cheerfully dug out the answers to many difficult questions and was kind enough to allow me to view films of those great World Series between the Dodgers and Yankees in the early fifties. Finally, I must say thanks to two old friends—writer Ford Hovis, who gave me valuable advice from the day I began writing to the day the job was done, and fellow Brooklynite Svein Arber, who's even more sentimental than I am about the lost era of Ebbets Field, if that's possible.

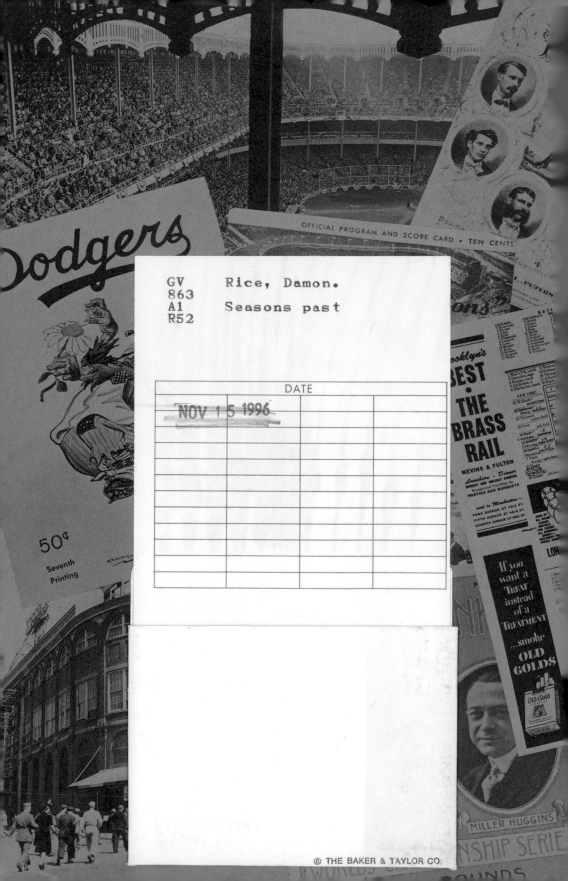

GV
863
A1
R52

Rice, Damon.

Seasons past